POPULAR TALES AND FICTIONS

ABC-CLIO CLASSIC FOLK AND FAIRY TALES

Jack Zipes, Series Editor

Collectors in the nineteenth and early twentieth centuries unearthed a wealth of stories from around the world and published them in English translations for the delight of general readers, young and old. Most of these anthologies have been long out of print.

The ABC-CLIO Classic Folk and Fairy Tales series brings back to life these key anthologies of traditional tales from the golden age of folklore discovery. Each volume provides a freshly typeset but otherwise virtually unaltered edition of a classic work and each is enhanced by an authoritative introduction by a top scholar. These insightful essays discuss the significance of the collection and its original collector; the original collector's methodology and translation practices; and the original period context according to region or genre.

Certain to be of interest to folklorists, these classic collections are also meant to serve as sources for storytellers and for sheer reading pleasure, reviving as they do hundreds of folk stories, both reassuringly familiar and excitingly strange.

OTHER TITLES IN THIS SERIES:

Creation Myths of Primitive America, by Jeremiah Curtin;
Introduction by Karl Kroeber

English Fairy Tales and More English Fairy Tales, by Joseph Jacobs;
Introduction by Donald Haase

Folktales from Northern India, by William Crooke
and Pandit Ram Gharib Chaube;
Introduction by Sadhana Naithani

Italian Popular Tales, by Thomas Frederick Crane;
Introduction by Jack Zipes

Old Deccan Days or Hindoo Fairy Legends, by Mary Frere;
Introduction by Kirin Narayan

Popular Stories of Ancient Egypt, by Gaston Maspero;
Introduction by Hasan El-Shamy

Popular Tales
and Fictions

Their
Migrations and Transformations

W. A. Clouston

Edited and with an Introduction by
Christine Goldberg

A B C  C L I O

Santa Barbara, California
Denver, Colorado   Oxford, England

Library of Congress Cataloging-in-Publication Data

Clouston, W. A. (William Alexander), 1843–1896
Popular tales and fictions / by W. A. Clouston ; edited and with an introduction by Christine Goldberg.
    p. cm. — (ABC-CLIO classic folk and fairy tales)
Originally published: Edinburgh : W. Blackwood & Sons, 1887.
Includes index.
    ISBN 1-57607-616-4 (hardcover); 1-57607-617-2 (e-book)
1. Folklore. 2. Fairy tales. 3. Tales. I. Goldberg, Christine. II. Title. III. Series.
GR65 .C413 2002
398.2′ 09—dc21

2002015519

06 05 04 03 02   10 9 8 7 6 5 4 3 2 1

This edition reprints in its entirety and retains the original chapter sequence of Popular Tales and Fictions, Their Migrations and Transformations, *collected and edited by W. A. Clouston, published by William Blackwood and Sons, Edinburgh and London, in 1887. The text of this edition has been altered only to fit an increased page dimension and to reflect contemporary typographical conventions.*

ABC-CLIO, Inc.
130 Cremona Drive, P.O. Box 1911
Santa Barbara, California 93116–1911

*This book is also available on the World Wide Web as an e-book.
Visit www.abc-clio.com for details.*

Contents

INTRODUCTION TO THIS EDITION

We do not know of any book more calculated to awaken an interest in the comparative study of popular tales than Mr. Clouston's [*Popular Tales and Fictions*]. We cannot imagine the most indifferent reader laying the book down without a desire to know more about the interesting questions suggested by it.

This well-disposed excerpt comes from a review of *Popular Tales and Fictions* in the first volume (published in 1888) of the *Journal of American Folk-Lore*. The reviewer, Thomas Frederick Crane, a professor of Romance Languages at Cornell University, was one of the founders of the American Folklore Society and the author of *Italian Popular Tales* (1885). *Popular Tales and Fictions* was also reviewed (anonymously, with a style and sentiments very much like those of Andrew Lang) more critically in the *The Athenaeum* (April 23, 1887: 541–542):

Mr. Clouston selects certain themes of popular literature, and illustrates them by a wide choice of variants, in the selection of which he draws freely upon the best modern European folk-tale collections, and shows considerable familiarity with mediaeval romance in all its ramifications, as well as—what might be expected from the editor of the "Bakhtyár Náma" and the "Book of Sindibád"—with Oriental story-books. Among the themes treated are invisible caps and cloaks, shoes of swiftness, inexhaustible purses, gold-producing animals, giants, trolls, dragons, &c., life tokens, tests of chastity, birdmaidens, forbidden rooms, fairy hinds, magic barks, thankful beasts, ring and fish legends, and magical transformations. Among the story groups examined are 'Aladdin,' 'The Enchanted Horse,' 'The Three Graziers and the Alewife,' 'The Four Clever Brothers,' 'The Heir of Linne,' 'Whittington,' 'The Merchant and the Folk of Falsetown,' 'The Robbery of the King's Treasury,' 'Little Fairly,' 'The Lady and Her Suitors,' 'The Three Hunchbacks,' 'The Pardoner's Tale,' 'The Miller's Son,' &c. Mr. Clouston tells his stories with point and spirit; he gives full and, where we have tested him, exact references. His work may thus be recommended to the reader who is simply in quest of entertainment, and to the professed student, who will find in it a number of facts set forth in simple and orderly arrangement by a conscientious scholar.

After this informative and positive beginning, this reviewer went on to criticize Clouston for being "of the school of Benfey," in that "he holds that the proofs of Asiatic origin of a very great number of our popular tales and fictions are abundant and conclusive." Modern readers will probably agree with this reviewer that many of Mr. Clouston's cases for the origin of the motifs and the tales are not actually proven. However, this failure in the argument need not detract from the reader's enjoyment of the retold tales. Any questions of ultimate origins require a thorough, modern study, and even then the answer must be qualified, "the evidence available suggests that. . . ."

Popular Tales and Fictions, first published in 1887, consisted of two volumes with a total of a thousand pages. It begins with an introduction explaining the author's position on the migration of folktales vis-à-vis the then-current theories. In this book, as elsewhere, Clouston's refrain is, There is nothing new under the sun, by which he meant that old tales are reproduced much more frequently than new ones are invented. Here, he describes the chief manuscripts that were responsible for conveying Indian, Persian, Arabic, and Hebrew tales to Europe from the period of the Middle Ages onward into the eighteenth century. The material in his initial illustrations is a potpourri of short narratives, religious, philosophical, sensational, and humorous. Then, several chapters are devoted to fairy-tale motifs (which the *Athenaeum* reviewer called "themes") such as magical invisibility, fantastic monsters, and speaking birds. Later chapters in volume 1 are devoted to tale types such as Aladdin and The Magician and His Pupil. Volume 2 covers humorous anecdotes, wisdom tales, and tales of tricks and of fate. Clouston invites the reader "to judge for himself of their common origin, and the transformations they have undergone in passing from one country to another." Some of the tales are familiar to modern readers (as they were to the original readership), but now as then, as Crane observed in his book review, "the greater portion will probably be quite new to the ordinary reader."

Why "popular tales and fictions"? *Popular* meant, then as now, "of the people," but the Victorian connotation was different from modern usage. The word implied "without individual authorship," "from the population" as opposed to "from a particular author." We might now see the contrast between *tales* and *fictions* as between narratives and non-narrative fancies, but this was not the distinction that Clouston was making. He was alluding to two different classes of folktales. Those based on magical motifs were the tales, and those based on real life were the fictions. Contemporary opinion held that these two genres of narrative came from different sources. Tales with magical motifs (as a genre) were thought to be universal, based as they were on animism, which was believed to be a primitive form of thought. Tales of real life, in contrast, were based on particular social norms and customs, and could (it was believed) be traced to the cultural level or region on which their point depended.

In general, this is the division between the German *Märchen* on the one hand and the so-called realistic *Novellen* (romantic tales) and *Schwänke* (jests) on the other. This distinction is the basis for the organization in the now-standard reference work *The Types of the Folktale,* and it is the reason that fairy tales with magical motifs are called "ordinary folktales" there. They are the true *Märchen,* while animal tales, which also contain fantastic elements (in real life, animals of course do not speak), usually, like *Schwänke,* depend on social usages. The idea that these are fundamentally different genres had great staying power. The influential Swedish folklorist C. W. von Sydow postulated a major differentiation between fantastic chimerates, which he thought were European, and realistic novellates, which he thought were Semitic.

The title *Popular Tales and Fictions* evokes Thomas Keightley's book, *Tales and Popular Fictions* (1834). Clouston credited Keightley's book with having "helped to promote a more wide-spread interest in the question of the origin and diffusion of folk-tales." Keightley and other early folktale researchers, according to Clouston, deserved

> all praise for having made the most of the materials within their reach. Those materials were, however, very scanty in comparison with the great mass that has since accumulated, by means of which the storiologist is enabled to "survey folk-tales from China to Peru." Not only have several of the oldest and most important Asiatic story-books been translated into English and other European languages, but oral tales and legends have been "taken down from the mouths of the people" in several parts of India. (p. xliv)

Tales and Popular Fictions was, as Richard M. Dorson remarked, a "pioneering effort." Moreover, its author had many other interests, and so did not devote his attention to this subject over a long period. Thus, that book suffers from inexperience in two important respects. The contrast between it and Clouston's work from fifty years later is marked: the one seems amateurish, and the other, competent, and even in parts professional.

The evidence that Clouston produced usually does point to an eastern origin of the tales he discussed. One reason for this is that, because of his knowledge of eastern literature, he chose to write about tales for which eastern sources exist. Indian story collections such as the *Pañca-tantra*, the *Jatakas*, and *The Book of Sindibád*; Persian collections such as the *Tales of a Parrot*; and Arabic collections such as the *Thousand and One Nights* all contain dozens or hundreds of tales, and date from times when few traditional tales had been documented in Europe. Moreover, while Greek and Roman philosophy tended to be abstract, and, following Plato's lead, hostile toward "old wives' tales," early eastern philosophy delighted in the use of parables, which added to its store of ancient traditional narratives. Therefore, given the fact that the tales which Clouston investigated were found in early eastern sources, the chances of there being earlier western examples would necessarily be small.

I do not believe that Clouston's repeated insistence on the eastern origin of European tales was intellectually dishonest. The problem comes from the desire to generalize from examples for which evidence has been presented, to examples for which evidence has not been examined and may not even exist. As the *Athenaeum* reviewer pointed out, results of studies based on old Oriental tales cannot be generalized to apply to all folktales, or even to all folktales known in Europe. Clouston's strongest generalizing statements were, for example, "By far the greater number of the apologues and stories which are common to all Europe have been current in Asia from a very remote period" (p. xlvii); and, "most of the popular tales of Europe are traceable to ancient Indian sources" (p. lxxxv). He aligned himself with German scholars (Theodor Benfey, Reinhold Köhler, and Felix Liebrecht) as well as Gaston Paris, who favored the idea that European folktales had migrated from western Asia, and against the British men (he named George Dasent and Sabine Baring-Gould) who believed that folktales should be considered survivals of primitive beliefs (p. xlvii). Some of this difference of opinion is due to different visions of the problem: the Germans were looking at whole complex tales, while the British tended to isolate single motifs.

William Alexander Clouston (1843–1896)

The author of *Popular Tales and Fictions* was a Scotsman, born in the Orkneys and later a resident of Glasgow. As a journalist he wrote feature articles for newspapers, but Clouston's real love was Oriental literature. The word *Oriental,* meaning "something that reached Europe from the East," is now considered to be in bad taste. However, for several centuries it filled a need, and synonyms are difficult to construct. European scholars who investigated ancient and medieval manuscripts and other aspects of culture quickly discovered that much of what those manuscripts contained had forerunners in Arabic, Persian, and Hindu or Sanskrit, plus Syriac, Armenian, Aramaic, Hebrew, Turkish, and possibly even Mongolian, Berber, Greek, or Egyptian. *Western Asia* and *Middle East,* as geographic terms, leave out India, which is one of the prime areas in question. "Oriental" referred to this group of interrelated cultures. It did not, in such a context, typically mean the Far East, China, Japan, etc., or Southeast Asia. While some of the work of the many important Asiatic or Oriental learned societies did and does pertains to those regions, the manuscript traditions that scholars like Clouston investigated did not extend to the Far East. Here, I use "Oriental" to refer only to literature, not to people or to culture.

Clouston repeatedly served as an editor of English translations of Oriental works. His first book was *Arabian Poetry for English Readers* (1881), which, like many of his books, was privately printed (370 copies) for "a few personal friends." In the preface, he mentions that he is engaged on his project of illustrating the migrations of popular European tales and fictions. One of the translators of the works in this anthology was Sir William Jones (see below). A short version of the Romance of Antar, a work that Clouston believed was the model for European chivalric romances, fills 125 of its pages. *The Bakhtyár Náma: A Persian Romance,* translated by William Ouseley and edited by Clouston, appeared in 1883. As in *The Book of Sindibád,* inset stories pertain to a criminal accusation in the frame tale. Here, the accused man, who is of course innocent, turns out to be the long-lost son of the king. Clouston's notes contextualize the exotic manners and customs.

Clouston's first really ambitious comparative study was *The Book of Sindibád, or, The Story of the King, His Son, the Damsel, and the Seven Vazirs* (1884). This is an Indian story collection that was translated into Arabic, Hebrew, Persian, and Syriac and, beginning in the twelfth century, into European languages, where it was called The Seven Wise Masters. Many of the motifs in its frame tale are present in other ancient story collections. At the birth of a much-longed-for only child, a prince, it is prophesied that in his twentieth year, his life will fall into grave danger. After all attempts to educate the boy have failed, the sage Sindibád succeeds in educating him in six months (as in the Pañca-tantra). Before the now-virtuous prince is restored to his father, another prophecy reveals that if he were to speak within the next week, he would die. One of the ladies (the "damsel") in the harem tries to seduce him, and, when that fails, accuses him of trying to seduce her (mot. K2111, as in the biblical tale of Joseph and Potiphar's wife and the ancient Egyptian tale of Anu and Bata). The prince cannot defend himself and the king would have him executed, but the execution is delayed (as is Shaharazad's death in *The Arabian Nights*) for seven days while seven philosophers relate tales concerning the treachery of women. Each night, the woman who accused the prince responds with a tale of her own (these inset tales are not the same in all the copies of the manuscript tradition). Finally, the prince explains what really happened and the evil woman is executed.

Clouston's volume includes synopses of two versions of this work, one Persian and one Arabic (see Perry 1959 and Belcher 1987 for recent work on this subject). A table compares eleven different manuscripts, Persian, Syriac, Greek, Spanish, Hebrew, Indian, and Arabic, showing which inset stories appear in each, and notes describe the main differences in the tales. The general content of pages missing from the two featured manuscripts is filled in with material from the others. The appendix, where Clouston discusses some of the tales as they appear in other sources, is over 150 pages long.

Shortly after *Popular Tales and Fictions* was published, Clouston added "Variants and Analogues of Some of the Tales in the Supplemental Nights" to Richard Burton's edition of *The Arabian Nights*. These include some of the best-known eastern tales, Aladdin (AT 561, see pp. 314–346), Ali Baba and the Forty Thieves (AT 676), and The Two Sisters Who Envied Their Cadette (AT 707).

Clouston was one of many scholars who worked on projects for Frederick J. Furnivall (1825–1910). Furnivall, a barrister and later a member of the British Academy, was a man of many enthusiasms: a Christian Socialist active in the establishment of the Working Men's College of London, he was also an avid oarsman who enjoyed the company of pretty girls. More to our purpose here, he founded several learned societies whose purpose was to publish material related to English literature, from ballads and Shakespeare to the poets Shelley and Browning. The primary sources that were published by these societies became the basis of twentieth-century scholarship on English literature. He also founded the project that became *The Oxford English Dictionary*. Frances James Child dedicated his *English and Scottish Popular Ballads* to Furnivall, noting that the publication of the Percy ballad manuscript had greatly enhanced this project. Two of these societies, the Early English Text Society and the Chaucer Society, published works by Clouston.

Many of Chaucer's *Canterbury Tales*, and also tales falsely purported to have been written by Chaucer, have close analogs in Indian, Persian, or Arabic sources, and Clouston happily found and described these parallels. In 1886, he furnished *Additional Analogues to the Wright's Chaste Wife*, a fifteenth-century English tale in which a married woman receives suitors but confines or humiliates them, thus keeping loyal to her husband (see pp. 443–448). Clouston divided this tradition into two parts, depending on whether it includes a chastity token, and traced it back through the Middle Ages (it appears in Boccaccio's *Decameron*) to two different stories in the Kathásaritságara (*The Ocean of the Streams of Story*). He found that Indian versions contained details preserved in the European versions, which were absent from Arabic tradition. This suggests that, insofar as it is different, the Arabic material is a later development.

In 1887, Clouston contributed analogs to *The Tale of Beryn*, edited by Furnivall and W. G. Stone. This spurious addition to *The Canterbury Tales* follows the first part of an Old French romance. The irresponsible hero, Beryn, exiled through the machinations of his stepmother, encounters trouble in Falseland: a series of dishonest citizens seek payment for alleged damages (false stepmothers and false court cases are common motifs in Oriental tales). An associate appears in court on Beryn's behalf, and turns each accusation around (see pp. 325–333). Clouston summarized the French romance and followed it with a version from *The Book of Sindibád*. As was the case with "The Wright's Chaste Wife," the Indian and the European material agreed, while an Arabic version stood out as substantially different.

Clouston's presentation of material for eight tales in the Chaucer Society's *Originals and Analogues of Some of Chaucer's Canterbury Tales* is admirably organized, in contrast to Furnivall's own haphazard section of that work. "On the Magical Elements in Chaucer's Squire's Tale"(1890b) is the longest of these projects. First this study treats the magical motifs:

automatic flying apparatus (mechanical horse, chariot, ship, carpet), magic mirror, magic ring, magic sword, and understanding the language of animals. Then Clouston describes analogues of the tale that Chaucer never finished, in which a mechanical flying horse is used to abduct a woman. He concludes that the original of this tradition was an Indian myth in which a man impersonated the god Vishnu flying on his garuda-bird. Even if this is merely the oldest extant (rather than the original) form of the tale, Clouston's material establishes the parameters for this tale type, which includes Turkish and Gypsy oral versions (it is now indexed under mot. D1621.1, Artificial flying horse). Western popular culture is much more familiar with the flying carpet than the flying horse, a distinction that Clouston attributed to the medieval interest in the notion of King Solomon's magic carpet.

In general, and regarding *The Canterbury Tales* in particular, twentieth-century work has not followed Clouston's example. Instead of attempting to trace the interrelationships of European and Asiatic stories, subsequent scholars, as epitomized in Brian and Dempster's *Sources and Analogues of Chaucer's Canterbury Tales* (1941), have restricted their interest to works that influenced Chaucer directly: his actual sources, or failing that, works that resembled those actual sources as closely as possible. This is a more practical but decidedly less ambitious project. Thus, Morris (1985) does not include Clouston's contributions to *Originals and Analogues* (although it does include his commentary on The Squire's Tale). Only when, as is the case of The Miller's Tale, no likely sources are extant, are later European folktales accepted as evidence. This newer perspective reflects the assumption that Chaucer's sources were European rather than foreign, in spite of Arabic influence in medieval Europe, and in France in particular.

The work on *Popular Tales and Fictions* was interspersed with a similar, smaller project on humorous tales relating to fools (1888). This is *The Book of Noodles: Stories of Simpletons; or, Fools and Their Follies* (the first phrase of its title turned out to be unfortunate). This work is arranged in large part geographically. Clouston began with ancient Greek tales of fools; then he covered English and German tales, Middle Eastern, Chinese, and Indian fools. Next comes the "silly son" in different national traditions. The book ends with a Tamil tale, Four Simple Brahmans, and multiple versions of the complex humorous tale, The Husband Hunts Three Persons as Stupid as His Wife (AT 1384).

Clouston's next works returned to Oriental subjects. In 1889, he published *A Group of Eastern Romances and Stories from the Persian, Tamil, and*

Urdu, with over a hundred pages of comparative notes. This was followed in 1890 with *Flowers from a Persian Garden and Other Papers,* which covers a miscellany of subjects, beginning with the Persian poet Saádí (d. 1291). There is a summary of *The Tales of a Parrot, the Túti Náma,* mentioned in several places in *Popular Tales and Fictions.* Anecdotes, clever retorts, aphorisms, and rules of conduct have been selected to convey Oriental humor, with Turkish, Persian, Arab, and even a couple of Chinese examples. Medieval Jewish parables and fables were taken from the Talmud, and a romantic tale of the lovers Majnún and Laylá came from Muslim (Persian and Turkish) sources. One chapter covers anecdotes about Latin gaffs made by ignorant medieval clergymen; another contains a humorous (but of course apocryphal) medieval biography of Aesop; and the last, a social history of beard-wearing. Throughout, Clouston reveals his interest in the use of narratives to convey moral lessons. Two subsequent books are more homogenous. *Some Persian Tales, from Various Sources* (1892b) includes substantial notes and analogues. *Book of Wise Sayings, Selected Largely from Eastern Sources* (1893a) contains maxims and proverbs from the Near and Far East.

Besides being an enthusiastic researcher, Clouston was also a bibliophile. In 1893, he came to the defense of Sir William Jones (1746–1794), who had been the subject of belittling remarks by a collector of rare books who failed to appreciate Jones's contributions to the British knowledge of Asiatic culture. Today, Jones is remembered chiefly for his discovery in 1787 that Sanskrit belonged to the same language family as Greek and Latin. This relationship is the basis for Indo-European philology, a discipline that made great progress in the following century. However, Clouston's admiration for Jones was for his foundation of the Bengal Asiatic Society in 1784 and for his pioneering translations of Sanskrit literature. As a student at Oxford University, Jones, already competent in French and Italian as well as Greek and Latin, had learned Arabic and Persian, and he continued mastering languages until he knew twenty-eight at least fairly well. From modest beginnings, he was helped in his career by powerful friends. For some years, his linguistic accomplishments were merely an avocation while he worked as a jurist in England. However, from 1783 until his death, he was the judge of the high court at Calcutta, and thus was able to make everyday use of his cross-cultural accomplishments. He was, for his time, unusually sensitive to cultural differences, and believed that while British law should apply to Britons living in India, the natives should be governed according to their own laws. At the time of his death he had organized a project of translations of Hindu (Sanskrit) and Islamic legal texts that could be used by the British for this purpose. Jones was universally credited with outstanding intelligence, personal character, and amiability. Clouston's admiration of such a man reflects well on the admirer.

In addition to Asiatic and narrative subjects, Clouston wrote on a few other topics. His "Notes on the Folk-Lore of the Raven and the Owl" (1893b) are chiefly European superstitions, interspersed with a few Indian ones. *Literary Coincidences; A Bookstall Bargain; and Other Papers* (1892a) is, as the title indicates, a miscellaneous work. The essay on riddles in wisdom tales covers, albeit lightly, material that in the twentieth century became the basis of important studies that shaped modern comparative folktale research (Thompson 1946, 158–163, 432–442; Chesnutt 1996). Other sections pursue some of the problems that Clouston encountered in his translations and comparative works. "Literary Coincidences and Imitations," part of *Literary Coincidences; A Bookstall Bargain; and Other Papers,* discusses cases in which different, sometimes far-flung, authors use the same expression. Here the reader can see Clouston's fascination with similarities among metaphors, similarities that were variously intended, unintentional, or coincidental. His book on hieroglyphic (rebus-style) bibles (1894) demonstrates the persistence of familiar stories stripped of their usual words, and, as usual, offers a history of the subject.

Richard M. Dorson, historian of the study of folklore in Britain, thought very highly of Clouston. He gleefully gave details of Clouston's "astute" critical remarks directed at his contemporaries' "errors of deduction and gaps of knowledge" (1968, 260) and summarized as follows:

> The Orkneyman belongs with the Great Team in his sensitivity to the science of folklore, his command of the vast literature, and his development of the work of the earlier English folklorists. . . . The achievement of William Alexander Clouston in rendering visible the network of popular tales and fictions between Asia and Europe has never received proper due, and that field today still remains largely his own. (258, 264)

It is not difficult to see why successors to Clouston's approach are scarce. As scholarship became more professionalized and academic in the twentieth century, researchers trained in western literatures came to feel that Indian, Persian, and Arabic works were outside of their expertise.

There has also been a tendency to assume that ethnic groups create their own folklore and literature rather than borrowing someone else's. This assumption has been reinforced by nationally named university departments of language and literature (English, German, Spanish, and so on). Divisions like these, which grew out of romantic nationalism, have been reconstituted in the modern "politics of identity." In addition, the initial excitement of sources and analogues criticism ran its course. The supply of new materials ran low, and researchers came to feel that few new analogues remained to be discovered and that few new ideas would be found through this method of interpretation. For all of these reasons, the study of the early connections between Asian and European literature is no longer a very popular subject of scholarship.

Dorson's idea that work like Clouston's was not continued in the twentieth century is, however, not entirely accurate. A few scholars with expertise in Asian literatures have continued to investigate the relationships between European and Asiatic tales. In England, one such person was N. M. (Norman Moseley) Penzer, whom Dorson considered a literary scholar rather than a folklorist. Penzer wrote comparative notes for the eleventh-century Indian tale collection, Somadeva's *Kathá sarit ságara,* and for Basile's seventeenth-century Neapolitan tale collection, *The Pentamerone.* Penzer was also the first comprehensive biographer of Sir Richard Burton, and the author of several other books, for example, one on the subject of harems. In Germany, Otto Spies researched and translated Turkish, Arabic, and Indian material with an eye on its European analogues. In particular, his short work on Oriental elements in Grimms' fairy tales (1952) covered a part of Clouston's subject and improved upon some of its particulars. Furthermore, Stith Thompson's folktale indexing systems are now widely used and are applied to many collections and catalogs of African and Asian folktales, thus drawing this material into a worldwide picture of traditional narratives. Oral versions of some of the tale types and motifs that Clouston investigated are listed in *Folk Traditions of the Arab World* (El-Shamy 1995) and in *Arabia Ridens* (Marzolph 1992).

The Intellectual Background of Popular Tales and Fictions

Where do folktales come from? was one of the many questions for which scholars in the nineteenth century sought an answer through scientific investigation. Following the example of Jacob and Wilhelm Grimm, people in many parts of Europe collected oral tales in published works that were read by adults as well as children. It immediately became evident that similar tales were known in different countries. Also at this time, old manuscripts of medieval romances were published, and Oriental works were translated into western languages. Between 1800 and 1900, a huge body of newly discovered tales that were either known or believed to be ancient became available to the reading public. The Grimms, in spite of Jacob's philological bent, had been content to cite domestic and foreign analogues to the folktales they published, without trying to sort out the logistics of the relationships among this material. Later in the century, however, scholars wanted to ascertain the routes through which the tales had been disseminated. This task was seen as a part of the task of writing a history of fiction (Dunlop 1888).

Today, the question of the origin of folktales is not a burning one. However, in the second half of the nineteenth century, "culture"—its nature and its origin—was a hot topic. Many people were of course distressed by Darwin's theory of evolution, according to which humans were closely related to lower animals. However, the accompanying notion of "social Darwinism," the survival of the fittest way of life, which validated the economic hierarchy of colonialism, was much more palatable to British citizens. Edward Burnet Tylor, in his *Researches into the Early History of Mankind* (1865), put forward the idea that myths were the philosophy of savage peoples, and surveyed international myth and folktale motifs including the markings on the moon, the world-tortoise, the sun-catcher, the fountain of youth, and the tail-fisher whose tail is cut off. He concluded that all of these were known in Native America, and that mythology was similar all over the world.

In *Primitive Culture* (1871), Tylor situated the source of mythological thought in animism, the notion that spirits help or harm human affairs. Animism was, he wrote, the most primitive form of religion. Thus, myths, fairy tales, and superstitions became evidence of primitive thought. The contrast between these fancies and the rational thinking of civilized peoples could be seen to attest to the superiority of the latter. However, as a counterpoint to this misguided cultural imperialism, it should be noted that many people, particularly writers and artists, also appreciated the poetic and symbolic qualities of mythological thought.

The discovery that primitive and ancient mythology, peasant fairy tales, and savages' superstitions were all similar (at least in contrast to rational Enlightenment learning) was an exciting one. To men whose education had emphasized classical studies (the languages and cultures of ancient Greece and Rome) this discovery was particularly intriguing. It helped explain how the Greeks, whose philosophy, mathematics, and (to a lesser extent) natural science were quite developed, also embraced myths and magic: even as great thinkers developed their rational thought processes, their culture had retained its universal primitive elements.

In 1878, the Folk–Lore Society of London was organized by intellectuals whose ideas had been stimulated by Tylor. Richard M. Dorson has chronicled their predecessors and their accomplishments in *The British Folklorists* (1968). He honored six men, Andrew Lang, George Lawrence Gomme, Alfred Nutt, Edwin Sidney Hartland, Edward Clodd, and William Alexander Clouston, by calling them The Great Team of Folklorists. Of these six, five subscribed to the notion of survivals, attributing folktales and superstitions to earlier stages of culture. The odd man out is Clouston.

No doubt the success of *Popular Tales and Fictions* was helped by the general interest in the new science of folklore. However, this book assigns the origin of its tales not to savage thought but to Oriental sources: manuscript tales from such places as Persia, Arabia, and India. In this notion, Clouston's predecessor was the German philologist Theodor Benfey (Cocchiara 1981, 296–305). Along with his translation (1859) of the Pañca-tantra, a Sanskrit collection of animal tales, Benfey wrote a 600-page introduction citing analogues. Because the Pañca-tantra is so old (ca. A.D. 500 or earlier), and because it has a long history of translations in the Middle East and in Europe (from the twelfth century onwards), the obvious conclusion was that the European tradition of those tales, and of new tales based on the same motifs, had come from India. Benfey also credited tales in China and Tibet to this tale collection, which had been carried in written form to Indonesia. Other folktale scholars who presented evidence for Indian origins of certain folktales include Reinhold Köhler in Germany and Emmanuel Cosquin and Marcus Landau in France.

Comparative Folktale Research Today

Since Clouston's time, comparative folktale study has become much more efficient. Clouston's dismay that "a single laborer" is limited in what he (or she) can accomplish was shared by others who solved much of this problem. Folktale scholarship in the nineteenth century was international but individual: researchers working alone made use of primary and secondary sources published in many different European countries. In the twentieth century, a forum for cooperative work was established. The Finnish folklorist Kaarle Krohn (Strömbak 1971, 11–33; Cocchiara 1981, 308–313) organized the Folklore Fellows (FF also stands for *Folkloristischer Forscherbund* and *Fédération des Folkloristes*) in 1907. This organization still publishes monographs, called Folklore Fellows' Communications (FFC): in 2000, this series passed number 270, making an average of three numbers per year. Many of these publications are reference works that direct folklore scholars to the material that they seek. Particularly since the amount of potentially relevant material is constantly expanding, centralized indexing is a much more efficient system than the previous situation, the one under which Clouston worked, in which each researcher had to depend on his own reading.

The need for folktale indexes is evident in the series "Tabulation of Folktales" published by the Folk-Lore Society of London beginning in 1889. However, the indexing system advocated in that tabulation was never widely employed. The scheme that was ultimately adopted for international folktales is that begun by Antti Aarne, another Finn, and explicated in the FFC series publication *Verzeichnis der Märchentypen* (1910). He was the author of numerous historic-geographic studies of folktales, and he adapted that method to study traditional riddles (Strömbak 1971, 35–43). Entitled *The Types of the Folktale*, Aarne's folktale index was revised (and greatly expanded) in 1928 and 1961 by Stith Thompson, and is now being revised yet again. The "AT" abbreviation in my references below honors Aarne and Thompson. Because of space limitations, *The Types of the Folktale* does not actually contain many references to printed texts of its tales. However, it does (when appropriate) direct readers to Bolte and Polívka's (1913–1932) *Anmerkungen* (notes) to the Grimms' tales, with their long lists of references, Clouston's among them.

Aarne's *Verzeichnis der Märchentypen* referred to Danish (from Svend Grundvig's) and German (the Grimms') texts and to unpublished texts in the Finnish folktale archive. Thompson's revisions were intended to broaden the region covered by the index to include the Old World culture area "from Ireland to India." This is sometimes taken to be "Indo-European," but that is definitely not what Thompson intended. He meant the phrase geographically, specifically including non-Indo-European traditions such as Finnish, Hungarian, Turkish, and Arab, that now occupy that region. The units in this index are whole tales.

In addition to whole tales, parts of tales, either incidents or striking details that petain to characters or objects, are also of interest to scholars.

Thompson created the *Motif-Index of Folk-Literature* (1955–1958), a six-volume work, for these. The *Motif Index* is meant to cover the entire world, and to cover traditional written literature and all traditional narrative genres (myths and legends as well as folktales). Section D in the *Motif Index*, for example, covers magic, including transformations, magic objects, and magic powers, and section K covers deceptions, which are frequently the basis of humorous anecdotes.

Researchers who seek more, or more recently published, material than these indexes provide make use of regional indexes of tale types or motifs (Uther 1996, 1997). Baughman's (1966) and Ashliman's (1987) indexes are particularly useful for English-speakers. The applicability of the Aarne-Thompson tale types to Asia is still an unresolved question, but many tale types certainly exist there too: indexes of Chinese, Japanese, and Persian tales have been published recently. Stith Thompson was an expert on the tales of North American Indians, and those have been included in both editions of the *Motif Index*. Wilbert and Simoneau's (1992) collections of South American Indian tales extend the use of motif numbers to a substantial amount of native material on that continent.

On a number of occasions, Clouston adduced modern Indian folktales, some of which he found quite similar to ancient Indian tales, suggesting that those traditions had remained stable over many centuries. The relationship of Indian to European oral tales is, of all Asiatic traditions, the easiest for Anglophone scholars to pursue. Thompson himself coauthored an index of Indian tale types and another of motifs (Ramanujau in Beck et al. 1987, xi–xxi). The folktale studies that have used this material show that tales that are relatively fixed in Europe are often less stereotyped in India.

In 1931, Krohn reviewed the results of historic-geographic folklore studies. In view of Krohn's suspicion of Benfey's bias, it is particularly interesting that Krohn himself concludes that many of the tales reviewed there originated in India (see also Thompson 1946 and Goldberg 1984). Relatively current information regarding studies of individual tale types is also to be found in the *Enzyklopädie des Märchens* (Ranke et al., 1977–), where the article "Erzähltypen" lists tale type numbers along with the name of the entry in which they are discussed. In addition, discussions of some of the most important folktale motifs can be found under obvious key words. This reference work is also valuable for its entries on the eastern story collections such as the Pañca-tantra that were the mainstays of Clouston's research.

Clouston's work was utilized by subsequent folktale scholarship. Thompson listed *The Book of Noodles* and *Popular Tales and Fictions* in the references in the tale type index, and in the Motif Index these appear along with *A Group of Eastern Romances and Stories from the Persian, Tamil, and Urdu*. Bolte and Polívka used these two same collections in their lists of analogues to the Grimms' tales, plus *Flowers from a Persian Garden and Other Papers*. A. M. Espinosa cited several of these books among his references in his *Cuentos populares españoles* (1947–1948).

The European material in *Popular Tales and Fictions* is now split between folklore, for tales with a substantial oral presence, and literary studies. The modern work in folklore most similar to *Popular Tales and Fictions* is Thompson's *The Folktale* (1946), which also gives summaries of traditional tales and describes their geographic distribution. Unlike *Popular Tales and Fictions, The Folktale* does not present multiple versions of each tale, nor do its retellings contain much detail. Thompson restricted himself in *The Folktale* to tales he believed had a substantial oral presence, while Clouston happily uses oral versions to support his arguments that are chiefly based on written texts. In spite of his efforts to broaden the material covered in each revision of *The Types of the Folktale,* Thompson never entirely escaped the northern-European basis of Aarne's 1910 *Verzeichnis der Märchentypen*. In contrast, Clouston deliberately favored Asian material, so the two books are also complementary in this respect.

Thompson maintained that his own and his Finnish colleagues' emphasis on oral variants resulted in a better technique and more conscientious studies than could be produced by scholars like Clouston (he mentioned Benfey and Cosquin in particular) who relied chiefly on material from written sources (1946: 428-430). In America, this category included Gordon Hall Gerould and Alexander Haggerty Krappe. In Europe, Albert Wesselski was the most vocal critic of the "Finnish School." Wesselski claimed that written texts were sufficient evidence for establishing the history of a tale, and that oral tradition was of little importance. This problem of the priority of written versus oral tradition was a matter of dispute for a long time. Recently, however, researchers have shown themselves to be willing to try to consider all evidence—written, oral, dramatic, and pictorial—of a tale type or of a motif (Bausinger 1996). Furthermore, the recent interest in contemporary folklore has directed attention to the kind of informal jests that were Clouston's forte. For these reasons, *Popular Tales and Fictions* should have more appeal now than it had fifty years ago.

References Cited

Aarne, Antti. 1910. *Verzeichnis der Märchentypen.* FFC 3. Helsinki.

———, and Stith Thompson. 1961. *The Types of the Folktale.* FFC 184. Helsinki (abbreviated "AT" followed by specific number).

Ashliman, D. L. 1987. *A Guide to Folktales in the English Language.* New York: Greenwood Press.

Baughman, Ernest. 1966. *Type and Motif Index of the Folktales of England and North America.* Indiana University Folklore series no. 20. The Hague: Mouton.

Bausinger, Hermann. 1996. Literatur und Volkserzählung. In *Enzyklopädie des Märchens,* edited by Kurt Ranke et al. (1977–), vol. 8: 1119–1137.

Beck, Brebda E. F., Peter J. Claus, Praphulladatta Goswami, Jawaharlal Handoo. 1987. *Folktales of India.* Chicago: University of Chicago Press.

Belcher, S. 1987. The Diffusion of the Book of Sindbád. *Fabula* 28 (1987): 34–58.

Bolte, Johannes, and Georg Polívka. 1913–1932. *Anmerkungen zu den Kinder- und Hausmärchen der Brüder Grimm.* 5 vols. Leipzig: Dieterich'sche Verlagsbuchhandlung.

Brian, W. F., and Germaine Dempster. 1941. *Sources and Analogues of Chaucer's Canterbury Tales.* Chicago: University of Chicago Press.

Chesnutt, Michael. 1996. The Great Crusader of Diffusionism, Walter Anderson, and the Geographical-Historical Method. *Studies in Folklore and Popular Religion* 1: 55–80.

Clouston, William A. 1881. *Arabian Poetry for English Readers.* Glasgow: privately printed.

———, ed. 1883. *The Bakhtyár Náma: A Persian Romance*, trans. William Ousley. Larkhall, Larnarkshire.

———. 1884. *The Book of Sindibád, or, The King, His Son, the Damsel, and the Seven Vazirs.* Glasgow: privately printed.

———. 1886. *Additional Analogues to The Wright's Chaste Wife.* Early English Text Society Publications no. 84. London: N. Trübner.

———. [1887]. Variants and Analogues of Some of the Tales in the Supplemental Nights, vol. 3. Pp. 552–652 in *Supplemental Nights* to the *Book of the Thousand Nights and a Night*, by Richard Burton, vol. 4. Bassorah Edition.

———. 1888. *The Book of Noodles: Stories of Simpletons; or, Fools and Their Follies.* London: E. Stock.

———. 1889. *A Group of Eastern Romances and Stories from the Persian, Tamil, and Urdu.* Glasgow: W. Hodge & Co.

———. 1890a. *Flowers from a Persian Garden and Other Papers.* London: David Nutt.

———. 1890b. On the Magical Elements in Chaucer's Squire's Tale, with Analogues. In *John Lane's Continuation of Chaucer's Squire's Tale,* ed. F. J. Furnivall.

Chaucer Society Publications. London: Kegan Paul, etc., 1888, 1890, pp. 263–478.

———. 1892a. *Literary Coincidences; A Bookstall Bargain; and Other Papers.* Glasgow: Morison Brothers.

———. 1892b. *Some Persian Tales, from Various Sources.* Glasgow: Bryce.

———. 1893a. *Book of Wise Sayings, Selected Largely from Eastern Sources.* London: Hutchinson and Co.

———. 1893b. Notes on the Folk-Lore of the Raven and Owl. In *Birds of Omen in Shetland,* by Jessie M. E. Saxby, 1982 (1893). New York: AMS Press.

———. 1893c. The Works of Sir William Jones. A Protest. *Bookworm* 6: 19–22.

———. 1894. *Hieroglyphic Bibles, Their Origin and History.* Glasgow: David Bryce and Son.

Cocchiara, Giuseppe. 1981. *The History of Folklore in Europe,* trans. John N. McDaniel. Philadelphia: Institute for the Study of Human Issues.

Crane, Thomas Frederick. 1888. Review. *Journal of American Folklore* 1: 87.

Dorson, Richard M. 1968. *The British Folklorists.* London: Routeledge and Kegan Paul.

Dunlop, John. 1888 (1814). *The History of Fiction.* New edition, revised and with notes by H. Wilson. London: George Bell and Sons.

El-Shamy, Hasan. 1995. *Folk Traditions of the Arab World.* 2 vols. Bloomington and Indianapolis: Indiana University Press.

Espinosa, Aurelio M. 1946–1947. *Cuentos populares españoles.* 3 vols. Madrid: Consejo Superior de Investigaciones Científicos.

Furnivall, F. J., Edmond Brock, and W. A. Clouston. 1875–1888. *Originals and Analogues of Some of Chaucer's Canterbury Tales.* Chaucer Society Publications, Second Series, nos. 7, 10, 15, 20, 22. London: N. Trübner.

———, W. G. Stone, and William Clouston. 1887. *The Tale of Beryn.* Chaucer Society Publications, Second Series, nos. 17, 24. London: N. Trübner.

Goldberg, Christine. 1984. The Historic-Geographic Method: Past and Future. *Journal of Folklore Research* 21: 1–18.

Krohn, Kaarle. 1931. *Übersicht über einige Resultate der Märchenforschung.* FFC 96. Helsinki.

Marzolph, Ulrich. 1992. *Arabia Ridens: die humoristische Kurzproza der frühen adab-Litteratur im internationalen Traditionsgeflecht.* Frankfurt am Main: V. Klostermann.

Morris, Lynn King. 1985. *Chaucer Source and Analog Criticism, a Cross-Referenced Guide.* New York and London: Garland Publishing.

Penzer, N. M., ed. 1924–1928. *The Ocean of Story, being C. H. Tawney's translation of Somadeva's Katha sarit sagara.* 10 vols. London: C. J. Sawyer.

———, ed. 1932. *The Pentamerone of Giambattista Basile.* 2 vols. London: John Lane.

Perry, Bed Edwin. 1959. The Origin of the Book of Sindibad. *Fabula* 3 (1959): 1–94.

Ranke, Kurt, et al., eds. 1977. *Enzyklopädie des Märchens*. Berlin: De Gruyter.

Spies, Otto. 1952. *Orientalische Stoffe in den Kinder- und Hausmärchen der Brüder Grimm. Beiträge zur Sprach- und Kulturgeschichte des Orients*, Bd. 6. Walldorf-Hessen: Verlag für Orientkunde Dr. H. Vorndran.

Strömbak, Dag, ed. 1971. *Leading Folklorists of the North*. Oslo etc.: Universitets Forlaget.

Thompson, Stith. 1946. *The Folktale*. New York: Dryden Press.

———. 1955–1958. *Motif-Index of Folk-Literature*. 6 vols. Rev. ed. Bloomington: Indiana University Press (abbreviated "Mot.," followed by the specific number).

Tylor, Edward B. 1871. *Primitive Culture*. 2 vols. London: John Murray.

———. 1878 (1865). *Researches into the Early History of Mankind*. 3d. ed. London: John Murray.

Uther, Hans-Jörg. 1996. Type- and Motif-Indexes: An Inventory. *Asian Folklore Studies* 55: 299–317.

———. 1997. Indexing Folktales: A Critical Survey. *Journal of Folklore Research* 34: 209–220.

Wilbert, Johannes, and Karin Simoneau. 1992. *Folk Literature of South American Indians, General Index*. Los Angeles: UCLA Latin American Center Publications, vol. 80.

Subsequent Scholarship
on Clouston's Tales

Like the reviewer for the *Athenaeum*, many Britons in the nineteenth century appreciated the dual nature of folklore books in then-current popular culture, the fact that the books could be used for research by the specialist scholar but still could be enjoyed by the general reader. For example, Joseph Jacobs's *English Fairy Tales* separates the tales (printed in fairly large type, for easy reading by or to children) from the comparative and source notes (printed in smaller type) with a charming picture that forbids children from reading the learned notes. Similarly, I hope that some modern readers of this edition of *Popular Tales and Fictions* will be happy just to read the tales. Others, however, may wonder what more is now known about the motifs and tales that Clouston describes here. The following notes indicate starting places where further references to additional texts or to research can be found. See the entry "Erzähltypen" in the *Enzyklopädie des Märchens* (EM) to locate the titles that are used there for the various tale type numbers.

Introduction

LIV–LV, Which is the true son? Mot. H486.2, Test of paternity: shooting at father's corpse. Cf. the better-known biblical motif, J1171.1 Solomon's judgment: the divided child.

LVI, Mot. J2112.1, Young wife pulls out his gray hairs; old wife his black. Marzolph, *Arabia Ridens*, no. 847. The different demands of the two wives form an extra twist on the idea in mot. J2112, Gray hair cured by pulling it out so that the person is bald.

LVI, Welcome to the clothes, AT 1558.

LVII, Mot. J1511.5, The wine-spilling host rebuked.

LIX, God's Justice Vindicated, AT 759. Haim Schwarzbaum, "The Jewish and Moslem Versions of Some Theodicy Legends," *Fabula* 3 (1960): 119–169.

LXIV, Mot. J1174.3, Girl screams when she is robbed.

LXV, The Matron of Ephesus, AT 1510. Peter Ure, "The Widow of Ephesus, International Comic Theme," *Durham University Journal* 49, N. S. 18 (1956): 1–9. Gerlinde Huber, *Das Motiv der "Witwe von Ephesus" in lateinischen Texten der Antike und des Mittelalters* (Tübingen: G. Narr, 1990).

LXVII, Mot. T327, Mutilation to repel lover.

LXIX, Mot. G313, Procrustes.

LXXVII, Mot. K402.1, The goose without a leg.

LXXIX, AT 1586, The Man in Court for Killing a Fly. Mot. J1193.1, Killing the fly on the judge's nose.

Chapters

Volume 1

1–30, Invisible Caps and Cloaks, Shoes of Swiftness, Inexhaustible Purse, etc. Fortunatus, AT 566. Devils (giants) fighting over magic objects which the hero gets by trickery is AT 518, and is also an episode in other tale types including AT 302, The Ogre's (Devil's) Heart in the Egg.

The tales where the hero is given food- or money-producing gifts, which he loses, and is then given a self-propelled cudgel, are AT 563, The Table, the Ass, and the Stick and AT 564, The Magic Providing Purse and "Out, Boy, Out of the Sack." Jes P. Asmussen, "Remarks on Some Iranian Folk-Tales Treating of Magic Objects, Especially AT 564," *Acta Orientalia* (Copenhagen) 28 (1965): 220–243. G. Calame-Griaule and V. Görog-Karady, "La calabasse et le fouet: le théme des 'objects magiques' en Afrique occidentale," *Cahiers d'Études Africaines* 12 (1972): 12–75. Michel L. Chyet, "Açil Sofram, Açil!: A Comparative Study of Middle Eastern Versions of AaTh 563," *Fabula* 28 (1987): 90–105.

AT 567, The Magic Bird-Heart. Christine Ohno, "Der Krautesel, eine Analyse der Motive und des Ursprungs dieses Märchen [AT 566] und des Märchentyps AaTh 567," *Fabula* 34 (1993): 24–44. Mot. J2073.1, Wise and foolish wish: keep doing all day what you begin. AT 569, The Knapsack, the Hat, and the Horn. AT 565, The Magic Mill.

31–36, Gold-producing animals. Mot. B100, Treasure animal. Mot. D876, Magic treasure animal killed, is attested around the world, in Europe, Asia, Indonesia, and native North America.

37–49, Adventures with Giants, Trolls, Ghúls, etc. AT 1640, The Brave Tailor.

50–57, Dragons and monstrous birds. Mots. B11, Dragon; B30, Mythical birds; B31.1, Roc, etc. AT 300, The Dragon Slayer.

58–66, Petrifying Victims, Life Tokens, Tests of Chastity. Mot. D231, Transformation: man to stone, refers to three tale types (AT 303, 471, and 516) and to countries literally from around the entire world. Mot. E761, Life token. Edwin Sidney Hartland, *The Legend of Perseus*, vol. 2 (London: D. Nutt, 1895), 1–54. Ruth Norton, "The Life-Index: A Hindoo Fiction-Motif," pp. 211–224 in *Stud-*

ies in Honor of Maurice Bloomfield (New Haven: Yale University Press, 1920). AT 303, The Twins or Blood-Brothers. Mot. H400, Chastity test.

67–72, Bird-Maidens. Mot. D361.1, Swan Maiden, appears in three tale types: AT 313, The Girl as Helper in the Hero's Flight; AT 400, Man on a Quest for His Lost Wife; AT 465, The Man Persecuted Because of His Beautiful Wife. There are also widely spread legends, for example, in Polynesia and in Arctic cultures, about supernatural wives who escape from their mortal husbands when they find their animal skins.

73–86, Subaqueous Fairy Halls, Forbidden Rooms, Cupid and Psyche Legends. Mot. F212, Fairyland under water. Alexander Haggerty Krappe, "Le Lac enchanté dans le Chevalier Cifar," *Bulletin Hispanique* 35 (1953): 107–125. Mot. C611, Forbidden chamber, refers to eight tale types including AT 311–312, Three Sisters Rescued; AT 314, The Youth Transformed into a Horse; AT 710, Our Lady's Child. AT 425, The Search for the Lost Husband. Jan Öjvind Swahn, *The Tale of Cupid and Psyche* (Lund: C. W. K. Gleerup, 1955).

87–92, Fairy Hinds, Magic Barks. Mot. N774, Adventures from pursuing enchanted animal (hind, boar, bird). Mots. D1121, Magic boat; D1123, Magic ship.

93–107, The Thankful Beasts; Secrets Learned from Birds. Mot. N452, Secret remedy overheard in conversation of animals (witches), in AT 432, The Prince as Bird, AT 516, Faithful John, and AT 613, The Two Travelers.

108–114, The Good Man and the Bad Man. The Two Travelers (Truth and Falsehood), AT 613. Reidar Th. Christiansen, *The Tale of the Two Travellers, or the Blinded Man* (Helsinki: FFC 24, 1916).

115–116, The Ungrateful Serpent. The Ungrateful Serpent Returned to Captivity, AT 155. Christine Goldberg, "The Ungrateful Serpent," *Fabula* 37 (1996): 248–258.

117–123, The Hare and the Tortoise. Hare and Tortoise Race: Sleeping Hare, AT 275A; Race Won by Deception: Relative Helpers, AT 1074.

124–130, The Four Clever Brothers. The Four Skillful Brothers, AT 653; The Rarest Thing in the World, AT 653A. Christine Goldberg, "Dilemma Tales in the Tale Type Index: The Theme of Joint Efforts," *Journal of Folklore Research* 34 (1997): 179–193.

131–147, Cumulative Stories. AT 2000–2340.

148–166, Aladdin's Wonderful Lamp. Aladdin, AT 561; The Spirit in the Blue Light, AT 562.

166–171, Life depending on some extraneous object. Mot. E765, Life dependent on external object or event. The Ogre's (Devil's) Heart in the Egg, AT 302.

James George Frazer, *The Golden Bough*, vol. 11 (London: Macmillan, 1919–1920), chapter 11, 95–225.

172–184, The Hunchback and the Fairies. The Gifts of the Little People, AT 503.

185–190, The Enchanted Horse. Mot. D1626.1, Artificial flying horse. H. S. V. Jones, "The Cléomadès and Related Folk-Tales," *Publications of the Modern Language Association* 23 (1908): 557–598.

191–200, The Demon Enclosed in a Bottle, Contracts with the Evil One, etc. The Spirit in the Bottle, AT 331.

201–209, "The Ring and the Fish" Legends; Men Living inside Monstrous Fish. The Ring of Polycrates, AT 736A. Mot. F911.4, Jonah. Fish (or water monster) swallows a man. James George Frazer, *Folk-Lore in the Old Testament*, vol. 3 (London: Macmillan, 1919), 82–83.

210–237, Magical Transformations. The Magician and His Pupil, AT 325. Mots. D671, Transformation flight; D672, Obstacle flight.

Volume 2

265–273, The Three Graziers and the Alewife. The Three Joint Depositors, AT 1591. Marzolph, *Arabia Ridens*, no. 1170.

274–280, The Silent Couple. The Silence Wager, AT 1351. W. N. Brown, "The Silence Wager Stories, Their Origin and Diffusion," *American Journal of Philology* 43 (1922): 289–317.

281–289, The Sharpers and the Simpleton. The Wager That Sheep Are Hogs, AT 1551.

290–295, The Cobbler and the Calf. Theft by Distracting Attention, AT 1525D. Marzolph, *Arabia Ridens*, no. 368. AT 1525 pertains to the cycle of tales about a Master Thief.

296–303, The Heir of Linne. The Treasure of the Hanging Man, AT 910D; cf. The Brother to Hang Himself, AT 740**.

304–311, Whittington and His Cat. Whittington's Cat, AT 1651.

312–316, The Tailor's Dream. The Tailor's Dream, AT 1574.

317–323, The Three Travellers and the Loaf. Dream Bread, AT 1626. Paull Franklin Baum, "The Three Dreams or 'Dream-Bread' Story," *Journal of American Folklore* 30 (1917): 378–410.

323–324, Sending One to an Older and the Oldest Person. The Oldest on the Farm, AT 726. Cf. mots. F571.2, Sending to the older, and H1235, Succession of helpers on quest. One helper sends to another, who sends to another, etc.

325–333, The Merchant and the Folk of Falsetown. Mot. J1162, Plea by admitting accusation and discomfiting accuser, including mot. J1162.1, Nurse's false plea admitted: child demanded; and mot. J1162.2, Robbers' false plea admitted: counteraccusation. Albert Wesselski, *Märchen des Mittelalters* (Berlin: H. Stubenrauch, 1925), 229, no. 40.

334–361, The Robbery of the King's Treasury. Rhampsinitus, AT 950. Mot. K315.1, Thief enters treasury through passage made by him as architect of building. This notion now circulates as a computer legend: a programmer is said to have left himself a secret entrance into an otherwise-secure computer network. Mot. K415, Marked culprit marks everyone else.

363–374, Llewellyn and His Dog Gellert, or Killheart. Llewellyn and His Dog Gellert, AT 178A. Stuart Blackburn, "The Bramahin and the Mongoose; The Narrative Context of a Well-Travelled Tale," *Bulletin of the School of Oriental and African Studies* 59 (1996): 494–507. Jan Harold Brunvand, *The Choking Doberman and Other "New" Urban Legends* (New York and London: W. W. Norton, 1984), 6–49.

375–379, The Lover's Heart. The Eaten Heart, AT 992. Francis James Child, *The English and Scottish Popular Ballads* (Boston and New York: Houghton, Mifflin, 1883–1898), no. 269. John E. Matzke, "The Legend of the Eaten Heart," *Modern Language Notes* 26 (1911): 1–8. J. D. Williams, "Notes on the Legend of the Eaten Heart in Spain," *Hispanic Review* 26 (1958): 91–98. References under mot. Q478.1 indicate similar tales among Native Americans.

380–388, The Merchant, His Wife, and the Parrot. Seventy Tales of a Parrot Prevent a Wife's Adultery, AT 1352A. Alexander Haggerty Krappe, "The Tuti-Nameh in Spanish Folk-Lore," *Hispanic Review* 1 (1933): 67–69.

389–398, The Elopement. Underground Passage to Paramour's House (Inclusa). R. M. Dawkins, *Modern Greek Folktales* (Oxford: Clarendon Press, 1953), 376–383, no. 60. Alexander Haggerty Krappe, "Studies in the Seven Sages of Rome XI, Inclusa," *Archivim Romanicum* 19 (1935): 213–226.

399–432, Little Fairly. The Rich and the Poor Peasant, AT 1535. Josef Müller, *Das Märchen vom Unibos* (Jena: Eugen Diederichs, 1934).

433–448, The Lady and Her Suitors. The Entrapped Suitors, AT 1730. Emmanuel Cosquin, *Études folkloriques* (Paris: Edouard Champion, 1922), 457–473.

449–451, The King's Life Saved by a Maxim. "Think Carefully before You Begin a Task," AT 910C. Jean-Pierre Pinchette, *L'Observance des conseils du maître* (Helsinki: FFC 250, 1991).

452–454, Irrational Excess of Sorrow. Mot. H1394, Quest for person who has not known sorrow, has this section of *Popular and Tales and Fictions* as its only reference. Cf. AT 844, The Luck-Bringing Shirt, and mot. N135.3.1, Feast for those who have not known sorrow.

455–457, The Intended Divorce. Mot. J1545.4, The exiled wife's dearest possession, is one of the components of AT 875, The Clever Peasant Girl.

458–472, The Three Knights and the Lady: The Three Hunchbacks, etc. The Three Hunchback Brothers Drowned, AT 1536B. Pillet, *Das Fabliau von les trois bossus menestrels* (1901). A. M. Espinosa, *Cuentos populares españoles* (Madrid: Consejo Superior de Investigaciones Científicos, 1946–1947), vol. 2: 153–157, nos. 31–32. Archer Taylor, Dane Hew, *Modern Philology* 15 (1917): 221–246, discusses this and other humorous tales regarding the disposal of a corpse.

475–478, The Advantages of Speaking to a King. Cf. mot. J689, Forethought in alliances—miscellaneous.

479–481, The Lost Purse. Mot. J1172.1, Not the same purse as was lost.

482–485, The Ungrateful Son. The Half Carpet, AT 980A.

486–503, Chaucer's Pardoner's Tale. The Treasure Finders Who Murder One Another, AT 763. Frederick Tupper, The Pardoner's Tale, in Brian and Dempster, *Sources and Analogues of Chaucer's Canterbury Tales*, 415–438. John Huston's film, *Treasure of the Sierra Madre* (1948).

508–517, The Lucky Imposter. Doctor Know-All, AT 1641.

518–524, Don't Count Your Chickens until They Are Hatched! Mot. J2061, Air-castle shattered by lack of forethought, has subdivisions for details such as selling a jar of honey, a basket of glassware, a pail of milk, and the hide of a deer. AT 1430, The Man and His Wife Build Air Castles. Gordon Hall Gerould, "Moll of the Prima Pastorum," *Modern Language Notes* 19 (1904): 225–230, defined subtypes according to whether the main character was a woman, a woman and a man together, or a man. In a Greek tale type (Dawkins, *Modern Greek Folktales*, 394–395, no. 63), a poor man who picks up a single chick-pea plans for storehouses to hold its eventual progeny, causing the king to believe him to be wealthy.

"Don't count your chickens until they are hatched," as a proverb, is first recorded in English in the fifteenth century. The notion that it is bad luck to count living things is traced to the Old Testament, 2 Samuel 24 where David is punished for ordering that a census be performed. James George Frazer, *Folk-Lore in the Old Testament*, vol. 2 (London: Macmillan, 1919), 555–563.

525–532, The Favourite Who Was Envied. Mots. K978, Uriah letter; K1612, Message of death fatal to sender.

533–537, The Miller's Son; or, Destiny. The Prophecy, AT 930.

538–541, Luckily, They Are Not Peaches. Thank God They Weren't Peaches, AT 1689.

POPULAR TALES AND FICTIONS

POPULAR TALES
AND FICTIONS

THEIR

MIGRATIONS AND TRANSFORMATIONS

BY

W. A. CLOUSTON

EDITOR OF 'ARABIAN POETRY FOR ENGLISH READERS;'
'BAKHTYÁR NÁMA;' 'THE BOOK OF SINDIBÁD,' ETC.

IN TWO VOLUMES
VOL. I.

WILLIAM BLACKWOOD AND SONS
EDINBURGH AND LONDON
MDCCCLXXXVII

TALES have wings, whether they come from the East or from the North, and they soon become denizens wherever they alight. Thus it has happened, that the tale which charmed the wandering Arab in his tent, or cheered the Northern peasant by his winter's fireside, alike held on its journey to England and Scotland.—
ISAAC D'ISRAELI.

Contents of the First Volume

CONTENTS

Contents

Preface

THE following papers are designed as a contribution to the history of European popular tales, the study of which—and it is both instructive and fascinating—has been, until within comparatively recent years, much neglected in this country, though its importance has long been recognised by eminent Continental scholars, the value of whose researches it would not be easy to overrate. The illustrations of the pedigree and modifications of our popular fictions adduced in these volumes are the result of many years' special as well as promiscuous reading, but, no doubt, they are in some instances very far from being exhaustive: it is little, after all, that a single labourer can accomplish in exploring so vast a field. I venture to think, however, that the papers will prove both useful to English students of comparative folk-lore and folk-tales and interesting to intelligent readers generally.

So far as I am aware, there is no work precisely similar to this in our country, in which variants of the same general stories are detailed—not merely indicated by their titles—thus enabling the reader to judge for himself of their common origin, and the transformations they have undergone in passing from one country to another, without the labour of consulting a great many different books, some of which are not readily accessible. Dunlop's 'History of Fiction,' though a remarkable work of research, was, even on its first publication, considered as very incomplete; and since then—indeed chiefly of late years—much light has been thrown upon the genealogy of our household tales, by the publication of such as are orally current in the different countries of Europe, as well as by the discovery of ancient Indian story-books and still older Buddhist collections, which has made it now somewhat out of date. An English rendering of Dr Liebrecht's notes to his German translation of Dunlop's work is much to be desired.

Keightley's little book, entitled 'Tales and Popular Fictions,' together with some able articles on the same subject which appeared in the 'Quarterly' and the 'Foreign Quarterly' Reviews shortly before it was published (about fifty years ago), must have helped to promote a more wide-spread interest in the question of the origin and diffusion of folk-tales; and the writers deserve all praise for having made the most of the materials within their reach. Those materials were, however, very scanty in comparison with the great mass that has since accumulated, by means of which the storiologist is enabled to "survey *folk-tales* from China to Peru." Not only have several of the oldest and most important Asiatic story-books been translated into English and other European languages, but oral tales and legends have been " taken down from the mouths of the people" in several parts of India: in the Panjáb and Kashmír, by Mrs Steel and Captain R. C. Temple; in Bengal, by Mr C. H. Damant and Rev. Lal Behari Day; in Southern India, by Pandit S. M. Natésa Sástrí.

Such a task as tracing through a great number of versions, or variants, the favourite story of Aladdin and his Lamp (in the first volume of this work—and a Buddhist version will be found in the Appendix); the Egyptian legend of the Robbery of the King's Treasury; the Irish legend of Little Fairly; the tale of the Lady and her Suitors; the story of the Three Knights and the Lady, and that of the Three Hunchbacks; and Chaucer's "Pardoner's Tale" (in the second volume)—was quite impossible in the time of Keightley, not to mention Dunlop. Of those two writers the former seems to have been as diffident of expressing an opinion regarding the probable extraction of a tale as the latter was unhesitating; the consequence of which is that neither is a safe guide to the young student of the history of popular fictions: Keightley being on the whole calculated to induce false theories of their transmission—in fact, he often appears to favour the absurd notion of their independent invention; while Dunlop, in his ignorance of the dates and sources of such Eastern story-books as he knew from translations, is very misleading, ascribing the originals of certain tales to works which are by no means either ancient or "original." Dunlop is perhaps to be trusted in his accounts of the romances of chivalry and the early Italian novels, but when he states their sources he is to be received with caution. Nevertheless, both Dunlop's book and that of Keightley (and the 'Fairy Mythology' of the latter may be included) are good pieces of work: a man cannot tell more than he knows or than is known at the time of his writing: and they can hardly fail of instructing the reader, and also of inciting him to pursue similar researches for himself. With greatly superior advantages in these days, when the results of the investigations of many learned and laborious scholars have been published, the present volumes are designed, not to bolster up any pet theory regarding the transmission of popular tales, but to supply materials from which those interested in the question may draw their own conclusions, as well as to furnish a collection of entertaining stories.

I may mention that a goodly number of the tales cited in this work appear in English for the first time, while by far the greater portion will probably be quite new to the ordinary reader. Some "discoveries" I believe I have made in the course of my researches: links which were wanted to unite European stories with their Asiatic originals or prototypes; and, occasionally, hitherto unknown sources, or at least Eastern variants, of our household tales. In a work such as this errors both of omission and commission are unavoidable; so frequently is one story found to run into another, with which it had originally no connection, that it is exceedingly difficult to "pigeon-hole" all semi-analogous incidents for the purpose of their being cited in their proper places. The tabulation, or classification, of folk-tales formed no part of my plan; that is being done by members of the Folk-Lore Society, and may be safely left in their able hands.

There are perhaps still some amongst us who think—and not so very long since they were in a small minority who thought otherwise—that our nursery and popular tales are utterly unworthy of consideration by "sensible, practical" men. But it has been well remarked that "any kind of writing, how trifling soever, that obtains general currency, and especially that early preoccupies the imagination of the youth of both sexes, must demand particular attention: its influence is likely to be considerable both on the morals and the taste of a nation." Sir John Malcolm's observation on the same subject is to the like effect: "He who desires to be well acquainted with a people will not reject their popular stories and superstitions." And I may add that a comparative study of folk-tales, apart from its great linguistic value, is calculated to enlarge the mind, and when assiduously prosecuted, broaden our sympathies, and enable us to recognise, more fully, perhaps, than could anything else, the universal brotherhood of mankind.

My task, if arduous, has been a most pleasant one—in truth, a labour of love; and I must not conclude these prefatory remarks without gratefully acknowledging my obligations to Dr Reinhold Rost, for the loan of scarce books from the Library of the India Office and important suggestions; to Mr F. F. Arbuthnot—author of 'Early Ideas: a Group of Hindoo Stories'—for the use of unpublished translations of Indian story-books; and to my learned and amiable friend Dr David Ross, Principal of the E. C. Training College, Glasgow, for much valuable assistance. I am also

greatly indebted to the courtesy of Mr E. B. Nicholson, of the Bodleian
Library, Oxford; to Mr F. T. Barrett, of the Mitchell Public Library,
Glasgow; and especially to Mr James Lymburn, of the Glasgow University
Library, who cheerfully helped me in my researches at that rich literary treasury.

W. A. C.

November, 1886.

~

Popular Tales and Fictions.

INTRODUCTION

———

SOLOMON'S oft-quoted dictum that "there is nothing new under the sun" may be safely applied to the popular tales and fictions of Europe; indeed, as an able writer has remarked, "to invent what has not been invented before may be no less difficult than it was, in Mr Shandy's opinion, to curse out of the comprehensive digest of Ernulphus." By far the greater number of the apologues and stories which are common to all Europe have been current in Asia from a very remote period; and it is certainly one of the most interesting chapters of the history of the human mind to trace those fictions, which furnished instruction as well as amusement to our simple ancestors, through their various forms, to ancient if not always to their primitive sources. Their independent invention and development, by persons living in countries and in times far apart, is, as Sir George Cox justly observes, "what no reasonable man could have the hardihood to maintain."

The question of their origin and diffusion has for more than half a century specially engaged the energies of distinguished European scholars, but there still exists very considerable diversity of opinion on the subject. In Germany, such eminent *savans* as Benfey, Gödeke, Köhler, Nöldeke, and Liebrecht maintain that our popular tales, which are current from Norway to Spain, from Italy to the West Highlands of Scotland, are simply secondary forms of Oriental originals, which were imported from Asia in different ways: for the south of Europe this was done through the Turks; for the north, by the Mongolians during their two hundred years of supremacy. In England, it is contended by Dasent, Baring-Gould, Cox, and other scholars, that they are survivals of primitive myths and legends, the common heritage of the whole Aryan race, and came to Europe with the tribes when they migrated westwards and northwards, at some very remote period—just as the languages of Europe are Aryan.

The "solar myth" theory is carried by some of our comparative mythologists to the verge of absurdity. For example, a writer in the 'Westminster Review,' in an article on Mr Swynnerton's 'Adventures of the Panjáb hero, Rájá Rasálú,' asserts that "no one at all acquainted with the science of comparative mythology can for a moment doubt" that King Rasálú is a solar myth. Thus, as the sun in his course rests not in toiling and travelling, so Rasálú's destiny forbade him to tarry in one place. And as the sun, after a battle, however tremendous, with the elements, shines forth clear and victorious, so Rasálú, after a series of magical thunderbolts hurled at him by the giants, is found, shortly after, calm and undaunted. Hence Rasálú is considered as merely another form of the fables of Indra, Savitar, Woden, Sisyphus, Hercules, Samson, Apollo, Theseus, Sigwid, Arthur, Tristram, and a host of other heroes, with one or other of whom every country, civilised and uncivilised, is familiar. These and similar fanciful analogies are, according to an acute Anglo-Indian scholar, simply imagination running riot: and "if comparative mythology is a science at all, it must at least show that its assertions are capable of proof. Is there," he asks, "a shadow of a proof, properly so called, of any of these statements? Can the history of the stories [of Rasálú] as told at the present day be carried back, step by step, to the solar myth and its development into ordinary folk-lore? Has anything regarding Rasálú been yet discovered which will give even a hint of such development? What if it can be shown that the stories our scientific comparative mythologist has thus strung together form merely a part of the stories told of the so-called solar hero, and that the same stories are not told of him in different localities, and that all those he has put into one category to suit his theory are not told in any one locality? What if it can be shown that some of the stories are the common property of every Indian village, and are told singly, in many a variant form, from Kashmír to Bombay? What if it can be shown that there is many another story of Rasálú, which the liveliest imagination could not twist into the battle of the elements, or the action of the sun, or moon, or dawn, or any other natural phenomenon that might occur to it, and that we have absolutely no reason for not receiving them as genuine tales about Rasálú, if we receive as such those quoted [by the reviewer]?" The ordinary mythologist, the same writer adds, "lets his imagination loose to follow its own way, and, presto! the thing is done and his point is proved. The hero beats his enemies—which, by the way, he usually does in a story—and it is the sun conquering the storm-clouds! He has one adventure after another, and it is the sun running his course across the sky. He is mortally wounded, and gets over it, perhaps miraculously, and it is the sun setting and rising. He has a long white beard, and it is the winter clothing of the forest. He has twenty sons, all minor heroes, and these are the lightning flashes. His wife runs away with somebody else, on whom he wreaks prompt vengeance, and it is the evening conquered by the night, who, in turn, is slain by the returning sun. What is simpler, and what more beautiful? 'No one at all acquainted with the science of comparative mythology can for a moment doubt' any of these, especially when they have been applied to story after story all the world over with signal success. Granting the beauty, the ingenuity, and the aptness of the ideas thus evolved, there are still those fortunately who are not satisfied with them, until it is proved, in the ordinary way, that any particular hero is a solar myth."[1]

That tales and legends of a more or less supernatural cast, dealing with magical arts (and the phenomena of physical nature, too, perhaps), in other words, our nursery fairy tales, which are found in almost identical forms, allowing for occasional local modifications and colouring, among peoples differing so much in their customs and modes of thought as the Norwegians and the Italians, are reflections or survivals of primitive Aryan traditions, which also continue current in Asiatic countries, may, I think, be to some extent granted. But the case is very different when we consider the question of the origin and diffusion of tales which have in them nothing of the supernatural—tales, namely, of common life. If we admit the theory as well founded that our fairy tales were, for the most part, brought to Europe when our remote ancestors, during the "childhood of the world," migrated from their Asian homes, most assuredly the storehouse of European folk-lore and folk-tales was largely augmented otherwise in more recent times.

Thanks to the assiduity of modern scholars, the proofs of the Asiatic origin of a very great number of our popular tales and fictions are abundant and conclusive. "The evidence adduced," says Dr H. H. Wilson, "has been of the most positive description. It is not built upon probabilities, upon general and indefinite analogies, or on partial and accidental resemblances, but upon actual identities. Although modifications have been practised, names altered, scenes changed, circumstances added or omitted, we can still discern the sameness of the fundamental outline,

---

[1] "Legends of Rájá Rasálú." By Captain R. C. Temple.—'Calcutta Review,' 1884.

and amidst all the multiplications of masquerade, lay our hands, without hesitation, upon the authentic individual. We can also, in many instances, follow the steps of the migration which the narratives have undergone, and determine when, and by what means, these Asiatic adventurers were naturalised in the different countries of Europe in which they are found."

It is not unusual for the first introduction of Asiatic fictions into Europe to be ascribed to the vast hordes of pilgrims and others who flocked to the East during the Crusades, and doubtless they helped considerably to swell the stock. But the transmission had begun at a much earlier date, and many apologues and narratives of Eastern origin had found their way to Europe long before Peter the Hermit and Walter the Penniless were born. From the early ages of Christianity down to the fifteenth century, the intercourse with the East, through commerce, literature, religion, and war, "was much more intimate and frequent," says Dr H. H. Wilson, "than it has ever been since. The greater proximity of Asia Minor to the countries of the south of Europe," he goes on to say, "was one especial cause of the more intimate intercourse that subsisted between them; and the greater parity of civilisation—in which indeed the Asiatics had rather the advantage—was another. The political relations of the divisions of the Eastern and Western Empire necessarily preserved the provinces of either in a communication with each other which could not speedily be forgotten; and although interrupted by the first violences of the Muhammedan conquest, it was readily resumed when the storm had passed, and the first Khalífs of the house of Abbas encouraged the resort of merchants and scholars, both from the east and the west, to Baghdád. Upon their decline followed the Crusades, and the interest which they attracted to the scene of their achievements, and the numbers that, as soldiers, or pilgrims, or traders, were constantly passing to and fro, continued to preserve that interest from decay, and were no doubt actively concerned in importing and disseminating the lighter Oriental fictions of domestic life as well as of chivalry and romance. . . . From the period subsequent to the establishment of the Khalífate, Europe received whatever literary articles were imported from the East through the medium of the Arabs. This did not imply that they were of Arab manufacture exclusively. The subjugation of Persia placed at the disposal of the Arabs whatever treasures they chose to spare from the destruction to which the mass was condemned; and it is upon record that the first Abbaside Khalífs, in the eighth and ninth centuries, from Al-Mansúr to

Al-Mamún, patronised in an especial manner the natives of India, and that Hindús of eminence in various branches of literature and science flourished at their courts."

Narratives of Indian, Persian, and Arabian origin were no doubt chiefly introduced into Europe orally; but some came through translations from Eastern books. Passing over the early spiritual romances, such as Barlaam and Josaphat, which were largely derived from Eastern, indeed Buddhist, sources, let us take, for instance, a work which was written, if not before the Crusades, certainly in the first years of the twelfth century, namely, the 'Disciplina Clericalis' of Peter Alfonsus, a Spanish Jew, who was baptised in 1106. This is a small collection of tales derived partly from the Hebrew Talmud—at all events several are found in that work, with which Alfonsus as a Jew was probably familiar—and partly from the Arabian fablers. To this work of Alfonsus the Trouvères, or minstrels of Northern France, were indebted for the groundwork of a number of their entertaining *fabliaux*, though it is very probable that they themselves brought from the East the substance of many of their tales, which were afterwards adopted by the early Italian novelists. A Greek translation of the celebrated Fables of Bidpai, or Pilpay, entitled 'Ichnelates and Stephanites,' was made by Symeon, son of Seth, about the year 1080, from an Arabic version, 'Kalíla and Dimna,' made from an old Persian translation of the Sanskrit original, which is lost. (About the year 1250, Rabbi Joel translated the Arabic version into Hebrew, from which John of Capua soon after composed a Latin version, 'Directorium Humanae Vitæ.') Next among translations from Eastern story-books may be mentioned 'Syntipas,' a Greek rendering of a Syriac version of the 'Book of Sindibád,' the prototype of our 'History of the Seven Wise Masters,' made probably during the last decade of the eleventh century. About the year 1184, what is thought to be the first European version, or rather imitation, of the 'Book of Sindibad'—soon followed by a host of others—was composed, in Latin prose, by a monk named Johannes of the Abbey of Alta Silva, in the French diocese of Nancy, under the title of 'Dolopathos; sive, de Rege et Septem Sapientibus' (Dolopathos; or, the King and the Seven Sages). The frame, or leading story, of this work corresponds with that of its Eastern original, but it has only one of the subordinate tales, though all of them are undoubtedly of Asiatic origin. In the thirteenth century this Latin prose 'Dolopathos' was rendered into French verse, under the same title, by a Trouvère named Herbers; and other Latin and French prose versions of the 'Seven Wise Masters' were afterwards produced.

li

Manuscripts of more than one early English metrical text of this widely popular romance are preserved in our great libraries.[2]

Thus, before the tide of Eastern fiction flowing into Europe had begun to be swelled by the Crusaders and pilgrims returning from the Holy Land, we see there existed at least two works of Asiatic origin which were not imported by oral tradition. But even in the case of the tales comprised in these and similar books, their dissemination among the people, as well as that of hundreds of other tales, must have been mainly through the pulpit, for the preachers in mediæval times liberally interspersed their sermons with stories, and not always stories of the most edifying tendency. Moreover, monks and other churchmen were constantly travelling about; and we may readily conceive that a jolly friar, or "clerk of Oxenford," when he sought and obtained a night's lodging at the hospitable domicile of some yeoman or simple rustic, would find he was doubly welcome if he had good store of marvellous, pathetic, and humorous tales to relate to those assembled round his host's cheerful fireside. By such means stories, which had their birth in the Far East more than two thousand years ago, spread into the remotest nooks of Europe; and jests, which had long shaken the shoulders and wagged the beards of grave and otiose Orientals, became naturalised from cold Sweden to sunny Italy. From oral tradition they were absorbed into literature, whence again they returned to the people; and after being, to all appearance, lost in the revolutions and political turmoils that followed the invention of printing, suddenly "turned up" again in the jest-books of the sixteenth and seventeenth centuries.

---

[2]The leading story of the 'Book of Sindibád,' or the 'Seven Wise Masters,' is briefly as follows: A young prince having resisted the importunities of one of his father's favourite women—his stepmother in the European versions—like the wife of Potiphar with Joseph, she accuses him to the king of having attempted her chastity. The king condemns his son to death; but the seven vazírs (or wise men) of the king, believing the prince to be innocent, and knowing that he is compelled by the threatening aspect of his horoscope to remain silent for seven days, resolve to save him till the expiry of that period, by each in turn relating to the king stories showing the depravity of women, and the danger of acting upon their unsupported assertions. This they do accordingly, but the woman each night counteracts the effect of their tales, by relating stories of the deceitful disposition of men; and so each day the king alternately condemns and reprieves his son, until the end of the seventh day, when the prince is free to speak again, and the woman's guilt being discovered, she is duly punished. A compendious account of the several Eastern versions of this romance is given in the Introduction to my editions (from the Arabic and Persian) of the 'Book of Sindibád,' and in the Appendix, abstracts of an early English text of the 'Seven Wise Masters' and the Latin 'Dolopathos.'

Much has been done of late years, especially by Continental scholars, towards elucidating the genealogy of popular tales, but more yet remains to be done in this field of research, which is indeed

> Exceeding rich, and long, and wide,
> And sprinkled with a sweet variety
> Of all that pleasant is to the ear or eye.

It is probable that fresh light would be thrown upon the means through which Oriental fictions were diffused over Europe, were more attention bestowed on the examination of the monkish collections of sermons and tales designed for the use of preachers. A very promising beginning, for English readers, has been made in this direction by Professor T. F. Crane, of Cornell University, N.Y., who, in March 1883, read before the American Philosophical Society a very learned, elaborate, and interesting paper on "Mediæval Sermon-Books and Stories," which has been reprinted from the 'Proceedings' of that Society. The first to regularly employ in sermons *exempla*, or narratives to instruct the people, as well as to keep up their attention when it was likely to flag, was Jacques de Vitry, who died at Rome in the year 1240. This eminent prelate and scholar took part in the Crusades during several years, and was made Bishop of Accon (Acre), in Palestine, in 1217; and there can be little doubt that he brought home from the East many of the tales with which his 'Sermones de tempore et sanctis' are so plentifully larded. Next in point of time was Etienne de Bourbon, a monk of the Dominican order, who died at Lyons about the year 1261; whose great collection of stories, usually called 'Liber de Donis,'[3] was specially designed for preachers' use. This work, as well as the 'Sermones' of Jacques de Vitry, is of earlier date than the 'Gesta Romanorum,'

---

[3]The full title of this work is 'Tractatus de diversis materiis prædicabilibus, ordinatis et distinctis in septem partes, secundum septem dona Spiritus sancti et eorum affectus, currens per distinctiones materiarum, per causas et effectus, refertus auctoritatibus et rationibus et exemplis diversis ad edificationem pertinentibus animarum,' by Stephanus de Borbone. The work is a treatise on the seven gifts of the Holy Ghost (Isaiah xi. 2, 3), *Timor, Pietas, Scientia, Fortitudo, Consilium, Intellectus,* and *Sapientia,* whence it is also called 'Liber de Septem Donis.' —M. Lecoy de la Marche has printed copious extracts from this work under the title of 'Anecdotes historiques, Légendes et Apologues, tirés du recueil inédit d'Etienne de Bourbon, dominicain du XIIIe siècle, publiés pour la Société de l'Histoire de France.' Paris: 1877. The editor's notes to the stories are not, as Professor Crane has remarked, so full as might be desired, and several of the most interesting parallels have been overlooked; nevertheless this selection of Etienne's *exempla* will prove most useful to the student of storiology.

that great storehouse of "moralised" tales—that curious jumble of classical, Oriental, and Gothic fictions and legends—which was first composed, according to Oesterley, in England, about the close of the thirteenth century, and upon it was based another Latin work, with the same title, done on the Continent, soon after. "The influence of the 'Gesta' on English poetry," says Sir Frederick Madden, in his introduction to an early English translation (made probably in the reign of Henry VI.), which forms one of the publications of the Roxburghe Club, "was very considerable during the reign of Richard II. and his successors, and quite equal to the effect produced on the Italian novelists by the original Latin compilation. The poems of Gower, Chaucer, Occleve, and Lydgate furnish many instances of their familiarity with the work. . . . Of the value of the 'Gesta' in illustrating the incorporation of Eastern fable and classical stories with the feudal institutions of Europe, no one can doubt who has studied its pages; and it is entitled to more than a usual share of consideration as the only instance of a compilation formed in the retirement of a cloister which has, mediately or immediately, furnished to Boccaccio his tale of the 'Two Friends,' to Gower and Chaucer their 'History of Constance,' to Shakspeare his 'Merchant of Venice,' to Parnell his 'Hermit,' to Walpole his 'Mysterious Mother,' and to Schiller his 'Fridolin.'"

The 'Sermones' of Jacques de Vitry and the 'Liber de Donis' of Etienne de Bourbon being prior to the 'Gesta Romanorum,' they are of considerable value in tracing the diffusion of popular tales; moreover, the authors of the 'Gesta' were indebted to both these works, as well as to the 'Disciplina Clericalis' of Peter Alfonsus, for a number of stories. For instance, the story of the legitimate son who was recognised by refusing to shoot an arrow at the body of his dead father, though his two brothers had no such scruple, which forms chapter xlv. of the Continental 'Gesta' (translated by Swan into English), has been taken from the 'Liber de Donis,' No. 160. The original form of the story is found in the Talmud thus: "A man overheard his wife telling her daughter that though she had ten sons, only one of them could fairly claim her husband as his father. After the father's death it was found that he had bequeathed all his property to one son, but the testament did not mention his name. The question therefore arose, which of the ten was intended. So they came one and all to Rabbi Benaah, and asked him to arbitrate between them. 'Go,' said he to them, 'and beat at your father's grave until he rises to tell you to which of you he had left his property.' All except one did so, and he, because by so doing he showed most respect for his father's memory, was presumed to be the one on whom the father had fixed his affection. He was accordingly supposed to be the one intended, and the others were therefore excluded from the patrimony."[4] In the 'Gesta' we are told, there was a certain wise king who had "a beloved but not a loving wife"; she had three illegitimate sons, who proved ungrateful and rebellious. In course of time she had another son, about whose legitimacy there was no doubt. When the king died, "there arose strife among his surviving sons about the right of succession." At length they agree to refer the matter to "a certain honourable knight of the late king," who bids them draw out their father's body from the sepulchre, set it upright as a mark for their arrows, "and whosoever transfixes the heart of his father shall obtain the kingdom." The arrow of the first son wounded the king's right hand; that of the second son entered his mouth; and that of the third son pierced the heart; but the fourth son broke forth into a lamentable cry, and with eyes swimming in tears said, "O my poor father, have I lived to see thee the victim of an impious contest?" etc. So, as he would not shoot, the knight decided that he was the true son, and he was seated on his father's throne. This version is obscure at the beginning; but in No. 21 of the selection of mediæval Latin stories, edited by Wright for the Percy Society: "There was a man who had, as he thought, three sons by his wife. One day they quarrelled, and the woman said to her husband, 'You think these boys are yours, but in truth only one of them is your son.'" After his death, the man's "lord" sets the sons to shoot at his body: the third son says, "Is he not my father? I will not shoot at his body for the whole world. Ye may have all his property rather than that I give him a single blow." Then the lord said to him, "You are his true son, and shall have his property and wealth." Wright remarks that the first part of this tale bears some analogy to one in the old French collection, 'Cent Nouvelles Nouvelles,' 51, "Le vrais pères."[5]

---

[4]Hershon's 'Talmudic Miscellany,' p. 142, par. 29.

[5]About the same date as the version of Etienne de Bourbon, if not earlier, is the *fabliau* entitled "Le Jugement de Salomon" (Barbazan, ed. Méon, iii. 440; Le Grand, ed. 1783, ii. 419), in which, as the title indicates, the sage Hebrew king is the umpire in this singular contest. Herrtage, in his notes to his editions of the 'Gesta' published for the Early English Text Society, cites versions from Alexander Neckam's book, 'De Natura Rerum,' cap. clxxvi. p. 313, end of the 13th century; and from Zuinger's 'Theatrum Vitæ Humanæ,' Basil, 1586 (vol. vii. lib. iv. p. 1910). It also occurs in the great collection of John Bromyard, 'Summa Prædicantium,' v. *Filiatio*, end of the 14th century; in Herolt's 'Promptuarium Exemplorum'; and in the 'Sermones Dominicales' of John Felton, 1431 (Harl. MS. 4, leaf 256). The incident is also found in the 'History of Friar Bacon' (see Thoms' 'Early English Prose Roman ces,' i. 319); and Geuelette has made use of it in his so-called 'Contes Tartares.' Lastly, it is the subject of a ballad, probably of the early years of the 17th century (reprinted in J. Payne Collier's 'Book of Roxburghe Ballads,' 1847), entitled, 'A Pleasant History of a Gentleman in Thracia, which had four

Both De Vitry and De Bourbon have the well-known story of the old man and his two wives, one of whom plucked out all his grey hairs, the other all his black ones, and thus left him entirely bald. This is also in the Talmud. Allan Ramsay makes it the subject of one of his rhymed fables, No. 18, beginning thus:

> In ancient tales there is a story
> Of ane had twa wives, Whig and tory.
> The carlie's head was now attired
> With hairs in equal mixture lyart.
> His wives (faith, ane might well sufficed)
> Alternately was aye ill-pleased.

And so on, in this doggrel fashion; the "moral" he deduces being that between the two great political parties the country's interests suffer, as "between two stools," etc. It is very curious to see how the story has become garbled among the Chinese: "A man whose beard was turning grey had ordered his second wife to pull out all the white hairs. She, seeing that the white hairs were very numerous, set about pulling them out. As she could not manage to separate them, she pulled out at the same time all the black hairs. The task finished, the husband looked at himself in the mirror, and was filled with astonishment. He sharply rebuked his second wife, who said to him, 'Since I was to pull out the more numerous [class of hairs], why should I not have plucked out the scarcer [class]?'"[6]

In the 'Liber de Donis' (No. 507) is a story to the effect that Homer (*sic*), having been forbidden to enter the king's palace while clothed in a mean dress, presented himself one day in rich garments, and was honourably received, and obtained what he asked; but instead of thanking the king for the favour, he thanked his clothes. This is also told, among many others equally spurious, of Dante, and it is current in another form, as one

---

sonnes, and three of them were none of his own: shewing how miraculously the True Heire came to his inheritance.' The affinity of this widely popular mediæval tale with the celebrated Judgment of Solomon as related in the First Book of Kings, ch. iii. 16ff., is very obvious; and the incident of the two women contending for the living child forms the subject of one of the *Játakas,* or Buddhist Birth-Stories: see Dr Rhys David's translation, vol. i. pp. xiv-xvi, and his remarks thereon, pp. xliv–xlvii.

[6]From a selection of Chinese Tales and Fables appended to the 'Avadánas' (Indian Tales and Apologues), translated from the Chinese into French by Stanislas Julien: Paris, 1859.

of the foolish things done by Giufà, the typical noodle of Sicily; of the Khoja Nasr-ed-Dín Efendi, in the collection of Turkish jests ascribed to that typical simpleton of the Ottomans; and of a learned man, in Gladwin's 'Persian Moonshee.'

Another of the entertaining stories in the 'Liber de Donis' (also in De Vitry's 'Sermones') is of an innkeeper who used to tip over his customers' wine, as if by mere accident, and then remind them facetiously that, according to the old saying, this accident was a sign of good luck (*"Hoc significat, abundanciam que veniet vobis, et bonam fortunam"*); but a pilgrim, to whom this had been done, privately opened the spigot of the cask, and repeated to the host his own favourite saying. This droll incident was made the subject of a *fabliau,* and from it adopted by the Italian novelists. It also forms No. 29 of the 'Novellette di San Bernardino,' and 372 of Pauli, 'Schimpf and Ernst.' The *fabliau* has been rendered by Way, from Le Grand, as follows:

> When Acre yielded to the hostile host
> ('Twas but a year or two ago at most),
> A pleasant chance in Normandy befell,
> Which, as my memory serves, I mean to tell.
>
> A needy bachelor had dwelling there,
> Of worldly means in sooth so passing bare,
> He once was fain his dinner-meal to make
> On the poor pittance of a farthing cake.
> To help this miserable morsel down,
> He hies him to a tavern in the town,
> And bade the vintner, as he meant to dine,
> To draw him straight a farthing's worth of wine.
> The vintner (one, it seems, of churlish kind,
> Who cared but little how his neighbour dined)
> From the next vessel filled his measure up,
> And, as he poured it thence into a cup,
> Slubbered with such ill-grace the business o'er,
> That half the draught was spilled upon the floor.
> To crown the deed, with supercilious pride,
> "You'll soon grow rich, Sir Bachelor," he cried;
> "Wine spilt, they say (be't true or falsely spoken),
> Some sequent good doth evermore betoken!"

The Norman deemed it were but labour lost
To chafe or wrangle with his boorish host;
His wit to artifice he wisely bent,
And thus devised the caitiff's punishment:

In his poor purse remained one farthing still;
This, with frank guise, as one who thought no ill,
He tendered to his host, so would he please
To furnish him a farthing slice of cheese.
Up to the loft, where all his cheeses lay,
The vintner hied, but muttering all the way;
That self-same instant turned the knight about,
And from the wine-cask pulled the spigot out;
Forth gushed the gurgling liquor, bright and good,
And the wide floor was deluged with the flood.
Back sped the host, and, furious at the sight,
First pegged his cask, and next assailed the knight;
But the strong Norman sternly shook the thrall,
Hurled back, and crushed the wine-pots with his fall;
And, but that entering neighbours quelled the fray,
The vintner then had seen his dying day.

The matter soon was to the king made known
(Count Henry of Champagne possessed the throne);
And first the plaintive vintner stoutly spoke,
And claimed redress—wine lost and vessels broke.
The Prince doomed not the knight to recompense,
But willed him first to argue his defence.
He the plain truth from end to end exposed,
Then with these words his frank recital closed:
"Great sire!" he said, "this worthy host of mine
Foretold much good would spring from spilling wine;
That I, forsooth, whose cup was half thrown down,
Should soon become the wealthiest wight in town.
My gratitude, I own, o'ercame me here,
And, weeping wealth might ne'er be bought too dear,
I strove to make him richer than myself,
And shed full half a cask to purchase pelf!"

He ceased: loud plaudits rang through all the court;
No tale was ever told so full of sport;
All ranged them seemly by the Norman's side,
While good King Henry laughed until he cried;
Then thus dismissed the parties and their suit:
"What's spilt is spilt, betide or bale or boot."

Dr Johnson said that a tavern chair is the seat of human felicity: "the more you call for, the more welcome you are;" and no doubt this is very true—when you have money to spend. But "mine host" can be very churlish as well as very obsequious; and certainly the poor gentleman in this tale did *not* "find his warmest welcome at an inn." There is a fine stroke of humour in representing the furious taverner, on discovering the wanton waste of his good liquor, as taking care to replace the spigot before falling foul of his enemy: he did not permit his anger to overcome his notions of economy!

Parnell composed his once very popular poetical tale of 'The Hermit' from chapter lxxx. of the 'Gesta Romanorum,' into which it was probably taken either from the 'Sermones' of Jacques de Vitry or the 'Liber de Donis' of Etienne de Bourbon. It should seem that the 'Gesta' story was not known to Thomas Bradwardine, confessor to Edward III., who died in 1349, a few weeks after he was consecrated Archbishop of Canterbury, since he cites it on the authority of De Vitry (Jacobus de Vitriaco) in his 'De Causa Dei contra Pelagium.' In this story, a hermit has begun to question the equity of God's providence—wicked men being permitted to prosper, and good men to be afflicted. To remove his doubts, an angel is sent from heaven, and they journey together. The first night they lodge in the house of a very pious man, and in the morning the angel takes with him from the house a great cup of gold. Next night they lodged in the house of another holy man, and in the morning the angel, before his departure, killed an infant in the cradle, who was the only son of their host. The third night they came to a house where they were also freely entertained, and when they departed in the morning, the master of the house sent with them his steward, whose fidelity he highly prized, in order to show them the way. As they were going over a bridge, the angel flung the steward into the river, and he was drowned. The fourth night they met with very untoward entertainment at a wicked man's house; yet next morning the angel gave him the cup of gold. Then he explained all his strange actions to the hermit: He had taken away the cup from the first

pious host, because, drinking from it every morning, he became somewhat unfit for his holy duties, though not so much that others or himself perceived it; and it was better for him to lose his cup than his
temperance. He had killed the only child of the second good man, because since it was born he had given but little to the poor, and become
eager to lay up money for his child; but now the child was taken to
heaven, the father would serve God better upon earth. The steward,
drowned by the angel, had plotted to kill his master the night following. And as for the wicked man, as he was to have nothing in the next
world, the angel gave him something in this, which, however, would
prove a snare to him, for he would become more intemperate.—The
story is also found in some recensions of the 'Vitae Patrum,' whence it
may have been taken by Jacques de Vitry, one version of which is regarded by M. Gaston Paris as the origin of the mediæval variants. It
reappeared in John Herolt's 'Sermones de tempore,' printed at Nurem-
berg in 1496. It also occurs, in a paraphrastic form, with some variations, and an interpolated incident, in Sir Percy Herbert's 'Certain
Conceptions or Considerations,' etc., published in 1652. The substance
of Herbert's narrative Howell copied in a letter "To my Lord Marquis
of Hertford," and printed in an early edition of his 'Epistolæ Ho-
Elianæ.' Besides transpositions and some alterations of the circumstances, which Bradwardine, after De Vitry, allotted to the four days,
Howell (eleventh edition, 1754) has the following addition: "The fifth
day they came to a great rich town, but some miles before they came
to it, they met with a merchant at the close of the day, who had a great
charge of money about him; and asking the next passage to the town,
the young man put him in a clean contrary way. The anchorite and his
guide being come to the town, at the gate they spied a devil, who lay
as it were sentinel, but he was asleep. They found also both men and
women at sundry kinds of sports, some dancing, others singing, with
divers sorts of revellings. They went afterwards to a convent of Ca-
puchins, where about the gate they found legions of devils laying siege
to that monastery." At the conclusion of the angel's *dénouement,* we are
informed that the merchant was misdirected that he might avoid a
band of ruffians prepared to rob and murder him; that the "great luxurious city is so much at Lucifer's devotion that he needs but one single sentinel to secure it, and even he may safely sleep upon his guard."
On the contrary, "to the monastery inhabited by so many devout souls,
in vain hath he brought so many legions to beleaguer it; for they bear

up against him most undauntedly, maugre all his infernal power and stratagems."[7]

The original form is found in the Talmud: Rabbi Jochanan, the son of Levi, accompanies Elijah, who had returned to earth, in his travels, and the incidents are: The only cow of a poor man drops dead, in response to Elijah's prayer; the saint causes a carpenter to repair the wall of a house, the master of which, a haughty and wealthy man, had treated them with little hospitality; entering a synagogue, Elijah called out, "Who is here willing to feed and lodge two poor men?" But none answered, and no respect was shown to them. In the morning he re-entered the synagogue, and embracing the members, said, "I wish that you may all become presidents." Next evening the members of the synagogue in another city sent them to the best inn, where they were entertained with honour; and in the morning Elijah, on parting with them, said, "May you have but one president." Rabbi Jochanan could no longer restrain his curiosity. "Tell me," said he to Elijah, "the meaning of all these actions which I have witnessed. To those who have treated us coldly, thou hast uttered good wishes; to those who have been gracious to us, thou hast made no suitable return." Then Elijah said, "We first entered the house of the poor man, who treated us kindly. It had been decreed on that very day that his wife should die. I prayed unto the Lord that the cow might prove a redemption for her; God granted my prayers, and the woman was preserved unto her husband. The rich man who treated us coldly, his wall I repaired, without a new foundation, and without digging into the old one; had he repaired it himself, he would have dug, and thus discovered a treasure which lies buried, but which is now for ever lost to him. To the members of the synagogue who were inhospitable I said, 'May you be all presidents,' for where many rule there can be no peace; but to the others I said, 'May you have but one president,' for with one leader no misunderstanding may arise. Now, if thou seest the wicked prospering, be not

---

[7]In the 'Contes Devots' we have one of the earliest European versions under the title of "L'hermite qu'un ange conduisit dans le siècle." Here the incidents are: a porcelain cup taken from the abode of a recluse, and afterwards given to a miser whose servant had sheltered the two travellers; a rich abbey set on fire by the angel, because the monks had become lazy, luxurious, and regardless of their religious duties: now they would rebuild their monastery in humbler style, and live frugally and piously; and the drowning of the son of a rich but good man. See Le Grand's 'Fabliaux, ou Contes, du XIIe et du XIIIe siècle;' Paris, 1781; tome v. pp. 211–223.

envious; if thou seest the righteous in poverty and trouble, be not provoked or doubtful of God's justice."[8]

Another talmudic legend is related of Moses while on Mount Sinai: Moses having complained of the impunity of vice and its success in this world, and the frequent sufferings of the innocent, the Lord took him to a rock which projected from the mountain, where he could overlook the plain of the desert stretching at his feet. On one of the oases he beheld a young Arab asleep. He awoke, and leaving behind him a bag of pearls, he sprang into his saddle, and rapidly disappeared from the horizon. Another Arab came to the oasis; he discovered the pearls, took them, and went away in the opposite direction. Now an aged wanderer, leaning on his staff, bent his weary steps towards the shady spot. He laid himself down and went asleep; but scarcely had he closed his eyes when he was rudely roused from his slumber: the young Arab had returned and demanded his pearls. The hoary man replied that he had not taken them. The other grew enraged, and accused him of theft. He swore that he had not seen the treasure, but the other seized him, and a scuffle ensued. The young Arab drew his sword, and plunged it into the breast of the aged man, who fell lifeless on the earth. "O Lord, is this justice?" exclaimed Moses in horror. "Be silent!" said the Lord. "Behold, this man, whose blood is now mingling with the waters of the desert, many years ago, secretly and on the same spot, murdered the father of the youth who has now slain him. His crime remained concealed from man: but vengeance is mine; I will repay."[9]

From some of the Arabian Jews it is probable that Muhammed derived the story, which he reproduces in the eighteenth chapter of the Kur'án, where it is told, with variations, of Moses and the prophet Khizar.[10] In the course of their wanderings they came to the seaside, where they went up into a ship, and Khizar made a hole therein. Then they met a youth, and he slew him. Coming to a city, they were refused food by the inhab-

---

[8]'The Talmud' (selections translated), by H. Polano, p. 313.

[9]Dr Weil's 'The Bible, the Koran, and the Talmud,' pp. 134, 135; note by English translator. See also Lane's 'Arabian Nights,' ii. 577.

[10]According to the Eastern legend, Khizar was despatched by an ancient Persian king to procure him some of the Water of Life. After a tedious journey, he reached the Fountain of Immortality, and having drank of its waters, they suddenly vanished. It is believed that Khizar still lives, and occasionally appears to favoured individuals, always clothed in green, and acts as their guide in difficult adventures. Khizar is often confounded with Moses, Elias, and even St George. The name Khizar signifies *green*. From my 'Book of Sindibád,' p. 41.

itants; and Khizar, seeing a wall that was ready to fall down, set it upright. Moses desires an explanation of these things, and he is told that the vessel belonged to certain poor men who did their business in the sea; and Khizar rendered it unserviceable because a king took every sound ship for his own use. As to the youth, his parents were true believers, and he, being an unbeliever, was slain, lest his parents should suffer from his perverseness and ingratitude. The wall belonged to two orphan youths in the city, and in it was a treasure hidden that belonged to them; their father was a righteous man, and the Lord was pleased that they should attain their full age, and take forth their treasure. In the Turkish book of the 'Forty Vazírs,' this Muslim version is reproduced as the Lady's 29th Tale.

Parnell's poems were first published by Pope in 1721, two years after the author's death. The invention of the tale of the 'Hermit' had been generally credited to Parnell till Goldsmith wrote his Life, prefixed to an enlarged edition of his poems, in 1773. From Pope, in Spence's Anecdotes, Goldsmith relates (and the opinion is adopted implicitly by Johnson) that the story was written originally in Spanish, whence, probably, Howell translated it into prose, and inserted it in his letters. He adds that "Dr Henry More, in his 'Dialogues,' has the very same story," and that he "had been informed by some that it is originally of Arabian invention." We have seen, however, that it is of Hebrew origin, so far as has been ascertained; and Parnell doubtless found it in the English translation of the 'Gesta Romanorum' published in 1703. Voltaire reproduces this famous story in his 'Zadig,' chapter xvii., where the "philosopher" accompanies an angel disguised as a hermit, who steals a gold cup from a man who was ostentatious of his wealth and hospitality, and gives it to a miserly old fellow; burns down the house of a man who had treated them kindly; and drowns the nephew of a widow who had entertained them most honourably. The angel explains to Zadig that the cup was taken from the owner in order to reform his pride, and given to the miserly man to excite his generosity; the good man finds a treasure beneath the ashes of his burned house; and the widow's son, had he lived another year, would have been her murderer. Some have supposed that Voltaire copied his apologue from Parnell; but the same story had previously been employed by Antoinette Bourignon the mystic. It is not unlikely that Jacques de Vitry, who seems to have first introduced it into Europe, heard the story while he was in Syria.[11]

---

[11] This legend has become a popular tale: see the 'Sicilianische Märchen' of Laura von Gonzenbach, No. 92, and De Trueba, 'Narraciones populares,' p. 65.

The stratagem employed by Sancho Panza, while governor of Bar-rataria ('Don Quixote,' ii. 45), to discover whether a young man had done violence to a certain woman, is found in Jacques de Vitry and Etienne de Bourbon. This is also in Wright's Latin Stories (No. 20), edited for the Percy Society, where it is thus related: I have heard of a certain woman, who was complaining before a judge of a certain young man, who, so she said, had overpowered and violated her. The youth denied the charge. "Give her," said the judge to him, "ten marks of silver, as a recompense for the violence you have offered her." Having got the money, she went off joyful. Then the judge said to the youth, "Follow her, and take the money from her." The young man tried to fulfil the command of the judge, and to take the money from her. But she began bravely to beat him off, and to call out, and many people running up, he was unable to hurt her. Both were again brought before the judge. "Woman," said he, "what is the matter with you? What do you want? Why were you clamouring so loudly?" She said, "Because, my lord, he was trying to take my money from me; but I beat him off bravely, and cried out so that he could not succeed." "Then," said the judge, "give the money back to the youth; for if you had beaten him off and called out so bravely before, he could never have violated you: you love money more than purity." This is imitated in the Italian novels of Malespini, Part ii. No. 56, and in the 'Cent Nouvelles Nouvelles,' 25, "Forcée de Gré." That the story is of Asiatic origin seems probable from its being one of the Pleasing Tales in Gladwin's 'Persian Moonshee,' and from its occurring in several Indian story-books.

The famous tale of the Widow who was Comforted which forms one of the stories of the 'Seven Wise Masters,' though it does not occur in the oldest European version of the romance, the Latin 'Dolopathos,' is found in the 'Sermones de tempore et sanctis' of Jacques de Vitry, and the 'Liber de Donis' of Etienne de Bourbon. A man who was very fond of his wife, while jesting with her one day, chanced to wound her slightly in the hand, at which he was so grieved that he died the following day. His widow was inconsolable; and after he was buried, she took up her abode beside his grave, and, refusing food, continued weeping and wringing her hands. When night came on, she made a good fire, for the weather was very cold. Now the bodies of three thieves were hanging on gibbets not far from the place, and a knight had to watch that they were not stolen by their friends, as quit-rent for his lands. Seeing the bright fire, he alighted from his horse, and approached to warm himself. He was both young and comely, and the widow was induced by his soothing speeches to abate somewhat of her excessive sorrow, and partake of some food which he pressed on her; then, fortified with a draught of wine, she yielded him her love. After a time, the knight quitted the widow whom he had comforted, and returned to his ghastly charge, when, to his dismay, he discovered that one of the bodies had been taken away. Going back to the widow, he told her that in consequence of this he should lose his lands. She bade him be of good cheer, for his heritage need not be lost for such a trifling matter; he had only to take up the body of her husband and hang it in place of that of the thief which had been stolen. But, says the knight, the thief had a great wound on his head. She replied, that he should make a similar wound on the head of her husband. Nay, quoth the knight, I could never strike a dead man; whereupon the widow took a sharp knife and wounded the head of her husband: and when the knight recollected that the thief had lost two of his front teeth, she immediately knocked out two of her husband's teeth with a stone. The body being hung on the gallows, the knight, according to some versions, sternly upbraided the widow for her levity and heartlessness, since her husband had died because he had accidentally shed a few drops of her blood, but she had not scrupled to mutilate his body, and so he would not unite himself to such a wanton.[12]

This was a favourite story of the *raconteurs* during the Middle Ages. The incident is the subject of a *fabliau* entitled "De la femme qui se fist putain sur la fosse de son mari," and Keller refers to many other versions in his "Einleitung," pp. CLIX–CLXVII, to the 'Romans des Sept Sages.'[13] It has been borrowed from the episode of the Matron of Ephesus, in Petronius Arbiter, where the grief-stricken widow, with her faithful maid, is represented as sitting in her husband's sepulchre with dishevelled hair and beating her bosom. The cause of her husband's death is not mentioned. Her relatives and friends in vain endeavoured to dissuade her from her

[12]In the 'Liber de Donis' of Etienne de Bourbon—who avowedly took the story from Jacques de Vitry—the body of the husband is not said to have been mutilated; but in another version of the same date, given by M. Lecoy de la Marche, in 'La Chaire française du moyen àge, spécialement au treizième siècle,' &c., in order that the body should correspond to that of the robber, a foot is cut off, an eye is plucked out, and the hair pulled off the head by "the widow who was comforted."

[13]It is found in the Talmud: When the widow is informed that the corpse has been taken away, she says, "Don't be alarmed; exhume the body of my husband, and hang it up instead." —(Hershon's 'Talmudic Miscellany,' p. 18, par. 30.) It occurs in the 'Cento Novelle Antiche,' the first collection of Italian tales. Eustace Deschamps reproduces it (14th century); St Evremonde, Lamote, and Fuselier each made it the subject of a comedy; it reappears in La Fontaine; it was taken into Æsop by Ogilvy; and Jeremy Taylor tells it in his 'Holy Dying.'

evident design of starving herself to death. All Ephesus bewailed the exemplary woman, who had been five days without food; when a soldier, who was guarding the bodies of some robbers crucified close by, observing the light of the lamp that burned in the tomb, was led to the spot by curiosity, and so on. The wounding of the husband's body does not occur. The story concludes with these verses:

> Give not your bark to the winds, nor your heart to the fair;
> More perfidious are they than the winds or the sea.
> They are all of them naught: if a good one was e'er,
> How a bad thing came good is a riddle to me.

Voltaire's tale of The Nose in 'Zadig' is similar to that of the Ephesian Widow, though he derived it from a different source: A lady had vowed she would not marry a second husband so long as the rivulet continued to flow past the grave of her lately deceased spouse, and was busy contriving to turn its course. Zadig's wife tells him of this, and professes her disgust at such heartlessness. Zadig, not long after, pretends to have died suddenly; his intimate friend visits the sorrowing lady, makes love to her, falls suddenly ill—the only cure is the nose of a dead man applied to the affected part; the lady takes a sharp knife, and repairs to her husband's tomb, with the intention of cutting off his nose, but Zadig gets up and scoffs at his wife's hollow professions of affection.

This Voltaire adapted from a tale related in Du Halde's 'Description of the Empire of China,' vol. ii. pp. 167–174. A philosopher called Chwang-tze had married three times: his first wife died; the second he divorced, because of her infidelity; the third is the subject of the tale, which is called 'Tyen,' from the lady's name. Chwang-tze having observed a widow fanning the earth over her husband's grave, he inquired of her the reason for such a strange proceeding, and she told him that she had promised her dying husband not to marry again before the earth of his grave was perfectly dry; "and now," she added, "as it has occurred to me that the surface of this ground, which has been newly tempered, would not very soon dry, I thought I would just fan it a little." The philosopher approved of her plan, and obtained her fan as a souvenir. Returning home, he told his wife of this adventure, and showed her the fan, which she snatched from him and tore into shreds, declaring the woman to be a heartless hussy;—for her own part, were he to die, she should never marry again. Shortly after this Chwang-tze became suddenly ill and died.

The lady was overpowered with grief. Preparations were made for the funeral; friends and acquaintances assembled at her house, amongst whom was a young and handsome student, attended by a servant. He informs the lady that he had purposed becoming a disciple of the late philosopher, and had come to attend his obsequies. The widow falls in love with him, and contrives to acquaint him of her passion through his old and faithful servant. After several objections which the student raised had been removed by the amorous widow, he consents to marry her, but suddenly falls into convulsions. His servant tells her that the only remedy is the brain of a man, recently dead, dissolved in wine. Quoth the lady readily, "My husband has been dead only a few days; open his coffin, and take the remedy from thence." The coffin was opened accordingly, when, to the consternation of the widow, the philosopher sat up, for he had only pretended to be dead, and had created all the scene by magical arts.[14]

Satirical tales of "widows' tears, which shrink, like Arno in the summer," are common in our old English jest-books. Thus in the 'Hundred Mery Talys' (the book referred to by Beatrice in "Much Ado about Nothing," when she says to Benedick, "Will you tell me who told you that I was disdainful, and that I had my good wit out of the Hundred Merry Tales?") is the story of the woman who followed her fourth husband's bier and wept, not because of his death, as she told a gossip, but because she was not this time, as on former occasions, provided with another husband; and in the same collection, we read of a woman kneeling at the mass of requiem, while the corpse of her husband lay in the chapel, when a young man whispered her "that he myght be her husband;" she replied, "Syr, by my trowthe, I am sorry that ye come too late, for I am sped all redy. For I was made sure yesterday to another man." And in 'Mery Talys and Quicke Answeres,' a young woman grieving sorely for the death of her husband, her father bade her cheer up, for he had provided another husband for her; but she said she would have him not. However, when they were all at dinner, she whispered to her father amidst her sobs, "Father, where is this same young man that is to be my husband?"

From the 'Vitae Patrum' Jacques de Vitry and Etienne de Bourbon took the story of the nun who tore out her eyes, and sent them to a king who had fallen in love with her beauty. This is the well-known tale of St

---

[14]This story is also given by Davis in his work on the Chinese. Abel Remusat made a French translation, somewhat fuller than that of Du Halde ('La Matrone du Pays de Soung'), and recently it has been reproduced, with an introduction, by M. E. Legrand.

Bridget (see 'Three Middle Irish Homilies,' by Whitley Stokes, p. 65); and it has its prototype in the great Indian story-book entitled 'Kathá Sarit Ságara'—Ocean of the Streams of Narrative—where it is related of a prince who abandoned his kingdom, and adopted the life of a wandering hermit. Entering the house of a merchant one day to ask alms, the young wife of the merchant, on seeing him, exclaimed, "How came such a handsome man as you to undertake such a severe vow as this? Happy is the woman who is gazed upon with such eyes as yours!" Upon this the begging hermit tore out one eye, and asked her what there was in it to be so attractive. He then told the lady a story of a hermit who conquered his anger, after which she bowed before him; and he, being regardless of his body, lovely though it was, passed on to perfection.

Liebrecht has shown that the biographies of Christian saints were largely indebted to Buddhist hagiology, in his essay on the sources of the spiritual romance of 'Barlaam and Josaphat.'[15] And a careful examination—but what a task it would prove!—of the mediæval sermon-books and *exempla*, as stories designed for preachers' use were styled, would probably result in the discovery that many of the monkish tales are traceable to Buddhist sources. After the fall of Buddhism in India, and even during its decline, according to Max Müller, the Bráhmans did not scruple to appropriate the beautiful tales and apologues of their enemies, and employ them for purposes of instruction. The Sanskrit book entitled 'Pancha Tantra'—Five Sections—to which our European versions of the Fables of Pilpay are closely allied, and very many of the tales in the 'Kathá Sarit Ságara,' are of Buddhist origin. Moreover, I conceive the germs of more than one of Lucian's amusing stories are found in the Buddhist writings. Nor is this at all improbable, since Indian fictions certainly began to spread both eastward and westward in the second century of our era; and fables and tales being the means employed for conveying the doctrines of Gautama to the minds of the people, we may well suppose that they would be readily taken up and "wafted from clime to clime," although the lessons they were designed to inculcate may have been ignored. But there is reason to believe that Buddhist doctrines had penetrated Western Europe long before the second century. As Dr J. W. Redhouse remarks eloquently, "When the Hindús had become disciples of Buddha [*i.e.,* Gautama], from the ninth century before Christ, the

[15]'Zur Volkskunde,' p. 441.

whole world of civilisation, from the Pacific to the Atlantic, caught many a maxim of grandeur, and especially mercy to others—the brightest gem of theoretical Christianity—from the followers of that mild sage, the greatest man, in some respects, that has ever lived on earth."

The monkish writers of mediæval times were indebted, directly or indirectly, for some of their stories to the Talmud, as we have already seen; and it appears that the compilers of that strange monument of human wisdom and human folly added to their own inventions narratives and apologues of Indian as well as Greek and Roman origin. For example, we are told that the infamous citizens of Sodom had a particular kind of bed for the use of the weary traveller who entered their city and sought shelter for the night: if he was found to be too long for the bed, they reduced him to the proper length by chopping off so much of his legs; and if too short, he was stretched to the requisite length. Here we have the old Greek legend of Procrustes, the robber of Attica, who was said to treat his victims in this manner. And some trace of the same tale seems to be found in an account of one of the adventures of Kurroglú, the robber-poet of Turkish-Persia (in Chodzko's 'Popular Poetry of Persia'), where the Princess Nighára, daughter of the Sultan of Turkey, playfully says to her bandit-lover, who had gained access to the harem in the disguise of a pilgrim, "I will fetch thee one of my father's robes; and if it should be too short for thee, I shall have thy legs chopped off just at the place where the robe will reach; and if it be too long, I shall direct a nail to be driven into each of thy heels, that thou mayest grow taller." Kurroglú replies that by so doing she should treat him after the code of Abú Hurayra, referring, apparently, to some Arab legend similar to that of Procrustes.[16] Another Greek legend reappears in the Talmud, as a citation from the Book of Jasher: "So light was Naphtali (the son of Jacob) that he could go upon the ears of corn without crushing them." This is "the fleet Camilla" in a Jewish gaberdine! And a farther instance of the familiarity of the Rabbins with classical literature is furnished in one of the numerous

[16]Abú Hurayra—"Father of a kitten." This was the *kunya*, or by-name, of one of Muhammed's most beloved disciples. He was so named by Muhammed from his carrying a kitten on his arm one day. He is the source of several traditions of the Prophet. The Abú Hurayra, whose "code," according to Kurroglú ("son of the blind," so called because his father had been blinded), was similar to that of the robber of Attica, must have been a very different man, and the story referred to seems now forgotten, like the tale of two women alluded to by the genie whom the Arabian fisherman liberated from the copper vessel in which he had been confined by Solomon: "Do not deal with me as did Umáma to Atika."

apothegms in the Talmud: "When love is intense, both [*i.e.,* man and wife] find room enough upon one bench; afterwards they may find themselves cramped in a space of sixty cubits." This seems derived from an anecdote in Athenæus, xii.: Python of Byzantium was a very fat man. He once said to the citizens, in addressing them, to make friends after a political dispute, "Gentlemen, you see how stout I am; well, I have a wife at home who is still fatter. Now, when we are good friends, we can sit on a very small seat; but when we quarrel, I assure you the whole house cannot contain us."

The famous Persian poet Hafiz seems also to have been acquainted with classical Greek and Roman literature. Stobæus (Flor. 36, 19) tells us that Zeno said to a youth who was more disposed to talk than to listen, "Young man, nature gave us one tongue, but two ears, so that we may hear just twice as much as we speak,"—a saying which Hafiz has thus reproduced:

> Two ears and but a single tongue
> By nature's law to man belong.
> The lesson she would teach is clear:
> Repeat but half of what you hear.

The origin of chivalric romance in Europe was the subject of keen controversy among English writers in the last century, and is still perhaps not satisfactorily ascertained. Percy contended that the spirit of chivalry existed among the northern nations long before the establishment of the feudal system, or the introduction of knighthood as a regular order; and that their fictions were carried from the North by the Scalds who probably accompanied the army of Rollo into Normandy. Warton, on the other hand, maintained that romantic fiction was introduced into Europe by the Saracens, who settled in Spain in the eighth century, and suggested that, even admitting the Gothic theory, yet as the Goths themselves came from the East, their fictions also had in all likelihood an Asiatic origin. There is much to be urged in favour of both theories. Many passages in European romances of chivalry, especially those describing the prowess of the heroes in battle, bear a very striking likeness to the narratives of the

---

[17]"A style various and elegant, reaching sometimes to the sublime; characters drawn with force, and skilfully sustained; render the Romance of Antar eminently remarkable: it may be termed the Iliad of the Arabians."—*Caussin de Perceval.*

exploits of the famous Bedouin poet-hero Antar, in the romance which purports to recount his adventures.[17] In the romance of Guy of Warwick, Sir Heraud, one of Guy's companions, is the prisoner of a king, who, having engaged in war, suffers defeat, and is at length besieged in his capital. It happens that an attendant of the king overhears the prisoner's complaints, and discovering that he is none other than the illustrious Heraud, the second hero of Christendom, acquaints the king of the name and rank of his prisoner. The king at once sends for Heraud and requests the aid of his sword, promising him his freedom and great gifts in return. Heraud consents, and by his invincible prowess turns the tide of affairs once more in favour of the king. A precisely similar incident occurs in the Arabian romance of 'Antar.' The hero is taken prisoner by Monzar, king of Híra, who, having offended his suzerain, Núshírván, king of Persia, the latter despatches an army to chastise his insolence, led by the famous champion Khosrewán. The king of Híra is defeated in the first battle, and recollecting his noble prisoner Antar, sends for him in his extremity, and requests him to lead his troops against the Persians on the following day. Antar consents, slays the champion Khosrewán in single combat, and the Persians are routed with great slaughter. In the romance of Sir Bevis of Hampton, we are told that Bevis, when only seven years old, knocked down two stout men with his cudgel; and while yet a boy, he slew sixty Saracen knights. The Bedouin hero Antar also exhibited extraordinary courage in his childhood: when he was but ten years old he slew a wolf that had dispersed his flock, and carried home the head and paws of the beast in a basket, and presented them as trophies of his prowess to his mother,—a bold exploit, which may be compared with that of David the Hebrew shepherd-boy: "Thy servant kept his father's sheep, and there came a lion and a bear, and took a lamb out of the flock: and I went out after him, and delivered it out of his mouth; and when he arose against me, I caught him by his beard, and smote him, and slew him. Thy servant slew both the lion and the bear; and this uncircumcised Philistine shall be as one of them." (1 Sam. xvii. 34–36.)

In the combat of Sir Guy with the Danish champion Colbrand are incidents analogous to some of Antar's hand-to-hand encounters with "foemen worthy of his steel." Colbrand threw three darts at Guy, two of which failed, and the third glided through his shield, and passing under his arm, went an acre before it fell to the ground. He dealt a stroke at Guy with his sword, missed him, but cut his horse in two. At last Guy gives Colbrand a stroke on the neck, smiting his head from his body, and sending it half a foot into the earth. Sir Bevis thus despatched an insolent citizen:

> To that burgess a stroke he sent,
> Through helm and hauberk down it went;
> Both man and horse in that stound
> He cleaved down to the ground.

King Arthur, dealing a heavy blow on the shoulder of a giant fifteen feet in height, divided him to the nave so accurately that his sides hung over his horse, and he was thus carried about the field to the great horror of the Saracens. Sir Guy cleaved Sir Gunter from the helmet to the pommel of his saddle. In the Romance of Antar the hero wards off the four darts thrown at him by the Greek champion, and catching the mace which he then hurled at him, he returned it with such force as to throw him off the saddle to the distance of twelve cubits, and broke his ribs and snapped his spine. In another encounter he smites his doughty antagonist with his irresistible sword Dhamí—a blade which may be compared with Morglay, Excalibar, Durandal, Balmung, Gram, Chrysaor, and others famed in European romance—cleaving both him and his horse to the ground, so that they fell each in two halves.

In the romance of Merlin (Part II.), King Arthur obtains his renowned sword Excalibar in this way: A miraculous stone was discovered before the church-door, and in the stone was firmly fixed a sword with these words engraved on its hilt:

> Ich am y-hote [called] Excalibore;
> Unto a king fair treasure.
> (On Inglis is this writing),
> Kerve steel, and yren, and al thing.

It was made law, that whoever should be able to draw out that sword from the stone, should be at once acknowledged as sovereign of Britain. Many strong and bold knights attempted to withdraw the sword in vain: at length Arthur came forward, and being at the time in want of a trusty blade, drew it forth with perfect ease. This incident seems to have been adapted from the (Norse) Volsung Tale. "The Volsungs," says Dr Dasent, "traced themselves back, like all heroes, to Odin, the great father of gods and men. From him sprang Sigi, from him Volsung. In the centre of his hall grew an oak, the tall trunk of which passed through the roof, and its boughs spread far and wide in upper air. Into that hall, on a high feast day, when Signy, Volsung's daughter, was to be given away to Siggeir, King of Gothland, strode an old one-eyed guest. His feet were bare, his hose were of knitted linen; he wore a great striped cloak and a broad flapping hat. In his hand he bare a great sword, which, at one stroke, he buried up to the hilt in the oak-trunk. 'There,' said he, 'let him of all this company bear this sword who is man enough to pull it out. I give it him, and none shall say he ever wore a better blade.' With these words he passed out of the hall, and was seen no more. Many tried, for that sword was plainly a thing of price, but none could stir it, till Sigmund, the best and bravest of Volsung's sons, tried his hand, and lo! the weapon yielded itself at once. That was the famous blade Gram."[18]

It is, to say the least, exceedingly curious to find a somewhat similar legend related in the Talmud regarding the manner in which Moses, the Hebrew lawgiver, became possessed of his famous rod—the same with which he divided the waters of the Red Sea and smote the rock in the wilderness, causing a stream of pure water to flow forth. According to the rabbinical narrative, this wondrous staff was created on the sixth day and given to Adam while yet in Paradise. Adam bequeathed it to Enoch, who gave it to Shem, the eldest son of Noah, from whom it descended to Isaac and Jacob. It was by the help of this staff that Jacob crossed the Jordan, and he took it with him to Egypt. Before his death he presented it to Joseph, at whose death it was taken, with the rest of his property, to Pharaoh's treasury, where Jethro, then one of the royal magicians, at once recognised its secret qualities, and on quitting the Egyptian court to settle in the land of Midian, he took it with him, and planted it in his garden, where no person was able to approach it, until the arrival of Moses, who had fled thither after slaying the insolent Egyptian, and having read the mystical words on the staff, pulled it out of the ground with ease.

The hero of chivalric romance is always possessed of a wonderful steed and a sword which nothing can resist. Rustam, the Persian champion of antiquity, had a horse called Raksh (lightning), with which, like some European heroes, he often conversed confidentially. The steed of Rasálú,

---

[18]Dasent's 'Popular Tales from the Norse'—Introd. pp. lxi, lxii. In the 'Saga of Gisli, the Outlaw,' we read of another famous blade "that would bite whatever its blow fell upon, be it iron or aught else; nor could its edge be deadened by spells, for it was forged by the Dwarfs, and its name is Graysteel."—Dr Dasent's Translation.

the hero of the Panjáb, warned him at a crisis not to touch him with whip or spur. Antar's horse Abjer was "dark-coloured, beautiful, and compact; of the race much prized by the Arabs; his hoofs were as flat as the beaten coin; his ears like quills; when he neighed he seemed as if about to speak." His sword Dhamí (which signifies "subduing") was forged out of a thunderbolt that had fallen and killed a camel. When it was finished, the chief who had employed the smith to forge it took the sword in his hand and asked him, "What name have you given it?" The smith replied:

> The sword is sharp, O son of the tribe of Ghalib,
> Sharp indeed; but where is the striker for the sword?

Then the chief waved the sword, saying, "As for the smiter—I am the smiter!" and struck off the blacksmith's head. The sword Dhamí descended from father to son, till the last possessor on his death-bed called his youngest son, and bade him privily hide it in the earth, so that it should not be seized with the rest of the family property by his grasping tyrannical brother. The youth hid the sword accordingly in the desert; but on the death of the chief, his elder son threatened to slay his brother if he did not deliver it up to him. They went together to the place, but the youth could not find it, and his brother drew his sword and would have slain him had not Antar opportunely arrived, and learning the cause of the quarrel, attacked and killed the tyrant, after which he sent the youth away. Then sitting down to rest himself, he was playing with the sand, when he came on a stone, which he removed, and lo! there lay the sword Dhamí which the youth had sought in vain.

Single combats between the champions of opposing armies are not only common in Asiatic as well as European romances, but seem to have been customary in actual warfare from the most remote times; and the historical books of the Bible furnish several instances. The combat between David and Goliath (1 Samuel xvii. 38–51) is a memorable example, and the battle between the men of Abner and the men of Joab (2 Samuel ii. 15, 16) is another. Such combats are of very frequent occurrence in the Romance of Antar, and, as in the European romances, the opposing champions invariably address each other in haughty tones. Thus Antar exclaims, when about to encounter the Greek champion, "I will break down the support of Greece from its foundations; I will sever Badramút's head with my scimitar! I am he whose might is uncontrollable in battle: I am of the race of Abs, the valiant lion of the cavern!" In like strain does a hero of the 'Shah Náma' (Book of Kings) of Firdausi, the Homer of Persia, vaunt himself:

> I am myself Hujer,
> The valiant champion, come to conquer thee,
> And to lop off that towering head of thine.

"Come to me," said Goliath to David, "and I will give thy flesh to the fowls of the air and to the beasts of the field."

It would appear, from the minute description of the arms and armour of the combatants in the Romance of Antar, that chivalry, in all essential particulars, was an institution in the East long before it was regularly established in Europe. The Persian satrap whom Antar encounters and slays is described as encased in a complete suit of mail "of Davidean workmanship,"[19] with plumed helmet, and armed with sword, mace, shield, etc., precisely like European knights. Nor can knight-errantry be said to have been unknown to Asiatic chivalry. Oriental historians mention a Persian knight who was surnamed Rezm Kha—"one who goes in quest of adventures;" and two famous Arabian knights-errant, one named Abú Muhammed El-Batal, who wandered everywhere in search of adventures and redressing grievances, and who was killed A.D. 738 (A.H. 121); and the other a great-grandson of the Khalíf Abú Bekr, named Jáfar Es-Sadik, a man eminent for his piety and extensive knowledge, as well as for his feats of arms, who died in the reign of Al-Mansúr, A.D. 764 (A.H. 147).

The rescue of distressed and imprisoned damsels is often accomplished by Antar. When the Bedouin hero is journeying to Mecca, accompanied by his half-brother Shibúb, they heard, in the calmness of night, a female voice crying out, evidently in sore distress; upon which Antar slackens his bridle and gallops in the direction whence proceeded the cries. He discovers a lady, who informs him that she is of the noble tribe of Kenda: her husband is As-hath, the son of Obed. A famine having visited their land, they were proceeding with their family to the country of Harith, where

---

[19]In the celebrated 'Burda,' or Mantle-Poem, of Kaáb the son of Zuhayr, recited by him before Muhammed, at Medina, in the 9th year of the Hijra (A.D. 619–30), after the conquest of Mecca, the warriors of the tribe of Kuraysh are described as "aquiline-nosed heroes; whose clothing, in combat, is of *shirts of the tissue of David*—bright and ample, interlaced with links like the tendrils of the Kafá plant, firmly wove together;"—that is to say, coats of mail. According to Arab tradition, David the Hebrew king was divinely taught, and very skilful, in the manufacture of link armour. '

they intended to settle, having a daughter married there, when they were attacked by a horseman of the desert, Sudam, the son of Salheb, with forty plundering Arabs, who had slain her three sons, wounded her husband, and taken herself and her three daughters captive; and that the brigands were about to convey them to the mountains of Tawayla, there to sell them as slaves. Consigning the ladies to the care of his brother, Antar grasps his spear, and turns to meet Sudam and his followers, whom he now sees hastily advancing towards him. The hero is assailed by several brigands at once, but he cuts them down on either side, and at length encounters Sudam, and striking him on the breast with his cleaving Dhamí, the chief falls to the ground dead, weltering in his blood. The three damsels and their mother crowd round their deliverer, kissing his hands and thanking him for having saved them from dishonour; and Antar, desiring the damsels to veil themselves, and having bound up the old shaykh's wounds, sat down to rest himself after the fatigue of his combats. The old shaykh, grateful for the good service rendered his family by Antar, offers him his choice of his three daughters, but the hero courteously declines the compliment, saying to the damsels, "Were my heart my own, I should desire nothing beyond you—it would covet nothing but you. But it loves what tortures it; where no word, no deed, encourages it." Never was European knight more "solicitous in the cause of women" than the Bedouin hero: when he rescued the tribe of Mazin, and learned that Oosack and his followers were plundering the women's quarter, he rushed with his warriors upon the dastards, scattering them to the right and left: "mighty was every act, and fate descended among them." It is certain that European chivalry owed much to the Arabs; and that many scenes and incidents from 'Antar' and other Arabian romances were appropriated by the early Spanish authors of similar works, which they had derived from their Moorish conquerors; and we may fairly consider 'Antar' as the prototype of European romances of chivalry.[20]

To return, after this long digression, to the subject of the origin and diffusion of popular tales. Mr Ralston has justly remarked that an unfamiliar joke is rarely met with in the lower strata of fiction. The same jests which amuse the Russian or Norwegian peasant are also well known to the vine-dressers of France and Spain, and to the Italian rustic; to the half-farmer–half-fisherman of Argyllshire; to the wandering Arab; to the luxurious Persian; to the peaceable Hindú; to the crafty Chinese. Who

---

[20]For some account of the Romance of Antar, see the Note at the end of this introductory paper.

has not heard of the Irishman who looked over the shoulder of a gentle-man while he was writing a letter in a coffee-house, and when the gentleman concluded with the words, "I have much more to say to you, but an impudent Irishman is reading every word I write," the Irishman exclaimed, "Upon my Bowl, I haven't read a word, sorr!" This was told many centuries ago in the 'Baháristán' of the Persian poet Jámí: A learned man being annoyed while writing a letter to one of his confidential friends at the conduct of a person who, seated at his side, glanced out of the corner of his eye at his letter, wrote: "Had not a hireling thief been seated at my side and engaged in reading my letter, I should have written to thee all my secrets." The man said, "By Allah, my lord, I have neither read nor even looked at thy letter." "Fool," exclaimed the other, "how canst thou, then, say what thou now sayest?"

Another familiar jest is that of the "pragmatical young fellow" who, sitting at a table opposite "the learned John Scott," asked him, "What difference is there between Scot and Sot?" to which he replied, "Just the breadth of the table." [21] This also occurs in Gladwin's 'Persian Moonshee' and several Indian collections of facetiæ: An indigent poet paid a visit to a rich man, and seated himself so near that there was not more distance than a span between them. Offended thereat, the rich man asked him, "What difference is there between you and an ass?" He answered, "The measure of one span."

The well-known story of the "natural" who ate a leg of a fowl intended for the laird's dinner may have been taken from Boccaccio's 'Decameron,' Day vi., novel 4. In our version the fool, on being accused of the theft, asserted that a fowl had only one leg, and being desired to prove this, he led the laird to a shed, where a number of fowls were standing with one leg tucked up, as is usual with fowls in wet weather; and when the laird cried, "Shooh! shooh!" the fowls all set down their legs. "Had you cried 'shooh!' to your hen," quoth the fool, "doubtless it would also have put down its other leg!" In Boccaccio it is a crane, a leg of which the cook had given to his sweetheart. It reappears in 'Tarlton's Newes out of Purgatorie,' under the title of "The Tale of a Cook, and why he sat in Purgatorie with a Crane's Leg in his Mouth."

One of the practical jokes of "the man who was called Howleglass" (a translation made about 1550, of the German jests of Tyl Eulenspiegel) is

---

[21]'A Collection of Jests, Epigrams, Epitaphs,' &c. Edinburgh: 1753.

his exhibiting "a strange animal which hath its head placed where its tail ought to be." This is found also in Gladwin's 'Persian Moonshee': A very poor man who had a horse, tied him in the stable with his head towards the part where it is usual to place the tail. He then proclaimed abroad, "O ye people! come and see a strange sight, a horse with his head where his tail ought to be!" All the people of the city crowded together, and from every one who wished to see the show he exacted a small piece of money, and gave them admittance; and they who went into the stable came back and said nothing. In the German version it is said: "As fast as they came in and found how wittily they had been deceived, they could not help laughing at the hoax, in which Howleglass joining, earnestly entreated them not to ruin his fortunes, and let those who had not paid laugh at them, by telling the secret to the townspeople on the outside. This they all promised, and as soon as they got home each advised his neighbour to go and see the great sight."

In 'Archie Armstrong's Banquet of Jests' is the following anecdote, which had long before been current in Europe: A fellow with one eye, being abroad about his business, his wife in his absence entertained her lover. But it so happened that her husband came home, and entered the room before the loving couple expected him. At whose presence the woman, greatly alarmed, rose up, and running to her husband, clapped her hand on the eye he could see with, saying, "Husband, I dreamt just now that you could see as well with the other eye as with this; pray tell me." Meanwhile her friend slipped out of doors.—This occurs in the 'Gesta Romanorum,' ch. cxxi.; and it is the eighth tale of Peter Alfonsus, where a vine-dresser wounds one of his eyes while working in the vineyard. In the meantime his wife is engaged with her gallant. On the husband's return, she contrives the lover's escape by kissing her spouse on the other eye. The story is also in the novels of Malespini (i. 44), and of Bandello (i. 23); in the 'Heptameron' of Margaret Queen of Navarre, who probably borrowed it from the first tale of the *fabliau* of the "Mauvaise Femme" (Le Grand, iv. 138, ed. 1781); and in the 'Elites de Contes' of the Sieur d'Ouville (Rouen, 1680, p. 284).

From Alfonsus the incident was probably adapted by the author of the old romance of 'Eurialus and Lucretia': The hero, Eurialus, is equerry to the Emperor Sigismundus, and the paramour of Lucretia, wife of the Senator Menelai. "One night, as he was at supper, the senator came in unexpectedly, and must have discovered Eurialus, had not Lucretia's wonted presence of mind saved him and herself from that disgrace. She went out to meet her husband, who had already got as far as the landing-place, and loaded him with the most tender reproaches for having left her to eat her supper alone. In vain did he protest to her that he had not eaten a morsel that day; she was not to be pacified, and falling on his neck, she bedewed the dear man with her tears. The senator, pleased at so rare an instance of her love, kissed off her tears, and comforted his loving wife in the most soothing language. Lucretia acted the farce long enough to give Eurialus time to get out at the window; then walking into the room arm in arm with her *cara sposa,* they sat down lovingly to supper."[22]

The original occurs in the Sanskrit book of tales and apologues, entitled 'Hitopadesa' (Friendly Counsel), Book i. fable 6: In the province of Gaur there is a city called Kausámbi. In it dwelt an opulent merchant named Chandanadasa. Being in the last stage of life, with his mind swayed by desire, he married a merchant's daughter named Lilavatí. She was young, resembling the victorious banner of Makara-Keta; consequently her aged partner was not to her liking. Still the old husband was dotingly fond of her. Now Lilavatí, through the impetuosity of youth, violating the honour of her family, became enamoured of a certain merchant's son. One day Lilavatí was sitting at her ease in familiar chat with the merchant's son, on a couch variegated with the lustre of strings of jewels, when, seeing her husband, who had approached unobserved, she rose up with precipitation, caught him by the hair, and vehemently embracing, kissed him. Meanwhile the gallant rose and escaped.

"Every schoolboy" knows the story of the blockhead who complained to the judge of being annoyed with flies, and being told that he was at liberty to strike them wherever he saw them, observing a big "blue bottle" alight on the judge's nose, delivered a blow with his fist on that useful member, and smashed it as well as the fly. This is also told of Giufà, the typical noodle of Sicily, in Pitrè's collection; and we have a different version of the incident in the Icelandic Tale of a Butter-Tub: An old woman, having privily eaten a whole tub of butter intended for use in winter, her husband was surprised to find the tub empty, and asked her if she knew how it had happened. Just then the old wife saw a big fly which had got into the open barrel, and she said, "Ah, there comes the wretched thief! Look here—this hateful fly has doubtless eaten all our butter from the tub." This, the old man thought, must be true, and ran off for the big

[21]'Bibliothèque Universelle des Romans.'

hammer with which he used to beat his dried fish, and would break the skull of the fly. He shut the door of the cottage, that the fly should not get out, and now chased the fly all over the place, knocking and beating at it, but never hitting save his own furniture and household chattels, which he broke to pieces. At last the old man, being tired, sat down in fury and despair. But then the fly came and sat on his nose. Then the earl begged his wife to kill the fly, and said, "Make haste, while it sits on the nose!"—which since has passed into a common saying. The old woman lifted up the hammer with all her might, and thumped it on the old man's nose, and broke his skull so well that he was dead on the spot; but the fly escaped with unbroken skull. It is unscathed yet. But the old woman is still wailing over her carl.[23] The incident seems to be of Buddhist origin, being found in two different forms in the 'Játakas,' or Birth-Stories, Nos. 44 and 45. In the former, a lad takes an axe to kill some mosquitoes that had alighted on his father's bald head, and cleaves the old man's skull. The other is as follows: A slave girl, named Rohini, was once pounding rice, when her aged mother came to the place and sat down. The flies came about her, and bit her as if they were running needles into her. She said to her daughter, "My girl, the flies are biting me; drive them off." She said, "I will, mother;" and raising the pestle, thinking, "I will kill and destroy the flies on my mother's body," struck her mother with the pestle, and killed her on the spot. Seeing that, she began to cry, "O mother! mother!"[24]

The really original tales in our collections of facetiæ are indeed but few. "In genuine home-grown humour," says Mr W. Carew Hazlitt, "English literature is by no means wealthy. We shine indeed, but it is with a borrowed light. Our jest-books are little beyond various readings to the Poggiana and other great stores of facetiæ: and if we should take away from the 'Hundred Mery Talys' and its successors what is merely imported mat-

[23]'Icelandic Legends.' Collected by Jón Arnason. Translated by George E. J. Powell and Eiríkr Magnússon. Second Series. London: 1866.

[24]Translations from the Páli of 'Játakas' 41–50, by the Lord Bishop of Colombo; in the 'Transactions' of the Royal Asiatic Society, Ceylon Branch. This is one of the Buddhist tales which have been adapted by the Bráhmans: In the First Book of the 'Panchatantra,' a prince sets his pet monkey to watch over him as he sleeps in a pavilion in his garden; a troublesome bee settles on the prince's face, in spite of the monkey's pains to drive it off, till the monkey, highly incensed, snatches up his master's sword, and making a blow at the bee, cuts off the prince's head. The apologue is reproduced in the 'Anvár-i-Suhaylí' (Lights of Canopus), a Persian version, by Husain Va'iz, of the Fables of Bidpai, and the modern Hindústaní version of the Persian work, by Abu-'l Fazel, 'Ayár-i-Dánish' (Touchstone of Knowledge), under the title of "The Gardener, the Bear, and the Fly." In this form it is an old European acquaintance.

ter, it is to be feared that the residue would be compressible into a very slender compass. There is scarcely a story which has not been told over and over again, with the change only of name, place, and circumstance. The germ and spirit are identical. Even the good things which the contemporaries of Sydney Smith applauded in that excellent man are in many cases discoverable in works which it is more probable than otherwise that he had read." And Mr J. O. Halliwell-Phillipps' remark is to the same purpose: "Nothing is more uncertain than the attribution of 'jests' to persons who have made themselves famous as wits, and we are occasionally favoured in the public prints with anecdotes concerning men of our own times that have long been familiar to us in slightly different forms in jestbooks of the sixteenth and seventeenth centuries."

Among the anecdotes told of Foote is this: Dining at Paris with Lord Stormont, the host descanted volubly on the age of his wine, which was served in very diminutive glasses. Foote, holding up his glass, said, "It is very little of its age." In Taylor's 'Wit and Mirth' (*temp.* James I. of England), the story is thus told: "A proper gentlewoman went to speak with a rich mizer that had more gowt than good manners. At her taking leave, hee requested her to taste a cup of Canara. Shee (contrary to his expectation) tooke him at his word, and thanked him. He commanded Jeffrey Starveling his man to wash a glasse, and fill it to the gentlewoman. Honest Jeffrey fil'd a great glasse about the bigness of the Taylors thimbles, and gave it to his master, who kist it to save cost, and gave it to the gentlewoman, saying that it was good Canara of six yeeres old at the least; to whom shee answered (seeing the quantitie so small): 'Sir, as you requested me, I have tasted your wine; but I wonder that it should be so little being of so great an age.'" This was probably adapted from Lucian, who tells how a lover brought his mistress a very small cask of wine, which he warmly commended as very choice and old, upon which she said drily: "It is very little of its age." The story is also told by Athenæus.

Queen Elizabeth, according to the tradition, once asked Sir Walter Raleigh whether he could tell the weight of smoke, and he at once undertook to do so. Having smoked a pipe of tobacco, he carefully weighed the ashes, and already knowing the weight of the tobacco, he informed the queen that the difference was the weight of the smoke. Raleigh may have imitated the philosopher in Lucian's story: "Some one, thinking to puzzle Demonax, asked him, 'If I burn a thousand pounds of fuel, how many pounds of it go into smoke?' 'Weigh the ashes,' he replied, 'and all the residue must be smoke.'"

Laird Braco, an ancestor of the Earls of Fife, was a very avaricious man. One day a tenant, who called upon him to pay his rent, happened to be deficient a single farthing. The amount could not be excused, and the farmer had to seek the farthing. When the business was adjusted, the farmer said to the laird, "Now, Braco, I would gie ye a shilling for a sight of a' the gowd and siller ye hae." "Weel, man," said Braco, "it sall no cost ye ony mair," and accordingly, having first received and pocketed the shilling, the laird exhibited several iron boxes filled with gold and silver coin. "Now," said the farmer, "I'm as rich as yoursel', Braco." "Ay, man," quoth Braco, "how can that be?" "Because I've *seen* it, and you can do nae mair."—A very similar story is current among the Chinese: A rich priest had hoarded a fine collection of jewels, to which he was constantly adding, and of which he was inordinately proud. Upon showing them one day to a friend, the latter feasted his eyes for some time, and on taking his leave thanked his host for the jewels. "How?" cries the priest; "I have not given them to you. Why do you thank me?" "Well," replied his friend, "I have at least had as much pleasure from *seeing* them as you can have, and the only difference between us, that I can see, is that you have the trouble of collecting them."[25]

And this is another well-worn jest which has also its parallel in China: Two fellows meeting, one asked the other why he looked so sad. "I have good reason for it," said the other; "poor Jack such-a-one, the greatest crony and friend I had in the world, was hanged but two days ago." "What had he done?" said the first. "Alas!" replied the other, "he did no more than you or I should have done on the like occasion: he found a bridle on the road, and took it up." "What!" says the other, "hang a man for taking a bridle! That's hard indeed." "To tell the truth of the matter," says the other, "there was a horse tied to the other end of it."[26]—The Chinese tell the story thus: A man was condemned to the cangue [a kind of portable pillory], and some of his friends seeing him asked him the cause of his punishment. He said to them, "As I happened to go along a road I saw a little cord on the ground; thinking it might be useful for something, I took it and went away. That is the cause of my misfortune." His friends replied, "Never has the theft of a cord led any one to such a torture." The thief said, "It is true there was something at the end of the

[25]'Folk-Lore in China, and its affinities with that of the Aryan and Semitic Races.' By M. B. Dennys. Hong-Kong: 1876. P. 151.
[26]'A Collection of Jests, Epigrams, Epitaphs,' &c. Edinburgh: 1753.

cord." They asked him what it was, and he replied, "It was only two little plough-oxen."[27]

The absurd decisions of judges or magistrates seem to have been favourite subjects of popular jests from remote times. In the Talmud the judges of the city of Sodom are represented as mockers and perverters of justice: A man having cut off the ear of his neighbour's ass, the judge said to the owner, "Let him have the ass till the ear is grown again, that it may be returned to thee as thou wishest." But it is not unlikely that the Talmudists produced stories of Asiatic Dogberries which had been current long before their days, and foisted them on the people of Sodom. However this may be, the sage decree finds a parallel in the 'Kathá Sarit Ságara:' A washerman complained before a magistrate that the wife of a Bráhman had beaten his donkey, and the animal, in running away, had fallen into a pit and broken its hoof. On the other side, the Bráhman accused the washerman of having assaulted his wife, and thereby caused her to miscarry. The magistrate ruled: "Since the donkey's hoof is broken, let the Bráhman carry the donkey's load till it is again fit for work; and let the washerman keep the Bráhman's wife till she is in the condition she was in before he beat her."—The Persian tale of the Kází of Emessa (the leading incident of which is the "pound of flesh" of Shakspeare's Shylock) furnishes similar examples of judicial wisdom. The people of that town (now called Hums) being noted for their stupidity—in popular stories, at all events—it is the Gotham of the East. Among other cases brought before the kází in this story, a man complained that the merchant in helping him to extricate his ass out of the mud, in which it had stuck fast, had pulled off its tail. "Well," says the kází, "fetch my ass, and let the man pull off its tail." The animal was brought accordingly, and the man exerted all his strength to avenge the insult which had been put upon his favourite. But an ass that had carried the kází was not likely to put up with such an indignity, and soon testified his resentment by several hearty kicks, which made the man faint. When he recovered he begged leave to decline any further satisfaction; but the kází said it was a pity he should not have his revenge, and he might take his own time. But the more he pulled the harder the vicious animal kicked, till at last the poor man, all bruises and blood, declared that he had accused the merchant falsely, for his own ass never had a tail. Then the judge mulcted him in 100 dínárs. Another man

[27]"Contes et Bon Mots, extraits d'un livre chinois, intitulé 'Sias li Siao,' traduit par M. Stanislas Julien," in the 'Journal Asiatique,' tome iv., 1824.

accused the merchant of having thrown a stone at his runaway mule, and knocked out one of his eyes, thus reducing the value of the mule by one-half—before it lost its eye the mule was worth 1000 dirhams. "This is a very simple case," said the judge; "take a saw, cut the mule in two, give him the blind half, for which he must pay you 500 dirhams, and keep the other side to yourself." But the man objected to this suggestion, and was therefore fined in 100 dínárs. Then two young men came forward and accused the merchant of having jumped from the roof of a house on to the street below, where there was a commotion, and lighting on their father, had killed him on the spot. The kází asked them whether they thought the roof of the court-house was about the height of the house that the merchant jumped from. They replied that they thought it was; upon which the kází decreed that the merchant should go to sleep on the ground, and that they should get upon the roof and jump down upon him: and that, as the right of blood belonged to them equally, they must take care to jump both at once. They accordingly went upon the roof; but when they looked below they felt alarmed at the height, and so came down again, declaring that if they had ten lives they could not expect to escape. The kází said he could not help that: they had demanded retaliation, and retaliation they should have; but he could not alter the law to please them. So they gave up their claim, but the kází mulcted them also in the sum of 100 dínárs. This last incident is often found in our own jest-books, thus: A Flemish tyler accidentally fell from the top of a house upon a Spaniard and killed him, though he escaped himself. The next of blood prosecuted his death with great violence against the tyler, and when offered pecuniary recompense, nothing could serve him but *lex talionis.* Hereupon the judge said to him, if he did insist upon that sentence, he should go up to the top of the same house, and fall down from thence upon the tyler.[28] In another version, a tailor, looking at two drunken fellows fighting in the street, fell out of the window and killed an old man, whose son caused him to be apprehended on a charge of murder. When the trial came on, the jury could not bring in a verdict of wilful murder, neither could they acquit him; so they referred the case to the judges, who in their turn referred it to the king; and the king asked George Buchanan's opinion, who said that the tailor should stand below and let the old man's son fall on him.[29]

[28] 'A Collection of Jests, Epigrams, Epitaphs,' &c. Edinburgh: 1753.

[29] "The Witty and Entertaining Exploits of George Buchanan, commonly called the King's Fool.' Leith: 1705.

Thus many of the tales in our jest-books, which are generally believed to be "racy of the soil," and many of the "good things" ascribed to wits of recent times, are also current as genuine in other countries of Europe, and winged their way from the Far East ages before "Joe Miller" became, what it purports to be, 'The Wits' Vade Mecum.' Perhaps the best jest in that popular jest-book is the name of Joe Miller on its title-page. It is a common practice in most countries to prefix to a new collection of old jokes the name of some man who was famed for his wit in his day and generation, and to credit him with clever or amusing things which he never did or said: as in the case of the Italian ecclesiastic Arlotto; the German arch-rogue Tyl Eulenspiegel; our English Skelton, George Peele, Dick Tarlton, and Archie Armstrong; the Turkish Khoja Nasr-ed-Dín Efendi; and the Indian Temal Ramakistnan, the Scogin of Madras. But it is said that Joe Miller, albeit a comedian by profession, was utterly incapable of making an "original" joke—that he was, in fact, a man of somewhat saturnine disposition: but no matter; the jest-book which has immortalised his name—which his stage career could never have done for him—contains some of the most diverting tales that are to be found in our own or any other language, although he had no more a hand in its compilation than he had in that of the Talmud!

The prototypes of—or, at least, parallels to-most European tales of the Gothamite class have been discovered, within quite recent years, in the 'Játakas' and other Buddhist works.[30] It would probably be going too far, however, to maintain that all such tales are of Buddhist invention. There must have existed in India, both orally and in writing, a great mass of stories and fables before the promulgation of Gautama's doctrines; and if the Bráhmans in later ages drew largely from the literary compositions of their enemies, perhaps they were, in some instances, only taking back their own. Nevertheless, there can be no doubt that Buddhist literature is peculiarly rich in original tales, apologues, and parables, which owe nothing to the fictions of the earlier Hindús.

But while most of the popular tales of Europe are traceable to ancient Indian sources, and the belief has been long general among scholars that India was the cradle-land of science and literature, the opinion is daily gaining ground that Egypt, not India, was the actual centre from which

[30]I have made a comprehensive collection of Stories of Noodledom, Asiatic as well as European, which is designed, like the present work, to illustrate the curious migrations of popular fictions; published by Mr Elliot Stock, London: 1886.

both the East and the West derived their civilisation. It cannot be denied
that there is much more certainty respecting ancient dates in connection
with Egyptian history than there is regarding those of any other country;
while on the subject of dates all through India, before the time of Alexander's conquest, there is a very inconvenient vagueness. But in Egyptian
history we have absolute dates for thousands of years before Christ. The
researches of modern Egyptologists have resulted in surprising and most
important discoveries, both in monumental inscriptions and in papyri;
and when the manuscripts recently unearthed in Egypt have been carefully examined by competent scholars, new facts may be brought to light,
to upset some of our present theories as to the origin and diffusion of literature and science.[31] That the Indian 'Vedas' and the grand epics
'Rámáyana' and 'Mahábhárata' are very old—though certainly not of such
high antiquity as was claimed for them by Sir William Jones and other
Sanskritists in the last century—is generally admitted by those best qualified to judge, but their date is not positively ascertained. In Egyptian literature, however, there is preserved among the papyri in the British
Museum a romance, or fairy tale, of singular interest, of two brothers
Anapú and Satú,—the first part of which presents a parallel to the Biblical incident of Joseph and the wife of Potiphar—which was composed
in the fourteenth century before Christ, when Pharaoh Ramses Miamun,
founder of Pithom and Ramses, ruled at Thebes, and literature, says
Deutsch, "celebrated its highest triumphs at his brilliant court." Nine
pre-eminent *savans* were attached to the person of that monarch, at
whose court Moses was educated. We have in this precious relic of antiquity, contemporary delineations of the manners and customs, the notions and views, of the Egyptians of 3000 years ago. And it is to be hoped
that much more will yet be discovered from the literary remains so mirac-

[31]"We know," says Sir Richard F. Burton, "that the apologue, the beast-fable proper, is neither Indian nor Esopic: to mention no others, the 'Lion and the Mouse' is told in a Leyden
papyrus. . . . From the Nile banks it was but a step to Phoenicia and Asia Minor, and thence,
with the alphabet, the fable went to Greece; while eastward it found a new centre of civilisation in Babylonia and Assyria, lacking, however, the alphabet. When the two great sources
were connected by Alexander of Macedon, who completed what Sesostris and Semiramis had
begun; when the Medo-Bactrian kingdom was founded, and when the Greeks took moral
possession of Persia under the Selucides, then the fable would find its way to India, doubtless
meeting there some rude and fantastic kinsman of Buddhistic 'persuasion.' The mingling of
blood would produce a fine robust race, and after the second century (A.D.) Indian stories
spread over the civilised world, between Rome and China."—'The Academy,' June 20, 1885.

ulously preserved beneath ruined temples, palaces, and sand-heaps, respecting not only the "learning of the Egyptians," but also their folk-lore.

NOTE.
THE ARABIAN ROMANCE OF ANTAR (pp. 39–49).

The *Kassas*, or story-tellers of the East, can be traced up to the first century of the Hijra. It is said that the first was Obeyd, the son of Omayr, in the time of Omar, who pursued his vocation at Mecca. The first story-teller in Egypt was Selim, son of Auz, A.H. 39 (A.D. 659). One of their favourite subjects was doubtless the romantic exploits of Antar, the father of Arab chivalry; but the work itself was not written till the sixth century of the Hijra, the author being Abu-'l Moyed Muhammed Ibn Es-Saygh, surnamed for this reason El-Antarí, or the Antarian. The year of his death is not known; but Abú Ossaibah, in his biography, mentions a letter which he addressed to Hajjet-ed-Dín Merwan, vazír of the Atabeg Zangui, son of Aksáikar, who died A.H. 540 (A.D. 1145). The Arabian biographer's account of him is, that he was a celebrated physician and scholar, and distinguished himself in philosophy and other branches of science. "The physician Sedid-ed-Dín Mahmúd ben Omar informed me," he says, "that the Antarí wrote at the beginning of his career traditions (tales) of Antar the Absite, and that he became celebrated through the attribute of this name." In one of the copies of the Romance the author is said to have been Sayyid Yusuf, son of Ismael, who procured most of his materials from writers versed in ancient traditions, especially from a learned contemporary of Hárún-er-Rashíd, named El-Asmay, to whom the work is sometimes attributed.[32]

Antar is no imaginary hero; he is well known as a famous warrior, and as the author of one of the seven prize poems (*Mu'allakát*) which were suspended in the Temple at Mecca before the time of Muhammed. That the Arabs possessed traditions of the warlike exploits of Antar long before they were reduced to writing, seems evident from a saying ascribed to Muhammed, who, while sternly prohibiting his followers from listening to the romances which had been brought from Persia, advised them to cherish the tales of the hero Antar, "that their hearts might become as

[32] 'Asiatic Journal,' vol. xxvii., 1838.

steel." The Romance of Antar is usually bound up in forty-five volumes; and it was from an abridged copy that Terrick Hamilton made a translation of the First Part—which treats of the hero from his birth to his marriage—which was published in four octavo volumes, 1819–20. An epitome of this part is included in my 'Arabian Poetry for English Readers,' 1881, from the appendix to which I may here cite my sketch of the characters in the Romance, the work being now out of print.

The hero Antar, the son of Sheddád, is always the central figure. His blackness of complexion, his homeliness—even ugliness—of feature, are forgotten in admiration of his prodigious strength of arm and his invincible courage; his lofty and impassioned verses; his greatness of soul and his tenderness of heart. A true knight, *sans peur et sans reproche:* bold as a lion when face to face with his foes; magnanimous towards an inferior antagonist; soft and gentle when he thinks of his beloved Abla, still more so when in her presence. Abla, the beauteous Abla, whose dark flowing tresses first ensnared the heart of the hero, and whose bright eyes completed the capture; a true Bedouin damsel: like Desdemona with the Moor, she saw Antar's beauty in his mind. And Antar—spite of his black complexion, spite of his base birth—"loved her with the love of a noble-born hero!" When the enemy approaches the tents of his tribe—when the time has come for sword-blows and spear-thrusts—his base origin is forgotten: his sword is then his father, and the spear in his right hand is his noble kinsman!

The other characters are of course subordinated to the hero and his achievements; yet each has an individuality which is strongly marked. Zuhayr, king of the tribes of Abs and Adnan, of Fazarah and Ghiftan—a prince possessing all the virtues and not a few of the failings of his age and race; chivalrous himself, he was not slow to recognise in the youthful son of Sheddád, the future hero. Prince Shas, naturally ill-tempered, proud and tyrannical, yet not without his good points, after adversity had tamed his spirit. Prince Malik, the brave but gentle son of Zuhayr; Antar's first friend and protector against the malice of his enemies; ever ready to plead eloquently in his favour, or to draw his sword when the hero was overwhelmed with numbers. Sheddád, the father of Antar; a bold fellow—"of a heavy-handed kin; a good smiter when help was needed"; proud of his pure blood as ever was hidalgo, yet yearning towards his brave son when his deeds were noised abroad, and bitterly lamenting his reported death. Zebíba, his simple-minded mother; like mothers of great men in general, did not appreciate her son's heroic achievements: thought he had much better stay at home and help her to tend the flocks. Malik, the father of Abla; crafty, calculating, sordid, perfidious, malicious, time-serving; withal a great stickler for the honour of his family. Amara, the Bedouin exquisite; proud, boastful; at heart a coward. Shibúb, the half-brother of Antar and his trusty squire; fleet of foot, and hence called Father of the Wind; a dexterous archer; ready with admirable devices for every emergency: never had gallant knight a more useful auxiliary.

With the noble lyric of the hero's death the curtain is appropriately dropped on the stirring drama: "They say that an old shaykh [his enemy], softened by the fate of the hero who had made himself illustrious by so many exploits, wept over his corpse, covered it with sand, and uttered these words: *Glory to thee, brave warrior! who, during thy life, hast been the defender of thy tribe, and who, even after thy death, hast saved thy brethren by the terror of thy corpse and of thy name! May thy soul live for ever! May the refreshing dews moisten the ground of this thy last exploit!*" Truly has it been said, "Happy is the warrior whose very enemies praise him." The moral of the story (for a moral there is to those who can read it aright) is, the triumph of a lofty mind and a resolute will over the clogging circumstances of humble birth and class-prejudice.

❧ INVISIBLE CAPS AND CLOAKS: SHOES OF SWIFTNESS: THE INEXHAUSTIBLE PURSE, ETC. ❧

A FAVOURITE ornament of popular fictions, remarks Price, in his edition of Warton's 'History of English Poetry,' "is the highly gifted object which is to supply the fortunate owner with the gratification of some particular wish, or to furnish him with the golden means of gratifying every want." Of this class of magical objects are the inexhaustible purse of Fortunatus and the wishing-cap and shoes of swiftness which so frequently figure in our fairy tales. The romance of Fortunatus, so long a nursery favourite in this country, and indispensable from the chapman's miscellaneous stock of penny story-books, ballads, and small-wares, is probably little known to juveniles of the present day, and copies have become so rare as to be considered as treasures by collectors of literary curiosities. The circumstance of the opening scene of the romance being the city of Famagosta, in the island of Cyprus, might suggest that it was of Venetian origin; but according to a copy in the British Museum, printed in 1682 (there is an imperfect copy dated six years earlier), it was "first penned in the Dutch [? German] tongue, thence abstracted, and was first put into English by T. C." —that is, by Thomas Churchyarde. Mr Ashton, in his 'Chap-Books of the Eighteenth Century,' says that the earliest notice he has found of the romance is 'Fortunatus Augsp. zu trucken verordnet durch J. Heybler, 1509,' and that it seems to have been popular, for there was a French edition, 'Histoire des aventures de Fortunatus, trad. de l'Espagn.': Rouen, 1656. As usual with chap-books, the title-page of an edition printed at Glasgow, so late as the year 1790, gives an abstract of the chief incidents of the tale: "The History of Fortunatus; setting forth his birth, life, travels, and adventures, in most parts of the world; how Lady Fortune appeared to him, and gave him a Rich Purse that never wanted money; and also in his travels how he got from the Soldan a Wishing Hat, that by putting it on his head he could convey himself immediately into whatever place he desired. With an account how Fortunatus on his deathbed declared to his two sons, Ampedo and Andolocia, the virtue of his Purse and Hat." Fortunatus, having quitted the service of the Earl of Flanders at the instigation of his fellow-chamberlain, who falsely represented to him that their master had a secret design to kill them both, proceeded from Venice to Calais, and thence to London, where, meeting with some merchants of Cyprus, he spent all his money in riotous living, after which he took shipping, and soon arrived at Picardy, in France. Being benighted in a wood, he lay down to sleep till the morning. "As soon as Fortunatus awoke, he saw standing before him a fair lady with her eyes muffled. 'I beseech thee,' said he, 'sweet virgin, for the love of God to assist me, that I may get out of this wood, for I have travelled a great way without food.' She asked what country he was of, and he replied, 'Of Cyprus; and I am constrained by poverty to seek my fortune.' 'Fear not, Fortunatus,' said she; 'I am the Goddess of Fortune, and by permission of Heaven have the power of Six Gifts, one of which I will bestow on thee, so choose for yourself; they are: Wisdom, Strength, Riches, Health, Beauty, and Long Life.' Said Fortunatus, 'I desire to have Riches, as long as I live.' With that she gave him a Purse, saying, 'As often as you put your hand into this purse, you shall find ten pounds of the coin of any nation thou shalt happen to be in.' Fortunatus returned many thanks to the goddess. Then she bade him follow her out of the wood, and so vanished." After this our hero returns to Famagosta, where he learns that his father and mother are both dead. He purchased his father's house, and pulled it down, and built on its site a stately palace; then he married Cassandra, the youngest daughter of a noble earl, by whom he had two sons, Ampedo and Andolocia. Twelve years after his marriage he resolved to travel once more, and taking leave of his wife and children, sailed for Alexandria, where he made acquaintance with the Soldan. "Fortunatus, after supper, opened his purse, and gave all the Soldan's servants very liberally. The Soldan, being pleased, told him he would show him such curiosities as he had never seen. Then he took him to a strong marble tower. In the first room were several very rich vessels and jewels; in the second he showed him several vessels of gold coin, with a fine wardrobe of garments, and golden candlesticks which shone all over the room, and mightily pleased Fortunatus. Then the Soldan showed him his bed-chamber, which was finely adorned, and likewise a small felt Hat, simple to behold, saying, 'I set more value on this hat than on all my jewels, as such another is not to be had, for it lets a person be wherever he doth wish.' Fortunatus imagined the Hat would agree very well with his Purse, and thereupon put it on his head, saying he should be glad of a hat that had such virtue. So the Soldan immediately gave it him. With that he suddenly wished himself in his ship, it being then under sail, that he might return to his own country. The Soldan, looking out at his window, and seeing the ship under sail, was very angry, and commanded his men to fetch him back, declaring that, if they took him, he should immediately be put to death. But Fortunatus was too quick for them, and arriving safe at Famagosta, very richly laden, was joyfully received by his wife, his two sons, and the citizens."

The Shoes of Swiftness of the renowned hero Jack the Giant-Killer possessed similar qualities to those of the wonderful Hat of Fortunatus. There can be no doubt that the tale of Jack and the Giants came to us from the North; and since the incidents are for the most part also found in Asiatic popular fictions, they may perhaps be considered as survivals of primitive Aryan myths, relating to conflicts with monstrous beasts, or hardly less brutal aboriginal races of men. The hero obtained his shoes of swiftness and other magical things in this wise, according to the vera-cious narrative of his exploits: King Arthur and his son were travelling about, and meeting with Jack, they joined company. The king being in want of money, Jack proposed that they should sup and sleep at the house of a "huge and monstrous" giant, who had three heads (none of which seems to have been of much account), and who could beat five hundred men in armour. So Jack goes to the house of this giant, and tells him that the king's son is coming with a thousand men, which would prove more than a match for him. "This is heavy news indeed," quoth the giant; "but I have a large vault underground where I shall run and hide myself." While the giant is thus in his self-imposed durance, Jack and the prince ate heartily at his expense, and slept soundly till morning, when they arose and took his money. Jack then goes to release the giant, who asked what he should give him for his care, seeing that his castle was not demolished. "Why," answered Jack, "nothing but your old rusty sword, the coat in the closet, and the cap and shoes which you keep at the bed-head." Quoth the giant readily, "Thou shalt have them with all my heart, as a just reward for thy kindness in protecting me from the king's son; and be sure that thou carefully keep them for my sake, for they are things of most excellent use: the *coat* will keep you *invisible;* the *cap* will furnish you with *knowledge;* the *sword* cuts whatever you *strike;* and the *shoes* are of extraordinary *swiftness.*"

These marvellously endowed objects play important parts in the romances and popular fictions of Northern Europe. The shoes of swift-ness were worn by Loke when he escaped from hell. Velent the smith, in the Edda of Sæmund, forged a "sword of sharpness," called Balmung in the Wilkina Saga, and it was so sharp that when Velent cleft his rival Œmilius with it, the blade seemed to the latter only like cold water running down his body. "Shake thyself," said Velent: he did so, and fell in two halves, one on each side of the chair. The coat of invisibility is identical with the *tarn-hut,* or hat of darkness, celebrated in the 'Nibelungenlied' and in the 'Nifflunga Saga,' and with the *nebel kappe,* or cloud-cap, fabled to belong to King Alberich and the other dwarfs of old German romance.—In the German fairy tale of "The Nose-Tree," three poor soldiers receive from a dwarf—one, a cloak, which, whenever the owner put it on his shoulders, accomplished anything he desired; the second, a purse, which was always full of gold, no matter how much was taken out of it; the third, a horn, that drew crowds around it whenever it played; and in the story of the "Dancing Shoes" (which is also domiciled in Portugal—see 'Portuguese Folk-Tales,' published by the Folk-Lore Society), a soldier is presented, by a little old woman, with a cloak which rendered the wearer invisible. Caps and coats having the same property are among the treasures which the conquered ogres lay before the hero Little Peachling, in Mr Mitford's 'Tales of Old Japan.' In the German story of Heads Off! Heinel, the hero, in the course of his adventures, "came to a hill where three giants were sharing their father's goods; and as they saw him pass, they cried out and said, 'Little men have sharp wits; he shall part the goods between us.' [In fairy tales giants are always foolish.] Now there was a sword that cut off an enemy's head whenever the wearer said, 'Heads Off!' a cloak that made the wearer invisible, or gave him any form he pleased; and a pair of boots that carried the owner wherever he wished to go. Heinel said they must first let him try these wonderful things, that he might know how to set a value upon each of them. So they gave him the cloak, and he wished himself a fly, and in a moment he was a fly. 'The cloak is well enough,' said he; 'now give me the sword. 'No,' said they, 'not unless you promise not to say, "Heads Off!" for if you do we are all dead men.' Then they gave it him, charging him to try it only on a tree. He next asked for the boots; and the moment he had all three in his power, he wished himself at the Golden Mountain, and there he was at once. So the giants were left behind with no goods to share or quarrel about." And in the Norse story of the Three Princesses of Whiteland, the wandering king comes upon three brothers on a moor, who were fighting for the possession of a hat, a cloak, and a pair of boots, which enabled the wearer to become invisible and to go wherever he pleased. "Why do you stand here," said the king, "fighting for ever and a day? Just let me try these things, and I'll give judgment whose they shall be." This they were very willing to do; but as soon as he had got the hat, cloak, and boots, he said, "When we meet next time, I'll tell you my judgment." And with these words he wished himself away.

This incident—which, as we shall presently see, is world-wide—also occurs in the Italian popular tale of Lion Bruno, which is of modern Greek extraction. The hero finds three robbers quarrelling in a wood, and is chosen to be their arbiter. They had stolen three things of great value, and could not agree about the division of them. These were: a pair of boots which had this virtue, that whoever put them on could run a mile faster than the wind; a purse which, by saying, "Open and shut," yielded a hundred ducats; and a cloak, which whoever put on saw and was not seen. The hero tries all three, and by aid of the boots gets safely off, leaving the robbers to quarrel among themselves, while he continues his journey.—In a Breton version, published in the first volume of 'Mélusine,' entitled, "Voleur avisé," the magical articles are: A cloak which, being put on, transported the owner to any place he desired to reach; a hat that conferred invisibility on the wearer; and gaiters that gave the power of walking as fast as the wind.[1]

So, too, in the Persian romance entitled 'Báhar-i-Dánish,' or Spring of Knowledge (which is, all but the frame, avowedly derived from Indian sources), two brothers dispute about an old fakír's cloak, which produced, when required, any quantity of rich clothes; a satchel, from which issued at will diamonds, pearls, and other precious gems; a kalender's bowl, which became full to overflowing with all sorts of delicious viands and

---

[1]"Some Italian Folk-Tales," by H. C. Coote, in 'The Folk-Lore Record,' vol. i. p. 211.—On the close affinity between the French and Italian popular mythologies, Coote remarks: "The same tales which have been told by Celtic crones in sequestered and misty Basse Bretagne, have been recounted in a more graceful tongue and under a better sky in sunny Tuscany, in the old Neapolitan kingdom, and elsewhere in the [Italian] peninsula, as familiar household words. No communication between the two countries can be reasonably supposed, since the disruption of the Western Empire. The simultaneous appearance of the tales in both countries, thus deprived of close intercourse, disposes of the Celtic ascription. Being found in a non-Celtic country as well as in a Celtic one, the common origin of the fictions cannot be Celtic merely. It should rather be sought in the free and unrestricted means of communication which existed between them when they were both parts of the same empire."—Ibid., pp. 212, 213.

A most remarkable *recipe* for making shoes of swiftness is found in an Icelandic story: "The giant told her that Hermódr was in a certain desert island, which he named to her; but she could not get thither unless she *flayed the soles of her feet and made shoes for herself out of the skin;* and these shoes, when made, would be of such a nature that they would take her through the air, or over the water, as she liked."—'Icelandic Legends,' translated by Powell and Magnusson. Second Series, p. 397.

liquors; and a pair of wooden clogs, which transported the wearer from one end of the world to the other in the twinkling of an eye. The hero is appointed arbiter, and shoots two arrows in different directions, which the disputants are to fetch him back, and he who returns first is to have the treasures, with which he decamps while they are running in search of the arrows. The same incident occurs in the Arabian tale of Hasan of Basra, which presents several points of resemblance to the charming Persian romance of King Bahrám Ghúr and the fairy Húsn Bánú. In the latter the royal hero receives from the lord of the second Káf the magical cap of Solomon, which enabled the wearer to see whom he pleased, but they could not see him; from the lord of the third Káf he obtained the staff of Solomon, which caused any door to fly open, no matter how strong it might be, and even if guarded by talismans and enchantments; and from the lord of the fourth Káf, Solomon's slipper, wrought with threads of gold, by which one might travel a journey of a hundred years without being weary, and the distance traversed would seem but a hundred steps.[2]

An invisible cap and boots of swiftness also figure prominently in the Kalmuk collection of tales, entitled 'Siddhí Kúr,' an English version of which, based upon Bergmann's German translation, was published many years ago by W. J. Thoms in his 'Lays and Legends of many Nations,' a work which was never completed, and the fasciculi that were printed are now become very scarce:[3]

"The Son of the Khán and his companion travelled along a river and arrived in a wood, where they found a number of children quarrelling one

---

[2]Muhammedans, like Christians before Copernicus, conceived the earth to be a vast plane of circular form, surrounded by a mountain of immense altitude, called by the Arabs *Káf*, and the Arabian lexicographers describe it as being composed of green emerald. In the 'Borham-i Kati,' a valuable Persian dictionary, we have the following description of it: "Káf, the name of the famous mountain which surrounds the four quarters of the earth. They say that its altitude is five hundred parasangs [nearly two thousand English miles!], and for the most part the sea washes the base of it."—*Duncan Forbes*. Káf was supposed to be the abode of genii, perís, and dívs, or giants—the mysterious region of enchantments. In Muslim legends, Solomon, the great Hebrew king, is represented as master of all magic arts, all the genii being under his control.

[3]Siddhí Kúr signifies a dead body endowed with supernatural powers, or a corpse into which a vampire has entered. These Relations of Siddhí Kúr are the Mongolian form of the ancient Indian work, 'Vetálapanchavinsati'—Twenty-five (Tales) of a Vetála, or demon. The first part of a book, published a few years ago under the title of 'Sagas from the Far East,' by Miss M. H. Busk, consists of the Tales of Siddhí Kúr, based, it is said, upon Professor Jülg's German translation; the second part, entitled Ardshí Bordshí (Rájá Bhoja), is the Mongolian form of another old Indian collection, 'Sinhásana Dwatrinsati,' or Thirty-two (Tales) of a Throne.

with another. 'Wherefore,' inquired they, 'do you thus dispute?' 'We have found a cap in this wood,' said the children, 'and every one desires to possess it.' 'Of what use is this cap?' 'The cap has this wonderful property, that whosoever places it on his head can be neither seen by demons nor men.' 'Now, go all of you to the end of the forest and run hither, and I will in the meanwhile keep the cap, and give it to the first of you who reaches me.' Thus spake the Son of the Khán, and the children ran; but they found not the cap, for it was upon the head of his companion. 'Even now it was here,' said they, 'and now it is gone!' And after they had sought for it, but without finding it, they went away weeping.

"And the Son of the Khán and his companion travelled onwards, and at last they came to a forest where they found a party of demons quarrelling one with another, and they said, 'Why do you quarrel one with another?' 'I have made myself master of these boots,' exclaimed each of them. 'Of what use are these boots?' inquired the Son of the Khán. 'He who wears these boots,' replied they, 'is conveyed to any country wherein he wishes himself.' 'Now,' said the Son of the Khán, 'go all of you that may, and he who first runs hither shall have the boots.' And the demons (*chadkúrs*), when they heard these words, ran as they were told; but the Son of the Khán had concealed the boots in the bosom of his companion, who had the cap upon his head. And the demons saw the boots no more; they sought them in vain, and went their way."

A much older version is found in the great collection of tales and apologues, entitled 'Kathá Sarit Ságara,' or Ocean of the Rivers of Story, composed in Sanskrit verse, by Somadeva, of Kashmír, in the eleventh century, after a similar work entitled 'Vrihat Kathá,' or the Great Story (of which no copy has hitherto been discovered), written by Gunadhya, in the sixth century:[4]

"As King Putraka wandered about [in the wilds of Vindhya], he saw two heroes engaged heart and soul in a wrestling-match, and he asked them who they were. They replied, 'We are two sons of the Asura Maya,[5] and his wealth belongs to us—this vessel, and this stick, and these shoes. It is

---

[4]This grand work, in which are found the originals of many of the tales of the 'Arabian Nights,' has been translated by Professor C. H. Tawney, and recently published at Calcutta, in fourteen fasciculi, or two large volumes. The best thanks of English students of comparative folk-lore are due to Mr Tawney for the service he has thus rendered them: his notes, giving references to variants of the tales, are very valuable as well as interesting.

[5]An *Asura* was formerly considered as a kind of deity, but latterly as a species of demon. The term *Maya* signifies "delusion."

for these that we are fighting, and whichever of us proves the mightier is to take them.' When he heard this speech of theirs, Putraka said with a smile, 'That is a fine inheritance for a man.' Then they said, 'By putting on these shoes one gains the power of flying through the air; whatever is written on this staff turns out true; and whatever food a man wishes to have in this vessel is found there immediately.' When he heard this, Putraka said, 'What is the use of fighting? Make this agreement, that whoever proves the best man in running, shall possess these treasures.' Those simpletons said, 'Agreed,' and set off to run, while the prince put on the shoes and flew up into the air, taking with him the staff and the vessel."

It is probable that this incident is of Buddhist origin, since it is found in the 'Avadánas' (No. 74), or, Indian Tales and Apologues, translated into French from the Chinese, by Stanislas Julien, in which, however, two Pisachas have *each* a magic coffer, staff, and shoe. "These two demons were always quarrelling, each wishing to have all those six things for himself. They passed whole days fighting with each other, without being able to agree. A man, who had witnessed this obstinate contention, asked them, 'What is there so rare in a coffer, a staff, and a shoe that you should fight so bitterly about them?' The demons answered, 'From this coffer we can take clothes, liquors, food—in short, all sorts of things needful for life and comfort. When we hold this staff, our enemies humbly yield to us, and no one dare withstand us. When we put on this shoe, we can walk as if we were flying, without encountering any obstacle.' On hearing this, the man said to them, 'Go a little way off; I am about to make a fair division.' At these words both the demons went aside. That man took the two coffers, the two staffs, and the two shoes, and made off with them. The two demons were dumfounded when they saw that there no longer remained anything for them. Then said that man to the demons, 'I have taken possession of everything, which leaves you both in the same plight, and I have removed from you all cause of jealousy and contention.'" The two Pisachas each possessing similar treasures seems a modification by the Chinese translator, but for which this might be considered as nearer the original form of the story.

The Mongolians have a curious legend of the origin of the Chinese nation, which is based upon the same incident of the contest for possession of a magical treasure:

There was once a poor Bandé. He had nothing to drink or to eat. The Bandé went on the road and met two men quarrelling over a precious stone as big as a sheep's eye. Bandé said to them that they should hand him the stone, and that he should run with it, and whoever first caught him should be given the stone. They prepared to race; then Bandé swallowed the stone and disappeared. He came to the territory of a certain Khán. In a poor tent lived an old man and an old woman; he lived with them; the old man adopted him as a son to his house. Bandé spat and vomited gold. The old man took the gold to the Khán, to ask him for his daughter for wife to Bandé. The Khán wished to see Bandé himself with his own eyes. Bandé vomited out some gold before the face of the Khán. The daughter of the Khán ordered him to be bound with a horse-girth, and giving him salt water, flogged him with a whip, and out flew the stone from him. The Khán's daughter seized the stone and swallowed it. Bandé returned to his old man, and said that he had lost the power of producing gold. "What are we to do now?" says the old man. "Make an ass's saddle and bridle," said Bandé. When the things were prepared, Bandé went to a tree and sat down. At that time the Khán's daughter, with twenty virgins, went out to play with the white tree. Then Bandé began to read a writing which had been read out to him in his sleep, when he in the time of his poverty slept in the road under the tree. By this reading the Khán's daughter, who was pregnant because she had swallowed the precious stone, was changed into a she-ass. Then the other maidens, seeing only the she-ass, and not seeing the Khán's daughter, were frightened; but Bandé saddled the ass and rode off. He rode for a month; then the ass was wearied out, and could go no farther. Bandé left her, and proceeded on foot to a certain town, where he became a lhama [*i.e.,* Buddhist priest]. The ass which he left behind gave birth to two boys—one good, the other evil. The following generations were all likewise twins. They all became rich; had much gold, silver, cloth, tea, etc. From them came the Chinese nation.[6]

In Steele and Temple's 'Wide-Awake Stories' from the Panjáb and Kashmír (tale of the King and his Seven Sons) there are four magical treasures: a wallet with two pockets, one of which will produce anything desired by the person who smells at it, except that it cannot make a man—the other pocket can even make a man; a staff, which can bring a dead man struck with it to life again three times; a brass pot, if properly cleansed, will give the person who cleanses it the thirty-six kinds of sumptuous food; and a pair of sandals, which convey the wearer wheresoever he pleases.

[6]'Folk-Lore Journal,' 1886, vol. iv. pp. 23, 24.

A Hindústaní version, in Miss Stokes's 'Indian Fairy Tales,' tells how four fakírs disputed with each other for the possession of four things left them by their late spiritual teacher, namely: a bed that carried whoever sat on it anywhere he wished; a bag that gave the owner of it whatever he wanted—jewels, food, or clothes; a stone bowl that gave as much water as was required, no matter how far one might be from any tank; and a stick and rope to which the owner had simply to say, "Stick, stick! beat as many men and soldiers as are here," and the stick would beat them, and the rope would tie them up. The hero of the story, of course, outwits the four foolish fakírs, and obtains possession of the wonderful bed, bag, bowl, and stick.—In the Rev. Lal Behari Day's 'Folk Tales of Bengal,' an indigent Bráhman received from Durga, the consort of Siva, a magic pipkin, from which flowed the most delicious sweetmeats; and when it was stolen from him, Durga gives him another pipkin, out of which issue fierce demons, who compel the thief to restore what he had stolen. A similar incident is found in Miss Frere's 'Old Deccan Days; or, Indian Fairy Legends.'

The magic stick figures also to the same purpose in the Norse tale of the Lad who went to the North Wind, some of the incidents of which closely resemble those of Miss Stokes's Hindú version. The North Wind having caught the Lad's meal, the hero immediately goes to him and demands it back. This the North Wind cannot do, but he gives the Lad in place of his meal a cloth, which provided him with everything he should want, when he said, "Cloth! cloth! spread yourself out and serve up all kinds of good dishes." This is stolen from him, so he goes back to the North Wind, who gives him a ram, which coined golden ducats as soon as he said to it, "Ram! ram! make money."[7] This also is stolen from him; so he goes back again to the North Wind, and gets a stick, which belaboured any one if the owner said, "Stick! stick! lay on;" and by means of this wonderful stick he recovers his cloth and his ram.[8]

The same story as this last is—*mutatis mutandis*—current among the people of Italy: A man named Geppone (*i.e.,* Joe) had a farm on the top of a hill, which was so buffeted by the North Wind that he could raise nothing. At last he goes to the North Wind and makes his complaint,

---

[7] Stories of Gold-producing Animals will be found compared in the following paper.

[8] Dasent's 'Popular Tales from the Norse.' Second edition, p. 263. A precisely similar story, under the title of "Jack's Luck; or, the Ass, the Table, and the Stick," is told in 'English Fairy Tales from the North Country,' by Dr A. C. Fryer.

and the North Wind gives him, by way of compensation, a box, which he has only to tap, at the same time calling out, "Bring wine, bread, and meat," when forthwith all sorts of eatables and drinkables are spread before him. He takes the box home, and his wife and children get a good dinner. Joe warns his wife to say nothing about his treasure to the prior, else he would want to take it for his own use. But she does tell the prior, who obtains the box, on promising to provide Joe with corn, wine, etc. The prior, however, does not keep his promise, so poor Joe goes again to the North Wind, acquaints him of how the prior had defrauded him, and receives this time a golden box. On his way home Joe taps the box and calls out "Provide," upon which out jumps a great big man with a stick in his hand, and belabours him within an inch of his life. Joe shuts up the box and resumes his journey. Having reached home, he was eagerly asked what he had got this time from the North Wind, to which he replied by producing the golden box, and calling out "Provide," when the big man came out of it, and thrashed Joe's wife and children till they cried for mercy. Joe then shuts the box, and bids his wife go to the prior and tell him that he has another box more beautiful than the first, which provides most sumptuous dinners. The prior is delighted to hear this news, and desires her to send her husband with the new box to him at once. Joe sets off accordingly; shows his treasure to the prior, who offers him the old box in exchange for it, which Joe accepts, at the same time cautioning the prior not to open the golden box until people were very hungry. "That will do," responded the prior; "I shall have the titular and many clergy-men to dinner, and I won't open the box before noontide." The morning comes; all the priests say mass, and afterwards some of them walk round about the kitchen. "To-day," they say, "the prior surely does not mean to give us any dinner. The fire is out, and there is nothing prepared." But the others, who had seen the effects of the first box, answered, "You will soon see: when dinner-time comes he opens a box, and makes all sorts of viands appear." When the dinner-hour arrived, the prior told all the priests to take their places, and they anxiously waited to see the miracle of the box. So the box is opened, and six men armed with sticks jump out, and belabour the whole company right and left. The box falls from the prior's hand, still open; but Joe, who is outside, picks it up and shuts it. He ever after retained both boxes, and never lent them to anybody, and became a great lord.[9]

[9]"Some Italian Folk-Tales," by H. C. Coote, in 'The Folk-Lore Record,' vol. i. pp. 204–206.

The 17th of Leger's collection of Slav Tales furnishes another interesting variant of the Norse story: A countryman had three sons, the youngest of whom was (as usual in fairy tales) considered as a blockhead. The eldest son hires himself to a farmer for a year, and receives as wages a snow-white sheep, from whose fleece a shower of gold fell whenever one said, "Sheep, help me." On his way home he tries his sheep in a wood, and obtains abundance of gold. He puts up at an inn, and tells the landlady to take care of his sheep, and allow no one to say to it, "Sheep, help me." But during the night she goes to the sheep, and having said these words, gets a shower of gold from its fleece. She then takes it away, and puts another sheep in its place. In the morning the youth goes home with this sheep, and in attempting to exhibit its gold-giving nature utterly fails, of course, and being laughed at by his friends, he beats the *spurious* sheep to death. The second son next goes and serves the same farmer for a year, and receives as his wages a napkin, to which one had only to say, "Napkin, serve me," and instantly it was covered with a sumptuous feast. He puts up at the same inn, and is cheated of his napkin, as his brother was of his sheep, and is ridiculed at home. Then the youngest son, whom everybody despised as a noodle, serves the same man, and at the year's end, on relating to him the misadventures of his two brothers, and expressing his wish to recover the sheep and the napkin, he gets from the farmer a stick, which when addressed, "Up, stick! down with the fellow!—*nab* him, slap him!" hits all round until it is recalled. He takes up his lodging at the inn, and gives the landlady the stick to take care of for him till the morning, warning her not to allow any one to say, "Stick! down with him!" But she determines to test the qualities of the stick as she had done those of the other things, and so at night she says to it, "Stick, stick, lay on!" etc.; whereupon the stick bangs her right and left till her yells and screams awoke the youth, who came to her rescue, but would not order the stick to cease beating her until she promised to restore the sheep and the napkin.[10]

A French version, "Jean a la Tige d'Haricot," current in Picardy, has the same incidents, with an ass that gave money whenever one said, "Ass, show your talent;" a table that was spread with all sorts of eatables and drinkables when one cried, "Table, do your duty;" and a kitchen rolling-

---

[10]'Contes Populaires Slaves.' Recueillis et traduits par L. Leger. Paris: 1882.

pin that compelled the restoration of the two other treasures, which had been stolen by the hostess.[11]

A variant orally current among the common people of Rome, possesses peculiar interest from the resemblance which the first part bears to an Indian story: The two sons of a poor man while in the woods one day saw a great bird alight and drop an egg, which, when the bird flew away, they picked up and discovered some writing on the shell. As they could not read, they took the egg to a farmer, who at once perceived that the inscription signified, "Who eats my head shall become emperor; who eats my heart shall never want for money;" but wishing to eat both the head and the heart himself, he told the youths that the meaning of the writing was, "Whosoever eats the bird shall make a very good dinner." "To-morrow, therefore," added he, "do you provide yourselves with a good stick, watch for the return of the bird, and knock her down. Then make a fire and cook the bird, and I will come myself and eat it along with you." The bird was accordingly killed next day, and put on a fire to roast. It happened that the head dropped into the fire, and the younger of the two brothers, thinking it too much burnt to set before the farmer, took and ate it; and soon after the heart also fell into the fire, and the elder brother ate it, as it was likewise sadly burnt. When the farmer came, he said he wished to have only the head and the heart of the bird, and great was his rage on learning what had become of them. On their return home the youths informed their poor father how they had unintentionally offended the farmer, at which he was much concerned, and told them there was no help for it, but they must go out into the world and seek their own fortunes. So they left the parental roof and set out on their travels. At night they came to an inn, and the landlord allowed them to sleep on some straw in the stable. What was the astonishment of the elder brother to discover a box full of sequins under his head when

---

[11]'Contes Français.' Recueillis par E. Henry Carnoy. Paris: 1885. See also a Tuscan parallel, p. 123 of 'Italian Popular Tales,' by Prof. T. F. Crane. London: 1885.—This is an ingenious "explanation" of the story of the Ass, Stick, &c., by one of our solar-mythologists: "The table is the all-nourishing cloud. The buck-goat [ass, or ram] is another emblem of the clouds, and the gold it spits is the golden light of the sun that streams through the fleecy coverings of the sky. The demon of darkness has stolen these things; the cloud gives no rain, but hangs dusky in the sky, veiling the light of the sun. Then the lightning-spear [*i.e.,* the Stick] of the ancient storm-god Odin leaps out from the bag that concealed it; the robber falls, the rain patters down, the sun shines once more."—'Curiosities of Indo-European Tradition and Folk-Lore.' By Walter K. Kelly. "Curiosities" indeed!

he awoke in the morning. Supposing that this was a device of the land-lord to try their honesty, the youths carried the box to him, saying that he must have left it in the stable inadvertently. The landlord, in his turn not a little astonished, took the box, treated them to a good breakfast, and gave them provisions for the day, after which they resumed their journey. The following night they slept in the stable of another inn, and in the morning again the elder brother found a box of sequins under his head. Believing the landlord of the preceding night had thus laid another trap for them, the brothers went back and gave him this second box, which he very willingly accepted, though wondering what it all meant. On the third night, when they were about to lie down in the sta-ble of another inn, the youngest expressed his doubts as to their first landlord being the real owner of the box of money, and he resolved to sit up and watch if the man came during the night. But he did not come, and in the morning there was a third box of sequins under the elder brother's head, so they were now satisfied that the treasure was intended for themselves. Continuing their journey, they reached a great city, the emperor of which had just died, and the inhabitants were at strife regarding the election of his successor. The younger brother, with the box of treasure on his shoulder, happened to be somewhat in advance of the other, and the guards at the city gates seized him, and when the peo-ple discovered the glittering contents of his box, they unanimously chose him for their emperor.

Meanwhile the elder brother entered the city unnoticed, and obtained a night's lodging in the house of a woman and her daughter. The box of sequins, which he found as usual beneath his head, when he awoke in the morning, enabled him to make handsome presents to the woman and her pretty daughter. But the girl wheedled out of him the secret of his wealth—his having eaten the bird's heart—and put an emetic into his wine at supper, which caused him to throw-up the money-giving heart, and he was then ignominiously turned into the street to shift as best he could. The poor youth wandered aimlessly till he came to the margin of a stream, where he lay down and began to weep and bewail his sad fate. Presently three fairies appeared, and hav-ing learned his story, gave him a sheep-skin jacket, the pockets of which, they told him, should be always full of money. Our hero then returned to the house of the fair but false demoiselle, with rich presents for herself and her mother. The girl, having ascertained the new source of his wealth, caused her maid to make a similar sheep-skin jacket,

which she substituted while he slept, and in the morning he left unsuspicious of the foul trick she had played him. He soon discovered it,
however, and seeking the stream once more, the fairies gave him a
wand, which, when struck on a table, would give him all he desired. Of
course, he returns again to the deceitful demoiselle, and of course she
steals the magic rod from him, and sends him about his business. He
revisits the stream and receives from the beneficent fairies a wishing-
ring, which they caution him to guard very carefully, since it is the last
gift in their power to bestow on him. Going back to the house of the
demoiselle, in answer to her inquiries he tells her that the ring on his
finger is a wishing-ring. "Then," says she, "do you wish that we may be
both together on the top of yonder mountain, and a sumptuous feast
spread out for us." The youth willingly complies, and in an instant they
are there, and find a grand feast spread out for them. The demoiselle
drugs his wine, and while he is asleep steals the ring, and by its virtue
is immediately back in her own house. What must have been the feelings of the poor youth when he awoke and found both his ring and the
treacherous demoiselle gone! After wandering about for three days
weeping, he took some herbs to assuage his hunger, when lo! he was at
once transformed into a donkey, with panniers hung over his sides. But
he still preserved his intelligence, and before beginning to descend the
mountain, he put some of the wonder-working herbs in his panniers.
When he reached the foot, he plucked some grass that grew there, and
behold! he was restored to his own proper form. Taking a quantity of
this grass also, he entered the city, and, disguised as a street-hawker,
with a basket of the herbs on his arm, he went under the window of the
false demoiselle and bawled out, "Salad, fine salad!" The maid, knowing her mistress was very fond of salad, took him into the house and
introduced him to the young lady, who no sooner began to test the
quality of the herbs than she was changed into the form of a donkey.
Our hero then drove her through the city, and cudgelled her so severely
that a citizen seized him, saying that he must answer for his cruelty to
the emperor. Now when he was brought, with the donkey, into the
emperor's presence, he at once recognised, in the person of the great
monarch, his younger brother, and desired the court to be cleared
before he entered into any explanations, which being done, he then told
the emperor his story, and the brothers fell upon each other's necks and
wept for joy. The emperor caused the wicked demoiselle in donkey-
shape to return to her house with our hero, and restore all the treasures

she had stolen from him, after which she was given some of the grass, and resumed her natural form.[12]

An Indian analogue of the incident of the eating of the bird's head and heart in this last story is found in the Manipurí tale of the two princes Turi and Basanta, who in the course of their wanderings rest for the night under a tree on which a pair of parrots are perched, and Turi, while his brother sleeps, hears the birds converse together. The cock-parrot calls to his wife, and asks her what will happen to the man who should eat her. She answers that at first he will experience great distress, and afterwards even greater happiness. The cock says that the man who should eat him will be made king. Turi kills both birds, and roasts them. By-and-by he feels very sleepy, and awaking his brother, desires him to keep watch for a short time. During the night Basanta, feeling hungry, eats the hen-bird, which is fated to bring sorrow upon him. In the morning Turi eats the other bird. Searching for water, the brothers lose sight of each other. Turi becomes a king, and Basanta, after a series of strange vicissitudes, is reunited to his brother.[13]

In another Roman popular story, an aged man on his deathbed bequeaths to his eldest son an old broken hat without a brim; yet such was its virtue, that "if you put it on, you can go in to dine at whatever inn you please, or sit down to drink at what wine-shop you please, and drink what you like, for no one will see you when you have it on." To his second son he gives a purse, "in which, whenever you put your fingers in, you will always find a scudo there, and after that another, and another, and as many as ever you wish—there will always be one." To his youngest son he gives a horn, telling him that whenever he wants anything he has only to sound it, and one [14] will come and bring whatever he wants—be it a dinner, a suit of clothes, a palace, or even an army. The second son—who, strangely, is the hero of this tale—is seen by a maid from a window, and invited to play at cards with the queen her mistress, who learns from him the secret of his wealth, and appropriates the magic purse. He borrows in succession his eldest brother's magic hat and his youngest brother's magic horn, both of

[12]'The Folk-Lore of Rome.' Collected from the mouths of the People. By M. H. Busk. London: 1874. Pp. 146–154.

[13]'Indian Antiquary,' 1875, vol. iv. pp. 260–264.

[14] By "one" we are to understand that the genie, or "slave," of the horn is meant.

which the greedy and unscrupulous queen also contrives to take from him. After this he went about disconsolate, and coming to a fig-tree he plucked and ate some of its fruit, when behold! his nose assumed an enormous length; but by-and-by, eating some cherries, his nose returned to its natural condition. Taking a quantity of these wonder-working figs and cherries, he gave some of the figs to the queen and her servants, whose noses, after their eating the fruit, became fearful snouts—that of the wicked queen was no less than twelve feet long. Then he went near the palace another day and cried, "Noses reduced in size!" So he was taken within, and, to convince the queen of his skill in this branch of surgical science, he reduced the noses of the domestics. When the queen saw this, she desired to have her own nose also reduced, but remarked to him that she possessed more wonderful things than his cure for long noses; and so saying, she showed him the magic hat, purse, and horn, explaining their respective qualities, upon which our hero clapped the hat upon his head, and, thus becoming invisible, then picked up the purse and the horn and went off—leaving the wicked queen still with her "twelve feet of nose."[15]

Still worse was the fate of the avaricious fellow in the 14th Tale of Siddhí Kúr ('Sagas from the Far East'): There were formerly two brothers, of whom the younger was very rich and very avaricious; the elder was exceedingly poor. One day the rich man gave a grand feast, and did not invite his brother; so, being reduced to absolute want, he went into the wilderness, intending to put an end to his wretched life. There he sees a party of Dakinis (male and female evil genii) assembled, who take from the cleft of a rock a bag, and a hammer with which they beat the bag, when lo! there issues from it a plentiful supply of food and drink; and thumping it a second time, they get from it silver and gold trinkets. After feasting to their hearts' content, they replace the sack and the hammer and disappear. Then the poor man comes out of his place of concealment and takes away these wonderful things. Of course, he soon becomes very rich, which his brother observing, he inquires the cause of his sudden prosperity, and is told the whole story. He sets off at once to the spot

[15]Miss Busk's 'Folk-Lore of Rome,' p. 129.—This story is also found in Grimm's 'Kinder und Hausmärchen.' The incident of the hero's transformation to donkey-form, by eating certain herbs, in the preceding Italian tale, is simply a variant of the "Nose" in this story. In the 46th chapter of an old English version of the 'Gesta Romanorum,' the hero, who had been tricked of three magic treasures by his leman, in his wanderings ate some fruit that made him a leper, and then came to a river the water of which healed him: returning to the city, he found the damsel leprous, cured her with some of the same water, and got back his treasures.

where the Dakinis were seen by his lucky brother, in hopes of being equally fortunate; but when the Dakinis discover him, they call out one to another, "This is he who stole our sack and hammer! Let us kill him." In the end they merely draw out his nose till it is four ells long, and then tie nine knots on it. The wretched man hides himself till it is dark, when he creeps home and frightens his wife by his appearance. How to get rid of his knotted nose perplexes him, till at length he sends for his brother, tells him how he had been treated by the Dakinis, and promises to give him half his wealth if he will cure his sore affliction by means of his magic hammer. The brother consents, and at each stroke of the hammer one of the knots disappears; but when eight of them have been thus removed, the wife of the avaricious one, thinking to save the money they had promised for the cure, seizes the hammer and runs with it into an inner room, where afterwards, attempting to do away the ninth knot on her husband's nose, she struck him such a blow with the hammer that he was killed outright.

The covetous man is always punished in fairy tales. Another instance is furnished in the Irish legend of Mick Purcell, who was reduced by a succession of bad harvests to take his only cow to market for sale. On his way he meets with—or is overtaken by—a strange-looking little grey man, who gives him in exchange for his cow a bottle, which, the little man assures him, would make him rich in a very short time: all he had to do was to go home, make his wife sweep the floor, spread a clean cloth over the table; then set the bottle on the ground, saying these words, "Bottle! do your duty"—and he would see the end of it. Mick goes home accordingly, and having strictly followed the little man's instructions, he had no sooner said, "Bottle! do your duty," when "two tiny little fellows rose like light from the bottle, and in an instant covered the table with dishes and plates of gold and silver, full of the finest victuals that ever were seen, and when all was done went into the bottle again. . . . Next day Mick went to Cork and sold his plate, and bought a horse and cart, and began to show that he was making money; and they did all they could to keep the bottle a secret: but for all that, their landlord found it out, and came to Mick one day and asked him where he got all his money—sure it was not by the farm; and he bothered him so much, that at last Mick told him of the bottle. His landlord offered him a deal of money for it, but Mick would not give it, till at last he offered to give him all his farm for ever. So Mick, who was very rich, thought he'd never want money, and gave him the bottle. But Mick was mistaken: he and his family spent money as if there was no end of it; and, to make the story short, they became poorer and poorer, till at last they had nothing left but one cow; and Mick once more drove his cow before him to sell her at Cork fair, hoping to meet the old man and get another bottle." Mick does meet the little old man again, and receives another bottle from him in exchange for his cow. Returning home in great glee, he at once begins to try the virtue of the bottle—the floor is swept, the table covered with a nice clean cloth, and then Mick sets his bottle on the ground and calls out, "Bottle! do your duty." In a twinkling, "two great stout men with bib cudgels issued from the bottle and belaboured poor Mick and his wife and all his family, till they lay on the floor, when in they went again." As soon as Mick was recovered from the effects of his beating, he got up, and tucking the bottle under his coat, sets off to the house of his landlord. "Well, what do you want now?" "Nothing," says Mick, "only I've another bottle." "Oh ho! is it as good as the first?" "A great deal better, as I will show you, before these ladies and gentlemen." "Come along then," says the landlord. So Mick sets it on the floor, saying, "Bottle! do your duty," and suddenly the landlord was tumbled on the floor; ladies and gentlemen, servants and all, were running and roaring and sprawling and kicking and shrieking. Wine-cups and salvers were knocked about in every direction, until the landlord called out, "Stop these two devils, Mick Purcell, or I'll have you hanged." "They'll never stop," says Mick, "till I get my own bottle that I see up there on the top of that shelf." "Give it down to him," says the landlord—"give it down to him before we are killed." Mick put his bottle in his bosom; in jumped the two men into the other bottle, and he carried them home. After this Mick got richer than ever, and his son married his landlord's only daughter.[16]

To the same wide cycle of folk-tales, in which the virtuous are rewarded and the greedy and avaricious are justly punished, belongs this Polish tale, from M. Leger's collection: An old man begs food of a woman called Blazkowa, who refuses him, saying merely, "God help you." He then applies for relief to a charitable woman named Janova, who takes from her children two buttered slices of bread which she had cut for them and gives them to the old man, saying, "May God give you something

---

[16] 'Fairy Legends and Traditions of the South of Ireland.' By J. Crofton Croker; edited by Thomas Wright: "Legend of Bottle Hill."

better; this is all I have in my hut." The beggar replies, "May God return it to you, kind woman, tenfold! May you ever have clothing for your children, and what you begin to do to-day may you be unable to finish to-night." She thanks him for his good wishes, and he goes off. But she has no food for her children, and what is she to do? She had lately spun some flax, of which the weaver had made twenty ells of cloth; it was her only wealth, and she was keeping it for winter clothing; but now she was compelled to sell a portion of it to a Jew, in order to obtain the means of support for herself and her children. So she begins to measure the cloth: ell succeeds ell, until she had measured a hundred and eight ells by sunset, and still she had not come to the end. Thousands of ells passed through her hands; time pressed; it is too late now to go to the Jew: she takes a few ells to her neighbour, the greedy woman, Blazkowa, who gives her but a trifling sum of money, which she took to feed her children. Next day Janova goes to the village fair, and her linen was found to be so fine that she had a good and ready sale, and returned home quite wealthy. Her neighbour Blazkowa is envious of her good luck, and invites her to her house. Over "a little glass" she learns the source of Janova's wealth, and the latter promises to send the old beggar-man to Blazkowa, should he come back again. A week later the beggar returns. Janova entertains him, and then sends him to Blazkowa. As soon as she saw him coming, she gave her children two slices of bread-and-butter, and when the old man entered she snatched them from the children and gave them to him. "May God reward you," says he; "and what you now do may you go on doing till sunset." She had got some linen and her ell-measure ready, when her children crying for water to drink, she ran with her pitcher to the well; but no sooner had she returned than she felt compelled to go again for another pitcherful, and so she kept on carrying water till sunset.[17]

An exact parallel story is current in China: Once upon a time Fo came down to this world to try the hearts of men, and was hospitably received by a kind widow. She sat up all night to make him a new shirt, and on leaving next day Fo pronounced this blessing, "May God reward you for what you have done to me, and may the first thing that you begin to do after I leave not cease till the sun sets." Thoughtless of the meaning of his words, the widow began to measure her cloth, to see how much was left, and she measured on till sunset before coming to the end of the piece. The

---

[17]'Contes Populaires Slaves.' Paris: 1882.

room was full of linen, and she had become a rich woman. A miserly neighbour, hearing of this good fortune, placed herself at her door in the hope of finding an equally profitable deed of charity. Fo appears in rags as before, and is treated by this woman in the same way as the other had done. On leaving next morning he gave her a similar blessing. Her pig at that moment began to grunt, and she thought to herself, "I shall be measuring linen and unable to feed the pig, so I had better give him some water before beginning." She took up her pail, and began to pour out some water, but soon found that she had not the power of stopping. There she stood and poured on and on till sunset, when the whole village was inundated, and she had to endure the ill-will of all her neighbours.[18]

In the collection of Sicilian popular tales by Laura Gonzenbach, we find a tablecloth, to which, when it is spread out, one has only to say, "Dear little tablecloth, give macaroni," or roast meat, and it supplies whatever is required; a purse, which furnishes as much money as may be wanted; and a pipe, which when played upon compels all who hear it to dance—like the marvellous pipe of the Pied Piper of Hamelin, and the magic violin of French and German fairy tales.[19]

Northern folk-lore is peculiarly rich in ingenious modifications of such wonder-working things. In Powell and Magnusson's 'Legends of Iceland' (second series), Hans, the Carl's Son, receives from a dwarf a stone which was of such a peculiar nature that, when one kept it in the palm of the hand, no one could see the holder of it; next he gave him a sword, saying, "It will cut, and it can be made so small that you can put it in your pocket, but it will grow to its full size when you like;" lastly, the dwarf gave him a ship, which he could carry in his pocket—"But when you like," said the dwarf, "you can have it as large as you need, even as large as seaworthy vessels; and it is one of its powers that it goes with equal speed against the wind and with it."

In the Norse tale of the Best Wish (Sir G. Dasent), three brothers are each bequeathed the accomplishment of a wish: the two elder brothers

---

[18]'National Review,' 1857, vol. v. pp. 398, 399.—The well-known Greek legend of Philemon and Baucis is of the same class: Hospitality Rewarded.

[19]In the romance of Huon of Bourdeaux, Oberon, king of the fairies, presents the hero with a bugle, one of whose virtues was to inspire whosoever heard it with such extraordinary mirth that they were utterly unable to repress the transports it occasioned. A similar magic pipe forms the chief subject of the old English tale of "The Frere and the Boy," printed, with a preface by Thomas Wright, from a manuscript preserved in Cambridge University Library.

wish that whenever they put their hands in their pockets they should find money there—a reflection, perhaps, of the legend of Midas. The youngest wished that every woman who saw him should fall in love with him, and then he sets out on his travels. An innkeeper's wife becomes enamoured of him, and presents him with a pair of scissors, which could of themselves cut out of the air the loveliest garments. Another hostess gives him a tablecloth, which covered itself with the finest kinds of food the moment it was spread. A third gave him a tap, from which, whenever he pleased, he could draw the best liquors. In another Norse tale, Katie Woodencloak—which presents several points of resemblance to the modern Greek story of Xylo-Marie—we read of a *wishing-bull*, in whose ear is a cloth, which, taken and spread out, furnishes as many dishes as may be desired. There can be little doubt that this is the wishing-cow of Hindu legend, which plays an important part in the great Indian epic 'Rámáyana.' In other Norse tales we find a blue belt, which gives super-human strength to the wearer, and a wishing-ring.—It was by means of an invisible ring that Angelica escaped the embraces of Rogero, in Ariosto's 'Orlando Furioso' (xi. 6, Rose's translation):

> Then softly to her mouth the hoop conveys,
> And, quicker than the flash which cleaves the skies,
> From bold Rogero's sight her beauty flies,
> As disappears the sun concealed in clouds.

So, too, in Berni's 'Orlando Innamorato' there is a ring, which, put on the finger, renders enchantment of no effect, and, placed between the lips, confers invisibility.[20] And in the 46th chapter of the Anglican 'Gesta Romanorum' we are told how a king bequeathed to his youngest son a ring, that won the wearer the love of all men; a brooch, which gave him whatever he wished for; and a cloth, that conveyed whoever sat upon it whithersoever he desired to go.[21]

---

[20]According to Plato, Gyges, a shepherd of Lydia, by means of a ring which rendered him invisible, introduced himself to the wife of Candaules, king of Lydia, murdered the latter, and got possession of the kingdom.

[21]Similar to the *bed* in the Indian story referred to on p. 10, and to the *carpet* in the Arabian tale of Prince Ahmed and the Perí Bánú. Muslim writers seem to have borrowed the idea of such a wondrous conveyance from the rabbinical legend of Solomon's carpet, on which he and his vast army were transported through the air great distances in a few minutes; and the rabbins may have adapted this from Indian fictions.

The youngest of a tailor's three sons, who leave home to seek their fortunes, in the German fairy tale (Grimm's collection), finds at the foot of a tree, in a great forest, a table that is covered with dainties the instant the desire for such is expressed. This he exchanges with a charcoal-burner for an old military knapsack, which has the quality, if knocked upon by the hand, of causing a corporal and six soldiers to appear, ready to obey any orders. Going farther, he summons the soldiers by means of the knapsack, and orders them to bring him back his wishing-table from the charcoal-burner, which is done immediately. He next meets with another charcoal-burner, who gives him in exchange for his table a hat, which has a very peculiar quality: if the wearer lift it up and turn it round above his head, a number of shots are fired, like a discharge of artillery, so that no enemy dare approach; and by means of this hat he again recovers his table, which once more he exchanges with a third charcoal-burner for a horn, which, when sounded near a town or village, causes fortresses, walls, houses, and all they contain, to be thrown down in one heap of confusion and ruin.

In a Bohemian variant (No. 2 of M. Leger's French collection of Slav tales), the hero takes from a giant's castle a table, upon which one has merely to strike thrice and say, "A royal meal!" and it is before him. The table he exchanges with an old man for a wonderful bagpipe, which when played upon sends forth any number of armed soldiers. By means of the bagpipe he recovers his table, of course, which he again exchanges with another old man for a sack, which produces any number of strong castles that may be necessary. The bagpipe causes its uhlans to bring back the table once more, after which the hero returns home with his treasures, and marries the king's daughter.

Now observe the close analogy which these two stories bear to this Kalmuk version from the Tales of Siddhí Kúr:

Next morning the man descended from the tree, and said to himself, "Last night there were in this spot many choice viands and liquors, and now they are all vanished." And while he was thus speaking he found a golden flask, and being thirsty he put it to his lips, when suddenly there sprang out meat and cakes, and other delicacies fit for eating. "This," cried he, "is of a surety a wishing-flask, which will procure him who has it everything he desires. I will take it with me." And, so saying, he continued his journey, until he met with a man holding a sword in his hand, and he asked him why he did so. The man answered, "This sword is called Kreischwinger, and when I say to it, 'Kreischwinger, there goes a

man who has taken such a thing from me; follow him and bring it back,'
—it goes forth, kills the man, and brings my property back again." To
this the other replied, "Out of this vessel springeth everything you can
desire; let us exchange." So they made an exchange, and when the man
went away with the flask, he who now owned the sword said, "Kreischwinger, go forth and bring me back my flask." So the sword went forth,
smote its former master dead, and brought the golden vessel back again.
And when he had journeyed a little farther, he met a man holding in his
hand an iron hammer. "Wherefore," said he, "dost thou hold that iron
hammer in thy hand?" The man answered, "When I strike the earth nine
times with this hammer, a great iron wall appears." Said the other, "Let
us exchange;" and when the exchange was made, he sent his sword after
the man to bring back his flask. After this he met another man, who carried in his bosom a goat-skin sack, and he asked him, "Wherefore keep-
est thou that sack?" And the man replied, "This sack is a very wonderful
thing. When you shake this sack, it rains; if you shake it very hard, it rains
very heavily." Hereupon the owner of the flask said, "Let us exchange,"
and they did so; and then the sword went forth and slew the man, and
returned to its master with the golden flask.

But the original form is the Buddhist story of "Sakka's Presents," which
is thus rendered by Dr T. W. Rhys Davids:

"Once upon a time, when Brahma-datta was reigning in Benáres, four
brothers, Bráhmans of that kingdom, devoted themselves to an ascetic
life, and having built themselves huts at equal distances in the region of
the Himálaya mountains, took up their residence there. The eldest of
them died, and was reborn as the good Sakka. When he became aware of
this, he used to go and render help at intervals every seven or eight days
to the others. And one day, having greeted the eldest hermit and sat
down beside him, he asked him, 'Reverend sir, what are you in need of?'
The hermit, who suffered from jaundice, answered, 'I want fire.' So he
gave him a double-edged hatchet. But the hermit said, 'Who is to take
this and bring firewood?' Then Sakka spake thus to him, 'Whenever, reverend sir, you want firewood, you should let go the hatchet from your
hand and say, "Please make me fire," and it will do so.' So he gave him
the hatchet, and went to the second hermit, and asked him, 'Reverend sir,
what are you in need of?' Now the elephants had made a track for themselves close to his hut, and he was annoyed by the elephants, and said, 'I
am much troubled by elephants; drive them away.' Sakka, handing him a
drum, said, 'Reverend sir, if you strike on this side of it, your enemies will

take to flight; but if you strike on this side, they will become friendly and surround you on all sides, an army in fourfold array.' So he gave him the drum, and went to the third hermit, and asked him, 'Reverend sir, what are you in need of?' He was also afflicted with jaundice, and said therefore, 'I want sour milk.' So he gave him a milk-bowl, and said, 'If you wish for anything, and turn this bowl over, it will become a great river, and pour out such a torrent that it will be able to take a kingdom, and give it to you.' And so he went away. But henceforward the hatchet made fire for the elder hermit; when the second struck one side of his drum the elephants ran away; and the third enjoyed his curds.

"Now at that time a wild boar, straying in a forsaken village, saw a gem of magical power. When he seized this in his mouth, he rose by its magic into the air, and went to an island in the midst of the ocean. And thinking, 'Here I ought to live,' he descended and took up his abode in a convenient spot under an *udumbara* tree. And one day, placing the gem before him, he fell asleep at the foot of the tree. Now a certain man of the land of Kási had been expelled from home by his parents, who said, 'This fellow is of no use to us.' So he went to a seaport and embarked in a ship as a servant to the sailors. And the ship was wrecked, but by the help of a plank he reached that very island. And while he was looking about for fruits, he saw the boar asleep, and going softly up, he took hold of the gem. Then by its magical power he straightway rose right up into the air. So, taking a seat on the tree, he said to himself, 'Methinks this boar must have become a sky-walker through the magic power of this gem. That's how he got to be living here. It's plain enough what I ought to do: I'll first of all kill and eat him, and then I can get away.' So he broke a twig off the tree and dropped it on his head. The boar woke up, and not seeing the gem, ran about trembling this way and that way. The man seated in the tree laughed. The boar, looking up, saw him, and dashing his head against the tree, died on the spot. But the man descended, cooked the flesh, ate it, and rose into the air. And as he was passing along the summit of the Himálaya range he saw a hermitage, and descending at the hut of the eldest hermit, he stayed there two or three days and waited on the hermit, and thus became aware of the magic power of the hatchet. 'I must get that,' thought he. And he showed the hermit the magic power of the gem, and said, 'Sir, do you take this, and give me your hatchet.' The ascetic, full of longing to be able to fly through the air, did so. But the man, taking the hatchet, went a little way off, and letting it go, said, 'O hatchet, cut off thou his head, and bring the gem to me.' And it went and cut off the hermit's head and brought the gem. Then he put the hatchet in a secret place, and went to the second hermit, and stayed there a few days; and having become aware of the magic power of the drum, he exchanged the gem for the drum, and cut off his head too in the same way as before. Then he went to the third hermit, and saw the magic power of the milk-bowl, and exchanging the gem for it, caused his head to be cut off in the same manner. And taking the gem, the hatchet, the drum, and the milk-bowl, he flew away up into the air."[22]

Such supernaturally endowed objects are common to the folk-lore of all countries, and are of ancient date. In the Greek legends there is the wondrous horn of Amalthea, which produced a never-failing supply of food. In early British romance we find the dish or napkin of Rhydderich the Scholar, which provided a splendid banquet, and the Horn of Bran, which produced whatever liquors were called for. In the Indian romance, 'Sinhásana Dwatrinsati' (Thirty-two Tales of a Throne), the magical objects are various and numerous: an inexhaustible purse; earth, which, when rubbed on the forehead, overcomes all enemies, and none dare oppose its possessor; a stick, which during the first part of the night furnishes ornaments studded with jewels, in the second part a beautiful girl, in the third part confers invisibility, and in the fourth part a deadly foe or death; a garland of flowers, which renders the possessor invincible and secures success; a lotus-flower, which produces a diamond each day, and never fades. In the Persian romance of 'Hatim Taï,' the hero obtains from the mouth of a dragon a pearl that restored sight to the blind, cured the bite of a snake, endeared the possessor to friend or foe, secured victory in battle, conferred profound wisdom and boundless wealth, and rendered all creatures obedient to his commands.[23] In the 'Kathá Sarit Ságara,' a poor woodcutter receives from a party of Yakshas

---

[22]'Buddhist Birth-Stories.' Translated, from the Pali text of V. Fausböll, by T. W. Rhys Davids. London: Trübner & Co. 1880. Vol. I. This is, according to the learned translator, the oldest extant collection of folk-tales, in which are found the germs of many Eastern as well as Western stories and apologues.

[23] Hatim was a chief of the Arab tribe of Taï, and flourished shortly before the promulgation of Islám. He was famed for his unbounded generosity, and even at the present day throughout the East no higher praise can be bestowed on a generous man than to say that he is "as liberal as Hatim." In the Persian romance, Hatim has been adopted for the hero solely because of his renown: the marvellous exploits which are there ascribed to him are purely imaginary, of course. The incidents in the romance—which is very entertaining, and of which an English translation by Duncan Forbes was published in 1830—are for the most part traceable to ancient Indian sources.

(a species of semi-celestial beings) a pitcher, from which, whenever he put in his hand, he could have an inexhaustible supply of food and drink; but should the pitcher be broken, it would at once and for ever disappear. For some time after this the woodcutter lived in happiness and prosperity, until one evening, while he was entertaining his friends, he took the pitcher and placed it on his shoulder, and began to dance and caper about, when suddenly the pitcher fell to the ground and was broken in pieces, and immediately it reverted to its former possessor, leaving "the last state of that man worse than the first," since he could not be content to enjoy his fortune reasonably.[24] The prototype of all inexhaustible vessels, bowls, flasks, &c., is the widow's cruse, of which we read in the First Book of Kings (ch. xvii. 14), although it possessed only a temporary virtue.[25]

According to Norse legend, King Frodi had a quern (or hand-mill, such as is still used in the East), which ground peace and plenty. Gold was so abundant, that golden armlets lay untouched from year's end to year's end on the king's highway. "In Frodi's house were two maidens of the old giant race, Fenja and Menja. These daughters of the giant he had bought as slaves, and he made them grind his quern, *Grotti*, out of which he used to grind peace and gold. . . . He kept them to the mill, nor gave them longer rest than the cuckoo's note lasted, or they could sing a song. But the quern was such that it ground anything that the grinder chose, though until then it had ground nothing but gold and peace. So the maidens ground and ground, and one sang their piteous tale, in a strain worthy of Æschylus, as the other rested. They prayed for rest and pity, but Frodi was deaf. Then they turned in giant mood, and ground no longer peace and plenty, but fire and war. Then the quern went fast and furious,

---

[24]This story reappears in the Persian romance, 'Tútí Náma' (Parrot-Book) of Nakhshabí, where it is interwoven with the tale of the Singing Ass. It is omitted in Káderi's abridgment of the 'Tútí Náma.' In Bartsch's Meklenburg stories a man gets possession of an inexhaustible beer-can, and immediately after telling how he got it, the beer vanished.

[25]During a famine in Ceylon, which continued for twelve years, a priest on a journey stopped at the house of a man named Sakka. "There remained of his store only one scanty meal of rice, which without hesitation he ordered to be dressed for his guest. His charity was rewarded: his little modicum became inexhaustible, and supported his family and all the country round as long as the drought and famine lasted. Though a Gowansè only, the people out of gratitude raised him to the throne, and as a perpetual memento they made the commencement of his reign an era, which is still in common use. The first year of Sakka corresponds with 621 of Buddha and with 78 of our era."—Davy's 'Account of Ceylon,' p. 298.

and that very night came Mysing, the sea-rover, and carried off the quern, and slew Frodi and all his men, and so Frodi's peace ended. The maidens the sea-rover took with him, and when he got on the high seas he bade them grind salt: so they ground, and at midnight they asked if he had not salt enough; but he bade them still grind on; so they ground, till the ship was full and sank—Mysing, maids, and mill and all—and that's why the sea is salt."[26]

The magic quern figures also in Icelandic story: A poor man having obtained from a mysterious individual a quern that would grind whatever it was ordered to grind, on repeating this charm—

Grind neither malt nor salt;
Grind in the name of the Lord.

Very soon his house was filled with all needful articles. At length it occurred to him that it would be a good thing to have some money to spend, although, in truth, he needed none, as he had plenty of everything. So he bade the quern grind gold; and the quern ground on, and ground pure gold. This was done time after time, so that he shortly became mighty rich in gold. Then said he to his wife, he fain would know how much gold they had. She answered that she deemed that not needful; she only knew they had plenty of it, as of everything else. But he had no peace till he found out by what means to measure his gold. As they themselves had no measure, he ran to his brother's house and asked him for one. The rich brother bade his wife to lend him the measure. She did so; but said to herself, "What, in the wide world, can they have to measure?" And, so saying, she took resin and smeared the measure with it, where the sides and bottom meet, and then gave it to her brother-in-law. He went home, and having measured his gold-dust gave back the measure. His sister-in-law took it and looked within, and saw that all round the bottom gold-dust clave to it. She then took it to her husband, and said, "Your brother measures gold, while we measure only rye."[27] So the rich man went and learned from his brother all about the wonderful quern, and offered to exchange his manor for it, to which the latter, being

---

[26] Dasent's 'Popular Tales from the Norse.'

[27] The reader will not fail to be struck with the resemblance which this incident bears to one in the Arabian tale of Ali Baba and the Forty Thieves; it is, indeed, of frequent occurrence in folk-tales everywhere.

already sufficiently wealthy, agreed. And the cottagefarmer moved to the manor, and took to himself all his brother's possessions. But the other bought himself a vessel, and embarked in it, taking nothing with him but his wife, his children, and his quern, thinking that he had made a marvellous gain by his bargain. When he was a good distance from the coast, he set to work to put the quern in trim, in order that it might grind them all they needed, and he repeated this verse—

> Grind neither malt nor salt;
> Grind in the name of the Lord!

But do and say whatever he would, the quern stood still and immovable, till at last he grew angry, and cried out, in a wild rage:

> Grind, then, both malt and salt;
> Grind in the name of the Lord!

Then the quern began grinding malt and salt, and in a short while overcharged the vessel, and as there were no means, anyhow, of stopping the quern, the end of it was that the vessel sank with all on board of it, and has never since been seen."[28]

The Norwegian version of this tale concludes differently: The elder brother, having obtained the quern, orders it to grind broth and herrings, but he did not know how to stop it, so the broth and herrings filled his house, and flowed over all his fields, and he gladly restored it to the hero, who sold it to a skipper. When the skipper was out at sea, he told the quern to grind salt for his cargo, and after the ship was filled, the quern continued to grind away till the ship sank and all were drowned; and as the quern still grinds, the sea is always salt.[29]

---

[28]Powell and Magnusson's 'Icelandic Legends,' second series, pp. 16–20.—There are some points of resemblance between this story and the Kalmuk tale of the Avaricious Brother, *ante*, pp. 101, 102. In the commencement of the Icelandic story, the rich brother kills an ox one day, and the poor one goes to ask him for a piece of the flesh, for he is in sore distress for want of food. At first he is refused by the rich brother, but in the end he gets one of the thighs of the ox, and is told, in a rage, to "go along with it to the devil." The poor fellow thinks his brother meant what he said, and sets off to deliver the meat to the fiend, and receives in return the magic quern, which, as we have seen, is the cause of the rich brother's destruction.—It is curious to observe in fairy tales of this kind that the possessor of a wealth-giving thing is always so foolish as to sell it *for money!*

[29]Dasent's 'Popular Tales from the Norse.'

We have thus seen that the purse and hat of Fortunatus, and the sword, shoes, coat, and cap of the renowned Jack, have their counterparts among "all peoples, and kindreds, and tongues," and to the numerous and varied magical objects which have passed under our review may be added, without by any means exhausting the list—the *lamp* of Aladdin, which (or rather, the "slave" of which) procured him everything he desired; the *purse* of Bedredden Hasan, which the fairy always kept filled for him; the *Sangreal*, which furnished the knights of Arthur's Round-Table with a grand banquet; and the *table* of the Ethiopians, which Herodotus tells us was covered with all kinds of dainties.

✌ GOLD-PRODUCING
ANIMALS ✌

SOMETIMES, in place of an inexhaustible purse, we find a tree, a beast,[1] a bird, and even the human person represented as producing in the same marvellous manner a daily supply of gold. Our nursery tale of the goose that daily laid a gold egg has its parallels in the folk-tales of Europe generally, and finds counterparts in Indian fiction. According to the Latin Æsop (ed. 1658): "He that seeketh to get more than he ought, ofttimes getteth nothing; as saith the fable of a man which had a goose that laid every day an egg of gold. The man, out of covetousness, commanded her that she should lay every day two eggs, and she said, 'Certainly, my master, I may not.' Whereupon the man was wroth with her and slew her, by means whereof he lost his profit, and afterward waxed very sorrowful."[2] But in our modern nursery version, the goose (it is a hen in some editions of Æsop) is killed in expectation of finding a lump of gold in her inside.[3] In the course of Jack the Giant-Killer's memorable adventures, he finds among the treasures of one of his "cousins" a gold-laying hen; and in the story of Jack and the Bean-stalk, the hero steals a wonderful hen that lays a gold egg as often as the possessor says " Lay."— In the 13th fable of Book iii. of the 'Panchatantra' we read of a bird that perched upon a tree and voided pure gold: she is captured by a huntsman, who presents her to the king, describing her wonderful qualities; but the king's foolish advisers persuade him to discredit the huntsman's story, and set the bird at liberty. In the noble

---

[1]Such as the *ram* and the *wishing-bull* of Norse tales, already mentioned, pp. 10 and 22.

[2]This fable is ascribed to Avian, a Latin writer of the fourteenth century, who imitated Phædrus.—It is thus briefly related by Babrius: "A bird once laid golden eggs. Wishing to take the gold from her, a lover of gold killed her, and lost the very great gift of fortune."

[3]Mr Baring-Gould says, "The golden egg laid every morning by the red hen is the dawn-produced sun." And Dr Rhys Davids thus explains the origin of the legend of the goose that laid golden eggs: "The word *hansa* (pronounce *hangsa*), generally translated goose, means more exactly a wild-duck; and the epithet golden, in description of its beauty of colour. But the word *hansa* is etymologically the same as our word goose (compare German *gans*), and the epithet golden, when applied to a goose, being meaningless as descriptive of outward appearance, gave rise to the fable of the goose with the golden eggs. The latter, therefore, is a true myth, born of a word-puzzle; invented to explain an expression which had lost its meaning through the progress of linguistic growth."—Both absurdly wrong!

Indian epic 'Mahábhárata,' it is related that King Srinjaya obtained as a boon from the sage Náráda that he should have a son whose nature was such, that all that issued from his body was of gold. The king's wealth in consequence increased enormously. The son was, however, carried off and killed by robbers, who hoped to get gold from his body, but were disappointed.[4] Here we seem to have the original of our nursery story of the gold-laying goose.

Serpents are celebrated producers of gold, and also of jewels of talismanic power, in fairy tales. In the Kalmuk 'Relations of Siddhí Kúr,' the son of the khán, after killing the yellow serpent, eats its head, and lo! he can spit out gold in any quantity; his companion eats the head of the green serpent, and can spit out emeralds. The 5th fable of Book iii. of the 'Panchatantra' is of the same class as our story of the goose that laid eggs of gold:

"In a certain country dwelt a Bráhman who reaped no benefit from the cultivation of his grounds. As he was reposing one day in the hot season under the shade of a tree, he dreamt that he beheld a large hooded snake, coiled upon an ant-hill, at a little distance; and waking from his dream, he concluded that the snake must be the tutelary deity of the spot, who was little pleased with him, as one from whom he had never received any veneration. The Bráhman determined therefore to worship him, and boiling some milk, he placed it in a vessel, and carried it to the ant-hill, exclaiming, as he laid the cup upon the ground, 'Lord of the soil, I have hitherto been ignorant of thy place of residence, and therefore have only forborne thy worship; forgive my negligence, and accept my oblation.'[5] So saying, he left the milk and went home. When he visited the ant-hill in the morning following, he found in place of the milk a *dínar,* and this was repeated daily. At last the Bráhman, having occasion to go to the village, appointed his son to present an oblation of milk in his absence. When the lad, upon the ensuing morning, found the *dínar* as usual, it occurred to him that the mound must be filled with coin, and that it would be the most eligible plan to kill its serpent owner, and seize at once upon the whole of the

---

[4] 'Metrical Translations from Sanskrit Writers,' by Dr John Muir, p. 27.—There are also birds that void gold in the 'Mahábhárata.' In La Fontaine's 'Contes et Nouvelles' there is a little dog "qui secoue de l'argent et des perreries;" and an ass with the same gift in the Signora von Gonzenbach's 'Sicilianische Märchen.'

[5] Regarding serpent-worship, see Tylor's 'Primitive Culture,' vol. ii. p. 217.

treasure.[6] Arming himself, therefore, with a stick, he lay in wait for the snake, as he was lapping the milk, and struck him on the head. The blow failed to kill the snake, and the animal, inflamed with wrath, bit the lad with his venomous fangs, so that he immediately died. The body was burnt by his people, who were at hand, and saw what had chanced. The father returned on the day following, and, when he had heard the cause of his son's death, was satisfied that the event was not unmerited, declaring that the vital elements will be ever snatched from those who show no tenderness to those living creatures that repair to them for preservation, as happened to the swans and their lake. The persons present asked him to explain this allusion, and he thus replied:

"'In a certain country reigned Chitraratha, in whose gardens was an extensive lake, guarded by his troops. In this lake were golden swans, who moulted a feather once in every six months. A large bird, having joined them, was refused admission to their troop, they claiming the exclusive occupation of the lake, by the fee of the moulted feather. After much discussion, the stranger-bird applied to the king, and said: "Sire, these swans have had the audacity to say, 'What have we to do with the king? We will not allow any one to preside here;' and it was to no purpose that I expostulated with them on the impropriety of such language, and threatened to bring it to your knowledge." The king, having heard this, commanded his servants to go and kill the birds, and bring them to him; and they set off with this intent. When they approached the lake, an old swan, suspecting their purpose, persuaded the rest to fly away; and thus, although they preserved their lives, they lost the residence which they refused to share with a guest.[7]

"Having related this tale, the Bráhman proceeded to worship the snake. But the serpent could not be tempted forth, but showing himself at the entrance of his hole, he thus spoke: 'Avarice brings thee hither, and

---

[6]It is a popular belief throughout the East that serpents and dragons are the guardians of concealed treasure. The notion was probably derived from the Hindús, although it also prevailed among the ancient Greeks; for example: the Scythian griffins that guarded the treasures coveted by the Arimaspians, and the dragon that watched the golden apples of the Hesperides. In the 'Nibelungenlied,' the dragon Fafnir keeps guard over a vast treasure of gold; Sigurd fights and slays him, and takes away all the treasure. And in Eastern fiction, whenever the adventurous hero comes to a valley strewed with diamonds and other precious stones—Sindbád's diamond-valley is not the only one!—the treasures are invariably found guarded (or, which is all the same, the place is infested) by multitudes of fierce serpents and similar creatures.

[7]But the king lost his half-yearly fee of a golden feather.

banishes all sorrow for thy son's fate, but there cannot be any cordiality between thee and me. In the insane presumption of youth, your son struck me; I have bitten him and killed him: how is it possible for me ever to forget his violence? How is it possible that you should ever forget his death? Take this jewel, then; depart, and never more approach this place.' Having thus spoken, and cast a gem of inestimable value to the Bráhman, he withdrew into his hole. The Bráhman took the jewel, but, considering its value very much inferior to what he might have acquired by long assiduous homage, never ceased to lament the folly of his son."[8]

This story seems to be an adaptation of the legend of the king's son in the 'Mahábhárata' already referred to; and it forms the 141st tale of Swan's, translation of the 'Gesta Romanorum,' as follows:

"In the reign of the Emperor Fulgentius, a certain knight named Zedechias married a very beautiful but imprudent wife. In a certain chamber of their mansion a serpent dwelt. Now the knight's vehement inclination for tournaments and jousting brought him to extreme poverty; he grieved immoderately, and, like one who was desperate, walked backward and forward, ignorant of what he should do. The serpent, beholding his misery, like the ass of Balaam, was on this occasion miraculously gifted with a voice, and said to the knight, 'Why do you lament? Take my advice, and you shall not repent it. Supply me every day with a certain quantity of sweet milk, and I will enrich you.' This promise exhilarated the knight, and he faithfully followed the instructions of his subtle friend. The consequence was that he had a beautiful son, and became exceedingly wealthy. But it happened that his wife one day said to him, 'My lord, I am sure that serpent has great riches hidden in the chamber where he dwells. Let us kill him, and get possession of the whole.' The advice pleased the knight, and at the request of his wife he took a hammer to destroy the serpent, and a vessel of milk. Allured by the milk, it put its head out of the hole, as it had been accustomed to do, and the knight lifted the hammer to strike it. The serpent, observing his perfidy, suddenly drew back its head, and the blow fell upon the vessel. No sooner had he done this than the knight's offspring died, and he lost everything that he formerly possessed." In the sequel, the knight's wife urges him to go to the serpent and humbly acknowledge his offence; he

---

[8]"Analytical Account of the Pancha Tantra," by Horace Hayman Wilson, in 'Transactions of the Royal Asiatic Society of Great Britain and Ireland.' Vol. i. 1827.

does so, but the serpent replies that he can never forget the blow aimed at him, and henceforward there could be no peace between them. The knight then departed, bitterly regretting that he had followed his wife's counsel.[9]

The story is told differently in the Latin Æsop, which was composed in the fifteenth century; the serpent does not give gold, but his presence is the cause of good fortune to a poor man:

"He that applies himself to do other men harm ought not to think himself secure; wherefore Æsop rehearseth this fable. There was a serpent which came into the house of a poor man, and lived of that which fell from the poor man's table, for the which thing there happened great fortune to this man, and he became rich. But on a day this man was very angry against the serpent, and took a sword and smote at him, wherefore the serpent went out of the house and came no more thither again. A little after, this man fell again into great poverty, and then he knew that by fortune of the serpent he was become rich, wherefore it repented him that he had driven away the serpent. Then he went and humbled himself to the serpent, saying, 'I pray thee that thou wilt pardon me the offence that I have done thee.' And the serpent said, 'Seeing thou repentest thee of thy misdeed, I forgive thee; but as long as I shall live I shall remember thy malice, for as thou hurtedst me, so thou mayest again.' Wherefore that which was once evil shall ever so be held: men ought therefore not to insult over him of whom they receive some benefit, nor yet to suspect their good and true friends."

In No. 17 of Dozon's collection of Albanian Tales[10] we have a similar story of a gold-producing lion: A poor man, who had a wife and one son, gained a scanty livelihood by carrying stones on asses to the neighbouring city. On one occasion he went a greater distance for stones than was his wont, and discovered a great lion sunning himself. The lion, on seeing him, rose up, at which the man would have fled, being much terrified; but the beast, as if to reassure him, lay down again, and he then drew somewhat nearer, when the lion dropped from his mouth a piece of gold

---

[9]One of the fables of Marie de France, who flourished in the middle of the 13th century, "Le Villain et le Dragon," was in all likelihood the direct source of the 'Gesta' story. (See Le Grand's 'Fabliaux,' ed. 1781, vol. v. p. 405.)—In a version from Bukhara cited by Rev. Dr Wolff in his journal (see 'The Morning Watch', 1832–33), the man's son attempts to kill the gold-giving serpent after his father's death.

[10]'Contes Albanais,' recueillis et traduits par Auguste Dozon. Paris: 1881.

of the value of 1000 piastres. The man hastened home and showed this windfall to his wife, who, like himself, was full of joy. He goes again next day, with the same result, and so for some days, when, by the advice of his wife, he erects an iron railing around the lion, with a gate for entry, and begins to feed the invaluable animal with 4 ocques of meat and 3 ocques of milk daily, receiving in return the same golden present each time he came with the food. The people soon begin to wonder at their neighbour's wealth, and somehow come to know about the lion; and the boys jeer at his son, calling him a booby, because he does not know that his father is really a mere carrier of stones, and that his wealth is obtained from a lion. Stung by their jeers and flouts, the lad goes to his mother, and worms out of her all the particulars, and insists upon going to see the lion, but she is afraid lest he should be killed, as the beast did not know him: ultimately she gives him the key of the cage, and he sets off on horseback, accompanied by a servant. He enters the cage, springs on the lion with a drawn sabre, and is instantly torn in pieces. The servant returns home and recounts the youth's fate to his parents, who are distracted with grief. The father erects a tomb for his son near the lion's cage, but the beast gives no more a piece of gold. At length he goes to the lion one day with his usual supply of food, and with tears begs him to renew his former gifts, for he is now become very poor. "Thou hast killed my son," says he, "but I bear thee no hatred on that account." To which the noble animal replied, "I shall give thee, it is true, the piece of gold, and thou shalt give me the usual ration: but none the less is our friendship at an end; for thou, seeing here the tomb of thy son, wilt curse me—hatred and fear will fill thy heart; and I, thinking on the blood which has flowed from my tail, shall wish to see thee no more. Yet, if thou continuest to feed me, I will give thee the piece of gold."

These stories of gold-producing animals, it will be readily perceived on comparing them, are each *alter et idem;* the " moral " being one that " runs at large," and thus neatly expressed in our own vernacular: "Don't kill the goose that lays the golden eggs!"

ADVENTURES WITH GIANTS, TROLLS, GHÚLS, ETC.

IN a former paper it is said that the story of Jack and the Giants came to us from the North, and that the Northern legends and tales of adventures with trolls and similar monsters are also found in Eastern fiction; and in order to prove this, let us take one or two of the renowned Jack's valiant exploits, from the veracious chap-book narrative.

Jack, we are told, "having got a little money, travelled into Flintshire, and came to a large house in a lonesome place; and, by reason of his present necessity, he took courage to knock at the gate, when, to his amazement, there came forth a monstrous giant with two heads, yet he did not seem so fiery as the former giants, for he was a Welsh giant." The story informs us that this giant was of a less savage disposition because of his breakfasting on a great basin of hasty-pudding. Our hero, having undressed himself, was about to lie down on the bed appropriated to him, when he heard the giant say to himself, as he walked towards another chamber—

> "Though here you lodge with me this night,
> You shall not see the morning light;
> My club shall dash your brains out quite."

"Say you so?" muttered Jack; "is that one of your Welsh tricks? But I hope to be quite as cunning as you, my friend." Then, looking about the room, he found a thick billet and laid it on the bed in his stead, and hid himself in a dark corner of the room. In the dead time of the night came the giant with his club, and struck several blows on the bed where Jack had craftily laid the billet, and then returned to his own room, supposing he had broken all Jack's bones. Early in the morning Jack came to thank the giant for his lodging. "Oh," said the giant, "did you see anything last night?" "No," said Jack; "but a rat gave me three or four slaps with its tail."[1]

---

[1] In a subsequent adventure Jack enters the castle of the giant Thondel, who speedily discovers his presence though he does not see him, exclaiming—

> "Fe, fa, fum!
> I smell the blood of an Englishman;

37

Compare this with the device practised by the giant Skrymer, when he accompanied Thor on his journey to Utgard, which is found related in the 12th chapter of the Edda of Snorro: At midnight the mighty son of earth laid himself to sleep beneath an oak, and snored aloud. Thor, the giant-killer, resolved to rid himself of his unsuspicious companion, and struck him with his tremendous hammer. "Hath a leaf fallen upon me from the tree?" exclaimed the awakened giant. The giant soon slept again, and snored, as the Edda says, as loudly as if it had thundered in the forest. Thor struck the giant again, and, as he thought, the hammer made a mortal indentation in his forehead. "What is the matter?" quoth Skrymer; "hath an acorn fallen on my head?" A third time the potent giant snored, and a third time did the hammer descend, "with huge two-handed sway," and with such force that Thor weened the iron had buried itself in Skrymer's temples. "Methinks," quoth Skrymer, rubbing his cheek, "some moss hath fallen on my face." Thor might well be amazed at the escape of the giant; but Skrymer had outwitted his enemy by placing an immense rock on the leafy couch, where Thor supposed he was sleeping, which received the blows of the hammer instead.

And in the Albanian story of the Bear and the Dervish, we read that the bear told his mother and his sister to sharpen the axe, for he must kill that man, he is so strong; but the bear's sister warned the dervish of this, so he concealed himself. During the night the bear made three or four

---

> Be he alive, or be he dead,
> I'll grind his bones to make me bread."

That our story of Jack and the Giants is older than the time of Queen Elizabeth seems evident from the occurrence of part of the giant's exclamation in Shakspeare's 'King Lear,' where Edgar, as Mad Tom, sings (Act. iii. sc. 5)—

> "Child Rowland to the dark tower came,
> His word was still, Fee, foh, and fum,
> I smell the blood of a British man."

It is curious to find a similar expression in Scandinavian stories, in which trolls, giants, and ogres exclaim, when the hero is concealed in the house, "I smell Christian flesh!" Thus also in French tales: "Femme, je sens la viande fraîche, la chair de chrétien!" In Italian stories of ogres, etc.—

> "Fum! fum!
> Sento odour di cristianum!"

And in Indian stories of rákshasas is the same formula as that of Jack's giant Thondel: "Fee, faw, fum! This room smells of man's flesh!"

strokes with his axe on the bed, and went back to sleep. In the morning he went out early for wood, and was surprised on his return to see the dervish alive and well. "Did nothing happen to you during the night?" asked he of the dervish. "Nothing, except that three or four fleas bit me."—Dozon's 'Contes Albanais.'

Jack, it will be remembered, having escaped being pulverised by the giant in the manner aforesaid, sits down to breakfast with his two-headed host. The giant placed a huge bowl of his favourite hasty-pudding on the table, and invited Jack to help himself. Jack had secretly fastened his scrip beneath his jacket, and instead of swallowing each spoonful he slipped a great deal into the scrip, and when at length the giant could eat no more, Jack told him that he could easily relieve his stomach without hurting himself, and thus be ready to eat as much more: so saying, he slit open the scrip with his knife, upon which the Welsh giant, exclaiming, "Hur can do that hurself," ripped himself open, and immediately expired.

This incident occurs in the Norse tale of the Youth who ate a match with a Troll. The young man has a soft new cheese in his scrip, and when the troll threatens to kill him, he takes it out, and in his turn threatens to squeeze the troll as he squeezes the water out of "this white *stone*." The troll is frightened, and makes his peace with the young hero. When it is supper-time the troll undertakes to make up the fire, while the lad goes to fetch water for their porridge, in his iron pails, which he could not so much as lift from the ground. "Pooh!" said he, "it isn't worth while to touch these finger-basins; I'll just go and fetch the spring itself." The troll can't afford to lose his spring, so he fetches the water himself. When the porridge was ready, the lad proposed they should eat a match, and hanging his scrip in front of him, he spooned more into it than he ate himself. At last the troll is quite gorged with the porridge he has supped, upon which the lad tells him that he ought to cut a hole in his paunch as he had done (in his scrip); and being assured that it didn't hurt, the troll cut his paunch open, and died on the spot.[2]

The Albanian story of the Bear and the Dervish, already cited, presents several points of resemblance to these incidents in the Norse tale: A shepherd being much annoyed by a bear that devoured five or six of his sheep every day, a dervish undertook to rid him of the pest, and, having

[2] See Dasent's 'Popular Tales from the Norse'; also Thorpe's 'Yule-Tide Stories': "The Boy who contended with the Giant in Eating" (Swedish version), pp. 245–249 of Bohn's edition.

obtained of the shepherd three skins of cream cheese, set off in quest of the bear, whom he soon met, when they began each to brag of his own strength. "I'll crush you as small as this stone," said the dervish, at the same time slyly taking a cheese from his wallet, and crushing it into powder. The bear tried to do the same with a stone, but failed, so he deemed it prudent to make friends with such a strong man. Supper-time drawing nigh, the bear proposed to the dervish that he should go and carry off an ox, while he went for wood. "Get an ox for yourself," quoth the dervish indignantly; "nothing less than a lion will do for me." Admiring his friend's prowess, the bear went and got an ox: meanwhile the dervish had gone to the wood and tied all the trees together, and when the bear returned he was astonished to see preparation made to tear up the whole wood at one pull, and he mildly observed, "One or two branches will be quite sufficient for us;" but the dervish said superciliously, "That isn't my way—all or none; *you* may take one or two branches, if that is all you want." The bear took two branches, and while the ox was being roasted the dervish went for water; but when he had filled the skin he could not carry it home, so he sat down and waited till the bear came, two hours after, to see what was detaining him. "I am considering," said the dervish, "how to convey this whole rock and the spring, for it would be a disgrace for such a man as I am to carry a skin of water." Hearing this, the bear took up the skin and carried it home. The death of the bear was not brought about in the same manner as that of Jack's friend the two-headed giant, and the Lad's friend the Troll: After the bear had wrestled with the dervish, and hugged him so that his eyes were starting from his head, but gave up when he heard the dervish say he was considering on which side he had better throw him; and the futile attempt to kill the dervish while he slept, as already related; the bear requested that his friend would make him as strong as himself. "Quite easy," quoth he; "a skin of boiled milk is all you need." The milk is boiled in a great cauldron, and the dervish told the bear to dip his hand into it thrice: at the third dip he tumbled the bear into the scalding liquid, and there was an end of him.

Similar incidents are found in the Sicilian story of the Brave Shoemaker (Gonzenbach's collection). The hero provides himself with some balls of plaster of Paris and cream cheese, and sets off to kill a fierce giant. When he hears the giant coming, he climbs into a tree; but the giant, having scented him, orders him to come down. The cobbler replies that if he does not leave him alone he will wring his head off; and as a proof of his strength, he crushes the balls of plaster of Paris between his hands, telling the giant they are marble. At this the giant is frightened, and invites the cobbler to his house. When they get there, the giant asks him to fetch some water in a pitcher from the well, and the cobbler says if the giant will give him a strong rope he will bring the well itself. The giant, in terror, takes the huge pitcher and draws the water himself. Then the giant requests him to cut some wood, but the hero asks him for a strong rope with which to drag the whole tree to the house. Next the giant proposes a trial of strength, to see which could carry a heavy stick the longer. The cobbler says the giant had better wind something about the thick end, for when he (the cobbler) turned a somersault with it he might hurt the giant. When they went to bed, the giant made the cobbler sleep with him; but the hero crept under the bed, leaving a pumpkin in his place. The giant, who was anxious to get rid of the cobbler, took an iron bar and struck at the pumpkin all night, believing it to be the cobbler's head. After he had beaten the pumpkin to pieces, the cobbler under the bed gave a sigh. "What is the matter with you?" asked the terrified giant. "A flea has just bitten my ear," replied the cobbler. Next day the cobbler proposed to the giant to cook a great pot of macaroni, and after they had eaten it, he would cut open his stomach to show that he had eaten without chewing it; the giant to do the same afterwards. The cobbler, of course, secretly tied a sack about his neck, and put his macaroni in it; then he took a knife and ripped open the bag, and the macaroni fell out. The giant, in attempting to follow the cobbler's example, killed himself. Then the cobbler cut his head off, carried it to the king, and obtained his daughter's hand in marriage.

In a Milanese story, a cobbler, being tired of cobbling, said to himself one day, "Now I will go and seek my fortune." So he bought a little cheese, and put it on the table. It got full of flies, so he took an old shoe and hit the cheese, and slew the flies. Then he counted them, and found 500 were killed and 400 wounded. After this he girded on a sword, and put on a cocked hat, and went to court, and said to the king, "I am the chief of warriors; 500 have I slain and 400 have I wounded." The king answered, "Since you are a warrior, you must be brave enough to climb yonder mountain, where there are two magicians, and kill them. If you do so, I shall give you my daughter." Then he gave him a white flag to wave when he had killed them. "Sound the trumpet," he added, "and bring me the heads of the magicians in a bag." So the cobbler departed and came to an inn, and the innkeeper and his wife were none other than the magicians. He asked for lodging and food and all he needed. Afterwards he went to his room, but before going to bed he looked at the ceiling, and there saw a great stone over the bed. Instead of getting into the bed, he got into a corner. When a certain hour struck, the magicians let the stone drop, and it crushed the whole bed. The next morning the cobbler went down and said he could not sleep for the noise. They told him they would change his room. The same thing happened the next night, and in the morning they told him they would give him another room. When it was a certain hour the man and his wife went to the forest to cut a bundle of faggots. Then the magician went home, and the cobbler, who had made ready a sickle, said, "Wait until I help you to take the bundle off your back," and gave the magician a blow with the sickle, and cut off his head. He did the same thing when the magician's wife returned. Then he unfurled his flag, and sounded his trumpet, and the band went out to meet him. After he had arrived at court, the king said to him, "Now that you have killed the two magicians, you shall marry my daughter." But the cobbler had got so used to drawing the thread that he did so in his sleep, and kept hitting his wife so that she could not rest. Then the king gave him a great sum of money, and sent him home.[3]

A Persian legend, related by the Shah's own storyteller to Sir John Malcolm, bears a striking resemblance to the Norse tale of the Youth and the Troll, as well as to our nursery tale. Amín of Ispahán, when he meets with a ghúl,[4] has in his pocket an egg and a lump of salt. He tells the ghúl that he has come out in search of ghúls, upon whom to try his strength and prowess. The ghúl says, "You don't appear to be very strong." "Perhaps not," says Amín, "but appearances are often deceiving; I will give you a proof of my strength. There," he continued, picking up a stone, "this contains a fluid; try if you can squeeze it so that it will flow out." The ghúl took the stone, but after a short attempt returned it, saying, "It is impossible." "Quite easy," quoth Amín, taking the stone and placing it in the hand in which he had before put the egg; "look there!" and the astonished ghúl, while he heard what he took for the breaking of the stone, saw the liquid run from between Amín's fingers, and this apparently without any effort. Aided by the darkness, Amín placed the stone

---

[3] 'Italian Popular Tales.' By T. F. Crane (London: 1885), p. 94ff.

[4] Ghúls (commonly written ghouls) are a species of demons, believed by Muslims to feed on human flesh, and to have the power of assuming any form they please, to decoy unwary travellers. They bear some resemblance to our ogres, the lamiæ of the Greeks, and to the rákshasas, vetílas, &c. of Indian mythology.

upon the ground, while he picked up another of darker hue. "This," said he, "I can see contains salt, as you will find if you can crumble it between your fingers." But the ghúl, looking at it, confessed he had neither knowledge to discover its qualities nor strength to break it. "Give it me," said Amín impatiently, and having put it into the same hand with the piece of salt, he instantly gave the latter all crushed to the ghúl, who, seeing it reduced to powder, tasted it, and remained in astonishment at the skill and strength of the wonderful man. Amín consents to stay with the ghúl all night. His grim host points to a bag made of the hides of six oxen, and bids him go and fill it with water, while he makes ready a fire. While the ghúl is absent in search of faggots, Amín with great difficulty drags the bag to the bank of a dark stream which issued from the rocks at the other end of the cavern. After some minutes' reflection he thought of a plan, and began digging a small channel from the stream towards the place where supper was being prepared. "What are you doing?" shouted the ghúl, as he advanced towards him. "I sent you for water to boil a little rice, and you have been almost an hour. Cannot you fill the bag and bring it away?" "Certainly I can," said Amín. "If I were content, after all your kindness, to show my gratitude merely by feats of brute strength, I could lift your stream if you had a bag as large as could hold it; but here," said he, pointing to the channel he had begun—"here is the commencement of a work in which the mind of man is employed to lessen the labour of the body. This canal, small as it may appear, will carry a stream to the other end of the cave, in which I will construct a dam that you can open or shut at pleasure, and thereby save yourself infinite trouble in fetching water. But, pray, let me alone till it is finished," and resumed his digging. "Nonsense," said the ghúl, seizing the bag and filling it; "I will carry the water myself: and I advise you to leave off your canal, as you call it, and follow me, that you may eat your supper and get to sleep. You may finish this fine work, if you like, to-morrow morning." . . . Amín places a large pillow in the middle of his bed, to make it appear as if he was still there, and retires to a concealed part of the cavern to watch the proceedings of the ghúl. The latter awoke a short time before daylight, and, without making any noise, went towards Amín's bed, where, not observing the least stir, he was satisfied that his guest was in a deep sleep; so he took one of his walking-sticks, which was in size like the trunk of a tree, and struck a terrible blow at what he supposed to be his head. He smiled at not hearing even a groan, thinking he had killed him outright; but to make sure he repeated the blow seven times. He then returned to rest, but had hardly settled himself to sleep when Amín, who had crept into bed, raised his head above the clothes, and exclaimed, "Friend ghúl, what insect could it be that has disturbed me by its tapping? I counted the flap of its little wings seven times on the coverlet. These vermin are very annoying, for, though they cannot hurt a man, they disturb his rest." The ghúl's dismay at hearing Amín speak at all was great, but that was increased to perfect fright when he heard him describe seven blows, any one of which would have felled an elephant, as seven flaps of an insect's wing. There was no safety, he thought, near so wonderful a man; and he soon afterwards arose and fled from the cave, leaving Amín its sole master. Having armed himself with a matchlock, which had belonged to some victim of the ghúl, Amín proceeded to survey the road. He had, however, only gone a short distance when he saw the ghúl returning with a large club in his hand, and accompanied by a fox. Amín's knowledge of the cunning animal instantly led him to suspect that it had undeceived his enemy, but his presence of mind did not forsake him. "Take that," said he to the fox, aiming a ball at him from his matchlock and shooting him through the head—"take that, for your not performing my orders. That brute," he said then to the ghúl, "promised to bring me seven ghúls, that I might chain them and carry them to Ispahán, and here he has only brought you, who are already my slave." So saying, he advanced towards the ghúl; but the latter had already taken flight, and by the aid of his club bounded so rapidly over rocks and precipices, that he was soon out of sight.[5]

The *motif* of all stories of this character is the superiority of intelligence to mere physical strength: the monsters that are tricked by clever little folks, whether giants, trolls, ogres, bears, lions, or tigers,[6] are invariably represented as being extremely stupid and credulous. In Steel and Temple's 'Wide-Awake Stories' there is a Kashmírí tale (which also occurs in the 'Suka Saptati,' or Seventy Tales of a Parrot, a Sanskrit collection), of which the catastrophe is similar to that of the Persian story of Amín and the Ghúl, last cited, and also finds parallels in European folk-lore: One day a farmer went to his field to plough with his bullocks. He had just yoked them when a tiger walked up to him and saluted him; the farmer returned the salute, when the tiger said that the Lord had sent him to eat

[5] Malcolm's 'Sketches of Persia,' ch. xvi.
[6] In fairy tales animals which play the parts of ogres and giants are simply the latter in other forms.

his two bullocks. The farmer promised that he would bring him a fine milch-cow instead. But his wife objected, and, putting on the farmer's best clothes, set off, man-fashion, on the pony to where the tiger was waiting. She called out, "I hope I may find a tiger in this field, for I have not tasted tiger's flesh since the day before yesterday, when I killed three." The tiger, on hearing this, turned tail and fled into the jungle, where he met a jackal, who asked him why he ran so fast, and was told that a tiger-eating demon was after him. The jackal tells him that it is only a woman; but the tiger is still afraid, and the jackal and he knot their tails together, in order that one should not escape at the other's expense. When the woman sees them she calls out to the jackal, "This is very kind of you to bring me such a fat tiger; but, considering how many tigers there are in your father's house, I think you might have brought me two." The tiger, more frightened than before, ran off, dragging the jackal after him, and the officious jackal was killed by being bumped against the stones.[7]

The same plan is adopted to frighten a dragon in No. 23 of Hahn's modern Greek stories: Lazarus the Cobbler having one fine day actually killed forty flies with a single blow, he made for himself a sword on which he wrote "Forty at a blow," and set off in quest of warlike adventures. He meets a dragon, who, *reading* these words, asked Lazarus to make friends with him, and introduces him to a number of other dragons, who, being afraid of his prowess, give him much gold to go away. The first dragon meets a fox, who undeceives him as to the pretended strength and courage of Lazarus, and the better to convince him, offers to conduct him to the cobbler. But when they come up with him, Lazarus, nothing daunted, cries to the fox, "I told you to bring me all the dragons, and you have only brought one," upon which the dragon scoured off, in terror for his life.

---

[7]A variant of this is found in the Chinese tales and fables appended to M. Stanislas Julien's French rendering of the 'Avadánas,' in which a tiger having seized a monkey was about to devour him, when the monkey, bethinking himself of some means of escape, suggested that he was too small to make a good meal for a tiger, and offered to conduct his captor to a neighbouring hill where a far more noble prey might be captured. This was a stag who, rightly assuming that the tiger had come for a most unfriendly purpose, concluded that his only chance was to put a bold face upon the matter, and accordingly addressed the monkey as follows: "How is this? You promised me ten tiger-skins, but you have only brought one—you still owe me nine." The tiger on hearing this became alarmed, and instantly decamped, saying that he never thought the monkey would be so treacherous.—See also my 'Book of Sindibád,' pp. 70, 71.

Another adventure with a stupid tiger—a substitute for the trolls and giants of Northern folk-lore—is related in the Santali story of two brothers, Kauran and Guja, translated by the Rev. F. F. Cole, in the 'Indian Antiquary,' vol. iv.: The brothers were in the jungle one day, as usual, for the purpose of digging up roots, on which they subsisted. They came to a tiger's den, and offered him some pieces of charcoal, pretending they were roots, and that they had kept the half-roasted ones to themselves. The tiger asks them a riddle: "One I will eat for breakfast, and another like it for supper." They answer, "Oh, uncle, we cannot tell; but we will ask you another riddle: One will twist the tail and another the ear." Hearing this, the tiger gets into a great fright, and is about to make his escape, when Kauran seizes his tail, which in the ensuing struggle is wrenched off. The tiger runs away in search of his tiger-friends, and comes back with a whole host of them to the tree up which the brothers have escaped. The tailless tiger proposes that they should stand one on another till they are high enough to reach the brothers, which is done; but in the meantime Kauran calls to his brother, "Give me the axe, and I will kill the tailless tiger." The latter, in great terror, struggled to make his escape, and in so doing upset the whole party, who were resting upon him, while they in their fall crushed the poor tailless tiger to death, and, overcome by terror, fled out of sight.

The concluding incident in the story of the Stupid Wolf, No. 18 of Leger's collection of Slav tales, is to the same effect: The wolf, after many attempts to satisfy his hunger, and getting nothing but kicks and blows till he could scarcely crawl, meets with a tailor, and tells him that he has been sent by the Lord to eat him. "What are you, who are going to eat me?" asked the tailor. "A wolf." "You lie: you're only a dog; you're too small for a wolf. Let me measure you." So saying, he seized the wolf by the tail, and turning him round in his hand, stretched him out till the wolf was out of breath, and his tail came off. "You're an *archine*[8] long," said the tailor. Overwhelmed with grief, the wolf escaped and went to his wolf-friends, to whom he related his misadventures, and they all set off after the tailor. When he saw them coming he climbed into a tree. "Brothers," said the stupid wolf, "I'll stand upright against the tree; do you mount one after the other upon me, making a staircase, and we shall take vengeance on that rascal! "So they got up, one upon the other. "Ah,

[8]Russian measure: 70 centimetres.

ah!" cried the highest, "wicked tailor, we've come to eat you!" "Little dears—my friends," said the tailor, "have pity upon me, and don't eat me!" "No, no, come down." "One moment; allow me at least to take a pinch of snuff." So he took a pinch and sneezed, *atchi! atchi!* The noodle, who was lowermost, imagined he said *archine, archine,* and that he was going to measure the wolves. Terror overcame him; off he set, down tumbled the wolves, who ran after him and tore him to pieces. So the tailor, having thus escaped, came down from the tree and went home.

The story of the Brave Little Tailor, in Grimm's collection, has incidents in common with several of those already cited of the tricking of monsters. The little tailor, having dashed a cloth among a swarm of flies and killed no fewer than seven of them, believed himself a man of great prowess, and resolved to go into the world and turn it to good account;[9] so off he went, wearing a girdle on which he had embroidered the device, "Seven at a blow." He meets a giant, and, pointing to his girdle, would persuade him that he was possessed of supernatural strength. The giant takes up a stone and squeezes it till water exudes from it. The tailor in his turn takes a soft cheese from his wallet, and makes the whey run out of it. Then the giant throws a stone up into the air so far that it went out of sight; upon which the tailor takes a live bird from his wallet and lets it go, and the giant believes it was a stone. Once more the giant would test the little man's strength: he bids him help to carry a great tree, and the tailor saying that he will take the end which has the branches, as being the heaviest, so soon as the giant has raised the root-end of the tree on to his shoulder, our hero slyly seats himself in the branches, and the giant staggers beneath his burden till he is forced to lay it down, quite exhausted. The little tailor then goes home with the giant, and at night, instead of going to bed, creeps into a snug corner, and the giant, intending to kill him, lays on the bed with an iron bar and breaks the bed: in the morning, when he finds the tailor unhurt, he flies off in a fright. The king, hearing of his prowess, sends him to kill two giants that were the terror of his subjects: he finds them both asleep beneath a tree; so filling his pocket with great stones, he climbs into the branches, and drops the stones on them, which causes them to awake; and each supposing the other had struck at him while he slept, they fell to blows and soon killed each other, and the brave little tailor was credited with having rid the

---

[9] Like the cobbler in the Italian (Milanese) story cited p. 41.

country of the two monsters. His next exploit was encountering a fierce unicorn: the animal, on seeing him, made a rush to destroy him on the spot; but our hero jumped behind a tree, and the unicorn, running at it full force, stuck his horn deep into the trunk, so that he could not withdraw it, on which the little tailor broke off the horn and led the unicorn into the king's presence. After an adventure with a wild boar, the little tailor is married to the daughter of the king.[10]

In a Chilian version (of Spanish extraction), a shoemaker having killed seven flies with his fist one day, dubs himself, Don Juan Bolondron,—killer-of-seven-with-one-fisticuff. The king sends him off to slay a ferocious boar that had killed many people. When Juan sees the boar, he runs back to the palace and hides behind the outer door. The beast runs after him into the courtyard, and is shot by the soldiers. Juan then comes forth, goes to the king, and says, "I not only wanted to kill the boar, but had brought him here alive so that you might see him, and these soldiers of yours have shot him." The king praises his prowess, and marries him to the princess.[11]

The two last-cited stories may be compared with the Kashmírí tale of Fattú Khán, the Valiant Weaver, in Steel and Temple's 'Wide-Awake Stories.' Fattú killed a mosquito one day, just as he was throwing the shuttle with his right hand. Being elated with his skill and bravery, he goes out to see the world, with his bundle, his shuttle, and a great loaf tied up in a kerchief. He reaches a city where a dreadful elephant came daily to make a meal of one of the inhabitants, against which many mighty warriors had gone out, but none of them ever returned. Hearing this, the valiant little man said to himself, "Now is my chance! To a man who has killed a mosquito with one blow of a shuttle, an elephant is mere child's play." So he went to the king, and announced that he was ready single-handed to slay the elephant. The king naturally thought he was mad; but when he persisted in his offer, he told him he was free to try his luck. So at the hour when the elephant usually appeared, Fattú Khán went out to meet him, armed with his shuttle. "It is a weapon I understand," said he to those who urged him to take a spear or a bow; "and it has done work in its time, I assure you." It was a fine sight to see Fattú

---

[10]Most of the incidents in the German tale of the Valiant Tailor and in the Norse tale of the Lad and the Troll reappear in the Gaelic story of Mac-a-Rusgaich: Campbell's 'Popular Tales of the West Highlands,' vol. i. p. 307.

[11]"Chilian Popular Tales," by Thomas M. Moore. 'Folk-Lore Journal,' vol. iii. p. 299.

Khán strutting out to kill the elephant, whilst the townspeople gathered
in crowds on the walls; but alas for the valiant little weaver! No sooner
did he see the elephant charging down on him than all his courage oozed
away. He forgot that he was Fattú Khán, dropped his bundle, his bread,
and his shuttle, and bolted away as hard as his legs would carry him. Now
it so happened that Fattú's wife had made the bread sweet and had put
spices into it, as she wanted to hide the taste of the poison she had used
with it,—for she was a wicked and revengeful woman, and wanted to get
rid of her tiresome, whimsical little husband. The elephant, as he charged
past, smelt the spices, and catching up the bread with his trunk, gobbled
it down without stopping a moment. Poor Fattú scuttled away ever so
fast, but the elephant overtook him. Then the little weaver, in sheer des-
peration, tried to double, and in doing so ran full tilt against the beast. As
luck would have it, just at that moment the poison took effect, and the
elephant fell to the ground dead. Now when the spectators who thronged
the city walls saw the monster fall, they could scarcely believe their eyes;
but they were more astonished when they ran up and found little Fattú
sitting quietly on the elephant's dead body, and wiping his face with his
handkerchief. "I just gave him a push," said he modestly, "and he fell
down. Elephants are big brutes, but they have no strength to speak of."
The king makes Fattú commander-in-chief of his army, and he undertakes to kill a fierce tiger that ranged the country. On seeing the tiger he
climbed a tree, and the tiger waited for him for seven days. Fattú tried to
slip away one day while the tiger was taking his noontide snooze. The
tiger jumps up with a roar, and Fattú's dagger falls down and enters the
tiger's mouth, and kills him. After this the king gives him his daughter—
as usual, in this cycle of stories—and very properly, since "none but the
brave deserve the fair"!

ᴖ DRAGONS AND
MONSTROUS BIRDS ᴖ

FROM giants and ghúls to dragons and basilisks the transition is easy; indeed they are all simply personifications of natural phenomena, if we adopt the theory that such tales or legends are survivals of primitive Aryan (solar) myths. The best-known dragon-story in Europe is probably that of St George, which is thus related in the 'Legenda Aurea,' or Golden Legend, of Jacques de Voragine:

St George, a tribune, was born in Cappadocia, and came to Lybia to a town called Silene, near which was a pond infested by a monster which had many times driven back an armed host that had come to destroy him. He even approached the walls of the city, and with his exhalations poisoned all who were near. To avoid such visits, he was furnished each day with two sheep to satisfy his voracity. If these were not given, he so attacked the walls of the town that his envenomed breath infected the air, and many of the inhabitants died. He was supplied with sheep till they were exhausted, and it was impossible to procure the necessary number. Then the citizens held counsel, and it was decided that each day a man and a beast should be offered, so that at last they gave up their children, sons and daughters—none were spared.

The lot fell one day on the princess. The monarch, horror-struck, offered in exchange for her his gold, his silver, and half his realm, only desiring to save his daughter from this frightful death. But the people insisted on the sacrifice of the maiden, and all the poor father could obtain was a delay of eight days in which to bewail the fate of the damsel. At the expiration of this time the people returned to the palace and said, "Why do you sacrifice your subjects for your daughter? We are all dying before the breath of this monster." The king felt that he must resolve on parting with his child. He covered her with royal clothes, embraced her, and said, "Alas, dear daughter, I thought to have seen myself re-born at your wedding; to have adorned you with royal garments, and accompanied you with flutes and tambourines and all kinds of music! Why did I not die before you?" Then she fell at her father's feet and besought his blessing. He accorded it her, weeping, and he clasped her tenderly in her arms. Then she went to the lake.

George, who passed that way, saw her weeping, and asked the cause of her tears. She replied, "Good youth, quickly mount your horse and fly, lest you perish with me!" But George said to her, "Do not fear. Tell me what you await, and why all this multitude look on?" She answered, "I see that you have a great and noble heart; yet fly!" "I shall not go without knowing the cause," he replied. Then she explained all to him, whereupon he exclaimed, "Fear nothing; in the name of Jesus Christ, I will assist you!" "Brave knight!" said she, "do not seek to die with me. Enough that I should perish, for you can neither assist nor deliver me, and you will only die with me."

At this moment the monster arose above the surface of the water, and the virgin said, all trembling, "Fly, fly, Sir Knight!" His only answer was the sign of the cross. Then he advanced to meet the monster, recommending himself to God. He brandished his lance with such force that he transfixed it and cast it to the ground. Then addressing the princess, he bade her pass her girdle round it, and fear nothing. When this was done, the monster followed like a docile hound. When they had brought it into the town, the people fled before it; but George recalled them, bidding them put aside all fear, for the Lord had sent him to deliver them from the dragon. Then the king and all his people, twenty thousand men, without counting women and children, were baptised, and George smote off the head of the monster.[1]

This renowned exploit of the saint of Cappadocia has its analogue in the legend of Perseus and Andromeda: Cassiope having boasted that she was fairer than the Nereides, Neptune, at their request, sent a sea-monster to ravage Ethiopia, the country of Cepheus, her husband. An oracle declared that the wrath of Neptune could only be appeased by exposing their daughter Andromeda to the fury of the monster, and she was accordingly chained to a rock on the seashore; but just as the dragon was advancing to devour the damsel, Perseus appeared, and plunging his dagger in the monster's right shoulder, destroyed it.

Legends such as these seem to have been common in both European and Asiatic countries from very ancient times. In the Danish ballad of "Svend Felding's Kamp med Risen," Svend is described as going on a pilgrimage to Rome, and on his way arriving at a city called Hövdingö, the princess of

---

[1] Baring-Gould's 'Curious Myths of the Middle Ages,' pp. 297–299. This legend, according to Mr Baring-Gould, is a solar myth. "The maiden," he says, "which the dragon attempts to devour is the earth; the monster is the storm-cloud; the hero who fights it is the sun, with his glorious sword, the lightning-flash." But he does not condescend to explain the signification of the men and beasts which the dragon had devoured previously.

which informs him that the land is being made desolate by a giant, who feeds only on women and maidens. Svend undertakes to encounter the monster, and a number of horses are led forth that he may select one qualified to bear him in the ensuing combat. The hero, of course, kills the giant.[2] So, too, in Ralston's 'Russian Folk-Tales' Ivan Popyalof encounters and slays a formidable serpent that had long devastated the country.

In No. 14 of M. Dozon's Albanian Tales, a lamia (or ogress) comes to a city once a year and devours many people. A damsel, disguised as a soldier, arrives just as the king is preparing to deliver up his son to the lamia, for she would not promise to stay away unless she was regaled on royal flesh. The damsel slays the lamia with one stroke of her sword, and the king, after some demur, rewards the supposed soldier with a wonderful horse, which plays an important part in the sequel.—A similar legend is known to the Chinese, according to Dr Dennys, in which it is related that a huge dragon devoured a maiden once every year, and the youngest of a magistrate's six daughters went off and successfully encountered the monster with a good sword and a dog.[3]

The slaying of dragons forms the subject of many Arabian and Persian tales. In the story of the King of Yemen and his Three Sons—one of the additional stories translated by Jonathan Scott, in vol. vi. of his edition of the 'Arabian Nights'—we are told of a dragon which on a certain day came to the city and demanded a beautiful virgin to be given up to him. The lot having fallen upon the king's daughter, the hero kills the monster, and is rewarded with the hand of the princess. Among the innumerable exploits ascribed to the Persian king Bahrám-i-Ghúr (i.e., of the Wild Ass) is his slaying, single-handed, an enormous elephant in India—whither he had gone in disguise—which had kept the inhabitants in a state of terror, and taken possession of the road between the jungle it inhabited and the city. And in Kashmírí folk-lore, two brothers, sons of a king, being ill-used by their step-mother, go abroad to seek their fortunes. The younger prince, having accidentally separated from his brother, comes to a cottage, where he finds a poor old woman evidently in great sorrow. She informs him that in the neighbourhood there was a fierce rákshasa (a species of demon) who every day compelled the inhabitants of

<hr />

[2]See Thorpe's 'Yule-Tide Stories,' p. 344, Bohn's ed.
[3]'Folk-Lore in China, and its Affinities with that of the Aryan and Semitic Races,' by N. B. Dennys, Ph.D. Hong-Kong: 1876.

the town to supply him with one cake, one goat, and one young man; and that the lot had at last fallen upon her only son. The prince undertakes to confront the rákshasa; and having obtained from the poor woman a cake of much greater size than usual, and the fattest goat she could select, he goes boldly to meet the monster, who, after gorging himself with the cake and the goat, falls asleep, when the prince cuts off his head.[4]

Indian fiction teems with similar incidents-generally encounters with rákshasas. There is a notable instance in the 'Kathá Sarit Ságara': Indívarasena received from the goddess Durgá a sword, by the power of which he should conquer all enemies, and whatever he should think of he should obtain, and by means of it gain the success he desired.[5] Thus armed, he journeyed onward, accompanied by his brother. The story goes on thus:

After he had travelled a long distance he found a great and splendid city, looking like the peak of Meru, on account of its golden houses. There he beheld a terrible rákshasa standing at the gate of the high street, and the hero asked him what was the name of the town, and who was its king. That rákshasa said, "This city is called Sailapura, and it is possessed by our lord Yamadanshtra, the slayer of his foes, king of the rákshasas." When the rákshasa said this, Indívarasena attempted to enter, in order to slay Yamadanshtra, but the rákshasa at the door tried to prevent him, upon which the mighty Indívarasena killed him, cutting off his head with one stroke of his sword. After slaying him, the hero entered the royal palace, and beheld inside of it the rákshasa Yamadanshtra, sitting on his throne, having a mouth terrible with tusks, with a lovely woman at his left hand, and a virgin of heavenly beauty on his right hand. And when Indívarasena saw him he went with the sword given him by Durgá in his hand, and challenged him to fight, and the rákshasa drew his sword and stood up to resist him. And in the course of the fight Indívarasena frequently cut off the rákshasa's head, but it grew again. Seeing that magic power of his, and having had a sign made to him by the maiden at the rákshasa's side, who had fallen in love with him at first sight, the prince, after cutting off the head of the rákshasa, being quick of hand, again cut it in two with a stroke of his sword. Then the

<hr />

[4]Steel and Temple's 'Wide-Awake Stories,' from the Panjáb and Kashmír.—See also Temple's 'Legends of the Panjáb,' vol. i. p. 17ff.

[5]Here we have a *wishing* as well as an all-conquering sword.

rákshasa's magic was baffled by contrary magic, and his head did not grow again, and the rákshasa died of the wound.[6]

According to Danish folk-lore (says Thorpe), when a cock is seven years old it lays an egg, from which, when hatched, there comes forth a basilisk—an ugly monster that kills people only by looking at them. It is said that the only method by which this creature can be destroyed is by holding a looking-glass before it; for it is so ugly that it cannot survive the sight of itself.[7] Thus in chapter 139 of Swan's 'Gesta Romanorum' a basilisk destroys the soldiers of Alexander the Great, without any visible wound; and a philosopher advises that a mirror be placed so as to confront the monster, which being done, it has the desired effect of causing its death. Berni has adopted this idea in his 'Orlando Innamorato,' in the story related by the lady to Rinaldo while he escorts her on a journey: a lover, in order to enter an enchanted garden, employs a mirror to drive away the Medusa by whom it was guarded. And in the Persian romance of 'Hatim Taï,' the hero comes to a village where he finds the people all lamenting and weeping bitterly. They inform him that "once every week a monster comes to our village and devours one of us; and if we do not appease him by the sacrifice of a human creature, he will raze our abodes to the dust. At present the lot has fallen on the son of our chief. On Thursday the monster will come, and the four days that intervene till that time are devoted to weeping and mourning. The youth's relations are at this moment standing around him, extolling his virtues and lamenting his fate." Hatim engages himself, of course, to face the monster in place of the chief's son. A sketch of the creature is shown him, upon which he said, "This must be the monster Haluka, who is invulnerable against all weapons; but if you follow my directions, I may be able to overcome him." Hatim then caused a huge mirror to be constructed, and placed in a certain spot outside the village. The monster came for his victim—in the shape of a great dome without hands or feet, having a terrible mouth in the middle of his body—and having approached within a few paces of the mirror, on seeing the reflection of his hideous form, he made the earth tremble with his roar, and, choking with rage, his confined breath so inflated his body that, like a crack of thunder, he burst, overspreading the surrounding district with his loathsome entrails.

[6]Tawney's translation of the 'Kathá Sarit Ságara,' Book vii. ch. 42, vol. i. p. 385.
[7]Thorpe's 'Northern Mythology,' vol. ii. p. 143, *note*.

The oldest known form of these legends of devouring monsters is found in a beautiful episode in the grand Indian epic, 'Mahábhárata,' which has been turned into graceful English verse by Dean Milman, under the title of "The Bráhman's Lament." Professor Monier Williams, in his 'Indian Epic Poetry,' gives the following outline of this ancient legend, which is called in the original "Bakabadha":

In the neighbourhood of Ekrachakra, a town in which the Pándavas had taken refuge after the treacherous attempt of their cousins to destroy them by setting fire to their dwelling, resided a fierce giant, named Baka, who forced the citizens to send him every day a dish of food by a man, whom he always devoured as his daintiest morsel at the end of the repast. The turn had come to a poor Bráhman to provide the rákshasa with his meal. He determines to go himself, but laments bitterly the hardness of his fate. Upon this his wife and daughter address him in language full of the deepest pathos, each in turn insisting on sacrificing herself for the good of the family. Lastly, the little son, too young to speak distinctly, with beaming eyes and smiling face, runs to his parents, and with prattling voice says, "Weep not, father; sigh not, mother!" Then breaking off and brandishing a pointed spike of grass, he adds in childish accents, "With this pike I will slay the fierce man-eating giant!" His parents (so proceeds the story), hearing this innocent prattle of their child, in the midst of their heartrending anguish felt a thrill of exquisite delight. The end of it is that Bhima,[8] who overhears the whole conversation, undertakes to convey the meal to the monster, and of course speedily despatches him.

"It is considered by some authors," remarks Henderson, "that these legends are figurative; that they grew up and around the memory of such monsters of cruelty as Attila or the infamous Baron de Retz, who are accordingly handed down to posterity with the outward lineaments of dragons and suchlike monsters. . . . Other writers see in the dragon only the huge serpent, the gigantic saurian, or other enormous creature, such as formerly disputed with man the mastery of the world, only by degrees disappearing before him. To others, again, all is pure allegory: in every tale of champion and dragon they simply see 'the ceaseless universal strife' between good and evil."[9]

---

[8] Bhima was one of the five Pándava princes. The name signifies "The Terrible."
[9] 'Notes on the Folk-Lore of the Northern Counties of England and the Borders.' By William Henderson. Second edition, printed for the Folk-Lore Society.

The notion is utterly absurd that "such monsters of cruelty as Attila and the Baron de Retz" are represented as dragons, etc., in these legends; while the solar myth theory is at last being considered by the most eminent comparative mythologists as quite untenable. That legends of encounters with fierce giants, ogres, and dragons are survivals of primitive traditions of contests between Aryan tribes and the savage aborigines of lands to which they migrated—or, going still farther back in the early history of the world, of combats between monstrous creatures and men—is, however, probable to the verge of certainty.

Enormous birds, which can as easily carry off an elephant as the eagle flies away with a lamb in its talons, frequently figure in popular fictions: of these the Roc (*rúkh*) of the 'Arabian Nights' is probably most familiar to the English general reader. Mention is made of this monstrous bird in the Norwegian story of the Blue Belt: A party of sailors landing on the coast of Arabia find "an egg the size of a small house." The hero splits it with his sword, when there issues from it a chicken as large as an elephant—an exact parallel to an incident in one of the voyages of Sindbád the Sailor.

"A *wundervogel*," remarks Wilson, "is the property of all peoples, and the Garuda of the Hindús is represented by the Eorosh of the Zend, the Simurgh of the Persians, the Anka of the Arabs, the Kargas of the Turks, the Kirni of the Japanese, the sacred Dragon of the Chinese, the Griffin of chivalry, the Phœnix of classical fable, the 'wise and ancient Bird' that sits upon the ash Yggdrasil of the Edda, and, according to Faber, with all the rest, is a representation of the holy cherubim that guarded the gate of Paradise. Some writers have even traced the Twelve Knights of the Round-Table to the Twelve Rocs of Persian poetry."[10]

Perhaps the earliest notice of a monstrous bird is found in 'Buddhaghosha's Parables,' in the story of Queen Samavati, where we read that, "in the Kosambi country King Parantapa was one day with his queen outside the palace. The queen being pregnant, the king made her put on a large scarlet cloak. Just then a Hatthílinga, a monstrous bird, flew down from the sky, and taking the queen for a piece of flesh, fluttered his wings with a tremendous noise. The king, hearing the sound, went inside the palace; but the queen, owing to her condition, being

---

[10]Dr Horace Hayman Wilson's 'Essays on Sanskrit Literature,' edited by Dr Reinhold Rost, vol. i. pp. 192, 193, note. To these monster birds may be added the Norka of Russian popular fictions.

unable to escape, was swept off by the bird, for the Hatthílinga has the strength of five elephants."[11]

In the 'Kathá Sarit Ságara' (B. v. ch. 26) Saktideva conceals himself in the back-feathers of an enormous bird of the vulture species, and is conveyed to the Golden City; in the Swedish tale of the Beautiful Palace East o' the Sun and North o' the Earth (Thorpe's 'Yule-Tide Stories') the Phœnix carries the hero on his back to the palace; and in No. 5 of Dozon's 'Contes Albanais' an eagle performs a similar service to a youth who had preserved her young from a serpent. But the largest of all the birds of Asiatic and European fictions must have been mere tom-tits in comparison with the Halcyon of Lucian's 'Vera Historia,' whose nest was seven miles in circumference!

[11]'Buddhaghosha's Parables': a commentary on the 'Dammapada,' or Path of Virtue. Translated from the Burmese by Captain T. Rogers; to which is prefixed a translation of the 'Dammapada' by Professor F. Max Müller, with an Introduction.

PETRIFYING VICTIMS: LIFE-TOKENS: TESTS OF CHASTITY

MAGIC performs a very important part in the folk-tales of Europe as well as in the fictions of all Asiatic countries, where belief in spells, talismans, enchantments, etc., has prevailed from the most remote period of which we possess any record. The classical fable of Medusa's locks, which turned into stone whoever looked on them, is paralleled in the Russian tale of Ivan Dévich: A Baba Yoga gives him one of her hairs, and bids him tie three knots on it, and then blow, which having done, both he and his horse become petrified.—In a Greek popular story, a young prince and his steed are partially turned into marble by an enchantress, but are restored to their natural condition through the instrumentality of a hermit.[1] A well-known instance of the power of enchanters to petrify their victims occurs in the 'Arabian Nights,' where a youth is discovered reading the Kurán, the lower half of his body having been turned into marble by the magical arts of his wicked wife. And in another Arabian tale—that of the Envious Sisters—the two princes, who successively go in quest of the Singing Tree, etc., which their sister had set her heart upon possessing, are both turned to stone (as had also been the fate of all former adventurers), because they looked back before securing the cage in which the wonderful bird was confined.

The prototype of such incidents seems to be the fate of Lot's wife, who, looking back to the burning Cities of the Plain—which she was expressly forbidden to do—was instantly turned into a pillar of salt (Gen. xix. 26). We are also reminded of the story of Orpheus in the regions of Pluto, who had consented to restore Eurydice to life on the condition that Orpheus did not look behind him until he had reached the upper world again; and on his violating the condition, Eurydice was lost to him for ever.

The welfare, or danger, of the heroes of many folk-tales is indicated by a magical flower, or some other object, which they leave behind with their friends, on setting out upon perilous adventures. In the Russian tale of Ivan Popyalof (Ralston's collection) the hero hangs up his gloves, and

[1] Story of "La Tzitzinæna" in 'Recueil de Contes Populaires Grecs,' traduits sur les textes originaux par Émile Legrand. Paris: 1881.

58

tells his two brothers that, should they perceive blood to drop from them, they must hasten to help him; and in another tale the hero leaves behind him a silver snuff-box which would turn black if any misfortune happened to him.

In the Arabian tale of the Envious Sisters, the elder prince gives his sister a dagger, which she is to draw out of its sheath every day while he is absent, and if the blade continue clear, it is a token that he is alive and well, but if it be stained with blood, he is dead; and the younger prince, when about to go in search of his brother, gives her a string of a hundred pearls, which if they would not run freely when she counted them, would then indicate that he had suffered the same fate as his brother.[2] A singularly close parallel to this Arabian tale is found in the Icelandic story of the Farmer's Three Daughters: The elder brother said to the younger that "if three drops of blood should fall from his knife at table while he was away, he must come at once to his rescue, for then it would be sure that he had fared like the others." This token being perceived one day, the younger brother goes off to help the elder, making the same arrangement with his sister as the other had made with himself.

In the Kalmuk tales of 'Siddhí Kúr,' six youths set out to travel, and arriving at the mouth of a great river, they agree to separate, and meet again a certain time after at the same place. They each plant a "tree of life," and should any one of their number be missing at the rendezvous, and his life-tree be found withered, they pledge themselves to search for him, wherever he might be. This idea is, however, much older than the Tartar tales. In the Indian romance of Chitrasekhara and Somasekhara a princess is held captive by a fierce giant, and one of the two heroes undertakes her liberation. Before setting out he gives his brother a flower, the withering of which would betoken that he was in danger, and required immediate assistance.[3]

In the popular tales of Madagascar, similar objects figure frequently. Thus in one story, the hero plants some *aruns* and plantain-trees, and says to his parents, "If these grow withered, then I am ill; and if they die, it will be a sign that I am dead." And in another, the hero tells his mother

---

[2] There is a variant of this tale in Jonathan Scott's edition of the 'Arabian Nights,' vol. vi. p. 161, in which the elder brother gives the younger a ring, which pressing hard upon his finger would betoken that the elder brother was dead.

[3] Descriptive Catalogue of the Oriental Manuscripts, &c., collected by Colonel C. Mackenzie.' By H. H. Wilson. Calcutta: 1828. Vol. i. p. 51.

that a certain banana-tree is to be a sign of his condition, according as it withered or died.[4]

To these "life-tokens" may be added the ring which, according to the Gaelic legend (beautifully versified by Leyden under the title of "The Mermaid"), Macphail of Colonsay received from his lady-love on his going to the wars:

> "When on this ring of ruby red
>   Shall die," said she, "the crimson hue,
> Know that thy favourite fair is dead,
>   Or proves to thee and love untrue."

The chief, in sailing home, was carried off by a mermaid while passing the Gulf of Corrivreckan, and they lived together in a grotto under the sea for several years. At length he grew tired of her society, and ardently wished to return to the Maid of Colonsay:

> But still the ring of ruby red
>   Retained its vivid crimson hue,
> And each despairing accent fled,
>   To find his gentle love so true.

One day the mermaid requested him to give her the ring, which he promised to do, if she would bear him near to Colonsay, and when they approached the shore he leaped on to the land, and was reunited to his "own true love."

Closely allied to these magical life-tokens is the nosegay which, in the Persian Tales of a Parrot ('Túti Náma'), a woman presents to her husband on his taking leave of her to enter the service of a nobleman, and which would remain fresh so long as she continued faithful to him. After some time the nobleman inquired of the soldier how he could thus procure a fresh nosegay every day in the middle of winter, and was informed that its continual bloom was a token of his wife's chastity. The noble sends his chief cook to attempt the woman's virtue, but she cleverly outwits and entraps him; and as he did not return to his master, the second cook was

---

[4] "Malagasy Folk-Tales," by Rev. Jas. Sibree, junior, in 'Folk-Lore Journal' (1884), vol. ii. pp. 52, 130.

despatched on the same errand, and met with a like reception. At length the nobleman himself, with his attendants (among whom was the soldier), visits the virtuous wife, who receives him courteously; and his two cooks, dressed as female slaves, to the infinite amusement of his excellency, wait upon him at supper. The happy soldier then returns his wife the nosegay, still fresh and blooming.

Tests of female chastity are the subjects of many old European romances and ballads. A rose is the test in the romance of Perce Forest; in Amadis de Gaul it is a garland that blooms on the head of her that is faithful, and fades on the brow of the inconstant; in 'Les Contes à rire' it is also a flower; in Ariosto's 'Orlando Furioso' the test, applied to both male and female, is a cup of wine which is spilled by the unfaithful lover —which also occurs in the romances of Tristan, Perceval, La Morte d'Arthur, and is well known in La Fontaine's "La Coupe Enchantée." In 'La Lai du Corn' it is a drinking-horn. Spenser has derived the girdle of Florimel from these sources, or, more immediately, perhaps, from the *fabliau,* "Le Manteau mal taillé," or "Le Court Mantel," an English version of which is found in Percy's 'Reliques,' under the title of "The Boy and the Mantle."[5]

In the metrical tale of "The Wright's Chaste Wife"—of which an analysis will be found in a subsequent paper, "The Lady and her Suitors" —edited by Dr F. J. Furnivall for the Early English Text Society, a rose-garland is the test. The 69th tale of the Continental 'Gesta Romanorum' tells how the mother-in-law of a carpenter gives him a shirt which had the singular property of remaining unsoiled, and could not be rent, so long as his wife and himself continued faithful to each other. So, too, in the North-German tale of the King and Queen of Spain (Thorpe's 'Yule-Tide Stories'), the queen gives her husband a shirt which would betoken her fidelity so long as it remained spotless.[6]

Another infallible indication of female chastity was the mirror presented by the king of the genii to Zeyn el-Asnám, in the Arabian tale, which reflected the form of the woman of whose spotless virtue he wished to be assured: if the mirror remained clear, she was chaste; but if dimmed, she was "no better than she should be," to employ the popular

[5] 'Essays on Sanskrit Literature,' by Dr H. H. Wilson, edited by Dr Reinhold Rost, vol. i. p. 218.
[6] Thorpe says that this story agrees in substance with the ballad of "Graf von Rom," in Uhland, and with the Flemish story of "Ritter Alexander aus Metz und seiner Fran Florentina."

phrase, which being interpreted signifieth that she was a great deal *worse* than she should be. Bandello has a somewhat similar contrivance in one of his Italian novels (Part I., nov. 21), where a Bohemian noble is possessed of a magic picture, which, by its colour, shows the fidelity or frailty of his wife. And in the 'Pentamerone' of Basile a fairy gives each of a king's three daughters a ring, which would break when its possessor quitted the path of virtue. Three distaffs take the place of these magic rings in the French fairy tale of "L'Adroite Princess," which is an imitation of Basile's story.

A flower is the test of marital fidelity in a story in the 'Kathá Sarit Ságara': When Devasmita is obliged to separate from her husband, the deity Siva gives each a red lotus, saying, "Take each of you one of these lotuses in your hands, and if either of you shall be unfaithful during your separation, the lotus in the hand of the other shall fade, but not otherwise."[7]—In the 115th tale of the Continental 'Gesta Romanorum' we read of an elephant which no one dare approach until it is lulled to sleep by two chaste virgins. The original of this story is probably found in the 'Kathá Sarit Ságara,' where it is related that a white elephant having fallen down apparently dead, a holy man declares that it can only be raised up by the presence of a perfectly chaste woman. All the women of the royal household, including the king's favourite wife, are called to put their virtue to this test, but each fails, and ultimately only *one* woman in all the city was found sufficiently chaste to restore the elephant to life![8]

A tank of water was the means by which the hermits ascertained the chastity of Sítá, the wife of Ráma, whose adventures are related in the great Indian epic, 'Rámáyana,' by Válmíki. When the hermits expressed their suspicions, Sítá said to them (according to the version of the inci-

---

[7]This, with analogous tokens of chastity, will be found more fully compared in a subsequent paper on versions of "The Lady and her Suitors."

[8]Heywood, in the Fourth Book of his 'History of Women' (ed. 1657, pp. 253, 254), relates out of Herodotus a very curious story, which bears a close resemblance to the above: On the death of Sesostris, King of Egypt, his son Pherones succeeded to the throne, and not long afterwards lost his sight. An oracle prescribed a peculiar remedy, in which a chaste matron was a *sine quâ non*,—"at which newes being much rejoiced, and presuming both of certain and sudden cure, he first sent for his wife and Queen," but all was in vain; "he sent next for all the great Ladies of the Court, one after one," and still his eyes fared no better; "but at length when he was almost in despaire, he hapned upon one pure and chaste Lady, by whose vertue his sight was restored, and he plainly cured." After relating how the king caused all those frail ladies to be put to a cruel death, "reserving only that Lady of whose loialty the Oracle had given sufficient testimony," whom he made his queen, Heywood has some uncomplimentary remarks on the ladies of his own times—which need not be reproduced, since they can have no application to those of *our* happy times!

dent given in the 'Kathá Sarit Ságara,' Book ix. chap. 51), "Reverend sirs, test my purity by any means that you know of, and if I turn out to be unchaste, let me be punished by having my head cut off." Hearing this, they experienced an emotion of pity, and said to her, "There is a famous bathing-place in this forest, called Títhibhasaras, for a certain chaste woman named Títhibhi, being falsely accused by her husband, who suspected her of familiarity with another man, in her helplessness invoked the goddess Earth and the Lokapálas, and they produced it for her justification. There let the wife of Ráma clear herself for our satisfaction." When they said that, Sítá went with them to that lake. And the chaste woman said, "Mother Earth, if my mind was never fixed, even in a dream, on any one besides my husband, may I reach the other side of the lake;" and after saying this, she entered the lake, and the goddess Earth appeared, and, taking her in her lap, carried her to the other side.[9]

In a Persian tale of an unfaithful wife, in Cardonne's 'Mélanges de Littérature Orientale,' her father-in-law cites her to the Tank of Trial, at Agra. The virtue of this water consisted in trying all kinds of falsehood. A woman, suspected of infidelity, swore she had been faithful, and was thrown into this tank: if she swore falsely she instantly sank to the bottom, but if truly she floated.[10] This wife, conscious of her guilt, devised a

[9]We find a curious parallel to this water-ordeal of Sítá in the Gospel of Pseudo-Matthew, chap. xii., in which both Joseph and Mary go through "the ordeal of jealousy " as ordained in the Book of Numbers, chap. v. 11–31: Joseph having done so in safety, the priests said to Mary, "This only we require of thee, that, since Joseph is pure regarding thee, thou confess who it is that has beguiled thee. For it is better that thy confession should betray thee, than that the wrath of God should set a mark on thy face, and expose thee in the midst of the people." Then Mary said, steadfastly and without trembling, "O Lord God, King over all, who knowest all secrets, if there be any pollution in me, or any sin, or any evil desires, or unchastity, expose me in the sight of all the people, and make me an example of punishment to all." Thus saying, she went up to the altar of the Lord boldly, and drank the water of drinking, and walked round the altar seven times, and no spot was found in her.—'Apocryphal Gospels, Acts, and Revelations,' translated by Alexander Walker, H.M.I.S.; Edinburgh: 1870; p. 30. (Vol. xvi. of Clark's 'Ante-Nicene Christian Library.')

[10]Our ignorant ancestors had the same plan for testing persons accused of witchcraft.—Heywood, in the Ninth Book of his 'History of Women' (ed. 1657, pp. 614, 615), says: "In Sardinia was a Water, in which if the Perjurer washt his eies, he was instantly struck blind, but the innocent departed thence purer in his fame, and more perfect in his sight (*Alex.*, lib. 5, cap. 10). Miraculous are those ponds in Sicilia, called Palici [Aristotle calls this fountain Acedinus], near the river Simethus, where Truths and Falsehoods are strangely distinguished: The Oaths of men and women being written in Tables, and cast in them, the Truths swam above water, and the Lies sunk down to the bottom. All such as forswore themselves, washing in these waters, died not long after, but others returned thence, with more validity and strength."

plan by which she should come through the ordeal scatheless: she bade her gallant counterfeit madness, and to seize her the moment she was to undergo the trial. The lover, solicitous to save the honour and life of his mistress, made no scruple to expose himself to the spectators, and found an opportunity to approach and embrace her, which he effected by subjecting himself to a few blows, being deemed insane by those who did not know him. The suspected wife advanced to the edge of the tank, and, raising her voice, cried, "I swear that I never touched any man but my husband and that madman who has just insulted me. Let this water be my punishment if I have sworn falsely." Having thus spoken, she threw herself into the tank. The water buoyed her up in sight of all present, who unanimously declared her innocent, and she returned triumphant to the arms of her husband, who had always thought her faithful.[11]

This incident has been taken from the 15th tale of the 'Suka Saptatí,' or Seventy Tales of a Parrot, a Sanskrit work; and it reappears in the mediæval "life" of Virgilius, with a metal serpent in place of the water-tank, as follows (the spelling is modernised):

"Then made Virgilius at Rome a metal serpent with his cunning, that whoever put his hand in the throat of the serpent was to swear his cause right and true; and if his cause were false he should not pluck it out again without harm doing. So it fortuned that there was a knight of Lombardy that mistrusted his wife; but she excused herself right nobly and wisely. And she consented to go with him to Rome to that serpent, and there to take her oath that she was not guilty of that that he put upon her. And thereto consented the knight: and as they were both in the cart, and also her man with her, she said to the man, that when he came to Rome he should clothe him[self] with a fool's coat, and disguise him[self] in such manner that they should not know him, and so did he; and when the day was come that he should come to the serpent, he was there present. And Virgilius, knowing the falseness of the woman by his cunning and necromancy, then said he to the woman, 'Withdraw your oath, and swear not;' but she would not do after him, but put her hand into the serpent's mouth; and when her hand was in she sware before her husband that she had no more to do with him than with that fool that stood by. And because she said truth she pulled her hand again out of the throat of the serpent, not

---

[11]A Mongolian variant is found in the tales of Ardshi Bordshi (the second part of 'Sagas from the Far East'), under the title of "How Naren Gerel swore falsely and yet told the truth," but the water-test is omitted.

hurt. And Virgilius, having thereat great spite and anger that the woman had so escaped, destroyed the serpent, for thus escaped the lady away from that great danger. And Virgilius said, that women be right wise to imagine ungraciousness, but in goodness they be but innocents"—*i.e.,* simpletons.

A similar stratagem is adopted by Queen Ysonde in the old metrical romance of 'Sir Tristrem.' Queen Ysonde, being (justly) accused of a *liaison* with Tristram, offers to prove her innocence by undergoing the fiery ordeal. A court is appointed to be held at Westminster, where the Queen is to bear red-hot iron in her hand, according to the ancient law of ordeal. Tristram joins the retinue, disguised as a peasant, in the most abject state of poverty. When they are about to cross the Thames, the queen pitches upon her disguised lover to bear her from the shore to the ship. Tristram designedly lets his fair burden fall upon the beach in such an indecent manner as to scandalise the attendants, who are about to drown him in the river, but are prevented by Ysonde, who imputes the accident to his feebleness, through want of food, and orders him a reward. When the queen is brought to her oath, she swears that she is "a guiltless woman," and that no one had ever familiarity with her person, excepting the king, and the peasant who bore her to the vessel, whose indelicate awkwardness had been witnessed by the whole of her retinue. The hot iron is then presented to Ysonde; but the uxorious king of Cornwall, resting perfectly satisfied with the equivocal oath of his consort, refuses to permit her to hazard this dangerous confirmation of her faith. Ysonde is proclaimed innocent, and is completely reconciled to her husband.[12]

The depravity of women is frequently the subject of satire in our old jest-books and other collections of stories; from which we must not suppose that they were formerly more vicious than the women of Europe at the present day. It is probable that, with the influx of popular fictions from the East, it became the fashion for European story-tellers to imitate the Asiatics in their low estimate of woman's virtue. Muslims have the authority of traditional sayings unfavourable to women, ascribed—falsely, let us trust—to Muhammed, such as, "I stood at the gate of paradise, and lo! most of its inmates were poor; and I stood at the gate of

[12]'Sir Tristrem; a Metrical Romance of the Thirteenth Century.' By Thomas of Erceldoune, called The Rhymer. Edited from the Auchinleck MS., by (Sir) Walter Scott. 4th ed., 1819: Argument; Fytte Second, st. 102–107.

hell, and lo! most of its inmates were women;" and that a man, if he would prosper in any undertaking, should do the contrary to what his wife advises. But sentiments unfavourable to the dignity of women are not peculiar to the Muslims. The writings of the Hindús contain remarks quite as spiteful and unjust, although there are also passages of great beauty, in which women are spoken of in terms of the highest praise. Among the northern nations of Europe, however, women seem to have been always held in great honour, and their influence contributed much to the martial superiority as well as the moral excellence of those peoples.

✌ BIRD ⁼ MAIDENS ✌

THE pretty superstition, which is the basis of so many folk-tales, that at certain times fairies put off their vesture and change their forms to those of swans, doves, or other birds, is perhaps one of those "primitive myths, the common heritage of the Aryan race;" although it is found current in almost all parts of the world. The forms which these beautiful imaginary beings assume are, of course, different in different countries. In the Farö Islands, says Thorpe, in his 'Northern Mythology,' "the superstition is current that the seal casts off its skin every night, assumes the human form, and dances and amuses itself like a human being until it resumes its skin and again becomes a seal. It once happened that a man passing during one of these transformations, and seeing the skin, took possession of it, when the seal, which was a female, not finding her skin to creep into, was obliged to continue in a human form; and being a comely person, the man made her his wife, had several children by her, and they lived happily together, until, after a lapse of several years, she chanced to find her hidden skin, which she could not refrain from creeping into, and so became a seal again." A similar notion prevailed among the people of Shetland regarding mermaids, who, it seems (according to Hibbert, quoted by Thorpe), are not naturally "flesh fishified" at their lower extremities, but resemble human beings, only are far more beautiful, and dwell in the depths of the ocean in halls of pearl and coral. "When they wish to visit the upper world, they put on the *ham,* or garb, of some fish; but woe to those who lose their *ham,* for then are all hopes of return annihilated, and they must stay where they are.[1] . . . It has happened that earthly men have married mermaids, having taken possession of their *ham,* and thus got them into their power."[2] It is the same story—*alter et idem*—everywhere.

---

[1] *Ham,* sub., skin: A. S. *hama.* Thus in Herrtage's 'Gesta,' published by the Early English Text Society, p. 385: "She left hire *name* with oute the stone, and anone she stode up a fayre woman."

[2] In the 'Nibelungenlied,' Sir Hagan, seeing a bevy of mermaids ("wise women") disporting in the waters of the Danube, seizes upon their raiment, in order to compel them to disclose his fate and that of his companions.—"The raiment of these mermaids," remarks Lettsom, the translator, in a note, "seems to have been the swan-raiment worn by the Valkyries, or Choosers of the Slain, which enabled its wearers to assume the shape of swans, or at least to fly away. Hagan had therefore good reason to begin with laying hands on the clothes of these water-nymphs. . . . In the traditions respecting Vœund, Wieland, or Wayland, the Smith, that hero captures a wife by a similar stratagem."

In the Persian romance of King Bahrám Ghúr and Husn Bánú, the royal hero obtains his fairy bride in like manner. Having been carried off by the Dív-i Safíd (White Demon) to the mountains of Káf, which are the boundaries of the world,[3] he is left in a magnificent palace, and after examining all its wonders his senses are overcome by slumber. The narrative thus proceeds: And while sleep possessed him, the fluttering of flying doves sounded in his ears, and, opening his eyes, he saw four doves sitting on a dome of gold, each of them as large as a sheep, and in colour like green emeralds; and the king was astonished at the sight of them. The doves flew off and lighted on the edge of the lake, and out of every dove came a perí, at whose beauty the reason was confused; and they put off their dress on the banks of the lake. Now there was one of these young beauties fair as a child of the húrí,[4] and when the eyes of the king fell upon her beauty he loved and yearned towards her with a thousand hearts; he fainted at the sight of her grace and loveliness. After some time he came again to himself, and saw that they had put down their dress on the banks of the lake, and were swimming and disporting themselves therein. Now the king had heard from the White Dív that if a portion of the garment on the body of a perí be in the possession of any one, she cannot escape from his power. Wherefore, as softly as he could, he stole towards the dress of the youngest fairy, and when he had possessed himself of it he hid himself in a cluster of roses. The fairies went on with their sport in the water till the youngest said to the others, "They say that the Dív-i Safíd has brought hither a king of the race of men, and that for grace and beauty his like was never seen amongst mankind;—let us assume our dove-form again, when we go out of the water, and go and look on him from a distance." Then said another, "It is even as thou sayest; there is not his like amongst the sons of men. Now we are young, and God forbid that the king's heart should incline to one of us, and we be unable to return his affection." The youngest sister said, "Sister, thou hast spoken rightly, and I myself have had a very troubled dream concerning him." "But," said the others again, "when we are disguised in the form of doves, he may think what he pleases." So they all three came out of the water, and sat in the same tree where they had been before. But the youngest missed her dress, and she drew a cold sigh, and

[3]See note, p. 6, for an account of the mountains of Káf.
[4]Húrí—commonly written in Europe houris—are the black-eyed nymphs of Paradise, according to the Kurán.

cried, "Ah, sisters, did I not tell you I had a troubled dream? See, here is the meaning of my dream!" Then they all took flight, and left her with a troubled heart and weeping eyes. The king, seeing this, came from the hiding-place he had chosen, and made his salám to her, and she, beholding the beauty of King Bahrám, inclined towards him, and loved his loveliness with a hundred thousand hearts.—The prince and the perí are forthwith married, and afterwards borne by 'Ifríts to the capital of Persia, where—to employ Shehrazád's formula in the 'Arabian Nights'—"they continued together in joy and happiness, until they were overtaken by the terminater of delights and the separater of companions."[5]

Hasan of Basra, in the 'Thousand and One Nights,' sees ten beautiful birds divest themselves of their plumage and plunge into the water as nymphs. They are the daughters of a powerful genie. Hasan contrives to steal the feathers of the youngest and prettiest of them, and having married her, takes her to his own country. Some years after, she discovers where her husband had concealed her feather-dress, and in his absence she puts it on, and escapes. Hasan is utterly wretched when he learns on his return that his fairy-wife had left him; but as she had considerately left her "address" with his mother, he at once begins his perilous and tedious journey to Jinnistán, the land of the Genii, to bring her back. On the way he obtains shoes of swiftness and other useful magical things, by means of which he reaches his journey's end, and is reunited to his wife—who, it seems, had met with but a scurvy reception from her relations on her returning to see them: her marriage with one of human race being considered by them as "disgracing the family." This is one of the best, as it is among the longest, stories in the 'Arabian Nights.'

The incident of stealing the garments of bathing fairies is often met with in Indian fictions. In the Santhalí folk-tale of Toria the Goatherd (translated by the Rev. F. T. Cole, in the 'Indian Antiquary,' 1875), the beauteous Daughters of the Sun were wont to bathe in a river, on the banks of which Toria fed his goats. Toria, having often beheld them sporting in the water, fell in love with one of them, and one day taking possession of her upper garment, she had no alternative but to follow him to his house and become his wife.—In the 'Kathá Sarit Ságara,' a hermit

---

[5] An Indian variant of this charming fairy-tale, of which the above is a mere extract, is found, under the title of "The faithful Prince," in Steel and Temple's 'Wide-Awake Stories' from the Panjáb and Kashmír.

says to a king's minister, "Go quickly and carry off the clothes of these [celestial] nymphs, and you will learn tidings of your master." He does so, and is successful, as was Sir Hagan with the mermaids in the 'Nibelungenlied.'[6] In the romance of 'Helyas, the Knight of the Swan,' in place of an upper garment or feather-dress, a golden chain is substituted: A young knight, in eager pursuit of a white stag, chased it into a deep and distant forest, where it escaped. In attempting to retrace his way, he came to a fountain in which a beautiful nymph was bathing; she held in her hand a chain of gold, in which lay her power: snatching away the chain, the knight seized the nymph, and she was constrained to become his wife.

"A hunter in Southern Germany," says Mr Baring-Gould, "lost his wife, and was in deep affliction. He went to a hermit and asked his advice; the aged man advised him to seek a lonely pool, and wait there till he saw three swans alight and despoil themselves of their feathers; then he was to steal one of the dresses, and never return it, but take the maiden whose was the vesture of plumes to be his wife. This the huntsman did, and he lived happily with the beautiful damsel for fifteen years. But one day he forgot to lock the cupboard in which he kept the feather-dress: the wife discovered it, put it on, spread her wings, and never returned.[7]

Traces of the same notion are found in a rather confused Albanian story (No. 12 of Dozon's collection), in which the hero gives his mother (a queen) the dress of his bride, the Beauty of the Earth, with strict injunctions not to let her have it during his absence. One day, however, she refused to dance unless she got her dress, and the queen's youngest daughter contrived to steal it for her, and so soon as she had put it on, she said to her maidens, "Farewell! Tell my husband, when he returns, that he need not hope to find me until he has worn out three pairs of iron shoes." The hero, in quest of his bride, comes upon twelve maidens bathing in a fountain, among whom was she whom he had sought so long, and seizing her dress he burned it. Her dress, in which lay her

⌇

---

[6] See *ante,* note, on p. 67.

[7] 'Curious Myths of the Middle Ages': "Swan-Maidens." This is the Arabian tale of Hasan of Basra, without his further adventures in quest of his fairy-wife.—In one of Ralston's 'Russian Folk-Tales' the hero discovers on the sea-shore twelve birds, which turn into beautiful maidens: he steals the shift of the eldest, and marries her.

[8] Dozon's 'Contes Albanais': "La Belle de la Terre."

power, being consumed, she could no longer escape, and therefore returned with her husband.[8]

A somewhat singular version is current in China: Once in olden time a man named Ming-ling-tzu, a farmer in poor circumstances, but without any family, had a well of delicious water near his house. He went one day to draw some, and when at a distance saw a bright light in the well: on approaching to see what it was, he beheld a woman diving and washing in the water, who had her clothes on a pine-tree. Being displeased at her shameless ways and at the well being fouled, he secretly carried off her dress. The garments were quite unlike Lew-chewan in their style, and were of a ruddy and russet colour, which excited his surprise, so that he cautiously came back to see what change would come about. The woman, finishing her bath, cried out in great anger, "What thief has been here in broad day? Bring back my clothes quickly." She then perceived the farmer, and threw herself on the ground before him. He began to scold her, and asked her why she came and fouled his water; to which she replied that both the pine-tree and the well were made by the Creator for the use of all. The farmer entered into conversation with her, and pointed out that fate evidently intended her to be his wife, as he absolutely refused to give up her clothes, while without them she could not get away. The result was that they were married. She lived with him for ten years, and bore him a son and a daughter. At the end of that time her fate was fulfilled: she ascended a tree during the absence of her husband [the narrator seems to have omitted to say that she had got possession again of her celestial garments], and having bidden her children farewell, glided off in a cloud and disappeared.[9]

The notion of Bird-Maidens is also prevalent in Japan. Thus in a lyrical drama, entitled "The Robe of Feathers," translated by Mr Basil Hall Chamberlain, in his 'Classical Poetry of the Japanese,' a fisherman discovers a feather-dress hanging from a tree, "on Miho's pine-clad shore," and resolves to take it home that it may be handed down as an heirloom. A fairy comes and claims it, saying that without it she "never more can

[9]Dennys' 'Folk-Lore in China.'—Dr Dennys remarks that he has found no trace of any similar story in China proper, though one may exist, and "the reappearance of the Keltic legend in a group of islands in the China Sea [*i.e.*, the Lew-chew Islands] is a noteworthy phenomenon." The idea of the story may, however, have been derived from India, where, as we have seen, it is generally current.

go soaring through the realms of air, never more can she return to her celestial home." The fisherman consents to restore it on the condition that she dance before him. She obtains the feather-dress, promising to dance after she has put it on, which she does, to the great delight of the fisherman; and the chorus describes her departure:

> But ah, the hour, the hour of parting rings!
> Caught by the breeze, the fairy's magic wings
> Heavenward do bear her from the pine-clad shore,
> Past Ukisháma's widely-stretching moor,
> Past Akisdaka's heights, and where are spread
> The eternal snows on Fusiyama's head;
> Higher and higher to the azure skies,
> Till wandering vapour hides her from our eyes.

Stealing the clothes of *human* damsels while they are bathing is a very ancient stratagem, and was doubtless often practised in our own country in more primitive times. In the Indian work entitled 'Prem Ságar,' or Ocean of Love, by Lallú jí lal Kavi, we read that Sri Krishnú—who is represented as an incarnation of Vishnu—purloined the garments of a party of pretty cowherdesses, who were bathing in the river Argun, and carried them to the top of a *kunduna*-tree. When the damsels discovered their loss, they set up loud lamentations, and espying Krishnú in his hiding-place, earnestly begged him to restore their clothes, which he refused to do except upon the condition that they should come out of the water one by one and claim their garments.—A similar trick is recorded of the celebrated pre-Islamite Arabian poet-prince Imra-el-Kays, according to the note prefixed to Sir William Jones' translation of his famous 'Mu'allaka,' or prize-poem, so called because it had the honour of being suspended in the temple at Mecca.

⌇ SUBAQUEOUS FAIRY HALLS: FORBIDDEN ROOMS: CUPID AND PSYCHE LEGENDS ⌇

THE dwellings of fairies, according to the folk-lore of most countries, are frequently splendid subaqueous halls or palaces, adorned with the most brilliant gems, and with couches of pure gold. "Mankind," it has been remarked, "have in all ages delighted to find their own image in all the parts of space. It is in consequence of this propensity that we find so frequently human beings, or divinities like men in form, represented as dwelling beneath the sea, or within the waters of rivers or fountains. In Homer the submarine cavern of Neptune at Ægæ is described in the 13th Iliad; and that in which Thetis and Eurynome concealed Vulcan, in the 18th. The only accounts given by the ancient poets of the descent of mortals into these aqueous abodes are, that of Hylas, of which the best account occurs in the 13th Idyllium of Theocritus, and that of Aristæus in the 4th book of the Georgics of Virgil."[1]

It is a very common occurrence for the heroes of popular tales to plunge boldly into a lake or fountain, and lo! they are in fairyland. In Berni's 'Orlando Innamorato,' the renowned and dauntless hero throws himself into a lake, and "finds himself in another world " (which has happened, in a different sense, to others, before and since!), standing upon a dry meadow, with the lake overhead, through which shone the beams of our sun, the meadow being on all sides surrounded by a crystal wall. After slaying his foe, Orlando discovers a gate in the crystal wall, and, having passed through the dark labyrinth, comes at last to where the place is lighted by a large carbuncle, the lustre of which was equal to that of day. This discovered to his view a river little less than twenty yards broad, and beyond this he saw a field as thickly covered with precious stones (the "flowers" of the fairy mead) as the sky is full of stars.

According to Irish legendary lore, there is (or was) in the south of Ireland a lake in which many young men were drowned, and, strange to say, their bodies were never recovered. On dark nights its waters seemed like

---

[1]Notes to Croker's 'Fairy Legends and Traditions of the South of Ireland.'

a flaming fire; horrid forms were seen to glide over it, and the air in its neighbourhood had then a sulphureous smell. In old times there dwelt, not far from this lake, a young farmer named Roderick Keating, who was about to be married to the prettiest girl in the whole district, who rejoiced in the name of Peggy Honan. It happened one day he had just returned from Limerick, where he had been to buy the wedding-ring, and was standing on the border of the lake, chatting with some young fellows of his own age, who began to "chaff" him about Peggy Honan, saying that his rival Delaney had won her affections and "put his eye out." Keating, knowing better, took the wedding-ring out of his pocket and showed it to them; but while he was toying with it, the ring slipped from his fingers and fell into the lake! Keating was greatly concerned at this accident, not because of the pecuniary loss, for that was a trifle, but because it was ominous of ill-luck. He offered five pounds to any one who would dive into the lake and fetch up the ring, but all the youths declined the venture, when a half-crazy fellow called Paddeen agreed to dive after it—not being able to resist so great a bribe. So he pulls off his coat and down he plunges head-foremost into the lake. What depth he went nobody knows, but he went down, down, down through the water, until it parted from him and he came upon dry land; and the sky, the sunlight, and everything was there just as it is here; and he saw fine pleasure-grounds, with an elegant avenue through them, and a grand house, with many steps going up to the door. When he had recovered from his wonder at finding the land so dry and comfortable under the water, he looked about him, and what should he see but all the young men that were drowned, working away in the pleasure-grounds as if nothing had ever happened to them. Some of them were mowing down the grass, and more were setting out the gravel-walks, and doing all manner of nice work as neat as if they had never been drowned. Well, when he had neared the door of the house, out walks a great fat woman, with teeth as big as horses' (!), and after mutual salutations, "What have you come here for?" asks this obese fairy. Quoth Paddeen, as bold as you please, "For Rory Keating's ring." "Here it is," says she, at the same time handing him the ring. "Will you please tell me," then says Paddeen, "am I to go back the same way as I came?" "Then," says the fairy, "you're not going to marry me?" "Wait till I come back again," says Paddeen, for he knew she had lost her power over him by parting with the ring; "I've got to get paid for bringing back this ring: but I'll be sure to come back and marry you." And here Paddeen began to edge away from the house, and at length he came to the water, and going up through it, he arrived safely at a rock on the borders of the lake.[2]

In the Persian romance which purports to recount the adventures of the celebrated Arab chief Hatim Taï, the self-denying hero, coming to a large city, finds the people all gathered round the mouth of a well. Inquiring the cause of their assemblage, he learns that the son of their chief magistrate had gone mad, and was in the habit of frequenting this well, and at length had thrown himself into it: "Three days have we looked for him here, but we have found no trace of him, and none of our people will venture into the well." Hatim readily undertakes to go down into the well in quest of the lost youth, and the people agree to remain there until he returns. No sooner has he leaped down ten feet than he finds himself on firm ground, and, looking about, sees no well, but an extensive plain. Coming to a garden, the doors of which stand invitingly open, he enters, and discovers in its midst a magnificent palace (in fact, such as are only to be found beneath enchanted wells), and within he sees fairies reclining upon couches which would beggar description. Conspicuous amidst all this splendour are two thrones of burnished gold, on one of which sat the fairy queen, on the other a young man of noble aspect. After Hatim had partaken of refreshments, the youth informed him that he was one day seated at the mouth of the well, when the heart-ravishing queen of the fairies appeared, and, bewildered with her beauty, he lost his reason (he probably had not much to lose), and for days lingered near the well, in hopes of seeing her fairy majesty once more, and being disappointed he plunged in, and on opening his eyes found himself in this paradise. Hatim prevails upon the fairy queen to allow the youth to return with him to his parents, and to promise to visit him personally; and so he restores the infatuated youth to his sorrowing relatives.[3]

In the 7th Tale of the ancient Indian romance, 'Twenty-five Tales of a Demon' (Vetala Panchavinsati),[4] the hero falls into the sea, and, looking about him, finds he is in a grand city, with palaces of gold, supported on pillars of jewels, adorned with gardens, in which were tanks with steps

[2]Adapted from Croker's 'Fairy Legends of the South of Ireland.'

[3]It is a popular belief in Persia that near the city of Kashan there is a well of unfathomable depth, at the bottom of which are enchanted groves and gardens.

[4]A Sanskrit work of very great antiquity, which is now incorporated with the 'Kathá Sarit Ságara,' and of which there exist versions in most of the vernacular languages of India—Bengalí, Hindí, Tamil, Mahratta, etc.

composed entirely of precious gems.—One of the earliest extant fairy tales of subaqueous halls is, perhaps, that contained in the 6th Fable of the second chapter of the 'Hitopadesa' (Friendly Counsel). Professor Johnson has translated it as follows: "One day as I was in the pleasure-garden I heard from a voyaging merchant that on the fourteenth day of the month, in the midst of the sea which was near, beneath what had the appearance of a kalpa-tree, there was to be seen seated on a couch variegated with the lustre of strings of jewels, a certain damsel, as it were the goddess Lakshmí, bedecked with all kinds of ornaments, and playing on a lute. I therefore took the voyaging merchant, and, having embarked in a ship, went to the place specified. On reaching the spot, I saw her exactly as she had been described, and, allured by her exquisite beauty, I leaped after her into the sea. In an instant I reached a golden city, where, in a palace of gold, I saw her reclining on a couch, and waited on by youthful sylphs. When she perceived me at a distance she sent a female friend, who addressed me courteously. On my inquiry, her friend said, 'That is Ratna-Manjari, the daughter of Kandarpa Keli, king of the Vidyaharas. She has made a vow to this effect: "Whosoever shall come and see the city of gold with his own eyes, shall marry me." Accordingly I married her by that form of marriage called Gandharva,[5] after the conclusion of which I remained there a long while delighted with her. One day she said to me in private, 'My beloved husband, all these things may be freely enjoyed; but that picture of the fairy Swarna-rekhá must never be touched.' Some time afterwards, my curiosity being excited, I touched Swarna-rekhá with my hand. For doing so I was spurned by her, although only a picture, with her foot beautiful as the lotus, and found myself alighted in my own country."

This last is not only curious as being one of the oldest specimens of fairy tales, but it is closely allied to stories of forbidden rooms, the entrance into which is immediately followed by severe punishment. The "Blue Chamber" in our nursery tale of the terrible Bluebeard (which came to us from the French—from Perrault's story of "La Barbe Bleue") will readily occur to the reader, first and foremost, among his reminiscences of forbidden rooms.[6] And numerous other instances might be

---

[5] In which the parties exchange flowers.

[6] "The treasure-house of Ixion, which none may enter without being either destroyed, like Hesioneus, or betrayed by marks of gold or blood, reappears," says Cox, "in a vast number of popular stories, and is the foundation of the story of Bluebeard."—'Mythology of the Aryan Nations,' vol. ii. p. 36.

cited from the fairy tales of Europe, especially those written in France during the seventeenth century, and afterwards translated into our own and other European languages. In No. 41 of Campbell's 'Popular Tales of the West Highlands' (vol. i. pp. 265–275) we have not only a "Bluebeard's Chamber," but also a curious example of "grateful animals": Three daughters of a poor man enter a forbidden room, which is full of dead gentlewomen, and get themselves stained knee-deep with blood; two of the sisters refuse to give the cat a little milk, and have their heads cut off; but the third makes friends with poor puss, who licks off the blood, and so she escapes detection.

In Eastern fictions, however, the forbidden chamber does not generally contain anything horrifying to the person whose curiosity has been unable to resist the injunction. A story in the romance of the 'King and his Seven Vazírs' has *two* forbidden rooms. A young man, having wasted his patrimony, enters the employment of ten old men who live together in a fine palace, until one after another dies, and the tenth, feeling his end near, calls the youth to his couch, and, bequeathing him the palace with all its wealth, warns him on no account to open a certain door, since if he did so he would repent it all his life. As usual, the young man's curiosity is not to be restrained. He opens the door, and finds himself in a long, dark passage, which leads him to the sea-shore, where a huge eagle, darting down, seizes him, and flying up high into the air, finally descends with him upon a desolate island. He is rescued by a passing vessel, and reaches a country, the queen of which offers him marriage, which he gladly accepts. The queen informs him that all her treasures are now at his disposal; but he must "avoid yonder door; if thou dost open it, thou wilt repent when it is too late." The new king lived happily with his lovely bride for some time, until, "tempted by the Evil One," he opens the fatal door, finds himself in a dark passage as before, and the same eagle which had borne him away from the palace of the old men sweeps down and carries him back to the spot where he had been first taken up. The rest of his life was spent in vain regrets. As the author says, "he never smiled again."

Perhaps among forbidden rooms in Eastern stories that which figures in the Arabian tale of the Third Royal Mendicant (or Calender, as in our common translation) is most familiar to the general reader. "We deliver to thee," said the fairies, when they were about to leave him for a season, "the keys of the palace, which are a hundred in number, belonging to a hundred closets. Open each of these, and amuse thyself, and eat and drink and refresh thyself, except the closet that hath a door of red gold;

for if thou open this, the consequence will be a separation between us and thee." After having opened all the other doors, and admired the rare splendour within each of the rooms, he had not patience to abstain from opening the forbidden closet; so he opened the door, and when he entered he found the place illuminated by golden lamps, and by candles, which diffused the odours of musk and ambergris. He saw there a black horse, saddled and bridled, and wondering at the sight, led him out and mounted him, and having struck him, "the horse uttered a sound like thunder, and expanding a pair of wings, soared with me to an immense height through the air, and then alighted upon the roof of another palace, where he threw me from his back, and by a violent blow with his tail upon my face, struck out my eye and left me."

These incidents were evidently imitated from the story of Saktideva, in the 'Kathá Sarit Ságara,' in which the hero's fairy bride, having to separate from him for a period, gives him strict charge never to ascend the middle terrace of the palace. Impelled by curiosity, however, he enters, sees much to marvel at, and, going out to the lake, a horse with a jewelled saddle: trying to mount it, he was struck with its heel, and flung into the lake. Rising up, to his astonishment he finds himself standing in the middle of a garden-lake of his own city of Vardhamana. And in the same work (story of Nágasvámin and the Witches), a Yakshiní, who had married the hero, commands him not to visit the middle block of buildings of her palace after she has gone away; but he does so, and there saw a horse, and going up to him, the horse kicked him, and immediately he finds himself in a temple of Siva.

Mr Ralston, in his 'Russian Folk-Tales,' has pointed out that in a modern Greek story (Hahn's collection, vol. ii. p. 197) the hero discovers in the 41st room of a castle belonging to a Drakos, who had given him leave to enter 40 of them, a magic horse, and before the door of the room a pool of gold, in which he becomes gilded. In another story (same collection), the 40th is the forbidden room, in which is a lake, and swan-maidens bathing therein. In a third story, the 40th room contains a golden horse, and a golden dog, which assist the bold liberator. And in a fourth story, he finds a fair maiden, shining like the sun, whom the demon-proprietor had hung up within by the hair.

In an Italian tale (from Pisa), cited by Mr H. C. Coote in 'The Folk-Lore Record,' vol. i. pp. 196, 197, a woodman receives from a lady in the forest an inexhaustible purse, on his consenting to give her one of his daughters for a companion. The eldest girl being sent, the lady takes her away to a magnificent palace. "See," said she, "thou art mistress here; I go away in the morning, and return in the evening. These are the keys of the whole palace; I only forbid thee to enter this room," and she showed a closed door. The girl's curiosity impels her to enter the forbidden room, where she sees the lady in a bath, and two damsels reading to her. She shuts the door again directly, but when the lady comes home she calls to her, saying, "Thou hast disobeyed. Let me hear what thou hast seen." The girl, being quite confounded, then related what she had seen, upon which the lady, without saying another word, took her, cut off her head, fastened it to a beam by the hair, and buried the body. The lady then gets the wood-man's second daughter to come, on the pretext of her being a companion to the other, and the same happens to her. But the third, though she also entered the fatal room, stoutly denied having seen anything. And when the lady saw that the girl was so obstinate, she made her put on again her peasant's clothes, and sent her into the forest to go about her business.[7]

Forbidden rooms occur frequently in the Norse tales; for example: In the story of the Widow's Son (Dasent's collection), the hero takes service with a man, who, on going away for eight days, warns him not to enter one of four rooms which he indicates to him;—if he did so, the man would take his life when he came back. But the youth, after his master has been gone a few days, goes into the first room, where he sees nothing but a bramble-bush rod on a shelf. When the man comes home, he soon discovers that the room had been entered, and gave the youth only a sound thrashing, as he pled hard for his life. Again the man goes away, and cautions him as before; but the youth could not resist the curiosity he felt to examine the second room, in which he finds a big stone and a pitcher of water on a shelf. On the return of his master, he found that the second room had been entered, and once more gave the hero a severe beating. He goes off a third time, and the lad looks into the third room, where he sees a trap-door in the floor, and on lifting it there was a great copper cauldron that bubbled and boiled away down below, but he could see no fire under it. He dips his finger into the broth, and when he drew it out, behold, it was gilded all over. He scraped and scrubbed it, but the

---

[7]This story seems imperfect; at least it is a very peculiar member of the "Forbidden Room" cycle of folk-tales.—In a Japanese story, the hero receives a casket which would give him everything he wished for, and even conferred on him immortal youth, so long as it remained unopened.

gilding would not go off, so he tied a rag round it: but when his master came back, he saw the rag on his finger, and tearing it off, at once saw where he had been. This time he gave our hero such a thrashing that he had to keep his bed three days, after which his master rubbed him over with some ointment, and he was as sound and fresh as ever. Once more the man goes away, and the hero entered the fourth room, where he saw a great black horse, tied up in a stall by himself, with a manger full of red-hot coals at his head and a truss of hay at his tail; so he changed them about, and put the hay at the horse's head. Then the horse told him that for this kindness he would enable him to escape; for should his master (who was a troll) come back and find him there, he would surely kill him. So, acting on the advice of the horse, the hero got into the cauldron in the third room, and came out feeling very strong; then taking from the other rooms the stone, the pitcher of water, and the bramble-bush rod, he got on the back of the horse and galloped off. The troll returns, and instantly pursues him, but the rod, stone, and water, thrown successively behind, raise a thicket, a mountain, and a great lake, and so the hero makes good his escape.[8]

Possibly some readers may be disposed to consider such wild tales as distorted traditions of the Fall of Man; others may see in them only dreams induced by hashish, or some other narcotic which forms the Paradise of Fools!

The beautiful story of Cupid and Psyche, which forms an episode of the 'Golden Ass' of Apuleius, and which has been so charmingly rendered into English verse by Mrs Tighe, has a near affinity with stories of forbidden rooms. Cupid consents to pass the nights with Psyche, on the condition that she does not attempt to see him; and for some time the lovers are happy in their reciprocal affection, until Psyche's two sisters, whom she acquaints of her happiness, at the same time of her never having seen her lover, urge her to break the condition, declaring their belief that her lover is a serpent. Psyche one night took a lamp to look at Cupid, and, in her agitation on beholding his beauty, allowed a drop of oil to fall upon him, which awoke him, and immediately Cupid and the palace disappeared, and Psyche found herself in the wilderness, where she was

---

[8]The reader will find this cycle of folk-tales ably treated in a paper by Mr E. Sidney Hartland, entitled "The Forbidden Chamber," in 'The Folk-Lore Journal,' vol. iii. pp. 193–242.

before her union with her lover.—Dunlop ('History of Fiction,' chap. iii.) has the jocular remark that Psyche ought to have had sufficient reason to know that her lover was not a serpent; but it seems to me that the suspicion, real or affected, of her sisters points to the Eastern origin of the story. In many Indian stories we read of a serpent-deity who, assuming the human form, took a mortal maiden for his wife, and disappeared each morning before daybreak; and sometimes the maiden, learning the nature of her lover, destroyed his serpent-skin while he slept, thus compelling him to continue in his human shape. On the other hand, European as well as Asiatic folk-lore abounds in stories of maidens being wedded to serpents and frogs, which the nuptial couch miraculously changed into handsome princes—they having been doomed to remain in such loathsome forms until espoused by beautiful damsels. Our nursery tale of Beauty and the Beast, and the German tale (in Grimm's collection) of the Frog Prince, are familiar instances.[9]

The first part of the Norse tale, "East o' the Sun and West o' the Moon," comprises exact parallels to these incidents in the Cupid and Psyche legend: A girl is married to a White Bear, who takes her to a grand palace, and when she has retired to rest she finds a man beside her;—"that was the White Bear, who threw off his beast-shape at night; but she never saw him, for he always came after the light was put out, and before the day dawned he was up and off again." After some time thus spent, the girl asks the White Bear's leave to visit her parents, which he grants, but warns her not to have any private conversation with her mother. But she could not resist her mother's importunity, and told her, one day, how a man slept beside her every night, but she had never seen him, for he always got up and went away before daylight. Her mother advises her to take a small piece of candle with her to bed, and light it while he was asleep; but she was to take care not to drop the tallow on him. The girl returns on the back of the White Bear, and in answer to his inquiries, stoutly denies having had any private conference with her mother. At night, when the man is fast asleep beside her, she lights the candle, and lets the light shine upon him"—"and so she saw he was the loveliest prince one ever set eyes on, and she fell so deep in love with him

[9]Another instance is found in Crane's 'Italian Popular Tales,' "Zelinda and the Monster": by her consenting to marry him, he becomes a very handsome youth.

on the spot, that she thought she should die if she didn't give him a kiss there and then. And so she did; but as she kissed him, she dropped three drops of hot tallow on his shirt, and he woke up." He then tells her that she has thus undone them both, for had she held out only that one year he had been freed—his step-mother having bewitched him, so that he was a White Bear by day and a man by night. "Next morning, when she woke up, both prince and castle were gone; and there she lay on a little green patch in the midst of the gloomy thick wood, and by her side lay the same bundle of rags she had brought with her from her father's home."[11]

This charming legend—the most delightful, perhaps, of all fairy tales, not even excepting that of Cinderella—is known all over the world, and is certainly very ancient. The following is a Sicilian version preserved to the present day by oral tradition: A man and his youngest daughter, gathering wild herbs, came to a garden, where the girl saw a fine radish and began to pull it up, when suddenly a Turk appeared and said, "Why have you opened my master's door? You must come in now, and he will decide on your punishment." They went down into the ground, more dead than alive, and when they were seated they saw a green bird come in and bathe in a pan of milk, then dry itself and become a handsome youth. He said to the Turk, "What do these persons want?" "Your worship, they pulled up a radish and opened the door of the cave." "How did we know," said the father, "that this was your Excellency's house? My daughter saw a fine radish, it pleased her, and she pulled it up." "Well, if that's the case," said the master, "your daughter shall stay here as my wife—take this sack of gold and go: when you want to see your daughter, come and make yourself at home." The father took leave of his daughter and went away. When the master was alone with her, he said, "You see, Rosella, you are now mistress here," and gave her all the keys. She was perfectly happy. One day, while the green bird was away, her (two) sisters took it into their heads to visit her, and asked her about her husband. Rosella said she did not know, for he had made her promise not to try to find out who he was. Her sisters, however, persuaded her, and when the bird returned and became a man, Rosella put on a downcast air. "What is the matter?"

---

[10]This incident reappears in the Danish story of "Prince Hatt under the Hill," in Thorpe's 'Yule-Tide Stories' (Bohn's ed., p. 23), and in No. 281 of Pitrè's collection of Sicilian tales.

[11]Dasent's 'Popular Tales from the Norse.' Second edition, pp. 27, 30, 31.

asked her husband. "Nothing." "You had better tell me." She let him question her a while, and at last said, "Well, then, if you want to know why I am out of sorts, it is because I wish to know your name." Her husband told her that it would be the worse for her, but she insisted on knowing his name. So he made her put the gold basin on a chair, and began to bathe his feet. "Rosella, do you really want to know my name?" "Yes." And the water came up to his waist, for he had become a bird and had got into the basin. Then he asked her the same question again and again, and again she answered yes, and the water was up to his mouth. "Rosella, do you really want to know my name?" "Yes! Yes! Yes!" "Then know that I am called THE KING OF LOVE!" And saying this, he disappeared, and the basin and the palace disappeared likewise, and Rosella found herself alone out in an open plain, without a soul to help her.[12]

A variant of this Sicilian form of the legend, current in Chili—brought thither, in all likelihood, from Spain—is to the following effect: One day an old man went to a forest to cut firewood to sell in the city. Chopping a very thick tree, he heard groaning inside; and suddenly a hideous black man appeared and threatened him with death. The poor old man humbly asked pardon, having offended unwittingly. Well, the black man will spare his life, on condition that he give him his beautiful daughter in marriage; and in the meantime he may split open the tree, and take out of it as much gold as he wished for the use of his wife and family. The old man loads his donkey with gold; and as he is about to return home, the black man tells him that eight days hence he will come to his house at night, and be married to his daughter in the dark. This takes place at the time appointed, and the damsel lived very happily, though her husband left her all alone every morning. He came each night, she met him in the dark, and just before daybreak he was off again. An old woman, a neighbour, asked her one day what sort of a man her husband was. She said she did not know, for she had never seen him. "Child," quoth the crone, "how knowest thou but thy husband may be a dog, or even Satan? It is needful thou shouldst see him. Take this match, and fear nothing. When thy husband is asleep, rub the match against the wall, and thou wilt see who he is." The damsel, when midnight came, struck the match, and looking at her husband, saw that he was so handsome that she became wonderstruck. She forgot all about the match, and a spark fell

[12]Crane's 'Italian Popular Tales,' p. 1ff.

upon his face. So he woke up, and blowing out the match, "Ungrateful wretch," said he, "thou hast broken thy word. Thou must know that I am a prince under a spell, and little was lacking for me to be freed from my enchantment; but now thou must wear out shoes of iron before thou shalt see Prince Jalma, thy husband, again; and my own pains will be still greater than thine." The damsel gets iron shoes made, and after long and weary travel discovers her husband, when the spell is broken, as in other versions.[13]

We find another parallel to the story of Cupid and Psyche in the old French romance of ' Parténopex de Blois': The fairy Meliora grants the hero her love on the condition that he does not attempt to discover her person until two years are expired, when they should be married. The mother of Parténopex, suspecting that he is under the spell of a wicked enchantress, gives him a magic lamp, by means of which he might behold his mysterious lady-love. Returning to the fairy palace, he enters the chamber of Meliora with the lamp in his hand, and while he is gazing with rapture on her beauteous form, she awakes and upbraids him for his perfidy, the consequence of which, she informs him, must be their immediate separation. The hero, however, is ultimately reunited to his fairy bride.

It seems to have been an article of very general belief (says Rose) that when a superior being received a mortal into favour, a test of obedience was required, in the resistance of some species of temptation; that the temptation was not usually resisted, and that the penalty of such disobedience was temporary, or, what was more rare, eternal banishment. Thus in the old French romance of 'Mélusine' the fairy Pressine becomes enamoured of a king of Albany (probably Scotland), and espouses him, on the condition of his never attempting to see her *pendant sa gésine*. She bears him three daughters at a birth—the first named Mélusine, the sec-

---

[13]"Chilian Popular Tales," by Thomas H. Moore, in 'Folk-Lore Journal,' vol. iii. pp. 293–299.—The second part of the Danish story of "Prince Wolf" is to the same purpose: After the heroine has been married for some time to her mysterious husband, she visits her parents, and her mother persuades her to take a little knife and stick it into the edge of the bedstead: when he gets in, he will give himself a slight scratch with the knife, and if he scream, he must be a troll, but if he only moans, he is a real man. The girl does this, and her husband moans, at which she is pleased; but next day the Wolf is lame in his right hind-leg. On her second visit home, her mother gives her a tinder-box and taper. She lights the taper, and beholding the loveliest prince, embraces him, at which he awakes, then springs from the bed and limps out into the woods.

ond Melior, and the third Palatine. The king, forgetful of his compact, enters her apartment during the period of her accouchement, and the fairy, after reproaching him with his breach of promise, quits him for ever, and retires with her daughters into the isle of Avalon.[14]

In the 'Lay of Sir Gruélan,' the hero sees a beautiful fairy bathing, who declares her love for him, and after passing some time in amatory converse—

> Lo! westward rolled, the sun, with slanting beam,
> Streaked the green mead and stained the glassy stream,
> Then the fond fairy bade the knight depart,
> Nor fear lest absence change her constant heart;
> Still veiled by secret law from human eyes,
> Clear to his sight alone her form should rise;
> Still loyal kind, while steadfast wisdom held
> His conscious lips inviolably sealed.[15]

And in the 'Lay of Lanval,' the hero is thus addressed by his fairy bride:

> "Whene'er thou call, thy joyful eyes shall see
> This form, invisible to all but thee.
> One thing I warn thee, let the blessing rest
> An unrevealed treasure in thy breast:
> If here thou fail, that hour my favours end,
> Nor wilt thou ever more behold thy friend."[16]

Asiatic fiction furnishes yet another instance in the Persian story of King Ruzvanshad and the fairy Princess Sheristáni. The fairy (or rather the queen of the Jinn, or Genii) marries the hero, on the condition that should she do anything in his presence that displeased him, he is not to blame or reproach her for it: if he do so, the consequence must be their separation. The princess, in due course, gives birth to a child, which (for good and prudent reasons, as afterwards appears) she casts into the fire, in the presence of her husband, who utters a cry of horror, upon which she vanishes, but finally returns and is reunited to her husband.

[14]Notes to W. Stewart Rose's rendering of 'Parténopex de Blois.'
[15]'Le Grand's 'Fabliaux,' ed. 1781, tome i. p. 132; Way's translation, ed. 1815, vol. ii. pp. 87, 88.
[16]Le Grand, iv. pp. 95, 96; Way, ii. p. 57.

Bryant, in his learned 'Analysis of Ancient Mythology,' offers the following interpretation of the esoteric signification of the Cupid and Psyche myth: "The most pleasing emblem among the Egyptians was exhibited under the character of Psyche. This was, originally, no other than the Aurelia, or Butterfly; but in after-years was represented as a lovely female child, with the beautiful wings of that insect. The Aurelia, after its first stage as an *eruca,* or worm, lies for a season in a manner dead, and is enclosed in a sort of coffin. In this state of darkness it remains all the winter; but at the return of spring it bursts its bonds, and comes out with new life, and in the most beautiful attire. The Egyptians thought this a very proper picture of the soul of man, and of the immortality to which it aspired. But they made it more particularly an emblem of Osiris, who, having been confined in an ark or coffin, and in a state of death, at last quitted his prison and enjoyed a renewal of life. This circumstance of the second birth is continually described under the character of Psyche; and as the whole was owing to divine love, of which Eros was an emblem, we find this person often introduced as a concomitant of Psyche. They are generally described as accidentally meeting and enjoying a pleasing intercourse, which is attended with embraces and salutes, and every mark of reconciliation and favour."

ᴣ FAIRY HINDS:
MAGIC BARKS ᴣ

A S the dryads and other mundane semi-deities were amongst the ancients an intermediate race between men and gods, so the fays, or fairies, of European romance, and the perís and yakshas of Arabian, Persian, and Indian fictions, were a kind of link between men and spirits. They were of two classes: those who, like the *nymphæ sorores*, possessed such amiable qualities as beauty of person, sweetness and gentleness of disposition, fondness for solitudes—sequestered spots, adorned with verdure, and flowers, and fountains, glassy lakes, or silent-flowing streams— and more especially for their *penchant* for mankind and the tenderness of their attachments to the sons of men; of the other class were those who seduced and held captive their lovers, such as the fairy Morgiana, and the female ghúls and the rákshasis of Asiatic romance, who assumed the forms of beautiful damsels to lure their victims to destruction.

A common device of a fairy enamoured of a bold and handsome knight was either to transform herself into a beautiful hind, or cause one to appear by her magic power, which he pursued eagerly, until in some "shady grove" it disappeared, when she discovered herself to the astonished chevalier. Thus, in the 'Lay of Sir Gruélan,' the brave Breton knight is riding along in melancholy mood one day,—

> When lo, all unawares, a spotless hind,
> More white than snow, the comeliest of her kind,
> Sprang up beneath his feet, then fled before,
> Yet seemed to pace with pain as wounded sore.
> Her timorous semblance and her limping flight
> Roused from his mournful muse the errant knight;
> Grief to a hunter's ardour now gave place,
> Fair was the game, and easy seemed the chase:
> She still with faltering steps appeared to toil,
> Just far enough before to feed the hopes of spoil,
> Till many a fruitless turn and circuit past,
> Into a flowery mead they came at last;
> And there she stopped; and there awhile she stood

By the green margent of a crystal flood.
Within that flood did bathe a dame so bright,
So prime in youth, of skin so dainty white,
That my poor wit, too feeble all, doth fail
With her sweet image to adorn my tale.
Rich was her raiment, all her robe was gold,
A neighbouring tree the costly charge did hold;
And, seated on the bank, two damsels sheen,
The ready handmaids of her will, were seen.[1]

Here, surely, was a scene sufficient to dispel Sir Gruélan's "mournful muse"! In the romance of 'Parténopex de Blois,' the hero is led to the palace of the fairy Meliora by pursuing a magic boar which she had caused to appear before him—even as Circe (in Ovid) decoyed Picus into her power. In the romance of 'Claris and Laris,' the two knights are led to the palace of the fairy Morgiana by two beautiful kids which skipped before them, seeming to invite them to follow their track through a luxuriant grove.

In the Irish 'Lay of the Chase' (Laoidh na Sealga), Fingal, with two of his dogs, is alone engaged in pursuit of a beautiful doe, which leads him from Almhaim, in the province of Leinster, to Slieve Guillin, or the mountain of Guillin, part of which is in Ulster and part in Armagh. Here he loses sight of the quarry, but in its lieu discovers a beautiful damsel, weeping, by the side of the lake, who proves to be an enchantress.[2]

We have in this last an exact parallel to a story in the Persian romance 'Sindibád Náma,' in which a young prince pursues a wild ass, leaving his attendants far behind, until it disappears as if the earth had swallowed it up, when he beheld near him "a charming lady, beautiful as a perí, her stature straight as a box-tree," and so forth—but she proves to be a female ghúl, who sought thus to get him into her power. And in the Persian Tales of the Dervish Mukhlis, the daughter of the king of the genii, Sheristáni, decoys the hero in the shape of a hind,—and they are married. (See *ante,* p. 85.)

According to Jewish legends, the arch-fiend sometimes adopts the same stratagem. The talmudists gravely relate that King David went out

[1]Le Grand's 'Fabliaux,' ed. 1781, tome i. pp. 130, 131; Way's translation, ed. 1815, vol. ii. pp. 84–86.
[2]See the original and a poetical English translation in Miss Brooke's 'Reliques of Irish Poetry.'

one morning to hunt, when Satan appeared before him in the form of a deer. David drew his bow, but missed him, and the deer ran off at the top of his speed. The king, with true sportsman's instinct, pursued the deer unwittingly into the land of the Philistines—whither it was Satan's design to lead him, in order that he should fall into the hands of Ishbi, the brother of Goliath, whose ignominious death Ishbi eagerly desired to avenge. But David is rescued by Abishai, one of his counsellors, who had learned of his mishap from a dove, and mounting upon the king's own horse (which he should not have ventured to do in any other circumstances), he was in a few minutes beside him, and the furious Philistine was baulked of his revenge.

But why multiply instances? The notion seems to be as universal as it is certainly very ancient.

Not least among the wonders in the land of faëry—where all is wonderful—are the gorgeously decked barks employed to convey the beloved knight to the palace of enchantments: to the bowers of exquisite bliss, where

> The swift-winged hours unnoticed fly;

golden galleys which have need of no "hands" to trim the sails and steer, for they are moved by magic power. It was one of these "craft" that the brave Sir Gugemer discovered, according to the Lai of Marie de France:

> A gallant bark, that with its silken sails,
> Just bellying, caught the gently rising gales,
> And from its ebon sides shot dazzling sheen
> Of silvery rays, with mingled gold between.
>
> . . .
>
> Now, by a strange resistless impulse driven,
> The knight assays the lot by Fortune given:
> Lo, now he climbs, with fairy power to aid,
> The bark's steep side, on silken cordage stayed,
> Gains the smooth deck, and wonders to behold
> A couch of cypress spread with cloth of gold;
> While from above, with many a taper bright,
> Two golden globes sent forth their branching light.
> And longer had he gazed, but sleep profound,

Wrought by the friendly fairy, wrapt him round;
Stretched on the couch the hunter lies supine,
And the swift bark shoots lightly o'er the brine.[3]

And in 'Parténopex de Blois':

'Twas eve; when from afar was heard the roar
Of hollow billows bursting on the shore;
And from those wilds, forth issuing on the strand,
He viewed a bark fast anchored by the land.
Gay was the hull, and seemly to behold;
The flag was sendal, purfled o'er with gold.
Scarce might he climb the deck, with toil foredone;
But in the shallop living wight was none.
While long and sore he mused, a gentle gale
Blew, rustling from the shore, and swelled the sail.
Self-steered, o'er sparkling waves the vessel flew,
The shore, receding, lessened from his view.[4]

The fiction of these enchanted vessels (Rose remarks, in the notes to his free rendering of 'Parténopex'), together with many other parts of romantic machinery, is to be found both in Grecian and in Celtic fable. In the 8th book of the Odyssey, Alcinous says to Ulysses (according to Pope):

So shalt thou instant reach the realm assigned
In wondrous ships, self-moved, instinct with mind;
No helm secures their course, no pilot guides;
Like men intelligent they plough the tides,
Conscious of every coast, and every bay,
That lies beneath the sun's all-seeing ray.

Macpherson has furnished an extract from an old Gaelic tale having a similar foundation; in which Sgeir, an ancient Druid, is wafted to a distant island in a self-moving boat, without any one else on board.

---

[3]Le Grand, tome iv. pp. 112, 113; Way's translation, vol. ii. pp. 104, 105.
[4]W. Stewart Rose's translation, canto i. p. 7: Le Grand, tome v. p. 256, "Parténopex, Comte de Blois: Roman de Fêrie."

One should suppose that Coleridge had forgot such wondrous vessels, when he compared his lost youth to the (then) new-fangled steamboats:

> Like those trim skiffs, unknown of yore,
>   On winding lakes and rivers wide,
> That ask no aid of sail or oar,
>   That fear no spite of wind or tide!
> Nought cared this body for wind or weather,
> When Youth and I lived in't together.

It would appear that no expense was spared in decorating royal galleys in mediæval times, if we may credit the following description of that which the messengers of Henry II. meet at sea, in the romance of 'Richard Cœur de Lyon':

> Such ne sawe they never none;
> For it was so gay begone.
> Every nayle with gold y-grave;
> Of pure gold was his sclave;
> Her mast was of yvery;
> Of samite her sayle wytly;
> Her ropes all of whyte silke,
> As white as ever was ony mylke.
> The noble shyp was, wythout,
> With clothes of gold spred about;
> And her loft and her wyndlace
> Al of gold depaynted was.

With this gaily-decked galley we may, finally, compare the faëry bark which conveyed the youth to the Land of Women (in the Arabian romance of the 'Seven Vazírs,' to which reference is made in the preceding paper): the youth having been carried through the air by a monstrous eagle and left on a small island, he remained a while motionless with terror; but recovering, began to wander about the island. "Suddenly a sail arose to his view on the waters, resembling a fleeting cloud in the heavens. He gazed, and the sail approached, till it reached the beach of the island, when he beheld a boat formed of ivory, ebony, and sandal-wood, the oars of which were made of aloes-wood of Comorin, the sails were of white silk, and it was navigated by beautiful maidens, shining like moons.

One of the ladies approached him with a parcel wrapped in rich damask, in which was a royal dress most superbly embroidered, and a crown of gold set with diamonds and pearls; and she assisted him to dress. The ladies then conducted him to the boat, which he found spread with elegant carpets and cushions of brocade. They hoisted the sails, and rowed with their oars, till they reached the land," where he was wedded to the Queen of the Land of Women, and might have been still living happily there—who knows?—but for his "fatal curiosity."

✣ THE THANKFUL BEASTS:
SECRETS LEARNED
FROM BIRDS ✣

IT is remarked by Lord Bacon, that "as the active world is inferior to the rational soul, so fiction gives to mankind what history denies, and in some measure satisfies the mind with shadows when it cannot enjoy the substance. And as real history gives us not the success of things according to the deserts of vice and virtue, fiction corrects it, and presents us with the fates and fortunes of persons rewarded and punished according to merit." In this, indeed, consists the chief charm of fiction, especially of those fairy tales which are the never-failing delight of wondering childhood, and not unfrequently the recreation of the sage, in which the good are ultimately extricated from their troubles and trials, and "live happily ever afterwards." A prominent characteristic of such tales is the befriending of animals, who subsequently evince their gratitude by rendering their benefactor signal services.

The story of Androcles and the Lion must be "familiar to every schoolboy," as well as to every one who has been a schoolboy. But perhaps the oldest and most widespread of stories of this kind is that of the traveller who rescued a man and several animals from a pit into which they had fallen; the man afterwards showing the basest ingratitude to his benefactor, while the animals are the means of his attaining wealth and honour. This story occurs in the 5th book of Gower's 'Confessio Amantis,' and the substance of his version is as follows:

Once on a time there was a great lord of Rome, whose name was Adrian, and while eagerly engaged in the chase he fell into a pit, where he lay helpless, until near night, when a poor faggot-maker, named Bardus, came past, leading his ass laden with sticks. Hearing a voice from the pit, Bardus drew near, and when the lord Adrian saw him, he cried, "Help me, I am the lord Adrian; and I will give thee the half of my wealth, by heaven and all the gods." Then Bardus untrussed his ass, and let down the rope wherewith his faggots were fastened together; but it chanced that an ape had also fallen into the pit, and when the end of the cord reached the bottom he seized it, and Bardus drew him up and he ran away. Seeing that it was an ape and not a man, he was sore afraid, for he thought it was witchcraft; but when the lord Adrian again cried for help, he once more let down the cord, and when he drew it up, a great serpent unwound itself and glided off. So Bardus, believing the voice "all phantom," called out, "What wight art thou, in God's name?" Quoth Adrian, "I am the same of whose goods thou shalt have half." Bardus now tried a third time, and pulled up Adrian, who did not even thank him, and was turning toward the city, when the simple faggot-maker "asked his covenant"; to which Adrian replied, that if he upbraided him of aught, he should be so revenged that it were better he was dead. So Bardus went home with his ass, and told his wife of this strange adventure, but he durst not say a word to lord Adrian. Next day he went with his ass to gather sticks, and coming near the pit he saw the ape, who had gathered faggots for him all ready to his hand; and this went on from day to day, until, "upon a time," he saw the serpent, who greeted him with reverence, and gave him "a stone more bright than cristall out of his mouth." Bardus took it up, astonished "that a beast should be so grateful, but a man's son not." Having shown the stone to his wife, they agree to sell it. The jeweller to whom he offered it gave him gold in payment, and home he went with joy. To his surprise, he finds the stone as well as the gold in his purse; shows them to his wife, saying he is sure that the jeweller had the stone; but he will go on the morrow to another place and sell it, and if it won't dwell with any buyer, but creep into his purse, he dare safely swear there is virtue in the stone. So he goes to another place and sells it for more gold; but when he gets home there is the stone, along with the gold, again in his purse, and this happened wherever he went to sell it; and the matter getting bruited in Rome, the emperor Justinian sends for him. Bardus tells his story, and of Adrian's false promise. The emperor will redress this matter; he sends for Adrian, who is compelled to give Bardus half of his goods:

> And thus of thilke unkinde blood
> Stant the memoire unto this day,
> Where that every wise man may
> Ensamplar him and take in minde,
> What shame it is to ben unkinde,
> Ayein [*i.e.,* against] the which reson debateth
> And every créature it hateth.

Under the year 1195, in the Chronicle of Matthew Paris—a monk of the Abbey of St Albans, who died in 1259—the story is related as a parable which Richard Cœur de Lion was wont to repeat after his return from the Crusades; in this version the animals are a lion and a serpent. In a later work, the 'Gesta Romanorum,' we find the same story—it is the 119th of Swan's translation—in which the animals are a lion, a monkey, and a serpent, and the man is a proud seneschal, while the man who rescues them is a faggot-maker named Guido. The story is not so well told in this version, I think, as in Gower. The seneschal having promised a rich reward to Guido if he drew him out of the pit, the wood-cutter sets off to the city and gets a long cord, with which he draws up successively the lion, the monkey, the serpent, and the seneschal, and—wonderful to say, or read—also the horse of the seneschal. Next day Guido goes to the palace for his promised reward, but receives, instead of money, a severe flogging for his presumption, which nearly deprives him of life. After a long and painful illness, he resumes his labours in the forest, where he meets ten asses laden with packs, and a lion driving them before him—the same that he had rescued. The lion, by gestures, signifies to Guido that they are meant for his acceptance; but being scrupulous about the matter, Guido causes the ten asses with their packs to be cried in church, and no one claiming them, he at length feels justified in appropriating them to his own use, and on opening the packs he found them all full of money. One should suppose that after this Guido had no cause to pursue his occupation; but we find him in the woods again, where, having forgot his axe, the monkey furnishes him with an ample load of faggots, and the serpent gives him a stone of three colours.[1] And here again the story becomes obscure: by means of this stone he obtains much wealth—but how so, we may guess from what follows, as well as from Gower's well-told tale. The emperor hears of this wonderful stone, and, wishing to see it, sends for Guido. When the emperor has inspected the jewel, he insists upon buying it, and Guido informs him that if the price is not paid, the stone will come back to him. So the emperor gives him 300 florins for it. Guido then tells the whole story, the seneschal is straightway crucified, and Guido installed in his place.

If King Richard of the Lion's Heart was wont to relate this "parable," he probably learned it in the East, where it had been current some four

[1] In one of the two texts of the 'Gesta' edited by Herrtage, for the Early English Text Society, Guido learns from a "stoner" (jeweller) that it possesses three virtues: bestowing evermore joy without heaviness; abundance without fail; and light without darkness.

centuries or more before his time. It is found in the 'Panchatantra,' 'Kalíla wa Dimna,'[2] and other texts of the celebrated collection of apologues and tales known generally throughout Europe as the Fables of Bidpaï, or Pilpay. In the later Syriac text (tenth or eleventh century) of 'Kalíla wa Dimna'—of which a translation, with a most valuable introductory account of the several versions of this wonderful work, by the Hon. Keith Falconer, has been recently published by the Cambridge University Press—it runs somewhat thus:

A pit having been dug in which to catch wild animals, it so chanced that a goldsmith fell into it, and afterwards a tiger, an ape, and a snake in like manner fell in. A traveller passing by saw them, and saying to himself that it would be a meritorious action to save these unfortunates, especially the man, he threw down a rope, which the ape at once laid hold of and was drawn up. Twice again did he let down the rope and rescued the tiger and the snake. The animals began to thank the traveller, and said to him, "Do not draw up the man out of this pit, for nothing in the world is worse than he." But he drew up the man also. Then the animals, having again expressed their gratitude, went away, and the goldsmith, after informing the traveller where he lived, and promising to requite his kindness, also departed. After some time it happened that the traveller was again passing the same place, when the ape met him, and presented him with choice fruits. He next met the tiger, who saluted him, saying, "Wait a little while, and I will contrive to repay what I owe you." So he went to the king's daughter, and killed her, and taking her trinkets brought them to the traveller, and said to him, "Take these trinkets, wherewith to supply your needs." But the traveller knew not whence he had brought them; so he proceeded to the goldsmith's house, and showing him the jewels, desired him to sell them, saying he should have part of the money for his trouble. But the ungrateful goldsmith, who at once recognised the trinkets as belonging to the king's daughter, took them to the palace, and being admitted to the king's presence, he said to him, "The man who killed your daughter and took these trinkets from her is staying at my house." The king commanded the traveller to be seized, scourged through the city, and afterwards crucified; and the snake he had rescued from the pit, seeing him hanging upon a cross, had pity on him, and, in

[2] A Greek translation of the Arabic 'Kalíla wa Dimna' was made by a Jew named Symeon the son of Seth, in A.D. 1080, through which the story, perhaps, first became known in Europe.

order to effect his deliverance, stung the king's son. Then the king assembled all his magicians and enchanters, but they could not cure the prince. But it was revealed to the prince in a dream that if the traveller who was crucified did not come and put his hand on his wound he would not recover, for the man had been unjustly condemned. So the king, on hearing this, ordered the traveller to be taken from the cross and brought before him, when he asked him to give an account of his circumstances, and relate what had brought him to that city. The traveller told his story from beginning to end, upon which the king said to him, "Grant recovery to my son from the bite of a snake, that the truth of all that you have told me may be confirmed." So the traveller, inwardly prayed to Heaven, and immediately the prince was cured. Then the king honoured the traveller, and gave him much wealth, but the ungrateful and false goldsmith he caused to be put to death.

Such is the later Syriac version, which differs from most of the other Eastern texts, in which the traveller is cast into a deep dungeon, where he is visited by the snake, who intimates to him that he intends to bite the king's son (or daughter), and then bring him a talisman (or herb) which would cure the wound, in order that when the king offers a great reward for his son's cure, the traveller should undertake and effect it, and thus obtain his liberty and many rich presents.[3]

A Páli variant, translated from the 'Rasaváhiní Jambudípa' story, in 'The Orientalist' for November 1884, may be cited, for purposes of comparison, in the following abridged form:

During a period of great drought a parrot descends into a pit in a forest, and, becoming heavy by drinking much water, is unable to rise. A snake and a man successively fall also into the pit. A man from Benáres draws all three out with a long creeper resembling a rope. The parrot informs his rescuer that he lives in the banyan-tree at the southern gate of Benáres, and should he at any time be in distress, to call "Parrot!" The snake tells the traveller that he lives in the ant-hill near the same banyan-tree. The man who had been rescued says he lives at such a house in Benáres, and desires his rescuer to come to him when in any difficulty. Some time after this the traveller is in sore want, and goes to the parrot. The king is bathing in a tank in a garden outside the city, and the parrot

---

[3]This is the form of the Siamese version given in Adolf Bastian's collection, and of a Tamil version, entitled "The Soothsayer's Son," in 'Folk-Lore of Southern India,' by Pandit Natésa Sástrí, now in course of publication at Bombay.

snatches up the jewels he had taken off, and conveys them to his benefactor, who deposits them with the man whom he had drawn out of the
pit. The king causes proclamation to be made of the lost jewels. The man
reports to the royal officers that the stolen jewels were in his house, and
his unlucky benefactor is immediately seized and led off to be impaled.
On the way to the place of execution he calls the snake to mind, upon
which the snake changes to human form, and appears before the officers,
saying, "Do not kill this man at present." Then in snake-shape he bites
the queen. Again assuming human form, he says to the royal officers,
"The man condemned to die knows antidotes for poison;" and to the
man, "When summoned, free the queen from poison by dashing on her
a quantity of water." The queen is cured accordingly, and the man then
tells the king the whole affair. He is richly rewarded, and the king builds
him a grand palace between the banyan-tree and the ant-hill, and he
enjoyed the friendship of the parrot and the snake the rest of his life.

Benfey pronounces the story Buddhist in origin, since it is found in the
'Rasaváhiní,' as above, and in another Buddhist work, 'Karmasataka'; but
it does not appear that he knew of its form in the 'Kathá Sarit Ságara'
(Book x. ch. 65), where a devotee rescues from a well a woman, a lion, a
golden-crested bird, and a snake. Some time after, the devotee, being
exhausted with hunger, is fed by the grateful lion with deer's flesh. And
being again in sore want of food, the golden-crested bird brought him a
casket of jewels. The devotee, while wandering about to sell the jewels,
came to the city where the woman he had rescued was living, and having
secretly deposited the jewels in the house of an old woman, he went to
market, and on his way met with the woman he had saved from the well,
and they fell into conversation. She told him that she was now one of the
queen's attendants, and asked him about his own adventures. So the con-
fiding man acquainted her of the jewels he had received from the golden-
crested bird, and, taking her to the house of the old woman, showed her
them. Now it happened that the bird had stolen this casket of jewels
before the queen's eyes, and the woman went at once to the queen and
told her that they were in the possession of the devotee. Then the king,
on hearing this, caused the devotee to be cast into prison, whither the
grateful snake came and said to him that he would coil about the king's
neck and not let him go until told to do so by the devotee. The snake
having coiled round the king's neck, and this being told to the devotee,
he offered to deliver him from the snake. The devotee was then sent for,
and saying to the snake, "Let the king go at once," the snake let the king

go, and the king gave the devotee half his kingdom, and thus he became prosperous in a moment.[4]

The story, moreover, occurs in a much older Buddhist work than either of those above mentioned, namely, the 'Játakas,' or Birth-Stories, where it is told in this wise:

King Bráhmadatta of Benáres had a son, named Prince Evil, of a cruel and vindictive nature. Bathing in the Ganges, he caused his slaves to carry him into the middle of the stream, where they kept him under the water, intending to drown him, and then went to the land. They told the king that they thought he had come to land before them. The prince, carried away by the stream, got on the trunk of a tree; a snake (formerly a rich landowner, who had buried in the shore of the river forty *kotis* of money), a rat (formerly a person of great wealth, who had buried thirty *kotis*), and a young parrot, successively also got on the trunk, because of the floods. In the middle of the night, the Bodisat [5] (reborn in the family of an Udicca Bráhman), a recluse, hears the bitter wailing of the prince, and, diving into the water, drags the log to the shore. He takes the prince, the snake, the rat, and the parrot to his hermitage, and restores them to strength. After some days the river floods begin to subside, and the hermit's guests take their leave of him. The snake offers him the forty *kotis* which he had concealed in a former birth; the rat offers the thirty *kotis* he had likewise hidden; and the parrot offers to furnish him—assisted by his relatives—with several cartloads of red rice. The king's son says to himself, "When he comes to see me, I'll murder him," but to the Bodisat, "When I become king, you must pay me a visit, and I will take care of you." Not long after this the prince became king, and the Bodisat thought to himself, "I'll make trial of these creatures." So he called out "Snake!" when the snake appeared before him, and renewed his offer of the forty *kotis* of gold; then to the rat, who again offered the thirty *kotis;* and then to the parrot, who

---

[4]Under the title of "Father Bruin in a Corner," in Dasent's 'Tales from the Fjeld,' we have a corrupted Norse version of this widespread story: A man digs a pit for wild beasts, and fastens near it a live young dog as a bait; in the course of the night a fox, a wolf, and a bear fall into the pit, and early in the morning an old woman coming past looks down and begins to jeer at the beasts thus entrapped, when she suddenly herself tumbles into the pit; by-and-by the man comes, and after drawing up the old woman, kills the three beasts from whose depredations he had suffered. It is significant that even in this garbled version it is a woman that falls into the pit, as in the 'Kathá Sarit Ságara.'

[5]The potential Buddha—*i.e.,* Gótama in one of his 550 births before attaining Buddhahood.

offered to supply him with any quantity of red rice. "Be it so," said he, "if I should have need." The Bodisat next goes to Benáres, takes up his abode in the royal gardens, and sees the perfidious prince go past on a richly caparisoned state elephant with a great retinue. The king, recognising his benefactor, at once gives orders to have him impaled. Accordingly the Bodisat is taken outside the city, where, before being impaled, he is severely bastinadoed, and at each blow he spoke this *gáthá:*

> Full truly this the wise declare,
> Indeed they do not err,
> Far better is a floating log
> Than a false ungrateful man.

On being questioned by the king's myrmidons whether he had ever done a service to the king, he tells them the whole story. Then the people, disgusted with the king's cruelty and ingratitude, put him to death, and place the Bodisat on the throne. But the Bodisat did not forget the three grateful animals whom he had rescued from the river: the snake and the rat give him the wealth which they had avariciously concealed in former births, and he deposited it in the royal treasury; the parrot again offered to furnish rice, and the Bodisat replied, "When I have need of it, I will accept of your kind offer." Then he caused a golden tube to be made for the snake's abode, a crystal cave for the rat, and a golden cage for the parrot. And so these four individuals lived together in peace and harmony as long as life lasted, and at their death passed away to be rewarded according to their deeds.[6]

Innumerable instances of the gratitude of befriended animals occur in the folk-tales of almost every country. Thus, in Steel and Temple's 'Wide-Awake Stories,' from the Panjáb and Kashmír, the son of a soldier, in quest of fortune, takes a thorn out of a tiger's foot, and is rewarded with a box which contains a manikin ("Sir Bumble"), who procures for him all he desires—food, sweetmeats, and even a beauteous princess for his bride. In the German tale of "The Fox's Brush," the hero's perilous adventures are brought to a successful issue through the aid of a fox, at which his two brothers (who preceded him) had shot, but he had

---

[6] See the "Saccankira Játaka," No. 73, translated by Rev. Dr R. Morris, 'Folk-Lore Journal' (1885), vol. iii. pp. 348–353.

humanely refrained.[7] And in the Norse story of "The Giant who had no Heart in his Body," a raven, a salmon, and a wolf, having been treated kindly by the young hero, enable him to encounter and slay the giant.

In Mr Mitford's 'Tales of Old Japan' little Peachling sets out for the Ogres' island, taking with him for his food some millet dumplings. On the way he meets first an ape, next a pheasant, and lastly a dog, to each of which, at their request, he gives one of his dumplings, and they follow him to Ogres' island, where, by their assistance, he enters the castle, puts the ogres to flight, and obtains all their vast treasures. But the hero of an Arabian tale, "The Prince of Sind and Fátima, daughter of Amir bin Naomán," received still more extraordinary aid from the creatures he had befriended. The young prince enters a desert, which is covered with an enormous flight of locusts, which had fallen from want of food. Pitying their distress, he orders meal to be strewed on the ground, and when the locusts had refreshed themselves they flew away. Some days afterwards he enters a thick forest, crowded with herds of wild animals of every description; but they did not attempt to attack him, although they were in a starving condition. He ordered some of his cattle to be killed and distributed to them for food. Presently he meets with an old man, of whom he inquires the way to the country of Amir bin Naomán, and learns that this prince has resolved that no one shall marry his daughter unless he can perform three tasks, which are so difficult as to surpass the ingenuity and power of man. When the prince demands the hand of Amir's daughter, he is led into a court where there is an immense vessel filled with three kinds of grain mixed together, which he is required to separate from each other, and put into different heaps before sunrise. This task is performed by the locusts which he had fed in the desert. His next task is to drain off before sunrise a large reservoir of water, which is done by the wild beasts he had fed in the forest, who came at night and drank up all the water. The third task is to construct, with materials provided by the king, a palace larger than that which he occupies. This is done by his friends the genii of the iron mountains, through which the prince had to pass on his way, whom he had sumptuously entertained; and the princess is accordingly won.

༄

[7]The Norse story of the "Golden Bird," in Dasent's 'Tales from the Fjeld,' is almost identical with "The Fox's Brush" in Grimm's collection; and a Servian variant is found in No. 19 of Leger's 'Contes Populaires Slaves.'

These incidents are of very frequent occurrence in the fairy tales of Europe. In the Danish story of Svend's Exploits, the king will not allow the hero to marry his daughter until he has separated seven barrels of wheat and seven barrels of rye which are lying in one heap, and this task is done for him by the ants, because he had once fed them.—In No. 12 of Dozon's Albanian Tales, the hero has a similar task done for him, also by grateful ants.

In No. 25 of Leger's collection of Slav Tales, the younger of two brothers sets out to seek his fortune, and comes upon a multitude of ants in a meadow, and shares his bread with them; farther on he sees a fish gasping on a river's bank, and throws it back into the water. Coming to a city, he learns from an innkeeper that the king's daughter is dangerously ill, and that whoever should restore her to health should marry her. The hero cures her with some wonderful water which his father had given him. But the princess refuses to marry him before he accomplishes certain tasks, one of which is to separate two sacks of poppy-seeds and two sacks of ashes which were mixed together: this is done by the thankful ants he had fed. Another task is to procure for her the most precious pearl from the bottom of the sea, which is given him by the fish he threw back into the river.

And in the Sicilian story of the beautiful Cardia, the hero has three tasks to perform in order to win his lady-love. First, he has to eat a cellarful of beans, which the ravens do for him; next, he has to dispose of a great number of corpses, which his friends the wild beasts quickly accomplish in their own way; lastly, he is enabled to stuff many mattresses with feathers by the help of the subjects of the king of the birds.

In the 'Kathá Sarit Ságara' a rákshasa first orders the hero to sow a great quantity of sesame-seed, which the demon's daughter performs for her lover by magic power; and when the demon finds it done, he bids him take up all the seed again, as a further task before he will give him his daughter, and she calls up an innumerable tribe of ants and makes them gather the sesame-seed together.

In the Tamil romance entitled 'Madana Kámarája Kadai' the hero of one of the stories, called Jagatalapratápa, wanders over mountains, and through forests and thickets, in search of his lost celestial wives. He spied a broad river before him, in which several ants were struggling for their lives. The ant-king also was among the sufferers, and he now called out to the hero and said, "Traveller, whoever you may be, if you relieve me from my danger, I shall relieve you also when you are in difficulty, whenever you think of me." These words excited the king's pity, so he entered the river and extricated all the ants. Then the ant-king thanked him and took his leave. Going a little farther, he found a frog dying in the midst of burning sand. He was the king of the frogs. And he called to the hero, begging him to take him into water, and promising to help him in return should he ever be in any strait. So he took the frog-king up and placed him in the nearest pond. At length he discovers his celestial wives bathing in a tank, and after he had upbraided them for deserting him, they take him up into Indra's paradise, to plead his case before the deity. Indra sets him certain tasks, which if he execute, his wives should be restored to him. Having caused his servants to reduce to the finest dust a tract of land, to scatter in it ten *kalams* of sesamum, and to plough it well a hundred times, he ordered the hero to heap up these ten *kalams* of seed without omitting a single grain, if he really deserved his daughters. The ant-king sets all his subjects to this task, which they accomplish perfectly. Then Indra throws his ring into a well inhabited by serpents, and the frog-king recovers it by compelling his subjects to jump into the well and become food for the serpents. Finally, the king is rewarded with the daughters of Indra in marriage.[8]

Sometimes the animals give the hero or heroine assistance out of mere goodwill, as in the case of Psyche, in the 'Golden Ass' of Apuleius: Venus takes wheat, barley, millet, poppy, vetches, lentils, and beans, and, mixing them all together, says to the unhappy bride of Cupid, "Separate this promiscuous mass of seeds, and having properly put each grain in its place, and so sorted the whole, give me a proof of your expedition by finishing the task before evening;" and a colony of ants, pitying her distress, speedily execute the otherwise impossible task.

M. Dozon, in a mythographical analysis of the story of Psyche, appended to his collection of Albanian Tales, pointing out that such tasks are common to both Eastern and Western folk-tales, remarks that they go back to the labours of Hercules or Bellerophon.

Cutting off a piece of one's own flesh and giving it to an animal to save the life of its intended victim, is always rewarded by the grateful creature thus rescued, and sometimes also by the other. In one of the Persian Tales of a Parrot, a younger son of a king saves a frog from a snake, and then gives the latter, in lieu of the prey of which he had been deprived, a piece

---

[8]'The Dravidian Nights' Entertainments: being a translation of Madanakámarájankadai.' By Pandit S. M. Natésa Sástrí. Madras: 1886. Pp. 109, 115–117.

of flesh from his own arm. The snake then assumed the form of a man, as did also the frog, and the prince by their help obtains a place of honour at the court of a foreign king, and marries his daughter.—The incident of a man supplying a snake or other animal with flesh from his own body is very common in Indian fiction, the snake, etc., being inferior deities, as in the foregoing story. In the 'Kathá Sarit Ságara' we read of a prince, in the course of his adventures, meeting with a rákshasa, and "not being able to obtain other flesh to give the demon to eat, he cut off with his sword some of his own flesh, and gave it to him." For this singular act of generosity the demon renders the prince great services. In the Persian romance of 'Hatim Taï,' the magnanimous hero, while journeying through a vast desert, discovers a wolf in pursuit of a milch-doe: he calls to the wolf to desist, and the wolf at once stood still—knowing that he who called was Hatim, since no one else could be so compassionate to rational and irrational creatures. The wolf, having thus allowed the doe to escape, then demands of Hatim something to eat. Hatim cuts a slice of flesh from his own thigh, and gives it to the wolf, who, in reward of his kindness, furnishes him with the information he requires to successfully accomplish the object of his journey.

Beasts and birds are often thus communicative, and occasionally their "secrets," which are of very great value, are overheard. Thus in the story of Vikrám Mahárájá (Miss Frere's 'Old Deccan Days; or, Indian Fairy Legends,' a delightful little work), a cobra had crept into the throat of the rájá, and could not be dislodged. His bride overhears the cobras talking, one of which tells the others that if certain nuts are pounded and mixed with cocoa-nut oil, set on fire, and burned beneath the rájá, the cobra would be instantly killed and drop to the ground. Moreover, if the same were done at the mouth of his hole, he, too, would be killed, and then they might find the treasure he guards. Needless to add that the rájá is cured and the treasure found. In like manner, Panch-Phul Rání (in the same work) learns from the conversation of two jackals the means to adopt for resuscitating her husband. And in the Danish tale of Svend's Exploits we read: "Just as he was going to sleep, twelve crows came flying and perched on the elder-trees over Svend's head. They began to converse together, and one told another what had happened to him that day. When they were about to fly away, one crow said, 'I am so hungry, where shall I get something to eat?' 'We shall have food enough to-morrow, when father has killed Svend,' answered the crow's brother. 'Dost thou think that such a miserable fellow dares fight with our father?' said another. 'Yes, it is probable enough that he will, but it will not profit him much, as our father cannot be overcome but with the Man of the Mount's sword, and that hangs in the mound, within seven locked doors, before each of which are two fierce dogs that never sleep.' Svend thus learned that he should only be sacrificing his strength and life in attempting a contest with the dragon, before he had become master of the Man of the Mount's sword;" which he obtained by means of a finger-stall that rendered him invisible, and with that resistless blade slew the monstrous dragon.—In a modern Greek version of the Cupid and Psyche legend, the King of the Birds (an enchanted prince) is cut in the feet with broken glass, by a device of the heroine's sisters, when he immediately disappears. The heroine sets off in quest of him. In the course of her wanderings she hears some snakes talking together about what had befallen their king. They say that the remedy for his hurts would be obtained by killing one of them and taking out his fat; and some birds say the same of themselves. She kills one of the snakes and one of the birds, takes the fat out of them, and applying it to the prince's feet, he is cured.

In the conclusion of Pandit Natésa Sástrí's 'Dravidian Nights,'[9] the prince and his clever companion, the son of the king's prime minister (who is the hero of this entertaining Tamil romance), are returning to their own country with their newly-acquired wives. They encamp for the night under a banyan-tree, and all are asleep excepting the ever-watchful minister's son, who hears a pair of owls conversing, and listens attentively to what they are saying one to the other—for he was well acquainted with the language of birds. Said the male bird, "My dear, the prince who is encamped under our tree is to die shortly by the falling on him of a big branch which is about to break." "And if he should escape this calamity?" quoth the female. "He will die to-morrow, then," replied the other, "in a river, in the bed of which he is to pitch his tent: the river will be dry at the time, but when midnight comes a heavy flood will rush down and carry him away." "And should he escape this second calamity also?" said the female. "Then," answered her mate, "he will surely die by the hands of his wife when he reaches his own city." "And should he escape this third calamity also?" "My dear love," said the male bird, "he cannot escape

[9]See note, p. 103.

it. But if he does, he will reign as a king of kings for hundreds of years;" adding, that any one who happened to know this secret and revealed it, his head should burst instantly into a thousand pieces. The three calamities and the curse on the person who should reveal them struck the minister's son with dismay. But he had no time to lose. So he rose up, and, going into the prince's tent, removed him, still sleeping, with his couch to a spot far from the tree. No sooner had this been done than the branch of the tree broke with a crash that aroused all the army as well as the prince, who exclaimed, "Surely I was sleeping in the very tent which that branch has crushed! How was I removed hither?" The minister's son simply said in reply, "I heard the noise of the breaking branch, and removed you out of danger."

At daybreak they resumed their journey, and near nightfall they reached the bank of a river-bed. All preferred to encamp on the embankment, excepting the prince, who insisted on having his tent pitched in the dry bed of the river. It was a fine moonlight night, and when all but the minister's son were fast asleep in their tents on the river's bank, he heard the roaring of waters in the distance, so he at once removed the prince with his couch to a place of safety. Down came the rushing flood with irresistible force. The noise awoke the prince, who, again wondering at his escape, thus addressed his friend, "Surely I was sleeping in the river-bed which is now deeply sunk in water! How is it that I am now here without injury?" The minister's son merely said that he had been wakeful, and hearing the sound of the coming flood, had removed him to the bank. The prince warmly expressed his gratitude to him for having repeatedly saved his life and watched over his safety.

When they reached their own city, the minister's son obtained a lodging for the prince and himself, with their wives, until other arrangements could be made. The minister's son, suspecting that the prince's wife did not love her husband, and purposed doing away with him, concealed himself at nights under the prince's bed. Now this lady had for her paramour a cripple fellow, who lived at some distance from her lodging, which was connected with his place of abode by an underground passage, by which she visited the cripple. Returning to her lodging one night, she went direct to the prince's chamber and cut her sleeping husband's throat. The minister's son, springing from his hiding-place—too late, however, to save his master—laid hands on the murderess, who, with wonderful presence of mind, at once called out that he had killed her lord. But when the king came, and the minister's son asked him whether, if he had wished to kill his friend, he did not have opportunities enough while they travelled together, the king was convinced of his innocence. The prince's body was laid on the funeral pyre, but the minister's son secretly removed it, and put in its place a quantity of bones, and taking the body home, deposited it in a large box. Meanwhile his own wife, who was as virtuous as the wife of the prince was vicious, went to the temple of Kálí to accomplish a vow she had made of sacrificing her right hand to the goddess, should her husband be acquitted of the charge of murdering the prince, and the minister's son, suspecting her movements, had followed her into the temple unseen. She was about to sever her right hand when the goddess stopped her, and said she was pleased with her devotion to her husband; and instead of requiring the sacrifice of her hand, she would confer on her right arm the power of raising the dead to life.[10] When the lady had regained her lodging, she found her husband (who had got home before her) apparently asleep, and shaking him, asked what presents he had brought her. He gave her his keys, bidding her open the large box and take out what she found there. The lady, having opened the box, thrust her right hand inside, upon which, to her amazement, the prince rose up, alive and well, but marvelling how he got into such a place. The prince's wife is put to death, before which, however, the minister's son was induced by the king and his courtiers to relate all the circumstances, which he had no sooner done than his head burst into a thousand pieces. All present exclaimed, "The great man of the world is gone for ever! We were fools in forcing him to relate the story!" But the wife of the minister's son joined the pieces together, and laying her right hand on his head, behold! like one awaking from sleep, he rose up to life.

[10]The power of resuscitating any dead creature is often ascribed to heroes of Hindú and Persian fictions—sometimes, as in the present case, conferred by a deity, but more frequently, perhaps, it is acquired by magical skill. This notion, as well as that of the power of making old persons young again, is one that seems to have captivated untutored minds in all ages, and examples of its prevalence in both European and Asiatic legends will be found in subsequent papers and notes.

↬ THE GOOD MAN AND THE BAD MAN ↫

WE find a remarkable example of benefits derived from overhearing the secret confabulations of birds in a story in the Brothers Grimm's 'Kinder und Häus Märchen"—a story, moreover, which, with variations, is known from Norway to India, and of which the following is an abstract:

A poor soldier, who had been robbed and. beaten by his comrades so severely as to be deprived of sight, and bound to the foot of a gallows, overhears the conversation of three crows perched high on a tree. The first crow observed to his companions that the princess was ill, and the king had vowed to marry her to whoever should perfectly cure her, which may be done by burning a blue flower and giving her the ashes to swallow. The second crow said that to-night such a dew would fall, that even a blind man, if he washed his eyes with it, would see. The third crow remarked that there was a great dearth of water in the city; but if they would take away the large square stone by the fountain in the market-place, and dig underneath it, the finest water would spring up. The soldier bathes his eyes in the dew, and his sight is at once restored. He then plucks the blue flower, and having burned it, takes the ashes, and proceeds to the king's court, and cures the princess. The king, however, refuses to give him his daughter unless he can find enough water for the use of the town. This he is able to do, and then obtains the hand of the princess. One day he meets the two wicked comrades who had robbed him, told them of his good luck and how it came about, forgave them the injuries they had done him, and took them to his palace and gave them food and clothes. But they resolved to go at night to the gallows-foot, in hopes of also hearing of something to their advantage. So off they went and sat under the tree, where they heard the crows saying to each other, "Some one must have heard us; for the princess is well; the flower is plucked and burned; a blind man has found his sight; and they have found the spring that gives water to the whole town." So they looked about them to see whether any one was eavesdropping, and discovering the two men below, they flew at them and pecked out their eyes.

A Norse version, entitled "True and Untrue," though similar in outline, differs somewhat in the details. Two brothers set out in quest of their fortunes. Untrue eats of the provisions in his brother's scrip until there is none left, then refuses his brother any share of his own store, flies into a rage, and plucks out his eyes. Poor blind True climbs up a tree till the night is over, for fear of the wild beasts. "When the birds begin to sing," said he to himself, "I shall know that it is day, and I can then try to grope my way farther on." Presently he heard some one approach the foot of the tree, and soon after some others; and when they began to greet each other, True found that it was Bruin the bear, Greylegs the wolf, Slyboots the fox, and Longears the hare. From their conversation he learns how the king of England may be cured of his blindness, his daughter cured of dumbness, how to find a spring of water in the palace-yard, and how to make the royal orchard fruitful. True first restores his own sight with the dew of the lime-tree, round which the quartette of sagacious animals had held their meeting, and then performs the other things and marries the princess. A beggar-lad comes into the hall during the wedding feast—it is the rascal Untrue: his brother recognises him, and after hospitably entertaining him, advises him to go to the lime-tree, where he also may learn some valuable secret. Untrue goes thither accordingly; the bear, the wolf, the fox, and the hare presently meet under the tree: he pricks up his ears to listen, but has the mortification to hear the bear say that since their conversation had evidently been overheard at their last meeting, they had better hold their tongues in future, and so they bade each other good night—"O most lame and impotent conclusion!"

In a Portuguese variant, a poor but very pious donkey-driver, after having given up to his irreligious comrade his donkey and merchandise, in token of his reliance upon Providence, takes shelter for the night in a cave, where he overhears some demons talking of a well which had been sunk in the neighbourhood, but without obtaining water, and how the owner had offered a purseful of silver money to any one who should cause it to flow into the well, and of the means by which this might be accomplished; also of the illness of the king's daughter, and how to effect her cure: but instead of marrying the princess after he has cured her, the donkey-driver contents himself with half of the king's revenue. His comrade is afterwards killed by the demons.

The Kabaïl of Northern Africa relate the story thus: Two men, one good, the other wicked, set out together on a journey. The good man shares his own food with his companion till it is all consumed, and the wicked man refuses to give him any portion of his store unless he part with one of his eyes, and afterwards with the other; and he then abandons the blinded man to his fate. The poor fellow is directed by a bird to take a leaf from an adjacent tree and apply it to his eyes, which he does, and his sight is at once restored. Arriving at a great city, he learns that the king of the country is blind, and after he has cured the afflicted monarch, he is rewarded with his daughter's hand in marriage.[1]

The story is found in a somewhat garbled form in the Kirghis tales contained in Radloff"s great collection of South-Siberian Folk-Tales ('Proben der Volks-litteratur der türkischen Stämme Süd-Siberians,' vol. iii. p. 344):

A good man and a bad man were travelling together, and the good man's food came to an end. Appealing to his companion for advice, he was recommended to cut off his ears and eat them, which he did. When they were consumed, he again appealed to his comrade, who persuaded him to have his eyes taken out, on which he lived for two days. Then his bad companion deserted him, leaving him alone in a dense forest. As he sat there, he heard a tiger, a fox, and a wolf holding converse together, and learnt that two neighbouring trees had the power of giving ears to the earless and eyes to the blind; that the bones of a certain rich man's black dog could bring back the dead to life; and that a hill not far off contained a mass of gold as large as a horse's head. Before long he had obtained from the trees new eyes and ears, and from the hill the mass of gold, with which he bought the rich man's dog. By means of its bones he restored to life a khán, who gratefully bestowed upon his reviver his daughter and half of his cattle. So he became rich and prosperous. One day his former companion came to see him, found out the secrets of his recovery and prosperity, and said, "O my good one, take me to the dark dense forest and leave me there! Perchance to me, as well as to thee, may it be given to

---

[1] 'Contes Populaires de la Kabylie du Djurdjura.' Recueillis et traduits par J. Rivière. Paris: 1882.—Q̲abá'il, or Kabá'il—incorrectly written in Europe *Kabyle* and *Kabylie*—is an Arabic word meaning *tribes*, the plural of *Qabíla*, a tribe. In all Muslim countries there are, quite distinct from townsmen, wandering tribes that move from pasture to pasture according to the season of the year, and those in Algiers are called Kabá'il, or tribesmen. —The stories collected by M. Rivière only exist orally among the Kabá'il, and thus possess a special value for the student of comparative folk-lore.

[2] From this it is evident that the good man's eating his ears and eyes (in the first part of the story) is a corruption of the usual incident—namely, his parting with his eyes to the bad man in exchange for some food.

become a man of mark. Thy two eyes did I take from thee, both thine ears did I take,[2] and I left thee in the forest: there didst thou become a right fortunate man. Now, then, do thou also put out my two eyes, cut off both my ears, and take me to the forest where I left thee, and leave me there." So the good man did as he was requested, and the earless, eyeless, bad man remained in the forest alone. But when "the fox, the wolf, and the tiger, all three together, examined the interior of the forest, there, at a certain spot, they found the bad man, and they all three ate him up. 'From good comes good, and from evil comes evil,' said they all three, and ate him up."[3]

In the Arabian tale of "Abou Neeut and Abou Neeuteen, or the Well-intentioned and the Double-minded,"[4] one of the additional tales translated by Jonathan Scott, in volume vi. of his edition of the 'Arabian Nights' Entertainments,' we have a different version from any of those above cited: The two friends travel together, and, coming to a well, Abou Neeuteen lets the other down for water, and, leaving him there, decamps with all his property. In the well are two Afreets[5] conversing together. One of them says that he has possessed the beautiful princess of Mosúl, and no one can drive him away, save by sprinkling an infusion of wormwood under her feet on a Friday during divine service in the great mosque. The other says that he has been equally fortunate, being in possession of such a hidden treasure of gold and jewels under a mound at Mosúl as cannot be computed, the talisman of which cannot be opened to any one unless by killing on the mound a white cock and pouring over it the blood. Having said this, they took their flight from the well. At daybreak Abou Neeut was delivered from the well by the arrival of a caravan, some of the followers of which went down to fill the water-skins.

---

[3] "Notes on Folk-Tales," by Mr W. R. S. Ralston, in 'The Folk-Lore Record,' vol. i. pp. 90, 91. Mr Ralston remarks that this story is very popular in Russia, Afanasief giving in his collection no fewer than seven different versions, in the introduction to one of which (vol. i. p. 10) considerable modern additions have been made. Two fellow-travellers dispute as to whether it is better to live honestly or dishonestly, and refer the question to a peasant, a merchant, and a lawyer whom they successively meet on their way, and who express themselves in favour of dishonesty, but the traveller who upholds honesty is still of the same opinion. After a time, in order to get a morsel of food, he is obliged to allow his antagonist to blind him. In his distress he prays to God: "O Lord, desert me not, thy sinful servant!" Then a voice is heard from heaven telling him what to do in order to recover his eyesight. After this the story proceeds in the usual way.—Ibid., p. 91.

[4] Dr J. W. Redhouse suggests for Abou Neeut and Abou Neeuteen: Abú Niyyet, father (or possessor) of a single resolution; Abú Niyyeteyn, father (or possessor) of two resolutions.

[5] Afreets (properly, 'Ifríts) are powerful evil genii (jinn), generally inhabiting wells and ruinous buildings.

Acting upon the information he had gained from the conversation of the Afreets, he dispossesses the princess, and obtaining the great treasure of gold and jewels from the mound where it was concealed, he is made prime minister, and marries the princess. After some time Abou Neeuteen comes to the city in woful plight; his old friend takes him to the palace, clothes and feeds him, and informs him of his good fortune. The envious fellow determines to try his luck also in the well; but no sooner is he down in it than the two Afreets, saying to each other that some person has fathomed their secrets, proceed to fill up the well which had been the cause of all their disasters, and hurling huge stones upon the head of Abou Neeuteen, crushed him to death.

This Arabian version is evidently of Indian origin, since it corresponds in all details with a Bengalí story, which Mr C. H. Damant has translated in the 'Indian Antiquary,' 1875, under the title of "The Two Bhúts."[6] A prince and a kótwal's son travel in company, and the latter lets his friend down into a well and abandons him. The prince hears two bhúts conversing, one about having possessed the king's daughter, and how she may be cured; the other, of his hoarded gold, and how it may be taken from him. The rest of the story is precisely the same as that of Abou Neeut and his treacherous comrade.

The Persian poet Hátifi (*ob.* A.D. 1520) relates the story, with additional incidents, in his romance of 'The Seven Faces' (*Heft Menzer*), which recounts the exploits of King Bahrám Ghúr, and how he built his Seven Pavilions, and placed in each "a beauty of the world":

Two youths left their native country to seek their fortunes; one was called Khayr (Good), the other Shár (Evil). After they had travelled together for some time, the provisions of Khayr were exhausted, and his companion, who had carefully hoarded his store of food and water, refused to give him any—not even a draught of water. Khayr offered him two precious gems which he had in his purse, but the wicked fellow would consent to give him to drink only on condition that he would part with his eyesight. Tormented at length by excessive thirst, Khayr bartered his eyes for a draught of water; but no sooner had Shár blinded him than he cruelly despoiled him of his clothes and other property, and left him, without so much as a drop of water, to mourn his misfortunes. It hap-

---

[6]Bhúts are malignant spirits, haunting cemeteries, lurking in trees and wells, animating carcases, and deluding or devouring human beings.

pened that near to the place where Khayr lay with his mangled eyes streaming blood a wealthy shepherd had taken up his station, and his daughter, passing by with a pitcher of water which she had drawn for the use of the family, heard his moans, and, discovering his wretched condition, first gave him some water to drink, and then tenderly bound up his eyes and led him to her father's dwelling. When the shepherd came home in the evening, and saw the poor youth whom his daughter had succoured, and learned that he had been deprived of his eyesight, he said that he knew of a certain tree, the leaves of which, made into a plaster, could restore his sight, and added that among the other wonderful qualities of this tree was that of curing the most inveterate epilepsy. The leaves were brought by the shepherd and applied by his beautiful daughter to the young man's eyes, and in a short time his sight was restored. After this, Khayr, beloved by all the household, and especially by the maiden, for some months assists in keeping the flocks, till at length he thought it proper to depart for his native place. When he intimated this intention to the shepherd and his family, they were all in consternation, and the old man made him an offer of his daughter in marriage, which he gratefully accepted, and they were wedded. Having resided for a year or two in the desert, Khayr visited the tree by the leaves of which his wonderful cure had been effected; and of each kind of leaves he took a quantity. About this time it was reported that the king's daughter was afflicted with severe epilepsy, for the cure of which all medicines had failed. Physicians from various countries had in vain exerted their skill; no remedy could be found. The king had made a condition that any person who succeeded in relieving the princess from the distressing malady should receive her in marriage, and ultimately succeed to the throne; but that whoever failed, after having seen his daughter's beauty, should inevitably lose his life. The heads of a thousand unsuccessful doctors had already flown off—townsmen and strangers; and yet the love of beauty and ambition of greatness and power were so irresistible, that adventurer followed adventurer with horrible swiftness. The rumour at length reached Khayr in his desert home. He undertakes the cure of the princess, marries her, and succeeds to the throne. Previous to his curing the princess, Khayr had cured the daughter of the chief vazír of blindness, and she became his wife; so that he was blessed at once with no less than three matchless wives, including his desert bride, who was, no doubt, "his first, his only love," the other marriages being *de convenance*. It happened, not long after he had settled in his new position, that while Khayr was walking in the garden of his palace he saw a man bargaining with a Jew, whom he recognised as his villanous fellow-traveller Shár. He gave orders to have him arrested and brought before him. On being asked his name, he said it was Mabesher Sefiri (the traveller who brings good tidings); and Khayr demanding his real name, and Shár persisting in concealing it, he declared himself, and condemned Shár to death. But Shár pleaded that he had simply acted in accordance with the decrees of God and with his own name, and that Khayr should act by him according to his name and renown.[7]

Another version is found in a beautiful legendary tale of Tévai—the classical name of the modern town of Rámnád, in the district of Madurá, Southern India—translated by S. M. Natésa Sástrí Pandit.[8] In this tale the principal characters are a king's son, whose motto is "Charity alone conquers," and his companion, the son of the king's prime minister, whose motto is "Absence of charity alone conquers." The wicked youth, in the course of their adventures, puts out the prince's eyes, and leaves him in a most deplorable condition. But his eyes are restored by the goddess Kálí, in whose temple he afterwards serves for some months. Meanwhile the daughter of the king of the Kávérí country has lost her eyesight, and the king has issued a proclamation that he will give his kingdom and his daughter to him who should cure her of her blindness. The goddess, in reward of his devotion, gives the prince a quantity of sacred ashes, which she instructs him to apply, for three consecutive days, to the eyes of the afflicted princess, and on the fourth day her sight should be restored. The prince accordingly proceeds to the Kávérí country, is successful in curing the princess, and obtains her in marriage together with the kingdom. In course of time his former companion, the minister's son, comes to the city, and earns a scanty livelihood by menial occupations. He is recognised by the young king, who sends for him, forgives his cruel conduct towards himself, and places him in a high and confidential position. But his evil nature soon shows itself; and in attempting the destruction of his benefactor, he is himself destroyed—learning, when too late, the truth of the prince's motto, "Charity alone conquers."—The tone of this story (which must not be judged from my meagre abstract) is decidedly Buddhistic, inculcating, as it does, the great Buddha's leading doctrine of "mercy to others."

[7]Abridged from "Fragments" appended to Sir Gore Ouseley's 'Biograpbical Notices of Persian Poets.'

[8]'Folk-Lore in Southern India,' p. 63.

❧ THE UNGRATEFUL SERPENT ❧

WHILE popular tales generally represent animals as grateful for kindness shown to them, occasionally they are exhibited as the very reverse. There is, for example, the world-wide story of the serpent that was found by a traveller fast bound to a tree, and after he had released it, the ungrateful reptile said it would sting him, such being its nature. A philosopher coming up and having had the affair explained to him, he pretended that he could not decide the question of whether the service rendered by the man to the serpent should not exempt him from being bitten, unless he saw the precise condition in which the serpent was before being set free. The serpent consented to be bound again to the tree, upon which the philosopher bids it loose itself, and on its answering that it could not, "Then," says he, "die, for your ingratitude."

This is the 4th tale of Peter Alfonsus, and the 174th of the Continental 'Gesta Romanorum.' It occurs in most versions of the Fables of Bidpaï: the 'Directorium Humanæ Vitæ' of John of Capua; the Arabic and Syriac 'Kalíla wa Dimna'; the Persian 'Anvár-i Suhayli'; in the old Indian story of King Vikrámaditya of Ujjain; Miss Frere's 'Old Deccan Days'; Steel and Temple's 'Wide-Awake Stories' from the Panjáb and Kashmír; and in the folk-lore of most countries of Europe.

The following is a translation of an Albanian variant, in Le Grand's useful collection:

Once a hunter passed by a quarry and found a serpent under a stone. The reptile called the hunter to his aid, who said, "I will not extricate you, for you will eat me." The serpent answered, "Deliver me; I will not eat you." But when the hunter had drawn away the stone from above him, the serpent sought to eat him. The hunter said, "Did you not promise that you would not eat me?" The serpent answered him, "Hunger will not keep that bargain." "But," replied the hunter, "if you are not right in eating me, will you still eat me?" The serpent said, "No." Then said the hunter, "Come, then, let us make it the subject of three different questions." So they went into a thicket, where they found a greyhound: they questioned him, and he said, "I was once with a master, and I caught hares, and when I brought them to his house he could not find meat good enough for me to eat. But now, when I cannot even catch tortoises, because I am old, he wishes to kill me. This is why I condemn thee to be eaten by the serpent, for whoever does good gets only evil in return." "Do you hear?" said the serpent to the hunter; "we've got a judge." They went farther, and met with a horse: they questioned him, and he also replied that the serpent would be right in eating the hunter. "For," said he, "I had a master, who gave me food as long as I could do my journey; but now, when I cannot, he wishes to kill me." And the serpent said to the hunter, "We have two judges." They went farther, and found a fox, to whom the hunter said, "Dear Reynard, you must come to my aid. Listen: I was passing a quarry, and under a great stone I found this serpent, almost dead. He asked me to help him, so I took him out, and now he wants to eat me." The fox replied, "Must I be the judge? Let us go then to the quarry, and see how you found the serpent." So they went thither, and placed the stone upon the serpent, and the fox then asked him, "Is that how you were?" The serpent said, "Yes." "Ah, well," said the fox, "just stay there always."[1]

In Dasent's second series of Norse Tales, entitled 'Tales from the Fjeld,' it is a dragon that is rescued by a wayfarer, and the fox who so cleverly entraps him again, having been granted by the man "the run" of his poultry-yard every Thursday, as a reward of his service, on his first visit for a supply of hens and geese is beaten almost to death, and he exclaims bitterly as he crawls off, "Such is the way of the world!"

In some Eastern versions the ungrateful animal is an alligator; in others a tiger, as in 'Wide-Awake Stories':

A tiger is caught in a trap that had been set for wild beasts, and cannot get out. A poor Bráhman comes by, and the tiger cries, "Let me out, O pious one!" "Nay," says the Bráhman, "you'd eat me if I did." "Not so," replies the tiger; "I should be for ever grateful, and serve you as a slave." At last the Bráhman lets him out, upon which the tiger seizes him, saying, "What a fool you are now! I shall eat you." The Bráhman pleads for his life, but all he could gain was a promise from the tiger to abide by the decision of the first three things he chose to question. The Bráhman refers his case to the *pípal*-tree, but it says men are ungrateful, and ought not to be allowed to live: "Don't I give them shade and shelter? And don't they tear down my branches, to feed their cattle on?" He next asks a buffalo. "No; man has no gratitude. When I gave milk they fed me; but now that I am dry they yoke me and half starve me." Last of all the question is put to a jackal, who wants to know how the tiger got into the trap, before giving his opinion. So the tiger enters the trap, where he is "left lamenting," or gnashing his molars in futile grief.

---

[1] See also Crane's 'Italian Popular Tales,' p. 150, for Sicilian and Italian parallels.

⤳ THE HARE AND
THE TORTOISE ⤳

IT may be safely asserted that there exists no apologue, in any language, which is better adapted to inculcate on the young the force of the aphorism, "the race is not always to the swift nor the battle to the strong," than is the familiar fable, commonly ascribed to Æsop, of the race between the hare and the tortoise. The moral lesson it teaches—that perseverance may achieve success in most untoward circumstances—ingenuous youth on the threshold of active life should "bind as a sign upon his forehead and as frontlets between his eyes." This is how the fable is generally told:

A hare insulted a tortoise on account of his slowness, and vainly boasted of her own great speed in running. "Let us make a match," replied the tortoise. "I'll run you five miles for five pounds, and the fox yonder shall be umpire of the race." The hare agreed, and away they both started together; but the hare, by reason of her exceeding swiftness, outran the tortoise to such a degree that she made a jest of the matter, and finding herself a little tired, squatted in a tuft of fern that grew by the way, and took a nap, thinking that if the tortoise went by, she could at any time fetch him up with all the ease imaginable. In the meanwhile the tortoise came jogging along at a slow but continued pace, and the hare, out of too great security and confidence of victory, oversleeping herself, the tortoise arrived at the end of the race first.

Analogues of this celebrated fable, in which a race is run between two creatures of very unequal swiftness and the slower is the winner, are known among widely-separated peoples; but in these the *motif* is different—the less swift animal succeeding by its superior cleverness in tricking its antagonist. Sir Alexander Gordon has furnished two interesting versions from Fiji, one of which is as follows:

The crane and the crab quarrelled as to their powers of racing. The crab said he would go the faster, and that the crane might fly across from point to point, while he went round by the shore. So the crane flew off and the crab stayed quietly in his hole, trusting to the multitude of his brethren to deceive the crane. And the crane flew from point to point, and seeing a crab-hole, put down his ear and heard a buzzing noise. "That slave is before me," said he, and flew on to the next point, where the same thing happened, till at last, on reaching a point above Serua, the crane fell exhausted, and was drowned in the sea.

In the other Fijian fable, the contest is between a crane and a butterfly. The latter challenges the crane to fly to Tonga, tempting him to do so by asking if he was fond of shrimps. The butterfly perches on the crane's back, without the crane being aware of it, and whenever the bird looks round and says to himself, "That low-born fellow is gone; I can rest and fly slowly now, without fear of his overtaking me," the butterfly leaves his back and flies a little way ahead, saying, "Here I am, cousin," till the poor crane dies from sheer exhaustion.

Several forms of the story are current among the natives of Madagascar. For instance: Once upon a time it was agreed between a frog and a wild-hog that they should race to the top of a hill. But just as the hog commenced to run, the frog leaped upon his neck, and the hog knew nothing about it, for he did not feel him at all, being big in the neck, while the frog was so light that his weight did not ruffle a hair. So the wild-hog ran, and raced, and galloped, and fumed; and just when he arrived at the goal, the frog leaped off, but the wild-hog did not see him, and so he was forced to say, "Why, you fellow, you have done it." Then he proposed that they should see which of them could leap best. "Just as you please," replied the frog. "Do your best, for if you don't exert yourself you will regret it, so don't have a stomach-ache for nothing." So the two came to the water-side to try who could leap farthest. And when they came there, and the wild hog was just about to do his best, the frog jumped again upon his neck. And again the stupid fellow knew nothing about it, for what good is it to be big if one has no sense? And so, when they were just at the goal, the frog leaped off again, and so he was first, upon which the wild-hog foamed at the mouth, and his eyes turned red. And again he was astonished to see the frog take it so easily, and said, "There is no getting the better of you, you rascal!"

In another Malagasy story the wild-hog reappears contending for superiority of speed with a chameleon: One day as a wild-hog was setting off to hunt, he met with a chameleon on the road by the side of a watercourse, and as he looked at the chameleon he exclaimed, "Dear me, what a strange way of walking you have, friend! Judging from the way you walk, one would think you could never get enough food, friend, for you walk so slowly. So take care lest some furious beast comes by and tramples you suddenly to death, for you are both weak and very slow in moving about. So I think we two will separate here at this watercourse; and although I don't walk quickly, but go along quite gently, just look, for when I have crossed over this valley you will even not have crossed the bed of this little stream." The chameleon replied, "True enough, friend, I seem to be very weak, and to go very gently indeed. At the same time, remember that we each possess what is most fitting for us; and so you are able to get food to satisfy you, and I also obtain food to satisfy myself." And then the chameleon spoke again, saying, "Excuse me, sir, for while I am but a little one challenging a big one, yet, if it would not make you angry, let us two play a little along this watercourse." The wild-hog replied, "But what sort of play would you like us to have?" The chameleon said, "Although you are certainly swift of foot, and I go very slowly, come, let us make a bet about our racing, elder brother." Then the wild-hog was inwardly angry, and said, "Come, then, let us two go up yonder a little higher to try our speed, for there is a spacious common, while it is boggy where we are just now; and if you should be struck even by the mud thrown up by my feet, you will be hurt. So let us go yonder to that spacious ground, and if you outrun me, then take me and all my family for your servants." Then the chameleon answered, "Why are you angry, elder brother? For you alone I cannot be a match, for you make me afraid; how much more, then, if I had all your family as my servants? But if it is only play we are to engage in, let us then go up yonder to try our speed." So they went up to the wide common, and agreed together, saying, "At yonder tree-trunk, where the long *véro* grass is growing, let us make our goal, to see who comes in first." And that being settled, they both arranged themselves in good order, the wild-hog saying, "Now shall we run off?" Then said the chameleon, "Wait a little first, that I may look well at yonder stepping-place." But the chameleon was crafty, and climbed up the long grass close to the mane of the wild hog, and when he was securely fixed in the mane, he said, "Now run, elder brother!" And as the wild-hog galloped away, the chameleon kept fast hold of his mane and tail; and when he came yonder to the appointed place, he leaped off on to the long grass. So, as the wild-hog stood looking behind him, the chameleon said, "Don't look behind for me, elder brother, for here I am in front of you." So the wild-hog was both astonished and angry, and ran off fast again. But the chameleon held fast by his mane as before. And so, after they had gone thus to and fro for a long time, the wild-hog was dead with fatigue, while the chameleon retained his shrewdness; for the wild-hog was "killed by his strength like the axe," and did not think of the cunning of his companion, but only of his own size.[1]

A different device was adopted by a tortoise in a competition with a lion, according to a Sinhalese version, translated by Mr W. Goonetilleke, in 'The Orientalist,' vol. i. p. 87:

Once a tortoise saw a lion on the bank of a narrow river, and said to him, "I lay a wager that I shall get to the other side of this river by swimming across it sooner than you can by jumping over it." The lion accepted the challenge, and a day was fixed for the trial of their speed. In the meantime the tortoise asked a relative of his to be on one side of the river on the day appointed, while he himself would be on the other side. Each was to have a bud of the *ratmal* flower in his mouth. On the day fixed the lion made his appearance, and said to the tortoise, "Are you ready?" "Yes, I am," answered the tortoise. "Well, then, let us begin," rejoined the lion. This being agreed to, the lion jumped to the other side, and was surprised to see the tortoise already there. They then agreed to continue the course till one of them should be tired and give up the wager. So the lion kept on jumping from that side to this, until at last he was so exhausted that he fell into the river and was drowned.

From Ceylon the story may have been imported into Siam, where, however, it is related in a form which seems to indicate an Indian extraction. Adolf Bastien has given it in his collection of tales, made by himself during a lengthened sojourn in Siam:[2]

It happened once that Phaya Kruth[3] was in search of nágas [*i.e.,* snakes] to fill his crop with, but could not find a sufficient number of them. He therefore came to a lake, and seeing a tortoise in it, thought of eating him up. But the tortoise cried out, "Before you devour me, let us run a race." Phaya Kruth agreed to the proposal, and proudly rose up high in the air. In the meantime the tortoise called together all his relatives and acquain-

---

[1] "Malagasy Folk-Tales," by the Rev. James Sibree, junior; in the 'Folk-Lore Journal' (1884), vol. ii. pp. 80, 81, 166–168.

[2] Translated by Mr Goonetilleke, in 'The Orientalist,' vol. i. p. 88, from the German version of Herr Bastien, reproduced in 'Orient and Occident,' band iii. s. 497.

[3] Phaya Kruth is Vishnu's vehicle, Garuda, who, at the direction of Kasyapa, rushed into heaven itself and carried off the Amrita from the gods in order to ransom his mother, who had been captured by the snakes.

tances—the whole generation of tortoises—and placed them in rows of 100, of 1000, of 10,000, of 100,000, of 1,000,000, and of 10,000,000, covering the whole ground. Kruth flew about with the whole strength of his wings, and the tortoise called out to him, "Well, let us begin. I beg your highness to fly along the sky while I move in the water. We shall see which of us will be the winner. If I lose I shall give myself up for a prey." Kruth flew forwards with all his might, and then stopped and called out to the tortoise; but to whichever side he flew, the tortoise always answered him from ahead. Kruth then flew again as fast as he could, but at every point the tortoise was in advance of him. He then flew and flew as far as the great mountain, the sacred Himaphan, and at last exclaimed, "Hear, O tortoise! you indeed understand how to run pretty fast," and giving up the race, he alighted on a *rathal*-tree, the place of his abode, to rest.

The story is most likely to be known to the Mongolian races, in common with other tales and fables of Buddhist invention or adaptation. In the incident of the Brave Little Tailor (in the German story, see *ante*, p. 151) seating himself among the branches of the tree, which he undertook to carry along with the giant, we seem to have a reflection of the device of the frog and the chameleon clinging to the neck of the wild-hog, in the Malagasy versions, and of that of the butterfly perched on the crane in the Fijian variant.

NOTE.

THE ORIGIN OF FABLES.

The term Fable is often indiscriminately applied to any kind of fictitious tale, but it properly signifies a moral narrative in which beasts, birds, or fishes are the characters. Although it is generally allowed that Fable was the earliest form of narrative designed to convey moral instruction, yet it is by no means agreed among the learned in what country of remote antiquity it had its origin. A modern German rabbi, Dr Landsberger, in his erudite little treatise, 'Die Fabeln des Sophos,' contends that the Hebrews were the first to employ fables for didactic purposes; and we have probably one of the oldest extant fables in the Book of Judges, ix. 8–15, related by Jotham to the people of Israel, of the trees desiring a king. Josephus informs us that Solomon "composed of parables and similitudes three thousand; for he spoke a parable upon every sort of tree, from the hyssop to the cedar; and in like manner, also about beasts, about all sorts of living creatures, whether upon earth, or in the seas, or in the air; for he was not unacquainted with any of their natures, nor omitted inquiring about them, but described them all like a philosopher, and demonstrated his exquisite knowledge of their several properties." Dr Landsberger asserts that the sages of India were indebted to the Hebrews for the idea of teaching by means of fables, probably during the reign of Solomon, who is believed to have had commerce with the western coasts of Hindústán. But this is mere conjecture.

"As far as relates to teaching by apologues," says Dr H. H. Wilson, "although there can be no doubt that it was a national contrivance [of the Hindús], devised by them for their own use, and not borrowed from their neighbours, yet there is no sufficient reason to suppose that it was originally confined to them, or at first communicated by them to other nations. It has been urged, with some plausibility, that the universal prevalence amongst the Hindús of the doctrine of the metempsychosis was calculated to recommend to their belief the notion that beasts and birds might reason and converse, and that consequently the plan of such dialogues probably originated with them; but the notion is one that readily suggests itself to the imagination, and an inventive fancy was quite as likely as a psychological dogma to have gifted mute creatures with intelligence. At any rate, we know that, as an article of poetical and almost of religious faith, it was known to the Greeks at an early date, for Homer is authority for the speech of horses. Without affirming the apocryphal existence of Æsop, we cannot doubt that fables such as are ascribed to him were current even prior to his supposed date; and we have an instance of the fact in the story of the Hawk and the Nightingale of Hesiod. Other specimens of the same class of compositions are afforded by the fable of the Fox and the Ape of Archilochus, of which a fragment is preserved by Eustathius; and by that of the Eagle and the Fox, which is attributed to the same writer, and is an established member of all collections of fables, both in Asia and in Europe. Roman tradition—it would have once been called history—furnishes at least one well-known instance of popular instruction by fable, which Menenius was not likely to have learnt from the Hindús; and various examples of this style of composition are familiarly known as occurring in Scripture. Although the invention was very probably of Eastern origin, we cannot admit that it was in any exclusive degree a contrivance of the Hindús, or that it was imparted originally by them to other Asiatic nations. If such a communication did take place, it must have occurred at a period anterior even to Hindú tradition."

The danger of attempting openly to administer reproof to absolute Asiatic potentates may have led to the invention of fables, in which the lessons intended to be imparted were veiled under ingenious fictions of animals. Oriental historians have preserved a curious anecdote of a tyrannical monarch having been reclaimed by such means. A wise and prudent vazír once related the following fable to his royal master: There was an owl in El-Basra and an owl in El-Mosul. And the owl of El-Basra said to the other one day, "Give me thy daughter in marriage to my son." Quoth the owl of El-Mosul, "I consent, on condition that thou give me as her dowry a hundred ruined villages." "That," replied the owl of El-Basra, "I cannot do at present; but if Allah spare the sultan another year, I will do what thou requirest." The sultan, deeply impressed by this simple fable, at once caused all the ruined towns and villages to be rebuilt, and henceforward studied to promote the well-being of his subjects, and to render his rule easy and acceptable to them.

✦ THE FOUR CLEVER
BROTHERS ✦

ACCORDING to one of Grimm's fairy tales of Germany, a poor man sent his four sons away, each to learn some craft by which he should earn his living. Having gone some distance together, they separate at four cross-roads, agreeing to meet at the same spot that day four years hence. The eldest learnt to be an expert thief, but "only of fair game"; the second was a skilful star-gazer, and received from his master, as a parting gift, a glass, by which he could see all that was going on in the sky and on the earth; the third had become an expert archer, under the tuition of a huntsman, who presented him with a bow, with which he was sure to hit whatever he shot at; and the youngest became so clever a tailor that his master gave him a needle with which he might sew anything, no matter how hard or how soft or brittle, so that no seam could be discovered. They each give proof of their skill before their father: the star-gazer tells by means of his magic telescope how many eggs are in a bird's nest high up in a tree; the thief takes the eggs from beneath the bird without its knowledge; the archer cuts all five eggs in two with one shot, although placed one at each corner of the table and the fifth in the centre; the tailor sews them up again with his wonderful needle: and when the birds are hatched, lo! each has only a little red streak across its neck, where they had been sewed together! Some time after this the king's daughter was carried off. The king promised her as the wife of the man who recovered her. The second son, by means of his glass, discovered her sitting on a rock by the sea and a fierce dragon guarding her. The king gave them a ship, and they sailed away till they came to the place. But the archer dared not shoot, lest he should kill the princess; so the thief stole her away while the dragon was asleep. They had not sailed far on their way back when the dragon awoke and flew after them; the huntsman shot him through the heart, but, unluckily, as he fell he upset the boat, and they had to swim upon a few planks. Then the tailor sewed the planks together with his wonderful needle, and they sailed about and gathered the pieces of their boat, which he also sewed together, and so they reached the ship and got home safe. They brought the princess to her father, and each of them claimed her: the second, because he had discovered where she was; the first, because he had stolen her; the third, because he had slain the dragon; and the youngest, because he had sewed the planks and thus saved all their lives. But it happened that the princess was attached to another person, so the father decided that she should be married to none of the sons. But the king gave each of them half a kingdom, and they lived contented and happy ever after.

A very curious version is found in the Albanian Tales, translated into French by M. Dozen, under the title of 'Le Pou' (No. 4 of his collection): The devil having whisked away to his grim abode the beautiful daughter of a king, the latter offered her hand in marriage to whoever should rescue her from the arch-fiend's clutches. Seven youths present themselves: the first could hear sounds at any distance; the second could cause the earth to open; the third could steal from any one without his knowledge; the fourth could throw an object to the end of the world; the fifth could instantaneously erect an impregnable and inaccessible tower; the sixth could bring down anything, however high, with a single shot; and the seventh could catch whatever fell from the sky, no matter how great the altitude. They set off; and having travelled some distance, the first youth laid his ear to the ground, and then said, "I hear him—command thou," addressing the second youth, "the earth to open at this spot," which being done, immediately the earth opened, and they descended into its bowels, where, guided by the loud noise of snoring, they came upon the fiend sound asleep, with the princess clutched to his breast. The third youth, by his art, removed the princess without awaking the sleeping fiend, at the same time putting a toad in her place. Then the fourth took off one of the devil's shoes and threw it to the end of the world, after which they all returned by the way they had come, and commenced their journey back to the king's dominions. But presently the arch-fiend awoke, and the grimy cavern resounded with his bellowing on his discovering that the princess was gone; and his rage was not less when he found that one of his shoes lay at the end of the world, since he well knew that his journey thither to fetch it (for apparently he had not any sons of St Crispin among his subjects to make him another) would give the fugitives a good start of him. Having, with his utmost diligence, recovered his precious shoe, he sped after the fugitives, who perceiving him in the distance, the fifth youth in a moment erected a lofty tower, in which they took refuge—and not an instant too soon, for hardly were they within, when the enraged fiend came up. Finding all his efforts to break into the tower futile, the crafty one told them that he would go away and trouble them no more if they would let him have one last look at the princess: they made a very small aperture through which he might see the lady, when, in "less than no time," he drew her through it, and flew with her high up into the air. The sixth youth now brought his special art into play, by drawing his bow and shooting the fiend, who, writhing with pain, dropped the princess, and the seventh youth caught her as she fell, so that she was uninjured. Resuming their journey, they in due time reached the palace in safety, and the king, delighted to have his daughter restored to him, desired her to choose one of the seven clever youths for her husband. "They have all contributed to my safety," said the princess, "especially he who caught me as I fell." Now the seventh youth was the youngest and best looking, so she chose him for her husband; but the others were all richly rewarded by the king.

In the Kalmuk tales of 'Siddhí Kúr' (Second Relation) a rich youth, an astrologer, a mechanic, a painter, a physician, and a smith go forth together into a foreign country, and coming to the mouth of a great river, each plants a tree of life, and, agreeing to meet at the same spot again, they separate, each following one of the branches of the river (the four cross-roads of the German tale). The youth marries a beautiful maiden, who is ravished from him by the khán, and he himself is murdered and buried beneath a rock. When the others meet at the place where they separated, they find the youth's tree of life withered. The astrologer discovers where his body lay; the smith breaks the rock, and draws it from beneath; and the physician, by means of a wonderful cordial, restores the youth to life. Then he informed them how the khán had stolen away his lovely wife, so they resolved to rescue her. And the mechanic constructed a wooden garuda,[1] which could move through the air like a living bird; and the painter decorated it in the finest colours. Then the youth seated himself within the wooden garuda, which flew up through the air, and hovering above the royal residence, the khán, astonished at the beauty of the bird, told his wife to go to the roof of the house and offer it all kinds of choice food. When she recognised the youth, she flew into his arms, and instantly seating her beside him, and turning the peg that guided the bird, he soon descended among his companions, who, on seeing the beauty of the damsel, began to quarrel for her possession, and drew their knives and slew each other.

[1]Garuda is the Bird of Vishnu in Hindú mythology.

A different form of the story is found in Nakhshabí's Persian Tales of a Parrot (Túti Náma); Night 34 of the MS., No. 2573 in the Library of the India Office: A rich merchant of Kábul had a beautiful daughter, named Zuhra (or Venus), who had many wealthy suitors, but declared that she would marry only a man who was completely wise or very skilful. Three young men presented themselves before the merchant, saying that if his daughter demands a man of skill for her husband, either of them was an eligible candidate. The first youth said that his art was to discover the whereabouts of anything that was lost, and to predict future events. The second could make a horse of wood, which would float in the air like Solomon's throne. And the third was an archer, and could pierce any object at which he might shoot with his arrow. The merchant having reported to his daughter the wonderful acquirements of her three new suitors, she promised to give her decision next morning. But the same night she disappeared, and the unhappy father sent for the three youths to rescue his daughter by the exercise of their arts. The first youth discovered that a dív (or demon) had carried the damsel to the summit of a mountain, which was inaccessible to men. The second made a wooden horse, and gave it to the third, who rode upon it, quickly reached the mountain, killed the dív with an arrow, and brought away the maiden. "Each of the three claimed her as his by right, and the dispute continued."

We find another variant in the unique Persian MS. text of the 'Sindibád Náma,' preserved in the India Office Library, where it forms the last of the tales related by the prince. A king's daughter, while sporting with her maidens in a garden, is carried away by a demon to his cave in the mountains of Yemen. The king offers the hand of the princess in marriage, and half his kingdom, to the man who should bring her back. Four brothers undertake the adventure: One is a guide, who had travelled over the world; the second a daring robber, "who would have taken the prey from the lion's mouth;" the third a warrior, like Rustam; and the fourth a skilful physician. The guide leads the others to the demon's cave; the robber steals the damsel, in the absence of the demon; the damsel being very ill, the physician restores her to health; while the warrior puts to flight a whole army of dívs who had sallied forth with huge clubs on their shoulders.

The Japanese seem to have been familiar with the story as early at least as the beginning of the tenth century, when their classical romance, 'Genji Monogatari,' was composed, in which one of the characters, speaking of a young lady whose father had entertained great hopes of her matrimonial success, exclaims, "Ah, she is a woman who is likely to become the Queen of the Blue Main!" On this the translator, Suyematz Kenchis, has the following note: "In an old Indian story, a certain king of ancient times had a beautiful daughter. Four neighbouring kings became her suitors. Suddenly the daughter was lost. Her parents made every search, and it was at last discovered that there was a dragon's castle at the bottom of the blue main. The dragon king had carried her off and placed her in his castle. The father and the four suitor kings went there together, and having rescued her, brought her back."—The circumstance that in the German version, as in the Japanese, it is a "dragon" that carries off the damsel, may perhaps indicate that this is one of the stories introduced into Europe by the Mongolians.

The Arabian tale of Prince Ahmed and the Peri Bánú is a familiar variant: Three princes are in love with their cousin, who is to be given to him that should bring the most wonderful thing. One obtains a magic carpet; another an ivory telescope; and the third an apple which could cure the person who smelt at it, even if at the very point of death. The youth with the telescope discovers that the princess is dying; the magic carpet carries all three from a distant country to the chamber of the lady; and the apple restores her to health.—With this the first part of the story of the Three Princes, in Powell and Magnussen's 'Icelandic Legends' (pp. 348–354), exactly corresponds, excepting that the apple, instead of being smelt at, is put in the arm-pit of the sick person. And, to go to the other extremity of Europe, we have also a parallel in Von Hahn's 'Neugriechische Märchen':[2] Three young men love the same girl; and in order to settle the question, which of them shall marry her, they agree to go away and return at a certain time, when whichever shall have learned the best craft shall have the girl. They all return after three years' absence. One is a renowned astronomer; the second can raise the dead; and the third can run quicker than the air, and be in a moment wherever he wishes. When they have all met, the astronomer looks at the girl's star, and knows from

[2]'Contes Populaires Grecs,' par J. G. Von Hahn, éditées par N. Pio: Athens et Copenhagen, 1879. No. II. p. 98.

its trembling that she is at the point of death. The physician—he who can raise the dead—prepares a medicine for the girl's recovery. The third runs off with the remedy, and by pouring it down her throat saves her life: her soul, which was at her teeth ready to depart, went down again.[2]

We have probably the original of all these different versions in the fifth of the 'Vetálapanchavinsati' (Twenty-five Tales of a Demon—see note, p. 6), where we read that a certain king's minister, named Harisvámin, had an excellent son, and also a beautiful daughter, who was rightly named Somaprabhá, or Moonlight. This damsel made her mother give the following message to her father and her brother: "I shall be married to a man possessed of heroism, or knowledge, or magic power; you must not give me in marriage to any other, if you value my life." Harisvámin was looking for a person possessed of one of these qualifications when the king despatched him on state business into the Dekkan, and while there a Bráhman, who had heard of the great beauty of Somaprabhá, came to him and sought her hand. Harisvámin informed him of the three qualifications, one of which his daughter had resolved her husband must possess, and the suitor replied that he had the power to construct a magic chariot that could fly in the air, and having convinced Harisvámin of this, he promised Somaprabhá to him, fixing the marriage for the seventh day from that time. Meanwhile his son had promised his sister to another Bráhman, who had satisfied him that he possessed wonderful skill in the use of missiles and hand-to-hand weapons, and, by advice of the astrologers, appointed the very same seventh day for the marriage. And at the same time his mother, who knew nothing of the engagement her son had entered into, gave her promise to a third person, who possessed supernatural knowledge, that Somaprabhá should be given to him in marriage on the same seventh day.—When Harisvámin came home, and told his wife and his son that he had promised Somaprabhá to a noble Bráhman in the Dekkan, and was informed by them of the engagements they had also made unknown to each other, his mind was filled with anxiety, and he knew not what course to pursue in such perplexing circumstances. On the wedding-day the three bridegrooms arrived—the man of knowledge, the man of magic power, and the man of valour; and just then it was discovered that Somaprabhá had mysteriously disappeared. "Man of knowledge," said Harisvámin, "tell me where my daughter has gone." He replied that a rákshasa had carried her off to his habitation in the Vindhya forest. On hearing this the father exclaimed, "Alas! how are we to recover her?" The man of magic power said, "Be of good cheer; I will take you in a moment to the place where the possessor of knowledge says she is;" saying which, he prepared a chariot that could fly in the air, provided with all kinds of weapons, and made Harisvámin, the man of knowledge, and the brave man get into it, and in a moment he carried them to the habitation of the rákshasa, who, on seeing them, rushed out in a rage, when the hero challenged him to fight. And in a short time the hero cut off the head of the rákshasa, after which they carried off Somaprabhá and returned in the magic chariot. When they reached Harisvámin's house a dispute arose between the man of knowledge, the man of magic power, and the man of valour, and while they were wrangling, each claiming Somaprabhá because of the share he had in her recovery, Harisvámin remained silent, perplexed in mind.

It is worthy of note that in this last, and oldest, form of the story, and also in the ' Túti Náma' version, the damsel is not represented as being ill, as in the 'Sindibád Náma' and the Arabian versions. According to Professor Tawney, the 47th tale of the 'Pentamerone' of Basile and "Das Weise Urtheil" in Waldau's 'Böhmische Märchen' closely resemble the Arabian story. Whence the Italian novelist obtained it we cannot say; but Galland's French translation of the 'Thousand and One Nights,' through which that work first became known in Europe, was not published till many years after the 'Pentamerone' was printed. The story may have come into Italy with Venetian merchants trading in the Levant.

❧ CUMULATIVE STORIES ❧

ONE should scarcely conceive that our prime nursery favourites the "House that Jack built" and the "Old Woman and the Crooked Sixpence" have their prototype in a sacred hymn in the Hebrew Talmud! Yet such is the case, and in order to show this, I must here reproduce the first-mentioned "story":

1 This is the House that Jack built.

2 This is the Malt
That lay in the House that Jack built.

3 This is the Rat,
That ate the Malt,
That lay in the House that Jack built.

4 This is the Cat,
That killed the Rat,
That ate the Malt,
That lay in the House that Jack built.

5 This is the Dog,
That worried the Cat,
That killed the Rat,
That ate the Malt,
That lay in the House that Jack built.

6 This is the Cow with the crumpled horn,
That tossed the Dog,
That worried the Cat,
That killed the Rat,
That ate the Malt,
That lay in the House that Jack built.

7 This is the Maiden, all forlorn,
That milked the Cow with the crumpled horn,
That tossed the Dog,
That worried the Cat,
That killed the Rat,
That ate the Malt,
That lay in the House that Jack built.

8 This is the Man, all tattered and torn,
That kissed the Maiden, all forlorn,
That milked the Cow with the crumpled horn,
That tossed the Dog,
That worried the Cat,
That killed the Rat,
That ate the Malt,
That lay in the House that Jack built.

9 This is the Priest, all shaven and shorn,
That married the Man, all tattered and torn,
That kissed the Maiden, all forlorn,
That milked the Cow with the crumpled horn,
That tossed the Dog,
That worried the Cat,
That killed the Rat,
That ate the Malt,
That lay in the House that Jack built.

10 This is the Cock, that cried in the morn,
That woke the Priest, all shaven and shorn,
That married the Man, all tattered and torn,
That kissed the Maiden, all forlorn,
That milked the Cow with the crumpled horn,
That tossed the Dog,
That worried the Cat,
That killed the Rat,
That ate the Malt,
That lay in the House that Jack built.

11 And this is the Farmer, sowing his corn,
That kept the Cock, that cried in the morn,
That waked the Priest, all shaven and shorn,
That married the Man, all tattered and torn,
That kissed the Maiden, all forlorn,
That milked the Cow with the crumpled horn,
That tossed the Dog,
That worried the Cat,
That killed the Rat,
That ate the Malt,
That lay in the House that Jack built!

The following is a translation of a mystical hymn in the "Sepher Hag-gadah" of the Talmud:

1   *A kid, a kid,* my father bought
    For *two pieces of money;*
                    A kid, a kid.

2   Then came *the cat,* and ate the kid
    That my father bought
    For two pieces of money;
                    A kid, a kid.

3   Then came *the dog,* and bit the cat,
    That ate the kid,
    That my father bought
    For two pieces of money;
                    A kid, a kid.

4   Then came *the staff,* and beat the dog,
    That bit the cat,
    That ate the kid,
    That my father bought
    For two pieces of money;
                    A kid, a kid.

5   Then came *the fire,* and burned the staff,
    That beat the dog,
    That bit the cat,
    That ate the kid,
    That my father bought
    For two pieces of money;
                    A kid, a kid.

6   Then came *the water,* and quenched the fire,
    That burned the staff,
    That beat the dog,
    That bit the cat,
    That ate the kid,
    That my father bought
    For two pieces of money;
                    A kid, a kid.

7   Then came *the ox*, and drank the water,
That quenched the fire,
That burned the staff,
That beat the dog,
That bit the cat,
That ate the kid,
That my father bought
For two pieces of money;

                    A kid, a kid.

8   Then came *the butcher*, and slew the ox,
That drank the water,
That quenched the fire,
That burned the staff,
That beat the dog,
That bit the cat,
That ate the kid,
That my father bought
For two pieces of money;

                    A kid, a kid.

9   Then came the *Angel of Death*, and killed the
butcher,
That slew the ox,
That drank the water,
That quenched the fire,
That burned the staff,
That beat the dog,
That bit the cat,
That ate the kid,
That my father bought
For two pieces of money;

                    A kid, a kid.

10   Then came the Holy One, blessed be He!
and killed the Angel of Death,
That killed the butcher,
That slew the ox,
That drank the water,
That quenched the fire,
That burned the staff,

That beat the dog,
That bit the cat,
That ate the kid,
That my father bought
For two pieces of money;

A kid, a kid.

This is the historical interpretation of the above curiosity of rabbinical literature, given by P. N. Leberecht, at Leipzic, in 1731:

1. The *kid,* which was one of the pure animals, denotes the Hebrews; the *father,* by whom it was purchased, is Jehovah, who represents himself as sustaining this relation to the Jewish nation; the *two pieces of money* signify Moses and Aaron, through whose mediation the Hebrews were brought out of Egypt.

2. The *cat* denotes the Assyrians, by whom the ten tribes were carried into captivity.

3. The *dog* is symbolical of the Babylonians.

4. The *staff* signifies the Persians.

5. The *fire* indicates the Greek Empire under Alexander the Great.

6. The *water* betokens the Romans—as the fourth of the great monarchies to whose dominion the Jews were subjected.

7. The *ox* is a symbol of the Saracens, who subdued Palestine, and brought it under the Khalífat.

8. The *butcher* that killed the ox denotes the Crusaders, by whom the Holy Land was wrested out of the hands of the Saracens.

9. The *Angel of Death* signifies the Turkish power, by which the land of Palestine was taken from the Franks, and to which it is still subject.

10. The commencement of this tenth stanza is designed to show that God will take signal vengeance on the Turks, immediately after whose overthrow the Jews are to be restored to their own land, and live under the government of their long-expected Messiah.

The stick, fire, water, and butcher of the Hebrew hymn play their parts in the story of the Old Woman and the Crooked Sixpence:

An old woman was sweeping her house and she found a little crooked sixpence. "What," said she, "shall I do with this little sixpence? I will go to market and buy a little pig." As she was coming home, she came to a stile, but piggy would not go over the stile.

She went a little farther, and she met with a dog. So she said to the dog, "Dog! dog! bite pig; piggy won't go over the stile, and I shan't get home to-night." But the dog would not.

She went a little farther, and she met a stick. So she said, "Stick! stick! beat dog; dog won't bite pig; piggy won't go over the stile, and I shan't get home to-night." But the stick would not.

She went a little farther, and she met a fire. So she said, "Fire! fire! burn stick; stick won't beat dog; dog won't bite pig" (*and so on, always repeating the foregoing words*). But the fire would not.

She went a little farther, and she met some water. So she said, "Water! water! quench fire; fire won't burn stick," etc. But the water would not.

She went a little farther, and she met an ox. So she said, "Ox! ox! drink water; water won't quench fire," etc. But the ox would not.

She went a little farther, and she met a butcher. So she said, "Butcher! butcher! kill ox; ox won't drink water," etc. But the butcher would not.

She went a little farther, and she met a rope. So she said, "Rope! rope! hang butcher; butcher won't kill ox," etc. But the rope would not.

She went a little farther, and she met a rat. So she said, "Rat! rat! gnaw rope; rope won't hang butcher," etc. But the rat would not.

She went a little farther, and she met a cat. So she said, "Cat! cat! kill rat; rat won't gnaw rope," etc. But the cat said, "If you will go to yonder cow and fetch me a saucer of milk, I will kill the rat." So away went the old woman to the cow.

And the cow said to her, "If you will go to yonder haycock, and fetch me a handful of hay, I'll give you milk." So away the old woman went to the haycock, and she brought hay to the cow. And as soon as the cow had eaten the hay, she gave the old woman milk, and away the old woman went with it in a saucer to the cat.

And as soon as the cat had lapped up the milk, the cat began to kill the rat, the rat began to gnaw the rope, the rope began to hang the butcher, the butcher began to kill the ox, the ox began to drink the water, the water began to quench the fire, the fire began to burn the stick, the stick began to beat the dog, the dog began to bite the pig, the little pig in a fright jumped over the stile, and so the old woman got home that night.[1]

---

[1] The Scotch version, entitled the Wife and her Bush of Berries, agrees very closely with this favourite English nursery tale—see Chambers' 'Popular Rhymes of Scotland.' An Aberdeenshire variant, "The Wifie and her Kidie," is given by the Rev. Walter Gregor in the 'Folk-Lore Journal,' vol. ii. pp. 277, 278.

Another of our English cumulative stories is one beginning—

> John Ball shot them all,
> John Scott made the shot,
> But John Ball shot them all.

We need not, however, parade Mr Ball and his numerous coadjutors, but shall proceed to cite similar stories from other languages. Mr Campbell, in his 'Popular Tales of the West Highlands,' gives the cumulative story of a couple named Moorachug and Menachaig, who went one day to gather fruit, but as fast as the man gathered his wife ate—his share as well as her own; so he went to a rod, and asked it to beat Menachaig for eating his share of the fruit, but the rod told him he must get an axe to dress it; so he went to the axe, but the axe told him he must get a stone to smooth it; so he went to a stone, but he must have water to wet it; so he went to the water, but he must first get a deer to swim it; so he went to the deer, but the deer says he must first get a dog to run him; so he went to the dog, but the dog says he must first have his feet rubbed with butter; so he went to the butter, but he must first get a mouse to scrape it; so he went to the mouse, but he must first get a cat to hunt him; so he went to the cat, but the cat must first get milk; so he went to the cow, but the cow must first get a wisp of hay from the barn-gillie; so he went to the barn-gillie, but he must first get a bannock from the baking-woman; so he went to the baking-woman, but she must have some water. "How shall I bring the water?" "There's nothing but the sowens-sieve," says the woman. But every drop of water he puts in it goes through. An old woman tells him to put in clay and moss, and so he brought in the water to the baking-woman, and he got a bannock for the barn-gillie—a wisp of hay from the barn-gillie for the cow—milk from the cow for the cat;—then the cat began to hunt the mouse—the mouse to scrape the butter—the butter to rub the dog's feet—the dog to hunt the deer—the deer to swim the water—the water to wet the stone—the stone to smooth the axe—the axe to dress the rod—the rod to beat Menachaig, and she eating his share of the fruit. But when Moorachug returned to Menachaig, she had just *burst!*

Such "accumulative " stories as these seem to be current in almost all countries. In Pitrè's Sicilian collection we find a parallel to our Old Woman and the Crooked Sixpence: Once upon a time there was a mother who had a daughter named Pitidda. She said to her, "Go sweep the house." "Give me some bread first." "I cannot," she answered. When her mother saw that she would not sweep the house, she called to the wolf, saying, "Wolf, go kill Pitidda, for Pitidda will not sweep the house." "I can't," said the wolf. "Dog, go kill wolf," said the mother; "for the wolf will not kill Pitidda, for Pitidda won't sweep the house." "I can't," said the dog. "Stick, go beat dog," and so on. Fire to burn stick; water to quench fire; cow to drink water; rope to choke cow; mouse to gnaw rope; and cat to eat mouse, and so on.—In another Sicilian variant, entitled the Sexton's Nose, the dog who has bitten his nose refuses a *hair* to heal it without getting some bread; so the sexton goes to the baker and asks for some bread, but the baker must first get some wood; so he goes to the wood-man, who must get a mattock; to the smith, who wants coals; to the collier, who must first get a cart; to the waggon-maker, who gives him a cart, which the sexton gives to the collier, who gives him coals, which he gives to the smith, who gives him a mattock, which he gives to the woodman, who gives him some faggots, which he gives to the baker, who gives him bread, which he gives to the dog, who at length gives the sexton a hair, which he applies to his nose, and the wound is cured.[2]

Traces of the Hebrew hymn are also found in the Norse story, How they brought Hairlock home: A certain dame had three sons—Peter, Paul, and Osborn Boots—also a nanny-goat, called Hairlock. Boots sets out to fetch the nanny-goat home—sees her high up on a crag—calls to her to come home, but Hairlock wouldn't. He tells his mother, who says, "Go to the fox, and bid him bite Hairlock." But the fox wouldn't blunt his snout on a goat's beard. His mother then sends him to ask Greylegs the wolf to tear the fox; but he wouldn't. To the bear, to slay Greylegs; but the bear wouldn't. To the Finn, to shoot bear; but the Finn wouldn't. To the fir-tree, to fall on the Finn; but the fir-tree wouldn't. To the fire, to burn fir-tree; but the fire wouldn't. To the water, to quench fire; but the water wouldn't. To the ox, to drink up water; but the ox wouldn't. To the yoke, to pinch ox; but the yoke wouldn't. To the axe, to chop yoke; but the axe wouldn't. To the smith, to hammer the axe; but the smith wouldn't. To the rope, to hang smith; but the rope wouldn't. To the mouse, to gnaw rope; but the mouse wouldn't. To the cat, to catch mouse. "Well," said the cat, "just give me a drop of milk for my kittens,

---

[2] Crane's 'Italian Popular Tales,' pp. 250–252.

and then"—That's what the cat said, and the lad said she should have it. So the cat bit the mouse, and the mouse gnawed the rope, and the rope hanged the smith, and the smith hammered the axe, and the axe chopped the yoke, and the yoke pinched the ox, and the ox drank the water, and the water quenched the fire, and the fire burned the fir-tree, and the fir-tree felled the Finn, and the Finn shot the bear, and the bear slew Greylegs the wolf, and Greylegs the wolf tore the fox, and the fox bit Hairlock, so that she sprang home and knocked off one of her hind legs against the barn wall. So there lay nanny-goat, and if she's not dead, she limps about on three legs.[3]

Another amusing Norse story of the same class, entitled the Cock and Hen a-nutting, closely resembles the Sexton's Nose, already cited: Once on a time the cock and the hen went into the hazel-wood to pick nuts; and the hen got a nut-shell in her throat, and lay on her back, flapping her wings. Off went the cock to fetch water for her; so he came to the spring, and said, "Dear good friend spring, give me a drop of water, that I may give it to Dame Partlet my mate, who lies at death's door in the hazel-wood." But the spring answered, "You'll get no water from me till I get leaves from you." So the cock went to the linden, and said, "Dear good friend linden, give me some of your leaves; the leaves I'll give to the spring, and the spring will give me water, to give to Dame Partlet my mate, who lies at death's door in the hazel-wood." "You'll get no leaves from me," said the linden, "until I get a red rib-bon with a golden edge from you." So the cock ran to the Virgin Mary, and said, "Dear good Virgin Mary, give me a red ribbon with a golden edge, and I'll give it to the linden, and the linden will give me leaves," etc. "You'll get no red ribbon from me," said the Virgin Mary, "until I get shoes from you." So the cock went to the shoemaker, but he must first get some bristles; to the sow, but she must first get some corn; to the thresher, but he must first get a bannock; to the baker's wife, but she must first get wood; to the wood-cutter, but he must first get an axe; to the smith, but he must first get char-coal; to the charcoal-burner, who took pity on the cock, and gave him a bit of charcoal, and then the smith got his coal, and the wood-cutter his axe, and the baker's wife her wood, and the thresher his bannock, and the sow her corn, and the shoemaker his bristles, and the Virgin Mary her shoes, and the linden its red ribbon with a golden edge, and the spring its leaves, and the

[3]Abridged from the version in Dasent's 'Tales from the Fjeld.'

cock his drop of water, and he gave it to Dame Partlet his mate, who lay there at death's door in the hazel-wood—and so she got all right again.[4]

In a third Norwegian cumulative story, the Death of Chanticleer, we find a very interesting analogue of one that is current at the present day among the children of the Panjáb and Kashmír. A cock fell one day into the brewing-vat of Yule ale and was drowned. His wife, Dame Partlet, when she saw this, lost her wits and flew about distracted, screaming and screeching. "What ails you?" said the hand-quern. "Goodman Chanticleer," said the hen, "has fallen into the ale-vat and drowned himself; that's why I am screaming and screeching, that's why I am sobbing and sighing." "Well," said the hand-quern, "if I can do nothing else I will grind and groan;" so it fell to grinding as fast as it could. When the chair heard this, it said, "What ails you, hand-quern, that you grind and groan so much?" "Why not?" said the hand-quern; "when goodman Chanticleer has fallen into the cask and drowned himself, and Dame Partlet sits in the ingle and sobs and sighs: that's why I grind and groan," said the hand-quern. "If I can do naught else," said the chair, "I will crack," and with that the chair fell to creaking and cracking. When the door heard this it said to the chair, "What's the matter with you, that you creak and crack?" "Why not?" said the chair; "since goodman Chanticleer has fallen into the ale-vat and drowned himself, and Dame Partlet sobs and sighs, and the hand-quern grinds and groans: that's why I creak and crack." "If I can do naught else," said the door, "I can rattle and bang, and whistle and slam," so it began to open and shut, and slam and bang. When the stove heard this it began to smoulder and smoke, and then the axe began to rive and rend about, and the aspen began to quiver and quake in all its leaves, and the birds began to pluck off all their feathers; and then the master, when he saw the feathers flying about like fun, and learned from the birds what had happened, he began to tear brooms asunder; and the goody, his wife, stood cooking porridge for supper, and seeing all this, she called out, "Why, man, what are you tearing all the brooms to pieces for?" "Oh," said the goodman, "Chanticleer has fallen into the ale-vat and been drowned, and so the Dame Partlet sobs and sighs, and the hand-quern grinds and groans, and the chair creaks and cracks, and the door slams and bangs, and the stove smoulders and smokes, and the axe rives and rends, and the aspen quivers and quakes, and the birds are pulling out all their feathers, so I am tearing

[4] See Dasent's 'Popular Tales from the Norse,' p. 437; and Thorpe's 'Yule-Tide Stories' (Bohn's ed.), p. 333.

the brooms to pieces." Then the goody began throwing the porridge against the walls; and that's how they drank the burial-ale after goodman Chanticleer, who fell into the brewing-vat and was drowned.[5]

The Panjábí tale of the Death and Burial of Poor Hen-Sparrow (Steel and Temple's 'Wide-Awake Stories') is clearly own brother to that of the Death of Chanticleer:

In days of yore there lived a cock-sparrow and his wife, who were both growing old. But the cock-sparrow was a gay bird, old as he was, and cast his eyes upon a lively young hen, and determined to marry her. So they had a grand wedding, but the old hen went out and sat disconsolately just under a crow's nest. While she was there it began to rain, and the water came drip, drip on to her feathers, but she was too sad to care. Now it so happened that the crow had used some scraps of dyed cloth in its nest, and when they got wet the colours ran and went drip, drip on the old sparrow, till she was as gay as a peacock. When she flew home, the new wife was dreadfully jealous of her old co-wife, and asked her where she had managed to get that lovely dress. "Easily enough," she replied; "I just went into the dyer's vat." "I'll go too," thought the new wife; "I won't have that old thing better dressed than I am." So she flew off to the dyer's, and went pop into the middle of the vat, but it was scalding hot, and she was half dead before she could manage to scramble out. Meanwhile the old cock, not finding his new wife at home, flew off distracted in search of her, and wept salt tears when he found her half drowned and half scalded, with her feathers away, by the dyer's vat. "What has happened?" he asked, and she replied:

> "My co-wife got dyed,
> But I fell into the vat."

So the cock took her up tenderly in his bill, and flew away home with her. Just as he was crossing a big river, the old hen-sparrow looked out of the nest, and when she saw her husband bringing his bride home in such a sorry plight, she burst out a-laughing and said:

> "One is vexed and one is grieved,
> And one laughing is carried on high."

At this the husband was so enraged that he could not hold his tongue, but shouted out, "Hush, hush! you old thing." Of course, when he opened

---

[5] Dasent's 'Tales from the Fjeld,' pp. 30–34.

his mouth to speak the poor draggled bride fell plump into the river and was drowned.[6] Whereupon the cock-sparrow was so distracted with grief that he pecked off all his feathers till he was as bare as a ploughed field, and went and sat quite naked on a *pípal*-tree and wept. Then the *pípal*-tree said to him, "What has happened?" "Don't ask me," said the cock-sparrow. "It isn't decent to ask questions when folk are in mourning." But the *pípal*-tree would not be satisfied, so at last, with sobs and tears, the poor bereaved sparrow said:

> "One hen painted,
> The other was dyed,
> And the cock loved her."

Then the *pípal*-tree was overwhelmed with grief too, and shed all its leaves on the spot. By-and-by a buffalo came, and asked the *pípal*-tree how it had lost all its leaves, and after much entreaty it answered:

> "One hen painted,
> The other was dyed,
> And the cock loved her,
> So the *pípal* shed its leaves."

On hearing this the buffalo was grieved, and shed his horns there and then. After a while the buffalo went to the river to drink, and the river asked him how he had lost his grand horns, so he said:

> "One hen painted,
> The other was dyed,
> And the cock loved her,
> So the *pípal* shed its leaves,
> And the buffalo his horns."

Then the river wept so sore that it became quite salt. By-and-by a cuckoo came to the river, and finding it salt, asked the reason, and was answered:

---

[6]This incident occurs in a great number of folk-tales, and its oldest form is probably the 'Játaka,' or Buddhist Birth-Story, of the Talkative Tortoise, which, with other variants—such as the Indian story of the Fools and the Bull of Siva, and the Russian story of the Old Man and the Cabbage-Stalk—will be found in my 'Book of Noodles.'

> "One hen painted,
> The other was dyed,
> And the cock loved her,
> So the *pípal* shed its leaves,
> And the buffalo his horns,
> So the river became salt."

Then the cuckoo plucked out an eye from actual sorrow, and went and sat by a tradesman's shop and wept bitterly. The tradesman wanted to know the cause of the bird's grief, and learned it thus:

> "One hen painted,
> The other was dyed,
> And the cock loved her,
> So the *pípal* shed its leaves,
> And the buffalo his horns,
> So the river became salt,
> And the cuckoo lost an eye."

At this sad news the tradesman wailed till he lost his senses. And when the king's servant came into his shop he gave her pepper when she asked for turmeric, and onion when she asked for garlic, and wheat when she asked for pulse. So the maiden asks what had thus distracted him, and after much persuasion he told her:

> "One hen painted,
> The other was dyed,
> And the cock loved her,
> So the *pípal* shed its leaves,
> And the buffalo his horns,
> So the river became salt,
> And the cuckoo lost an eye,
> So Bhagtu went mad."

Then the maid went into the palace, saying dreadful things, because of her sorrow, and the queen asking what had happened, the maid told her:

> "One hen painted,
> The other was dyed,

> And the cock loved her,
> So the *pípal* shed its leaves,
> And the buffalo his horns,
> So the river became salt,
> And the cuckoo lost an eye,
> So Bhagtu went mad,
> And the maid took to swearing."

Then the queen danced till out of breath, and her son asked the reason:

> "One hen painted,
> The other was dyed,
> And the cock loved her,
> So the *pípal* shed its leaves,
> And the buffalo his horns,
> So the river became salt,
> And the cuckoo lost an eye,
> So Bhagtu went mad,
> And the maid took to swearing,
> So the queen took to dancing."

And then the queen's son became so deeply grieved that he took his tambourine, and began to play on it, when in comes the king himself and learns all about it:

> "One hen painted,
> The other was dyed,
> And the cock loved her,
> So the *pípal* shed its leaves,
> And the buffalo his horns,
> So the river became salt,
> And the cuckoo lost an eye,
> So Bhagtu went mad,
> And the maid took to swearing,
> So the queen took to dancing,
> And the prince took to drumming."

When the king hears this sad story, he began to lay upon the zithar:

> "One hen painted,
> The other was dyed,

And the cock loved her,
So the *pípal* shed its leaves,
And the buffalo his horns,
So the river became salt,
And the cuckoo lost an eye,
So Bhagtu went mad,
And the maid took to swearing,
So the queen took to dancing,
And the prince took to drumming,
So the king took to thrumming."[7]

From Madagascar we have a singular cumulative story, which is well worth reproducing, as follows: Once upon a time Ibotíty went and climbed a tree; and when the wind blew hard the tree was broken, whereupon Ibotíty fell and broke his leg. So he said, "The tree is indeed strong, for it can break the leg of Ibotíty." Then said the tree, "I am not strong, for it is the wind that is strong." Then said Ibotíty, "The wind it is which is strong; for the wind broke the tree, and the tree broke the leg of Ibotíty." "I am not strong," said the wind; "for if I were strong, should I be stopped by the hill?" "Ah, it is the hill which is strong," said Ibotíty; "for the hill stopped the wind, the wind broke the tree, the tree broke the leg of Ibotíty." "Nay, I am not strong," said the hill; "for if I were strong, I should not be burrowed by the mice." "Ah, it is the mouse which is strong," said Ibotíty; "for the mouse burrowed into the hill, the hill stopped the wind, the wind broke the tree, and the tree broke the leg of Ibotíty." "Nay, I am not strong," said the mouse; "for am I strong who can be killed by the cat?" "Ah, it is the cat which is strong," said Ibotíty; "for the cat killed the mouse, the mouse burrowed into the hill, the hill stopped the wind, the wind broke the tree, and the tree broke the leg of Ibotíty." "Nay, I am not strong," said the cat; "for am I strong who am caught by the rope and cannot escape?" "Ah, it is the rope which is strong," said Ibotíty, etc. "Nay, I am not strong," said the rope; "for am I strong and am cut by the iron?" "Then it is the iron which is strong," said Ibotíty, etc. "Nay, I am not strong," said the iron; "for am I strong which

---

[7]A somewhat similar series of catastrophes are recounted in a Roumanian folk-tale: Two old folks have a mouse which, to their intense sorrow, is scalded to death in boiling milk; whereupon a magpie pulled out all its feathers as a sign of its grief; an empress on hearing the news fell out of a balcony and was killed; and the emperor her husband became a monk in the cloister of Lies on the other side of Truth.

am softened by the fire?" "Ah, it is the fire which is strong," said Ibotíty, etc. "Nay, I am not strong," said the fire; "for am I strong and am put out by water?" "Ah, it is the water which is strong," said Ibotíty, and so on. But it would be tedious to give every detail; suffice it to say that the greatest power is shifted successively from the water to the canoe, from the canoe to the rock, from the rock to mankind, from mankind to the sorcerer, from the sorcerer to the *tangéna* (poison ordeal), and from the *tangéna* to God; the last and complete paragraph reading thus: "Nay, I am not strong," said the *tangéna*, "for God overcomes me." "Ah, it is GOD who is strong," said Ibotíty; "for God overcame *tangéna*, *tangéna* killed the sorcerer, the sorcerer overcame man, man broke the rock, the rock broke the canoe, the canoe crossed the water, the water quenched the fire, the fire softened the iron, the iron cut the rope, the rope caught the cat, the cat killed the mouse, the mouse burrowed into the hill, the hill stopped the wind, the wind broke the tree, and the tree broke the leg of Ibotíty." So Ibotíty and all things agreed that God is the strongest of all, and governs all things in this world, whether in heaven above, or on the earth beneath, or underneath the earth, or to the verge of the sky; for God will bear rule for ever and ever.[8]

Lastly, here is a Singalese variant of our Old Woman and the Crooked Sixpence, from the first part of 'The Orientalist,' vol. ii., 1885:

Once upon a time a bird laid two eggs in a cleft between two large stones. Through some movement of the stones this cleft became closed up, and the bird could not gain access to her nest.

So she begged a mason to split open the stones again, in order that she might get to her eggs. But the man would not.

She then went to a wild boar, and asked him to enter the paddy-field and eat the mason's corn, because the mason would not split open the stones, and she could not get to her two eggs. But the wild boar would not.

She then went to the hunter, and asked him to shoot the wild boar, because the wild boar would not eat the mason's paddy; the mason would not split open the stones; and she could not get to her two eggs. But the hunter would not.

She next went to the elephant, and begged him to kill the hunter,

---

[8]'Malagasy Folk-Tales,' by the Rev. James Sibree, junior: 'Folk-Lore Journal' (1884), vol. ii. pp. 136–138.

because the hunter would not shoot the wild boar; the wild boar would not eat the mason's paddy; the mason would not split open the stones; and she could not get to her two eggs. But the elephant would not.

She then went to the *katussá* ("bloodsucker" lizard), and asked it to crawl up the elephant's trunk into his brain, because the elephant would not kill the hunter; the hunter would not shoot the wild boar; the wild boar would not eat the mason's paddy; the mason would not split open the stones; and she could not get to her two eggs. But the *katussá* would not.

She then asked a jungle-hen to peck and kill the *katussá*, because the *katussá* would not crawl up the elephant's trunk; the elephant would not kill the hunter; the hunter would not shoot the wild boar; the wild boar would not eat the mason's paddy; the mason would not split open the two stones; and she could not get to her two eggs. But the hen would not.

She then went to a jackal, and begged him to eat the jungle-hen, because the jungle-hen would not peck the *katussá*; the *katussá* would not crawl up the elephant's trunk; the elephant would not kill the hunter; the hunter would not shoot the wild boar; the wild boar would not eat the mason's paddy; the mason would not split open the stones; and she could not get to her two eggs.

And the jackal was too glad to eat the jungle-hen; so he immediately set off after her: and the jungle-hen began to peck the *katussá*; and the *katussá* began to crawl up the elephant's trunk; and the elephant went to attack the hunter; and the hunter took his bow and arrows to shoot the wild boar; and the wild boar began to eat the mason's paddy; and the mason, seeing the turn things had taken, split open the stones; and so the bird at last got back to her two eggs.

It is the opinion of several learned continental scholars that the Hebrew mystical hymn, "A kid, a kid, my father bought," etc., is a comparatively modern interpolation in the Talmud. Be this as it may, it is very probable that accumulative rhymes and stories were common in the East, long before the rabbins first reduced their traditionary lore to writing and loaded it with their own fanciful commentaries.

⁓ ALADDIN'S WONDERFUL
LAMP ⁓

A Second Chapter on the Thankful Beasts.

TO most general readers the charming tale of Aladdin and his Lamp, as related in our common English version of the 'Arabian Nights'— which was made, early in the last century, from Galland's selections, rendered into French—is doubtless a typical Eastern fiction. It does not, however, occur in any known Arabian text of 'The Thousand and One Nights' (*Elf Laila wa Laila*), although the chief incidents of the tale are found in many Asiatic fictions, and it had become orally current in Greece and Italy before it was published by Galland. A popular Italian version, which presents a close analogy to the familiar story of Aladdin (properly 'Alá-'u-'d-Dín, signifying, "exaltation of the Faith"), is given by Miss M. H. Busk in her 'Folk-Lore of Rome,' under the title of "How Cajusse was married," of which the following is an abstract:

A good-natured-looking old man one day knocks at the door of a poor tailor out of work; his son opens the door, and is told by the old man that he is his uncle, and he gives the lad a piastre to buy a good dinner. When the tailor comes home—for he was absent at the time—he is surprised to hear the old man claim him as a brother; but finding him so rich, he won't dispute the matter. After the good old man had lived some time with the tailor and his family, liberally defraying all household expenses, he finds it necessary to depart, and, with the tailor's consent, takes the boy Cajusse with him, in order that he may learn some useful business. But no sooner are they outside the town than he tells Cajusse it is all a dodge. "I'm not your uncle," he says. "I want a strong daring boy to do something I am too old to do. I'm a wizard—don't attempt to escape, for you can't." Cajusse, not a bit frightened, asks him what it is he wants him to do, and the wizard raises a flat stone from the ground and orders him to go down, and when he gets to the bottom of the cave, to proceed till he comes to a beautiful garden, where he will see a fierce dog keeping watch—there's bread for him. "Don't look back when you hear sounds behind you. On a shelf you'll see an old lantern; take it down and bring it to me." So saying, the wizard gave Cajusse a ring, in case anything awkward should happen to him after he had got the lantern, when he had only to rub the ring and wish for deliverance. Cajusse finds precious stones hanging like fruit from the trees in the garden underground, and fills his pockets with them. Returning to the entrance of the cave, he refuses to give up the lantern until he has been drawn out; so the wizard, thinking merely to frighten him, replaces the stone. Cajusse, finding himself thus entrapped, rubs the ring, when instantly "one" [the slave of the ring] appears, and the youth orders "Table laid for dinner!" He then calls for his mother and father, and they have all an unusually good meal. Some time after Cajusse returned home the town was illuminated one day, and he learned it was because the daughter of the sultan was to be married to the grand vazír's son. He sends his mother to the palace with a basket of priceless jewels as a present to the sultan, and to demand his daughter in marriage to her son. The sultan is astonished at the beauty of the gems, and says he will give his answer in a month. At the end of the same week, however, the vazír's son is married to the princess. Cajusse rubs his lantern and says, "Go to-night, and take the daughter of the sultan and lay her on a poor pallet in our outhouse." This is done, and Cajusse, placing a naked sabre in bed between himself and the princess,[1] begins to talk to her, but she is far too frightened to answer. The same thing occurs three consecutive nights, and at last the princess tells her mother how she is conveyed in some mysterious way to a poor hovel, and so on. The sultan learns of this from the mother of the princess, and he does not know what to make of such a strange business. The son of the vazír complains to his father that his wife disappears every night, and comes back just before the dawn. Cajusse now sends his mother to the sultan with a present of three more baskets full of jewels, and the sultan tells her he may come and see him at the palace. Having received this message, Cajusse rubs his lantern, and gets a dress of gold and silver, a richly caparisoned horse, four pages with

---

[1] This incident of the naked sword, it will be remembered, occurs also in the story of Aladdin; and in one of the genuine tales of the 'Arabian Nights,' that of Sayf el-Muluk and Badía el-Jamal, the hero adopts the like "precaution" while he and the Princess of Hind are drifting over the sea on a raft. The practice, with many other chivalric observances and customs, seems to have been early brought from the East to Europe, and is often employed in mediæval romances, *e.g.*, the Older Edda, in the case of Sigurd and Brynhild; in 'Sir Tristrem'; and in 'Amis and Amiloun,' which, with the heroes' names changed to Alexander and Ludovic, is interwoven with the story of The Ravens in the old English prose version of 'The Seven Wise Masters.' Scott says "it was, in the middle ages, an acknowledged and formal emblem of the strictest continence betwixt persons who, from whatever cause, were placed in circumstances otherwise suspicious;" and he cites a historical instance, on the occasion of Louis, county palatine of Waldenz, acting as the Duke of Austria's proxy in marriage with the Princess of Burgundy.—See notes to Scott's edition (1819) of the Romance of Sir Tristrem, p. 345.

velvet dresses, to ride behind him, and one to go before, distributing money among the people and crying, "Make way for the Signor Cajusse!" To be brief, he is married to the princess (she having been duly divorced, doubtless, by the vazír's son), and they live together in joy and happiness, in a most magnificent palace reared and furnished by means of his all-bestowing lantern. But by-and-by the old wizard hears of all this, and resolves to obtain the lantern by hook or by crook. So dressing himself as a pedlar, he comes near Cajusse's palace and bawls out, "Old lanterns taken in exchange for new ones!" Cajusse is from home, unluckily, and the princess sends a servant out with the lantern, for which the wizard very gladly gives a bran-new one in exchange, and immediately causes the palace to be transported to an island in the high seas. When Cajusse returns and finds what has happened, he rubs his ring (which he always wore on his finger) and is conveyed to where the palace now was. He sounds his horn; the princess, hearing it, is delighted, goes to the window, and tells Cajusse that she won't marry the old man. He gives her this advice: "Make a feast to-night; say you'll marry him if he'll tell you what thing would be fatal to him, and you will guard him against it." The princess wheedles out of the wizard the fatal secret. "One must go into a far-distant forest," he tells her, "where there is a beast called hydra, and cut off his seven heads. If the middle head is split open, a leveret will jump out and run off. If the leveret is caught and his head split open, a bird will fly out. If the bird is caught and opened, in its body is a precious stone, and should that be placed under my pillow I shall die." Cajusse accomplishes all these things, and gives the life-stone to the princess, together with a bottle of opium. The princess drugs the magician's wine, and when he had laid his head on his pillow (under which was the stone), he gave three terrible yells, turned himself round three times, and was dead. After thus ridding themselves of their enemy, the hero causes his enchanted palace to be transported to where it was before, and he and his beautiful princess passed their days in joy and happiness.[2]

⟡

[2]It does not seem very likely that this Roman popular version of our nursery favourite was derived from any written source, since Miss Busk states that the old woman who told it to her was almost quite illiterate; moreover, the life of the magician being represented as depending upon a precious stone, to obtain which the hydra and other creatures within it have to be killed, is sufficient evidence of the oral transmission of the tale.—See Note at the end of this paper "Life Depending on Some Extraneous Object."

Aladdin's adventure with the African magician at the enchanted cave has its parallel also in the Meklenburg tale of the Blue Light (Grimm's German collection): A soldier, discharged from service and journeying homeward, obtains shelter one night in the hut of an old woman, who proves to be a witch, and compels him to dig her garden and chop a cartload of wood for his two-days' lodging. On the third day she exacts from him a solemn promise to get her the blue light which burned at the bottom of a well. She lets him down with a long rope, and having found the blue light, he makes a signal to be drawn up. When the witch had pulled him up near enough to be within her reach, "Give me the light," she says, "and I will take care of it;" but the soldier suspected treachery on the part of his hostess, and so he answered that he would not give her the light till she had drawn him quite out of the well. At this the old witch flew into a rage, and let him drop again to the bottom. There the poor fellow lay for a while in utter despair, till at length recollecting that his pipe happened to be in his pocket, and half full of tobacco, he thought he might as well smoke it out; so he lit it, and began to puff away. All of a sudden a black dwarf appeared before him; he had a hump on his back and a feather in his cap. "What do you want of me, soldier?" said he. "Nothing at all," replied the soldier. "I am bound to serve you in everything," quoth the dwarf, "as lord and master of the blue light." So the soldier first desired to be taken out of the well, which being done, he next ordered that the old witch should take his place in the well—and there she may be still; who knows? He then plundered the house of the wicked crone, and took away as much gold and silver as he could carry. The dwarf, before "taking himself off," tells him that if at any time he should want his services, he has only to light his pipe at the blue light, and he will instantly appear before him, ready to obey any commands. After a variety of adventures, the soldier marries the king's daughter.[3]

Most of the other versions, European as well as Asiatic, may be considered as belonging to the Thankful Beasts cycle of popular fictions—a circumstance which would seem to indicate that the tale is of Buddhist origin. The following is the substance of a Bohemian variant, given in M. Leger's collection of Slav Tales, No. 15:

[3]Mr Taylor, the translator of a selection of Grimm's Fairy Tales (Bohn's edition), says that this is also found in a collection of Hungarian stories, by Georg von Gaal, under the title of "The Wonderful Tobacco Pipe."

There was once a rich man, who had three sons, the eldest of whom he sent away to go the round of the world; and after an absence of three years he returned home superbly dressed, and a great feast was held in his honour. The same happened to the second son. But as for the youngest, who was called Jenik (or Johnny), he was despised as being weak-minded; for he did nothing but soil himself with the ashes of the stove.[4] Yet, seeing the success of his brothers, he, too, wished to go away and seek his fortune in the wide, wide world. "*You* go, noodle!" exclaimed his father. "What will you pick up on the way, I wonder?" Jenik persists, however, and at last is allowed to go—indeed they were all so glad to get rid of him that they actually gave him some money. In the course of his wanderings Jenik meets in succession crowds of people who were going to kill a dog, a cat, and a serpent. He intercedes for them, gets them as presents, and they follow him in single file: Johnny, dog, cat, and serpent. By-and-by the serpent says to him, "Come with me. In the autumn we serpents hide in our holes, and my king will be angry at my delay; but I'll tell him of the danger I was in when you rescued me. So do you ask for your reward the watch which hangs on the wall: by rubbing it you may have whatever you want." Jenik accompanies the serpent, and gets the enchanted watch.[5] He rubs it, and a sumptuous meal is before him in the twinkling of an eye. By the same means he gets a supper and a bed in the evening. Next day he returns home, expecting a feast from his father, but instead of this he is abused for coming back in rags. So Jenik takes once more to his favourite amusement of grubbing in the ashes. On the third day he has grown weary, and goes out. He rubs the magic watch, and gets a three-storey house, fine furniture, silver plate, and so forth. He invites his father, and relatives, and friends to a grand banquet. After the first course, he desires his father to go and fetch the king and his daughter, and for this purpose provides him with a coach-and-six. But the father will not enter so royal a carriage; he goes on foot, and invites the king and his daughter. Jenik, by means of his magic watch, has the road laid for six

---

[4]In fairy tales there are commonly three brothers, the youngest of whom ("Boots," as Dr Dasent aptly styles him in his Norse Tales) is invariably believed by the family to be a mere idiot, good for nothing but raking among the ashes—Cinderella is his female counterpart. Yet for him alone has Dame Fortune reserved her favours: he accomplishes tasks which his brothers have attempted in vain, and generally comes home with incalculable wealth, and a beautiful princess for his bride.

[5]"Montre Enchantée," according to Leger—a local modification, doubtless, of the talisman of Eastern fairy tales.

miles with polished marble, and a new house instantly erected, four storeys high, furnished finer than any royal palace. The king gives his daughter in marriage to Jenik, and there is a splendid wedding. But the princess does not love Jenik, and having wormed out of him the secret cause of his wealth, she steals the magic watch, rubs it, and off she goes in a coach-and-six to her father's, where, having provided herself with a number of servants, she then proceeds to the sea-shore. By the power of the watch she has a palace erected in the middle of the sea, connected with the land by a bridge, over which having passed into her palace, she causes it to disappear.

Meanwhile poor Jenik is mocked by everybody and without friends, excepting the cat and the dog whose lives he had saved, and with them for his companions he goes away—far, very far, on and on, through great deserts, till one day he sees two crows fly to a mountain, and a third comes up to him. So Jenik asks this crow why he is so late, since winter has come on; and the crow tells him that he flew over a palace in the sea, so beautiful that he could not but linger and admire it. Jenik then goes to the sea-shore and discovers the palace, which he knows to be that of the faithless princess. "Dog," says he, "you can swim; Puss, you are nimble—sit on doggie's head, and he'll carry you to that great house in the middle of the sea. Conceal thyself near the gate, and get secretly into the bed-room of the princess, and take away my watch." So the dog carries the cat through the sea to the palace, and when the princess saw the cat, she at once suspected what her business was, so she put the watch in a box in the cellar. But the cat gnaws a hole in the box, seizes the watch in her mouth, and waits the coming of the princess to see that all is safe. At last the door opens—crack! away puss bolts with the precious watch. When the cat seats herself on the dog's head to return to Jenik, she says to him, "Be careful not to speak to me during the passage." The dog keeps silent till near the shore, when he can't help asking, "Have you the watch?" The cat says nothing, afraid of dropping the watch. When they come to a rock, the dog asks again, "Have you the watch?" "Yes," says the cat, and so the watch falls into the sea.[6] Upon this follow mutual recriminations. Presently the cat grabs a passing fish, and is going to kill him, when he exclaims piteously, "I have nine children—spare the life of the father of a

---

[6] From the same cause was poor Hen-Sparrow drowned—see *ante*, p. 141. Truly saith the Preacher, "There is a time to keep silence, and a time to speak."

family!" Says the cat, "So be it; but you must get us our watch," which the fish does, and is then allowed to go away. When Jenik gets back his wonder-working watch, he rubs it, and lo! the wicked princess and her fine palace disappear beneath the waves; then he returns home, and he, and his dog, and his cat lived happily together the rest of their days.

In the 9th of M. Dozon's 'Contes Albanais,' the hero, having saved a serpent's life, is rewarded with a marvellous stone, which he rubs accidentally, like Aladdin with the ring and the lamp, when a black man appears, ready and able to do whatever the possessor of the talisman should desire or command. He immediately erects a magnificent palace, and the hero marries the king's daughter, of course. On the wedding-night, a Jew, who was among the guests, secretes himself in a closet, and, while the happy pair are sound asleep, steals the wonder-stone, with which he summons the black man, whom he commands to take the hero and lay him at the king's gate, and then convey the palace with the princess and all else in it to the sea-shore. In the morning the hero is discovered by the king's guards and thrown into prison. One day he happened to look out, and saw a man with a cat, which he bought, and fed with part of his own victuals till it grew to a great size, and burrowed a passage under the prison walls, by which the hero and his four-footed friend made good their escape. Arrived at the spot to which the Jew had caused the palace to be removed, the cat threatens to destroy a colony of mice unless they procure the talisman. One of their number is selected for the task. The Jew slept every night with the gem in his mouth, so the mouse tickles his nose with her tail, which causes the Jew to sneeze violently, and so the talisman falls out of his mouth.[7]

But more closely resembling the Bohemian version is a popular Greek tale in Hahn's collection: A poor boy saves the life of a snake which some other boys were bent upon killing. The snake, in requital of the lad's kindness, induces his father to give him a seal-ring. "If thou art in need of anything," says the old snake, "lick this seal, and a black man will appear. Command him to do whatever thou wilt, and he will perform it." The lad goes home and bids his mother look into the cup-

---

[7]Cf. "Three years without wages," in Dasent's 'Tales from the Fjeld,' where the animals are a puppy, a kitten, and a lizard.

board. He licks the ring, and sure enough a black man appears, is ordered to fill the cupboard with eatables, and when the old woman opens it, there they are. The mother and her son live on in this way for some time, until one day the lad says to her, "Go to the king and tell him he must give me his daughter in marriage." She naturally objects, but, as her son insists, at length goes to the king and delivers her message. The king laughs, and says, "If he is able to build a castle larger than mine, he shall have my daughter in marriage." The same night the lad licks the seal, and commands the black man to build the castle, and in a moment he finds himself in a castle far bigger and handsomer than the king's. Next morning the mother is sent again to require the king's performance of his promise. But the king says, "If he is able to pave the way from his castle to mine with gold, then he shall have my daughter." When the lad hears of this new condition, he once more summons the black man, who does what is required of him, and on the following morning the old woman announces to the king that the way from his castle to that of her son is now paved with gold. So the king at last consents to the marriage. All the princess requires of her father is a black man for her servant, and she is supplied with one. After the marriage the widow's son and the princess lived happily together, until he told her the secret of the ring, when she stole it from him while he was fast asleep, and ran off with the black man to an island on the sea. There, by the power of the ring, she has a castle built, in which she lives with her sable paramour. When the widow's son learns of his misfortune he is distracted with grief; but his cat tells him she will recover the ring if he will allow his dog to be her companion, to which he consents very willingly, as may be supposed. So the cat gets on the dog's back, and the dog swims with her over the sea to the castle of the princess. It appears the black man keeps the ring in his mouth, under his tongue. In spite of this, the cat obtains the ring, and after some adventures on the way back, restores it to her master, who immediately licks it, and at his command the castle is removed from the island to where he stands. He then kills the sable paramour, and lives thenceforth happily and contentedly with his princess.

We find the same fundamental outline, though with incidents from other folk-tales introduced, in a Danish member of the Aladdin cycle: A poor peasant, named Hans, who had one son and three daughters (triplets), received from an old man one day a wishing-box, on condition that he gets his three daughters when they are three years of age. Hans has a fine mansion built by the power of his magic box, gets coaches, horses, and servants galore, and lives in great style. At the end of three years the three little girls are taken away, no one knows where or by whom, in a grand carriage. The mother is inconsolable, and ere long dies of grief, and soon after her husband dies also. Hans is the heir of all their wealth and grandeur. But the stewards and servants rob him right and left, and in two years' time the king's bailiff comes and seizes everything, and poor Hans is turned adrift. He takes with him an old sheepskin cloak, which he thought suitable to his altered fortunes, and discovers in one of the pockets the very wishing-box that had, unknown to him, made his father a rich gentleman. Presently a great black fellow appears before him, and desires to know his commands. Hans wishes to have a fiddle, which when played upon causes everybody to dance. He then enters the service of a king as shepherd. The king's daughter is charmed by the music of the magic fiddle, and jestingly gives him her written promise that she would marry him. When Hans claims the hand of the princess, she laughs at him, and says it was all a joke. But the king insists upon her keeping her word—a written promise, too—and so they are married. Hans, by means of his wishing-box, gets a gold chariot with six horses, and a castle some two miles distant, where he and his royal bride live together for a time. But the princess is discontented, keeps her own apartments, and seldom speaks to her husband. So Hans goes out shooting every day, always carrying the wishing-box with him. By-and-by a young cavalier comes to the castle, and finds favour in the eyes of the princess. He is greatly puzzled at what he sees: riches and splendour reigned throughout the house; no stint in anything; and yet there was no visible source of income. He talks this over with the princess, but she couldn't account for it. So he advises her to worm out of her husband the secret of his wealth. This she does by assuming an affectionate demeanour towards him, and when she learns of the wishing-box, she persuades him to leave it in her care when he goes out shooting, lest he should lose such a precious treasure. Next morning the princess took leave of him very lovingly, and wanted to know when he would be coming home, as she would come and meet him. But no sooner was Hans gone than she sent for the young cavalier, showed him the box, and related to him all she had learned about its wonderful properties. They soon decided what to do. The cavalier took the box and tapped it, and out sprang the black man, saying, "What are my new lord's commands to-day?" "I command you to take this castle just as it stands and hang it by four golden chains in mid-air over the Red Sea." No sooner said than done. And of all the splendour and grandeur not a trace was left, as poor Hans found on his return in the evening. So he begins to wander about anywhere, and he sees a young woman washing linen, and speaks to her. She turns out to be one of his sisters, who is married to a man who is in the form of a bear all day, but for six hours of the night he is a man. Going farther, he finds a second of the sisters, who is married to a prince transformed into an eagle; and still farther, he discovers his third sister, who is married to a prince enchanted into the form of a huge fish. By the help of his brothers-in-law Hans gets back his box, causes the black man to destroy the princess and her paramour the young cavalier, and then to transport the castle to where it stood before. Finally, his enchanted brothers-in-law are restored to their human forms, and they all lived happily ever after.[8]

Although Galland's tale of Aladdin and his Lamp is not found in any Arabic text of 'The Thousand and One Nights,' yet a most interesting variant of it occurs in an inedited MS. text of that fascinating story-book, which was brought from the East—from Constantinople, it is believed—by Mr Wortley Montague, and is now in the Bodleian Library, Oxford. This story has been translated as follows, by Dr Jonathan Scott, in the sixth volume of his edition of the 'Arabian Nights,' published in 1811:

A fisherman's son having in company with his father caught a large fish, the latter proposed to present it to the sultan, in hopes of receiving a great reward. While he was gone home to fetch a basket, the son, moved by compassion, returned the fish into the water, and, fearful of his father's anger, fled from his country and repaired to a distant city, where he was entertained by a person as a servant. Strolling one day in the market, he saw a Jew purchase of a lad a cock at a very high price, and send it by a slave to his wife, with orders to keep it safely till his return home. The fisherman's son, supposing that as the Jew gave so great a price for the cock it must possess some extraordinary property, resolved to obtain

<hr>

[8] Abridged from Miss Jane Mulley's translation of the story from 'Danske Folkeäventyr," etc., by Professor Grundtvig, in the 'Folk-Lore Record, vol. iii. part 2, pp. 203–213.

it; and, accordingly, having bought two large fowls, carried them to the Jew's wife, whom he informed that her husband had sent him for the cock, which he had exchanged for the fowls.[9] She gave it him, and he, having retired, killed the bird, in whose entrails he found a magic ring, which being rubbed by his touch, a voice proceeded from it demanding what were the commands of its possessor, which should be immediately executed by the genii who were servants of the ring.

The fisherman's son was rejoiced at his good fortune, and while meditating what use he should make of his ring, passed by the sultan's palace, at the gates of which were suspended many human heads. He inquired the reason, and was informed that they were those of unfortunate princes, who, having failed to perform the conditions on which the sultan's daughter was offered them in marriage, had been put to death. Hoping to be more fortunate than they by the aid of his ring, he resolved to demand the princess' hand. He rubbed the ring; the voice asked his commands; upon which he required a rich dress, and it was instantly laid before him. He put it on, repaired to the palace, and being introduced to the sultan, demanded his daughter to wife. The sultan consented, on condition that his life should be forfeited unless he should remove a lofty and extensive mound of sand that lay on one side of the palace, which must be done before he could wed the princess. He accepted the condition, but required an interval of forty days to perform the task. This being agreed to, he took his leave, and having repaired to his lodging, rubbed the ring, commanded the genii to remove the mound, and erect on the space it covered a magnificent palace, and to furnish it suitably for a royal residence. In fifteen days the task was completed; he was wedded to the princess, and declared heir to the sultan.

In the meanwhile the Jew, whom he had tricked of the cock and the magic ring, resolved to travel in search of his lost treasure, and at last arrived at the city, where he was informed of the wonderful removal of the mound and the erection of the palace. He guessed that it must have

---

[9]This recalls a diverting Italian story, related in Leigh Hunt's 'Indicator,' of two rogues in Bologna, who having seen an old doctor of laws purchase a silver goblet and take it home, resolved to obtain possession of it for themselves. With this object they buy a fine lamprey, and one of them goes with it to the doctor's house, after they had observed him go out, and tells his good lady that he had been sent with it by the doctor, as he had invited some friends to dinner, and that she was to give the bearer his new silver goblet, in order to have his arms engraved on it. The rogues having got the cup, by another plausible story get back the lamprey—and the tale shook the shoulders in Bologna for many months after.

been done by means of the ring, to recover which he planned the following stratagem: Having disguised himself as a merchant, he repaired to the
palace and cried for sale valuable jewels. The princess, hearing him, sent
an attendant to examine them and inquire their price, when the Jew
asked in exchange only old rings. This being told to the princess, she recollected that her husband kept an old shabby-looking ring in his writing-
stand, and, he being asleep, she took it out and sent it to the Jew, who,
knowing it to be the one he had so long sought for, eagerly gave for it all
the jewels in his basket.[10] He retired with his prize, and having rubbed the
ring, commanded the genii to convey the palace and all its inhabitants,
excepting the fisherman's son, into a distant desert island, which was
done instantly.

The fisherman's son, on awaking in the morning, found himself lying
on the mound of sand, which had reoccupied its old spot. He arose, and
in alarm lest the sultan should put him to death in revenge for the loss of
his daughter, fled to another kingdom as quickly as possible. Here he
endured a disconsolate life, subsisting on the sale of some jewels which
he happened to have upon his dress at his flight. Wandering one day
through a town, a man offered him for sale a dog, a cat, and a rat, which
he purchased and kept, diverting his melancholy with their tricks and
uncommon playfulness together. These seeming animals proved to be
magicians, who, in return for his kindness, agreed to recover for their
master his lost prize, and informed him of their intention. He warmly
thanked them, and they all set out in search of the palace, the ring, and
the princess. At length they reached the shore of the ocean, after much
travel, and descried the island on which the palace stood, when the dog
swam over, carrying on his back the cat and the rat. Being landed, they
proceeded to the palace, when the rat entered, and perceived the Jew
asleep upon a sofa, with the ring laid before him, which he seized in his

---

[10]This familiar Aladdin-incident reappears in an Italian story, cited by Mr H. C. Coote, in
'Folk-Lore Record,' vol. iii. part 2, p. 189: A princess, after agreeing to surrender her young
daughter to a magician, regrets her promise and shuts her up in the palace, not permitting her
ever to go out. The magician, thus baffled, has recourse to the following expedient—to use
the words of the tale itself: "The magician was not a magician for nothing. He pretended to
be a hawker, and went through the streets crying out, 'Women, women, who will exchange
rings of iron for rings of silver?' The princess' maids all ran down-stairs. The magician prof-
ited by the opportunity, carried off the young princess, and took her away to an enchanted
palace."—"La Fanciulla e il Mago": De Gubernatis' collection, 'Novelline di Santo Stefano di
"Calcenaia,'" p. 47.

mouth and then returned to his companions. They began to cross the sea as before; but when about half-way over, the dog expressed a wish to carry the ring in his mouth. The rat refused, lest he should drop it; but the dog threatened, unless he would give it to him, to dive and drown them both in the sea. The rat, alarmed for his life, complied with his demand; but the dog missed his aim in snatching at the ring, which fell into the ocean. They landed, and informed the fisherman's son of his loss; upon which he, in despair, would have drowned himself, when suddenly a great fish, with the ring in his mouth, swam close to shore, and having dropped it within reach of the desperate youth, miraculously exclaimed, "I am the fish which you released from captivity, and thus reward you for your generosity." The fisherman's son, overjoyed, returned to his father-in-law's capital, and at night, rubbing the ring, commanded the genii to convey the palace to its old site. This being done in an instant, he entered the palace and seized the Jew, whom he caused to be cast alive into a burning pile, in which he was consumed. From this period he lived happily with his princess, and on the death of the sultan succeeded to his dominions.

It will be observed that this Turco-Arabian form of the story comprises some elements of Galland's version and also of those in which grateful animals recover the stolen talisman. Through the Ottomans the story seems to have spread into Greece and Albania, while it was probably brought to Northern Europe by the Mongolians, since it forms one of the Relations of Siddhí Kúr:

A youth sets out on a trading expedition with three bales of merchandise, which he parts with to save a mouse, a young ape, and a young bear from being tortured by parties of boys. These animals henceforward become his attached friends, and one of them procures for him a talisman, or wishing-stone, from the bottom of a river, where he had seen it glittering. The youth wishes that, by virtue of the talisman, he might find in the morning a flourishing city in the plain where he had pitched his tent, and in the midst of the city a shining palace, with plenty of horses, food, and all good things. When he awakes, he finds everything that he had wished for, and lives there for a time very happily, until a caravan of merchants come to the district. The leader of the merchants expressed his astonishment at seeing a city and a palace where last year was nothing but a desert, when the youth explained all to him, and showed him the talisman, by means of which these wonders had been performed. Perceiving the guileless nature of the youth, the chief of the caravan offered him all his own and his fellow-merchants' goods, money, and jewels, in exchange for the talisman, which he accepted, and behold! next morning the city, and the palace, and all therein had vanished, and the youth finds himself lying on a barren island. His four-footed companions recover the talisman in this wise: Having ascertained where the merchants were residing, they proceed thither. The mouse creeps through the keyhole into the room where the chief of the merchants is asleep, and finds the talisman guarded by two fierce cats, chained close to it. He returns and relates this to his companions, and, acting on the advice of the ape, goes in again, and gnaws the sleeper's hair, which annoyed him so much that he causes the cats to be chained to his pillow the next night, thus leaving the talisman unguarded; and, aided by the ape outside, the mouse contrives to drag it through the keyhole and restore it to the despairing youth.

We have thus traced the tale of Aladdin and his Wonderful Lamp through several European versions to a Mongolian form; but it has not, I think, been hitherto pointed out that a very similar fiction is also current in Southern India. This I am now enabled to do, through the courtesy of my friend Pandit S. M. Natésa Sástrí, of the Government Archæological Survey, Madras, who has favoured me with an early copy of his translation of the Tamil romance, 'Madana Kámarája Kadai,' from the second story of which I present the following abstract:

Alakésa, king of Alakápurí, dying prematurely, left behind him a young son and a very good wife, with whom he had lived happily. The king's younger brother acted as regent during the minority of his little nephew; but after a time, fired by ambition, he turned the young prince and his mother adrift. The ex-queen goes to her father's house and obtains a hundred pagodas, which she gives to her son, telling him to lay the money out in some sort of goods for sale, and thus make his own livelihood. The youth sets off, and meets a farmer with a cat and her kittens in a gunny-bag, which he means to get rid of, as they were a nuisance. Inquiring the price of the kittens, he is told by the unprincipled husbandman, perceiving his simplicity, that he wants 500 pagodas; but when the youth says that he has only 100, he lets him have one kitten for the money, "as a great bargain." The lad returns home, and shows his purchase to his mother, who is vexed at his stupidity, but goes back to her father and gets another 100 pagodas, which she gives her son, cautioning him to be more careful this time. He goes away once more, and meets with a snake-charmer carrying two baskets full of snakes suspended at the ends of a long bamboo rod across his shoulders. Among these snakes was the son of Adisésha, the king of the serpents, who had left his palace in the lower regions and come to see the world, and had been captured by the snake-charmer. The simple-minded lad purchases the snake-prince with his second 100 pagodas, and his mother is deeply grieved to find how he has again thrown away his money. After this he goes about begging from door to door, sharing his food with the cat and the serpent, until his mother bids him get rid of the serpent, as it is the enemy of mankind. So he takes the serpent into a wood, and explains to him that he must abandon him in obedience to his mother's order. The snake invites his benefactor to his father's palace, and Adisésha, the king of the snakes, gives him a ring, which he has only to put on his finger, and extolling Paramésvara, think of what he wants, and it will be instantly before him.

Highly delighted with his treasure, the young prince went into a thick jungle, and thinking of the deity Paramésvara, the supreme lord of the world, he exclaimed, "May this forest to a distance of 500 *kós* round about me, with all things in it, excepting myself, be burnt to ashes! May those people who protected me during my misfortunes come here and be my subjects! May there rise here dwellings to accommodate them with their families! May they have fields, gardens, pleasure-villas, and everything that they had in their own towns! May broad rivers run throughout the year in this country! May my mother and cat join me here! May I have a palace for my own use, a minister, a commander, and every other officer of a royal household! And may this kingdom be known as Nishadadésa!" No sooner had he uttered these words than the whole forest was burnt down with everything therein, except himself. The people who protected him, his mother, and his cat appeared before him. Palaces, mansions, pleasure-villas, temples, tanks, and all other requisites sprang up. Rivers began to flow through the land. And thus, by the power of the ring which he obtained from Adisésha, in a moment a thick jungle was converted into a populous country. Those who, taking pity on the prince, had formerly supplied him with food, were now very glad to become his subjects, and he was equally pleased to be their sovereign. His mother, who had been so much grieved at his stupidity in having bought a snake for 100 pagodas, now thanked the gods for his good fortune.

One moonlight night, after some years of peace and plenty and prosperity, the prince, who was now in the prime of youthful manhood, was lying awake, and thought by the power of his ring as to whom Paramésvara designed for his consort. Closing his eyes for an instant in deep contemplation, he found that at a distance of 500 *kós* from his city there was another called Svarnapurí, ruled over by a king named Svarnésa, and that his daughter was destined to be his queen-consort. So he said, "May that princess be lifted with her couch, without disturbing her slumber, and brought here immediately!" And lo! the couch descended and the princess was before him. The prince touched her gently, and she opened her eyes, and discovered that she had been mysteriously transported from her own chamber into another country. She was very prudent as well as intelligent, so she said to the prince that she was convinced she was destined for his wife, and begged him to defer their nuptials for a few days, in order that she should communicate the matter to her father. Then kissing her future lord, she stood before him respectfully, as if waiting his orders. The prince, highly gratified with the prudent advice of the young lady, sent her back on her couch to her own chamber in her native country by the power of his ring. Next day the prince despatched ambassadors to Svarnapurí, requesting the hand of his daughter in marriage, and after all preliminaries had been properly arranged, the nuptials were celebrated with unexampled splendour.

Now the princess was very fond of sea-bathing, so she desired her lord to construct an underground passage from her bed-chamber to the seashore, which was at once accomplished by the power of the ring, and the princess always used this secret passage when she went to take her bath. One morning after she had bathed a hair fell from her head, and, collecting itself into a ball by the dashing of the waves, was lying on the shore. The king of Kochchi [*i.e.*, Cochin] chanced to ride past, and perceived the hair-ball. He took it up and examined it, and unrolling it found it to consist of a single hair ten *bhágams*[11] long. By his knowledge of the art of discovering the beauty and nature of human beings from anything belonging to them, the king of Kochchi at once concluded that the woman from whose head the hair had fallen must be a paragon of

[11] A *bhága* is equal to two yards.

beauty, and he resolved to obtain her as his wife.[12] He offered a great reward to any person who should accomplish his desire. An old double-bent woman undertook the task, and ascertaining the place where the hair was discovered, she proceeded thither. Collecting some pieces of wood, she heaped them in a pile, and setting fire to it, sat down and began to weep. The queen of Nishada came, as was her custom, for her morning bath. Hearing a woman crying, she was greatly affected, and looking about her, perceived the old trot mourning over the funeral pile, and ran to console her. The old woman, when the beautiful princess drew near, threw her arms round her neck and exclaimed, "My daughter, you left me in my old age but a few hours ago for the other world. I am astonished to see that you have returned again!" These words, of course, excited the queen's pity, and thinking that the poor woman had lost a daughter of her age and had mistaken her for that daughter, she consoled her with appropriate words. The queen then inquired into her history. "I had an only daughter," replied the old woman; "and as we were going to a neighbouring village she suddenly died, and hence my sorrow." So the queen took her to the palace, and caused a room to be prepared for her use. The old hag pretended to be devoted to the queen and all the other female members of the palace; and even Nishadésa liked her, and believed her to be a woman of great piety and virtue. One day, when it was not the season for mango-fruits, the old woman earnestly begged the queen to gratify her by procuring one, and on the queen's acquainting her royal consort of this request, he at once said aloud in the crone's presence, "Let there be a mango-fruit by the power of this ring," when it appeared; and she readily understood that if she could but get the ring into her pos-

[12] An analogous incident is related in No. 4 of the Rev. Lal Bahari Day's 'Folk-Tales of Bengal': "The first day they went to bathe, one of [Princess] Keshavati's hairs came off, and as it is the custom with women never to throw away a hair unaccompanied with something else, she tied the hair to a shell which was floating on the water, after which they returned home. In the meantime the shell with the hair tied to it floated down the stream, and in course of time reached the *ghat* [or bathing-place] at which Sahasra Dal and his companions were in the habit of performing their ablutions. The shell passed by when Sahasra Dal and his friends were bathing; and he seeing it at some distance said to them, 'Whoever succeeds in catching hold of yonder shell shall be rewarded with a hundred rupees.' They all swam towards it, and Sahasra Dal, being the fleetest swimmer, got it. On examining it he found a hair tied to it. But such a hair! It was exactly seven cubits long. 'The owner of this hair must be a remarkable woman, and I must see her,' said Sahasra Dal, and he went home from the river in pensive mood."

session, it would be an easy matter to secure the queen for the king of Kochchi. So, with this design, she pretended, a day or two afterwards, to have a severe headache. All sorts of remedies were applied, but without effect. At last she called the queen to her side and said, "My daughter, there is only one remedy that can possibly cure my headache and save my life, and that is your husband's ring. Get that for me, and I shall return it after wearing it on my finger for a few seconds." The queen procures the ring and takes it to the infamous old hag, who had no sooner put it on her finger than she ascended into the sky and disappeared, leaving the queen in a state of utter despair.

The old woman reached Kochchi in the twinkling of an eye, and having placed the ring before the king and received the promised reward, she told him that if he thought of the lady he admired, with the ring on his finger, he should have her by his side instantly. As the king was dying for love, he thought of the lady; and lo! the queen of Nishada, who was pining away in sorrow for the loss of the ring, was suddenly lifted into the sky and placed before him. Delighted at the power of the ring, he then desired that the king of Nishada should become mad, and that his kingdom should be burnt to ashes, both of which great misfortunes took place accordingly. But the unhappy queen obtained leave of the king of Kochchi to keep an eight-days' fast before the celebration of their nuptials, during which she should distribute money and food to the poor. Thousands flocked daily to the palace, amongst whom came her own husband, formerly king of Nishada, now a poor lunatic, wandering about the land with his cat, and begging his bread. The queen observed him take his seat with other beggars; and when the leaves were spread out (to serve as plates), the mad king fought with the leaf-spreader to have one laid also before his cat. She remonstrated with the leaf-spreader on his refusal to give food to the cat, which had life as well as men; and her sorrow knew no bounds to see her husband sitting among beggars voraciously eating the food placed before him; and when he had satisfied his hunger he lay down and slept, while his faithful cat perched upon his bosom.

Some refuse-leaves had been thrown near the spot where the king of Nishada slept, and a number of rats began to eat them. Among these was a stout rat, who, by his prominent appearance and the respect paid to him by the others, was evidently the rat-king. The cat, who was pitying his master all the while, and wished to try his best to reinstate him in his kingdom, sprang on the rat-rája, and seizing him by the neck, spoke to him thus: "If you are able to do me a service which I require, I will set you at liberty. My master, who lies there asleep, had a ring which is now in the possession of the king of this country. If you do not bring it, I shall certainly eat you." The rat promised to procure the ring, and sent his subjects to examine the king's treasure-chests. To their great joy, they found the ring in a box near which the king of Kochchi was himself sleeping, and brought it to the cat, who then liberated the rat-rája. The cat, having awoke his master by placing the ring on his breast, related how it had been lost and recovered; and when the king put the ring on his finger, behold! his senses were restored to him. Wishing himself and his queen back in Nishada, and everything to be as it was before, he then wished Kochchi to become insane and his kingdom destroyed, and all these things were accomplished. Thus reclaiming every good thing which he had lost by means of his faithful cat, the king reigned many years over his loyal subjects.

The story of Aladdin and his Lamp and three or four others in Galland's ' Mille et une Nuits' were, on the first publication of that work, generally considered as his own inventions; and when in after-years several Arabic texts of the 'Elf Layla wa Layla' preserved in the great European libraries were examined and none of these tales discovered in any of them, it was almost concluded that they were not of Asiatic extraction. Yet Galland was surely the last man to attempt such an imposture, even had he possessed the ability—which there is no reason to suppose—for constructing from his own fancy tales at least equal to those which are admitted to be of Arabian composition; and indeed his literary integrity is now satisfactorily vindicated. Mr H. C. Coote, in an interesting paper on "The Sources of some of M. Galland's Tales," published in the 'Folk-Lore Record,' vol. iii. part 2, has shown that the chief incidents of the stories of Aladdin, Ali Baba, Prince Ahmed, and the Two Envious Sisters were known in Italy before Galland's work appeared, and is of the opinion that the equivalents of these four tales found their way into Italy through Byzantine Greece, European and Asiatic, but that Galland probably heard them at Constantinople and Smyrna, where he sojourned many years. It does not appear that Mr Coote knew of the Turco-Arabian (or Turco-Egyptian) version presented in the story, cited in the present paper, of the Fisherman's Son, or of the Mongolian form, in both of which the fundamental outlines are similar to several European variants, more especially the incident of the recovery of the talisman by grateful animals, which Galland may have thought advisable to modify to suit the taste of his readers. So far indeed was Galland from inventing these four stories, that they all occur in Asiatic collections, and a fifth, Zeyn el-Asnám, my learned friend Mr E. J. W. Gibb informs me he has found in a Turkish story-book, by 'Alí 'Azíz.

NOTE.

LIFE DEPENDING ON SOME EXTRANEOUS OBJECT (p. 150)

This is a characteristic of many folk-tales all over the world, and some of our comparative mythologists have attempted to explain its signification with very considerable ingenuity.[13] Miss Busk, in a note on the death of the wizard in her story of Cajusse, cites a parallel from a Hungarian tale, in which the hero, István (or Stephen), after a series of strange adventures, is returning home with his bride, a king's daughter, and having drawn the king of the dwarfs out of a ditch, is himself thrust into it by the ungrateful monster, who then decamps with the princess. István sets out to recover his bride. He meets with a frog whose life he had saved, and who gives him important aid, and leads him through further heroic adventures, in which he renders services to other animals, who conduct him to the palace of the dwarf-king. Here exactly the same scene occurs between István and his bride as between Cajusse and the sultan's daughter, and they lay the same plan. But the dwarf-king is more astute than the magician, for he at first tells her that his life's safety lies in his sceptre, on which she persuades him to give her the sceptre, that she may take care of it, but really intending to give it to István. When he sees her so anxious for his safety, he tells her it is not in his sceptre; but he does not yet tell the truth, for he next says it is in the royal mantle, and then in the crown. Ultimately he confides to her that his life is in a golden cockchafer, inside a golden cock, inside a golden sheep, inside a golden stag, in the 99th island. She communicates all this to István, who overcomes these golden animals by the help of the beasts he had lately succoured, and thus recovers his bride.

[13] See Cox's 'Aryan Mythology,' vol. ii. pp. 36, 330; De Gubernatis' 'Zoological Mythology,' vol. i. p. 168; and an able paper in the 'Folk-Lore Journal,' 1884, vol. ii. p. 302, on "The Philosophy of Punchkin," by Mr Edward Clodd.

In the Russian story of Koshchei the Deathless (Mr Ralston's collection), Prince Ivan's mother says to him, "Whereabouts is your 'death,' O Koshchei?" He answers, "My death is in such and such a place. There stands an oak, and under the oak is a casket, and in the casket is a hare, and in the hare is a duck, and in the duck is an egg, and the egg is my death." By-and-by Prince Ivan went to look for Koshchei's death. He went on his way a long time without eating or drinking. At last he felt mortally hungry, and thought, "If only something would come my way." Suddenly there appeared a young wolf, and he determined to kill it. But out of a hole sprang the she-wolf and said, "Don't hurt my little one, and I'll do you a good turn." Says Prince Ivan, "Very good," and he let the young wolf go. After this he befriends in succession a crow and a pike, and these grateful animals help him to get Koshchei's "death."—In another version Koshchei attempts to deceive his fair captive by pretending that his death resides in a besom or in a fence, both of which she adorns with gold in token of her love. Then he confesses that his death really lies in an egg, inside a duck, inside a log, which is floating on the sea.[14]

So, too, in one of Campbell's 'Tales of the West Highlands,' there is a flag-stone under the threshold, a wether is under the flagstone, in the wether is a duck, in the duck an egg, and in the egg is the giant's soul. And in Dasent's 'Norse Tales' the princess learns from the giant who had no heart in his body, that "far, far away, in a lake lies an island, in that island is a church, in that church is a well, in that well a duck is swimming, in that duck is an egg, and in that egg is my heart, you darling!"

The same notion occurs, with local modifications, in a great number of Hindú folk-tales. To cite a few examples: In Miss Frere's 'Old Deccan Days' (story of Punchkin), a magician says, "Far, far away, hundreds of thousands of miles from this, there lies a desolate country covered with jungle. In the midst of the jungle grows a circle of palm-trees, and in the centre of the circle stand six chattís full of water, piled one above another. Below the sixth chattí is a small cage, which contains a little green parrot. On the life of that parrot depends my life, and if the parrot is killed I must die." A rákshasa, in another story, says, "Sixteen miles away from this place is a tree; round the tree are tigers and bears and scorpions and snakes; on the top of the tree is a great flat snake; on the snake's

---

[14]Cf. Delilah's attempts to wheedle out of Samson the secret of his strength: how he told her, first, that if bound with seven green withs, he should be weak and be as another man; next, if he were bound with new ropes; then, if the seven locks of his head were fastened to the pin of the weaving-beam; and how he confessed at last the fact that if his head were shaven his strength should depart.—Book of Judges, xvi. 4–20.

head is a little cage; in that cage is a bird; and my soul is in that bird." In Miss Stokes' 'Indian Fairy Tales' the daughter of a demon tells a king's son, "On the other side of the sea is a great tree; in that tree is a nest; in that nest is a maina [hill-starling]; and if one kills that maina, my father will die." In No. 1 of the Rev. Lal Bahari Day's 'Folk-Tales of Bengal' the life of a young prince is bound up, from his birth, in that of a *boal* fish, which is in a tank in front of the palace. In the heart of the fish is a small box of wood, in the box is a necklace of gold, and in that necklace is the prince's life. And in No. 4 a captive princess one night feigns anxiety as to what she shall do when her "friend" the rákshasi (female demon) shall die, to which she responds that "in a tank close by, deep down in the water, is a crystal pillar, on the top of which are two bees. If any human being can dive into the water and bring up these two bees in one breath, and destroy them so that not a drop of their blood falls to the ground, then we rákshasas shall certainly die; but if a single drop of their blood falls to the ground, then from it will start up a thousand rákshasas." In a Kashmírí tale, entitled "The Shipwrecked Prince," contributed by the Rev. J. Hinton Knowles to the 'Indian Antiquary' for September 1885 (p. 250), an ogre confides to his fair captive that there is in a certain tree a honeycomb, and that his life is in the queen-bee there. In his cave is a stool which would convey any one who sat upon it to the honeycomb (or anywhere else), but the bees are so fierce that they would sting to death the person who should attempt to seize their queen-bee; so the ogre considered himself as quite safe.

In the Arabian story of Sayf el-Muluk and Badía el-Jamál, the princess of Hind asks the genii who has stolen her where his soul abides, in order that she might watch over it, and he tells her that it is in the crop of a sparrow; the sparrow is shut up in a box; the box is in a casket, which is within seven other caskets, and these again are within seven chests, laid in an alabastrine coffer, which is buried in the margin of the earth encircling the sea.

But the life of the demon or giant Mairávana, who carried off and confined Ráma and Lakshmana, depended on no less than five separate objects. According to a Telegu version of the story (the Sanskrit original of which is said to form a part of the 'Jaimini Bhárata'), Hanumán, the monkey-deity, having killed all the giant's guards and carried the two princes out of the castle, set to work to demolish the fortifications, which brought Mairávana against him. He overthrew but could not kill the giant, and on marvelling at the cause, is informed by Dordandi (the giant's sister) that the five vital airs of the giant are on a mountain 60,000 *kós* remote, in the form of five black bees. Hanumán immediately travels thither, and catches and kills the bees, on which Mairávana perishes.[15]

The comparatively novel theory—which is entertained by Sir R. F. Burton and other eminent European scholars—that Egypt was the centre of the world's civilisation, and that even the most ancient Hindú apologues and fictions were derived, mediately or immediately, from that country, seems to be supported to some extent by the circumstance that the notion of an individual's heart existing apart from his body is found in an Egyptian romance, written 3000 years ago, to which reference has already been made in my introductory chapter (pp. liv, lv), and of which an account is furnished, in a paper on Hieratic Papyri, by Mr C. W. Goodman, in 'Cambridge Essays,' 1858: Satú tells his brother Anapú that he will take his heart and place it in the flowers of an acacia-tree. If at some future time the brother desires to renew communication with him, he must search for his heart, and, when found, place it in a vessel containing wine or some other liquor, with certain ceremonies. Satú will then appear to him, and answer any questions he may put. . . . Ra, the sun-god, says to Núm, the creator, "Wilt thou not make a woman for Satú, that he may not remain alone?"[16] Núm accedes to this request, and forms for him a consort more beauteous than all the women in Egypt, for all the gods endow her with gifts. He takes the beautiful creature to his house, and she remains at home while he employs himself industriously in hunting. One day he says to her, "When thou goest out to walk, beware lest the river seize thee, for I could not deliver thee, being a woman even as thou art [he had been emasculated himself, when his brother sought to slay him on a false accusation of his (Anapú's) wife]; for my heart is among the flowers of the acacia." He then explains his history to her. The daughter of the gods loses no time in going to the acacia-tree to search for her husband's heart, when she perceives the river overflowing his banks and advancing towards her. A lock of her richly perfumed hair floats down the river as she escapes, and it is taken to the king of Egypt, who seeks for her far and wide, as did another Egyptian king, Psammeticus, according to Ælian, for Rhodope (the prototype of Cinderella), whose shoe was carried off by an eagle while she bathed, and dropped into his lap. When the daughter of the gods is at length discovered to be the owner of the tress of perfumed hair, and brought before the king, she at once induces him to cut down the acacia-tree in order to get rid of her husband Satú; then the heart falls and Satú dies. He is, however, afterwards resuscitated, by his brother Anapú finding his heart and steeping it, as he had been instructed, in

[15]'Descriptive Catalogue of the Mackenzie MSS., &c.,' by H. H. Wilson; vol. i. p. 329.

[16]Cf. Gen. ii. 18: "It is not good that the man should be alone; I will make him an help meet for him."

a vessel full of wine. The resemblance between the incident of the tress of per-fumed hair in this oldest of fairy tales and that of the hair-ball in the Tamil member of the Aladdin-cycle, cited in the foregoing paper (p. 163), is proba-bly not merely fortuitous.[17]

[17]The "life-trees," etc., which figure in many folk-tales (see *ante,* p. 59) are evidently near akin to the idea exemplified in the ancient Egyptian story and its derivatives.

♈ THE HUNCHBACK
AND THE FAIRIES ♈

IT is well known that fairies are (or rather were, for, alas! they are no more) a very merry but capricious race of beings: well was it for such as found favour in their sight—woe to those who in any way offended them! In proof of this there is an amusing story in Thoms' 'Lays and Legends of France,' to the following effect: Once upon a time a hunchback minstrel, returning from a merry-making, fell asleep on fairy-ground, and awaking at midnight he discovered a large party of fairies disporting themselves, so he played to them on his instrument, while they danced to their hearts' content. Before they departed, the fairies asked the minstrel to name his wish, and it would be gratified, as a reward for his excellent music. He requested that his hump should be removed, which was done instantly, and he returned to his village straight in body, without the ugly protuber-ance on his back. One of his neighbours, a surly fellow, who had also a hump, became envious of his good luck, and on learning how he had got rid of his hump, secretly went at night to the spot where the fairies were wont to dance. When they discovered him, they desired him to give them some music, but this he could not do; so, by way of revenge, they took the minstrel's hump, and clapped it on that of the ill-natured fellow, who was ever after the laughing-stock of his townsmen.

A different form of this story is given in Grimm's 'Kinder und Haus Märchen': One evening a tailor and a hunchbacked blacksmith were return-ing from a town where they had been working at their respective trades. As night came on, they saw the sun setting behind the hills, and presently, as the moon rose, came the sound of distant music, which grew more distinct as they advanced on their way. The tones were somewhat unearthly, but so charming that they forgot their fatigue, and went forward with rapid steps. After walking some little distance they reached the hill-side, and caught sight of a crowd of little men and women, holding each other's hands and dancing merrily in a circle to the strange music they had heard. In the cen-tre was a little old man, with a coat of many colours, and a snow-white beard spreading over his breast. The hunchbacked blacksmith, being a bold fellow, stepped in to take a share in the merriment; but the tailor at first held back, the ring again closed, and the pixies resumed their dancing. After they had ended, the old man took a knife, sharpened it on a stone, and looked at the strangers so that they trembled. He then seized the smith, and with one stroke shaved his hair and beard clean off, and afterwards treated the tailor in the same manner. Then he slapped them on the shoulder, and said they had done wisely not to resist; and pointing to a heap of coals, signed to fill their pockets. Both did so, and took leave of the pixies; and as they passed through a valley they heard the hour of midnight tolled from the church tower, upon which the music ceased, and the pixies disappeared. The travellers put up at a wayside inn, where they had to be content with a bundle of straw for a bed, and in the morning they discovered their pockets filled with gold in place of the coals they had taken the preceding night, and, not less wonderful, their hair and beards were grown again. The smith, who was a very avaricious man, and had filled both his pockets, was not content, but proposed to go again the next night; the tailor, however, was quite satisfied with what he had got from the pixies, but consented to wait for his companion at the inn. As night drew on, the smith, having provided himself with two large sacks, went to the meadow where the pixies had held their revels the previous night, and found the same company assembled. The old pixie, who knew the sort of fellow he had to do with, signed to him to take as much coals as he pleased, so the smith filled his two sacks, and returned to the inn. But in the morning he found he had nothing save coals; his hair and beard were permanently removed; the hump on his back had grown larger; and he had ever afterwards to wear a cap to cover his bald head.

In an Italian version entitled "I due Fratelli Gobbi," the Two Hunchbacked Brothers, given by Miss Busk in her 'Folk-Lore of Rome,' the magic stick reappears for the hero's benefit: There was once a man, who had one son, who married a widow, who had also one son, and both were hunchbacks. The wife took very good care of her own son, but the son of her husband she used to put to hard work, and gave him scarcely anything to eat. Her son, too, used to follow her example, and sadly ill-used his stepbrother. After ill-treating him for a long time, she at length sent him away from the house altogether. The poor little hunchback wandered without knowing whither to go. On, on he went, till he came to a lonely hut on a wide moor. At his approach a whole host of little hunchbacks came out and danced round him, chanting plaintively—

> Sabbato!
> Domenica! [1]

[1] Saturday, Sunday.

a great number of times. At last our little hunchback felt his courage stirred, and, taking up the note of their chant, chimed in with—

Lunedi! [2]

Instantly the dancing ceased: all the hunchbacked dwarfs became full-grown, well-formed men, and, what was better still, his own hump was gone too, and he felt that he also was a well-grown lad. "Good people," said he, "I thank you much for ridding me of my hump, and making me a well-grown lad. Give me some work to do among you, and let me live with you." But the chief of the strange people answered him and said, "This favour we owe to you, and you are not indebted to us; for it was your chiming in with the right word on the right note that destroyed the spell that held us all. And in testimony of our gratitude we give you this little wand, and you will not need to work as you did formerly. Go back and live at home, and if any one beats you as heretofore, you have only to say to it, 'At them, good stick!' and you will see what it will do for you." So the youth goes home again, and when his step-mother learnt how he had got rid of his hump, she sent her own son to the hut of the strange folk. When he saw a party of hunchbacked dwarfs dancing and chanting—

Sabbato!
Domenica!
Lunedi!

he chanted, all out of tune,

Martedi! [3]

and was rewarded with a drubbing and a hump on his breast, besides the one he already had on his back. Coming home, his mother, seeing his plight, sets upon her step-son; but he takes his magic stick and cries, "At 'em, good stick!" and the old woman gets a sound rib-roasting, until she begs for mercy; and ever after this he lived at home in perfect peace. [4]

There is a version from the south of Ireland which presents a very close analogy to the main incidents in the foregoing Italian story: In olden times

[2] Monday.
[3] Tuesday.
[4] A Tuscan version given by Mr Crane in his 'Italian Popular Tales,' p. 103, agrees generally with the above: there is, however, no step-mother; the two hunchbacks reside together after the catastrophe; and the magic stick does not figure in the story.

there lived a poor little hunchback, who was nicknamed lusmore, from his always wearing a sprig of the fairy-cap, or lusmore (the foxglove), in his straw hat. One evening he was returning from the town of Cahir towards Cappagh, and it was quite dark when he came to the old moat of Knock-grafton. Tired and weary, he sat down under the moat to rest himself, and began looking mournfully upon the moon. Presently there rose a wild stream of unearthly melody: he listened, and thought he had never heard such ravishing music before. It was like the sound of many voices, each mingling and blending with the other so strangely that they seemed to be one, though all singing different strains, and these were the words of the song:

> Da Luan,
> Da Mort,
> Da Luan,
> Da Mort,
> Da Luan,
> Da Mort;[5]

when there would be a moment's pause, and then the sound of melody went on again. Lusmore listened attentively, scarcely drawing his breath lest he should lose the slightest note. He now plainly perceived that the singing was within the moat, and though at first it had charmed him so much, he began to get tired of hearing the same round, sung over and over so often without any change; so, availing himself of the pause when

> Da Luan,
> Da Mort,

had been sung three times, he took up the tune and raised it with the words,

> Augus da Cadine;[6]

and then went on singing with the voices inside of the moat,

> Da Luan,
> Da Mort;

finishing the melody, when the pause again came, with

> Augus da Cadine.

The fairies within Knockgrafton—for the song was a fairy melody—when

---

[5]Monday, Tuesday.
[6]And Wednesday.

they heard this addition to their tune, were so much delighted, that with instant resolve it was determined to bring the mortal amongst them whose musical skill so far exceeded theirs, and little Lusmore was conveyed into their company with the eddying speed of a whirlwind. The greatest honour was paid him, for he was put above all the musicians, and he had servants to wait on him, and everything to his heart's content. By-and-by Lusmore saw the fairies engaged in consultation, and he felt frightened, in spite of their civility, till one of them stepped forward and said—

> "Lusmore! Lusmore!
> Doubt not, nor deplore;
> For the hump which you bore
> On your back is no more:
> Look down on the floor,
> And view it, Lusmore!"

When these words were said, poor little Lusmore felt himself so happy and so light, that he thought he could have bounded at one jump over the moon; and he saw, with inexpressible pleasure, his hump tumble from his shoulders to the ground. At last he fell into a sound sleep, and when he awoke he found it was broad daylight, the sun shining brightly and the birds singing merrily, and that he was lying at the foot of the moat of Knockgrafton, with the cows and sheep grazing peacefully about him. He put his hand behind to feel for his hump, but it was gone, sure enough, and he had now become a well-shaped, dapper little fellow: moreover, he was clothed in a bran-new suit, doubtless the gift of the fairies. When he returned to Cappagh, not a soul knew him at first, such was the alteration in his person. The story soon spread far and wide, and one day an old woman came up to him as he sat by his cabin door, and told him that the son of her gossip had got a great hump on his back, and she had come to learn the charm that could effect its removal. Lusmore gave her all particulars, which she duly communicated to her gossip's hunchbacked son, a peevish and cunning creature, whose name was Jack Madden. He was driven by his friends in a car, and just at nightfall they left him under the old moat of Knockgrafton. Jack Madden had not sat there long when he heard the tune going on within the moat, much sweeter than before; for the fairies were singing it the way Lusmore had settled their music for them, and the song was going on,

> Da Luan,
> Da Mort,
> Augus Cadine,

without ever stopping. Jack Madden, who was in a great hurry to get rid of his hump, never thought of waiting till the fairies had done, so out he bawls without minding the time, or how he could bring in the words properly,

> Augus da Cadine,
> Augus da Hena,[7]

thinking that if one day was good, two were better, and that if Lusmore had one new suit of clothes given him, he should have two. But the words had no sooner passed his lips than he was taken up and whisked into the moat with prodigious force, and the fairies came crowding about him in great anger, screaming, "Who spoiled our tune? who spoiled our tune?" and twenty of the strongest fairies brought Lusmore's hump and put it upon Jack's own hump, where it became firmly fixed. In the morning his friends found him half-dead, lying at the foot of the old moat, with a double hump on his back, and they carried him home, but he died of vexation soon after, leaving his heavy curse, they say, on all who should go and listen to fairy tunes again.[8]

From this Irish legend it is probable that Parnell composed his fine "Fairy Tale, in the ancient English style," of which the opening verses are as follows:

> In Britain's isle and Arthur's days,
> When midnight fairies danced the maze,
>   Lived Edwin of the Green;
> Edwin, I wis, a gentle youth,
> Endowed with courage, sense, and truth,
>   Though badly shaped he'd been.

> His mountain-back mote well be said
> To measure height against his head,
>   And lift itself above:
> Yet, spite of all that Nature did
> To make his uncouth form forbid,
>   This creature dared to love.

---

[7] And Thursday.

[8] Crocker's 'Fairy Legends and Traditions of the South of Ireland': "The Legend of Knockgrafton."

He felt the charms of Edith's eyes,
Nor wanted hope to gain the prize,
   Could ladies look within.
But one Sir Topaz dressed with art,
And if a shape could win a heart,
   He had a shape to win.

Distraught with his love, poor Edwin wanders one night near an enchanted court; he enters and lays himself down, hoping to banish his woes for a season in slumber. Suddenly a hundred bright tapers illumine the ruined hall, and he hears the patter of many feet and the sound of many strange voices. From his corner he discovers a gay procession of little folk pranking along the floor. Presently one who seemed the chief of the fairies (for such they were) calls out, "What mortal infests the balmy air with his doleful sighs?" Edwin comes forward and tells his sad tale without reserve:

"'Twas grief for scorn of faithful love
Which made my steps unweeting rove
   Amid this nightly crew."
"'Tis well," the gallant cries again:
"We fairies never injure men
   Who dare to tell us true.

"Exalt thy love-dejected heart;
Be mine the task, or ere we part,
   To make thy grief resign.
Now take the pleasure of the chance,
Whilst I with Mab my partner dance,
   Be little Mabel thine."

The dancing is followed by some of the merry pranks of Robin Goodfellow, and, says the poet,

Here ended all the phantom play;
They smelt the fresh approach of day,
   And heard the cock to crow:
The whistling wind that bore the crowd
Has clapped the door and whistled loud,
   To warn them all to go.

When Edwin awoke at daybreak he found his hump gone. Edith sees and admires him on his return home. Sir Topaz, having heard of the fairy revels, goes to witness them. His presence is of course discovered by the fairies, who demand to know his business there. Sir Topaz replies that he had lost his way, but the fairies know full well that such was not the fact, so they punish him for his falsehood by fixing Edwin's hump on his back; and we may well suppose that Sir Topaz after this no longer found favour with the beauteous Edith.

The story, says a writer in the 'Quarterly Review,' NO. LXIII, is told in Spain very nearly as it is in Ireland: A humpbacked man hears some small voices singing—

Lunes y Martes y Miercoles, tres,[9]

and he completes their song by the addition of

Jueves y Viernos y Sabado, seis.[10]

The fairies, who were the songsters, are so pleased at this, that they immediately relieve him from his hump and dismiss him with honour. A stupid fellow, afflicted with the same deformity, having got wind of this story, intrudes upon them, and offers a new addition to their song in

Y Domingo, siete.[11]

Indignant at the breach of rhythm, or at the mention of the Lord's Day, which is a tender subject with fairies,[12] they seize the intruder, and according to received genii-practice, overwhelm him with a shower of blows, and send him off with his neighbour's hump in addition to his own. Hence *"Y Domingo, siete"* is a common Spanish comment upon anything which is said or done *mal-à-propos*.

The following. Breton story—cited by Keightley in his 'Fairy Mythology' (1850), from an article in a work entitled 'Tracts for the People'—presents several points of resemblance to the Italian and Irish versions:
The valley of Goel was a celebrated haunt of the korred [*i.e.,* fairies].

---

[9]Monday and Tuesday and Wednesday, three.
[10]Thursday and Friday and Saturday, six.
[11]And the Lord's Day, seven.
[12]In the Italian version, however, the fairies themselves chant "Domenica."

It was thought dangerous to pass through it at night, lest one should be forced to join in their dances, and thus perhaps lose his life. One evening, however, a peasant and his wife thoughtlessly did so, and they soon found themselves surrounded by dancing sprites, who kept singing—

> Lez y, lez hon,
> Bas an arer zo gant hon;
> Lez on, lez y,
> Bas an arer zo gant y.[13]

It seems the man had in his hand the *fourche,* or short stick which is used as a plough-handle in Brittany, and this was a protection, for the dancers made way for them to go out of the ring.

When this became known, many persons, having fortified themselves with a *fourche,* gratified their curiosity by witnessing the dance of the korred. Among the rest were two tailors, Peric and Jean, who, being merry fellows, dared each other to join in the dance. They drew lots, and the lot fell upon Peric, a hump-backed, red-haired, but bold and stout little fellow. He went up to the korred and asked permission to take share in their dance. They granted it, and all went whirling round and round, singing—

> Dilun, Dimeurs, Dimerc'her.[14]

Peric, weary of the monotony, when there was a slight pause at the last word, added—

> Ha Diriaou, ha Digwener.[15]

"Mat! mat!" (good! good!) cried they, and gathering round him, they offered him his choice of beauty, or rank, or riches. He laughed, and only asked them to remove his hump and change the colour of his hair. They forthwith took hold of him, and tossed him up into the air, throwing him from hand to hand till at last he lighted on his feet with a flat back, and fine long black hair.

---

[13] Let him go, let him go,
For he has the wand of the plough;
    Let her go, let her go,
For she has the wand of the plough.

When Jean saw and heard of the change, he resolved to try what he could get from the potent korred; so a few evenings after he went and was admitted to the dance, which now went to the words as enlarged by Peric. To make his addition, he shouted out—

Ha Disadarn, ha Disul.[16]

"What more? what more?" cried the korred, but he only went on repeating the words. They then asked him what he would have, and he replied, riches. They tossed him up and kept bandying him about till he cried for mercy, and on coming to the ground he found he had got Peric's hump and red hair.

It appears that the korred were condemned to this continual dancing, which was never to cease till a mortal should join in their dance; and after naming all the days of the week, should add, "Ha cetu chu er sizum" (and now the week is ended). They punished Jean for coming so near the end, and then disappointing them.

In a version from Amiens, given by M. Henri Carnoy in 'Mélusine' (1878),[17] tome i., c. 241, we find a curious variant of the Slav and Chinese stories of Hospitality Rewarded—see *ante*, pages 18–21: A peasant woman, while engaged collecting dead wood in a forest, comes upon three fairies dancing and chanting—

Dimanche, lundi,
Après mardi,
Ensuite mercredi,
Avec jeudi.[18]

She joined in the dance, and chimed in—

Vendredi, samedi,
La semaine est fini,
Dieu l'a dit.[19]

---

[16] And Saturday, and Sunday.

[17] 'Mélusine: revue de mythologie, littérature populaire, traditions, et usages; dirigée par H. Gaidoz et E. Rolland.'—The publication of this excellent journal, after having been discontinued for six years, was resumed in 1885. It would be difficult to over-rate its value to story-comparers.

[18] Sunday, Monday, after Tuesday, follows Wednesday, with Thursday.

[19] Friday, Saturday, the week is ended, God says it.

"What you'll do to-morrow on rising," said one of the fairies, "you'll do the whole day. That is the reward which we accord you for having finished our song."

Next morning when she arose, thinking little of what the fairies had said, her husband asked her for two sous to get some beer. She put her hand in her pocket, and was astonished to find it full of money; and she continued from morning till night taking money out of her pocket. A neighbour, whom she had called in to help her to count her treasure, learns from her the secret of her great luck, and goes off to the wood, where she discovers the fairies and joins in their dance, and adds to their chant the same refrain as her gossip had done. The fairies also promise her that what she'd do in the morning she'd do all the day. Returning home, she slipped a six-sous piece into her pocket, expecting to take out a large quantity of similar coins on the morrow. But alas! so soon as she arose in the morning she found it necessary to relieve nature, and so she continued doing all that day.

Mr Ralston, in an interesting paper on Sicilian Fairy Tales in 'Fraser's Magazine' for April 1876, cites a somewhat singular version from Dr Pitrè's collection:[20] A hunchbacked shoemaker once passed a night in a haunted house. At midnight down dropped from the ceiling of the room in which he kept watch *quattru pupi*—four puppets,[21] who began to sing—

Luni, Marti, Miércuri, Juòvidi, Vennire, e Sabutu![22]

Hearing this, the hunchback lifted up his voice and joined harmoniously in the song. Delighted to find he was not frightened, they took off his hump and hung it upon the wall. Before the day dawned they disappeared. Great was the astonishment of the neighbours, when they came in the morning to see how the shoemaker had fared at the hands of *li diavuli,* to find him happy and humpless.

Now there was among them an old woman who had a hump larger than his had been, and when she had heard his story she determined to try her luck with the *diavuli.* So next night she kept watch in the haunted house. At midnight appeared the *pupi,* and began to sing as before. The old woman joined in the song, but very badly; and the puppets, seeing

[20]'Fiabe, novelle, e racconti popolari siciliani.' Raccolti ed illustrati da Giuseppe Pitrè. Palermo, 1875.

[21]Enchanted puppets are a striking characteristic of Sicilian folktales; they occur seldom in Northern fictions.

[22]Monday, Tuesday, Wednesday, Thursday, Friday, and Saturday.

that she was not inclined to sing cheerfully, took down the shoemaker's hump from the wall and fastened it on to her breast. So she had a couple of them, one before and one behind, and the sight of her next day made the neighbours right cheerful.

Another adventure with the fairies is the subject of a Breton ballad: One Friday night, Paskou, a tailor out of work, enters a fairy grotto, digs up a crock of treasure, and makes off with it, pursued by the korred right into his courtyard, dancing and singing full lustily, "Monday, Tuesday, Wednesday, and Thursday and Friday." Finding the door shut, they clamber on to the roof, break a hole in it, through which they get into the house, where they resume their dance and song, calling out to poor Paskou, who lies trembling under the bed-clothes—

> Hilloa! tailor, Master Snip!
> Show us but your nose's tip;—
>
> Come, let's have a dancing bout,
> We will teach you step and shout!
>
> Tailor—little tailor, dear,
> Monday, Tuesday, Wednesday—hear!
>
> Tailor thou, and robber too,
> Wednesday, Thursday, Friday, too!
>
> Come again—come back to us,
> Little tailor villainous!
>
> You shall dance until you crack
> Every sinew in your back;—
> *Fairies' coin doth virtue lack!*

If Paskou had but had enough sense to complete their song, by adding "and Saturday," no doubt all had been well; as it was, his stolen treasure was turned into stones, like the gold of the blacksmith in the German story. In another version the thief is a baker, who, with more cunning than the tailor, strews hot ashes round his house, so that when the fairies come, they scorch their feet, for which indignity, however, they take ample vengeance by breaking all his pans and ovens.[23]

[23]'Foreign Quarterly Review,' 1844, vol. xxxiii., pp. 171–3.

We have thus seen that the story of the hunchbacks and the fairies is known over Europe; and among the Japanese it is current in a form which strikingly resembles the first French version, and which is given as follows by Mr Mitford, in his entertaining 'Tales of Old Japan,' under the title of "The Elves and the Envious Neighbour":

Once upon a time there was a certain man who, being overtaken by darkness among the mountains, was driven to seek shelter in the hollow trunk of a tree. In the middle of the night a large company of elves assembled at the spot; and the man, on peeping from his hiding-place, was frightened out of his wits. After a while, however, the elves began to feast and drink wine, and to amuse themselves by singing and dancing, until at last the man, caught by the infection of the fun, forgot all his fears, and crept out of his hollow tree to join in the revels. When the day was about to dawn, the elves said to him, "You're a very jolly companion, and must come out and have a dance with us again. You must make us a promise and keep it." So the elves, thinking to bind the man over to return, took a large wen that grew upon his forehead, and kept it in pawn; upon this they all left the place and went home. The man walked off to his own house, in high glee at having passed a jovial night and got rid of his wen into the bargain. So he told all his friends, who congratulated him warmly on being cured of his wen. But there was a neighbour of his who was also troubled with a wen of long standing, and when he heard of his friend's luck, he was smitten with envy, and went off to hunt for the hollow tree, in which, when he found it, he passed the night. Towards midnight the elves came, as he had expected, and began feasting and drinking, with songs and dances, as before. When he saw this, he came out of his hollow tree, and began dancing and singing, as his neighbour had done. The elves, mistaking him for their former boon companion, were delighted to see him, and said, "You're a good fellow to recollect your promise, and we'll give you back your pledge." So one of the elves, pulling the pawned wen out of his pocket, stuck it on the man's forehead, on the top of the other wen which he already had. And so the envious neighbour went home weeping, with two wens instead of one.

It will be observed that the only difference between the Japanese story and the first French version is, that in the former the elves do not increase the envious man's protuberance in anger. The result is the same in all the numerous versions above cited.

❧ THE ENCHANTED HORSE ❧

THE civilising influence of the Moors is still traceable in the manners and customs, the literature and arts, of Spain. From Moorish sources the Spanish romances of chivalry were largely derived, and from Spain tales and fictions, originally imported from the East, spread into France, furnishing rich materials for many *fabliaux* of the Trouvères. In the thirteenth century a French poet, named Adans, or Adènis, styled *Le Roi*, from his position as chief of the minstrels, composed, in honour of the Princess Mary of Brabant, on her becoming queen of France, a romaunt in verse, entitled 'Cléomades,' of which Count Tressan published an *extrait* in the 'Bibliothèque Universelle des Romans.' This work was originally written in Spanish verse, and afterwards rendered into prose, French as well as Spanish. Its Eastern extraction is unquestionable, and it was probably brought by the Moors to Spain in the eleventh or twelfth century. Another title of the French metrical version of this romance is 'Le Cheval de Fust' (the Wooden Horse), from the important part which a steed of that description plays in it—in fact, it is the tale of the Enchanted Horse in the 'Arabian Nights,' though there is reason to believe that that fascinating story-book was not then composed, at least in its present form.

The story seems to have spread rapidly over Europe. Chaucer introduces the Magic Horse in his Squire's Tale—the "half-told tale of Cambuscan bold;" but in place of a wooden steed it is (quoth Milton) "a wondrous horse of brass, on which the Tartar king did ride." The qualities of this steed are thus described by the ambassador who presented it in his royal master's name to Cambynskan,[1] seated on his throne and surrounded by "all his liege men so noble of birth":

> He saide: The King of Araby and Inde,
> My liegè lord, on this solempne[2] day
> Salewith[3] you as he best can or may,
> And sendith you, in honour of your feste,
> By me, that am redy at al your heste,

[1] Not Cambuscan, as Milton writes the name.
[2] *Solempne:* solemn; important.
[3] *Salueth:* salutes.

This Stede of Brass, that esily and well
Can in the space of a day naturell,
That is to say, in four and twenty hours,
Where so you listè,[4] in droughte or in shours,
Berin your body into every place
Into which your hertè willith to pace,
Withoutin wem[5] of you, through foule or faire;
Or if you list to flein in the aire
As doth an Egle, whan him list to sore,
This same stede shall bere you evirmore,
Withoutin harme, till you ben there you lest,
Though that you slepin on his bake and rest,
And tourn agen with writhing of a pin.
He that it wrought couth full many a gin;[6]
He waited many a constellation,[7]
Ere he had don this operation,
And knew ful many sele and many bond.

. . .

And aftir supper goth this nobill king
To sene this Horse of Brass, with all his rout
Of lordis and of ladies him about.
Soch wondring there was on this Horse of Brass,
That sithin[8] the grete siege of Troyè was,
There as men wondrid on an horse also,
Ne was there such a wondrin as was tho.[9]
But finally the king askith the knight
The vertue of this coursere and the might,
And prayid him to tell its governaunce.
The horse anon gan forth to trip and daunce,
Whan that this knight laid hold upon his reine,
And seidè, Sir, there is no more to seine,
But when you list to ridin anywhere,

---

[4]*Listè:* please; choose.
[5]*Wem:* harm; risk; danger.
[6]He that made it knew full many an ingenious contrivance.
[7]He observed the motions of the heavenly bodies until a certain conjunction, a lucky hour arrived, which enabled him to endow it with the required magical qualities.
[8]*Sithin:* since.
[9]*Tho:* then.

You motè[10] trill a pin stant in his ere,
Which I shall tellin you between us two,
Ye motè nempnè'[11] him to what place also,
Or to what contrè, that you list to ride.
But when you come there as you list t' abide,
Bid him descend, and trill anothir pin
(For therin lyth th' effect of all that gin),
And he wol down descend, and don your will,
And in that place he woll abidin still,
Though all the world had the contráry sworne,
He shall not thennis[12] be throwin, ne borne.
Or if you listin bid him thennis gone,
Trill this pin, and he woll vanish anon
Out of the sight of every mannere wight,
And come agen, be it by day or night.
Whan that you list to clepin[13] him agene,
In sock a gise, as I shall to you seine,
Betwixtin you and me, and that full sone;
Ride when you list, there is no more to done.

Chaucer, apparently, did not finish the story, or if he did so, the greater part of it is now lost. So far as it goes, it has the elements of a charming tale;—the magic horse; the mirror that foreshadowed coming evil; the ring that enabled the wearer to understand the language of birds; and the sword that cured wounds which itself had made.[14] Very probably the Tartar king's younger son Camballo had an adventure with the "steed of brass" similar to that of the bold Cléomades, who wooed and won the fair Claremonde, daughter of Cornuant, king of Tuscany, as related in the old Hispano-French romaunt, and to that of the prince in the Arabian tale.[15]

[10]*Motè:* must.
[11]*Nempnè:* name.
[12]*Thennis:* thence.
[13]*Clepin:* call.
[14]The magic mirror may be compared with the ivory tube in the Arabian story of Prince Ahmed and the Perí Bánú. Many Asiatic tales turn upon a knowledge of the language of birds and beasts, which Solomon the sage Hebrew king is said to have possessed in the highest degree. Chaucer may have derived the idea of the magic sword from the legendary spear of Telephus.
[15]In the romance of Cléomades, three great princes arrive at Seville as suitors for the three daughters of King Marchabias. They were not only powerful monarchs, but were deeply

The Polish wizard Towardowski in later times is popularly credited with riding on a painted horse of his own contrivance, which carried him through the air wheresoever he wished to go. But our own country can boast of a wizard as good—or bad—as Towardowski. Leland, in his Itinerary, informs us that in ancient times one Rutter, "a man in great favour with his prince, desired to have reward of him of as much land as he could ride over in a day upon a horse of wood; and he did ride over as much as is now Rutlandshire by art-magic, and was afterwards swallowed into the earth." The usual fate of magicians is to come to a violent end. The Polish wizard aforesaid was carried up the chimney by the arch-fiend when his "time" was come.

There is reason to think that the Arabian tale of the Enchanted Horse was derived from the Persians, who, in their turn, may have adopted the idea of such a steed from Indian fiction. The story of Maliík and Shírín in the Persian Tales of a Thousand and One Days, ascribed to the Dervish Mukhlis of Ispahán, in which a flying-machine plays a leading part, and that of the Labourer and the Flying Chair in Jonathan Scott's 'Tales from the Arabic,'[16] are certainly clumsy substitutes, as Dr H. H. Wilson has remarked, for the original Indian fiction, in which an adven-

---

versed in astronomy, and well skilled in the art of magic. One was Melicandus, king of Barbary; the second was Bardigans, king of Armenia; the third, whose name was Croppart, was king of Hungary. This last was ugly and hump-backed; his soul was as deformed as his body, and his tongue was pregnant with falsehood. These three kings had met together before they set out for Seville, and had agreed that each should give such a present to the king and queen as would entitle him to ask a gift in return. On their arrival they were received with all becoming honours. King Melicandus presented the royal pair with a man of gold, who held in his hand a trumpet formed of the same metal, made with so much art, that if treason lurked even within a considerable distance of him, he put the trumpet to his mouth and blew a loud and piercing blast. King Bardigans presented a hen and six chickens of gold, so skilfully formed that they seemed to be alive. He placed them on the ground and they instantly began to run about, to peck, and to clap their wings. The hen flew up on the queen's knee, cackled, and laid a fine pearl in her lap. "She will do the same every third day," said Bardigans. All present were lost in admiration of these wonderful gifts. King Croppart now came forward with a large wooden horse,' magnificently caparisoned, with pins of steel on his head and shoulders. "Sire," said he, in a harsh and discordant voice, "with the horse which I offer you, one may mount in the air, cross the seas, and travel at the rate of fifty leagues an hour." There can be little doubt that Cervantes borrowed the idea of the famous steed Clavileño Aligero ("Wooden-pin Wing-bearer"), which figures so ludicrously in 'Don Quixote,' from the Spanish version of this romance, not, as he seems to hint, from that of Peter of Provence and the Fair Magalona, in which there is no such magic horse.

[16]Translated from a fragment of an Arabic manuscript of the 'Thousand and One Nights,' procured in Bengal. The story of the Flying Chair does not occur in any of the three printed texts of the 'Nights,'—the Búlák, Breslau, and Calcutta.

turer, in love with a princess, personates the deity Vishnu, and appropriately rides on a wooden effigy of Garuda, guided by a pin and moving by magic[17]—the prototype of the Enchanted Horse of the Arabian tale, and of other self-moving machines of celebrity in oriental and chivalric romance.

Sir Richard F. Burton, however, says that the flying horse of the 'Arabian Nights' "is Pegasus, which is a Greek travesty of an Egyptian myth, developed in India." If this be so, we must consider the wooden Garuda (which reappears in the Kalmuk tales of Siddhí Kúr—see *ante*, p. 126) as an Indian "development" of the Egyptian myth, and also the enchanted horse referred to in connection with Forbidden Rooms (p. 78), together with its Arabian imitation in the story of the Third Calender. It is a popular belief among the Singalese that in the country of the Himálayas, the land of wonders, there are horses and elephants which possess the power of flying through the air.[18]

But more simple things than wooden horses have been endowed with self-moving powers by "art-magic" in times of old: for instance, the pestle, in Lucian's 'Philopseudes' ('The Liars' in Francklin's translation), which Pancrates, in want of a servant, caused to fetch water and perform other useful domestic duties. When the Egyptian sorcerer was absent one day, his pupil tried to perform the trick; but he did not know the charm for stopping the water-carrying pestle, and the house was soon flooded. In despair, he chopped the pestle in two with an axe; but this only made matters worse, for both halves then set to work to bring water. This incident has been versified by Goethe, and also by Barham in his 'Ingoldsby Legends.' It reappears, under the title of "The Master and his Pupil; or, the Magic Book," in Dr A. C. Fryer's 'English Fairy Tales from the North Country.' And with it may be compared the conclusion of the Norwegian tale of the Magic Quern (*ante*, p. 29), which two of its possessors did not know how to stop.

In the 'Kathá Sarit Ságara' we read of a demi-goddess who had mechanical dolls made of wood and magically endowed. One of these, on a pin in it being turned, went through the air at her orders, fetched a garland of flowers, and quickly returned; another brought water at will;

[17]'Pancha Tantra,' Book I, Fable 5.—Garuda, the vehicle of Vishnu, is represented as half-man, half-bird; having the head, wings, talons, and beak of the eagle, and the body and limbs of a man; his face is white, his wings red, and his body golden.

[18]See Davy's 'Ceylon,' p. 197.

another danced; and yet another conversed. It is curious to find the magic pestle of Lucian's story reproduced in the Edinburgh tradition of one Major Weir, who had the unenviable reputation of being a wizard, and after his death, at the stake, his house long remained unoccupied: the major's walking-stick, it seems, answered the purpose of a man-servant, opening the door to visitors, and even going to the tobacconist's to procure snuff for its master!

✥ THE DEMON ENCLOSED IN A BOTTLE: CONTRACTS WITH THE EVIL ONE, ETC. ✥

Few readers I presume, are unfamiliar with the Arabian tale of the fisherman and the Genii, whom the poor man fished up in his net, confined in a copper vessel by the power of Solomon's magical signet; how the genii, having been unwittingly released by the fisherman, threatened to destroy his liberator, and the latter adopted a clever plan to entrap the ungrateful monster once more. "How wast thou in this bottle?" asked the fisherman. "It will not contain thy hand or thy foot; how then can it contain thy body?" "Dost thou not believe that I was in it?" answered the genii. The fisherman said, "I will never believe thee until I see thee in it." Upon this the genii shook, and became condensed, and entered the bottle by little and little, until he was all enclosed.

This idea of a demon being confined in a bottle is derived from a Muslim legend, adapted from the Talmud, regarding the loss and recovery of Solomon's signet-ring. According to the Talmudic legend, when the building of the Temple was finished, the king of the Demons begged Solomon to set him free from his service, and promised in return to teach him a secret he would be sure to value. Having cajoled Solomon out of possession of his signet-ring, he first flung the ring into the sea, and then taking up Solomon himself, cast him into a foreign land some 400 miles away, where for three weary years he wandered up and down as a vagrant, begging his bread from door to door. In the course of his rambles he came to Mash Kernin, and was so fortunate as to be appointed head-cook at the palace of the king of Ammon. While employed in this office, Naama, the king's daughter, fell in love with him, and determining to marry him, eloped with him for refuge to a distant land. One day, as Naama was preparing a fish for dinner, she found in it a ring, and this turned out to be the very ring which the king of the Demons had flung into the sea, and the loss of which had bewitched the king out of his power and dominion. In the recovery of the ring the king recovered both himself and the throne of his father David.

The Muhammedan traditionists give the tale with several curious additions, including the Demon in the Bottle. After Solomon had obtained possession of his celebrated magical signet-ring, in which were four jewels presented to him by the lords of the heavens, the air, earth, and water, he first subdued the demons and genii, all but Iblís (Satan), to whom Allah had promised perfect independence till the day of judgment, and the mighty demon Sakhr, who was concealed in an unknown island of the ocean. It happened that Solomon, in one of his wars against an idolatrous nation, had taken captive the beautiful daughter of the king; and on his return to Jerusalem he placed her in his harem, where she soon acquired such ascendancy over him that he worshipped her false gods, for which great sin he was sorely punished. One day, before going to the bath, he intrusted his signet-ring to the care of his pagan concubine, which being observed by the demon Sakhr, who was hovering about the harem unseen, he at once assumed the form of Solomon, and thus obtained the ring from the lady. Solomon's features, it seems, had in the meantime undergone such a metamorphosis that his courtiers did not recognise him, and drove him from the palace with every mark of indignity; and while Sakhr sat on the throne, doing all kinds of wickedness, the sage king of Israel, after wandering through foreign lands, took service with a fisherman. At length the conduct of Sakhr—so unlike the mild and beneficent rule of the real Solomon—aroused the suspicion of the royal counsellors that he must be an evil spirit who had assumed the form of their beloved monarch; and it was resolved to put him to the test, by reading in his presence some passages of the book of the law. Barely had the sacred scroll been opened, and the reading begun, when Sakhr, uttering loud shrieks, flew out of the palace, and, after throwing the magical signet into the sea, was seen no more. Not long after this occurrence, Solomon, having received from his master two fishes as his day's wages, on cutting open one of them found in its stomach his signet-ring, and was thus enabled to subdue the demon Sakhr, whom he compelled to enter into a copper vessel, which, having sealed it with his signet-ring, he cast into the sea, where the demon will remain till the last day.[1] Muslim writers often allude to this wonderful exploit of Solomon. For instance, in the Persian poetical version of the 'Book of Sindibád' (A.D. 1375) we read: "By predominant might he put the demon in the bottle; the genii howled and whined on account of him;" and again, in the same work: "No sooner had he mounted, than—like a demon that leaps from the bottle—like a lion

---

[1] The tale of the Emperor Jovinian, ch. lix. of the 'Gesta Romanorum,' and that of King Robert of Sicily, reproduced by Swan in his notes to the 'Gesta,' seem both to have been derived from the Jewish or the Muslim legend of Solomon's temporary abasement.

rushing from the thicket—the elephant darted off with the monarch, and flew with the speed of lightning over hill and dale."

In China the same notion prevails, as we learn from Mr Giles' 'Strange Stories from a Chinese Studio,' where more than one instance occur of demons being enclosed in vessels from which they cannot escape without external assistance. In the story, for example, of the Painted Skin, a female demon hires herself as maid-of-all-work in a certain family; but her real nature is discovered by a priest, who strikes her with his magic sword, upon which she falls down and becomes a hideous devil. The priest then strikes off her head, and she becomes a dense column of smoke curling up from the ground, when he takes an uncorked gourd and throws it into the midst of the smoke: a sucking noise is heard, and the whole column is drawn into the gourd; after which the priest corks it up closely, and puts it in his pouch.[2]

From the Eastern fabulists, no doubt, European story-tellers derived this idea of confining an imp or demon. In the Norse tale of the Master-Smith, the hero, who had sold himself to the devil, contrives to outwit the arch-fiend by the same device as that adopted by the fisherman with the genie. "Is it true," asks the master-smith of the devil, when he came to carry him away—"is it true that you can make yourself as small as you please?" The devil answers that it is quite true, and to gratify the curiosity of his "friend," creeps into the smith's steel purse, where he is confined until he promises never to come back any more.—In Grimm's 'Kinder und Haus Märchen,' an old soldier possesses a wonderful knapsack, into which everything must fly which he wishes there. He spends a night in a castle haunted by nine demons, who attack him, and endeavour to expel him, but he wishes them all in his knapsack, and immediately they are there sure enough. Next day, as he trudges along, he comes to a black-

---

[2] In Icelandic folk-lore, the "Sending"—a ghost raised up by sorcery for the purpose of learning from it the mysteries of the future state, and for sending it on malignant missions against an enemy—"is sometimes induced to assume the form of some small beast or insect, either by taunts or flattery, and to creep into a bottle or into an empty marrow-bone; and, once there, he is corked up tight for his folly. Sendings thus entrapped are generally cast into morasses, or stowed away in secret hiding-places, where no inquisitive fingers are likely to grope. Woe betide him who, unsuspecting, finds the marrow-bone or bottle subsequently, and uncorks it! The goblin gains ten times his original force by being imprisoned, and ten times his old malignity. Like the genie in Solomon's lead-sealed urn, which the fisherman, in the 'Arabian Nights,' found and opened, he is apt to treat his liberator with scorn and revenge."
—Powell and Magnusson's 'Legends of Iceland.' Second series. Introd., p. lxxvii.

smith's shop, and placing his magical knapsack on the anvil, he asks the smith and his man to strike it with all their strength with their great hammers. "The imps set up a fearful screech, and when all was quiet the knapsack was opened. Eight of them were found quite dead, but the ninth, who had laid himself in a fold, was still living. He slipped out when the knapsack was opened and escaped."

This ludicrous incident is related in a different form in the Norse tale of the Lad and the Deil (Dasent's collection): Once on a time there was a lad who was walking along a road cracking nuts, so he found one that was worm-eaten, and just at that very moment he met the Deil. "Is it true now," said the lad, "what they say, that the Deil can make himself as small as he chooses, and thrust himself in through a pin-hole?" "Yes, it is," said the Deil. "Oh, it is, is it? Then let me see you do it, and just creep into this nut," said the lad. So the Deil did it. Now, when he had crept into the worm's hole, the lad stopped it up with a pin. "Now I've got you safe!" he said, and put the nut into his pocket. So when he had walked on a bit, he came to a smithy, and he turned in and asked the smith if he'd be good enough to crack that nut for him. "Ay, that'll be an easy job," said the smith, and took his smallest hammer, laid the nut on the anvil, and gave it a blow, but it wouldn't break. So he took another hammer, a little bigger, but that wasn't heavy enough either. Then he took one bigger still, but it was still the same story; and so the smith got wroth, and grasped his great sledge-hammer. "Now I'll crack you to bits," he said, and let drive at the nut with all his might and main. And so the nut flew to pieces, with a loud bang that blew off half the roof of the smithy, and the whole house creaked and groaned as though it was ready to fall. "Why! if I don't think the Deil must have been in that nut!" said the smith. "So he was; you're quite right," said the lad, as he went away laughing.

In a Bohemian version (No. 21 of M. Leger's collection of Slav popular tales), the hero having "bagged" all the demons who haunted a nobleman's castle, including Satan himself, whom he had beaten at dice, takes his sack to a smith's shop, and after they have been well hammered, and promise never to return, sets them at liberty. For many years after this adventure he lived very happily, but at length Death came to fetch him away: folk who are happy do not die willingly, however, so Death was sent into the sack. A strange result followed;—people and the beasts multiplied like the moss in woods; everybody wondered what had become of Death; a great famine occurred, and men shrank up, but did not die. The hero pitied their misery, so he allowed Death to go about his business again, after making him swear never to call for him. In course of time, however, he got tired of life, and set out for heaven. Arrived there, St. Peter refused to admit him, because he had preferred, when he had three wishes to be granted, earthly wealth to the joys of Paradise. "Go along," said the saint, "and find those with whom you played at dice." So he took his way to the nether regions, but when he reached the gate of the infernal city he met one of the devils whom he had formerly put into his sack, and whom the smiths had so terribly mauled. This guardian uttered the most awful cries, which roused all his brother devils, and they at once doubled the watchmen at the gate, with orders not to allow the enemy to enter. What was now to be done? The hero was perplexed. Finally, he returned to St. Peter, and by dint of prayers and tears, the celestial porter admitted him—and he now acts as Peter's lieutenant.— An Italian variant is found in the 'Novellini di S. Stefano,' in which the hero, Bippo Pipetta, forces Death to enter his magic sack, and keeps him there for a year and a half, during which period there was great joy among the doctors, for none of them lost a patient.

A prune-tree is substituted for the magic sack in one of M. Carnoy's collection of French popular tales, entitled "La Mort Jouée," the substance of which is as follows: In a village of Artois there was an old lady whose greatest pleasure was to relieve the distressed;—no beggar ever quitted her door without some money and white bread. One day a great saint visited this good dame, and told her that he was empowered to grant her any wish that she should form. After considering a long time, she said, "I have a fine prune-tree in my garden, and wish that whosoever shall climb up into it shall remain there as long as I please." "Your wish is certainly a very odd one," rejoined the saint; "but so be it," and bidding the old lady adieu, he returned to heaven. Ten years after this Death came to the charitable dame—she being now, as he reflected, wellnigh eighty years old; and when she saw him, "Oh, is it you, Death?" she said quietly. "I have waited for you long, and shall take my departure without regret. But ah! I had forgot: I should like to eat some prunes before leaving this world." So the King of Terrors very obligingly went into the garden, climbed the prune-tree, and having gathered a quantity of prunes, was about to come down, when the old lady exclaimed, "It is my will that Death shall not descend without my permission." In vain did Death threaten and pray by turns; he could not come down. During six months no one died. The sick who were racked with pain besought Death to put an end to their misery, but Death was helpless. And most unhappy of all were the doctors, who could not contrive to bring Death to release their patients. One of them, a great friend of Death, went to help him down from the tree, but he too was firmly fixed beside him! At length the dame took her embargo off the King of Terrors, and down he came to resume his old business. Finally, the old lady, becoming very feeble, called for Death, and was straightway admitted into Paradise.[3]

Another story in M. Carnoy's collection (Part ii., No. 12), 'Les trois Souhaits,' is a variant of the Bohemian tale of the Happy Shepherd cited above: A soldier named Tholomé obtains from his captain three months' furlough, together with a present of three pounds of bread and six liards. On the way homeward he is accosted by an old woman, who asks him for alms, and he gives her a pound of bread. Next an old man comes up to him, saying he has not eaten anything for two days, and Tholomé gives him a pound of bread, and the remainder he bestows on a third beggar. Meeting with three other mendicants in succession, he gives each two liards. Then the last of these (perhaps we are to understand that all six were one and the same individual) changed himself into a bright genie, and appearing before Tholomé, told him that in reward of his charitable deeds he should have three wishes accomplished.[4] "In that case," says the soldier, "I wish in the first place that any one who shall sit on the bench at the door of my house shall remain there as long as I please; secondly, that whosoever mounts our cherry-tree shall continue there until I give him leave to come down; and thirdly, that I may confine any person I please in my purse." "So be it," said the genie, and disappeared. Tholomé then resumed his journey, and reaching home, warmly embraced his grandfather (both his parents were dead), and soon after married one of his fair cousins. His three months' leave of absence having expired, one fine day comes a gendarme to conduct him back to his regiment. "I am quite ready to go with you," says Tholomé; "only suffer me to bid my poor grandfather farewell;—meanwhile do you rest yourself on this bench." When Tholomé came out the gendarme attempted to rise from the bench, but found himself fixed to it; and he had to promise Tholomé six months' additional leave before being released. When his second furlough was

---

[3] 'Contes Français.' Recueillis par E. Henri Carnoy. Paris: 1885.

[4] The obtaining by supernatural means of the accomplishment of *three wishes* is a favourite subject of popular fictions, and the various forms in which the notion is treated are very numerous. Perhaps the oldest form is found in the several Eastern texts of the 'Book of Sindibád,' where a dervish is granted three wishes, and, acting by his wife's advice, finds himself, when his third wish is accomplished, no better than before.

expired there came another gendarme to fetch Tholomé, who desired him to go and help himself to some cherries from the tree in the garden, while he embraced his grandfather; and he had to grant Tholomé a year's leave before he was allowed to descend from the tree. At the end of the year, a third gendarme came, who had the wonderful and very useful power of elongating his body so that he could reach the top of the cherry-tree standing on the ground. "This is very clever," says our hero; "but can you also make yourself as small as you please?" Upon this the gendarme changed himself into a fly, and alighted on Tholomé's arm, who instantly clapped him into his purse. "Let me out! let me out!" cried the gendarme, "and you shall have unlimited leave of absence." So Tholomé set him free, and after this lived many years in peace and happiness.[5]

A Dutch version of the same story occurs in a work entitled 'The Gondola,' by Harry Stoe Vandyck, published at London in 1827: One dark evening in winter a tall stranger entered the hut of Jan Schalken, a kind-hearted fisherman, and sought a night's lodging, to which he was made welcome. In the morning, when the "mysterious stranger" was about to depart, in requital of Jan's hospitality, he promised him the gratification of three wishes. Jan had little faith in his promise, but thought he might as well put it to the test. So he first desired that he and his wife Mietje should live fifty years longer than nature had designed. "It shall be done," said the stranger. Whilst he was puzzling his brain for a second wish, he bethought him that a pear-tree, which was in his little garden, had been frequently despoiled of its fruit, to the no small injury of the tree and grievous disappointment of the owner; so he said, "For my second wish, grant that whoever climbs my pear-tree shall not have power to leave it until my permission be given." This was also assented to. Now Schalken was a sober man, and liked to sit down and chat with his wife of an evening; but she was a bustling body, and often jumped up in the midst of a story that she had heard only a dozen times, to scrub the table or set their clay platters in order. Nothing disturbed him so much as this, and he was determined, if possible, to prevent a repetition of the annoyance. With this object in view he approached the stranger, and in a low whisper told him his third and last wish, that whoever sat in a certain chair in his hut should not be able to move out of it until it should please him so to order. This wish was also agreed to by the traveller, who, after many greetings,

[5] A parallel to this and the preceding tale is found in Miss Busk's 'Folk-Lore of Rome,' pp. 180–183.

departed on his way. Years passed on, and Jan had often fully gratified his two wishes, by detaining thieves in his tree and his wife in her chair, till the time came when he was seventy-nine and his wife seventy-three years of age. Death arrived at the hut one evening, dressed like a gentleman, and told them that by rights they should both be his on that day, but since a fifty years' respite had been granted, he should not call again till that period was expired. For the next fifty years Jan and his wife lived on as quietly as before, and when the fatal day at length arrived, Death kept his appointment. As Jan and Mietje were accompanying Death, they passed by the pear-tree in the garden, and Jan persuaded Death to climb the tree and gather some fruit for their journey, but there he was stuck fast till he granted that they should live another half century. When Death came again, he was induced to sit down in the enchanted chair, and was only released on promising a further respite of fifty years, at the end of which period Jan Schalken and his wife died peacefully in their bed.

In stories of this class, the wishes are granted indifferently by Jesus, St. Peter, or the Evil One; in the last case, the Arch-Enemy is to have the soul of the possessor of the wishes at the expiry of a certain period, but his crafty devices are invariably turned to his own discomfiture. Thus in a Tuscan version a smith contracts with the devil to sell his soul for two years of life, and is granted that whosoever should sit on a bench near the fire must stay there so long as the smith pleases; that whosoever should look out of the window cannot go away without the smith's leave; and that whosoever should climb his fig-tree must remain there till the smith permits him to come down. When the two years are expired, the devil comes to fetch the smith away, and is asked to sit on the bench till the smith has finished the job at which he is working, which the devil unthinkingly does; and the smith blew up such a fire that even the devil could not endure it, and he was fain to grant two more years to the smith in order to be set free. The same happens when he comes again and is asked to look out of the window; and when he returns a third time and is induced to climb the fig-tree, be has perforce to cancel the contract and sign a new one, by which it is solemnly agreed that the smith and he should never meet again.[6]

There is a curious Italian variant, also from Tuscany, entitled "Grand-father Misery," in which Jesus and St. Peter having received from the

---

[6]This story finds its exact parallel in an Irish legend, related (I think) in one of Carleton's books.

hero some polenta, he is granted in return three favours: the bench near the fire; the fig-tree; and finally, out of regard to St. Peter, the salvation of his soul. Death comes, and is invited to sit by the fire, and he would soon be ready. But Death, thin as he is, could not stand the heat; so he granted him a hundred years more of life. When Death again comes to fetch him, he is induced to climb the fig-tree to pick a few figs for the journey, and is not allowed to come down till he consents to another lease of a century to the hero. The third time Death comes, "Give me time," says his intended victim, "to say an Ave Maria." "You shall have it," says Death. But the old fellow seemed in no hurry to begin or finish his Ave Maria, and Death bade him make haste. "You have given me *time,* and I am taking it," said Grandfather Misery, who still lives, for Misery never ends.[7]

It was formerly believed by Muslim doctors that evil spirits could be subdued and confined in bottles by means of fasting and prayers. This notion had its origin, doubtless, in the Rabbinical legends of Solomon's power over demons and genii (*jinn*); and the Rabbins borrowed most of their wild tales of *diablerie* from the Zoroastrians of ancient Persia, and perhaps partly also from the Hindús. According to the *Vinculum spirituum,* a work of Eastern extraction, Solomon, having discovered the secret of subduing demons, confined no fewer than three millions of them, together with seventy-two of their kings, in a bottle of black glass, which he then threw into a deep well near Babylon.[8] But it happened that the citizens of Babylon, descending into this well, in expectation of finding treasure, and breaking the bottle, liberated the demons.—Le Sage borrowed the leading idea of his well-known novel, 'Le Diable Boiteux,'[9] from a Spanish work, by Guevara, entitled 'El Diable Cojuelo,' written in 1641, in which a student, named Don Cleofas, "having accidentally entered the abode of an astrologer, delivers from a glass bottle, in which he had been confined by the conjuror, the demon called Diable Cojuelo,

---

[7]See Crane's 'Italian Popular Tales,' pp. 221, 222, and notes.

[8]The magic of Babylon is frequently alluded to by Muslim writers; the poets speak of the "Babylonian witchery" of a beautiful woman's eyes; and it is believed that the two wicked angels, Hárút and Márút mentioned in the Kurán (see chap. ii. and Sale's note), are still hanging, head downwards, in a well at Babel, and will instruct any one who is bold enough to go and solicit them. Setting idle legends aside, it is highly probable, as Sir W. Ouseley remarks, that at Babylon the Persians learnt the arts of magical incantation from the conquered Chaldeans.—Notes to my privately-printed edition of the 'Bakhtyár Náma.'

[9]The English translation is entitled 'The Devil upon Two Sticks.'

who is a spirit nearly of the same description as the Asmodée of Le Sage, and who, in return for the service he had received from the scholar, exhibits to him the interior of the houses of Madrid." Mr J. O. Halliwell (now Halliwell-Phillipps), in his 'Fugitive Tracts and Chap Books,' printed for the Percy Society (vol. xxix.), describes a very rare tract which was evidently also derived from the Spanish romance. It is entitled "The Devil upon Two Sticks, or the Town Until'd [*i.e.,* unroofed]; with the comical humours of Don Stulto and Seignor Jingo; as it is acted in Pinkeman's booth in May Fair. Printed by J. R., near Fleet Street, 1708." The tract, we learn, consists of only four leaves, and the title is illustrated by a woodcut of Don Stulto escaping from an intrigue, and finding himself in the chamber of an astrologer at Madrid. "He saw books and papers in confusion on the table, spheres and compasses on the one side, and vials and quadrants on the other. Presently he heard a deep sigh break out just by him, which a little startled him. He took it at first for a nocturnal illusion or imaginary phantom, but hearing a second sigh, it made him cry out, 'What devil is it which sighs here.' "'Tis I, Seignor Stulto,' answers a voice; 'I have been three years enclosed in one of these bottles. In this house lives a skilful magician, who, by the power of his art, has kept me so long shut up in this close prison.'" The demon is liberated, and represented as "a very surprising figure, about three feet and a half high, resting upon two crutches, with goat's legs and a long visage, sharp chin, a yellow and black complexion, a very flat nose, and eyes that seemed like two lighted coals."

↬ "THE RING AND THE FISH" LEGENDS: MEN LIVING INSIDE MONSTROUS FISH ↬

SOLOMON'S recovery of his magical signet-ring from the stomach of a fish, according to the Talmudic legends, finds many parallels in the popular tales of Europe, and the Rabbins perhaps borrowed the idea from the classical story of Polycrates, which must be so generally known that it need hardly be cited here, excepting for its connection with similar stories. Polycrates, king of Samos, having made a treaty of alliance with Amasis, king of Egypt, the latter, terrified by his continued prosperity, advised him to chequer his enjoyments by relinquishing some of his most cherished possessions. Polycrates complied by throwing into the sea a magnificent ring, the most valuable of his jewels. The voluntary loss of so precious an object afflicted him for some time, but a few days after he received a present of a large fish, in whose stomach the jewel was found. Amasis no sooner heard of this than he rejected all alliance with Polycrates, observing that sooner or later his good fortune would be reversed.

The plot of the noble Hindú drama of 'Sakúntála,' by Kalidasa, turns upon the same incident. In Act vi. a fisherman offers for sale a ring "bright with a large gem," on which the king's name is engraved, and, being arrested by the police, tells them that "one day, having caught a large *róhita* fish, I cut it open, and saw this bright ring in its stomach." The ring had been given by the king to Sakúntála, whom he had married by the Gandharva form while on a hunting expedition, and after his return to his capital, altogether forgot her, and its recovery at once brings her back to his recollection, and the lovers are finally united.[1]

A story is told in the Talmud of a wealthy but irreligious man, who was informed by an astrologer that all his riches should one day come into the possession of his neighbour Joseph, a poor man, but very strict in his observance of the Sabbath. Resolved to set the stars at defiance, this man disposed of all his property, and purchased with the proceeds a large diamond, which he sewed into his turban, and then embarked in a vessel

---

[1] In the 'Mahábhárata'—Last Days of the Sons of Pándu—we read that a piece of iron was found in the belly of a fish and made into an arrow-head, with which Krishna was slain.

bound for a distant country. Standing on the deck, his turban was blown into, the sea,—and how he fared after the loss of all his wealth the Talmudist does not inform us; but it happened shortly after this accident that the pious Joseph, having bought a fish and taken it home to have it cooked on the Sabbath eve, found in its stomach the very diamond which his neighbour had lost with his turban.

The legend of Kentigern, or St Mungo, the patron saint of the city of Glasgow, is another of the ring legends which abound in European folklore. "A queen, having formed an improper attachment to a handsome soldier, put upon his finger a precious ring which her own lord had conferred upon her. The king, made aware of the fact, took an opportunity, in hunting, while the soldier lay asleep beside the Clyde, to snatch off the ring and throw it into the river. Then, returning home along with the soldier, he demanded of the queen the ring he had given her. She sent secretly to the soldier for the ring, which could not be restored. In great terror she then despatched a messenger to ask the assistance of Kentigern. He, who knew of the affair before being informed of it, went to the river Clyde, and having caught a salmon, took from its stomach the missing ring, which he sent to the queen. She joyfully went with it to the king, who, thinking he had wronged her, swore he would be revenged upon her accusers; but she affecting a forgiving temper, besought him to pardon them, as she had done. At the same time she confessed her error to Kentigern, and solemnly vowed to be more careful of her conduct in the future."[2]

A poor man finds a valuable diamond in a fish, in a North German legend entitled "The Three Gifts." Three students becoming acquainted with a poor weaver, gave him a hundred dollars. He did not even tell his wife of his good fortune, but concealed the money among some old rags, which his wife one day sold to a rag-collector. When a year had passed, the three students came again, and finding the man poorer than before, when they expected he would be in comfortable circumstances, they asked him the reason, and he informed them of his misfortune. Warning him to be more careful for the future, they gave him another hundred dollars. Now he resolved to be more prudent, and so, without saying a word to his wife, he hid the money in the dust-tub, the contents of which his wife exchanged with the dustman for a few pieces of soap, in her husband's absence. Another year having passed, the three students came for

[2] Chambers's 'Book of Days,' vol. i., pp. 105, 106.

the third time, and found the weaver in rags and misery. They said to him, at the same time throwing a piece of lead at his feet, "Of what use is a nutmeg to a cow? To give thee money again would prove us greater fools than thou art." Thereupon they went away in anger, and the weaver picked up the piece of lead and placed it in the window-sill. By-and-by his neighbour, a fisherman, came to him, and inquired whether he could lend him a piece of lead, or anything heavy, as a sinker for his net. He gave the fisherman the bit of lead which the students had thrown at his feet, and was promised the first large fish he caught. He received from the fisherman a fish of four or five pounds weight, and when he opened it he found in its stomach a large stone, which in the dark shone like the sun.[3] It was a diamond, and the weaver sold it to a merchant who chanced to be passing for 1000 dollars, and then became the richest man in the village. His wife would have it that his good fortune was entirely due to her having thrown away the money twice.[4]

An exact parallel to this legend is found in the Arabian tale of the poor ropemaker, whom two benevolent gentlemen wished to assist in his business. One of them, believing that without money no one could attain wealth, gave the poor man twice a sum of money. Of the first sum, he spent a portion in buying hemp, and wrapped the remainder in his turban, which a kite snatched off his head one day; of the second sum given him the following year, when the two friends came to see how the money had been spent, he again used a part in the purchase of hemp, and placed the balance in a pot, which he then filled with sand. His wife sold the sand, pot and all, to a sand-merchant. The third year the two friends came again, when he told them of his second mishap, which the gentleman who gave the money did not believe. The other, who was of opinion that it is vain to strive if destiny is not in our favour, gave the ropemaker a piece of lead. As in the German tale, a fisherman borrows the lead as a sinker for his lines, and gives him by way of acknowledgment a fish, which contains a splendid diamond. This the ropemaker sells to a Jew, who lived next door, for a great sum of money, and he now begins business on a "large scale." At the end of the fourth year the two friends come again, and find that he has "removed to more commodious premises." He tells them the cause of his success in trade, and before they leave, strange to say (that is, outside of an oriental romance), his turban

[3]See Note, "Luminous Jewels," p. 209.
[4]Thorpe's 'Yule-Tide Stories,' p. 463 of Bohn's edition.

with the money is found in a tree, the kite having made a nest of it, and the pot of sand with the money originally placed in it has again found its way into his own warehouse, thus proving the truth of his stories.

Strange things are certainly found sometimes in the stomachs of large fish, occasionally even rings and gems—for they greedily seize and swallow any glittering object; but the ring-legends of all countries are for the most part mere inventions. The story of Kentigern is an evident imitation of Christ's miracle, of causing a fish to be caught, in whose stomach was found money wherewith to pay tribute to Cæsar.[5]

If such tales as those above cited, of wonderful "finds" in the maws of fish, may be admitted to be probable or possible, the equally wide-spread and ancient legends of men having been swallowed by monster fish and escaping after living therein—not merely the "three days and three nights" of the prophet Jonah's similar experience, but sometimes for several years—are so incredible that we must conclude, either that they had originally an esoteric signification, and are variants of a "nature myth," or that they are the mere offspring of the untutored fancy. Stories of this class are common to the folklore of Asiatic countries, but they were not unfamiliar in medieval Europe, if we may judge from a specimen found in one of the early English versions of the 'Gesta Romanorum.' The king of Naples sends his daughter in a ship to be married to the son of the Emperor of Rome:

"And whenne thei were in the shippe, and hadde passid fro the londe, there rose vp a gret horribill tempest, and draynt all that were in the ship, except the mayde. Thenne the mayde sette all hire hope strongly in God; and at the laste, the tempest sesid; but ther folowid strongly a gret whale, to devoure this maide. And whenne she saw that, she moche dradde; and whan the nyght com, the maide dredyng that the whale wolde haue swolowide the ship, smot fire at a stone, and had gret plenté of fire. And as long as the fire laste, the whale dorst come no nere, but abowte cockis crowe the mayde, for gret vexacion that she hadde with the tempest, fell on slepe, and in hire slep the fire went out. And when it was out the whale com nye, and swolowid both the ship and the mayde. And when the mayde felte that she was in the wombe of the whale, she smot, and made

[5]The old ballad of 'The Cruel Knight and the Fortunate Farmer's Daughter' turns upon the discovery of a ring in the stomach of a fish; a legend which is alluded to in Lyson's 'Environs of London,' and which forms the basis of a novel entitled 'Dame Rebecca Berry; or, Court Scenes in the reign of Charles II.,' published at London in 1827.

a gret fire, and greuously wondid the whale with a littill knyfe, in so moche that he drowe to the lond, and deyde. For that is the kynde, to drawe to the londe when he shall dye. And in this tym they was an Erle namyd Pirius, and he walkid in his disport by the see, and afore him he sawe the whale come toward the lond. He gaderid gret helpe and strenght of men; [and] with diuerse instrumentis thei smote the whale in euery part of hym. And when the damesell hurde the gret strokys, she cryde with an hye voys, and saide, Gentill siris, havith pite of me, for I am the dowter of a king, and a mayde haue y-ben sith I was borne. Whenne the Erle hurde this, he merveilid gretly, and openyd the whale, and toke out the damesell. Thenne the maide tolde by ordr how that she was a kyngys dowter, and howe she loste hir goodes in the see, and how she sholde be maryed to the Emperour. And when the Erle hurde theise wordis, he was glad, and helde the maide with him a gret while, till tyme that she was wele confortid; and thenne he sent hire solemply to the Emperour."[6]

To say the least, this "story" is not very consistent in its details: all those on board the ship were drowned, excepting the maiden, after which both she and the vessel were swallowed by "a great whale"; but how the others came to be drowned without the ship being broken in pieces the credulous monkish chronicler does not condescend to inform us: and since the maiden told the noble who rescued her from the animal's internal economy that she had lost all her goods by the misadventure, we must suppose that the whale had digested ship and cargo.

The story may have been suggested by Lucian's 'Vera Historia,' Book i., where a monster fish swallows a ship, and the crew discover extensive countries in the creature's inside.[7] Sindbád, of 'Arabian Nights' celebrity, among other perils he encountered in his frequent voyages to unknown parts, narrowly escaped the like fate: his vessel was surrounded by enormous fish, one of which darted down to swallow the ship and all that was in her; but a tempest drove her on a reef and broke her to pieces—the hero reaching the shore, as usual, with the aid of a plank. It is surprising that the historian of Sindbád's trading career has not represented him as

[6]Herrtage's 'Gesta Romanorum' (Early English Test Society), pp. 297–299.

[7]Possibly Rabelais had this most veracious incident in mind when he represented the renowned Pantagruel as eating a salad one day, and unwittingly taking into his mouth half a dozen pilgrims who had sheltered themselves under the leaves. By skipping about with their staves the unlucky pilgrims manage to avoid contact with his grinders, till at last one of them chances to strike the cleft of a decayed tooth; the pain which this occasions makes him search his mouth, and the devotees are delivered.

having been actually swallowed—himself, at least—by the sea-monster that thus threatened the destruction of the ship and all that was in her;—the incident could hardly fail of proving to most readers an interesting addition to the marvels so minutely described by the Arabian story-teller.

More judicious was the Hindú author in his story of Saktideva's adventures in quest of the Golden City. That hero sets out in the vessel of a merchant with whom he had scraped acquaintance, and this is what happened to him: "When they had but a short distance to travel, there arose a black cloud with rumbling thunder, resembling a roaring rákshasa, with flickering lightning to represent his lolling tongue. And a furious hurricane began to blow like Destiny herself, whirling up light objects and hurling down heavy.[8] And from the sea, lashed by the wind, great waves rose aloft like the mountains equipped with wings, indignant that their asylum had been attacked. And that vessel rose on high one moment, and the next moment plunged below, as if exhibiting how rich men are first elevated and then cast down. And the next moment that ship, shrilly laden with the cries of the merchants, burst and split asunder, as if with the weight. And the ship being broken, that merchant its owner fell into the sea, but floating through it on a plank, he at last reached another vessel. But as Saktideva fell, a large fish, opening its mouth and neck, swallowed him without injuring any of his limbs. And as that fish was roaming at will in the midst of the sea, it happened to pass near the island of Utsthala; and by chance some servants of the king of the fishermen, Satyavrata, who were engaged in the pursuit of small fish, came there and caught it. And those fishermen, proud of their prize, immediately dragged it along to show their king, for it was of enormous size. He too, out of curiosity, seeing that it was of such extraordinary size, ordered his servants to cut it open; and when it was cut open, Saktideva came out

---

[8]That is to say, Destiny often elevates the worthless, and hurls down men of worth.—Compare Defoe, in his scathing reply to Lord Haversham's Vindication of his Speech: "Fate makes footballs of men; kicks some up-stairs and some down;—some are advanced without honour, others suppressed without infamy; some are raised without merit, some are crushed without crime;—and no man knows, by the beginning of things, whether his course will issue in a peerage or a pillory." And these passages from the drama of "Mrichchakata," or the Toy-Cart (Dr H. H. Wilson's 'Theatre of the Hindús'):

"Fate views the world
A scene of mutual and perpetual struggle;
And sports with life as if it were a wheel
That draws the limpid water from the well;

alive from its belly, having endured a second wonderful imprisonment in the womb."[9]

A similar accident befell Ahlá, the celebrated Bundel'-khand hero: "The Banaphals went once to Hardwar to hunt. When they arrived near the hunting-ground, Ahlá went into the Ganges to bathe, and was then and there swallowed by a monstrous fish. His friends searched for him. While they were lamenting, Machhlávatí, the daughter of the king Ragho Machh of Hardwar, came there with her companions to bathe. Hearing the lamentations of Ahlá's friends, she sent for a fisherman, who, throwing his net into the river, brought the fish to land. On its belly being split open, Ahlá issued therefrom unhurt. Thereupon they all set out for Machhlávatí's house, and Ahlá engaged himself to marry her and her friend Subhna."[10]

But a proud king, in a Kashmírí tale, who had lost his kingdom, and was swept away by a swift river which he attempted to wade across, had a sojourn of many years inside a great fish. Meanwhile his two little sons had been found on the banks of the river, and adopted by a kind-hearted fisherman and his wife. "One day it happened that an enormous fish threw itself on the bank of the river, and could not get back into the water. Everybody in the village went to see the monster and cut off a slice of it. A few people also went from the neighbouring villages, and amongst them was a maker of earthenware. His wife had heard of the great fish, and urged him to go and get some of the flesh. Accordingly he went, although the hour was late. On arriving he found nobody there, as all the people had satisfied themselves and returned. The potter took an axe with him, thinking that the bones would be so thick as to require its aid before they could be broken. When he struck the first blow a voice came out of the fish, as of some one in pain. The potter was very much

---

For some are raised to affluence, some depressed
In want, and some are borne awhile aloft,
And some hurled down to wretchedness and woe."

"O Fate! thou sportest with the fortunes of mankind,
Like drops of water trembling on the lotus-leaf."

[9]'Kathá Sarit Ságara,' chap. xxv.—In another story, chap. lxxiv., a Bráhman named Sankhadatta relates how he was swallowed by a very large fish in the Ganges, and remained for a long time inside "the capacious habitation of its stomach," eating its flesh, which he cut off with a knife, until the waves cast the fish upon the bank, and some men, having killed it, drew him out.

[10]"Legend of Ahlá," in 'Indian Antiquary,' September 1885.

surprised. 'Perhaps,' thought he, 'the fish is possessed by a bhút. I'll try again;' whereupon he struck another blow. Again a voice came forth from the fish, saying, 'Woe is me! woe is me!' On hearing this the potter thought, 'Well, this is not a bhút evidently, but the voice of an ordinary man. I'll cut the flesh carefully. May be that I shall find some poor distressed person.' He began to cut away the flesh carefully, and presently he descried a man's foot; then the legs appeared; then the body, all entire. 'Praise be to God!' he cried aloud, 'the soul is in him yet.' He carried the man to his house as fast as he could, and there did everything in his power to recover him; and the joy of the potter and his wife was great when they saw that the stranger was revived."[11] This was the once-proud king, who had lived so long in the inside of the monster fish.

In one of Miss Stokes' 'Indian Fairy Tales,' the heroine, "Loving Lailí," lives twelve years in a Rohita fish; and in another, in the same entertaining story-book (which is rendered so useful to story comparers by Mr Ralston's learned Introduction to it), a crocodile is substituted for a fish (No. 12): A man started off to the river, and began drawing up water in a bucket. "Stop, stop!" cried an alligator, who was the king of the fishes; "you are taking all the water out of the river, and my fishes will die." The man replied, "I want money, and I can find none; so I am taking the water out of the river in order to get some" [by selling it]. "You shall have some in a minute," said the alligator; "only do stop drawing the water." Then a great wave of water dashed on to the land, and dashed back into the river, leaving behind it a heap of gold, which the man picked up joyfully. The next day he came again, and night and day he drew water out of the river. At last the alligator got very angry and said, "My fishes will all die for want of water. Once I gave the man a heap of gold, and yet he wants more. I won't give him any," and the alligator thrust up his head out of the river and swallowed the man whole. For four days and four nights the man lived in the alligator's stomach. At the end of the fourth night the king of the fishes said to him, "I will let you get out of my stomach on condition that you tell no man what has happened to you. If you do, you will die instantly." The man jumped out of the alligator's mouth and walked towards his house. On his way he met some men, and told them what had happened to him; and as soon as he got home he told his wife

---

[11] "Pride Abased: a Kashmírí Tale," by the Rev. J. Hinton Knowles, in 'Indian Antiquary,' June 1886.

and children, and the moment he had done so he became mad and dumb, and blood came out of his mouth, and he fell down dead.

NOTE.

LUMINOUS JEWELS (p. 203)

In the 'Gesta Romanorum,' chap. cvii., a carbuncle supplies the place of sunlight. "Whether a carbuncle doth flame in the dark," says Sir Thomas Browne, in his 'Vulgar Errors,' "or shine like a coal in the night, though generally agreed on by common believers, is very much questioned by many." (Why did not Sir Thomas satisfy himself, by experiments?) This absurd notion of luminous jewels is of frequent occurrence in Eastern fictions and legends. In the Talmud it is said that Noah and his family while in the Ark had no light besides what was sent forth by diamonds and other precious stones. And Abraham, who, it seems, was very jealous of his wives, built for them a city, the walls of which were so high as to exclude the light of the sun!—an inconvenience which he easily remedied by means of a large basin full of pearls and other gems, which shed a light equal in brilliancy to that of the "eye of day." It is related that over the gable of the palace of Prester John were placed, at the two extremities, two golden apples, in each of which were two carbuncles, so that the gold might shine by day and the carbuncles by night. In the Pseudo-Callisthenes it is said that Alexander found in the belly of a fish a precious stone, which he set in gold, and used at night as a lamp. In Lucian's 'De Deâ Syriâ,' on the head of the statue of the goddess was a stone, "which they call the Lamp, from its lustre; by night it shines with such splendour as to light the whole temple." In the 'Forty Vazírs' we read of a dome composed of a carbuncle six feet in diameter, which served instead of the sun in an underground palace. Jewel-lamps are often mentioned in the 'Kathá Sarit Ságara.'

꙳ MAGICAL
TRANSFORMATIONS ꙳

THE stem of what Mr Baring-Gould terms the "Magical-Conflict Root" has spread its branches far and wide in the shape of popular fictions in which two or more persons, possessing nearly equal powers of changing themselves into whatever forms they please, engage in a life-or-death struggle. It seems to me that popular belief in men being capable of acquiring such powers should sufficiently account for the universal prevalence of stories of this class, without seeking for their origin in primitive conceptions of the phenomena of physical nature, such as sunrise, sunset, clouds, lightning, and so forth. However this may be, there certainly is no cycle of folk-tales of which the members, everywhere present a more striking resemblance to each other, or indicate more clearly a common origin. In this case especially is independent invention of the same incidents in different countries and ages altogether out of the question, as I hope to prove conclusively in the course of the present paper.

Readers familiar with the 'Arabian Nights'—and who is not?—must remember the terrible conflict which occurs in the story of the Second Calender: He had been changed into an ape by an evil genie; and while a beautiful young princess is performing magical rites for restoring him to his natural form, the genie appears as a fierce lion, upon which the princess changes herself into a keen-edged sword and cuts the lion in two. Then the genie becomes a scorpion and the princess a serpent, in which form she vanquishes her enemy, who flees away as an eagle, and is pursued by the princess as a larger eagle. The succeeding metamorphoses are: a black cat, chased by a wolf; the cat becomes a worm, which, piercing a pomegranate, causes it to burst, when the wolf becomes a cock, and begins to pick up the seeds; one of the seeds rolls into the canal and becomes a fish, and then the cock turns himself into a great pike; finally, the princess and the genie are seen enveloped in flames, and both are reduced to ashes.—This catastrophe is, so far as I am aware, peculiar to the Arabian version of the Magical Conflict; in the other versions the person who acts the same part as the princess is usually victorious.

Keightley, in his 'Tales and Popular Fictions,' published more than half a century ago—an interesting little book, though now obsolete with comparative storiologists—has pointed out Italian and German tales "which have some resemblance" to the foregoing, "though probably an accidental one." This is Keightley's abstract of a story in the 'Pleasant Nights' of Straparola:[1]

A magician, named Lactantius, followed the trade of a tailor. He takes an apprentice, who, happening to overhear his incantations, loses all relish for tailoring, and his father takes him home. Lactantius, however, receives him again, and sets him now only to common work, and the father takes him away once more. As they were very poor, the son said to his father, "I will turn myself into a fine horse. Do you then sell me; but be sure to keep the bridle, and not to let it go with me, or else I cannot come back." Lactantius, seeing the horse, knows who it is. He buys him, and persuades the father to let him have the bridle along with him. Having got the horse into his possession, he ties him up, beats him, and abuses him. One day the daughters of the magician led the horse to water, when suddenly he turned himself into a little fish, and dived down. Lactantius hastened to the spot, and becoming a large fish, pursued the little one, who jumped, in the form of a ruby set in a gold ring, into the basket of the king's daughter, who was gathering pebbles at that place. She takes him away with her, and he shows himself to her in his true form—that of a handsome youth. She loves him, and keeps him with her as a ring. The king falling sick, Lactantius comes as a physician, cures him, and for his fee demands a ruby-ring which his daughter has, and with which he was well acquainted. The princess refuses to give it up; but when at last she is compelled to surrender it, the youth tells her to throw it against the wall before the magician. She does so, and as soon as the ring falls to the ground it is turned into a pomegranate, which bursts, and scatters its seeds about. The magician converts himself into a cock, and picks them up; but one hid itself from him, and becoming a fox, catches him by the neck and bites his head off. The king then gives the young man his daughter in marriage.

In the German version cited by Keightley (the tale of the Gaudeif, or Thief, in Grimm's collection), the pupil is sold, in like manner, as a horse, the father also parting with the bridle. When he gets the bridle off, he changes himself into a sparrow, and is pursued by his master, also as a sparrow. They then become fishes: finally, the master is a cock, and the

---

[1] 'Piacevoli Notti di M. Giovan Francesco Straparola la Caravagio,' etc., first printed at Venice in 1550.

pupil, as a fox, bites his head off.—In all Austrian version, the last metamorphosis of the master is into a grain of oats, which is gobbled up by the pupil, in the form of a cock, and thus an end of the magician.

"There are, it will be seen," remarks Keightley, "some points of resemblance in these different tales, but perhaps hardly sufficient to justify an assertion of one being borrowed from another. Yet possibly," he adds, "the Arabian story had reached Venice." (Pp. 123, 124.)

That many Eastern fictions were imported into Italy in the 16th century there is every reason to believe; but I do not think this was one of them, since the first incident, the selling of the horse with the bridle, is found in a separate tale in the 'Arabian Nights,' as Keightley himself was aware; while not only in Germany and Austria, but in Denmark and Norway also, the "magical conflict" is current in a form similar to that of Straparola's story; and I am rather disposed to consider that it was introduced into the south of Europe by the Norsemen, than that it travelled from the South to the North.

The "bridle" incident occurs in the Arabian tale of Julnar of the Sea and her Son. Queen Láb, a sorceress, having attempted to transform King Badr Bassim and failed, because he had taken precautions by the advice of Abdallah the grocer, who was skilled in "white" magic (which is not regarded as unlawful by Muslims), and who had also instructed him how to turn the tables on her, the story thus proceeds, according to Sir R. F. Burton's new translation:

Badr Bassim took water in his palm and threw it in her face, saying, "Quit this human form and take that of a dapple mule." No sooner had he spoken than she found herself changed into a she-mule, whereupon the tears ran down her cheeks, and she fell to rubbing her muzzle against his feet. Then he would have bridled her, but she would not take the bit. So he left her, and going to the grocer, told him what had passed. Abdallah brought out for him a bridle, and bade him rein her forthwith. So he took it to the palace, and when she saw him, she came up to him, and he set the bit in her mouth, and mounting her, rode forth to find the shaykh. But when the old man saw her, he rose and said to her, "Almighty Allah confound thee, O accursed woman!" Then quoth he to Badr, "O my son, there is no more tarrying for thee in this city; so ride her, and fare with her whither thou wilt; and beware lest thou commit the bridle to any." King Badr thanked him, and farewelling him, fared on three days without ceasing till he drew near another city, and there met him an old man, grey-headed and comely, who said, "Whence comest thou, O my son?" Badr replied, "From the city of this wretch." And the old man said, "Thou art my guest to-night." He consented, and went with him; but by the way, behold! they met an old woman, who wept when she saw the mule, and said, "Verily this mule resembleth my son's she-mule, which is dead, and my heart acheth for her. So, Allah upon thee, O my lord, do thou sell her to me." He replied, "By Allah, O my mother, I cannot sell her." But she cried, "Allah upon thee! do not refuse my request; for my son will surely be a dead man except I bring him this mule." And she importuned him till he exclaimed, "I will not sell her save for a thousand dinars;"[2] saying in himself, "Whence should this old woman get a thousand gold pieces?" Thereupon she brought out from her girdle a purse containing a thousand ducats, which when King Badr Bassim saw, he said, "O my mother, I did but jest with thee. I cannot sell her." But the old man looked at him and said, "O my son, in this city none may lie; for whoso lieth they put to death." So King Badr Bassim dismounted and delivered the mule to the old woman, and she drew the bit from her mouth, and taking water in her hand, sprinkled the mule therewith, saying, "O my daughter, quit this shape for that which thou wast aforetime." Upon that she was straightway restored to her original semblance, and the two women embraced and kissed each other. So King Badr Bassim knew that the old woman was Queen Láb's mother, and that he had been tricked, and would have fled, when the old woman whistled a loud whistle, and her call was obeyed by an Ifrít, as he were a great mountain;[3] whereat Badr was affrighted and stood still. Then the old woman mounted on the Ifrít's back, taking her daughter behind her and King Badr Bassim before her, and the Ifrít flew off with them.[4]

[2] About five hundred pounds.

[3] Demons of this species often figure in Arabian romances, and we have met with them more than once in the preceding papers. A Persian poet has thus graphically sketched the likeness of one of these formidable beings:

He was an Ifrít, created from mouth to foot by the wrath of God.

His hair like a bear's, his teeth like a boar's. No one ever beheld such a monster.

Crook-backed and crabbed-faced, he might be scented at the distance of a thousand parsangs.

His nostrils were like the ovens of brick-burners, and his mouth resembled the vat of a dyer.

For a full account of the nature of the jinn, ifríts, etc. see Lane's 'Arabian Nights,' vol. i. pp. 26–33.

[4] "A Plain and Literal Translation of the "Arabian Nights Entertainments," now entituled "The Book of the Thousand Nights and a Night." With Introduction, Explanatory Notes on the Manners and Customs of Moslem Men, and a Terminal Essay upon the History of "The Nights." By Richard F. Burton. [In ten volumes.] Benares: MDCCCLXXXV. Printed by the Kamashastra Society for Private Subscribers only.' Vol. vii. pp. 304, 305.

❧

To return to the "magical conflict." In the Norwegian version, the pupil of Farmer Weathersky, having become what his mother wished, "the master of all masters," she wouldn't rest till he gave a proof of his magical skill. So when the fair came round the lad changed himself into a horse, and told his father to lead him to the fair. "Now when any one comes," he said, "to buy me, you may ask a hundred dollars for me; but mind you don't forget to take the headstall off me—if you do, Farmer Weathersky will keep me for ever, for he it is who will come to deal with you." So it turned out. Up came a horsedealer who had a great wish to deal for a horse, and he gave a hundred dollars down for him; but when the bargain was struck, and Jack's father had pocketed the money, the horsedealer wanted to have the headstall. "Nay, nay," said the man, "there's nothing about that in the bargain; and, besides, you can't have the headstall, for I've other horses at home to bring to town to-morrow." So each went his way; but they hadn't gone far before Jack took his own shape and ran away, and when his father got home, there sat Jack in the ingle. Next day he turned himself into a brown horse, and told his father to drive him to the fair: "And when any one comes to buy me," said he, "you may ask two hundred dollars for me—he'll give that, and treat you besides; but whatever you do, and however much you drink, don't forget to take the headstall off me, else you'll never set eyes on me again." So all happened as he had said: the man got two hundred dollars for the horse, and a glass of drink besides, and when the buyer and seller parted it was as much as he could do to remember to take off the headstall. But the buyer and the horse hadn't got far on the road before Jack took his own shape, and when his father got home, there sat Jack in the ingle. The third day it was the same story over again; the lad turned himself into a black horse, and told his father some one would come and bid him three hundred dollars for him, and fill his skin with meat and drink besides. But however much he ate or drank, he was to mind and not forget to take the headstall off, else he'd have to stay with Farmer Weathersky all his life long. "No, no, I'll not forget—never fear," said his father. So when he came to the fair, he got three hundred dollars for the horse; and as it wasn't a dry bargain, Farmer Weathersky made him drink so much that he quite forgot to take the headstall off, and away went Farmer Weathersky with the horse.

Now when he had gone a little way, he thought he would just stop and have another glass of brandy; so he put a barrel of red-hot nails under his horse's nose, and a sieve of oats under his tail, hung the halter upon a hook, and went into the inn. So the horse stood there, and stamped and pawed, and snorted and roared. Just then came a lassie, who thought it a shame to treat a horse so. "O poor beastie!" she said; "what a cruel master you must have to treat you so!" and as she said this, she pulled the halter off the hook, so that the horse might turn round and taste the oats. "I'm after you!" roared Farmer Weathersky; but the horse had already shaken off the headstall and jumped into a duck-pond, where he turned himself into a tiny fish. In went Farmer Weathersky after him, and turned himself into a pike. Then Jack turned himself into a dove, and Farmer Weathersky became a hawk, and chased and struck at the dove. But just then the princess stood at the window of the palace and saw this struggle. "Ah, poor dove!" she cried, "if you only knew what I know, you'd fly to me through this window." So the dove came flying in through the window, and turned himself into Jack again, who told her his own tale. "Turn yourself into a gold ring," said the princess, "and put yourself on my finger." Quoth Jack, "Nay, nay, that'll never do; for Farmer Weathersky will make the king sick, and then there'll be no one who can make him well again till Farmer Weathersky comes and cures him; and then for his fee he'll ask that gold ring." The princess replied, "Then I'll say I had it from my mother, and can't part with it." So Jack turned himself into a gold ring, and put himself on the finger of the princess; and so Farmer Weathersky couldn't get at him. But then followed what the lad had foretold: the king fell sick, and there wasn't a doctor in the kingdom who could cure him till Farmer Weathersky came and asked for the ring off the princess' finger for his fee. So the king sent a messenger to the princess for the ring; but she said she wouldn't part with it, for her mother had left it her. When the king heard that he flew into a rage, and said he would have the ring, whoever left it her. "Well," said the princess, "it's no good being cross about it. I can't get it off, and if you must have the ring, you must take my finger too." "If you'll let me try, I'll soon get the ring off," said Farmer Weathersky. "No, thanks; I'll try myself," said the princess, and flew to the grate and put ashes on her finger. Then the ring slipped off, and was lost among the ashes. So Farmer Weathersky turned himself into a cock, and scratched and pecked after the ring in the grate till he was up to the eyes in ashes. But while he was doing this, Jack changed himself into a fox, and bit off the cock's head; and if the Evil One was in Farmer Weathersky, it is all over with him now.[5]

[5] Dasent's 'Popular Tales from the Norse.' Second edition, pp. 335–339.

In the Danish version the lad's master in magic is a Troll-man, and his first exploit is to change himself into a beautiful little dog, which his father sells for a considerable sum to the occupants of a fine carriage that came rolling past; at the same instant the son changes his father into a hare, and in the form of the dog chases it, and both disappear in a wood, when father and son assume human forms and return home. After all the money was spent, the youth said to his father, "Now I will turn myself into a boar, and you must put a cord round my leg and take me to Horsens market for sale; but remember to throw the cord over my right ear at the moment you sell me, and then I shall be home again as soon as you." The peasant did as his son directed him, and went to market; and there at length sold the boar at a high price to an old man (who was none other than the magician), taking care to throw the cord over its right ear as the lad had told him, and in the same moment the animal vanished, and when he reached his own home again, there was his son sitting at the table. They now lived a merry life until all their money was spent, and then again set out on fresh adventures. This time the lad changed himself into a bull, first reminding his father to throw the rope over his right horn as soon as he was sold. At the market he met with the same old man, and soon came to an agreement with him about the price of the bull. While they were drinking a glass at the alehouse, the father threw the rope over the bull's right horn, and when the magician went to fetch his purchase it had disappeared, and the peasant on reaching home again found his son sitting beside his mother at the table.

The lad next turned himself into a horse, and the magician was again in the market and bought him. "Thou hast already tricked me twice," said he to the peasant, "but it shall not happen again;" and before he paid down the money he hired a stable and fastened the horse in, so that it was impossible for the peasant to throw the rein over the animal's right ear. The old man, nevertheless, returned home, in the hope that this time also he should find his son; but he was disappointed, for no lad was there. The magician in the meantime mounted the horse and rode off. He well knew whom he had bought, and determined that the lad should pay with his life for the deception he had practised upon him. He rode the horse through swamps and pools, until at length he himself was tired and went home. When he arrived there, he put a magic bridle on the horse and shut him in a dark stable, without giving him anything to eat or drink. After some time had elapsed, he said to the servant-maid, "Go out and see how the horse is;" and when she went into the stable the horse began to moan piteously, and begged her to give him a pail of water. She did so, and on her return told her master that the horse was well. Some time after, he again desired her to go and see if the horse was not yet dead. When she entered the stable the poor animal begged her to loose the bridle and the girths, which were strapped so tight that he could hardly draw breath. The girl did as she was requested, and no sooner was it done than the horse was changed into a hare and ran out of the stable.

The magician, who was sitting at the window, was immediately aware of what had happened on seeing the hare go springing across the yard, and, in a moment changing himself into a dog, went in pursuit of it. When they had run many miles over corn-fields and meadows, the hare's strength began to fail, and the magician gained more and more upon him. The hare then changed into a dove, but the magician as quickly turned himself into a hawk and renewed his pursuit. In this manner they flew towards a palace where a princess was sitting at a window. When she saw a hawk in chase of a dove she opened the window, and immediately the dove flew into the room, and then changed itself into a gold ring. The magician now became a prince, and went into the apartment for the purpose of catching the dove. When he could not find it, he asked permission to see her rings. The princess showed them to him, but let one fall into the fire. The Troll-man instantly drew it out, and in so doing burnt his fingers, and was obliged to let it fall on the floor. Then the ring became a grain of corn, and at the same instant the magician turned himself into a hen in order to eat the corn, but scarcely had he done so than the lad became a hawk and killed him. He then went to the forest, fetched all the magician's gold and silver, and from that day lived in wealth and happiness with his parents.[6]

A similar but briefer conflict is waged between the hero and a species of griffin, called the Tree Lion, in the Gaelic story of the Fair Gruagach, son of the king of Eirinn: "When they were on forward a short distance, whom saw they coming but the Tree Lion. He became a bull; the Fair Chief became a bull before him, and the first blow he struck him he laid his head on his side, and the Tree Lion gave out a roar. Then he sprang as an ass; the Fair Chief sprang as an ass before him, and at the first rush he gave towards him he took a mouthful between flesh and skin. The Tree Lion then sprang as a hawk in the wood, and he took the heart and liver out of him. The Fair

[6]Thorpe's 'Yule-Tide Stories,' Bohn's edition, pp. 336–339.—The incident, in the Norse version, of the horse having a pan of red-hot nails at his head and a bushel of oats at his tail occurs in a different Norwegian story in Thorpe's collection, "The Widow's Son," p. 295.

Chief fell down afterwards; Fionn seized him, and he put him into the napkin [as had been previously arranged between them], and he cut a turf, and he put the napkin under earth and the turf upon it, and he stood on the turf. The wife of the Tree Lion came, and the book of witchcraft was on her back in a hay-band. 'Eeen, son of Connal, man that never told a lie, who killed my comrade?' 'I know not, *above earth*, who killed thy comrade. And she went away in her weeping cry, and she betook herself to distance. He caught hold of the Fair Chief, and he lifted him with him, and he reached the castle in which was the Dame of the Fine Green Kirtle."[7]

The oldest European form of the Magical Conflict is doubtless found in the legend of the birth of Taliesin, a famous Welsh bard, who flourished in the sixth century, as given in the last of the 'Mabinogion,' translated by Lady Charlotte Guest:

Ceridwen, the wife of Tegid Voel, having prepared a magical concoction in order to render her ugly son Aragddu all-knowing, and thus compensate him for his physical defects, she set the cauldron containing it upon the fire, and put Gwion Bach, the son of Gureang, to stir the ingredients, and a blind man named Morda to kindle the fire beneath the cauldron, charging them on their peril not to suffer it to cease boiling for the space of a year and a day. All went well until near the end of the year, when Ceridwen being absent one day culling plants of magic virtue, three drops of the Water of Inspiration flew out of the cauldron and fell upon the finger of Gwion Bach, and by reason of their great heat he put his finger to his mouth, and instantly perceived all that was to happen, and that he must guard against the wiles of Ceridwen. So he fled towards his own land. The cauldron burst into pieces and the charmed liquor was all lost. When Ceridwen returned and saw what had happened, she struck blind Morda on the head with a billet of wood, upon which he declared himself guiltless, and then she knew it was Gwion Bach who had done it.

And she went after him, running. And he saw her, and changed himself into a hare and fled. But she changed herself into a greyhound and turned him. And he ran towards a river and became a fish. And she in the form of an otter chased him under the water, until he was fain to turn himself into a bird of the air. She, as a hawk, followed him, and gave him no rest in the sky. And just as she was about to stoop upon him, and he was in fear of death, he espied a heap of winnowed wheat on the floor of a barn,

---

[7] Campbell's 'Tales of the West Highlands,' vol. ii. p. 423.

and he dropped among the wheat and turned himself into one of the grains. Then she formed herself into a high-crested black hen, and went to the wheat and scratched it with her feet, and found him out and swallowed him. And, as the story says, she bore him nine months; and when she was delivered of him, she could not find it in her heart to kill him, by reason of his beauty. So she wrapped him in a leathern bag and cast him into the sea to the mercy of God, on the twenty-ninth day of April.[8]

If this cycle of folk-tales be, as some comparative mythologists maintain, survivals of a primitive Aryan myth, then the foregoing Cymric story, so far as it relates to the Magical Conflict, probably reflects more or less faithfully the very tradition which the tribes carried with them when they first began to migrate to Europe. "It might, I think," says Lady Charlotte Guest, "be shown that the Cymric nation is not only, as Dr Prichard has proved it to be, an early off-shoot of the Indo-European family, and a people of unmixed descent, but that, when driven out of their conquests by the later nations, the names and exploits of their heroes and the compositions of their bards spread far and wide among the invaders, and affected intimately their tastes and literature for many centuries, and that it has strong claims to be considered as the cradle of European romance." No doubt the mediæval romances of Europe were largely derived from ancient British sources, though they also owed much to the Sagas of Scandinavia, and to Arabic fictions; but it is not at all likely that the Cymric story of the magical contest between Ceridwen and little Gwion Bach was the direct source of the Norse tale of Farmer Weathersky and his pupil, or Straparola's version, with which it so closely corresponds. We must conclude that the resemblance between these two versions is due to transmission from the North to the South, or *vice versá;* or that the story, like so many others, reached Scandinavia through the Mongolians, and Italy through the Turks.[9] Observe the exact parallel

---

[8]'The Mabinogion.' From the Welsh of the 'Llyfr Coch o Hergest' (The Red Book of Hergest), in the Library of Jesus College, Oxford. Translated, with Notes, by Lady Charlotte Guest. London: Quaritch, 1877. (Last edition.) Pp. 471–473.—The term "Mabinogi," Professor E. B. Cowell has informed me, means "juvenility," from *mab*, a child; then "juvenile amusement," "a youth-tale." It is properly the title of four only of Lady Charlotte Guest's tales—viz., "Owyll," "Branwen," "Manawyddan," and "Math," which all form one romance; but the name in the plural, "mabinogion," has been improperly applied to all the rest. Properly, these four are *the* 'Mabinogion.'

[9]Many learned Icelanders visited even remote parts of the East during the middle ages, and they probably carried back with them some of the fictions which have long been domiciled in the north of Europe, and which are demonstrably of Asiatic extraction.

which is presented to both the Norse and the Italian stories in the following version from Leger's 'Contes Albanais':

Once upon a time a man sent his son away among the devils to learn
their art, and at the end of a year he had learned it so thoroughly that he
knew more of it than his masters; so his father went for him and brought
him home. Then he said to his father, "To-morrow I intend to become a
horse, with every quality valued in that animal. You will sell me at a price
proportionate to my value, but take particular care not to give away the
bridle with me." So next day he changed himself into a horse, and his
father took him to market and sold him for I know not how many thousand piastres, taking care to keep the bridle. But the youth, resuming his
proper form, fled from the buyer's house and came home. Next day there
was a new metamorphosis, this time into a mule; and his father again set
out to sell him at the market. The devils with whom the youth had studied came and asked the father what he wanted for his mule, and having
agreed on the price, they paid him the money. Then quoth the father to
them, "Observe, I do not give you the bridle." The devils replied, "But we
must have it," and thereupon a dispute arose. The mule took advantage
of it to scamper off, and the devils bolted in pursuit. Seeing that he could
not escape, the mule at once became a hare, and then the devils changed
themselves into dogs and coursed the hare. When the hare was about to
be caught, he became an apple, which fell upon the queen's table. The
dogs then took the forms of dervishes and said to the queen, "In the
name of Heaven, give us that apple which has just fallen on your table!
For many days have we sweated blood and water to obtain it." The queen
replied, "You shall not be disgraced by a refusal. What! is it for this apple
you have suffered so much? There it is—take it, and go in peace," and
she tossed them the apple, which instantly became millet, and spread all
over the ground. Upon this the dervishes changed themselves into fowls
and began to pick up the grain. Then the millet became a fox, which
crunched up the fowls. So well had the youth learned the devils' art, that
he devoured those who had taught him.[10]

In the frame-story of the Relations of Siddhí Kúr,[11] we have a Kalmuk
version, from an older form of which it is possible the Norse story may

[10]As the story occurs also in the Turkish romance of the 'Forty Vazírs,' it is highly probable that the Albanians derived it from the Ottomans.

[11]See note on page 6.

have been derived—for that work, as it now exists, is generally considered as of comparatively recent date:

In the kingdom of Magadha there once lived seven brothers who were magicians. At the distance of a mile from their abode lived two brothers, sons of a khán. The elder of these went to the seven magicians, saying, "Teach me to understand your art," and abode with them seven years. But though they were always setting him to learn different tasks, yet they never taught him the true key to their mystic knowledge. His brother, however, coming to visit him one day, by merely looking through a crack in the door of the apartment in which the seven brothers were at work, acquired perfectly all magical science. After this they both went home together; the elder, because he perceived he would never learn anything of the magicians, and the younger, because he had learned everything they had to impart. As they went along, the younger brother said, "Now that we know all their art, the seven magicians will probably seek to do us some mischief. Go thou, therefore, to our stable, which we left empty, and thou shalt find there a splendid steed. Put a bridle on him, and lead him forth to sell him—only take care thou go not out in the direction of the dwelling of the seven magicians; and having sold him, bring back the price thou shalt have received." When he had made an end of speaking, he transformed himself into a horse, and went, and placed himself in the stable awaiting his brother's arrival.

But the elder brother, knowing that the magicians had taught him nothing, stood in no fear of them. Therefore he paid no heed to the words of his brother, but saying to himself, "As my brother is so clever that he could conjure this fine horse into the stable, let him conjure thither another if he wants it sold—this one I will ride myself." So he saddled and mounted the horse; but all his efforts to guide him were vain, and in spite of his best endeavours, the horse, impelled by the power of the magic of those from whom the art had been learned, carried him straight to the door of the magicians' dwelling. Once there, he was equally unable to induce him to stir away; the horse persistently stood before the magicians' door. When he found he could not in any way command the horse, he determined to sell it to them, asking a great sum for it. The magicians readily knew that it was a magic horse, and said among themselves, "If our art is to become thus common, and everybody can produce a magic horse, no one will come to our market for wonders. We had best buy the horse up and destroy it." Accordingly they paid the high price required, and took possession of the horse and shut it up in a dark stall. When the time came to slaughter it, one held it down by the tail, another by the head, other four by the four legs, so that it should in no wise break away, while the seventh bared his arm ready to strike it with death. When the khán's son who was transformed into the horse perceived what was the intention of the magicians, he thought, "Would that any sort of living being would appear into which I might transform myself!" Hardly had he formed the wish when a little fish was seen swimming down the stream; into this the khán's son transformed himself. The seven magicians knew what had occurred, and immediately transformed themselves into seven large fish and pursued it. When they were very close to the little fish with their mouths wide open, the son of the khán said within himself, "Would that any sort of living being would appear into which I might transform myself!" Immediately a dove was seen flying in the air, and the khán's son became a dove. The seven magicians, seeing what was done, transformed themselves into seven hawks, and pursued the dove over hill and dale, and they were near overtaking the dove when it took refuge in Land Bede [*i.e.,* Tibet].

Southward in Bede was a shining mountain, and a cave in it called Giver of Rest. Hither the dove took refuge, even in the very bosom of the Great Master and Teacher Nágárguna.[12] The seven hawks, following fast after the dove, at the entrance of the cave changed themselves into men wearing cotton garments. The son of the khán then became a bead of the master's chaplet, and when the men humbly requested the master to give them the holy chaplet, he, who knew the whole affair, loosened the string, and putting in his mouth the son of the khán transformed into one of the beads, handed them the chaplet; and then dropping the bead out of his mouth, it instantly became a man armed with a great stick, and the son of the khán slew the pretended devotees but real magicians.

The story is well known to the people of Southern India, and a version occurs in the Tamil romance 'Madana Kámarája Kadai,' which bears considerable resemblance to the European variants, and of which this is an abstract:

One of the sons of a rája, who has lost his kingdom and is reduced to poverty, having been instructed in magic by a Bráhman, who is afterwards eager for his destruction, said to his father one day, in order that they should procure the means of subsistence, "There lives in this city a

___

[12]The 17th Patriarch in Buddhist succession, who died B.C. 212.

rich merchant who has an only son. I shall assume the shape of a *pan-chakalyáni* horse,[13] and do you walk with me to the tank where the merchant's son will come in the morning for his bath. He will take a liking for the horse and ask his price. You had better demand a thousand pagodas. After you have parted with me, I shall contrive to escape and return to you." So saying, the prince transformed himself into a horse, and stood before his father whinneying pleasantly, who took him to the side of the tank, and sold him to the merchant's son for a thousand pagodas. But the prince's instructor in magic recognised in the horse his former pupil, and by making the merchant's son believe that the animal was vicious and most dangerous to ride, bought him of him for the same sum that he had just paid for him, and then rode him about till he was almost dead with fatigue.

The transformed prince, perceiving his old master intended to kill him, became a fish in a tank, which, when the master discovered, he caused all his pupils to draw off the water in the tank and kill all the fish afterwards. The prince then entered the carcase of a buffalo which some skinners had left on the bank of the pond while they went to fetch their knives, and began to run away. Seeing this, the master made the skinners give chase, when the prince entered the dead body of a parrot[14] which he saw in a tree. Then the master took the form of a kite, and followed him at a furious speed over mountains and through jungles, until at length they came to a city. The parrot flew towards the palace, and entered through an open window into the chamber of the princess, who was seated on a couch unloosing her hair, and alighted in her lap. She was delighted at the sight of the beautiful bird, and taking it up, kissed it and pressed it fondly to her bosom. Then she placed the parrot in a golden cage, and fed it with dainties. One night, when the princess was lain down on her couch, the young prince assumed his own form, and told her how he was persecuted by his former master, who would return shortly as a rope-dancer, and having pleased the king her father with his performances, as his sole object was to kill him (the prince), would demand the parrot. She had

[13] A horse whose four feet and forehead are white.

[14] This is not transformation, but voluntary transmigration—the exercise of the magical art of transferring one's soul into any dead body, on which is based the frame-story of the Indian romance of Vikrámaditya of Ujjain, which is imitated in the 'Bahár-i Dánush,' the Persian 'Thousand and One Days,' and the Turkish 'Forty Vazírs.' It is evident this Tamil version is garbled: the prince here takes no precaution that the body he is represented as quitting should not be discovered and burnt; and indeed we find him afterwards simply transforming himself, like the persecuted pupil in other versions.

better at first refuse, but when her servants come a second time she should break the neck of the parrot and then give it to them. "Don't be afraid of having killed me," added the prince; "for I shall instantly become a pearl of your necklace. The servants will come once more, saying that your father requires your necklace. Do you then scatter the pearls in the courtyard, after which you will see something very wonderful." All happens as the young prince had forecast, and when the pearls fell into the courtyard they were all changed into worms. The magician saw that one of these was the prince, and at once assumed the form of a cock, and began to devour the worms, whereupon the prince changed himself into a cat, and pouncing upon the cock, caught it by the neck. The cock in human voice calls out for help, and the king now interfering, learns the whole story from the prince, on whom the king most willingly bestows his lovely daughter. The magician repents of his crimes and is reconciled to the prince, who afterwards drove the usurper of his father's throne out of the country, and ruled over it many years in peace and prosperity.[15]

It will be very evident on a comparative analysis of the several stories above cited, that they have all been derived, mediately or immediately, from one source. Although they are found to differ more or less one from another in the several metamorphoses and their sequence, yet they all possess some incidents in common. Thus, the transformation into a *horse* occurs in the Italian, German, Austrian, second Arabic (a she-mule), Norse, Danish, Albanian, Kalmuk, and Tamil. The *fish*, in the first Arabic, Italian, German, Austrian, Norse, Welsh, Kalmuk, and Tamil. The *hare and hound*, in the Danish, Welsh, and Albanian. The *bird and hawk*, in the Norse, Danish, Welsh, Kalmuk, and Tamil. The *grain of seed*, in the Italian, Austrian, and Welsh; the *worm*, in the first Arabic and the Tamil; the *ring*, in the Italian, Norse, and Danish; the *cock and fox*, in the Italian, Norse, Albanian, and Tamil. The pursued bird flies in at the palace-window in the Norse, Danish, and Tamil; into the cell of a devotee, in the Kalmuk; and in the form of an apple in the Albanian version.

Akin to the Magical-Conflict cycle are stories in which the hero is pursued by a fierce giant, or demon, and escapes by means of certain objects which, thrown behind him on his track, are instantly transformed into

[15]S. M. Natésa Sástri's 'Dravidian Nights,' pp. 8–18.

obstacles difficult or impossible to be overcome by the enemy. Sometimes the hero is running away with a giant's beautiful daughter who has become deeply enamoured of him, and it is through her supernatural skill that he is enabled to baffle the giant's repeated attempts to re-capture him. Of this class is the Gaelic story, in Campbell's collection, entitled "The Battle of the Birds," in which a king's son wishes to marry the youngest daughter of a giant, and having accomplished, by the help of the damsel herself, three difficult tasks which the giant sets him to do before he will give his consent, at night the giant's daughter tells the prince that they must fly, or her father would kill him. So they mounted on the grey filly in the stable. But before starting the daughter cut an apple into nine shares: she put two at the head of the bed, two at the foot, two at the door of the kitchen, two at the house-door, and one outside the house. The giant awoke and called, "Are you asleep?" several times, and the shares answered "No." At last he went and found the bed empty and cold, and pursued the fugitive couple. At the break of day the giant's daughter felt her father's breath burning her back. She told the prince to put his hand in the horse's ear, and fling what he found behind him. He found a sprig of sloe, flung it behind him, and produced a wood twenty miles long. The giant had to go back for his axe and wood-knife. In the middle of the day the prince finds in the horse's ear a piece of gray stone. This produces twenty miles of gray rock behind him, and the giant has to go back for his lever and mattock. When the giant has cut his way through this second obstacle, the next thing the prince finds in the filly's ear and flings behind him is a bladder of water, which produces a fresh-water loch twenty miles broad, and in it the giant is fortunately drowned.[16]

A horse takes the place of the giant's daughter as mentor in a similar adventure of the hero of a Norse tale, to which reference has been already made in comparing stories of Forbidden Rooms, pp. 79–80. The widow's son having, by the horse's advice, taken the whip of thorn, the stone, and the water-flask, he mounted his equine friend and rode off at a rapid rate. After riding some time, the horse said, "I think I hear a noise; look round, can you see anything?" The youth answered, "A great many are coming after us, certainly a score at least." Quoth the horse, "That is the Troll; he is coming with all his companions." They travelled on for some time until their

[16]Campbell's 'Tales of the West Highlands,' vol. i. pp. 32–34.

pursuers were gaining on them. "Throw now the thorn-whip over your shoulder," said the horse, "but throw it far away from me." When the youth had done what the horse desired, there sprang up a large thick wood of briars. Then the youth rode a long way, while the Troll was obliged to go home for something wherewith to hew a road through the wood. After some time the horse again said, "Look back, can you see anything now?" The youth replied, "Yes, a whole multitude of people, like a church congregation." Quoth the horse, "Ah, that is the Troll; now he has got more with him; so throw out the large stone, but throw it far from me." The youth did so, and instantly there arose a large mountain behind them. So the Troll was obliged to go home for something with which to bore through the mountain; and while he was thus employed the youth rode on a considerable way. But now the horse again bade him look back; he then saw a multitude like a whole army—they were so bright that they glittered in the sun. "Well, that is the Troll with all his friends," said the horse. "Now throw the water-bottle behind you, and take good care to spill nothing on me." The youth did so, but notwithstanding his caution, he happened to spill a drop on the horse's hips. Immediately there appeared a vast lake, and the spilling of a drop caused the horse to stand far out in the water; nevertheless he at last swam to the shore. When the Trolls came to the water they lay down to drink it all up, and they gulped and gulped it down till they all burst.[17]

A very striking resemblance to these incidents is found in a story in the 'Kathá Sarit Ságara,' chap. 39. The daughter of a rákshasa having performed for her lover the tasks which her father appointed him (see *ante*, p. 102), the demon, in order to cause the hero's destruction, despatches him to his fierce brother, who lived at two yojanas (about sixteen miles) distant, to invite him to his daughter's marriage. The damsel gives him, before setting out, some earth, some water, and some thorns, bidding him deliver his message, and at once return at full gallop, but look often behind him, and should he see the demon coming after him, throw these things successively in his way. The youth rode off, and after delivering his

---

[17]Thorpe's 'Yule-Tide Stories' (Bohn's ed.), pp. 295, 296.—Similar incidents occur in one of Powell and Magnusson's 'Icelandic Legends.' In Carleton's 'Traits and Stories of the Irish Peasantry,' a sprig, a pebble, and a drop of water produce a wood, a rock, and a lake. And in the Sicilian story of Fata Morgana, a prince is pursued by her and two lions. He throws successively three pomegranates behind him: one produces a river of blood, the second a thorny mountain, and the third a volcano.

message, fled from the place at full speed. And as soon as he turned his head and looked round, he saw the demon coming after him, so he quickly threw the earth behind him, and immediately produced a great mountain. When he saw that the rákshasa had, with much labour, climbed over the mountain and was coming on, he threw the water behind him, and it produced a great river in his path with rolling waves. The rákshasa with difficulty got across it, and was coming on, when the youth quickly scattered the thorns behind him, and they produced a dense thorny wood in the rákshasa's path. When the demon emerged from it, the prince threw the fire behind him, which set on fire the path with the herbs and the trees; and the demon, seeing that it was hard to cross, returned home tired and terrified.

In the Magical-Conflict cycle of stories the metamorphoses are effected by the combatants in their own persons. It now remains to notice some other kinds of transformations, in which sorcerers or magicians change their victims into the forms of various animals, and of which we have already had one example, from the 'Arabian Nights,' in the case of King Badr Bassim and Queen Láb (p. 212). The Arabic language has distinct terms for various metamorphoses: *naskh* is change from a lower to a higher form, as beast to man; *maskh* is the reverse; *raskh* is from animate to inanimate (see *ante,* p. 58); and *faskh* is wasting away. The methods adopted in fictions to effect such changes are various. For instance, in the 'Kathá Sarit Ságara' a witch teaches a young woman two spells, by reciting one of which a man can be changed in a moment into an ape, if a string is fastened round his neck, and on unloosing the string and reciting the other spell, he becomes a man again; and by sticking a pin in a man's head, at the same time uttering certain words, he is transformed into a bird, resuming his proper shape when the pin is withdrawn.[18]

---

[18] In No. 16 of the 'Decisions of Princess Thoo-Dharma Tsari,' a Burmese story-book, translated by Capt. T. P. Sparks (Maulmain, 1851), two sisters having quarrelled about the possession of a young man at length are reconciled and agree to let him go, but not in his own form: "They fastened a magic thread round the young man's neck, whereupon he was transformed into a small parrot, and flew away back into his own country, and settled in the king's garden, where he lived upon the fruit." The bird-catchers are employed to snare the parrot, and having succeeded, as he was so beautiful, they presented him to the king's daughter. "The princess, continually playing with the parrot, one day noticed the thread, and taking it off, he instantly became a handsome young man; and when she put it on again he was changed back into a parrot." This discovery, however, led to consequences which proved rather awkward for the amorous princess.

Sometimes we find certain fruits or grasses producing like changes of form, as in the Roman popular tale cited on p. 15, where the hero by eating some herbs that grew on a hill becomes a donkey. A very close parallel to this is found in the 'Madana Kámáraja Kadai': A young prince, who had been treacherously abandoned on an island by a dancing-girl and her mother (who decamped with his four magical treasures), climbed a mango-tree which had only four branches, and on eating the fruit of one of these he was turned into a black ape; the fruit of another changed him into a kite; that of a third transformed him into an old woman; and on eating of the fourth branch he was restored to human form. In the 'Bahár-i Dánush,' a young man, having escaped from a demon who lived on men's flesh and sheep—as Ulysses escaped from Polyphemus, by blinding him with a red-hot iron spike—travelling through a forest for several days without food, found a nest containing seven eggs of the size of a gourd, and each of a different colour. Having ate one, he continued his journey for seven days, when, having eaten the seventh egg, suddenly beautiful feathers of many colours, and at length wings, covered his body, and he was able to fly. One day, after soaring through the air, he alighted on a tree round which was a great multitude of people, to whom he addressed himself as they were going to shoot him. On hearing his adventures, they had compassion, and took him under their protection. With them he remained seven years, at the expiry of which his wings and feathers fell off, and he returned safely to his own country.[19]

Certain waters also effect wonderful changes, mental as well as physical, in those who drink of or bathe in them. From Greek and Roman classical sources Boiardo probably adapted in his 'Orlando Innamorato,' and Ariosto in his 'Furioso,' the idea of the two magic fountains, one of which inspired love, the other disdain, which reappear in the old Spanish

[19]Dr Jonathan Scott's translation, vol. iii. pp. 288–291. The 'Bahár-i Dánush,' or Spring (season) of Knowledge—Scott renders it 'Garden of Knowledge'—was composed in Persian by 'Inayatu-'lláh of Delhi in the year of the Hijra 1061 (A.D. 1650). In the author's introduction, which is a florid imitation of the charming preface to the 'Gulistán,' or Rose-Garden, of the celebrated Persian poet Saádí, it is said that "this heart-enticing story" was communicated to him by a young Bráhman; in other words, both the leading story and the tales interwoven are adapted from Indian sources, which are now well known. Scott's version leaves much to be desired, albeit he justly claims that it is fuller and more faithful to the original than that of Dow: he was unable to give in English the Persian names of flowers, which so frequently occur in the romance; his mode of transliteration is objectionable and antiquated; and he gives only brief abstracts of a number of stories in an appendix, which might have been translated, with a few modifications, and inserted in their proper places.

romance of 'Diana,' by Montemayor. In the 14th chapter of Swan's 'Gesta Romanorum' a princess by bathing in a certain fountain becomes a leper.—In all the Eastern texts of the Book of Sindibád, a prince on his way to be married to the daughter of a mighty monarch, came to a fountain, of which he drank, when lo! he instantly became a woman, and his companion the vazír abandoned him to his fate in the desert. He meets with a wandering horseman, who directs him to another fountain, the waters of which restore his proper sex, and he is duly united to his betrothed.—We read of pools and lakes having similar properties in several Indian story-books. Thus, in the 'Sinhásana Dwatrinsatí' (or Thirty-two Tales of a Throne), a monkey descends from a tree, and bathing in a well close by, is changed into a woman whenever a "pious" hermit comes to converse with her, and by dipping into the same well she becomes a monkey again—"till farther orders." And in a romance which recounts the adventures of two sons of a king, named Somasekhara and Chitrasekhara, one of them on a journey sees a monkey in his gambols plunge into a pool and come out a man; and a little farther on he leaped into another pool, and issued from it a monkey as before. The prince carries off some of the waters which produced these changes, and afterwards getting into his power a rascally giant who had stolen his brother's bride, by means of some of the water of the second pool changes him into a monkey, and sells him to a beggar, who compels him to perform tricks for his benefit.

Belief in witchcraft—that most deplorable of popular delusions, that most heart-hardening phase of the "madness of crowds"—was strong throughout Europe during mediæval times, and indeed long after intellectual darkness was supposed to be dispelled by means of the printing-press. King James I. of England, yeleped by his flatterers "the Scottish Solomon," and by men of better judgment "the wisest fool in Christendom," was a firm believer in witchcraft, and encouraged witch-hunting in all parts of his dominions. It is horrifying and blood-curdling to read of the tortures which were inflicted upon decrepit old wretches—often absolutely innocent, and generally the victims of mental disease—in order to compel them to confess their intimate connection with "the devil and all his works." The stories of magical transformations related so minutely by grave authors as having occurred in different parts of Europe, are all derived, as also belief in witchcraft itself, directly or indirectly, from Eastern sources. Heywood, in his curious and entertaining 'History of Women,' devotes a chapter to anecdotes "of witches who have either changed their own shapes or transformed others." After copious references to eminent authorities for the fact that some men can change themselves into wolves—such being called by the Germans *werwolff;* by the French *loups garous;* by the Greeks *lukanthropous,* or *mormolukias;* and by the Romans *versipelles,* turn-skins—he thus proceeds: "Saint Augustine, in his book, 'De Civitate Dei,' lib. 18, caps. 17 and 18, tells us of divers hostesses or innkeepers, practised in these diabolical arts, who put such confections into a kind of cheese they made, that all such travellers as guested with them, and ate thereof, were presently metamorphosed into labouring beasts, as horses, asses, oxen, all which they employed either in drawing or bearing of burdens, or else let them out for hackneys to gain profit by their hire; and when their work was done and they had made of them what benefit they could, they restored them to their pristine shape.

"Ranulphus and Gulielmus, 'De Regib.,' lib. 20, relate a history of two such witches that lived in the roadway to Rome: A minstrel or piper travelling that way, tasted of this cheese, and was presently changed into an ass, who, notwithstanding he had lost his shape, still retained his natural reason; and (as one Banks here about this city taught his horse to show tricks, by which he got much money) so this ass, being capable of what was taught him, and understanding what he was bid to do, showed a thousand several pleasures (almost impossible to be apprehended by any unreasonable creature) to all such as came to see him and paid for the sight, insomuch that he was sold by these witches to a neighbour of theirs for a great sum of money; but at the delivery of him saith one of the witches, 'Take heed, neighbour (if you mean to have good of your beast), that in any case you lead him not through the water.' The poor trans-shaped piper this hearing, apprehends that water might be the means to restore him to his former human figure, purposing in himself to make proof thereof at his next best opportunity. Careful was the new merchant of the charge given, and watered him still in a pail, but would never let him drink from the river. But the master travelling by the way, and, to ease his beast, alighting and leading him in his hand, the ass on the sudden broke his bridle, ran out of sight, and leaped into the next river he came near, where, leaving his saddle and furniture behind, he waded out in his own shape. The man pursues him with all the speed he can, and follows him the way he took. The first he meets is the piper, and asks him if he saw not such a kind of beast, and describes him to a hair. The fellow acknowledgeth himself to have been the same ass he bought of the witch. The master wondereth, and relates this to his lord; his lord acquaints this novel to Petrus Damianus, a man of approved knowledge and wisdom, and numbered amongst the greatest scholars of his age; he examines the master, the piper, the witches, and such as saw him leap into the river a beast and return a man, and informs Pope Leo VII. thereof. All their examinations and confessions were taken, and a disputation of the possibility thereof held in the presence of the Pope, before whom the truth thereof was acknowledged and recorded. The same history is told by Vincentius, in 'Speculo,' lib. 3, cap. 109, and Fulgentius, lib. 8, cap. 11.

"We read in Gulielmus, archbishop of Tyrus, whom Sprangerus, the Great Inquisitor, citeth to the same purpose: An English soldier, being in Cyprus, was by a witch transformed into an ass; and when all his mates went on shipboard, he following them, as loath to lose their fellowship, was, by his own friends and countrymen, that gave him [up for] lost, beaten back with clubs and staves. They put to sea without him. He, having no other owner, returned back to the witch's house that had trans-shaped him, who employed him in all her drudgeries, till at length he came into the church when the bishop was at divine service, and fell on his knees before the altar, and began to use such devout gestures as could not be imagined to proceed from a brute beast; this first bred admiration, and then suspicion. The witch was called before the judges, examined, and convicted, after condemned to the stake, having before restored him to his former shape after three years' transformation.

"Answerable to this we read of Ammonius the philosopher, of the sect of Peripatetics, who hath left recorded that an ass came usually into his school at the time of reading, and with great attention listened to his lecture. Merchants have delivered that nothing is more frequent in Egypt than such trans-shapes, insomuch that Bellonius, in his observations printed at Lutetia, saith that he himself in the suburbs of Cairo (a great city in Egypt) saw a comedian that desired conference with the ass that he himself rode on, who, wondering what he then intended, gave him liberty of free discourse; where they seemed to talk with great familiarity (as having been before acquainted), where the ass by his actions and signs seemed to apprehend whatsoever was spoken to him: when the one protested with the hand upon his breast, the other would strike the ground with his foot; and when the man had spoke as if he had told some jest, the ass would bray aloud as if he had laughed heartily at the conceit, appearing to him not only to apprehend and understand whatsoever was spoken, but to make answer to such questions as were demanded him."[20]

[20]Heywood's 'History of Women,' ed. 1657, lib. 8, pp. 573–575.

We should nowadays require even better authority than that of Saint Augustine, Ranulphus, and Gulielmus, archbishop of Tyre, combined, to induce us to credit such stories, which are simply Arabian and Indian fictions in European masquerade. The ass seems to have been the form of animal, according to popular belief, into which witches and magicians generally changed those whom they got into their power;[21] and this notion is the basis of a diverting Italian tale, ascribed, on slight grounds, to Michele Colombo, the substance of which is as follows:

A poor labourer, named Gilbert, cultivated a small enclosure, gathered faggots in a wood close by, brought them home on his ass, and conveyed them to the neighbouring market-town. He was a very simple fellow, who could be made to believe almost any absurdity. One day he left his ass tied to a tree in the outskirts of the wood, and went farther into the interior. Two monks of St. Francis, Father Antony and Father Timothy, having rambled over the adjacent districts, begging for the good of their convent, were returning heavily laden, and, seeing the ass, Timothy threw his wallet and that of Antony on the beast, loosed the halter, and, placing it round his own neck, bids Antony to lead the ass to their convent, and tell the brethren that he had been suddenly attacked by fever, and had taken refuge in the house of a benevolent peasant, who had lent him the ass, which was to be returned next week. When Gilbert came with his faggots and saw who it was that stood in the animal's place, he crossed himself, and was about to run away. Timothy tells him that for his sins he had been transformed into an ass, but he was now restored to his own proper form. On hearing this wonderful story, Gilbert says, "And can you, good father, ever forgive me the blows which you have had from my hands, and the curses, moreover, which you have often heard from my lips?" But Timothy assures him that the blows were salutary castigation, according to the will of Heaven: "Take, then, thy wood upon thy shoulder and go; and may peace attend thee." The monk, however, is easily persuaded to put up for the night at Gilbert's cottage, as the hour is waxing late. During supper he ogles Gilbert's comely wife, which the woodcutter observing, he warns the monk to be circumspect, lest his former punishment again befall him. Next day Father Timothy returns to his convent, and informs the prior that

---

[21] In the 'Golden Ass' of Apuleius, when the sorceress Pamphile turns herself into an owl, Apuleius asks her maid Fotis to change him also into an owl, in order to follow her; but she by mistake turns him into an ass, in which form he sees and hears many curious things, and he is at length restored to human shape by eating some roses.

Gilbert had made a present of his ass to the convent; so they resolve to sell the beast, and send a trusty person with it to the fair. Gilbert happened to be there, and at once recognised his own ass, from the circumstance of its having one ear cropped. Going up to the ass, he put his mouth close to its ear and whispered softly, "Alas, good father, the rebellious flesh, then, has played thee another trick! Did I not forewarn thee that this would happen?" The ass, feeling a breathing and tickling in his ear, shook his head, as if not assenting. "Deny it not," resumed Gilbert; "I know thee well: thou art the self-same." Again the ass shook its head. "Nay, deny it not—lie not," rejoined the worthy Gilbert, raising his voice somewhat—"lie not, for that is a great sin: thee it is; yes, in spite of thyself, it is thee." The bystanders, seeing a man thus holding a conversation with an ass, believed him to be crazy, and gathering round him, began to put questions, some about one thing, some about another, and Gilbert advanced the strangest and most unaccountable facts, always maintaining that this was not his ass, but in truth a poor miserable Franciscan, who, for his carnal frailties, was now uncomfortably a second time transformed into this shape. Then he told from beginning to end all the story of the incontinent friar metamorphosed into a beast of burden. His narrative was greeted with bursts of laughter. Poor Gilbert was all day the butt of the fair. At last he was induced to buy the unlucky animal again; and taking it home, believing it to be no ass but the friar again transformed, he would not employ it to carry his faggots, but fed it until, like Jeshurun, it "waxed fat and kicked."

Alexis Piron has told the same story in French verse, under the title of "Le Cordelier Cheval," which, together with the Italian novel and translations of both, was published at London in 1821.[22] In the preface, the translator, G. H., gives the following account of the novel: "The Italian novel, which I believe to be now for the first time printed, existed in manuscript in the collection of the late Count Borromeo of Padua, at the sale of which, in 1817, it fell, among other trifles, to my lot. It stands thus in the catalogue of that sale: 'No. 250, Novella di Gianni andato al Boscoa far legna, &c., in 4to, MS., inedita'; and it is there, upon what authority I know not, attributed, together with some preceding articles of the catalogue, to Michele Colombo. It attracted my notice from its resemblance

---

[22]'Tales of the Cordelier Metamorphosed, as narrated in a manuscript from the Borromeo Collection, and in Le Cordelier Cheval of M. Piron, with Translations.' London, 1821. 4to, 54 pages. The tales are illustrated with a number of clever etchings.

in the principal incidents of the story to 'Le Cordelier Cheval,' or, as it is sometimes entitled, 'Le Moine Bride,' of Alexis Piron, a tale which I have always esteemed as not the least pleasant of that author's facetious effusions; and suspecting that Piron, like La Fontaine before him, often gathered his subjects from some older record, I have looked in vain among the earlier novelists for an original hint of this story. Whether the Italian which I now present be such, or merely an imitation, or whether both the narratives be not borrowed with variations from preceding collections of facetiæ, I will not pretend to determine. Of Colombo as a writer I have not met with any notice, but it would seem that in Tiraboschi's time he was possessed of some curious books at Padua. Without better information, one may reasonably doubt whether he was the author of the articles which Borromeo attributed to him."

In Piron's version a man named Blaise was returning from market, where he had profitably disposed of his oats and hay, and bought a horse to carry him home. After riding some distance, the weather being frosty, he dismounts in order to warm himself by walking, and while he is trudging along, leading his palfrey by the bridle, he is seen by two monks, who steal the horse, as in the Italian story. When Blaise (he is called Ralph in the English rendering) turns round to mount his horse again, what was his surprise to perceive the monk with the bridle round his neck! Father Peter explains that as a penance for having indulged his carnal desires, he had been condemned for seven years to live in the form of a horse, and his time was now expired. Ralph (or Blaise) replies that he can't understand why his purse should have to pay for the monk's misdeeds; but Heaven is just: he himself had also sinned and must do penance in his turn; the only difference between them being that the monk's mulct is paid, while his own has but begun. "You've been seven long years a horse, and it might come to pass that I should be an ass for a similar period." However, the twenty marks that he paid for the monk as a horse won't ruin him—"Go to your convent, and beware for the future."

> The monk, with reverence profound,
> Thrice clasped his knees, thrice kissed the ground;
> Then gaily and with quickened pace
> Made off; while Ralph, with rueful face,
> Light purse, and bridle dangling loose,
> Sneaked homeward, like a truant goose.
> He kept his counsel; not a word,

You may be sure, had e'er been heard
From him of his adventure rare,
Had he not one day at the fair
Espied his well-known horse, and nigh it
Stood Gregory about to buy it.
Ralph stared, but, laughing in his sleeve,
Whispered, "Friend Gregory, by your leave,
This way—a word—that horse don't buy—
I know him, and a good reason why!
Don't buy that horse, you'll sadly rue
Your bargain one day, if you do.
Some morning, when you think on't least,
Parading bravely on that beast
(A beast to look on not amiss),
You'll find yourself—remember this—
Hey, presto! pass than lightning fleeter
Mounted astride on Father Peter.
"Astride on Peter! O you jeer!"
"Not I, indeed; you'll find him there,
With cord and cowl and chaplet meet,
A fat, gray Cordelier complete."

Ralph then began to tell his tale—
The purchase—storm—Franciscan frail—
The penitence and all the rest;
What happened since he shrewdly guessed:
"Look you," said he, "this child of sin,
His lesson fast forgetting quite,
Has given the bait another bite;
So here he is." "And here may be,
By th' mass," quoth Gregory, "for me.
Pox take him and his liquorish story,
And his new lease of purgatory!
Ralph, but for thee, I'd lost my chink;
'Tis ten pounds saved—let's drink!"[23]

[23]Peste! interrompt Grégoire,
Qu'il aille an diable avec son hameçon,
Et ses sept ans de nouveau purgatoire!
Vraiment, sans toi, j'etois joli garçon;
C'est cinq cens francs que je gagne—allons boire!

The story is also found in 'Facetiæ Cantabrigienses,' 1825, p. 10, and in Bohn's edition of 'Joe Miller's Complete Jest Book,' printed in 1841 (No. 151): "Three or four roguish scholars, walking out one day, espied a poor fellow near Abingdon asleep in a ditch, with an ass by him laden with earthenware, holding the bridle in his hand. Says one of the scholars to the rest, 'If you will assist me, I'll help you to a little money, for you know we are bare at present,'" and so on. When the poor fellow sees his ass offered for sale at the fair, "Oh," said he, "have he and his father quarrelled again already? No, no, I'll have nothing to say to him."

The original of these three tales is perhaps found in the Búlák and Calcutta printed Arabian texts of the 'Thousand and One Nights,' where the story is thus related:

A simple countryman was walking along, dragging his ass after him by the halter, which a brace of sharpers observing, one said to his fellow, "Come with me, and I will take the ass from that man." He then quietly advanced to the ass, unloosed it from the halter, and gave the beast to his confederate, who went off with it; after which the sharper passed the halter round his neck, and allowed the man to drag him along until the other rogue with the ass was out of sight, when he suddenly stopped, and the man having tugged the halter several times without effect, he looked back, and, amazed to behold a man in place of his beast, exclaimed, "Who art thou?" The sharper answered, "I was thy ass; but hear my story, for it is wonderful. I have a virtuous and pious mother, and one day I came home intoxicated. Grieved to see me in such a condition, she reproved me; but, instead of being overwhelmed with remorse, I beat her with a stick, whereupon she prayed to Heaven, and in answer to her supplication I was transformed into an ass. In that shape I have been in thy service until this day, when, as it appears, my mother has interceded for me, and I am restored to the human form." The simpleton, believing every word of this story, raised his eyes to heaven, and said, "Of a truth there is no power or strength but from Allah! But pray forgive me for having used thee as I have done." The sharper readily granted forgiveness, and, taking leave of the simpleton, went off to rejoin his companion and to dispose of the ass; while the countryman returned home, and showing his wife the halter, told her of the wondrous transformation which had taken place. His wife, in hopes of propitiating Heaven, gave alms, and offered up many prayers, to avert evil from them, since they had used a human being as a beast of burden. The simpleton, having remained idle at home for some weeks, went one day to purchase another beast at the market, and on entering the place where the animals were all fastened, he saw with amazement his own ass offered for sale. Putting his mouth to its ear, he whispered, "Woe to thee, unlucky! Doubtless thou hast again been intoxicated; but, by Allah, I will never buy thee!"

The English version does not appear to have been derived from the French or the Italian, since its conclusion corresponds more closely with the Arabian tale: the poor hawker's exclamation, "Oh, have he and his father quarrelled again already? No, no, I'll have nothing to say to him," having its exact parallel in that of the Arab simpleton, "Doubtless thou hast again been intoxicated; but, by Allah, I will never buy thee!"[24] In the Italian story Gilbert buys his beast once more out of pity for Father Timothy; while in Piron's version the original owner dissuades a friend from purchasing his horse. It is not at all probable that Piron adapted his tale of 'Le Cordelier Cheval' from the Italian novel, since he represents the simpleton as leading his horse by the bridle, like the Arab countryman with his ass; while in the Italian story the animal was fastened to a tree when it was discovered by the two monks. The story may have been brought to France by some Trouvère from the East;—it is precisely such a tale as would have been readily appropriated by the professors of the "gay science," and from a *fabliau* it may have become orally current among the people. Its appearance in Italy is no more remarkable than that of many other stories which occur in the 'Arabian Nights,' considering the close commercial relations which were once maintained by the Venetians with Syria and Egypt, the countries where that famous storybook almost certainly had its origin.

[24]Yet, so far as I am aware, the Arabian tale had not been rendered into English when the Cambridge Jests were published.

✤ APPENDIX ✤

I. THE INEXHAUSTIBLE PURSE, ETC.

A VARIANT of the story of the four young fakírs and the magical treasures left them by their teachers, cited in p. 10, from Miss Stokes's 'Indian Fairy Tales,' is found in the Tamil romance, 'Madana Kámarája Kadai,' translated by Mr Natésa Sástrí, under the apt title of 'The Dravidian Nights,' p. 129. The youngest of two brothers, in the course of his wanderings, went one day to a tank to wash himself. While there he saw at a short distance from him an old *sanyási* (religious mendicant) breathing his last. The sage was surrounded by four of his disciples, to whom he was thus speaking: "My students, I have had possession for a long time of four objects which are as dear to me as life. They are: a bag, which yields to one whatever he may want; a cup, which serves up newly cooked meals whenever you require them; a cudgel, which would belabour all your enemies if you aim it at them; and a pair of sandals which takes you wherever you wish to go. First bury me, and then take these things for yourselves." So saying, the sage expired, and his disciples buried him close by, under a tree. Then they quarrelled over the four things, and at length agreed to place them in the hollow of an old tamarind-tree, and go to the town in search of an arbiter. The youth was observing from a distance what was passing, and as soon as they went away he proceeded to the spot and took possession of the four treasures. But fearing that without the permission of the departed soul of the sage these things would be of no benefit to him, he went to the grave of the *sanyási* and there said, "My respected *sanyási*, your disciples fought over these rare treasures and carelessly put them in the hollow of a tree; I have taken them out, and with your kind leave will make use of them." Then this answer came out of the grave: "You did very well in taking possession of these objects, which will be of more service to you than to those envious fellows."

An analogue of the German, Bohemian, Kalmuk, and Buddhist tales cited in pp. 22–26 is found in the same Tamil romance ('Dravidian Nights,' p. 149 ff.): The prince, in quest of the *parijáta* flower, having, by the directions of the third sage, who opened his eyes every third watch, won the love of a celestial maiden, she gives him a guitar on which he had only to play, when she would appear and set before him abundance of the most delicious viands. He goes back to the third sage, and playing on his guitar, the damsel appears with food as she had promised. The sage persuades the prince to exchange his guitar for a cudgel that would put to death a vast army in the twinkling of an eye. By means of the club, which goes back and kills the sage, the prince recovers his guitar, which he exchanges with the second sage for an inexhaustible purse, and with the first sage for magic sandals, each time recovering it by means of the all-powerful cudgel, which here performs the part of Kreischwinger in the Kalmuk version and of the hatchet in the Buddhist Birth-Story of Sakka's Presents.—In the German version, the hero twice recovers his magic table by means of the article for which he exchanges it—a knapsack and a hat; and in the Bohemian story, a bagpipe brings it back to him after exchanging it for a sack of wonderful virtue.

II. "WHO EATS MY HEART," ETC.

In the story cited in p. 13 ff., from Miss Busk's 'Folk-Lore of Rome,' one of the brothers, by eating the head of a bird, becomes emperor, and the other, by eating the heart, is never without money, of which incident an Indian analogue is given in p. 16. In the same tale from the 'Dravidian Nights' cited in the preceding note, the two brothers enter a dense wood, in which is an extraordinary mango-tree that yields one fruit once in a hundred years. To obtain that fruit a sage was practising penance before the tree, and just as the youths entered the wood the fruit dropped down at the feet of the sage, who left it where it fell, and went off to bathe before touching it. The younger brother, without being observed by the elder, picked up the fruit and concealed it in the midst of his rice-ball. The sage, on returning from his ablutions, was distracted to find the fruit was gone, and overtaking the brothers, asked them whether they had seen a mango-fruit on the ground, to which they replied in the negative. Then the sage began to weep and tear his long beard. "What special property is there in that fruit," asked the younger brother, "that you should so much lament its loss?" Said the sage, "My dear son, he who eats the skin of that fruit will become a king, and he who eats the seed, gems will drop from his mouth every time he laughs."[1] The youths then resumed their

[1]In No. 5 of Rev. Lal Behari Day's 'Folk-Tales of Bengal' a fisherman brings a young merchant a fish, which if any one eats, when he laughs the most precious gems will fall from his mouth, and when he weeps pearls will drop from his eyes. Ill-used step-daughters are often thus endowed in European fairy tales. In the Relations of Siddhí Kúr we find a gold-spitting

journey. In the evening they sat down beside a stream, and the younger gave the elder some rice and the skin of the mango fruit, and himself ate the seed, with the results predicted by the sage.—I have before remarked (p. 227) that this story in the sequel very closely resembles Miss Busk's tale of 'The Transformation Donkey.'

III. THE GOOD MAN AND THE BAD MAN—p. 108.

My conjecture that this story is of Buddhist extraction (p. 114) seems borne out by the existence of a version current in Ceylon. Under the title of the "Two Peasants," S. Jane Goonetilleke gives a translation of it in 'The Orientalist,' 1885, pp. 150–152. In this version two peasants left their native village to seek their fortune. At the outset one of them said to the other, "Friend, if you provide out of your purse for both of us, I will do like wise when your money is all spent." To this his companion agreed, and whenever he cooked his rice he always gave his friend half of it. When his stock of money was exhausted, he asked his companion to give him some of his food, but he refused. After being without food for some days, the poor peasant at last consented to part with one of his eyes for a spoonful, and soon afterwards the other eye was also taken out by his wicked comrade, who then left him at the foot of a tree and went his own way. The blinded peasant overhears a party of rákshasas who were in the tree conversing together. One said, "All are not aware of the rare qualities of this tree. Any blind man will have his sight restored to him, if he will only rub his eyes with some of its juice." "That is not all," said another: "if a man should eat one of these leaves, he would not get hungry for seven days and seven nights." "More than that," said a third: "if a man eat the fruit of this tree, he will become a king in seven days." When the rákshasas had gone away, the poor man contrived to scrape away part of the bark of the tree, and thus obtained a little of its juice, which he at once applied to his eyes and he immediately recovered his sight. When he had eaten some of the leaves he felt quite strong, and then climbing to the top of the tree he ate of the fruit, convinced that be should become king in

---

prince—see p. 32 of the present volume. In Gonzenbach's 'Sicilianische Märchen,' a girl drops pearls and precious stones from her hair whenever she combs it, to which Dr Köhler gives many parallels in a note on this tale. In Coelho's 'Contos Portuguezes,' No. 36, pearls drop from the heroine's mouth. In a Norse story gold coins fall from the mouth of the heroine whenever she speaks; and in a Swedish tale, a gold ring.

seven days. He set off and reached a town on the seventh day, and during all the time he did not once feel the pangs of hunger. Seating himself outside a rest-house (for the company within would not have such a dirty and ragged fellow amongst them), the late king's elephant came past to choose a successor, and kneeling down before the peasant, he was at once acknowledged and crowned king.[2] Now his false friend had before arrived at the same city, and married the daughter of the prime minister, and when he saw the new king he was struck with his resemblance to the man he had so cruelly blinded; but fearing to ask a direct question, he one day said to him, "Sire, is it possible for a blind man by any means to recover his sight?" The king answered, "It is not impossible. If a man only sought it he would find a remedy even for blindness." So the prime minister resolved to get some one to treat him as he had done his comrade, and set out from the city with his wife, having instructed her how to act. First the man provided food for both, and when his stock of money was all spent, his wife treated him in the same way he had treated his friend, and finally left him bound under a tree. Before parting she told him where he would find her when he had become king. The woman went on till she came to a shepherd's hut, and obtained leave to stay there for seven days till her husband the king came to take her away. Seven days passed, but there was no sign of the king, and when other seven days had elapsed, the shepherd lost all patience, upon which the woman told him the whole story. The shepherd repaired to the spot to find out what had happened to the man, and there he found his carcase surrounded by eagles and other ravenous birds and animals. Returning home, the would-be queen eagerly questioned the shepherd as to the fate of her husband, and asked him whether be had indeed been crowned king. "Oh, yes," replied he, "I found him surrounded by so many of his subjects, that I could not exchange one word with him, and tell him of your welfare, but now you can go and see for yourself." So saying, he drove her out of his house as an adventuress.

IV. ENCOUNTERS WITH OGRES, ETC.

The beautiful episode "Baka-badha" which occurs in the first book of the 'Mahábhárata,' and which has been done into English verse by Dean

---

[2] This singular mode of choosing a successor to the throne occurs in many Indian tales, and it seems to have been actually practised at one time.

Milman, under the title of the "Bráh-man's Lament" (see p. 55), seems adapted in one of the Rev. Lal Behari Day's 'Folk-Tales of Bengal,' pp. 73–77:

Two youths, Champa Dal and Sahasra Dal, arrived one evening at a village, and became guests in the house of one of its most respectable inhabitants. They found the members of the family in deep gloom. Evidently there was something agitating them very much. Some of them held private consultations, and others were weeping. The eldest lady of the house, the mother of its head, said aloud, "Let me go, as I am the oldest. I have lived long enough; at the utmost my life would be cut short only by a year or two." The youngest member of the house, who was a little girl, said, "Let me go, as I am useless to the family; if I die, I shall not be missed." The head of the house, the son of the old lady, said, "I am the head and representative of the family; it is but reasonable that I should give up my life." His younger brother said, "You are the main prop and pillar of the family; if you go the whole family is ruined. It is not reasonable that you should go; let me go, as I shall not be much missed." The two strangers listened to all this conversation with no little curiosity. They wondered what it all meant. Sahasra Dal at last, at the risk of being thought meddlesome, ventured to ask the head of the house the subject of their consultations, and the reason of the deep misery but too visible in their countenances and words. He answered, "Know then, worthy guests, that this part of the country is infested by a terrible rákshasi,[3] who has depopulated all the regions round. This town, too, would have been depopulated, but that our king became a suppliant before the rákshasi, and begged her to show mercy to us his subjects. The rákshasi replied, 'I will consent to show mercy to you and your subjects only on this condition, that you every night put a human being, either male or female, in a certain temple for me to feast upon. If I get one every night I will rest satisfied, and not commit farther depredations on your subjects.' Our king had no alternative but to agree to this condition; for what human beings can ever hope to contend against a rákshasi? From that day the king made it a rule that every family in the town should in its turn send one of its members to the temple as a victim to appease the wrath and satisfy the hunger of the terrible rákshasi. All the families in this neighbourhood have had their turn, and this night it is the turn for one of us

[3]Female demon of the rákshasa species.

242

to devote himself to destruction. We are therefore discussing who should go. You must now perceive the cause of our distress." The two friends consulted together for a few minutes, after which Sahasra Dal said, "Most worthy host, do not any longer be sad. As you have been very kind to us, we have resolved to requite your hospitality by ourselves going to the temple and becoming the food of the rákshasi. We go as your representatives." The whole family protested against the proposal. They declared that guests were like gods, and that it was the duty of the host to endure all kinds of privation for the comfort of the guest, and not the duty of the guest to suffer for the host. But the strangers insisted on being proxy for the family, who at length reluctantly consented to the arrangement.

Immediately after candle-light, Sahasra Dal and Champa Dal, with their horses, installed themselves in the temple and shut the door. Sahasra told his brother to go to sleep, as he himself was determined to sit up the whole night and watch against the coming of the terrible rákshasi; and Champa was soon sound asleep, while his brother lay awake. Nothing happened during the early hours of the night; but no sooner had the king's gong announced the hour of midnight than Sahasra heard a sound as of a rushing tempest, and immediately concluded, from his knowledge of rákshasas, that the rákshasi was nigh. Presently he beard a thundering knock at the door, followed by these words:

> "How, mow, khow!
> A human being I smell;[4]
> Who watches inside?"

Sahasra Dal replied,

> "Sahasra Dal watcheth,
> Champa Dal watcheth,
> Two winged horses watch."

On hearing this the rákshasi turned away with a groan, knowing that Sahasra Dal had rákshasa blood in his veins. An hour after she returned, and again at two o'clock and at three o'clock, and made the same inquiry,

---

[4]This is the "Fe, fo, fum!" of our nursery tale of Jack and the Giants. Ogres and such-like monsters readily scent the presence of a human being. See the note in p. 37.

and obtaining each time the same answer, went away with a groan. After three o'clock, however, Sahasra Dal felt very sleepy; he could no longer keep awake; so he roused his brother, told him to watch, and strictly enjoining upon him, in reply to the query of the rákshasi, to mention his (Sahasra's) name first, he went to sleep. At four o'clock the rákshasi again returned, thundered at the door, and said,

> "How, mow, khow!
> A human being I smell;
> Who watches inside?"

As Champa Dal was in a great fright, he forgot for the moment his brother's injunction, and answered:

> "Champa Dal watcheth,
> Sahasra Dal watcheth,
> Two winged horses watch."

On hearing this reply the rákshasi uttered a shout of exultation, laughed as only demons can laugh, and with a dreadful noise broke open the door. The noise roused Sahasra, who in a moment sprang to his feet, and with his sword, which was as supple as a palm-leaf, cut off the head of the rákshasi. The huge mountain of a body fell to the ground, making a great noise, and lay covering many an acre.

V. 'CUPID AND PSYCHE' LEGENDS.

The eighth of the Rev. Lal Behari Day's 'Folk-Tales of Bengal' presents, in the second part (the first belongs to the "Outcast Child" cycle), some resemblance to the modern Greek version of the 'Cupid and Psyche' legend cited in pp. 104, 105, in connection with stories of secrets learned from birds. A young lady is married to a mysterious youth, Prince Sobur,[5] who had sent her a box containing a looking-glass and a fan, and when she had shaken the fan, he stood before her. The six sisters of the bride, envying her good fortune, determined to cause the death of the prince. They broke some bottles, reduced the fragments to a fine powder, and scattered it on the nuptial couch. The prince had no sooner laid him-

---

[5]Query—Pers. *sabr,* meaning "patience"?

self down than he felt the most acute pain, for the fine glass-powder had penetrated all his body. As he was writhing and shrieking, his attendants hastily took him away to his own country. The young bride, on discovering that her husband had been spirited away, was distracted with grief, and though she had never seen his country, she determined to seek it out, however far distant it might be. So she put on the dress of a religious mendicant, and set out on her journey. She soon became weary, and sat under a tree to rest. On the top of the tree was the nest of the celestial bird Bihangama and his mate. They were absent at the time, but two of their young ones were in the nest. Presently they gave a loud scream, and the pretended mendicant looking up discovered a monstrous snake climbing the tree, and in a moment she cut the snake in two with a dagger which she carried. Soon after this the parent birds return, and their young ones relate how the mendicant at the foot of the tree had killed a snake that was climbing up to destroy them. The Bihangama then said to his mate that they must do her a service, for the person under the tree was not a *sanyási,* but a woman who had been married last night to Prince Sobur, who a few hours after, on laying himself down on his bed, had been sorely injured with fine particles of glass which had been spread there by his envious sisters-in-law, and was now in his native country and at the point of death. The bird then goes on to explain to his mate that if their dung, which is lying about the tree and is hardened, be reduced to powder and applied with a brush to the body of the prince after bathing him seven times with seven jars of water and seven jars of milk, he will certainly get well, adding that he himself will carry her on his back to the capital of the province. The poor girl, having heard this conversation, begged the Bihangama to carry her to the prince, and he readily consented. Before mounting the bird, she gathered a quantity of the specific, and arriving at the palace of the prince, applied it to his body as the bird had directed, and he was perfectly cured.

VI. ALADDIN'S WONDERFUL LAMP.

Another Arabian Variant

The variant of Galland's story found in the tale of Marúf—the last in the Búlák and Calcutta printed Arabic texts of the 'Book of the Thousand and One Nights'—had escaped my memory for the time, else I should have added an abstract of it to the tale of the Fisherman's Son (p. 157 ff.), from the Wortley Montague MS. of 'The Nights.' The story of

Marúf is evidently composed of incidents taken from a number of separate tales, and I shall confine my abstract to the portion which resembles Galland's tale of Aladdin:

Marúf having married the sultan's daughter "under false pretences"—he had given out that he was a wealthy merchant and daily expected the arrival of his grand caravan—the chief vazír, who had all along asserted that he was an impostor, at length prevailed upon the king to urge his daughter to wheedle out of him the real facts of the case. So one night Marúf confessed to her that he was not a merchant, and that the caravan had no existence. Upon this the princess, who was fondly attached to Marúf, said that, should this come to her father's knowledge, his death was certain, and he had better fly at once to a distant land, and at her father's death she would send for him. She then gave him a purse of gold, together with a mamlúk's dress, and before dawn Marúf disguised himself and left the city undiscovered by any one. In the morning the princess informed her father that Marúf having yesterday received a letter from the chief of his caravan stating that it had been plundered by a gang of Arabs to the extent of two hundred bales of merchandise, he had set off with the messenger to bring the caravan safely into the city, and thus defeat the vile machinations of the vazír. The sultan believed the story, and joined with his daughter in reviling the minister, who, trembling for his head, was forced to bear all in silence.

Meanwhile Marúf fared on, he knew not whither, till, about mid-day, he came near a village, and seeing in a field a peasant guiding a plough drawn by oxen, he approached and asked him for some food. The man, supposing him to be one of the sultan's mamlúks, readily answered that he would at once proceed home and fetch such as his house could furnish. So saying, he left his plough and oxen, and hastened to the village. Left to his own reflections, Marúf thought that since the man had quitted his work to oblige him, the least he could do was to continue it for him. Scarcely had Marúf ploughed a furrow before the ploughshare struck against something hard in the ground, and while endeavouring to disengage it, he discovered a large ring of iron fixed in a marble slab.[6] His curiosity was strongly excited. He pulled the ring with all his strength, and raised up a slab, which turned on a hinge. A few steps were then dis-

---

[6]This incident occurs in several Eastern stories—*e.g.*, the tale of Abdúllah of Khurasan, in Malcolm's 'Sketches of Persia,' ch. xi.

covered, which having descended, Marúf entered a cavern about the size of a bath, and heaped on all sides with gold, emeralds, rubies, and other gems, beyond all price. This place led to other chambers containing vast riches, and the suite terminated in an apartment in which was nothing more than a coffer of crystal, enclosing a little box made of one entire diamond. Curious to know what it contained, Marúf opened the box, and discovered a gold ring, quite plain, except that around it some mysterious talismanic characters were engraved. As he was fitting this ring on his finger he heard a voice exclaiming, "What wouldst thou—what wouldst thou, master?" and he beheld at his side a hideous figure, with a most extraordinary countenance, who continued to address him in these words: "What are thy commands?—speak; I obey thee. What land shall I cover with flowers? what kingdom shall I ravage? what army shall I cut in pieces? what king shall I slay? what mountains shall I level with the valleys? what sea shall I lay dry?—speak; I obey. I am thy slave, by permission of the Master of spirits, the Creator of day and night!" "What art thou?" asked Marúf. "I am," replied the figure, "a genie, the slave of this ring, and of the powerful Name thereon engraved. To the possessor of this ring I must submit myself, and execute his commands. Nothing exceeds my power, for I am a king among the genii and command seventy-two tribes, each of which is composed of twelve thousand genii of my species, called *ún*. Each ún has under his command one thousand *ifríts;* every *ifrít,* one thousand *shaytans;* and every shaytan, a thousand inferior genii. Over all these I rule; but, mighty as I am, I submit to thee and this ring. I obey thee with all I possess, and am thy devoted slave. Command! I hear thee and obey; with the rapidity of lightning I fulfil thy orders. When thou requirest my succour, be thou on land or on sea, rub this ring, invoke me by the power of the name engraved thereon, and thou shalt instantly behold me."

Marúf then desired that the treasures should be transported to the surface of the earth, and in an instant the floor of the cave opened, and two young boys of great beauty appeared, bearing on their heads baskets of gold, which they proceeded to fill with the precious stones that lay scattered around. "Can you procure mules and coffers to transport this treasure?" asked Marúf. "Nothing is more easy," replied the genie, and uttering a loud cry he summoned all his children, who were as beautiful as the first two. At the command of their father, some of these transformed themselves into mules, some into mule-drivers, and others into mamlúks mounted on superb horses, to guard the caravan. Three hundred mules were soon laden with cases, containing the most precious gems and pure gold. Marúf then commanded his new slaves to pitch tents and form a camp, to raise him a pavilion and serve up a repast.

At this moment the peasant arrived with a dish of lentils, some black bread, and a bag of barley. When he saw the camp and pavilion and the crowd of mamlúks and mules, he imagined the sultan had arrived, of whom Marúf had been the *avant-courier.* "Holy Prophet!" said he to himself, "wherefore did I not kill and cook my two hens? The sultan will cut off my head in return for this sorry fare!" Marúf, having perceived him, ordered one of the mamlúks to desire his presence in the pavilion. "What hast thou got there?" he asked. "Your dinner and that of your horse," replied the villager. "But I pray you, pardon me: had I known that the sultan would have halted here, I would have killed two hens which I have at home, and stewed them in butter." "Set down your lentils," replied Marúf; "I am so hungry that I shall eat them with pleasure. The sultan is not here; but I am his relation. You treated me well, though you knew me not; therefore I shall not forget to be grateful." Marúf made his dinner of the humble plate of lentils, notwithstanding that the genie, to tempt his appetite, served up the most delicious meats, of such rich flavour that the villager stood amazed at the sight. As soon as Marúf had devoured the last lentil with much appearance of appetite, he heaped the plate with gold and precious stones, and returned it to the astonished peasant, who, declaring he was enriched for life, then returned to the village with his plough and oxen, fully convinced that his guest was the son of the sultan.

Thus far after the style of the 'Arabian Nights,' but the sequel must be related with brevity. Marúf having passed the night in feasting and beholding the dances of the daughters of the genie, whom he had sum-moned to amuse him, early next morning set out for the sultan's capital, with 700 mules laden with rich merchandise and attended by 500 mam-lúks. The vazír had just been declaring to the sultan that Marúf was an impostor and he would never see his face again, when a genie, disguised as a messenger, arrived, to intimate the approach of the sultan's son-in-law at the head of his grand caravan. "May Allah confound thy beard, traitor that thou art!" exclaimed the sultan, turning fiercely to his vazír. "Art thou not at last convinced, wretch, of the grandeur of my son-in-law?" The vazír, terror-struck, threw himself on his knees, and the sultan gave orders to illuminate the city. On the arrival of Marúf, he caused the royal treasury to be filled with gold and gems and silks, and other pre-cious stuffs. The princess met her husband with joy, and having embraced him and kissed his hands, said with a smiling countenance, "You have amused yourself, my lord, at my expense, by your tale of poverty; you wished, doubtless, to put my affection to the proof. Thanks be to Allah, you are happily restored to me; for whether rich or poor you are not less dear; I love yourself, not your wealth." When the 700 mules and the 500 mamlúks were found to have disappeared the following morning, the suspicions of the vazír were once more aroused—Marúf could certainly be no merchant. So he advised the sultan to ascertain the cause of his great wealth, lest he should prove dangerous to his government. "Invite him to a banquet, ply him with wine, and then question him concerning his treasures." The sultan accordingly invited Marúf to a grand feast, and when he was warmed with wine, asked him to relate his adventures. So Marúf in an evil hour told the whole story. "I pray thee, my son," then said the sultan, "show me this ring of wonderful power." Marúf drew the ring from his finger, and gave it to the vazír, to lay it before the sultan; but as soon as the vazír touched the ring, he summoned the genie and commanded him to convey Marúf to some desert and there leave him to perish. The genie immediately obeyed the order of the new possessor of the ring. Then the vazír again summoned the genie and ordered him to convey the sultan to the same spot where he had left Marúf, which being done, he assembled the divan and compelled them to acknowledge him as sultan. The next step of the vazír was to insist on marrying the princess, who, being threatened with death if she should refuse compliance, had no resource but in stratagem. At a banquet in the evening, she pretended that she had long secretly loved him, but she was afraid of a genie whom, she had been informed, he held captive in a ring, and if he would consent to divest himself of that terrible companion, she would be his slave for life. Deceived by her flattering words, the vazír drew the ring from his finger and flung it to a distance. The princess then presented him with a cup full of wine, which she had first pressed to her own lips, and he continued to carouse till his senses were utterly intoxicated, after which the princess seized the ring, summoned the genie, and commanded him to secure the vazír and restore her husband and father. The moment Marúf and the sultan were brought back to the palace the latter caused the vazír's head to be struck off; but when he desired his daughter to give him the ring, she replied that men who carouse over wine-cups are not to be trusted with unlimited power, and so she should give it neither to him nor her husband, but keep it in her own possession.

ᴣ

In this version, as in Galland and the Story of Cajusse (p. 148 ff.), the talisman is not recovered by means of grateful animals, which was most probably the original form of the story, since they play the principal parts in the European variants, in the Arabian tale of the Fisherman's Son, and in the Mongolian and the Tamil versions, a circumstance which, as I have before remarked, would seem to indicate that the tale is of Buddhist extraction;[7] and this conjecture is strengthened by the existence of a Burmese version in a story-book translated by Captain T. P. Sparks, under the title of 'The Decisions of Princess Thoo-dhamma Tsari,' printed at Maulmain in 1851, which is as follows:

Burmese (Buddhist) Version.

During the era of Gaunagóng,[8] a prince, a young noble, a rich man's son, and a poor man's son were being educated together in the country of Tekkatho.[9] Having learned as much as they wished, they asked their teacher to discourse to them upon the benefits resulting from a good quality to its possessor. Their teacher then related to them the following story:

Soon after the commencement of the world, there dwelt in Gahapati Waytha four very rich men, between whom there existed the warmest friendship, so that each sought only the interest of the others. After a time one of them died, leaving an only son, to whom his mother said, "My dear boy, your father, my husband, is dead, you are therefore now in his place and are entitled to his estate; but you are still very young; go, therefore, to your father's three friends, and learn from them wisdom and prudence." Thus saying, she gave him three hundred pieces of money, and dismissed him.

The youth started on his way to his father's friends, with a retinue of attendants befitting his station. As he was journeying, he met a man with

[7]Although the Fisherman's Son is represented as purchasing the dog, the cat, and the rat in order to divert his melancholy by their tricks, and "these seeming animals proved to be magicians," we must regard this as a corruption of the Mongolian story, in which the hero buys the three animals to save them from being tortured. The alteration of the Arabian compiler is very clumsy, and spoils the story to some extent.

[8]The twenty-fifth Buddha.

[9]"The Páli name of Tekkatho is Tekkathela or Tekkasela, and we know that *kha* corresponds to the Sanskrit *ksha*, so the Sanskrit name is Tekshéla, which is the famous Taxila of Ptolemy, in the time of Alexander the Great 'the largest and wealthiest city between the Indus and the Hydaspes.'"—'Notes on the Ancient History of Burmah,' by the Rev. F. Mason.

a dog. "Hey, fellow," said he, "will you sell your dog?" The man replied, "If you want to buy him, give me a hundred pieces for him." The youth gave the sum demanded, and sent the dog back to his mother, with an account of what he had done. Supposing that her son had obtained the sanction of her late husband's friends to his purchase, she fed and tended the dog with the greatest care. Another day, after his mid-day meal, he was walking along when he fell in with a man who had a cat, which he asked him whether he would sell. "You may have her for a hundred pieces," said the man. The lad paid the money and sent the cat to his mother as before, and she, under the same impression as in the previous case, treated the cat with the same attention as she did the dog. Another day he met a man with an ichneumon, which he inquired whether he would part with. The man said he would, and on being asked the price, demanded a hundred pieces. The rich man's son paid the money, and sent the ichneumon to his mother, who, supposing as before, received and fed it.

Now the dog and the cat being domestic animals, she kept them in the house without any fear, but the ichneumon, being a wild animal, she was in such dread of it that she wasted away. Her spiritual teacher coming to her house to receive his meal of cooked food, she went down to give it to him, when, on seeing her, he exclaimed, "Why, my disciple, how thin you have grown!" He then recited the eight accidents to which human life is liable.[10] The rich man's widow replied, "The only reason is this: having given my son three hundred pieces of money and sent him to his father's three friends to learn how to manage his affairs with prudence, one day he sends me a dog, on another, a cat, and on a third, an ichneumon, for each of which he paid a hundred pieces. Now the dog and the cat are domestic animals, and I am not afraid of them; but the ichneumon is a wild animal, and if I only look at it even, I am so frightened that my body, limbs, and eyes are all wasting away." The priest told her to let the ichneumon loose in the jungle, and it being wrong to disobey the commands of one's teacher or one's parents, she turned it loose, giving it at the same time some food smeared over with oil for its subsistence.

On arriving at the jungle, the ichneumon said to himself, "The rich man's son gave a hundred pieces for me, and since I have been in his possession he has had me well fed and taken care of, and has been the cause of my obtaining life and liberty. I will repay the obligation I am under to

---

[10]These are: (1) Success in one's undertakings; (2) dignity and splendour; (3) honour and fame; (4) happiness; and their four opposites.

my benefactor." Thus meditating, he took up in his mouth a ruby ring which he found in the jungle, and carrying it to the rich man's son, gave it to him, saying, "This is no common ring; it possesses the power of gratifying every wish of its owner. Wear it constantly, therefore, on your finger, and on no account allow any one else to wear it. The ichneumon then returned to the jungle. And the rich man's son wished, and during the night a palace with a pinnacled roof rose up in front of his house. All the people of the country, from the king downwards, came to see this sight, and the king gave him his daughter in marriage.

Soon afterwards the princess' teacher came to see if he could discover the prince's talisman. He looked, but could see nothing except the ring. Watching his opportunity, on one occasion when the prince had gone out, he entered the palace, and after making flattering speeches to the princess, asked her whether her husband loved her. "How can you ask such a question as that?" replied she. "He is only a rich man's son, while I am the daughter of the king." "If he loves you so much, you have been, perhaps, allowed to wear his ring?" insinuated the Bráhman. "If I have not worn it," returned she, "pray who should?" After this the Bráhman retired. A day or two later, the princess asked her husband to let her wear his ring, and he, being extremely attached to her, took it off and gave it to her, at the same time charging her not to show it to any one, but to wear it constantly on her finger.

One day, when the rich man's son had gone out, the Bráhman came again and addressed her with his usual smooth phrases. She said, "I have got the ring you spoke about the other day." "Have you?" cried he. "Where is it?" "Here," she replied, displaying it. He begged of her earnestly to take it off and let him examine it; and at last, on her nurse, who was present, persuading her to yield to her teacher's importunity, she took it off and gave it to him. The instant the Bráhman received it he changed himself into a crow and flew away to the middle of the ocean, whither no one could follow him, and there dwelt in a pinnacled palace.

When her husband returned, and heard that the Bráhman had taken the ring, he said to her, "You showed the ring, although I particularly charged you not to do so; and the consequence is that it is now in the midst of the sea, where I can never recover it" After speaking these words, he remained brooding over his loss.

One day a party of the daughters of the Nats[II] came to bathe in a tank covered with water-lilies, not far from the place where the rich man's son dwelt, and having taken off their necklaces they laid them down on the bank; there the cat found them, and picking them up, ran away and hid them. The daughters of the Nats came to the cat and begged her to return the necklaces, saying they were only fit for Nats, not for mortals. The cat said, "If I do, you must make a road for me to travel to the place where the Bráhman is living in his palace in the midst of the ocean; on this condition only will I restore them."[12] So the daughters of the Nats made the road, and the cat crept stealthily along it until she arrived at the palace, where she found the Bráhman asleep, with the ring on his finger. She then slipped off the ring, brought it back, and delivered it to her master, in return for his kindness, saying, "You paid a great price for me, and have fed and taken care of me ever since." As for the Bráhman, he fell into the sea and was drowned; while the rich man's son, being once more in possession of the ring, had every wish he formed gratified.

After a time a band of five hundred robbers came to kill the rich man's son and take away his ring. The dog, perceiving that they had come to kill his master, who had purchased him at so high a price and treated him so kindly, flew at the leader of the band and bit him to death, and threw his body down a well. Seeing this, the rest of the robbers fled in dismay.

Next morning the dog said to his master, "I had no sleep last night; I had hard work to do"; and on being asked to explain, he related how the robbers came to slay his master, and how he had killed their chief, and thereby put the rest to flight, adding, "In return for the many favours you have conferred upon me, I have preserved your life and your property." "Ah," replied the rich man's son, "all men reviled me for giving a hundred pieces for you who are but an animal, but I owe all my prosperity to three animals, each of whom I purchased at that price." Thus saying, he went into the jungle, brought back the ichneumon, and kept him in the house.

Now the ichneumon, the dog, and the cat each asserted it had a right to eat before the others. The ichneumon, because he was the first to give the ring to their master. The cat, because, when the gift which the ichneumon had made to their master had fallen into the hands of the Bráhman, she, by taking the necklaces of the daughters of the Nats, and by means of the road which they made for her, had recovered the ring, and

---

[11]The inferior celestial regions are inhabited by Nats, beings who occupy the same place in Buddhist belief that fairies, genii (*jinn*), dívs, perís, yakshas, etc. hold in European, Arabian, Persian, and Hindú superstitions.

[12]Maidens of this order of semi-celestial beings cannot leave the earth, apparently, without their necklaces, like the daughters of the *jinn*, when their garments are seized by a human being.

was thus the cause of their master's happiness. The dog, because, when five hundred robbers came to strip the rich man's son of what the others had given him and to take his life, he killed their chief, and cast him into the water, whereupon the rest of the band fled. "And thus," said the dog, "I am the preserver not only of our master's wealth, but of his life also."

Thus disputing, they agreed to submit their cases to the decision of the Princess Thoo-dhamma Tsari, the daughter of King Dhammarít, who dwelt at Madarít, in the kingdom of Kambautsa, in a pavilion with one pillar in the centre,[13] who possessed a perfect acquaintance with the ten laws,[14] and was deeply versed in the civil and criminal codes, the fame of whose wisdom had spread to the eight quarters of the world,[15] so that the illustrious of every nation came to her for judgment.

The three animals having appeared before the princess, the ichneumon opened the case: "A rich man's son paid a hundred pieces of money for me, fed and tended me well, and gave me my liberty in the jungle. Bearing this in mind, and because he was my benefactor, I gave him a ruby ring, by means of which he obtained a pinnacled palace which sprang up out of the earth; therefore I am entitled to take precedence of, and eat before, the dog and the cat." The cat, in turn, related how that when the Bráhman had gained possession of the ring which the ichneumon had given their master, she recovered it, and so was the cause of his present good fortune. After her, the dog stated his case, saying, "When robbers came to take from our master the ring which the ichneumon had given him, and which, when lost, was restored to him by the cat, I killed their chief, and the remainder of the band fled. Thus I preserved not only my master's wealth but his life also, and therefore I ought to have precedence over the two others."

When they had ended, Princess Thoo-dhamma Tsari thus pronounced her decision: "The dog, in addition to saving his master's treasures, also prolonged his life; therefore he is entitled to the first place among you; but verily among animals there are none who understand how to repay a debt of gratitude as you do."

---

[13]Pavilions of this form are only allowed to certain females of the Burmese royal family.

[14]These are: (1) To make religious offerings; (2) to observe the Five Precepts; (3) to be charitable; (4) to be upright; (5) to be mild and gentle; (6) not to give way to anger; (7) to be strict in the performance of all religious ceremonies; (8) not to oppress; (9) to exercise self-restraint; (10) not to be familiar with inferiors. The Five Precepts of Buddha referred to in the second of these ten laws are: (1) not to do murder; (2) not to steal; (3) not to commit adultery; (4) not to drink intoxicating liquors; (5) not to do anything evil.

[15]The four cardinal points, and North-East, North-West, South-East, and South-West are called the "eight faces," or quarters, of the world.

ↄ

Thus ends the story of the dog, the cat, and the ichneumon, from which you may learn, that although man is superior to animals, yet kindness towards them does not go unrequited.

As almost all Burmese story-books are translations from the Páli,[16] we may consider the foregoing as representing the Buddhist prototype of Galland's tale of Aladdin. Here, as in the Mongolian, first-cited Arabian (the Fisherman's Son), Bohemian, Albanian, and Greek versions, the number of befriended and grateful animals is three. In the Tamil story there are but two—the snake, through which the hero obtains the talisman, and the cat, which recovers it from the king of Cochin-China. It is interesting to see how the chief incidents are reproduced in the several versions. In Aladdin the princess parts with the "old" lamp for a new one; in the Fisherman's Son, the ring is exchanged for a basket of jewels; in the Mongolian story, the hero very foolishly barters his talisman for the merchants' goods and money. But in the Bohemian, Greek, and Danish versions, the princess, who does not love the hero, her husband, steals the talisman; this is done by a Jew in the Albanian; in the Tamil, by an old hag, who, like the Bráhman in the Burmese story, artfully obtains possession of it from the princess. In all the versions, with the exception of the Burmese, the magically-constructed palace is transported to a great distance—to the heart of Africa, an island in the midst of the sea, or to the sea-shore. The underground cave in the story of Marúf has its counterpart in that of Aladdin, while the wicked vazír plays the part of the African magician—with a difference. From whatever source Galland may have derived his tale, it is very evident, from the Bohemian, Albanian, and Greek variants, that it came to Europe in a form closely resembling the Mongolian, Tamil, and Burmese versions.

VII. THE MAGICAL CONFLICT.

My friend Mr E. J. W. Gibb has kindly furnished me with the following Turkish version of the Magical Conflict (referred to in p. 220), from his forthcoming translation of the romance of 'The Forty Vazírs':

[16]The translators have a curious method of doing their work. Instead of composing continuously in their vernacular (says Captain Sparks), a few words of Páli are written, and then their meaning in Burmese; then a few more Páli words, followed by their interpretation, and so on through the whole book, after the fashion called at school "construing."

It is related that there was a woman in the city of Cairo, and that woman had a worthless son, who, no matter to what trade she put him, did no good. One day the woman said to the youth, "My son, what trade shall I give thee?" The youth replied, "Take me along with thee, let us go; and whatever trade I like, to that do thou give me." And that woman and her son went to the bazaar, and while they were walking about they saw a geomancer, and the youth observed that geomancer and liked him. Thereupon the woman made him over to him, and the geomancer took the youth and began to show him the principles of geomancy. After some days the master said to the youth, "To-morrow I will become a ram; sell me, but take heed and give not my rope." The youth said "Very good." The master became a ram, and the youth took and led him to the bazaar and sold him for a thousand aspres; but he gave not the rope, but took it away with him, and returned. When it was evening his master appeared. After some days the master said, "Now, youth, to-morrow I will become a horse; take and sell me, but take heed and give not my headstall." And he became a horse, and the youth took him and sold him, but gave not the headstall; and he took the money and went to his own house. When it was evening his master came to his house and saw the youth was not there, and he said, "He will come in the morning," and went to bed. On the other hand, the youth went to his mother and said, "O mother, to-morrow I will become a dove; sell me, but take heed and give not my key." And he became a dove without peer; and the woman put the dove up to auction, and the bidders began to raise their bids at the rate of five piastres. But this dove, which spake the language of the people of that city, acquired such fame as cannot be described. Now, as every one was speaking of the qualities of this dove, his master heard and came; and as soon as he saw him he knew him to be the youth, and he said, "Out on thee, misbegotten wretch, thou doest a deed like this and I whole; now see what I will do to thee." And he went and bought him from the woman. The woman said, "I will not give the key." Quoth the master, "Take fifty piastres more, and go and buy another key such as thou pleasest." And he gave her the whole sum; and the woman was greedy and took it, and drew the key from her girdle and threw it on the ground. As soon as the key fell, it became a pigeon and began to fly, and the master became a hawk and pursued the pigeon. While these were flying along, the king was seated in the plain taking his pleasure; and the youth looked and saw no escape, and he became a red rose and fell in front of the king. And the king wondered and said, "What means a rose out of season?" and he took it in his hand. Then the master became a minstrel, and he came to the king's party, with a mandolin in his hand, and sang a stave with a sweet voice. And the king marvelled and said to the minstrel, "What desirest thou from me?" The minstrel answered, "What I desire from thee is the rose that is in thy hand." The king said, "The rose came to me from God; ask something else." The minstrel was silent; then he sang another stave, and again the king said, "What desirest thou from me?" Again the minstrel asked the rose; and this time the king stretched out his hand to give it him, whereupon the rose fell to the ground and became millet. Then the minstrel became a cock, and began to pick up the millet. One grain of the millet was hidden under the king's knee; and that grain became a man, and seized the cock and tore off its head. And the king and the nobles wondered, and they asked the youth of these matters, and he explained them to them.

It will be observed that this version differs materially from all others in some of the details, especially in representing the master, not the pupil, as turning himself into a ram and a horse for sale. The rope and the bridle, however, as in the Norse and Italian variants, are not to be given into the bargain. For the apple in the Albanian story we have here a red rose. The grain of millet and the cock are metamorphoses which occur in most of the versions. But there is some obscurity in the transformation of the key—of the dove's *cage?*—into a "pigeon." What became of the wonderful dove (the youth thus self-changed) after the master had bought it? The incident of the woman's casting the key on the ground, with its result, has its parallel in Straparola's story, in which, by the hero's counsel, the princess dashes the ruby ring against the wall, when it turns into a pomegranate, which bursts, and the seeds are scattered about; also in the Albanian version, in which the queen tosses the apple to the pretended dervishes, when it instantly becomes millet. In the Tamil version (p. 224), the hero, having changed himself into a pearl of the princess's necklace, when the latter is required of her, she scatters the pearls in the courtyard, and they at once become worms—an incident to which that of the rosary in the Mongolian variant bears some analogy. The grain of millet, in the Turkish version, becoming transformed into a man, who kills the cock, seems a reflection of the catastrophe of the Mongolian story (p. 222), from an earlier form of which it was probably derived.

POPULAR TALES

AND FICTIONS

THEIR

MIGRATIONS AND TRANSFORMATIONS

BY

W. A. CLOUSTON

EDITOR OF 'ARABIAN POETRY FOR ENGLISH READERS;'
'BAKHTYÁR NÁMA;' 'THE BOOK OF SINDIBÁD,' ETC.

IN TWO VOLUMES
VOL. II.

WILLIAM BLACKWOOD AND SONS
EDINBURGH AND LONDON
MDCCCLXXXVII

How many uncles, aunts, brothers, sisters, and cousins of all degrees a little story has, and how few of those we hear can lay any claim to originality!

—BARING-GOULD.

Contents of the Second Volume

Contents

APPENDIX

Contents

ༀ POPULAR TALES AND FICTIONS ༀ

Having, in the preceding volume, traced through various countries stories which, from their magical or supernatural elements, were the delight of our simple-minded ancestors in remote times, and still enchant wondering childhood, "when Love and all the world are young," we now come to treat similarly stories of common life, which have little or nothing improbable in their details, and while all of them may be true, some are certainly "founded in fact."

ༀ THE THREE GRAZIERS AND THE ALEWIFE ༀ

THE story of Attorney-General Noy and the Three Graziers is a well-worn "Joe Miller," and furnishes a curious instance of the migrations and modifications of popular fictions and tales. In a foot-note to the article on William Noy (1577–1634) in Chalmers' 'Biographical Dictionary of Eminent Persons' (vol. xxiii. pp. 267, 268), it is cited as follows, from Lloyd's 'State Worthies':

"Three graziers at a fair had left their money with their hostess while they went to market: one of them calls for the money and runs away; the other two come upon the woman and sue her for delivering that which she had received from the three before the three came and demanded it. The cause went against the woman, and judgment was ready to be pronounced, when Mr Noy, being a stranger, wisheth her to give him a fee, because else he could not plead; and then moves, in arrest of judgment, that he was retained by the defendant, and that the case was this: The defendant had received the money of the three together, and confesseth was not to deliver it until the same three demanded it; therefore the money is ready: let the three men come, and it shall be paid; a motion which altered the whole proceedings."[1]

Strange to say, the very same anecdote is also related of Lord Chancellor Egerton (1540–1617) in the same work, vol. xii. pp. 71, 72, note. Noy is, however, invariably connected with it in the popular mind. Yet it is found in an old English jest-book, printed at London half a century before Noy was born and ten years before Egerton. It is thus told in 'Tales and Quicke Answeres, very Mery and Pleasant to Rede,' first printed in 1530:

"There were two men on a time, the whiche lefte a great somme of money in kepyng with a maiden on this condition, that she shulde nat delyuer hit agayne, excepte they came bothe to gether for hit. Nat lang after, one of them cam to hir mornyngly arayde, and sayde that his felowe was deed, and so required the money, and she delyuered it to hym. Shortly after came the tother man, and required to haue the moneye that was lefte with her in kepyng. The maiden was than so sorowfull, both for lacke of the money and for one to defende her cause, that she thought to hange her selfe. But Demosthenes, that excellent oratour, spake for her and sayd: Sir, this mayden is redy to quite her fidelite,[2] and to deliuer agayne the money that was lefte with her in kepynge, so that thou wylt brynge thy felowe with the [*i.e.,* thee] to resceyue it. But that he could nat do."

This version has been taken directly from Valerius Maximus, who is said by some authors to have flourished about the middle of the third century of our era, and by others in the early years of the first century. In place of a "maiden," we find it is an old woman whose cause is so *astutely* defended by Demosthenes; but the story of Valerius is probably as baseless as that of Lloyd himself.[3]

---

[1]Lloyd, says honest Anthony Wood, "wrote many books, which, being without quotation or authority, were little esteemed by intelligent men."

[2]That is, discharge or acquit herself of her trust.

[3]Demosthenis quoque astutia mirifice cuidam aniculæ succursum est, quæ pecuniam depositi nomine a duobus hospitibus acceperat ea condicione ut illam simul utrique redderet. Quorum alter interjecto tempore tamquam mortuo socio squalore obsitus deceptæ omnis nummos abstulit. Supervenit deinde alter et depositum petere cœpit. Hærebat misera et in maxima pariter et pecuniæ et defensionis penuria jam de laqueo et suspendio cogitabat: sed opportune Demosthenes ei patronis adfulsit. Qui ut in advocationem venit, "Mulier," inquit, "parata est depositi se fide solvere, sed nisi socium adduxeris, id facere non potest, quoniam, ut ipse vociferaris, hæc dicta est lex, ne petunia alteri sine altero numeraretur."—'Valeri Maximi Factorum et Dictorum Memorabilium Libri Novem. Julii Paridis et Januarii Nepotiani epitomis adjectis recensuit Carolus Halm.' Lipsiæ in ædibus Teubnerianis, MDCCCLXV. Lib. vii. cap. iii. §5.

The story reappears in another old jest-book, entitled 'Jacke of Dover, His Quest of Inquirie, or His Privie Search for the Veriest Foole in England,' printed in 1604, where the woman defends her own case without assistance from a lawyer—not to mention Demosthenes! And again we find it reproduced in the 'Witty and Entertaining Exploits of George Buchanan, commonly called the King's Fool,' where we read that three pretended pedlars left a pack of goods with a "widow woman": two of the rogues return together, and informing her that their other partner had gone to a certain fair, where they were to meet him, request her to deliver up the pack to them, which she does without hesitation. The third fellow brings an action against the poor widow, and George, putting on an attorney's gown, goes to the court and wins her cause.

A somewhat elaborate variant occurs in the notes to Rogers' poem of 'Italy.' He says it was told him by a cardinal who had heard it when a boy, and "you may not be unwilling to hear it," quoth his eminence, "for it bears some resemblance to the 'Merchant of Venice.'" The outline of this Italian version is as follows: A widow lady, of the family of Lambertini, in the fourteenth century, was reduced to keep an inn at the foot of the Apennines. Three cavaliers, who had come to the inn for refreshment, desired her to take charge of a bag of gold until all three returned together, and then rode away; presently one of the cavaliers returned, saying that he had not affixed his seal to the bag as the others had done, and, having received the bag, while pretending to seal it, the lady was called away by some of her guests, and the cavalier decamped with the money. The two others sued the lady for recovery of the bag of gold. She consulted the most eminent lawyers in Bologna, and their unanimous opinion was that she must lose the cause; but a young advocate, her daughter Gianetta's lover, undertakes her defence, and is triumphantly successful; becomes, in consequence, famous and wealthy, and duly marries the lovely Gianetta.

Wright, in his introduction to an old English metrical text of the 'Seven Wise Masters,' printed for the Percy Society, states that he had met with the story among the Latin tales of the thirteenth and fourteenth centuries, but could not call to mind in what collection: it is found, he adds, a little varied in detail, in the 'Nouveaux Contes à rire,' Amsterdam, 1737, under the title of "Jugement subtil du Duc d'Ossone contre deux Marchands." Apparently Wright was not aware that the story in this form occurs in one of the novels of Le Sage, 'The History of Vanillo Gonzales,' ch. xvi., which was published in 1734. The hero, while a page to the Duke of Ossuna, governor of Sicily, is met on the street one day by a young citizen of Palermo, who, recognising by his dress that he is in the duke's service, tells him that his old father will be ruined unless the governor's influence is secured in his behalf, and prevails upon Gonzales to go home with him and hear the story from his father's own lips, which the old man relates as follows:

"About six months ago, Charles Azarini, Peter Scannati, and Jerom Avellino, three merchants, all of them my intimate friends, came to this house, accompanied by a public notary, and bringing with them the sum of ten thousand crowns in gold, informed me that they had agreed to make me the depositary of this money, which they intended to export whenever an advantageous opportunity happened. Delivering it into my possession, they desired me to give them an undertaking in writing that I would not deliver it, or any part of it, to any one of them except in the presence of the other two; and I accordingly entered into this engagement by executing a document which the notary prepared for this purpose. We carefully preserved the money thus deposited for the parties concerned whenever its delivery should be required. But a few nights ago, Jerom Avellino knocked loudly at my door, and on its being opened, hastily entered my room, in great agitation. 'Signor Giannetino,' said he, 'if I break in upon the hours of repose, you must excuse the interruption from the importance of the business which occasions it. Azarini, Scannati, and myself have learnt that a Genoese vessel, richly laden, is just arrived at Messina, from which, if despatch be used, we have an opportunity of deriving great advantage, and have therefore resolved to employ the ten thousand crowns which are in your hands. Make haste, if you please, and deliver them to me; my horse is waiting at the door, and I burn with impatience to reach Messina.' 'Signor Avellino,' said I, 'you seem to forget that I cannot part with them unless—' 'Oh no, no,' interrupted he; 'I very well recollect that it is expressed in the agreement that you are not to deliver them unless the three parties be present; but Azarini and Scannati are ill, and could not accompany me to your house; they, however, absolve you from that condition, and desire that you will deliver me the money immediately. Every moment is of consequence. Come, you have nothing to fear. You have long known me. I have always maintained the character of an honest man, and I hope you will not, by any unjust suspicion of my integrity, disturb the friendship which has subsisted between us, and be the cause of our losing the present advantageous opportunity. Do, do make haste,' continued he; 'deliver me the money instantly, or I am fearful I shall be too late at Messina.' A secret apprehension of danger, which Heaven no doubt inspired for my safety, made me hesitate a long time; but Avellino, the villain Avellino, supplicated, pressed, and tormented me in such a way that my resistance at length failed, and I foolishly delivered to him the deposit, with which he immediately disappeared."

The old man, as he uttered these words, recollecting his imprudence, burst into a flood of tears. Gonzales' heart melted at his distress. "Do not afflict yourself," said he, endeavouring to console him; "his excellency the viceroy has much in his power. Avellino will have great difficulty to escape his vengeance." "Avellino, alas!" said the son of the old citizen, "is already at a great distance; and what is more afflicting, no sooner were Azarini and Scannati informed of the trick their associate had played, than they instantly commenced a suit against my father for the money confided to his care. This cause will be heard in the course of two days, and my poor father will in all probability be condemned to restore ten thousand crowns to the complainants." "The cause is not yet decided," exclaimed Gonzales; "and I have no doubt that the viceroy, upon being informed of the facts and circumstances, which he shall be this very day, will choose to try it himself."

Gonzales made a faithful report of this case to his excellency, who, after great attention, said to him, smiling, "I shall give such a judgment in this case as will make some noise in the world." On the following day he summoned the parties to appear before him; and when the plaintiffs had pleaded their cause, he addressed the defendant: "Giannetino," said he, "what answer have you to make to this demand?" "None, sir," replied Giannetino, elevating his shoulders and resting his chin upon his breast.—"He is right, gentlemen," said the viceroy, addressing himself to Azarini and Scannati; "he has no answer to make to your charge. He acknowledges all that you have said, and is ready to pay you the ten thousand crowns which were deposited in your hands. But as he cannot, by the terms of the agreement, deliver them unless the three parties be actually present, do you bring Avellino into court, and you shall have the money." The numerous auditory which attended this trial no sooner heard the judgment than the court resounded with peals of applause, and it became the subject of conversation throughout Sicily.[4]

꒰

[4]The novel of 'Vauillo Gonzales' is said by the editor of Le Sage's works to be of Spanish extraction—"tirée de l'Espagnol"; but this may mean no more than that Le Sage took the general plan of it from a similar Spanish novel, as in the case of his 'Diable Boiteux.'

But the story, so long a favourite throughout Europe, appears to be of Eastern origin, and it was in all likelihood among the earliest to migrate westward along with other Indian tales. It is found in nearly all the Eastern texts, or texts directly derived from Eastern sources, of the Book of Sindibád, of which some account will be found in another paper. The following is a prose rendering of the story from the Persian 'Sindibád Náma':

Once on a time three persons agreed among themselves to enter into partnership, have everything in common, and share one another's secrets. One was a farmer, another a merchant, and another a dealer in grain. When they had amassed a sum of money, they agreed to deposit it with an old woman of approved honesty, but on this condition, that none should ask it back unless all the three were present. One of them was an expert sharper. Being with his companions in the street, he pretended that he was going to ask from the woman some clay and other substances for the bath. He approached her window, and begged her to hand him out, not what he had mentioned, but the purse. She asked, where were his two partners? He said, "They are at hand. Look from the window, and see that they are both witnesses." The woman, seeing them, gave him the purse, while his companions never suspected any mischief. The man immediately on receiving it fled to the desert, and went to another kingdom. The two friends, after waiting some time in the street, and not finding their companion return, began to suspect what had happened, and hastening in alarm to the house of the old woman, demanded the deposit. She replied, that their partner had received the money by their order and in their presence; upon which they took her before the kází, who commanded her to restore the deposit. She begged a delay of three days, which was granted. She departed weeping, and a child five years of age, whom she met in the street, inquired the cause of her distress. Upon her relating it, the child smiled and said, "Tell the kází to-morrow that when he produces the three partners before you, you are ready to restore the money." Next day she did as the child had suggested to her. The kází, in astonishment, asked her "who had pierced this pearl" [*i.e.,* who had solved this difficult question]? She at first claimed the merit to herself; but as the kází would not believe that a woman could possess such wisdom, she confessed the truth; and whenever in future a difficulty occurred, the kází referred to that child for a solution."[5]

[5] See Note, "Precocious Children," at the end of this paper.

In the Greek text ('Syntipas') three merchants put their gold and silver in *three* purses. In a manuscript copy of the 'Thousand and One Nights,' preserved in the British Museum, which, though imperfect, contains the 'Seven Vazírs,' the number of merchants is *four;* they possess a thousand dínars, which they put into *one* purse, and as they are travelling they enter a garden, in which was a running stream, and having sat down and refreshed themselves, they say one to another, "Come, let us bathe in this river." So they leave their purse with the woman who was keeper of the garden, and put off their clothes and go into the water. One of the four, who had not yet put off his clothes, said to his friends, "We have no comb; let us ask the woman for one." The others saying, "Go, then, and ask her for one," he went to her, and said, "Give me the purse." But she said, "When thy companions come all together and ask for it, as they gave it me together." The man then called out to his friends in the river, "Are you willing she should give it me?" They answered, "Yes; give it him," think-ing he meant the comb. So she gives him the purse, and off he goes with it, flying as fast as possible. At length the bathers became impatient, and putting on their clothes, they went to the woman and said, "Where is he to whom thou gavest the comb?" She said, "What comb? He asked me for the purse; and I was not willing to give it him till he cried out to you, and you told me to give it to him, and he took it and is gone." The conclusion is the same as that of the Persian version above quoted.—The story is well known in India at the present day: in a Canarese collection of tales it is related of four sharpers who found a purse on the road, and disputing about its possession, they agree to deposit it, in the meantime, with a respectable merchant. It also occurs in Gladwin's 'Persian Moonshee' (No. 7 of "Pleasing Stories"), where two sharpers leave their money with an old woman; by-and-by one of them returns and gets the money; the other sues the old woman, and the kází is credited with the sagacity which in the 'Sindibád' is ascribed to a child of five years.—And now we may regard the story of Valerius Maximus with suspicion, and that of Lloyd as absolutely untrue, so far as William Noy's alleged share in the "case."

NOTE

PRECOCIOUS CHILDREN (p. 270)

Absurd as it seems to represent a child of five years as exhibiting such sagacity, yet this occurs in all versions of the Book of Sindibád in which the story is found. It is indeed far from uncommon in Eastern tales to find children credited with solving difficulties which had puzzled grave and reverend seigniors, and otherwise showing wonderful precocity of intellect. A well-known instance occurs in the story of the pot of olives as related in the 'Arabian Nights,' which finds some curious parallels in the tales of 'Ardshí Bordshí,' the Mongolian form of the Indian romance entitled 'Sinhásana Dwatrinsati,' Thirty-two Tales of a Throne:

A merchant intrusted his friend with a jewel to give to his wife, but the man sold it, and used the proceeds for his own purposes, and afterwards declared that he had duly delivered it. When the merchant brought his case to trial, his false friend produced two witnesses who asserted that they had seen him give the jewel to the merchant's wife, and judgment would at once have been given in his favour but for the interposition of a boy, who advised that all four should be confined in separate rooms, and each be given a piece of clay, out of which they were to make models of the jewel. But when their models were examined, only those of the merchant and his false friend were found to correspond, while those of the two suborned witnesses, who had never seen the jewel, were each different, and neither of them at all like the others. Thus was the twofold crime of the false friend made manifest by the sagacity of a boy.—A similar incident is related in Gladwin's 'Persian Moonshee' (No. 14 of "Pleasing Stories"), where a king is substituted for the boy.

In the same Mongolian collection we read of a youth who went to the wars, and, after two years' absence, he sent his father notice of his approaching return. The father made preparations for his reception, but when he arrived there appeared at the same time a person exactly like himself in form, features, and voice, who declared himself to be the true son, and the other to be an impostor. In vain was he tested regarding his knowledge of family affairs; he knew more than the real son, and there seemed no alternative but to receive him into the family, when a boy undertook to settle the question decisively. A water-jug was brought, and the boy said that the true son should be able to go inside of it. On hearing this, the son, saying that such a thing was impossible, was turning sadly away, when his "double"—who was, as the boy suspected, Shimnu, or the devil—suddenly compressed himself, and triumphantly entered the jug (like the genie in the Arabian tale), upon which the boy clapped down the lid and imprisoned him; and the father had no longer any doubt as to the identity of his son.

Another example of juvenile shrewdness is found in the 'Kathá Sarit Ságara,' book ii. chap. xiv.: A child of five years, who was neglected by his stepmother, resolved to punish her, and with this view he said to his father one day, "Papa, I have two papas," which made the man suspect his wife had a lover, and he refrained from visiting her. The lady, surmising that her husband's altered conduct was caused by something that her stepson had said to him against her, deemed it good policy to mollify the clever but spiteful child, so she gave him dainty food, and taking him in her lap, asked him what he had been saying to his father about her. He answered that he would say a great deal worse if she did not treat him as she did her own children, and she promised to do so in future. When his father came home, the child held a mirror before him, and, showing him his reflection, said, "That is my second father." Upon this the man dismissed his suspicions, and was immediately reconciled to his wife, whom he had blamed without cause.

❧ THE SILENT COUPLE ❧

COULD any one suspect that the popular and highly humorous Scotch song, "The barrin' o' the door," had for its subject an Oriental origin, and that it is only the treatment of the subject—which is indeed admirable—that is peculiarly Scotch? The song informs us that about "Martinmas time" a goodwife was busy making puddings, and the cold wind blowing through the open door, her husband desires her to close it; but she bids him do it himself, as her hands are busily occupied: hereupon they have an altercation, until it is at length agreed that whichever of them first spoke should "get up and bar the door." For some time both remain obstinately silent; by-and-by, two travellers, passing by, see the open door, and enter the house. Having repeatedly addressed the silent couple without receiving any reply, one says to his companion:

> "Do you tak' aff the auld man's beard,
> While I kiss the gudewife."

Upon this the husband starts up, and indignantly demands to know whether they would dare to kiss his wife before his face and scald himself with "puddin' bree." The gudewife then "gives three skips o'er the floor," and exultingly exclaims:

> "Gudeman, ye've spoke the foremost word,
> Rise up and bar the door!"

This song was recovered by Herd in 1776, and included in the second edition of his collection of Scottish Songs and Ballads. It is an improved version of an ancient song entitled "Johnie Blunt," which is found in Johnson's 'Scots Musical Museum,' published in 1790, vol. iv. p. 376, and which thus begins:

> There lived a man in yonder glen,
>   And John Blunt was his name, O;
> He maks gude maut, and he brews gude ale,
>   And he bears a wondrous fame, O.
>
> The wind blew in the hallan ae nicht,
>   Fu' snell out o'er the moor, O;

274

"Rise up, rise up, auld Luckie," he says,
"Rise up and bar the door, O."

They made a paction 'tween them twa,
They made it firm and sure, O;
Whae'er sud speak the foremost word,
Should rise and bar the door, O.

By-and-by *three* travellers, who had lost their way, come in, and begin to use freedoms with the wife, which Johnie resents by an expression "not fit for ears polite," when she cries:

"Aha! Johnie Blunt, ye hae spoke the first word,
Get up and bar the door, O!"

The date of this song—which is evidently imperfect —does not seem to be known, but it is believed to be of considerable antiquity.

A musical entertainment by Prince Hoare,[1] entitled 'No Song, no Supper,' written in 1790, has for its plot the same incident: Crop orders his wife Dorothy to shut the door, which he had left open on coming in, "because his hands were full," and she flatly refuses: ultimately they agree that "whoever speaks the first word shall shut the door." So they sit doggedly silent, until a seafaring acquaintance, named Robin, comes in, and finding he cannot get either to utter a word, he tells the husband, "A good ducking at the yard-arm would put your jawing-tackle aboard, and be well employed on you—wouldn't it, mistress?" To which she replies, "Ay, that it would—oh, I forgot!" Upon this the husband bursts into a guffaw, and says, "Now, Dorothy, go and shut the door."

If this idea was not derived from some current English jest, it may have been taken from 'Le Notte Piacevoli' (the Pleasant Nights) of Straparola, printed at Venice in 1550, where the story forms the eighth Novel of the first Night, in which, as in the English dramatic piece, only one person comes in, and the husband is victorious.—The story is orally current among the Venetians as follows:

---

[1] Not a "prince" of the blood-royal, but a very respectable gentleman nevertheless, who wrote a considerable number of light comic pieces for the stage, some of which were very successful in their day; and a fine sea-song, 'The Saucy Arethusa,' which even Dibdin might have been proud to own. He was born in 1755, and died in 1835.

There was once a husband and wife. The former said to the latter, "Let us have some fritters." She replied, "What shall we do for a frying-pan?" "Go and borrow one from my godmother." "You go and get it; it is only a little way off." "Go yourself. I will take it back when we are done with it." So she went and borrowed the pan, and when she returned she said, "Here is the pan, but you must carry it back." So they cooked the fritters, and after they had eaten, the husband said, "Now let us go to work, both of us, and the one who speaks first shall carry back the pan." Then she began to spin, and he to draw his thread (for the man was a shoemaker), and all the time keeping silence, except that when he drew his thread he said, "Leulerò, leulerò," and she spinning said, "Piccicí, piccicí," and they said not another word. By-and-by a soldier came in and said to the man, "Cut me a girth for my horse." But he went on working away, saying, "Leulerò, leulerò," and she spinning away, saying, "Piccicí, piccicí." Then said the soldier, "Cut me a girth for my horse, or I'll cut your head off." But they both paid no heed to him, but went on as before. The soldier, now quite enraged, seized the man and was about to cut off his head, when the wife called out, "Ah, don't, for mercy's sake!" Upon this the man exclaimed, "Good! good! Now do you go and carry the pan back to my godmother, and I will go and cut the horse's girth."—In a Sicilian variant, the husband and wife fry some fish, and then set about their respective work, and the one who finishes first is to eat the fish. While they are singing and whistling respectively, a friend knocks at the door, and finally walks in; speaks to the silent couple; but gets no answer; so he sits down and eats up all the fish.[2]

This droll incident is the subject of several Eastern stories. In the Arabian tale of Sulayman Bey and the Three Story-Tellers, a hashish-eater, having married his pretty cousin, gave the customary feast to their relations and friends. "When the festivities were over," he goes on to relate, "I conducted my relations and guests to the door, but, from absence of mind, I neglected to shut it before returning to my wife. 'Dear cousin,' said my wife to me when we were alone, 'go and shut the street door.' 'It would be strange indeed if I did,' I replied. 'Am I just made a bridegroom, clothed in silk, wearing a shawl and a dagger set with diamonds, and am I to go and shut the door? Why, my dear, you are crazy—go and shut it yourself.' 'Oh, indeed!' she exclaimed, 'am I, young, robed in a satin dress,

---

[2]Crane's 'Italian Popular Tales,' pp. 284, 285.

with lace and precious stones—am I to go and shut the street door? No, indeed; it is you who have become crazy, and not I. Come, let us make a bargain,' she continued, 'and let the first who speaks go and fasten the door.' 'Agreed,' I replied, and straightway I became mute, and she too was silent, while we both sat down, dressed as we were in our nuptial attire, looking at each other, and seated on opposite sofas. We remained thus for one-two hours. During this time thieves happened to pass by, and, seeing the door open, entered and laid hold of whatever came to their hands. We heard footsteps in the house, but opened not our mouths; the robbers came even into our room, and saw us seated, motionless and indifferent to all that took place. They continued their pillage, therefore, collecting together everything valuable, and even dragging away the carpets from beneath us; they then laid hands on our own persons, which they despoiled of every article worth taking, while we, in fear of losing our wager, said not a word. Having thus cleared the house, the thieves departed quietly, but we remained on our seats, saying not a syllable. Towards morning a police officer came round on his tour of inspection, and, seeing our door open, walked in. Having searched all the rooms and found no one, he entered the apartment where we were seated, and inquired the meaning of what he saw. Neither my wife nor I would condescend to reply. The officer became angry, and ordered our heads to be cut off. The executioner's sword was just about to perform its office, when my wife cried out, 'Sir, he is my husband, spare him!' 'Oh, oh!' I exclaimed, overjoyed and clapping my hands, 'you have lost the wager; go and shut the door.' I then explained the whole affair to the police-officer, who shrugged his shoulders and went away, leaving us in a truly dismal plight."

To the same effect is another Arabian story, in Beloe's 'Oriental Apologues,' translated for him by Dr Russel, from a manuscript collection of tales which the latter had procured at Aleppo: A man comes home one night and asks his wife to prepare his supper. She places before him some dry, stale bread. "Why, my dear," says he, "who on earth can eat such dry, hard bread as this?" "Get up and moisten it, then," replied the wife. "No, you must do it," said he. "I'll do nothing of the sort," rejoined his loving spouse; "I'm tired, and shan't budge an inch." So they went on, growing more and more obstinate. At length they determined, by mutual consent, that whoever should speak the first word should get up and moisten the bread. In this interesting situation they remained for a considerable time, when one of their neighbours accidentally dropped in. "Good evening," said the visitor. They said nothing. "What's the matter?" continued he;

"why are you silent?" They said nothing. "You are a man," said he to the husband; "why don't you speak?" He said nothing. He kissed his wife, but the man said nothing. He gave him a blow on the cheek, but the man said nothing. Irritated, he at length went to the kází, and complained that he could not make the man speak: he was committed to prison; still he said nothing. Next morning he was again brought before the kází; still he said nothing. The kází ordered him to be hanged for contumacy. When the sentence was on the point of being executed, the wife appeared, and in the most pitiable tone exclaimed, "Alas, my unfortunate husband!" "You devil," said he, "go home and moisten the bread."

There is a Turkish version, in which only men are the principal actors, in the romance of the 'Forty Vazírs';[3] and for the following rendering of it I am indebted to my friend Mr E. J. W. Gibb (author of 'Ottoman Poems,' the 'Story of Jewád,' etc.), who is preparing for publication a complete English translation of that interesting collection:

Some bang-eaters,[4] while out walking, found a sequin. They said, "Let us go to a cook, and buy food and eat." So they went and entered a cook's shop, and said, "Master, give us a sequin's worth of food." The cook prepared all kinds of food, and loaded a porter with it; and the bang-eaters took him without the city, where there was a ruined tomb, which they entered and sat down in, and the porter deposited the food and went away. The bang-eaters began to partake of the food, when suddenly one of them said, "The door is open—stay, do one of you shut the door, else some other bang-eaters will come and annoy us; even though they be friends, they will do the deeds of foes." One of them replied, "Go thou and shut the door," and they fell a-quarrelling. At length one said, "Come, let us agree that whichever of us first speaks or laughs, shall rise and fasten the door." They all agreed to this proposal, and left the food and sat quite still. Suddenly a great number of dogs came in: not one of the bang-eaters stirred or spoke, for if one spoke he would have to rise and shut the door, so they spoke not. The dogs made an end of the food, and ate it all up. Just then another dog leapt in from without, but no food remained. Now one of the bang-eaters had partaken of everything, and some of the food remained about his mouth and on his beard. That

[3]See Note, "Book of the Forty Vazírs," at the end of this paper.
[4]Bang is a preparation of hemp and coarse opium. In the East hemp is a soft fibreless plant, of no textile value, saturated with narcotic juice, from which hashish is made.

newly-come dog licked up the particles of food that were on the bang-eater's breast, and while he was licking up those about his mouth, he took his lip for a piece of meat and bit it. The bang-eater did not stir, for he said within himself, "They will tell me to shut the door." But to ease his soul he cried "Ough!" inwardly cursing the dog. When the other bang-eaters heard him make that noise, they said, "Rise, fasten the door." He replied, "'After loss, attention'; now that the food is gone and my lip is wounded, what is the use of shutting that door? Through negligence and folly ye have let this great good slip." And crying, "Woe, alas!" they each went away in a different direction.

Perhaps the germ of the foregoing versions is to be found in the Indian tale of the Four Simple Bráhmans,[5] in which the noodles dispute with each other the palm for superior *stupidity,* and, before a duly constituted court, each in his turn gravely relates the most foolish thing he has done in the course of his life. The Third Bráhman recounts how he one night peevishly told his wife that all women were babblers, to which she retorted that she knew some men who babbled quite as much as women. Taking this remark as meant for himself in particular, he wagered a betel-leaf (an article of no value) that she would speak before he did. To this she agreed, and both went to sleep. Next morning they remained in bed till an advanced hour; and their relations, having knocked at their door and received no response, sent for a carpenter to break it open, fearing that they were both sick—perhaps dead. On the door being broken open, the relatives, discovering them both in good health, inquired the reason of such extraordinary conduct, but they remained silent. So they concluded that both were possessed with demons, and sent for a celebrated magician to exorcise them; but the fee he demanded was so great that one of the relations, suspecting the real state of the affair, undertook himself to cure them both of their dumbness, and thus save all expense. Taking a small bar of gold, and heating it to a very high degree, he applied it successively to the husband's forehead, arms, breast, legs, and the soles of his feet; but all this excruciating torture he heroically endured without even uttering a cry of pain. Proceeding next to the woman, no sooner had the hot bar come in contact with her tender epidermis than she screamed, "Enough! enough!" Then, turning to her husband, "There," said she, "is your leaf of betel." The exulting husband exclaimed, "Did I not tell you

[5]Translated from the Tamil, in the Abbé Dubois' 'Description of the People of India.'

that you would be the first to speak, and that you would prove by your own conduct that I was right in saying last evening that women are all babblers?" When the relations were informed of the whole affair, "Never," said they—"never in the whole world was there seen such folly!"

Every popular tale has its history, according to Baring-Gould; but this is not always ascertainable. The story of the Silent Couple was probably introduced into Europe and diffused orally at first, and if so, its Western history must be sunk in the sands of time. Possibly it may be found in one of the immense Latin collections made by monkish writers in mediæval times—when some future enthusiastic story-hunter undertakes the Herculean labour of searching into them!

NOTE

THE BOOK OF THE FORTY VAZÍRS (p. 278)

This Turkish collection of tales, entitled 'Qirq Vazír'—the frame of which is similar to that of the Book of Sindibád—is said to have been composed, during the reign of Sultan Murád II., by Shaykh Záda, after an Arabian work entitled 'The Forty Mornings and Evenings.' Shaykh Záda is not a proper name; it signifies, simply, the offspring of a shaykh, and, employed by an author, it must be considered as a *nom de plume,* indicating, however, the quality of his parentage. In the early years of the last century a portion of this collection was translated into French by Petis de la Croix, from which it was rendered into English, and included in Weber's 'Tales of the East.' Of the Arabian original nothing seems to be known. It is thought that the original work was of earlier date than the 14th century. Des Longchamps, in his 'Essai sur les Fables Indiennes,' etc., has pointed out the close resemblance between one of the tales of the 'Forty Vazírs' and the fifth Novel of the tenth Day of Boccaccio's 'Decameron,' and observes that its presence in the latter proves that the Arabian original of the 'Forty Vazírs' was anterior to the 14th century, or that its author had gone to some more ancient collection. The story to which he refers forms one of the Twenty-five Tales of a Demon—the tenth of the version incorporated in the 'Kathá Sarit Ságara'—and is probably of Buddhistic origin. The Franklin's Tale of Dorigen, in Chaucer's 'Canterbury Tales,' is similar to Boccaccio's novel; indeed, the story is known all over the world. In a forthcoming publication, for the Chaucer Society, I have given many analogues, from Sanskrit, Burmese, Persian, Hebrew, Turkish, Italian, Gaelic, etc.

↬ THE SHARPERS AND THE SIMPLETON ↬

ANDREW BORDE, a Carthusian monk before the Reformation in England, afterwards one of the physicians to Henry VIII.—and an eccentric, mirth-loving good fellow he seems to have been from all accounts—is the putative author of a collection of *facetiæ* entitled 'The Jests of Scogin,' or Scogan, one of which is the following:

"Scogin and his chamber-fellow, lacking money, Scogin said, 'If thou wilt be ruled after me, we will go to Thame[1] market, where we shall overtake, going or coming, some that drive sheep: now do as I shall tell thee, and we will get some money.' And as they went to Thame they did see a man drive sheep. Then said Scogin to his fellow, 'Go thou before, and make bargain with him that the sheep be no sheep, but hogs; and when that thou hast made a full bargain, ask by whom the matter shall be tried; and then say thou, by him that shall next overtake us.' The scholar did overtake him that drove the sheep, and said, 'Well overtaken, my friend; from whence hast thou brought these fine hogs?' 'Hogs!' quoth the fellow, 'they be sheep.' Said the scholar, 'You begin to jest.' 'Nay, sir,' said the fellow, 'I speak in good earnest.' 'Art thou in earnest?' said the scholar. 'Thou wilt lay no wager with me to the contrary?' 'Yes, by the bone of a pudding, I will lay all the money in my purse.' 'How much is that?' said the scholar. The fellow said, 'I have two shillings.' Said the scholar, 'That is nothing. Wilt thou lay half thy hogs and two shillings, and I will lay as much against it? Strike hands, and he that loseth shall pay.' 'Be it so,' said the fellow. 'Now,' said the scholar, 'by whom shall we be tried?' The fellow said, 'We shall be tried in the town of Thame.' 'Nay,' said the scholar, 'Thame is out of my way; let us be tried by him that shall next overtake us.' 'Be it so,' said the fellow. By-and-by Scogin did overtake them, saying, 'Well overtaken, good fellows.' 'Welcome, master,' said the scholar and the fellow. 'Master,' said the fellow, 'here is a scholar of Oxford hath made a bargain with me of two shillings and half of my sheep that they be hogs that I do drive before me.' Scogin did set up a laughing, saying, 'Alack, good fellow, dost thou think these be sheep?' 'Yea, sir,' said the fellow. 'Alack, good fellow, thou hast lost thy bar-

---

[1] Thame, in Oxfordshire.

281

gain,' said Scogin, 'for they be fair hogs. Then said the scholar, 'Give me my money and divide these hogs, for I must have half of them.' 'Alack,' said the fellow, 'I bought these for sheep, and not for hogs; I am undone.' 'Nay,' said Scogin, 'I will be indifferent between you both; let the scholar have the two shillings, and take thou the hogs away with thee.' The fellow said, 'Blessed be the time that ever you were born! Hold, scholar, there is two shillings.' The fellow was glad he lost not his hogs, which were sheep."

The story again appears, with some variations, in 'The Sacke-Full of Newes,' probably printed, says Mr W. C. Hazlitt, as early as 1558, where the man is represented as driving *hogs,* and the two sharpers persuade him they are sheep, the first "coney-catcher" wagering his coat against one of the "sheep," and, unlike Scogin and his comrade, he selects the fattest of the hogs. "What became of him [*i.e.,* the hoggard] afterwards I cannot tell; only this much I know, that he was deceived by those two crafty fellows of one of his hogs. But they immediately met one the other again, and sold the hog for money, and rejoiced that they fared so well, not knowing how to have otherwise sustained their wants." And in a manuscript of the time of Charles I., printed by Mr J. Payne Collier in his 'Extracts from the Registers of the Stationers' Company,' the exploit is ascribed to George Peele, the dramatist, and John Singer, the actor. This is in verse, and does not differ materially from the version in the 'Sacke-Full of Newes.'

In a note on the jest of Scogin, Mr Hazlitt says he does not know "whether this tale is to be found in earlier books, or related of any one before Scogin's time." Variants of the same story, in which the fundamental outline is clearly discoverable, are, in fact, found in the folk-tales of nearly every European country.

One of the tales of the Anglican 'Gesta Romanorum,' edited for the Roxburghe Club by Sir Frederick Madden, is to this effect: A physician named Averoys is successful in curing the emperor of an obstinate disease, and is rewarded by his royal patient with fair gifts, and retained in the palace as one of the imperial household. Three other doctors, envious of his great good fortune, conspire to ruin Averoys. They go out of the city, and station themselves on the road along which he usually passed on his visits to patients in the suburbs, a mile or so apart from each other. As Averoys passes the first doctor, he is told that he is a leper. The second and the third successively make the same observation to him; and Averoys, now thoroughly frightened, hastens home, and informs the emperor that he is smitten with leprosy. But the emperor, instead of causing him to be thrust from the city, as his enemies anticipated, expresses his concern, and assures him of his continued friendship. Averoys then takes a bath of goats' blood, and finds that the leprosy was only in his imagination. He informs the emperor of the wicked trick that had been put upon him by the three envious doctors, who are then, by the emperor's orders, dragged to the gallows at the tails of horses, and hanged—without benefit of clergy.[2]

A droll variant occurs in the old English jest-book, 'Merry Tales and Quick Answers,' No. lviii, entitled "Of the fool that thought hym selfe deed"; this is how it goes:

"There was a felowe dwellynge at Florence, called Nigniaca, whiche was nat verye wyse, nor all a foole, but merye and iocunde. A sorte[3] of yonge men, for to laughe and pastyme, appoynted to gether to make hym beleue that he was sycke. So, whan they were agreed howe they wolde do, one of them mette hym in the mornynge, as he came out of his house, and bade hym good morowe, and than asked him if he were nat yl at ease? No, quod the foole, I ayle nothynge, I thanke God. By my faith, ye haue a sickely pale colour, quod the other, and wente his waye. Anone after, an other of them mette hym, and asked hym if he had nat an ague, for your face and colour (quod he) sheweth that ye be very sycke. Than the foole beganne a lyttel to doubt, whether he were sycke or no, for he halfe beleued that they sayd trouth. Whan he had gone a lytel farther, the thyrde man mette hym and sayde: Jesu! manne, what do you out of your bed? Ye loke as ye wold nat lyue an houre to an ende. Nowe he doubted greatly, and thought verily in his mynde that he had hadde some sharpe ague; wherfore he stode styll and wolde go no further; and, as he stode, the fourth man came and sayde: Jesu! man, what dost thou here, and arte so sycke? Gette the home to thy bedde, for I perceyue thou canst nat lyue an houre to an ende. Than the fole's harte beganne to feynte, and [he] prayde this laste man that came to hym to helpe hym home. Yes, quod he, I wyll do as moche for the as for myn owne brother.

"So home he brought hym, and layde him in his bed, and than he fared with hym selfe, as thoughe he wolde gyue vp the gooste. Forth with came the other felowes, and saide he hadde well done to lay hym in his bedde. Anone after, came one whiche toke on hym to be a phisitian; whiche,

---

[2]Madden, No. xx. p. 57; Herrtage, p. 67. The story is much abridged in the text translated by Swan.

[3]Knot or party.

touchynge the pulse, sayde the malady was so vehement, that he could nat lyue an houre. So they, standynge aboute the bedde, sayde one to an other, Nowe he gothe his way; for his speche and syght fayle hym; by and by he wyll yelde vp the goste. Therfore, lette vs close his eyes, and laye his hands a crosse, and cary hym forth to be buryed. And than they sayde lamentynge one to an other, O! what a losse haue we of this good felowe, our frende!

"The foole laye stylle, as one [that] were deade; yea, and thought in his mynde, that he was deade in dede. So they layde hym on a bere, and caryed hym through the cite. And whan any body asked them what they caryed, they sayd, the corps of Nigniaca to his graue. And euer as they went, people drew about them. Among the prece[4] ther was a tauerners boy, the whiche, whan he herde that it was the cors of Nigniaca, he said to them, O! what a vile beastly knaue, and what a stronge thefe is deed! by the masse, he was well worthy to haue ben hanged longe ago. Whan the fole harde those wordes, he put out his heed and sayd, I wys, horeson, if I were alyue nowe, as I am deed, I wolde prone the a false lyer to thy face. They, that caryed him, began to laugh so hartilye, that they sette downe the bere and wente theyr waye.

"By this tale ye may se, what the perswasion of many doth. Certaynly he is very wyse, that is nat inclined to foly, if he be stered therevnto by a multitude. Yet sapience is founde in fewe persones: and they be lyghtly[5] olde sobre men."[6]

But more akin to the version in the 'Jests of Scogin' is one of the tricks of the renowned German rogue, Tyl Eulenspiegel, a work which, according to Görres' 'Folksbücher,' was first published in the Lower Saxon dialect in 1485, and of which an English translation was printed by William Cop-

---

[4]Crowd.

[5]Usually.

[6]'Mery Tales, Wittie Questions, and Quicke Answeres, very pleasant to be Readde.' Imprinted at London by H. Wykes, 1567.—This quaint little work is reprinted, with useful and interesting notes, in the First Series of 'Shakspeare Jest-Books,' edited by Mr W. Carew Hazlitt (London: 1864).—The story was probably taken from the Facetiæ of Poggius, where it is entitled "Mortuus Loquens," which was reproduced by Grazzini in his collection, which was not printed till after his death. There are many modern variants of the story. In the Turkish jest-book which purports to relate the witless sayings of the Khoja Nasr-ed-Dín, he is persuaded that he is dead, and allows himself to be stretched on a bier and carried to the cemetery. On the way, the bearers, coming to a miry place, said, "We will rest here," and began to talk together, upon which the Khoja, raising his head, remarked, "If I were alive, I would get out of this place as soon as possible"—an incident which is also found in a Hindú story-book.

land at London about the year 1550, under the title of 'A Merrie Jest of a Man that was called Howleglas. The story referred to is entitled, "How Howleglas, by False Witnesses, obtained a new piece of Cloth." Howleglas goes to a fair, and seeing a peasant purchase a piece of green cloth, begins to consider how he might obtain it for his own use. He presently meets with a priest of his acquaintance, and his companion, "a malicious rogue like himself," and they agree, for a consideration, to bear him out in his proposed assertion to the countryman, in order to induce the poor fellow to make a wager that his piece of cloth was not green, but blue. The arch-rogue then goes up to the peasant and asks him where he bought that fine blue cloth, to which the man replies that the cloth is green, as any one who had eyes might see for himself. To be brief, a wager is laid, and the question is to be decided by the first man who passes. The priest's companion then comes up, and on the question being referred to him, he pronounces the cloth to be blue. Upon this the peasant roundly asserts that "they are both in a tale," but he consents to abide by the judgment of the priest, who now approaches. The churchman, of course, declares for the blue colour, and the poor rustic, though still unconvinced, at length surrenders the cloth, which the rogues cut up into winter garments for themselves.

A similar exploit to this of the German rogue is related in the Spanish work 'El Conde Lucanor'; and, according to Dunlop, in the eighth novel of the Italian Fortini, "a countryman is persuaded at market, by the repeated asseverations of the bystanders, that the kids he had for sale were capons, and disposes of them as such." In a variant current in Mecklenburg, a farmer is induced, in the same way, to believe that the calf he was leading to market is a goose. And there is an Arabian version in the tale of "The First Sharper in the Cave"—vol. vi. of Jonathan Scott's edition of the 'Arabian Nights Entertainments'—in which forty butchers at market combine to persuade a youth that the calf he had brought thither for sale is a she-goat; but he is afterwards amply revenged upon them.[7]

Under the title of "Ass or Pig?" in Miss Busk's 'Folk-Lore of Rome,' we seem to have a variant of the Arabian story last cited: A countryman was

[7]A tale in the Turkish jest-book seems imitated from the Arabian version: The Khoja had a lamb, and his friends devised a plan to get a share of it. One of them met him, as if by accident, and said, "What do you intend to do with this lamb, O Khoja? To-morrow is the Last Day; come, let us kill and eat it." The Khoja paid little attention to him. A second companion came up, and said the same; in short, they all came up, and said the same, till at length the Khoja professed to believe them. "Since it is thus," quoth he, "be welcome, my friends; let us go to-day into the fields and kill the lamb, and pass our last moments merrily in a little

going along a road driving a pig. "Let's have a bit of fun with that fellow," said the porter of the monastery to the father superior, as they saw him approaching. "I'll call his pig an ass," continued the porter, "and of course he'll say it's a pig; then I shall laugh at him for not knowing better, and he will grow angry. Then I'll say, 'Well, will you have the father superior to settle the dispute? and if he decides I am right, I shall keep the beast for myself.' Then you come and say it is an ass, and we'll keep it." The father superior agreed with a hearty laugh, and as soon as the rustic came up, the porter did all as he had arranged. The countryman was so sure of his case, that he willingly submitted to the arbitration of the father superior, but great was his dismay when that holy man decided against him, and so he had to go home without his pig. But he resolved to have his revenge. So, disguised as a girl, he obtains admittance into the monastery, and is allowed to sleep all night in the superior's chamber. Early in the morning he gives the superior a severe drubbing, crying at each blow, "Don't I know an ass from a pig?" In the course of the same day he returns to the monastery disguised as a doctor, and undertakes to cure the superior of his wounds and bruises, on the condition that the community all go out in search of a certain herb; and while they are absent he whacks the superior more soundly than before. On the return of the brethren the superior penitently confesses his fault, and causes the pig to be restored to the countryman.[8]

꒰꒱

---

feast." They all agreed, and took the lamb and went into the fields. "Oh, my friends," said the Khoja, "do you all amuse yourselves while I cook the lamb." So they all took off their cloaks and turbans, laid them beside him, and went away to stroll about the plain. Without delay the Khoja lighted a great fire, threw all the clothes into it, and began to cook the lamb. Shortly afterwards his friends say to one another, "Let us see what the lamb is like, and eat it." They approached, and seeing that the Khoja had thrown all their clothes into the fire, "Art thou mad?" cried they. "Why hast thou destroyed our clothes?" "Oh, sirs," answered the Khoja, "do you not, then, believe your own words, with which you have persuaded me? If to-morrow be the Last Day, what need have you of clothes?"

[8]In a Norse story (Dasent's 'Tales from the Fjeld') an old hunks cheats a poor lad out of his pig, by giving him only fourpence for it, pretending that was all it was worth. The lad, in revenge, puts on a beard, and a stout rope and whip in his pocket, goes to see the old rascal, and offers himself as a builder. As the "builder" requires a big tree, they both go into the forest, where the lad selects a tree, and bids old hunks go to the other side of the tree to see if their hands can meet. When hunks has embraced the tree with both arms, the lad fastens his hands to the tree with the rope, and then gives him a rare thrashing, exclaiming, "This is the lad that sold the pig!" Next day he visits him in the capacity of a doctor, but no one is to be present while he cures hunks: should he cry, his people are not to mind him, for the more he cries the sooner he will be well, and so he thrashes him again, saying, "This is the lad that sold the pig!"

The story is of Eastern origin, and seems to have been brought to Europe by Jacques de Vitry (Jacobus de Vitriaco), who was made Bishop of Accon (Acre) in Palestine, 1217, where he took an active part in the Crusades, and who died at Rome in 1240. From the 'Sermones' of de Vitry it was taken into the 'Liber de Donis' of Etienne de Bourbon, a member of the Dominican order, who died in 1261, from which the story of the envious physicians in the 'Gesta Romanorum' was probably imitated. It reappears in a later collection, 'Dialogus Creaturarum,' by an otherwise unknown author, Nicolaus Pergamenus, which, according to Græsse, cannot be earlier than the middle of the fourteenth century. This work was first printed in Latin, at Gouda, in 1480, and an English translation of it, entitled 'Dialogues of Creatures Moralised,' was printed in 1518. In the latter the story is thus related (the spelling modernised):

"On a time a rioter said to his fellows, when he saw a poor man bear a lamb to the market to sell, 'Will ye have the lamb that he beareth to market?' And they said, 'Yea, with good will.' And he ordained his fellows to stand in divers places as the poor man should come, and each of them should ask if he would sell the dog that he bare. And when the first asked him, he answered and said, 'It is not a dog, but a lamb.' And when they had met with him all, and asked so, the simple man believed that the lamb was a dog, and so let them have it for little or nought."

It also occurs, in a slightly different form, in the selection of mediæval Latin Stories edited by Wright for the Percy Society, No. 27, "De Rustico et Agni," which may be translated as follows:

"A certain countryman brought a lamb to the market. On his entering into the town six crafty hirelings met him, one of whom said to the others, 'We can well have that lamb from the rustic if we wish.' And when they asked the way, he said, 'Let us separate ourselves mutually through six streets, so that none of us may be with another, and let each one of you ask if the countryman wishes to sell his dog.' This was done, and they accosted him in turn. And when the rustic swore that it was a lamb, the other said that it was a dog. At length, compelled by shame, because it had been said so often, and by so many, that it was a dog, he says to the sixth, 'I don't wish to sell it, but accept it for nothing, and don't envy me any more (in the name of God).'"[9]

---

[9]In the 'Liber de Donis,' No. 339, the sharpers are three in number, and the rustic is persuaded by them to believe his lamb is a dog, and gives it to them. The story is reproduced in the 'Nights' of Straparola, N. 1, Nov. 3; in the 'Facétieux devis et plaisant contes, par le Sieur du Moulinet'; and also in Gueulette's Tartar Tales (the "Young Calender"), an interesting story-book, written in imitation of the 'Arabian Nights.'

We must now turn to the Eastern source of this widely diffused tale—namely, the Fables of Bidpaï, or Pilpay. In the oldest Sanskrit collection of these celebrated apologues, the 'Panchatantra,' it is the third fable of the third section; and in its abridged form, the 'Hitopadesa' (ch. iv. fab. 10), it is thus told, according to Professor Johnson's translation:

In the forest of Gautama was a Bráhman ready for a sacrifice, who, having gone to another village and purchased a goat, laid it upon his shoulder, and as he was returning he was seen by three rogues, who having agreed that, if by any contrivance that goat could be got possession of, it would be the height of cleverness, seated themselves by the foot of three trees, by the wayside, along that Bráhman's path. Presently the Bráhman was thus accosted by one rogue, "O Bráhman, how is it that you carry a dog on your shoulder? " "It is not a dog," replied the Bráhman; "it is a goat for sacrifice." Soon afterwards the same was repeated by the second rogue, stationed at the distance of a *kos*. On hearing that, the Bráhman laid the goat on the ground, and after looking at it again and again, he replaced it on his shoulder, and walked on with a mind waving like a swing. The Bráhman, on hearing the address of the third rogue, feeling convinced of his mistake, abandoned the goat, washed himself,[10] and went home. The goat meanwhile was taken and eaten by the rogues.

The Arabic, Hebrew, Greek, Syriac, Persian, and Latin versions of the Fables of Bidpaï have also the story; this is how it is related in the later Syriac Arabic text of 'Kalíla wa Dimna':

"It is said that a certain ascetic bought a fat ram to offer as a sacrifice. As he was leading it home, there met him three rogues who lay in wait for him at three different places. The first one said to him, 'What are you going to do with that dog, which you are leading along by a cord?' The next one said to him, 'Do you want to hunt game, O ascetic, with that dog?' And the third one met him and said to him, 'Ascetics and hermits truly do not use dogs; so this man is no ascetic.' When the poor ascetic heard these words from those rogues, he let go the sheep and left it in their hands, saying within himself, 'Perhaps those who sold me this sheep bewitched my eyes, and instead of a sheep gave me a dog.'"

The story is also found in the 'Kathá Sarit Ságara,' Book x. ch. 62, where the Bráhman is "seen by many rogues": first one comes up to him, next two others, and finally three more—six in all, which is the number

[10]Because he had touched, as he believed, a dog, which is considered, both by Hindús and Muhammedans, as an unclean animal.

of "hirelings" in the second of the Latin versions cited above; the victim is cheated by three rogues in the several versions of Bidpaï's Fables, in Tyl Eulenspiegel, and in the 'Gesta' imitation; by only two in our old English jests: the number of "rioters" is not mentioned in the 'Creatures Moralised.' In three versions—namely, Tyl Eulenspiegel, the Arabian, and our second Latin tale—the rustic is not deceived, although he yields up, in one case, his cloth, in the second his calf, and in the third his lamb.

We have thus traced Scogin's jest as far back as the 5th century, the date of the 'Panchatantra,' according to Dr H. H. Wilson; but since Professor Benfey has shown that the outlines of most of these fables are of Buddhistic origin, the story of the Bráhman and the Sharpers may be older than the present era.

It is curious to find Macaulay giving a very garbled version of the Bráhman and the Goat (which reappears in our English rendering of the 'Fables of Pilpay,' the sixth edition of which was published in 1789, and is now before me) in his scathing criticism of Robert Montgomery's so-called Poems: He represents one of three sharpers as coming up to a Bráhman, and *pulling a dog out of a sack*, offering him *this fine sheep* for sale. The second and third rascals come up in succession, and declare the dog to be a sheep; at length the Bráhman, believing that he must be under the influence of an optical delusion, purchases the dog, and discovering on going home that he has been tricked, he is "smitten with a sore disease in all his joints!"—Possibly Macaulay thus perverted the story to render it apposite: the *sharpers* were the venal reviewers; the *dog* was Robert Montgomery's twaddle, which they asserted was true poetry; and the *Bráhman* was the public, who were gulled by false knaves!

↬ THE COBBLER AND THE CALF ↬

IN a fragment of an old magazine—most probably printed about the year 1820—the title of which was wanting, I found the following diverting story, which has its parallels among divers peoples:

A butcher having purchased a calf at the town of Lewes, in Essex, was riding home with it strapped before him, when he stopped at a wayside tavern and called for a draught of ale. A droll cobbler, who happened to be lounging at the door, offered to the landlord to steal the calf from the butcher for sixpenny-worth of grog, which, being agreed to, he set off, and dropped one new shoe in the path, near the middle of a wood, through which the butcher had to pass, and another shoe about a quarter of a mile farther on. When the butcher came to where the first shoe lay, he did not think it worth the trouble of picking up; but coming upon the other, he thought that he might as well have a pair of new shoes for nothing as any one else, and accordingly dismounted, and, tying his horse to the hedge, went back to pick up the first shoe. Meanwhile the crafty cobbler unstrapped the calf, took a short cut across the fields to the tavern, and gave it to the landlord, who placed it in his barn. The butcher returned in a state of great excitement, and informed the landlord of the loss he had just sustained. The landlord offered to sell him a calf to replace the one that had been stolen from him, and the butcher unwittingly bought his own calf of the landlord, and rode off with it. The cobbler, having under-taken to steal it again, hastened to the wood, where he hid himself till the butcher approached, when he imitated the cry of a calf so well that the butcher, thinking it to be the one he had lost, got off his horse and began to search the wood: meanwhile the cobbler again unfastened the calf, and had returned to the tavern before the butcher had arrived to tell of his second misfortune, which he ascribed to downright witchcraft. The whole affair was then explained to him, and the good-natured butcher laughed heartily at the joke, and paid for a crown's worth of punch, of which he himself partook with mine host and the clever son of St. Crispin.

In most versions of this tale the hero is a clever young thief, as in the Gaelic story of the Shifty Lad, whose first master, called the Black Rogue, he very soon surpasses in skill and adroitness:

At the end of a few weeks there was to be a wedding in the neigh-bourhood; and it was the custom of the country, when any who were well

off were asked, that they should send some gift or other to the people of
the wedding. There was a rich tenant, and he was asked; and he desired
his herd to go to the mountain moor and bring home a wether for the
people of the wedding. The herd went up the mountain and he got the
wether, and he was going home with it; and he had it on his back when
he was going past the house of the Black Rogue. Said the Shifty Lad to
his master, "What wager wilt thou lay that I do not steal the wether from
the back of that man yet before he reaches the house?" Said the Black
Rogue, "I will lay thee a wager of a hundred marks that thou canst not:
how shouldst thou steal the thing that is on his back?" "Howsoever I do
it, I will try it," said the Shifty Lad. "Well, then, if thou dost it," said the
Black Rogue, "I will give thee a hundred marks." "It is a bargain," said the
Shifty Lad; and with that he went away after the herd.

The herd had to go through a wood, and the Shifty Lad took the ground
that was hidden from him until he got before him; and he put some dirt
in his shoe, and he set his shoe on the road before the herd, and he himself went in hiding. And when the herd came forward and saw the shoe,
he said, "But thou art dirty, and though thou art, if thy fellow were there I
would clean thee;" and he went past. The Shifty Lad lifted the shoe, and
ran round about and was before the herd, and he put his other shoe on the
road before him. When the herd came forward and saw the other shoe on
the road before him, he said to himself, "But there is the fellow of the dirty
shoe." He set the wether on the ground, and said to himself, "I will return
now, and get the dirty shoe, and clean it, and I shall have two good shoes
for my trouble;" and he ran swiftly back again. The Shifty Lad ran swiftly
and stole the wether, and took with him the two shoes; and he went home
to the Black Rogue, and got a hundred marks from him.

The herd went home and told his master how it had befallen him. His
master scolded him; and the next day he sent him again up the mountain
to seek a kid instead of the wether he had lost. He went away to the hill,
and got hold of a kid and tied it; then he put it on his back and went
homeward with it. The Shifty Lad saw him, and went into the wood; and
he was there before the herd and went in hiding, and began bleating like
the wether. The herd thought that it was the wether that was in it; and
he put the kid off his back and left it at the side of the road and went to
seek the wether. At the time when the herd was seeking the wether, the
Shifty Lad went and stole the kid and went home with it to the Black
Rogue. When the herd went back to where he had left the kid, it was
gone, and when he could not find it, he went home and told his master

291

how it had befallen him. And his master scolded him, but there was no help for it.

On the next day the tenant asked his herd to go up the mountain and bring home a stot, and to be sure that he did not lose it. The herd went up the mountain and got a good fat stot. And as he was driving it home the Shifty Lad saw him, and said to the Black Rogue, "Come along, and we will try to steal the stot from the herd when he is going through the wood with it." The Black Rogue and the Shifty Lad went away to the wood before the herd. And when the herd was going through the wood with the stot, the Black Rogue was in one place baa-ing, and the Shifty Lad in another place bleating like a goat. The herd heard them, and thought that he would get the wether and the kid again. He tied the stot to a tree, and went all about the wood seeking the wether and the kid; and he sought them till he was tired. While he was seeking the wether and the kid, the Shifty Lad went and stole the stot, and took it home with him to the house of the Black Rogue. When the herd came back to the tree where he had left the stot tied, the stot was not there, and he knew that it had been stolen. He went home and told his master how it had happened, and his master scolded him, but there was no help for it. The next day his master asked him to go up the mountain and bring home a wether, and not let it off his back till he should come home, whatever he might see or hear. So the herd went away and got a wether, and he succeeded in taking it home.[1]

Possibly the direct source of the Gaelic story is to be found in the Norse tale of the Master-Thief, in which a youth, in order to qualify himself as one of a gang of robbers, undertakes to steal an ox from a man as he drives it to market, without the man's knowledge, and without doing him any personal injury. The youth set off, and took with him a pretty shoe, with a silver buckle on it, which lay about the house; and he put the shoe in the road along which the man was going with his ox; and when he had done that, he went into the wood and hid himself under a bush. So when the man came by he saw the shoe at once. "That's a nice shoe," said he; "if I only had the fellow to it I'd take it home with me, and perhaps I'd put my old dame in a good humour for once." (For you must know he had an old wife so cross and snappish, it was not long between

[1] Campbell's 'Tales of the West Highlands,' vol. i. pp. 324-327.

each time she boxed his ears.) But then he bethought him that he could do nothing with the odd shoe unless he had the fellow to it; so he went on his way, and let the shoe lie on the road. Then the youth took up the shoe, and made all the haste he could to get before the man by a short cut through the wood, and laid it down before him in the road again. When the man came along with his ox, he got quite angry with himself for being so dull as to leave the fellow to the shoe lying in the road instead of taking it with him; so he tied the ox to the fence, and said to himself, "I may just as well run back and pick up the other, and then I'll have a pair of good shoes for my old dame, and so perhaps I'll get a kind word from her for once." So he set off, and hunted and hunted up and down for the shoe, but no shoe did he find, and at length he had to go back with the one he had. But meanwhile the youth had taken the ox and gone off with it. The poor man returns home and takes another ox to sell, and this the clever youth contrives by another ingenious trick to steal also. Home again the man goes and takes his third and only remaining ox, which the youth also undertakes to steal; and this he does by means of the same trick as that employed by the cobbler of our English story in his second exploit. The youth conceals himself in the wood until the man approached, when he set up a dreadful bellowing, "just like a great ox." The man, thinking it was the cry of one of his two stolen animals, ties up his third ox by the roadside, and runs off to look for the others in the wood, but meantime the youth goes away with the third ox.[2]

These incidents also occur in No. 24 of Legrand's collection of modern Greek popular tales, where a youth is adopted by his uncle, an arrant rogue, in whose thievish tricks he takes part: the youth sees a man carrying a lamb to market, and drops first one slipper in advance of the man, then another still farther on his road; and when the man goes back for the first slipper the uncle seizes the lamb. After a time the man returns with another lamb; the youth hides himself and imitates the cry of a lamb, and while the man is seeking for the lost one, the second is also stolen. Another time they discover a man with two oxen drawing a cart. The lad goes near him and exclaims, "Wonderful! wonderful!" Thinking

---

[2] Dasent's 'Popular Tales from the Norse.'—In a Suabian analogue (tale of Clever Martin, No. 55 of Mein's collection) the thief places separately on the road the contents of his luncheon-case; and in another German version (Wolf's 'Hausmärchen,' p. 398) Hans Küh- stock deposits singly a sword and its sheath.

a great treasure has been discovered, the man leaves his oxen and goes up to the youth and asks him what he means by his cries. "Is it not a wonder," says the youth, "to see a cart drawn by a single ox?" The man returns and finds one of his oxen is stolen.

Most probably the story is of Asiatic extraction. The Arabs have a proverb, "The boots of Hunayn," which is used in reference to any one who has lost more than he gained by a bargain; and the saying had its origin in the following incident, related by Baron de Slane in the notes to his translation of Ibn Khallikán's great biographical dictionary of the eminent men of Islám:

A desert Arab, mounted on his camel, entered a town, went to the bazaar, and bargained for a pair of boots. Not being able to conclude with the dealer, whose name was Hunayn, he flew into a passion, gave him foul names, and quitted the shop. Having made his other purchases, he got upon his camel, left the town, and took the road leading to the tents of his tribe. The bootmaker was so highly offended at the Arab's insulting language, that he resolved upon being revenged. Taking up the boots, he ran to the road by which the Arab had to pass, and threw one of them on the ground. A mile or two farther on he threw the other, and hid himself to see the result. The Arab observed the first boot as he was riding along, and said to himself, "There is one of the boots of Hunayn; if the other were along with it, I should dismount and pick them up." About half an hour after he perceived the other boot, and regretted not having picked up the first. So he got off his camel, not wishing to fatigue it too much; and having fettered it with a cord, picked up the boot which was lying there, and ran back to take up the other. As soon as he disappeared, Hunayn went off with the camel and the baggage. When the Arab returned, his camel was missing, so he went home on foot. On reaching his tent, he was eagerly asked what he had brought back, and he replied dolefully, "The boots of Hunayn!"

Much farther east than Arabia, however, the same story is known. In a Bengalí version, the trick is played by one thief on another, who had decamped with their joint stock of stolen treasure on the back of a cow. The older thief determined to overreach his comrade in his turn. He invested all his money in a costly pair of shoes covered with gold lace; and walking very fast, avoiding the public road, and making short cuts, he soon discovered the younger thief trudging on slowly with his cow. He went before him in the highway a distance of about 200 yards, and threw down on the road one shoe. Then he walked on another 200 yards and threw the other shoe, at a place near which was a large tree, and amongst the thick leaves of that tree he hid himself. The younger thief coming along the road saw the first shoe, and said to himself, "What a beautiful shoe is this! It is covered with gold lace, and would have suited me in my present circumstances, now that I have become rich; but what shall I do with one shoe?" So he passed on. Presently he came to the place where the other shoe was lying. The younger thief said within himself, "Ah, here is the other shoe! What a fool I was, that I did not pick up the one I first saw! However, it is not too late. I'll tie the cow to yonder tree and go for the other shoe." So he tied the cow to the tree, and, taking up the second shoe, went for the first, which was lying at a distance of about 200 yards. In the meantime the elder thief got down from the tree, loosened the cow, and drove it towards his native village, carefully avoiding the highway.[3]

Surely no one could be so infatuated as to consider the incidents of these several versions of the same story as mere accidental resemblances. The exploit of the Norwegian rogue is performed with but one shoe, which is doubtless a corruption of the original story; but our English version has the advantage of the others, insomuch as the jolly son of St. Crispin plays his clever tricks with no evil intention, while the others are represented as actual thefts—and very heartless ones, besides.

[3]Rev. Lal Behari Day's 'Folk-Tales of Bengal,' pp. 167, 168.

ᘒ "THE HEIR OF LINNE" ᘒ

DUNLOP thought the concluding portion of the fine old ballad of "The Unthrifty Heir of Linne" to have been suggested by one of the Italian novels of Cinthio, who died in 1573: but there is certainly no ground for such a conjecture. According to the ballad, after the Heir of Linne had—like Núr-ed-Din in the Arabian tale—wasted all his patrimony in riotous living, and having in vain solicited pecuniary assistance from the boon companions who had shared in his prosperity—

> One, I wis, was not at home;
> Another had paid his gold away;
> Another called him "thriftless loon,"
> And bade him swiftly hie away—

he resolves, in accordance with his father's testamentary injunctions, in the event of his being reduced to penury, to go to the "lonely lodge," where he should find means of release from his misery. There he discovers a rope with a noose at the end, dangling from the roof; and putting it round his neck, he takes the fatal leap, when suddenly he falls to the ground; and on recovering from the shock, he looks towards the roof, where he perceives a golden key, to which is attached a billet, informing him that his father had feared his conduct would sooner or later lead to this, and that he would find additional treasure in the lodge, which he hoped he would use with more prudence.

A prose version of the story was widely popular in England last century, in the form of a chap-book, the elaborate title of which is as follows: 'The Drunkard's Legacy. In four parts. Giving an account, First, of a Gentleman having a wild Son, and foreseeing he would come to poverty, had a cottage built with one door to it, always kept fast. His father, on his dying bed, charged him not to open it 'till he was poor and slighted, which the young man promised he would perform. Secondly, of this young man's pawning his estate to a Vintner, who, when poor, kicked him out of doors. Thinking it time to see his Legacy, he broke open the door, when, instead of money, he found a Gibbet and Halter, which he put round his Neck, and jumping off the Stool, the Gibbet broke, and a Thousand Pounds came down upon his head, which lay in the Ceiling.

Thirdly, of his redeeming the Estate, and fooling the Vintner out of Two Hundred Pounds, who, for being jeered by his neighbours, cut his own throat. And Lastly, of the young man's Reformation.'—There can be little doubt, I think, that this chap-book version was adapted from the Scotch ballad of "The Heir of Linne."

Cinthio's story, to which Dunlop refers, is the eighth of the ninth decade of his 'Hecatommithi,' and tells how a widow lady concealed a treasure in her house during the siege of Carthage: A daughter of the Roman soldier who had obtained this house being disappointed in love, determined to hang herself; but in tying the rope she removed a beam, which discovered the hidden treasure, and completely consoled her for all misfortunes.[1]

And not very remotely allied to this tale of Cinthio's is the following—from an old magazine, the name of which I omitted to "make a note of," thus disregarding the maxim of the immortal Captain Cuttle: An Italian, named Antonio Batistei, having lost five hundred crowns in a ship that was wrecked, resolved to hang himself, and entered an uninhabited house for the purpose; but as he was about to fasten the rope to the beam, he discovered a treasure of one thousand crowns, and very gladly exchanged the halter for the hoard and went away. Shortly after he was gone, the owner came to look at his gold, and finding it to be stolen, he straightway hanged himself with the halter which was left in its place.

In the Persian tales of 'The Thousand and One Days,' however, we have a striking parallel to the ballad:

Al Talmulk,[2] who was styled the Sorrowful Vazír, relates that when his father, a rich jeweller, was at the point of death, he called him to his bedside and cautioned him to take care of the great wealth which he was to inherit. "If you are so unhappy," he continued, "as to squander it away idly, be sure to have recourse to the tree which is in the middle of the garden; tie the fatal rope to one of the branches, and by that means prevent the miseries which attend poverty." After his father's death he keeps open house, and in a short time dissipates all his wealth in feasting his companions and sycophants. At length he remembers his father's advice, and goes

---

[1] This story was reproduced in Paynter's 'Palace of Pleasure,' first published in 1556.

[2] Perhaps for Áletu-'l-Mulk: instrument, or insignia, of the kingdom; or for 'Áliyetu-'l-Mulk: high purpose, or aim, of the kingdom.

to the tree, fastens a rope to one of the branches, places the other end in a noose round his neck, and, springing into the air, expects to end his misery; but the branch gives way, and on his rising from the ground he discovers that the branch was hollow, and filled with diamonds and other precious stones. This was a prudential stratagem of his father, who had suspected that he would misspend his wealth in a life of pleasure.[3]—The same story is found in the 'Forty Vazírs,' the only variation being that the father directs his son to a wooden ring hanging from the roof of a room, to which he is to attach a rope, when he has become penniless, and hang himself.

There is a singular version in the text of 'The Thousand and One Nights,' printed at Breslau,[4] under the editorship of Habicht and Fleischer, from a manuscript procured in Tunis, where it forms one of a series of 28 tales related to Shah Bakht by his vazír, Er-Rahwan[5]—Nights 875–930: A man on his deathbed counsels his son, should he ever come to want, not to ask relief of any one, since he would find a treasure laid up for him in a chamber, which he indicated, but which he was not to open until he stood in need of a day's food. After his father's death, the youth had not patience to wait till he had spent all the great wealth he had inherited, but opened the chamber, and found it empty save that some bricks lay on the floor, and from the middle of the ceiling dangled a rope with a noose at the lower end, and there was a scroll which directed him to beg not of any, but to hang himself forthwith. Seeing this, the youth said, "Here in sooth is a goodly legacy!" and went forth and feasted and

---

[3]These Persian Tales are not, as many have supposed, mere French imitations of Eastern fictions. In the preface to Petis de la Croix' translation ('Les Mille et Un Jours'), which was published after his death, it is stated that they were taken by a dervish of Ispahán, named Mukhlis, from a collection of Hindú comedies, a Turkish translation of which, entitled 'Alfaraja Badal Shidda,' or Joy after Affliction, is preserved in the Paris Library. Mukhlis transformed these comedies into tales, inserted them in a frame-story, after the plan of the 'Arabian Nights,' and entitled his work, 'Hazár ú Yek Rúz,' or the Thousand and One Days. In 1675 Mukhlis allowed Petis to take a copy of it, and it is said that in the translation Petis was assisted by Le Sage—which is certainly far from being an additional guarantee of its fidelity to the original—and that "nearly all" of the tales were afterwards transformed into comic operas (!), which were performed at the Théatre Italien. Early in the last century Ambrose Phillips made an English version from the French, under the title of 'Persian Tales,' which is reprinted in Henry Weber's 'Tales of the East,' published, in 3 vols., in 1811. Of the genuineness of these Tales there can be no doubt, since Sir William Ouseley brought from Persia a manuscript which comprised a part of the 'Hazár ú Yek Rúz'—see his 'Travels,' vol. ii. p. 21, *note*; and, in the same place, his interesting remarks on "a thousand and one" being a favourite number in the East.

[4]It occurs in no other printed text of the 'Nights.'

[5]See Note at the end of this paper, "Story of King Shah Bakht and his Vazír."

revelled with his companions till all his wealth was gone. After being two days without food, he sold a handkerchief for two dirhams (about a shilling), with which he bought milk and bread, and leaving some of it on a shelf, went out. During his absence, a dog came and ate up all the bread and milk. When he discovered his loss on returning home, he was distracted, and again going out, he met an old friend to whom he related his misfortune; but his friend would not believe his story, and abused him. Then the youth returned to his house, and opening the fatal chamber, piled the bricks one upon another, put the halter round his neck, and kicked away the bricks, upon which the rope gave way, and he fell to the ground, while a shower of gold fell upon him from the ceiling. And now he understood the lesson his father meant to impart to him. He at once bought back the lands and houses he had sold, and one day invited his former boon companions to a feast, when he entertained them with the following "story": "We had some bread, and locusts ate it all up, so we put in its place a stone, a cubit long and a cubit broad, and the locusts came and ate the stone, because of the smell of the bread that had formerly been there." One of his friends—even he who had refused to credit his story of the dog eating his bread and milk on a shelf—remarked, "This is no wonder; for locusts do more than that." Then said the youth in wrath, "Get you back to your own houses. In the days of my poverty, I was called a liar because I said that a dog had climbed up to a shelf and eaten my bread and milk there; but now that I am once more a wealthy man, you pretend to believe me when I tell you that locusts devoured a great stone!"[6]

Part of the plot of an ancient Roman comedy, entitled 'Thesaurus,' by

[6]Many variants of this last incident are current in Europe. The following is given by Professor Crane, in his 'Italian Popular Tales,' from Pitrè's Sicilian collection: A peasant one day conversing in the farmhouse with his master and others happened, while speaking of sheep and cheese, to say that he had had a present of a little cheese, but the mice had eaten it all up. Then the master, who was rich, proud, and fat, called him a fool, and said that it was not possible that the mice could have eaten the cheese; and all present said the master was right and the peasant wrong. What more could the poor man say? Talk makes talk. After a while the master said that, having taken the precaution to rub his ploughshares with oil, to keep them from rusting, the mice had eaten off all the points. Then the friend of the cheese broke forth, "But, master, how can it be that the mice cannot eat my cheese if they can eat the points of your ploughshares?" But the others began to cry out, "Be silent, you fool! The master is right, the master is right!"—The original is probably found in the fable of the mice that ate iron, and the hawk that carried off a boy, which occurs in most versions of the Fables of Bidpaï, and from which La Fontaine adapted his fable of 'Le Dépositaire Infidèle.' From the Fables of Bidpaï it was doubtless taken into the 'Kathá Sarit Ságara,'—see Tawney's translation, vol. ii. pp. 41, 42.

Lucius Lavinius, based upon a Greek play by Menander, bears some analogy to the ballad of the Heir of Linne. It is thus sketched by Dunlop, in his 'History of Roman Literature': An old man, by his last will, commanded his son to carry, ten years after his death, libations to the monument under which he was to be buried. The youth, having squandered all his fortune, sold the ground on which the monument stood to an old miser. At the end of the ten years the prodigal sends a servant to the tomb with due offerings, according to the injunctions of his deceased father. The servant applied to the new proprietor to assist him in opening the tomb, in which they discovered a hoard of gold. The miserly owner of the soil seizes the treasure, and retains it on pretence of having deposited it there for safety during a period of commotion. It is claimed, however, by the young man, who goes to law with him; and the remainder of the comedy consists chiefly of the progress of the suit.

It is very evident that the idea of the 'Heir of Linne' was not taken from the plot of this Roman play. But the resemblance between the ballad and the Persian and Turkish tales is so close, that we must conclude all three have been indirectly derived from a common source.[7] In the ballad, however, there are incidents which give the story additional interest. The "unthrifty heir" had sold all his lands—all save the "lonesome lodge"—to his factor, yclept John o' the Scales, who, as is unfortunately usual in such cases, drove a hard bargain, well knowing he was dealing with a man who was sorely in need of money. When he found, so strangely, the hidden treasure in the lodge, he went to the house of John o' the Scales—erstwhile, alas! his own paternal home—and, looking in at the "speere," or hole in the door or window, there he saw—

> Three lords upon a row
> Were drinking of the wine so free.

---

[7] In our ballad and the Eastern prose versions the "hanging" business was designed—together with the sudden accession to wealth to induce the prodigal to reform his way of life. In the Græco-Roman play the father seems to have intended the same moral lesson (without any incipient hanging), apparently never dreaming that his spendthrift heir would pour the libations by proxy. The analogy between the play and the ballad is, however, closer than may appear at first sight: for the sacred tomb we have the "lonesome lodge," which the son is on no account to sell. It is curious to observe that in the Arabian version the reading of the scroll in the chamber—unlike his brethren in the other versions, he still has lots of money—does not deter him from his extravagant courses: we may safely regard this as a corrupted version, like many other stories in the text of 'The Nights' in which it occurs.

And John himself sat at the board's head,
　　Because now lord of Linne was he.
I pray thee, he said, good John o' the Scales,
　　One forty pence for to lend me.

Away, away, thou thriftless loone,
　　Away, away, this may not bee;
For Christ's curse on my head, he sayd,
　　If ever I trust thee one pennìe.

Then bespake the heire of Linne,
　　To John o' the Scales his wife spake he:
Madame, some almes on me bestowe,
　　I pray, for sweet saint Charitìe.

Away, away, thou thriftless loone,
　　I swear thou gettest no almes of mee;
For if we should hang any losel heere,
　　The first we wold begin with thee.

Then bespake a good fellàwe,
　　Which sat at John o' the Scales his bord:
Sayd, Turn agayne, thou heire of Linne,
　　Sometime thou wart a well good lord;

Sometime a good fellow thou hast been,
　　And sparedst not thy gold or fee;
Therefore Ile lend thee forty pence,
　　And other forty if need be.

And ever, I pray thee, John o' the Scales,
　　To let him sit in thy companìe:
For well I wot thou hadst his land,
　　And a good bargain it was to thee.

Up then spake him John o' the Scales,
　　All wood [*i.e.*, enraged] he answered him againe:
Now Christ's curse on my head, he sayd,
　　But I did lose by that bargàine.

And here I proffer thee, heir of Linne,
    Before these lords so faire and free,
Thou shalt have it back againe better cheape,
    By a hundred marks, than I had it of thee,—

I drawe you to record, lords, he said.
    With that he cast him a gods pennìe;
Now by my fay, sayd the heire of Linne,
    And here, good John, is thy monìe.

And he pullèd forth three bagges of gold,
    And layd them down upon the board;
All woe begone was John o' the Scales,
    So shent he could say never a word.

He told him forth the good red gold,
    He told it forth with mickle din:
The gold is thine, the land is mine,
    And now I'm again the lord of Linne.

Sayes, Have thou here, thou good fellòwe,
    Forty pence thou didst lend mee;
Now I'm again the lord of Linne,
    And forty pounds I will give thee.

The ballad concludes with the lamentation of Joan, wife of John o' the Scales, at this sudden reverse of fortune, and the Heir of Linne's expression of his resolution to take good care of his gear henceforward. Percy, who gives the ballad in his 'Reliques of Ancient English Poetry,' says that it is found in his folio MS., and that, "from Scottish phrases here and there discernible, it should seem to have been composed beyond the Tweed"; but he assigns no approximate date.

NOTE

STORY OF KING SHAH BAKHT AND HIS VAZÍR (p. 298)

Er-Rahwan, prime minister of Shah Bakht, "had many enemies, who envied him his high place, and still sought to do him hurt, but found no way thereunto; and God, in His foreknowledge, decreed that the king dreamt that his vazír Er-

Rahwan gave him a fruit from off a tree, and he ate it and died." The king sends for a celebrated astrologer, in order that he should learn what his dream imported. But the vazír's enemies had privately besought the sage to slander him to the king, promising him much wealth therefor; and so the sage told the king that his vazír would slay him within a month from that day, and bade him hasten to put the vazír to death. The king then sends for his vazír Er-Rahwan, and frankly tells him of his dream and the sage's interpretation thereof; and the vazír, seeing it was a wicked device of his enemies to destroy him, expresses his willingness to be put to death;—"But if the king," he adds, "see fit not to put me to death till to-morrow, and will pass this night with me, and take leave of me, when the morrow cometh, the king shall do what he will." That same night the vazír related a story to the king, which so pleased him that he respited the vazír for another day; and in this way he entertained Shah Bakht each night until the fatal month was past, when the wickedness of the vazír's enemies was made manifest.—This romance, with its twenty-eight subordinate tales, belongs to the sporadic part of the 'Sindibád' family.

～ WHITTINGTON AND HIS CAT ～

THAT Lord Mayor Whittington was the poor ill-used boy he is represented to have been in the popular tale seems quite impossible, since, according to the accurate Stow, he was the son of the Worshipful Sir William Whittington, Knight. The story was current in Europe in the 13th century: In the chronicle of Albert, abbot of the convent of St Mary at Slade, written at that period, it is related that there were two citizens of Venice, one of whom was rich, the other poor. It fortuned that the rich man went abroad to trade, and the poor man gave him as his venture *two* cats, the sale of which, as in our tale of the renowned Dick Whittington, produced him great wealth.

In the Facetiæ of Arlotto, a celebrated character in Tuscany in the 15th century, the story is told of a Genoese merchant who presents two cats to the king of a foreign land, who rewards him with rich presents. Arlotto's version was reproduced in the 17th century by a Florentine nobleman, Count Lorenzo Magalotti, in a letter to his friend Ottavio Falconieri, in which he tells how a merchant named Ansaldo degli Ormanui (*temp.* Amerigo Vespucci), after three successful voyages, on the fourth was driven to an island named Canary. The king received him graciously; but he noticed that all present at the dinner-table had long staves in their hands to drive away the countless numbers of mice which attacked the viands. Ansaldo sends to his ship for two cats, a male and a female, which he presents to the king. On his return home, a friend hearing the story, and thinking, if the king gave much wealth for a pair of cats, he would give still more for precious gems, sailed to the Canaries, and presented his majesty with some valuable jewels, and received in return, what the king supposed to be a gift of the highest value, a *cat,* offspring of Ansaldo's pair.—In a description of Guinea, published in 1665, it is related that Alfonso, a Portuguese, being wrecked on the coast of Guinea, was presented by the king with its weight in gold for a cat to kill their mice, and for an ointment to kill their flies: this he improved within five years to six thousand pounds in the place, and returning to Portugal, after fifteen years' traffic, became not, like Whittington, the second, but the third man in the kingdom.

The story is common to all Europe. In Norway it is thus told: A poor woman's little boy, having wrapped his jacket round a stone which looked wan with the frost, found under it next day a box full of silver money, which he emptied into the tarn; but one silver piece floated, which he kept, believing it to be "honest." His mother is angry at his folly, and sends him off to earn his own living. After wandering about for some time, he obtains employment in a merchant's kitchen, carrying wood and water for the cook. It comes to pass that the merchant has to make a voyage to foreign parts, and so he asks his servants what he should bring home for each of them, and when it is the turn of the poor boy, he gives the merchant his silver penny to purchase something for him. So the merchant sailed away, and when he had unloaded his ship and taken in a fresh cargo, he bought what he had promised the servants, and just as he was about to weigh anchor he recollected the poor boy's penny, and bought with it a cat from an old woman. On the voyage home the ship was driven out of her course and arrived at a strange country. The merchant went up into the town, and at the inn he observed that the table was laid with a rod for each man who sat at it, and when the meat was put on the table he soon saw what the rods meant, for out swarmed thousands of mice, and each one who sat at the table had to beat them off with his rod. The merchant in astonishment asked them if they did not keep cats, but they knew not what cats were; so he sent for the cat he had bought for the poor scullion, and she soon made the mice scamper off into their holes. Then he sold them the cat for a hundred dollars, and soon after sailed off again. But what was his surprise to see the cat sitting on the main-mast-head! And all at once there came on foul weather, and the ship was driven to another strange port, where the mice were more numerous than at the former place. So he sold the cat to the people for two hundred dollars; but when he got to sea again, there was the cat sitting on the mast as before, and a great storm carried the ship to a third country, where the people suffered from swarms of rats. So he sold them the cat for three hundred dollars; but when the merchant was once more at sea, he began to think how much the poor lad had made out of his penny, and resolved to keep part of the money to himself; but no sooner had he formed this wicked resolution, than there arose such a storm that all on board the ship believed they must perish. So the merchant made a vow that the poor lad should have every penny, and immediately the weather became calm, and the ship soon reached home in safety. And when the merchant got to land he gave the lad the six hundred dollars, and his daughter besides; and after that the lad sent for his mother and treated her kindly, and he lived all his days in mirth and jollity.[1]

In a Breton popular tale, entitled "Les Trois Frères; on, le chat, le coq, et l'échelle," which M. F.-M. Luzel has given in 'Mélusine,' 1876, c. 154–8, we find our story of Dick Whittington in another form:

A certain man had three sons, and when their mother died they demanded of him each their share of patrimony, in order that they should go into the world and seek their fortune. The eldest of the brothers, Yvon, gets for his share a cat, and sets off towards the seaside. He comes to a mill, near which is a grand castle, with lofty towers. Yvon enters the mill, carrying his cat on his left arm. There he sees four men in their shirt-sleeves, armed with sticks, and very busy running after mice, which were scampering about on all sides. "How much trouble you are taking for a trifling matter!" says Yvon. "A trifling matter?" echo the men. "Don't you see that, if we allowed them, these accursed beasts would eat both the corn and the meal, and we should starve?" "Well," says Yvon, "here is a little animal," showing his cat, "who, alone, in less than an hour, will do more work than you could do in a year: he will very quickly free you from the mice." Quoth the men, "That little animal!—you are surely joking. He hasn't a wicked look at all. What do you call it?" (In that country they had never seen a cat.) "He is called Monsieur le Chat," says Yvon. "Do you wish to see him working?" "Yes; let us see what he can do." Hereupon Yvon let go his cat, who was very hungry. The mice, never having seen a cat, were not at all afraid of him, and were in no hurry to run into their holes; so the cat soon made great havoc among them. The four men looked on, quite thunderstruck, and in less than an hour the whole floor of the mill was covered with dead mice.

The miller and his men could not think enough of it, and so one of them runs to the castle, and says to the lord, "Make haste, my lord, and come to the mill, where you will see what you never saw in your life." "What's that?" asks he. "There has arrived a man, we don't know from what country, with a little animal which has a very quiet look, yet in the twinkling of an eye it has killed all the mice against which we have had so much trouble to protect your corn and meal." "I wish that were true,"

[1] "The Honest Penny" in Dasent's 'Tales from the Fjeld.'—In a Danish version, a man in Jutland had made much money by unlawful means, and dying, left it to his three sons. The youngest—usually the favourite of Fortune in folk-tales—threw his share into the sea, and only one small copper coin floated, with which he bought a cat, which he sent as a venture on board a ship, like Whittington in our story.

cries the lord, and he runs to the mill, and looking at the work of the cat, remains in admiration, with his mouth and eyes wide open. Then perceiving on the arm of Yvon the author of all this havoc, who sat quietly, with eyes half shut and purring away like a wheel, he asks, "Is that the animal with so mild a look that has done so bravely?" "Yes, my lord, that is he," said the men. "What a treasure is this creature!" then says the lord. "Ah, if I could only possess it! Will you sell it to me?" he asks Yvon. "With pleasure," replies Yvon, stroking his cat. "How much do you want for it?" "Six hundred crowns, with board and lodgings; for my friend the cat will not work well if I don't remain with him." "Agreed," cries the lord; and there and then they strike hands upon it. Yvon is at once installed in the castle, where he has nothing to do but eat and drink, walk about, and go from time to time to see the cat at the mill. He becomes the friend of the lord of the manor as well as of his daughter, for he was a pretty fellow. With the young lady indeed he is on such good terms, that he gets from her all that he wishes—gold and diamonds galore. At length he gathers his wealth together, secretly mounts the best horse in the stable, and rides back to his father's house.[2]

This is how the story is told in Russia: A poor little orphan served a rich man for three years, and received for his wages three copecks (a copeck is worth about one-third of a penny), with which he bought from some mischievous boys a cat which they were tormenting. He then hired himself to a merchant, whose business at once began to increase wonderfully. By-and-by the merchant prepared to go on a long trading voy-

[2]Dr Reinhold Köhler, in a note appended to the Breton story of "Les Trois Frères," compares with it No. 10 of 'Le Grand Parangon des Nouvelles,' composed by Nicolas de Troyes, and published from the original manuscript by E. Mabille, at Paris, 1869; No. 70 of the Brothers Grimm's 'Kinder und Haus Märchen;' and a tale in Waldau, 'Böhmisches Märchenbuch,' Prague, 1880, p. 176 ff.—In the collection of Nicolas de Troyes, the youngest of the three brothers sells his cat to a king who was so much pestered with rats and mice that, whether at dinner or supper, or other repast, he had a great crowd of gensdarmes to drive away the vermin. When the lad had gone a little distance on his way home, a messenger is sent after him by the king to ask him what the cat will eat besides rats and mice, and he answers that it will eat anything ("Si luy fut dit qu'elle mengeoit de tout"). The king is affrighted at this, and orders the cat to be killed, but it makes its escape. In the German version, the cat, having destroyed an immense number of mice, becomes thirsty, and cries "mew! mew!" upon which the king, in fear of the cat, bombards his castle, but the cat escapes through a window. In the Bohemian version (translated from the Tchéque), the youth, on being asked what they should give the cat after it has eaten all the mice, replies, "Yourself."—A similar story is told of the Schildbürgers, the Gothamites of Germany: see chap. iii. of my 'Book of Noodles.'

age, and he took the poor boy's cat with him, in order that she might keep down the mice on board ship. When the merchant reached his destination in a far-distant country, he took up his lodgings at an inn. The landlord, seeing that he was very wealthy, put him into a bedroom infested with swarms of rats and mice, hoping that the vermin would make an end of him during the night. But when the landlord came into the merchant's room next morning, much to his surprise, he discovered the floor heaped with dead rats and mice, and the cat placidly purring in the merchant's arms. The landlord buys the cat for a sackful of gold; and when the merchant had despatched all his business, he sailed homeward. On the way he thought it would be the height of folly to give the orphan lad so much money, and determined to keep it to himself. Suddenly a great storm arose, and the vessel was in danger of sinking. The merchant, knowing that this was because of his wicked purpose of robbing the poor orphan, prayed to heaven for forgiveness, when the sea immediately was calmed, and the ship duly arrived at port in safety. The merchant faithfully paid over to the orphan all the great wealth he had received for the cat, and the first thing the lad did afterwards was to buy a large quantity of incense, which he scattered along the shore and burned in honour of God.[3]

Such is the outline of the Russian version of "Whittington and his Cat." But it may be maintained by some readers, who firmly believe in the "genuineness" of all our British household tales, that the Italians, Bretons, Norwegians, and Russians all borrowed the story from us, and dressed it up to suit themselves. This is, perhaps, possible, though far from probable. But what will they say when they learn that the story is found in the pages of a grave Persian historian, who wrote at the end of the 13th century, sixty years before Richard Whittington was born? In the history of Persia, by Abdulláh, the son of Fazlulláh, a native of S-hiráz, whose poetical name was Wásif, or the Describer, entitled 'Events of Ages and Fates of Cities,' the story is thus related:

Kays, the eldest son of a man named Kayser, having spent the whole of his patrimony at Siráf, and disdaining to seek for service in a place where he had once lived in opulence, passed over to an island (from him called Kays) opposite to the city, with his two brothers, in a small skiff, and left his widowed mother behind, helpless and forlorn. The brothers built a

---

[3]"The Three Copecks": Ralston's 'Russian Folk-Tales.'

dwelling with the branches and leaves of trees, and supported life with dates and other fruits, the produce of the island. It was customary for the masters and captains of ships to ask the poorest people for some gift when they were setting out on a trading voyage, which they disposed of to the best advantage at the port to which they were bound; and if the trip proved prosperous, and they ever returned, they repaid the amount of the gift or venture, with the profit upon it, and a present besides, proportionate to the good luck with which, in their opinion, the prayers of the poor had blessed their concerns.[4] It so happened that the captain of a vessel bound to India from Siráf applied for a gift to the poor old widow of Kayser, who gave him the only property which the extravagance of her sons had left her—a cat. The captain, a kind-hearted man, received the old lady's present gratefully, although he did not consider it as the best kind of venture for a foreign port. Heaven had ordained otherwise. After the ship had anchored at an Indian port, the captain waited on the sovereign with costly presents, as is usual, who received him graciously, and invited him to dinner in a kind hospitable manner. With some surprise he perceived that every dish at table was guarded by a servant with a rod in his hand; but his curiosity about the cause of this strange appearance was shortly satisfied without asking any questions, for on looking about he perceived hundreds of mice running on all sides, and ready to devour the viands, whenever the vigilance of the domestics ceased for a moment. He immediately thought of the old woman's cat, and on the following day brought it in a cage to the palace. The mice appeared as usual, and the cat played her part amongst them to the astonishment and admiration of the monarch and his courtiers. The slaughter was immense. The captain presented the cat to his Majesty, mentioned the case of the old lady, and the motive for bringing so strange, but, as it turned out, so acceptable a freight with him, on which the king, happy at his delivery from the plague of mice, not only rewarded the captain with splendid presents, but loaded his ship with precious articles of merchandise, the produce of his kingdom, to be given to the mistress of the cat, with male and female slaves, money, and jewels. When the vessel returned to Siráf,

---

[4]We have an instance of this in the tale of "Muhammed the Lazy" (see Lane's 'Arabian Nights,' vol. ii. p. 366), where the youth's mother gives the captain of a ship that was about to sail five pieces of silver in her son's name. In the Norse version of our story, also (see *ante*, p. 305), the like practice is observed: the poor scullion gives his silver penny to the merchant as his "venture."

the old lady came down to the landing-place to ask about the fate of her cat, when, to her great joy and astonishment, the honest and worthy captain related to her the fortunate result of her venture, and put her in possession of her newly acquired wealth. She immediately sent for her son Kays and his brothers to share her opulence; but as they had collected a large settlement in their island, she was soon persuaded by them to accompany them to it, where, by means of her riches, they formed more extensive connections, purchased more ships, and traded largely with India and Arabia. When Kays and his friends had sufficiently added to their wealth by commerce, they by a signal act of treachery having murdered the crews of twelve ships from Omán and India, then at anchor there, seized the ships and property in them. With this addition to their fleet they commenced a series of outrageous acts as pirates, and successfully resisted every attempt of the neighbouring states to suppress their wicked practices. Every year added to their power and wealth, and at length a king was elected to the chief government of the island of Kays. This monarchy lasted for nearly 200 years, until the reign of Atábeg Abubaker, A.H. 628 (A.D. 1230), when the descendants of Kays were reduced to vassalage to the court of Persia.[5]

This "plain, unvarnished" narrative of the Persian historian—the incident, it will be seen from the concluding sentence, is said to have occurred in the 11th century[6]—reads rather tamely in comparison with our own veracious 'History of Sir Richard Whittington, thrice Lord Mayor of London, showing how he came up a poor boy to London, and was received as a scullion by a merchant; his sufferings and afflictions under a cruel cook-maid; how he bought a cat for a penny, and sent her a venture beyond sea, for which he got great riches in exchange; and lastly, how he married his master's daughter, and was made thrice Lord Mayor of London.' How Whittington came to be adopted as the hero of the English version of this romantic tale is not very apparent. Even in the absence of direct evidence regarding its first appearance in England, we should conclude that the story must have been composed long after the parentage of Whittington had passed out of the popular memory. A

---

[5]'Biographical Notices of Persian Poets,' etc. By Sir Gore Ouseley.

[6]Morier, who gives the story in his 'Second Journey to Persia,' as it was told him by the Persian ambassador, says that the date of the occurrence was the 700th year of the Hijra, or about A.D. 1300. He does not appear to have known of its being found in Wásif's History.

rather significant circumstance is mentioned by Granger, in his 'Biographical History of England,' with reference to the common print of Sir Richard Whittington. He says that "the cat has been inserted, as the common people do not care to buy the print without it. There was none originally in this plate, but a skull in place of it."

With regard to the Russian version, Mr Ralston thinks there can be little doubt as to its origin—"such a feature as the incense-burning pointing directly to a Buddhistic source"; and he is probably right in this conjecture,[7] notwithstanding the circumstantial and unembellished narrative of the Persian historian, to which, however, he makes no reference. The original Buddhist story—or a variant of it—may well have reached Russia *viâ* China. Yet nothing at all like our story has hitherto been found in Indian fiction, so far as I am aware, which is strange, since we have seen that it has been so long domiciled in Persia as to become one of the historical traditions of that country. But if the facts be not as the Persian historian relates them—and indeed there is much that is purely fictitious in the historical works of Asiatic writers—whence came the story into Persia? From India, unquestionably; and we may trust that the Buddhist original will yet be discovered. One thing is very clear, however—namely, that this is one of those tales which came to Europe in two different and independent ways: by the Mongolians to the North; through the Ottoman Turks to the south;—and our nursery tale of Dick Whittington—like that of Jack and the Giants—was almost certainly imported from the North.

[7]Another incident in this version seems also to indicate its Buddhist origin, that of the poor boy's purchasing with his three copecks a cat which some mischievous boys were tormenting. Compare with this the Mongolian and Tamil versions of "Aladdin's Lamp," vol. i. pp. 335, 337, 338; and the Bohemian, Albanian, and modern Greek variants, pp. 321, 324, 326.—I cannot but think the Norse version of our story also shows traces of its Buddhist extraction in the incident of the poor boy's covering a "frost-bitten" stone with his jacket, and finding under it next day a box full of silver money, only one coin of which he keeps, and with it his master purchases the cat which is the source of the boy's fortune. The reappearance of the cat twice after being sold the first time, and the storm which frightened the greedy merchant into a resolution to be just towards his poor scullion, are incidents which appear to me also essentially Buddhistic.

ꝯ THE TAILOR'S DREAM ꝯ

THE propensity of tailors to appropriate to their own purposes part of their customers' cloth is a frequent subject of satire in the popular literature of Europe. In one of the early volumes of 'Chambers's Edinburgh Journal' (No. 29, January 1837) there is an amusing story, entitled "John Hetherington's Dream," beginning thus: "In a certain small town in the West of Scotland there lived several years ago a decent old tailor." The story goes on to say that he was greatly addicted to "cabbaging," and that one night, after a plentiful supper, he dreamed that he was in the "lower regions," where Satan unrolled before him a long web of patchwork of all colours, consisting of pieces of cloth which he had cabbaged in the course of his business. The poor tailor awakes in great fright, and virtuously resolves to "cabbage no more"; and next morning, telling his foreman of his appalling dream, he requests the man, should he see him at any time inclined to yield to his besetting sin, to remind him of it. For some time after this all goes well with the reformed tailor, until one day he receives from a customer a piece of fine scarlet cloth to be made into a coat for a fox-hunter; and, unable to resist the temptation of a fine "off-cut," he is about to apply the scissors, "on cabbaging thoughts intent," when his foreman, as requested, reminds him of his terrible dream. "Ay, ay," quoth John, "I mind the dream; but I mind, too, that there was nae clout o' this colour in the wab."[1]

This story is simply a modernised and localised version of an old European popular tale, and "John Hetherington" is a mere myth. In order to gird at the English Puritans of his day, Sir John Harrington (1561–1612) made it the subject of the following humorous verses:—

Of a Precise Tailor.
A tailor, known a man of upright dealing
(True, but for lying, honest, but for stealing),
Did fall one day extremely sick by chance,
And on the sudden was in wondrous trance.
The fiends of hell, mustering in fearful manner,

---

[1] The tale so circumstantially related in 'Chambers's Edinburgh Journal' had been told long before in 'Joe Miller.'

Of sundry coloured stuffs displayed a banner,
Which he had stolen, and wished, as they did tell,
That he might find it all one day in hell.
The man, affrighted at this apparition,
Upon recovery grew a great precisian.
He bought a Bible of the best translation,
And in his life he showed great reformation:
He walkéd mannerly, he talkéd meekly,
He heard three lectures and two sermons weekly.
He vowed to keep no company unruly,
And in his speech to use no oath but truly;
And, zealously to keep the Sabbath's rest,
His meat for that day on the eve was drest.
And lest the custom which he had—to steal—
Should cause him sometimes to forget his zeal,
He gives his journeyman a special charge,
That if the stuff, allowance being large,
He found his fingers were to filch inclined,
Bid him to have the Banner in his mind.
This done (I scant can tell the rest for laughter),
A captain of a ship came three days after,
And brought three yards of velvet and three-quarters,
To make venetians down below the garters.
He, that precisely knew what was enough,
Soon slipped aside three quarters of the stuff:
His man, espying it, said in derision,
"Master, remember how you saw the vision!"
"Peace, knave," quoth he, "I did not see one rag
Of such a coloured stuff in all the flag!"

But the tailor's multi-coloured banner is met with in the writings of a
Scottish poet of earlier date than Sir John Harrington. William Dunbar,
a man of remarkable genius, who flourished from about 1460 to 1520, in
his humorous description of an imaginary tournament between a tailor
and a shoemaker, the scene of which is also laid in the "lower regions,"
says of the tailor-knight that

His banner borne was him before,
Wherein were clouts a hunder score,

Ilk ane of divers hue;
And all stolen out of sundry webs;—
For while the sea flood fills and ebbs,
Tailyors will never be true.

And in a curious 16th-century tract, entitled 'The Wyll of the Deuyll [*i.e.,* Devil] and Last Testament' is the following: "Item. I geue to euery Tayler, a Banner, wherein shall be conteyned al the parcelles of cloth and sylkes, etc., as he hath cast them into hell.[2] The late Mr J. Payne Collier thought this was "most likely borrowed from the 'Facetiæ' of Piovano Arlotto, originally printed in 1520, and often afterwards; but it is the first notice of it in English;" and that from the 'Wyll' "it may have found its way into Sir John Harrington's Epigrams, published in 1615, and from thence into later jest-books." Dunbar, however, anticipated, as we have seen, this reference to the infernal "banner" in the 'Wyll'; and while it is likely he got the idea from Arlotto, it is perhaps more probable he had it from some old monkish collection of *exempla*.

The story of the Tailor's Dream appears to be of Asiatic extraction. It is thus told in Cardonne's 'Mélanges de Littérature orientale,' extracted from Arabic, Persian, and Turkish manuscripts:

A tailor, being dangerously ill, had an extraordinary dream. He saw, floating in the air, an ensign of immense extent, composed of all the pieces of different stuffs he had purloined. The angel of death bore this ensign in one hand, and in the other an iron club, with which he chastised the tailor. Starting from his sleep, he made a vow that in case of his recovery he would deal more honestly for the future. His health returned, and, as he distrusted his own memory, he told one of his men to remind him of his dream whenever he was cutting out a garment. For some time the tailor paid regard to this admonition of his servant; but a great man having sent him some costly cloth to be made up, his virtue was not proof against so strong a temptation. In vain did his servant remind him of the ensign in the air. "You tire my patience," said the tailor, "with harping on my dream; there was no such stuff as this in the standard."[3]

---

[2] This tract, with some others, has been reprinted, edited by Dr F. J. Furnivall, as a supplementary fasciculus of the publications of the Ballad Society.—The repository for remnants of cloth is, I understand, called "hell" by journeyman-tailors both in this country and in Germany.

[3] In almost identical terms, the jest is found in 'Sottisier de Nasr-ed-Dín Hodja, Bouffon de Tamerlan, suivi d'autres facéties turques, traduits sur les manuscrits inédits.' By J. A. Decourdemanche. Brussels, 1878.—It is amusing to find this old story reappear in a collection of

✑

Apropos of tailors' "cabbage," a unique black-letter history, in verse, of the renowned Robin Goodfellow is given by Mr J. Payne Collier, in his introduction to the prose version, entitled 'Mad Pranks and Merry Jests of Robin Goodfellow' (ed. 1628—Percy Society publications), in which a ludicrous incident is related. Robin is apprenticed to a tailor, and they have a maid's wedding-gown to make:

> His master then the gown did take,
>   And to his work did fall;
> By that time he had done the same
>   The maid did for it call.
> Quoth he to Robin, "Goe thy wayes
>   And fetch the remnants hither
> That yesterday we left," said he,
>   "We'll break our fasts together."
>
> Then Robin hies him up the staires,
>   And brings the remnants downe
> Which he did know his master saved
>   Out of the woman's gowne.
> The Taylor he was vext at this—
>   He meant remnants of meate,
> That this good woman ere she went
>   Might there her breakfast eate.
>
> Quoth she, "This is a breakfast good,
>   I tell you, friend, indeed;
> And, to requite your love, I will
>   Send for some drinke with speed;
> And Robin he must goe for it
>   With all the speed he may."
> He takes the pot and money too,
>   And runs from thence away.

Scottish anecdotes published about the year 1873, and the compiler gratefully acknowledging his indebtedness to a correspondent, whom he names, for "this *original* anecdote"!

And readers of 'Don Quixote' will remember, among the various instances of shrewdness exhibited by Sancho during his brief governorship of the island of Barrataria (several of which appear to be of Talmudic origin), how a man brought a tailor—don't suppose, good reader, that I would insinuate a *tailor* is not also a *man!*—before Sancho, complaining that he had given him a piece of cloth to make up into six caps, and that the rascally Snip had sent him half-a-dozen caps (produced) that fitted the tips of his fingers and kept the rest of the cloth to himself; and how the tailor stoutly asserted that he had made up all the cloth into these caps; finally, Sancho—finding the case "abstruse," as the priest remarked of Paddy and the stolen chicken—sagaciously decrees that the man shall keep the caps, and the tailor shall have nothing for his labour.

THE THREE TRAVELLERS
AND THE LOAF

OUR old English jest-books generally represent Welshmen and Frenchmen as arrant simpletons or noodles; for these, in our modern collections of *facetiæ*, the raw Highlander and the blundering Irishman are often substituted. Occasionally, however, the Irishman is exhibited as a particularly shrewd fellow—turning the tables on would-be practical jokers, as in the "Joe Miller" of the Englishman, the Scotsman, and the Irishman who were travelling together and had but one loaf, which it was agreed should be eaten by him who had the most wonderful dream during the night. In the morning the Englishman and the Scotsman related their (concocted) dreams, after which the Irishman coolly informed them that he "dreamt he was hungry, and so got up and ate the loaf." This forms the third novel of the first decade of Cinthio's 'Hecatommithi' (16th century), in which a soldier is travelling with a philosopher and an astrologer, and the wise men mistake him for a simpleton. They had but a single loaf, and resolved to cheat him out of his share. Accordingly they propose that it should belong to the person who had the most delightful dream during the following night. The soldier, suspecting their design, rose while they were sound asleep, ate the loaf, and in the morning told them with an ingenuous air that he "dreamt" he had eaten the loaf.

Cinthio probably borrowed the story from the 'Gesta Romanorum,' where the first traveller dreams that he ascended to heaven on a golden ladder; the second, that devils with iron implements dragged his soul from his body, and plunged him into flames; the third, that an angel led him to the gate of paradise, where he saw one companion (the first) with abundance of good things to eat and drink, and the other companion he saw in the nether regions, but still with plenty of bread and wine, and so the angel said to him, "Do you rise up and eat the bread, since you will see neither of your comrades again."[1]

꒰

---

[1]This is also the subject of a *fabliau*, "Les Deux Bourgeois et le Vilain"—see Le Grand, ed. 1781, tome ii. p. 328.

I am not aware that the story has yet been discovered in any of the great monkish collections of earlier date than the 'Gesta'; but its first appearance, in European literature, was in the 'Disciplina Clericalis' of Petrus Alfonsus, where it is thus related:

Two citizens and a rustic, going to Mecca, shared provisions till they reached that place, and then their food failed, so that nothing remained save so much flour as would make a single loaf, and that a small one. The citizens, seeing this, said to each other, "We have too little bread, and our companion eats a great deal. Wherefore we ought to have a plan to take away from him part of the loaf, and eat it by ourselves alone." Accordingly a plan of this sort proved acceptable: to make and bake the loaf, and while it was being baked to sleep, and whoever of them saw the most wonderful things in a dream should eat the loaf alone. These words they spake artfully, as they thought the rustic too simple for inventions of the kind. They made the loaf and baked it, and at length lay down to sleep. But the rustic, more crafty than they thought, whilst his companions were asleep took the half-baked loaf, ate it up, and again lay down. One of the citizens, as if terrified out of his sleep, awoke, and called his companion, who inquired, "What is the matter?" He said, "I have seen a wondrous vision, for it seemed to me that two angels opened the gates of Paradise and led me within." Then his companion said to him, "This is a wondrous vision you have seen. But I dreamed that two angels took me, and, cleaving the earth, led me to the lower regions." The rustic heard all this, and pretended to be asleep; but the citizens, being deceived, and wishing to deceive, called on him to awake. But the rustic replied cunningly, as though he was terrified, "Who are they that call me?" Then they said, "We are your companions." But he replied, "Have you returned already?" To this they rejoined, "Where did we go, that we should return?" Then the rustic said, "Now it seemed to me that two angels took one of you, and opened the gates of heaven and led him within; then two others took the other, and opened the earth and took him to hell: and, seeing this, I thought neither of you would return any more, and I rose and ate the loaf."[2]

---

[2] A similar tale occurs in the 'Toldoth Jeśu,' a scurrilous Jewish "Life" of Christ, the Hebrew test of which, with a Latin translation and elaborate notes, was published at Leyden in 1705: 'Historia Jeschuæ Nazareni, à Judæis blasphemè corrupta, ex Manuscripto hactenus inedito nunc demum edita, ac versione et notis (quibus Judæorum nequitæ propius deteguntur, et authoris asserta ineptiæ ac impietatis convicuntur) illustrata à Joh. Jac. Huldrico, Tigurnio.'

In the following Latin rendering of the Jewish version of our story it will be observed that, in place of a loaf, the prize to be "dreamt" for is a little roasted goose:

Going still farther afield, we find our "Joe Miller" also, though in a somewhat different guise—*alter et idem*—in a fable which occurs in the introduction to a Persian poetical version of the ancient Book of Sindibád ('Sindibád Náma'), the only known copy of which is an illuminated—but unfortunately imperfect—manuscript preserved in the Library of the India Office (No. 3214):

An old wolf and fox, intimate friends, were once travelling together. A short way before them they saw a camel, who joined them, and the three together took the road to the village of camels. Their only provision for the journey consisted of a pumpkin. They travelled on for a long time, up hill and down dale, till, exhausted by the heat of the road, their eyes became black with thirst. At length they reached a pond full of water, and sat down on its brink. The pumpkin was produced, and after some discussion it was agreed that the prize should belong to him who was eldest among them. First the wolf began, "Indian, Tájik, and Turk,[3] know that my mother bore me one week before God created heaven and earth, time and space; consequently I have the best right to the pumpkin." "Yes," said the old and crafty fox, "I have

---

Venerunt itaque inde in diversorium. Quærit ibi Jesus ex hospite, "Est ne tibi unde hi edant?" Resp. hospes, "Non mihi suppetit nisi anserculus assatus." Sumit ergo Jesus anserem illisque apponit, aiens, "Anser hic exiguus nimis est, quam ut à tribus comedi debeat. Dormitum eamus, et ille qui somniarit somnium optimum, comedit anserem solus." Decumbunt igitur. Tempesta vero nocte surgit Jehuda et anserem devorat. Mane itaque illis surgentibus, Petrus ait, "Somnio mihi visus fui assidere solio Filii Dei Shaddai." Jesus ait, "Ego sum Filius ille Dei Shaddai; et somniavi te proprope me sedere. Ecce ergo me præstantius quid somniasse te; quare meum erit anserem comedere." Jehuda tandem aiebat, "Ego quidem ipsemet in somnio comedi anserem." Quærit ergo anserem Jesus, sed frustra, Jehuda enim devorabat illum.

Jehuda, the person who in this version plays the part of the rustic in Alfonsus' story, was, according to the 'Toldoth Jeśu,' a rabbi—a most malignant scoundrel he appears in the narrative—who pretended to be a disciple of Jesus in order the more surely to betray Him, which he did shortly after this adventure at the inn.—If Alfonsus adapted his story from the above—and it is not unlikely he was acquainted with the 'Toldoth Jeśu' before he became a convert to Christianity—it must be allowed that he has greatly improved upon his model.

In the following Latin rendering of the Jewish version of our story it will be observed that, in place of a loaf, the prize to be "dreamt" for is a little roasted goose:

There is a Sicilian variant in Pitrè's collection, in which a monk, who was an itinerant preacher, is represented as being accompanied on a journey by a very cunning lay-brother. One day the monk received a present of some fish, which he wished to eat himself, and so he proposed to his companion that the one of them who dreamed the best dream should have all the fish: the monk is outwitted by his lay-brother.

[3]The term "Tájik" is used for "Persian"; thus in Mírkhánd's history, "Turk ú Tájik," Turk and Persian. As employed above, the phrase is equivalent to "all the world," or "all civilised men."

nothing to object on this account; for on the night your mother bore you, I was standing by in attendance. That morning it was I that lit the taper, and I burned beside your pillow like a morning taper." When the camel had heard their speeches to an end, he stalked forward, and bending down his neck, snapped up the pumpkin, observing, "It is impossible to conceal a thing so manifest as this—that, with such a neck and haunches and back as mine, it was neither yesterday nor last night that my mother bore me."

The original form of this fable is probably found in the "Culla Vagga" portion of the 'Vinayapitaka,' one of the oldest parts of the Buddhist sacred books, which Professor E. B. Cowell, who has made the following translation of it, thinks can hardly be later than the third century B.C.:

Long ago, there was a great banyan-tree on the slope of the Himálya mountains, and three friends dwelt near it—a partridge, a monkey, and an elephant. They were disrespectful and discourteous to one another, and did not live harmoniously together. Then it occurred to them: "Oh, if we could know which of us is the eldest, we could honour him, and respect him, and show him duty and reverence, and abide by his exhortations." Then the partridge and the monkey asked the elephant, "What is the oldest thing, friend, that you remember?" "Friends," he replied, "when I was a child I used to walk over this banyan-tree, keeping it between my thighs, and its topmost shoot touched my belly. This is the oldest thing that I remember." Then the partridge and the elephant asked the monkey, "What is the oldest thing, friend, that you remember?" "Friends, when I was a child I used to sit on the ground and eat the topmost shoot of this banyan. This is the oldest thing that I remember." Then the monkey and the elephant asked the partridge, "What is the oldest thing, friend, that you remember?" "Friends, in yonder place there was once a certain great banyan-tree; I ate a fruit from it, and voided it in this spot, and from it sprang this banyan. Therefore, friends, I am older than either of you." Then the monkey and the elephant thus addressed the partridge, "You, friend, are the oldest of us all; we will honour and respect you, and will show you duty and reverence, and will abide by your exhortations." Then the partridge stirred them up in the five moral duties,[4] and also took those duties upon himself. They were respectful

[4] The five moral duties, or the Five Precepts of Buddha, are: (1) Not to do murder; (2) not to steal; (3) not to commit adultery; (4) not to drink intoxicating liquors; (5) not to do anything which is evil.

and courteous to one another, and lived harmoniously together, and after the dissolution of their bodies they were reborn happily in heaven.[5]

The same fable occurs in the 'Avadánas,' translated from the Chinese into French by Stanislas Julien; another version is found in the 'Játakas,' or Buddhist Birth-Stories, recently translated by Dr T. W. Rhys Davids; and a curiously distorted variant occurs in the "Uttara Kanda" of the Sanskrit epic, the 'Rámáyana,' in which an owl and a vulture dispute about the possession of a certain cave, each claiming it to be his by ancient right. They refer the matter to Ráma, who decides in favour of the owl, because the cave had been his ever since the earth was first adorned with trees, while the other had only known it since men first came into being.

A Mongolian version presents a striking analogy to the fable as found in the Persian 'Sindibád Náma,' though, as in the variant last cited, the number of the disputants is but two:

The wolf and the fox found on the road a skin full of fat. "Hand it over; let us eat it," said the wolf. "That won't do here," answered the fox. "Here are people going backwards and forwards; so we must carry it to the top of a mountain and eat it there." "Do thou carry it." So the wolf carried the fat to a great mountain. Then said the fox, "There is not enough fat for us both, and it is not worth dividing; let one of us eat the whole." "Which of us?" asks the wolf. "Let the elder eat it," replied the fox; "pray how old art thou?" The wolf thought a while, and determined to invent a lie, so as to cheat the fox. "When I was a youngster," said he, "the Mount Sumérn was only a clot of earth in a bog, and the ocean only a puddle." The fox lay down and wept. "Why weepest thou?" "I weep," said the fox, "because I once had two cubs, and the youngest was just your age." So the fox cheated the wolf, who was so ashamed that he ran away.[6]

---

[5] The partridge, monkey, and elephant are, of course, men reborn in these forms.—A variant of this apologue is known to the Northern Buddhists: "Some Bhikshus asked the Lord what claims an elder person had to the veneration of the younger. The Lord said, During the reign of Brahmadatta there lived at Benáres four animals,—a francoline partridge, a hare, a monkey, and an elephant, who all honoured an elderly banyan-tree. On account of the merits of this good work, there was always abundance of rain and plenty of everything."—From 'The Sanskrit Buddhist Literature of Nepal,' by Rájendratála Mitra, LL.D. Calcutta, 1882. Pp. 70, 71.

[6] 'Folk-Lore Journal,' 1886, vol. iv. p. 29.—In Rivière's 'Contes populaires de la Kabylie du Djurdjura' (I. iii. 4), a lion, a jackal, and a boar possess jointly a jar of butter. One day they all go to plant beans. The jackal gets hungry, and pretends he is called away. "Who calls thee?" asks the lion. "My uncle—there's a marriage at his house, and so I'm off to the feast." The jackal goes and eats half the butter. When he comes back, "Have you had a good feed?" the

∽

Variants of the Buddhist legends of the oldest animals seem to have come to Europe at an early period. "Readers of the 'Mabinogion,'" says Professor Cowell,[7] "will remember the curious legend which is found in the story of Kilhwch and Olwen. We read there how Arthur's ambassadors went successively in search of tidings about Mabon the son of Modron, to the ousel of Cilgwri, the stag of Redynvre, the owl of Cwm Cawlwyd, the eagle of Gwern Abwy, and, finally, the salmon of Llyn Llyw, and each of them gave some fresh proof of its greater age than its predecessors, but still referred the question to some animal of still more venerable antiquity than itself.[8] Ap Gwilym, however, alludes to another version of the story, which, I am inclined to think, preserves an older form of this widespread piece of folk-lore. In his poem 'Yr Oed,' where he describes himself as waiting and waiting under the thorn for his faithless mistress, he says:

> A thousand persons and more liken me
> To him who dwelt in Gwern Abwy;
> In truth I should not be an eagle at all,
> Except for my waiting for my lady three generations of men;—
> I am exactly like the stag
> In Cilgwri, for my beloved;
> Of the same colour, gray, to my thinking,
> As my bedfellow (the owl) in Cwm Cawlwyd.

Here we have only three animals, instead of the five in the 'Mabinogi'; and, as far as I can trace the story in Eastern literature, three is the usual number given, however the species of the animals themselves may vary."

---

others ask. "Yes, yes—God bless them!" Next day he goes off on a similar pretended errand, and eats the rest of the butter. After some time they invite all their friends to a grand feast, and on discovering the butter-jar empty, the lion and the boar, exclaiming, "You ate it—ah, you scoundrel!" tear the jackal in pieces.—With a different catastrophe, the Icelandic story of the Butter-Tub (in Powell and Magnusson's collection) closely resembles the Kabaïl fable: An old man and his wife set apart for the winter a tub of butter, and the old woman, pretending on three occasions that she is invited to a christening, goes secretly and eats up all the butter. For the sequel, see vol. i. of the present work, pp. 55, 56.

[7] In an interesting paper, "The Legend of the Oldest Animals," in 'Y Cymrodor' (Welsh Society's Journal), October 1882.

[8] See Note at the end of this paper, "Sending one to an Older and the Oldest Person."

It would be interesting to ascertain how the Buddhist legend of the oldest animals came to be transformed into the popular jest of the Three Travellers and the Loaf. The fable of the Wolf, Fox, and Camel, in the Persian 'Sindibád Náma,' and the Mongolian variant of the Wolf and the Fox—in both of which the disputants are still animals, but with a pumpkin introduced in the one and a skin of fat in the other, as the objects of contention—may be considered as transition forms, some version of one of which was doubtless known to the author of the 'Toldoth Jeśu,' whence, through Alfonsus, it seems to have spread over Europe in its existing form.

NOTE

SENDING ONE TO AN OLDER AND THE OLDEST PERSON (p. 322)

The incident of one aged individual sending an inquirer to another who is older occurs in many fairy tales. To cite a few instances: In the Albanian tale of the Jealous Sisters (No. 2 of Dozon), the hero, in quest of a flower from the Belle of the Earth, meets with a *lamia,* who not only refrains from eating him, but kindly directs him to go to her elder sister, who may tell him where the place is of which he is in search, and she again refers him to the eldest sister, from whom he obtains the wished-for information. In Laura Gonzenbach's Sicilian Tales, a prince is sent by an "Einsiedler" to his brother, who sends him to an older brother, and he again to one older still. In the Swedish tale of the Beautiful Palace East of the Sun and North of the Earth (Thorpe's 'Yule-Tide Stories'), the hero, in quest of the palace, is sent by an old woman to her old sister, who in turn sends her to an older sister, dwelling in a small ruinous cottage on a mountain. In the 'Kathá Sarit Ságara' (Book v. ch. xxv.) Saktideva, in quest of the Golden City, is sent by a hermit, who had lived 800 years in the same place and had never heard of it, to an elder brother; and most readers will remember a similar instance in the Arabian tale of Hasan of Basra. But in the tenth story of Natésa Sástrí's 'Dravidian Nights' (translation of the Tamil romance, 'Madana Kámarája Kadai'), instead of to older persons, the hero, in quest of the *párijáta* flower for his betrothed, is sent by a devotee, who opened his eyes every watch, to another, who opened his eyes every second watch, and he sends him to a third devotee, who opened his eyes every third watch.

In Thoms' 'Longevity of Man' the following is quoted from Clarkson's 'History and Antiquities of Richmond' (in Yorkshire): "There had been some legal dispute in which the evidence of 'Old Jenkins,' as confessedly the oldest inhabitant, was required, and the agent of Mrs Wastell, one of the parties, went to visit the old man. Previous to Jenkins going to York (says Mr Clarkson), when the agent went to find out what account he could give of the matter in dispute, he saw an old man sitting at the door, to whom he told his business. The old man said he could remember nothing about it, but that he would find his father in the house, who perhaps could satisfy him. When he went in he saw another man sitting over the fire, bowed down with years, to whom he repeated his former question. With some difficulty he made him understand what he had said, and after a little while got the following answer, which surprised him very much: That he knew nothing about it, but that if he would go into the yard he would meet with his father, who perhaps could tell him. The agent, upon this, thought that he had met with a race of antediluvians. However, into the yard he went, and to his no small astonishment found a venerable man with a long beard and a broad leathern belt about him, chopping sticks. To this man he again told his business, and received such information as in the end recovered the royalty in dispute. "The fact is," adds Mr Thoms, "that this story of Jenkins' son and grandson is only a Yorkshire version of the story as old or older than Jenkins himself, namely, of the very old man who was seen crying because his father had beaten him for throwing stones at his grandfather." Mr Thoms does not seem to have been aware, however, of the incident of sending an inquirer to older and oldest persons being both ancient and common to the folk-lore of most countries.—In Dasent's second series of Norse popular tales (entitled 'Tales from the Fjeld'), a traveller comes to a house and asks a night's lodgings; he is referred by son to father successively until he comes to the head of the house, the oldest of seven old men and a five-fold grandfather, who had shrunk to the bulk of a baby, and was literally laid on a shelf! Something like this I remember having met with in an Indian story-book. The idea is probably a survival of some primitive myth, suggested by the physical and mental imbecility of extreme old age—"second childhood."

❧ THE MERCHANT AND THE FOLK OF FALSETOWN ❧

IT is probable that few besides special students of Chaucer are acquainted with the old metrical "History of Beryn," which is foisted in a unique manuscript of the 'Canterbury Tales.' Assuredly it is none of Chaucer's,[1] although it is of considerable importance to such as are interested in the genealogy of popular fictions. In the folio edition of the works of Chaucer, by John Urry, London, 1721, "The History of Beryn" is given as the Merchant's Second Tale, the prologue to which is "The mery adventure of the Pardonere and Tapstere at the Inn at Canterbury," and both, it is stated in a prefatory note, "were never before printed, and are taken out of a MS. borrowed from the Honourable Lady Thinn, and not to be met with in any of the other MSS. which Mr Urry had perused." That unique manuscript, which is described in the preface to Urry's edition of Chaucer as imperfect at the beginning and end, is now in the possession of the Duke of Northumberland, and the "Pardoner's Adventure" and the "Tale of Beryn"—re-edited by Dr F. J. Furnivall and Mr Walter G. Stone, with side-notes giving the substance of the narratives—were published for the Chaucer Society in 1876, as a first fasciculus of a volume of Supplementary Canterbury Tales; and an introduction and appendix of analogues are likely to be issued shortly. The following is the outline of the Tale of Beryn:

A Roman knight of great worth and wealth, named Faunus, had a son born to him after many years of wedlock, who was named Beryn. His parents indulged this only son in his every whim, the result being that he grew up idle and dissipated, a dicer and frequenter of ribald assemblages. His mother died when Beryn was still a youth, and some time after his father married again, and doted on his second wife, who set his heart against his spendthrift son, and Faunus one morning, after a colloquy with his wife, refused him further supplies of money. Beryn, after upbraiding his father for being so completely under the influence of his new wife, in despair went out of the house, and wandering without aim, came to the church in which his mother was buried, entered it, and gave

---

[1]It would seem, from a couplet at the end of the Tale, that it was written by a monk of Canterbury: Nomen Autoris presentis Cronica Rome Et translatoris, Filius ecclesie Thome.

vent to his grief—now thoroughly repentant—on his mother's tomb. Meanwhile his step-mother, fearing that she should be blamed by the citizens for causing Beryn to be disinherited, induced his father to search for him, and he was brought home. Faunus made several proposals to Beryn, but he would be nothing but a merchant, and ultimately his father purchased five ships, and having laden them with rich merchandise, Beryn sailed away to foreign shores. After a dangerous voyage, he arrives with his five ships all safe at a strange city, where he falls into the toils of the knavish inhabitants: (1) He plays at chess with a burgess, who makes it a condition that the loser shall do whatsoever the other may require of him; and Beryn, having lost the game, is required to "drink up all the salt water that is in the sea," and compelled to pledge his ships for his performance of the task. (2) Another induces him to discharge into his store-houses the cargoes of his ships, lest they should be forfeited as well as the ships, promising to reload them with any kind of goods he might choose. (3) A blind man accuses him of having borrowed his eyes many years before, and failed to restore them, according to agreement. (4) A woman accuses him of deserting her, his wife, and their child. (5) Lastly, a knave persuades him to purchase a peculiar knife which he possesses, in order to present it to the judge, who had long desired it, by way of bespeaking his favour on the morrow, when all the charges against him are to be heard; and then accuses Beryn in court of having murdered his (the knave's) father seven years before, when he left for Rome, the knife being then in his possession. On the following day Beryn and his accusers appear before the judge ("steward"), and by the cleverness of a man who was a native of Rome, and desired to return thither, he comes out of his troubles not only scatheless, but with considerable profit. His first pursuer is required to stop the fresh water from flowing into the sea, and then Beryn will drink all the salt water. But as this is impossible, the burgess is heavily fined because of the trouble and anxiety the accused had suffered through him. The second, having made away with the goods, is required to load the five ships with butterflies. The blind man is challenged to produce Beryn's eyes, that they should be exchanged for those which Beryn has at present. The woman is asked to accompany Beryn to Rome, but she declines—fearing, perhaps, that she might be drowned on the way thither. Finally, the knave is answered that Beryn found the knife sticking in his own father's body, and that it was the knave's father who was his murderer. All, therefore, had to pay large sums of money to Beryn for having brought false accusations against him; and Beryn, having thus doubled his property, returns with his able advocate to his ships in great joy and solace. Presently five damsels come with rich presents to Beryn from the Duke Isope: a cup of gold, a fine sword, a purple mantle, a cloth of gold, and a palm. Next day he visits Isope, by whom he is received most graciously, and the Duke bestows on him the hand of his fair daughter in marriage.

The Tale of Beryn—which is told with spirit throughout—has evidently been taken from the first part[2] of an old French romance, of which two manuscripts are known to exist, one in the National Library at Paris,[3] the other in the Imperial Library at Vienna. This romance was printed early in the 16th century;[4] and a copious *extrait* of it is found in 'Mélanges, tirés d'une grande bibliothèque,' Paris, 1780, tome viii. 225–277. Our English version ends, as we have seen, with the marriage of Beryn to the daughter of Duke Isope, who is called Cleopatra in the French romance, and it goes on to relate: That a chevalier named Logres, who had loved Cleopatra, and had pretensions to the crown of Blandie— the scene of our Beryn's troubles and triumphs—enraged that a foreigner should have deprived him of the one and his chance of the other, sent a challenge to the "Roman merchant." They fight; Berinus is victor, and Logres quits the field covered with shame. Esope, the emperor, dies some time after, and Berinus succeeds to the throne of Blandie; but the army give him up at length to his old rival Logres, who generously allows him to return to Rome, with five richly laden ships. So Berinus sails away from Blandie, with his wife Cleopatra, their son Aigres, and their daughter Romaine. For three days all goes well, but on the fourth the ships are irresistibly drawn towards a huge rock, which the older mariners know to be called the Rock of Adamant, and soon the vessels are all stuck to it— no efforts of the crews avail to free them. To be brief, they learn from an inscription on the rock that if one of their number consent to be left behind, and throw a ring which is there into the sea, the ships should be freed. They draw lots, and Aigres, the son of Berinus, is the allotted one. He goes upon the rock, and throws the ring into the sea, when instantly the vessels are freed and resume their voyage. Aigres gets off the rock

---

[2]Not the second part, as Dunlop says—'History of Fiction.'

[3]This MS. is of the 15th century, Professor Gaston Paris has informed me.

[4]With the spelling modernised, the title runs thus: 'L'Histoire du noble Chevalier Berinus, et du vaillant et trés-chevalereux Champion Aigres de l'Aimant, son fils; lequel Livre est tant solacieux qu'il doit être sur tout autre nommé le vrai Sentier d'Honneur, et l'Ex-emplaire de toute Chevalerie; nouvellement reduit de langage inçonnu au vulgaire langage François.' À Paris, par Jean Jannot. [? 1521.]

after some time, by informing the crew of the next ship attracted to it how to free themselves, and carries with him a fine horse, a sword, and armour which he found in a vessel that had long before been attracted by the fatal rock. Here follow the chivalric adventures of Aigres; and the rest of the romance comprises a version of the ancient legend of the Robbery of the King's Treasury, which must form the subject of a separate paper.

A story similar to that of the adventures of Beryn in Falsetown is found in all the Eastern derivatives of the Book of Sindibád, including versions derived directly from Eastern texts—namely, the Greek ('Syntipas'), which was translated from the Syriac, and the old Castilian ('Libro de los Engannos,' etc.), which was made from an Arabic text now lost. The Arabic version (the 'Seven Vazírs'), which forms a member of the 'Elf Layla wa Layla,' or Thousand and One Nights, is probably not more than 400 years old, if not even of later date in some texts of that famous story-book.

In the Persian metrical version ('Sindibád Náma), a merchant, on arriving in the city of Káshgar, is first victimised by a rogue who induces him to believe that the sandal-wood he has brought for sale was of no value—the fact being that it was worth its weight in gold—and purchases all his stock, promising to give him in return a certain measure of "whatever else he should choose." He plays with a citizen at draughts, the condition being that the loser shall do whatever the winner should require;[5] and being beaten, he is required to "drink up the waters of the sea." He is next accosted by a one-eyed man, who accuses him of having stolen his other eye. Lastly, another rogue produces—for some reason not mentioned in the MS.—a stone, and says to him, "Make me from this piece of marble a pair of trousers and a shirt." The merchant having acquainted the old woman with whom he lodged of all these entanglements, she advises him to disguise himself and go to such a place in the evening, where all the rogues of the city assembled to recount their exploits of the day to their chief,[6] a blind old man, who was noted for his sharpness of intellect, and attend carefully to his remarks. He goes thither accordingly, and sits among the numerous

---

[5] A favourite practice in the East, especially among the Arabs, is to impose upon the loser of a game, instead of a pecuniary payment, the obligation of doing whatsoever the winner may command him.

[6] "Every Muslim capital," says Sir R. F. Burton, "has a Shaykh of Thieves, who holds regular levées, and will restore stolen goods for a consideration; and this has lasted since the days of Diodorus Siculus."—Notes to his Translation of 'The Nights'; see also his 'Pilgrimage to Meccah and el-Medínah,' vol. i. p. 91.

cheaters unobserved. To him who had related the bargain for the sandal-wood the blind old man said, "You are a fool; for instead of this merchant asking a measure of silver or gold, he may require you to give him a measure of male fleas, with silken housings and jewelled bridles, and how will you do this?" To the draught-player he said, that his opponent might express his readiness to drink up the waters of the sea, provided the rivers were first stopped from flowing into it. To the one-eyed man he said, "The merchant may propose that one of his eyes and your only eye be taken out and weighed, to prove whether they are the same, and in such a case you would be totally blind, while the other would still have one eye." And to the man who required a pair of trousers and a shirt to be made of a piece of marble, he said, that the other might ask him to first make an iron thread to sew them with. The disguised merchant, having attentively heard the blind old man's remarks, returned to his lodging, and next day, when the parties appeared before the kází, he made to each of his claimants the reply which their chief had suggested, so that all were confounded—the rogue who had cheated him out of the sandal-wood having to restore it, and pay the merchant several bags of gold by way of compensation.

In the Arabic version the merchant, after disposing of his sandal-wood, is accosted by the one-eyed man, and obtains a day's respite, on finding surety; his shoe having been torn in the scuffle, he takes it to a cobbler, saying, "Repair it, and I will give thee what will content thee"; then he plays at dice with a fourth sharper, and losing the game, is required to drink up the sea, or surrender his wealth. The blind old man tells the cobbler that the merchant might say to him, "The sultan's troops have been victorious, and the number of his children and allies is increased—art thou content?" to which he dared not reply in the negative; and the dice-player might be required to hold the mouth of the sea and hand it to him. In the Greek, Hebrew, and old Castilian versions, the "stopping the rivers" is the old man's suggestion, and the incident of the cobbler does not occur.

It has not, I think, been hitherto noticed that the story, in a somewhat varied form, is orally current in India—whence, indeed, it first set out upon its travels many ages ago. The following is abridged from a version given in a little-known but very entertaining collection of Indian stories and anecdotes:

A merchant, on his deathbed, warns his son not to venture into the region of the Himályas in his trading journeys, since the people there were very artful and dishonest; but should he neglect this warning and go thither, and fall into trouble, he should go to Gholab Sing, the chief of that place, and mention his (the father's) name, and he would help him out of his difficulties. The young man, after his father's death, resolves, out of curiosity, to visit the prohibited country, and accordingly sets off, with a large stock of valuable goods. Arriving there after two months' tedious journey, instead of firing his gun in the air to notify the fact (as usual), he shot at and killed a heron that was sitting quietly on the bank of a large piece of water. A washerman, engaged in cleansing clothes hard by, seeing this, accused him of having killed his father, who had been re-born in the form of that bird, and demanded that he should restore his father (the heron) to life, or pay him 400 rupís. Presently a man came up who was blind of an eye, and said to the merchant, "Your father (peace be to his spirit!) traded in all kinds of things, took a fancy to my eyes, and bought one of them for 600 rupís, promising to pay me on his next visit hither. I forego the interest due me for many years, but you must pay me the principal, or restore the eye to me." While this man and the merchant were disputing there came up a woman bearing a child in her arms, who said that she was a wife of the young merchant's father, and had borne him that child; and that when he left her, he bade her borrow such sums of money as she should require for her maintenance during his absence, which he should duly refund on his return: she therefore desired him to pay off the debts she had incurred during the past two years and six months, to save his father's credit. The young merchant, confounded by such strange demands, bethought himself of his father's advice, and desired all three claimants to accompany him to Gholab Sing, their chief, by whose decision he would be bound. To this proposal they willingly agreed; and when the merchant had, in a private audience, stated the several claims made upon him, the chief advised him to repel them in this wise: To the washerman he should say that his own father had been re-born as a fish, which the washerman's father, the heron, had swallowed: "Restore my father to life, and I will then resuscitate your father." To the one-eyed man he should say that it was true his father dealt largely in eyes, but in order to find out which of those in his stock belonged to him, he must take out his remaining eye to have it weighed.[7] And to the woman

---

[7]Among the Kashmírí traditions regarding Akbar is the following: The emperor went out one night into the outskirts of the city, disguised as a fakír, and Bír Bal, his minister, meeting and recognising him, the two went on together, till a one-eyed man came up to them and said to Akbar, "You have taken out my eye. Either pay me 1200 rupís or restore my other eye."

he should say that he admitted the truth of her statement, his father having often spoken to him of the circumstance, and indeed had on his deathbed desired him to give her one of his sandals, which she was to put on and then mount the funeral pyre.[8] The young merchant acted upon these suggestions, and having thus defeated his claimants, they were sent to prison loaded with chains, and he was afterwards permitted to trade in that place without further molestation.[9]

We might well suppose that the adventures of Beryn in Falsetown were derived from the Greek 'Syntipas,' and that the variations in the former were made by the author. But the case is altered when we have before us an Indian version of the story which has two incidents in common with the Tale of Beryn, not found in any of the 'Sindibád' versions: (1) the woman and her child; (2) the charge of having murdered a man's father, which in the Hindú story has its representative in the washerman accusing the merchant of having killed his father in shooting a heron. On the other hand, the 'Sindibád' versions have two incidents in common with the Tale of Beryn, neither of which is found in the Indian story: (1) "the waters of the sea;" (2) the aloes-wood swindle, for which the rogue is required to give a measure of "harnessed fleas," which has its equivalent in Beryn's being cheated out of his cargoes and requiring the cheater to reload his ships with butterflies. But the Indian version has one incident in common with all the others—the one-eyed man: in Beryn he is totally blind. Thus, it appears, the Tale of Beryn—that is to say, his adventures in Falsetown—was derived neither from any known 'Sindibád' version nor from the only Indian version at present known. We must therefore conclude that a version having the elements of both was the source of the Tale of Beryn. As to the long narrative of Beryn's froward youth, that may

---

Akbar was taken aback by such a demand, but Bír Bal was equal to the occasion. "Yes," said he, "it is quite true. We have your eye, and if you will come to-morrow we will return it to you." The man agreed, and left. Bír Bal sent to the butcher's for some sheep's eyes, and put each one separately in a wooden boa by itself. When the man came in the morning, Bír Bal told him that the king had several eyes, but it was impossible to say which was his eye: he must therefore submit to have his other eye taken out and weighed, and the man was blinded for life.—See Knowles' 'Dictionary of Kashmírí Proverbs,' pp. 88, 89.

[8]When a Hindú died away from his family, a messenger was despatched to his house with one of his shoes to intimate his death and cremation; his wives then performed *sattí* (or voluntary death by burning), with his shoes in place of his body.

[9]'The Hermit of Motee Jhurna; also Indian Tales and Anecdotes.' By C. Vernieux. Calcutta: 1873.

have been an invention of the author, or adapted by him from another tale—no unusual thing, whether in the case of written or oral fictions. To conclude this critical inquiry—which may by some, perhaps, be considered as "wasted labour" on a trifling subject: but let that pass—it is observable that in all the 'Sindibád' versions the merchant, by the advice of another, learns from the remarks of the blind old shaykh of the thieves how to answer his opponents: in the Tale of Beryn, he is advised by a pretended cripple called Geoffrey—an incident which does not appear in my brief abstract of the story—to go and listen to what the rogues should say of their cases to Duke Isope, who, like the thieves' shaykh, is blind but very clever; and when Beryn declines to do so, Geoffrey goes himself: in the Indian story, the advice is obtained directly from a prince, Gholab Singh.

A jest similar to the reply, in the Persian version of our story, to the man with the piece of marble is found in the Talmud—where many wise and witty as well as foolish and absurd things occur—in the story of an Athenian who, walking about the streets of Jerusalem, and seeing a tailor on his shop-board busily at work, picked up a broken mortar and facetiously asked him to be good enough to put a patch upon it. "Willingly," replied the tailor, taking up a handful of sand and offering it to the witling—"most willingly, if you will first have the kindness to make me a few *threads* of this material." The "stopping of the rivers" is the reply made by the German rogue, Tyl Eulenspiegel, when asked to state the quantity of water in the sea; and this question also occurs in one of Sacchetti's novels, though the answer is somewhat different; but in the nineteenth Tale of Madden's edition of the 'Gesta Romanorum' we find, to the question of how many gallons of salt water there be in the sea, the answer: "Let all the passages of fresh water be stopped, and I shall tell thee." Such "hard questions," or *posers,* are very common in the early popular literature of Europe. Thus, in the ballad of King John and the Abbot of Canterbury, the latter is required to answer the king "questions three," and failing to do so, "his head should be smitten from his bodíe,"—which is similar in outline to one of Eulenspiegel's exploits and to the novel of Sacchetti already referred to.[10] In a

[10]The Norse story of "The Priest and his Clerk," in Dasent's 'Tales from the Fjeld'; "The Cook" and the "Thoughtless Abbot," in Crane's 'Italian Popular Tales'; and the "Three Priests and the Khoja," in the Turkish collection of pleasantries ascribed to Khoja Nasr-ed-Dín Efendí, also correspond, *mutatis mutandis,* with our fine old English ballad of 'King John and the Abbot.'

small tract preserved in the British Museum, entitled 'Demands Joyous,' are such *posers* as: "Why doth a dog turn himself about three times before he lieth down? *Ans.* Because he knoweth not his bed's head from its foot." Again: "How many straws go to a goose's nest? *Ans.* None; because they be all carried." Again: "How many calves' tails would it take to reach the moon? *Ans.* But one, if it be long enough." Goldsmith may have had this last jest in mind when, Johnson and he supping on rumps and kidneys one night at the Mitre Tavern, the literary dictator remarked to his friend, "These rumps are very fine things, sir;" to which Goldy replied, "Yes, sir, but it would take a great many of them to reach to the moon." "To the moon!" echoed Johnson; "that, sir, I fear, exceeds your calculation." "I think I could tell," answered Goldy. "Pray, then, sir, how many?" Quoth Goldy—at the same time probably hitching beyond arm's length of the irascible Doctor—"Only one, if it were long enough." For a little, Johnson, saith the veracious Boswell, sate sulky, but at length recovered his good-humour, and said, "I deserved it, sir."—In another book of facetiæ, entitled 'The Scots Piper's Queries, or John Falkirk's Cariches' (*i.e.,* Catechism): "What time is a scolding wife at her best? *Ans.* When she is fast asleep." "Who was the good-man's muckle cow's calf's mother? *Ans.* The muckle cow herself." "What is the likest thing to a man and a horse? *Ans.* A tailor and a mare." "What is the hardest dinner that ever a tailor could lay his teeth to? *Ans.* His own goose, ever so well boiled or roasted." With such "hard questions" did our simple ancestors exercise their wits, and pleasantly pass the long winter evenings, in the absence of higher intellectual amusements—and of halfpenny newspapers with "piping-hot" tidings from the farthest ends of the earth!

༈ THE ROBBERY OF
THE KING'S TREASURY ༈

WHETHER it be true, as Butler asserts in his 'Hudibras,' that "the pleasure is as great of being cheated as to cheat," there can be no doubt that mankind in all ages have delighted in stories of expert thievery. Indeed, in some Eastern countries at the present day theft is a regular profession, and no disgrace attaches to it—except perhaps upon detection. It often appears in folk-tales that boys and youths are apprenticed to the thieving craft, as in the Norse tale of the Master-Thief, and the Gaelic tale of the Shifty Lad. Even the sons of kings formerly added to the ordinary accomplishments of princes perfect skill in jugglery and theft, if we may credit the Indian romance which recounts the adventures of the princes Somasekhara and Chitrasekhara, who cleverly effected their entrance into the palace of Vikráma, king of Lilavatí, and in spite of every precaution plundered, unknown to them, the king, the queen, and the princess of their jewels, and stripped them and the maids of honour of their garments— leaving a written paper stating that they would not cease their depredations until the king consented to give his daughter in marriage to one of them, and threatening, if he withheld his consent, to carry off the princess. The exploits of European sharpers in modern times are tame compared with those of their brethren in the East, especially in Egypt, which breeds the cleverest thieves in the world; but all combined are "as nothing, and less than nothing, and vanity," in comparison with the achievements of the hero of a hundred stories (he is one and the same clever youth under all disguises)—stories which are spread through every country, from the shores of Argyleshire to the plains of Mongolia, from Ceylon to the pine-clad hills of Norway—variants (brothers and sisters and cousins) of an ancient Egyptian legend which Herodotus has related (Euterpe, 121):

Rhampsinitus, king of Egypt, to secure his vast treasures, caused a strong room to be built of hewn stone. The architect erected the building in exact accordance with the king's orders, but left a stone loose, yet so nicely adjusted that it could not be discovered by any one who was not aware of the fact; while it could be readily removed and replaced by two persons, or even one, if necessary. When the architect was on his deathbed, he acquainted his two sons of this secret provision he had made for their future maintenance, whereby they could, without fear of detection, supply themselves with gold from the royal treasury. The elder brother is at length caught in a snare set by the king's orders near his coffers, when he discovered that his treasure was fast growing less, and the younger cuts off his head and carries it home. The king causes the headless body to be suspended from the outer wall of his palace, with a guard of soldiers near. The mother of the dead man induced her surviving son to devise some plan of removing the body, and with this purpose he thus proceeded: Having loaded some asses with skins of wine, he drove them towards the place where the soldiers were on guard; and as he drew near, he contrived to partially unloose the necks of several skins, thus permitting the wine to run out, upon which he began to make loud lamentations over the misfortune. The soldiers, hearing his cries, and seeing so much good wine running to waste, quickly ran with vessels to save some of it for themselves. At this the pretended wine-dealer seemed in a still greater rage; but as they answered him in soothing terms, he affected to become gradually pacified, and having secured the wine that remained, he made them a present of a full skin, which they thankfully accepted, and insisted on his joining in their carouse. At midnight, when the soldiers were all dead drunk, the youth shaved the right side of the guards' beards, then removed his brother's body, and placing it on one of his beasts, returned home. In the sequel the king sends his daughter in the capacity of a courtesan, in hopes of her being able to discover the thief; and on the youth's visiting her, when she had heard from him an account of his exploit with his brother's body (she had made it the condition of her granting her love to such as related the most extraordinary thing that had happened to them), the lady attempted to lay hold of him, but the youth had, in expectation of this, provided himself with the fresh hand of a dead man, which he put into her hand, and escaped. When this new exploit was reported to the king, he was amazed at the versatility and boldness of the man, and at last caused proclamation to be made in all the cities that he would grant a pardon and add to it a valuable reward if the thief would come into his presence. Trusting to his promise, the thief went before Rhampsinitus, who was much astonished, and gave him his daughter in marriage, as to one who surpassed all men in knowledge; for, as they say, the Egyptians surpass all mankind, while he surpassed the Egyptians.—A similar legend is found in Pausanias, ix. 37, relating to the treasury of Hyrieus, built by Trophonius and Agamedes, architects of the temple of Apollo at Delphi, which corresponds with the story in Herodotus so far as the cutting off of the brother's head, caught in the snare, but, according to Pausanias, the earth opened and received Trophonius—and so the story ends.

This legend seems to have been first introduced into European literature in the 12th century, in the oldest version of the romance of the 'Seven Wise Masters,'—a work written in Latin prose, and entitled 'Dolopathos; sive, de Rege et Septem Sapientibus.' After the king discovers that his treasury has been robbed, he takes counsel of a wise old man, who had formerly been himself a great robber, but, though now deprived of sight, often gave the king excellent advice. The old man suggests that a quantity of green grass should be taken into the treasury and set on fire; then closing the gate, the king should walk round the building, and observe whether smoke escaped through any part of the walls. This the king does, and perceiving smoke issuing from between stones which had not been cemented, the precise place where the robbers had gained entrance was at once ascertained. The youth's device of stealing his father's body is peculiar: The king, still acting by the old man's advice, causes the corpse to be guarded by twenty horsemen in white armour, and twenty in black. The youth disguises himself, one side in white and the other in black, so that he is mistaken as he rides past the two lines of horsemen by each as belonging to the other party, and thus reaches the body and carries it away.

The story as found in one of our Early English versions of the 'Seven Sages'—probably derived from the French—being put into the mouth of the queen, whose object is solely to prejudice the king against his son, ends with the incident of the father's decapitation:

A certain king's counsellor, having wasted all his wealth and become reduced to poverty, breaks into the royal treasury, with the assistance of his son, and takes away a great quantity of gold. The king, on discovering the robbery, placed a large vessel filled with pitch close to where the breach had been made in the wall, in order to entrap the robber when he next came there. The counsellor, having again fallen into poverty, went one night with his son to procure a fresh supply of gold, and on entering the treasury as before, fell up to his neck in the pitch. Calling to his son, and informing him of what had happened to him, he warned him not to attempt his release, for it was quite impossible; but desired him to draw his sword and cut off his head and carry it away, so that he should not be recognised and his family disgraced. The son accordingly cuts off his father's head, takes it home, and recounts the whole particulars of the adventure.—In the Latin prose version

of the same work, entitled 'Historia Septem Sapientum Romæ,' the robber
of the king's treasury is a knight, who had spent all his wealth at tourneys,
and similar idle sports. After the son had taken home his father's head, the
king is informed of the headless body found in his treasury, and orders it to
be drawn at the tails of horses through the principal streets to the gallows,
charging his soldiers to bring before him any persons whom they observed
affected with excessive grief. As the body was drawn past the knight's house,
one of his daughters uttered loud cries of sorrow, upon which the son
quickly drew his knife and wounded his hand, causing the blood to flow
freely. The soldiers entered the house, and inquired the cause of the loud
cries they had just heard, when the son, showing his wounded hand, said
that his sister had been alarmed at seeing his blood, on which the soldiers,
satisfied with this explanation, quitted the house.[1]

From the version in 'Dolopathos' it is probable Ser Giovanni derived
the story as found in his 'Pecorone,'—a work written about 1378, but not
printed till 1578,—where it is related of an architect named Bindo, who
stole a golden vase from the treasury of the Doge of Venice, who adopts
the plan of burning straw in order to discover how the thief had entered.
The son of Bindo recovers the headless body, which was guarded by a
party of soldiers, in this manner: He hires twelve porters and disguises
them in the black habits of monks, and himself in a vizard, and his horse
in a black cloth, and proceeding thus at night to where the soldiers were
stationed, so frightened them that they made no attempt to resist, and
reported next morning that the body had been carried off by demons.
Finally the Doge proclaims that he will give his daughter in marriage to
the clever robber, and the son of Bindo accordingly reveals himself.

In a Sicilian popular version, given in Pitrè's collection, the youth steals
the body, after drugging the guards, but it is recovered; and he next borrows a flock of goats, sticks lighted candles in pots between their horns,
which terrify the soldiers, who run away, and the youth steals the body
once more. Next day proclamation is made, fixing a high price for meat,
and ordering all old women to come to the palace. A hundred come: they
are to find out who was cooking meat—the king thinks only the thief
could afford to buy meat at the price. The thief does buy meat. An old

---

[1] An Armenian version of the 'Seven Wise Masters,' written at Ispahán in 1687, of which a
Russian translation appeared at Moscow in 1847, has the story in much the same terms, with
the addition that the father's corpse was hung on a tree.

woman comes begging, and gets from his mother a piece of meat;—she is met by the thief, who suspects the trick and throws her into the well. On the following day, when the old women assemble at the palace, one is missing. The king ascertains that only one person had purchased meat, so he at last issues proclamation that the man who had done such wonders should have his daughter.

A modern Greek popular version (No. 24 of Legrand's collection) is, I think, singular in preserving the incident in the Egyptian legend of the dead man's hand:

The "Thief by Nature" goes, with his rascally uncle, to break open the king's treasury: taking a sack, some ropes, and two grappling-irons, he climbs on to the roof, then helps his uncle to ascend, removes a plate, and thus gains access to the treasury, and having filled the sacks with gold, the two rogues get home in safety. In this manner they rob the royal treasury on thirteen different nights. At length the king, discovering that his store of gold was becoming rapidly less, consulted an old and expert thief who was in prison, and was advised by him to close all doors and other openings, in order to find where any light comes in, and thus the loose plate is discovered. The prisoner then directs that a cauldron of boiling pitch be placed immediately below the loose plate; and next time the uncle and nephew visit the treasury for a further supply of gold, the youth smells the pitch, and will not go down, but the uncle goes and falls into the pitch; his nephew cuts off his head, and taking it home, tells his aunt not to betray herself by excessive grief. The man in prison next advises that the headless body be exposed in the market-place, and men concealed to watch if any persons weep at the sight of it. The youth bids his aunt take some glasses of sour milk to market, and, if she must see her husband's corpse and give vent to her feelings, to let the glasses drop on the ground, and then sit down and cry ostensibly for the loss of her glasses and milk: this she does accordingly, and is not suspected, but the old thief says she ought to have been detained. He next counsels the king to put some gold coins under the dead body—the confederate is sure to come for them; but the youngster gets a boy to play with him at horses, and each time he passes the body he clutches some of the coins, and in the evening the soldiers in charge are censured for their carelessness. After this another expedient is adopted to detect the dead robber's accomplice: A camel laden with precious stones is driven through the city, in hopes of attracting the thief; but the youth goes to a cheap wine-seller, and procures a quantity of wine, with which he makes the guards drunk, then shaves off half their hair and beards, takes away the jewels, kills the camel, from which his mother obtains two pots of grease. Then an old woman is sent through the city to procure camel's grease, gets some at the old woman's house, and marks the door, but the young thief similarly marks all the doors in the city. At last the experienced thief in prison tells the king that the dead robber's associate is much more clever than himself, and he can advise nothing further. The king offers, by public proclamation, the hand of his daughter in marriage to the man who had so cleverly escaped detection, and the youth comes boldly forward; but when the king called to his soldiers to arrest him, he leaps amongst them, as if trying to arrest some one, like the others, and thus escapes once more. In the sequel the king again makes public offer of his daughter to the clever man, and the young thief, providing himself with a dead man's hand, presents himself before the princess, and when she has heard his story and calls for help to arrest him, he runs off, leaving her holding the dead man's hand; and the king, seeing that he can make nothing of the youth with all his devices, gives him the princess in marriage.

In the collection of Albanian Tales by M. Dozon (No. 13) we find a most extraordinary version: The youngest of three brothers joins a party of twelve robbers, and they all set off to rob the king. Having broken a hole in the stable-wall, the twelve robbers go inside; but the youth remains outside to watch, and resolving to have no part in the robbery, but on the contrary, to kill them, he calls out, "Save yourselves—you are discovered," and as they come out, one by one, he cuts off their heads, then sticks his knife in the ground, and goes away. In the morning the king is astonished to see the twelve dead bodies and the knife; and in order to discover the person who had thus saved him from being robbed, he causes an inn to be erected at cross roads, at which all travellers are to be lodged and fed free of charge, on condition of their relating all, good and bad, they had done in their lives. The hero, among others, comes to the inn, where he tells of the intended robbery of the royal stables, which being communicated to the king, he gives him his daughter in marriage.[2]

---

[2]This seems a distorted reflection of the device of Rhampsinitus in exposing his daughter to public hire on the like condition. It reappears in a Hungarian tale, cited by Miss Busk in her 'Folk-Lore of Rome' (pp. 167–169): The hero, István, comes to a castle which is besieged by three giants to obtain possession of the king's three beautiful daughters. István kills them by stratagem, takes three tokens of his having been there, and returns to his two brothers. They continue their wanderings till they come to an inn where the three princesses and the

The story as related in the old French romance 'L'Histoire du Chevalier Berinus'—the first part of which, his adventures in Falsetown, is the subject of the preceding paper[3]—is indebted but little to Herodotus: When Berinus arrived at Rome, he found that all his father's property had been seized by the emperor, and it was not long till the wealth he brought with him from Blandie was all spent, and he was in sore straits for the means of subsistence. And now a man called Silvain, whom he had taken off the Rock of Adamant, when his own son Aigres was left there in order to free the ships from its influence (see *ante*, p. 327), informed Berinus that his father was the architect who built the tower where the emperor kept his treasure, and had taken care in the course of its construction to make a secret entrance for his own use. "It is marked with a stone, which is not cemented like the others, but which joins itself to them so perfectly that one could not suspect it is loose. I know this entrance," he added, "and have been more than once into the tower before I quitted Rome. I will go there again on your account, and will restore to you, without knowledge of the emperor, a portion of what he has taken from you." Berinus hesitated a long time before acquiescing in Silvain's proposal, and scarcely had he given his consent than shame and remorse took firm hold of him. But without any means in the midst of Rome, even obliged to conceal his name, he saw Cleopatra his wife and Romaine his daughter, the one the offspring of a sovereign, the other born whilst he was himself one,—he saw them both condemned to die of hunger; and he could not endure the prospect. "Take me there," said he to Silvain—"I agree to everything." He lodged in an isolated house not far from the treasury of Philip, to which Silvain made several visits, so that Berinus was enabled to live in a state of comfort, but he was prudent enough to have no one in the secret. Cleopatra and Romaine, knowing that they had been formerly rich, were not astonished that he should find in Rome some means of subsistence. They asked him no questions of this matter, because his absolute silence announced that he did not wish that they should do so.

The emperor Philip, intending to give his barons rich presents on their departure from court after the Feast of Pentecost, went into his treasury,

---

king their father have established themselves in disguise, and make all who pass that way to tell the story of their lives, in order to discover who it was that delivered them from the giants. They make themselves known, and the king bestows his daughters on them.

[3]The romance is really composed of three parts, which have very slight connection one with another: (1) Berinus at Falsetown; (2) his son the Chevalier Aigres l'Aimant's knightly adventures; (3) Berinus at Rome: robbing the treasury of Philip.

and perceiving his wealth considerably diminished, he accused the ten treasurers who guarded it of the robbery, and threw them into prison. One of them offered to the emperor to discover the thief, if he would keep the matter of the robbery a profound secret, to which Philip consented, and both repaired to the tower. The treasurer lighted a great fire in it, and closed all the windows and the door, and when the smoke issued from the sides of the loose stone they discovered how the robbery had been effected, finding it could be displaced and replaced easily. In order to capture the robber, they placed close to the stone a vessel filled with a glutinous composition. Silvain was now dead. Berinus determines to visit the treasury once more, and never return to it again. He goes, and is caught in the trap laid for him. Just then his son Aigres, surnamed L'Aimant, from his adventure on the Rock (who had come to Rome some time before), is returning from a visit to the palace, and passing the tower observes the aperture left by the removal of the stone, and is proceeding to seize the robber, when he hears a voice exclaiming, "Alas, I have lost my own honour, and have disgraced my family!" "Who are you, unhappy one?" cried Aigres. "Approach, my son," responded the same voice. "Come and save the honour of your father!" Aigres entered, and found it impossible to extricate his wretched parent. In short, after much entreaty, Aigres cuts off his father's head, and, carrying it away, buried it in a neighbouring wood. Next day the headless corpse was exposed in the city, and guarded by forty horsemen and a great number of foot-soldiers. Aigres, resolved to save his father's corpse from such degradation, attacks the guards, and having routed them, carries off the body and buries it. In fighting, he had shouted the name of Nullie, the emperor's daughter, of whom he was deeply enamoured. When this was made known to the emperor's Seven Sages, they advised that all the barons should be ordered to sleep in beds round the hall, with the Princess Nullie in the midst. This is done accordingly. During the night, when all the rest are sound asleep, Aigres kisses Nullie's hand. She marks his forehead with a black preparation, and on his speaking she recognises her lover, and tells him in a broken voice that she has signed his death-warrant, whereupon Aigres marks all the other barons on the forehead.[4] In the morning the Seven Sages are perplexed; but Geoffrey, the old advocate of Berinus at Falsetown, who has just returned to Rome, says that the man with the small thumb-mark

---

[4] See the Note, "Marking a Culprit," at the end of the present paper.

is the culprit, even Aigres. Geoffrey, however, having been promised a boon by the emperor on his finding out the guilty man, demands the pardon of Aigres, who is then banished from Rome. On the death of Philip, Aigres returns, becomes emperor of Rome, and re-establishes his mother Cleopatra as queen of Blandie.

Under the title of "Le Voleur Avisé," M. F.-M. Luzel gives, in "Mélusine," 1876, c. 17 ff., a Breton version, as related by a workman of Morlaix, in which are interpolated several incidents from other popular tales; and it is unique, inasmuch as the thief performs his exploits, not by his own skill, but by magical means:

There was once a poor man who had a son named Efflam, and a daughter named Hénori. The father sent Efflam to seek his fortune in Paris; and he walked and walked, always setting one foot before the other, till, in passing through a forest, he was overtaken by night, and climbed into a tree, to secure himself from wild beasts and to await daylight. Presently three robbers, laden with booty, arrived at the tree, and raising a stone, deposited their spoil in a cavern, the entrance of which it covered. Then they sat down under the tree to eat and drink, and to talk over their exploits. Efflam listened attentively to what they said to each other. Quoth one of the robbers, "I have a wonderful mantle which can carry me through the air wherever I wish to be." Said another, "And I possess a hat which renders me invisible, and when I put it on my head I can do anything I please without being seen." Then said the third robber, "And I have gaiters with which I can march as fast as the wind when I have them on my legs." Efflam, thinking it would be fine if he had these magical things, quickly devised a plan by which he might obtain them. Dropping down, by means of a long branch of the tree, into the midst of them, and roaring out, "Ah, robbers!" they were seized with fright, believing that the devil or the gensdarmes had come after them, and ran away, leaving behind the mantle, the hat, and the gaiters.[5] Efflam took possession of these talismans, and putting on the gaiters was instantly in Paris, where, by the aid of his hat of invisibility, he contrived to plunder several shopkeepers, and lived merrily on the proceeds of the stolen goods.

It happened one day, while he was walking through the city, he overheard three men talking about the king's treasury, and lamenting that it was so well guarded, upon which he resolved that thick walls and watch-

[5]This device occurs again and again in folk-tales, as we shall see in a subsequent paper.

ful soldiers should be no obstacles to himself. So when night came on, Efflam went to the foot of the tower, and having spread his mantle on the ground and seated himself upon it, and putting on his magic hat, he said, "Mantle, do your duty, and take me immediately into the royal treasury;" and he was there in an instant, without the guards or any other person being aware of it. He returned in the same manner with his pockets filled with gold and silver. The next night and several nights following he went again to the treasury, and always with the like success. Having now become very wealthy, Efflam bought a fine palace, and sent for his father and sister to come to him. The day on which they were to arrive, he went to meet them in a fine carriage drawn by two horses. When he reached the outskirts of the city he discovered his father and sister on the road, on foot, and poorly clad. So he bade his coachman return on one of the horses to his house, and bring him a box which he had left on the table in his private chamber. Efflam then retired to a house on the roadside with his father and sister, and gave them rich vestments which he had brought with him in the carriage, and to each a purse full of gold, so that the coachman should not recognise the poor peasants. When the coachman returned and told his master that he could not find the box, "No," replied Efflam, "I had it in the carriage all the time, and was not aware of it."

One day the father asked Efflam how he had become rich so soon. "It is by robbing the king's treasury," replied he. "If you please," then said the old man, "I will go with you, and we two can carry away a great sum." To this Efflam consented, and the next night they both seated themselves on the mantle, placed their heads under the hat, and were at once transported inside the royal treasury, where, having taken much gold and silver, they returned in the same manner. But the king now began to perceive that his treasury was being robbed, at which he was greatly astonished, since he never confided the key to any one, and could see no trace of an opening having been made in the walls. In order to catch the robber, he placed traps close to the vessels containing his gold and silver, and on the following night the father was caught by one of the traps. "Cut off my head," said he to his son, "and carry it away, with my clothes, so that no one may recognise me." Efflam accordingly cut off his father's head, and carrying it away, buried it in his garden.[6]

[6]This is the only version, I think, in which the father directs his clothes to be carried off as well as his head.

In the morning, when the king visited his treasury, he was pleased to see the dead body, but on examining, it, was astonished to find it headless. He caused proclamation to be made that the robber was taken at last, and ordered the body to be drawn through each quarter of the city. Four soldiers, two in front and two behind, accompanied the corpse, with instructions to observe if any one wept or lamented in the course of their passage through the streets. Efflam cautioned his sister not to weep or lament when their father's body was drawn past, else both he and herself should lose their lives. She does cry, however, and Efflam, drawing his poignard, wounds her in the hand. So when the soldiers come in and ask the cause of the outcry, he tells them that his sister, playing with his dagger, had wounded herself, and they went away quite satisfied.

This stratagem of the king having failed, he caused the robber's body to be suspended from a hook in the palace-wall, and placed guards near it, persuaded that the parents or the friends of the robber would come at night to remove the corpse. When Efflam saw this, he disguised himself as a wine-merchant, loaded an ass with wine in which he had put a narcotic, and, accompanied by his sister, came to the place where his father's body was exposed. He artfully tumbled one of the casks off the ass, and the soldiers coming to assist him, he gave it to them, still half-full, for their trouble, and drinking the drugged wine they soon fell asleep. Then Efflam takes the body down, and going to an abbey in his assumed capacity of wine-merchant, he there obtains lodging for the night. The abbot and all the monks drink freely of Efflam's wine, and when they were sound asleep, Efflam and his sister buried their father's body in consecrated ground. He then strips the garments off the sleeping monks, and does likewise with the soldiers, clothing the monks in the soldiers' dresses and the soldiers in the robes of the monks.

"This is certainly a very clever robber," said the king, when he heard of this exploit; "but nevertheless I shall yet find him out." Then he published that he would expose in a public place a beautiful white kid, which should be the property of him who should steal it away. The king himself sat in his balcony, with his queen and courtiers, and soldiers guarded the white kid. Efflam put on his magic hat, and stole the kid without being seen by any one. The king now thought the robber must be a great magician. Efflam took the kid to his house, and gave it to his sister to cook, charging her not to bestow any of it in charity on a mendicant or any other person. "We shall eat the kid between our two selves alone," said he. The king employed a blind man to go through the city begging, and should he get flesh of a kid at any house, he must mark the door with chalk. The beggar gets some of the kid's flesh from Efflam's sister, and marks the door. The king then despatched his guards to arrest all that were in the house; but Efflam having observed the mark on his door, questioned his sister, and learning of the blind beggar's visit, goes at once and marks all the doors in the street, thus foiling the soldiers. "What a man this is, to be sure!" said the king. He next exposes his royal crown, which Efflam steals by the aid of his invisible hat. And now the king reflected that it would be wise for him to attach the clever man to his own interests, so he exposed his daughter in a public place, and proclaimed that whoever should take her away, in spite of his guards, should marry her. Efflam's magic hat enabled him to carry off the princess, after which he took her to the king's palace, and confessed that he was the son of the treasury thief. The marriage of Efflam and the princess was celebrated with great pomp, and the old king at the same time made Efflam's sister Hénori his queen.

A Gaelic variant is found in the story of the Shifty Lad, in Campbell's 'Popular Tales of the West Highlands': The shifty lad remarks to his master the wright, that he might get plenty from the king's storehouse, which was near at hand, if only he would break into it. The two eventually rob it together. But the king's people missed the butter and cheese and the other things that had been taken out of the storehouse, and they told the king how it had happened. The king took the advice of the Seanagal about the best way of catching the thieves, and the counsel that he gave them was, that they should set a hogshead of soft pitch under the hole where they were coming in. This was done, and the next day the shifty lad and his master went to break into the king's storehouse. The consequence was that the wright was caught in the pitch. Thereupon the lad cut off his head, which he carried home and buried in the garden. When the king's people came into the storehouse, they found a body without a head, and they could not make out whose it was. By the advice of the Seanagal, the king had the trunk carried about from town to town by soldiers on the points of spears. They were directed to observe if any one cried out on seeing it. When they were going past the house of the wright, the wright's wife made a tortured scream, and swift the shifty lad cut himself with an adze, and he kept saying to the wright's wife, "It is not as bad as thou thinkest." He then told the soldiers that she was afraid of blood, and therefore the soldiers supposed that he was the wright and she his wife. The king had the body hung up in an open place, and set soldiers to watch if any person should attempt to take it away, or show pity or grief for it. The shifty lad drives a horse past with a keg of whisky on each side, and pretends to be hiding it from the soldiers. They pursue him, capture the whisky, get dead drunk, and the shifty lad carries off and buries the wright's body. The king now lets loose a pig to dig up the body. The soldiers follow the pig, but the wright's widow entertains them. Meanwhile the shifty lad kills the pig and buries it. The soldiers are then ordered to live at free quarters among the people, and wherever they get pig's flesh, unless the people could explain how they came by it, to make a report to the king. But the shifty lad kills the soldiers who visit the widow, and persuades the people to kill all the others in their sleep. The Seanagal next advises the king to give a feast to all the people. Whoever dared to dance with the king's daughter would be the culprit. The shifty lad asks her to dance; she makes a black mark on him, but he puts a similar black mark on twenty others. The king now proclaims that if the author of these clever tricks will reveal himself, he shall marry his daughter. All the men with marks on them contend for the honour. It is agreed that to whomsoever a child shall give an apple, the king is to give his daughter. The shifty lad goes into the room where they are all assembled, with a shaving and a drone, and the child gives him the apple. He marries the princess, but is killed by accident.

Dr Reinhold Köhler, in his review of Campbell's Gaelic Tales in 'Orient and Occident,' bd. ii., cites a considerable number of versions, mostly German, which present no very important variations from those given above. Thus in an old Dutch poem entitled 'Der Dieb von Brügge' (the Thief of Bruges), we are told that two great thieves, of Paris and Bruges, rob the king of France's treasury. By the advice of an aged knight the opening made by them is discovered, as in 'Dolopathos' and other versions, by means of a fire of straw, and a kettle of pitch is set under it. The Paris thief falls into it, and has his head cut off by the thief of Bruges. When the corpse is dragged round, and the wife of the deceased breaks into lamentation, the thief of Bruges hacks his hand, and on the servants of the king informing him and the knight of this, the latter is convinced that that must be the culprit, and sends the servants back again to that house, but they find it empty. Now the king, by the advice of the knight, has the corpse hung on the gallows and watched by twelve warders. The thief loads a cart with provisions, a cask of wine drugged, and a dozen monks' cowls, and drives at night to the gallows. The warders take his meat and drink and fall asleep, whereupon he puts on them the cowls and steals away the body. After this follows the incident of the princess sleeping in a general room, her marking the thief, and his marking all the others in the room, and the marriage of the princess and the thief.

In a Tyrolese variant (Zingerle's 'Kinder und Hausmärchen aus Süddeutschland,' p. 300), two thieves, of Prussia and Poland, rob the treasury of a lord, by digging a subterranean passage. As in 'Dolopathos,' a blind old thief is the lord's mentor, and suggests the placing of an iron trap on the hole. The Prussian thief is caught in it, and his head is cut off by his companion, who recovers the body from the gallows in the same manner as did the Bruges thief. After this a stag with gilded horns is driven through the streets: the thief contrives to steal it. A beggar is sent about and gets venison-broth at the thief's house, and marks the door; the thief on discovering this rubs it out, and marks the lord's house. And now the lord offers a reward to the person who has performed these tricks, upon which the thief declares himself.

In Denmark (Etlar's 'Eventyr og Folkesagen fra Jylland,' p. 165) the tale is told of Klaus, a schoolmaster, who must really have lived in the 14th century, when Count Geert governed Jutland. He broke into the count's treasury. The mason who had built the treasury discovers through the issuing smoke of a straw-fire the place through which Klaus broke in. A tar barrel is set under the place, and at the next entry Klaus' son falls into it. Klaus cuts off his head. Next day the body is dragged through the streets, and Klaus' wife would have betrayed the matter by her cries had not Klaus quickly cut her hand with the knife with which she had just been cutting bread. The tale then runs into another which has no special connection with it.[7]

A Russian version is cited by M. Leger, in 'Mélusine,' 1878, from a paper by Professor Vesselovsky, of the University of St Petersburg, in the 'Revue Russe,' 1877. The robber is called Chibarca. After having drugged

---

[7]It is nothing unusual to find popular tales, especially oral versions, comprising incidents which properly belong to other tales, as in the Breton version of our story which begins with an adventure of the Hat of Fortunatus class of stories. And in this Danish version the process is reversed; with the story of the Treasury is fused a quite different one. So far as it goes, it seems to have been orally recited by one who had a confused recollection of the story: instead of the mason who built the treasury being the thief, he is the detective; and it is the thief's son, not himself, who falls into the trap!

the guards he steals his uncle's body. The king sets precious stones in the horns of an ox, which he causes to be led through the streets of Moscow, directing his soldiers to arrest whoever should regard it with astonishment (the king's idea being, of course, that the thief would thus betray himself). Chibarca puts some fine birds in a cage, which he offers for sale as rare foreign birds. The soldiers insist upon seeing them; he refuses; they break open the cage, and the birds fly away. While they are pursuing the birds, Chibarca leads off the ox; prepares the flesh at home; kills an old beggar-woman who comes to his house (presumably sent to get some of the flesh); takes her body during the night to the palace gates, and placing the horns (without the gems, we may suppose) on her breast, leaves it there. In the morning the guards report that an old woman who had brought the horns had been found dead near the palace. The next stratagem of the king is to supply wine and beer *ad libitum* at the taverns, in front of which silver is scattered abundantly, and his soldiers are to arrest any one who should stoop to pick up the money. But Chibarca puts adhesive matter on the soles of his boots, to which as he walks along the pieces of money stick, after which he goes into a tavern and gets drunk. The soldiers, to identify him, shave off half his beard. Chibarca, on waking, does likewise to all in the tavern while they in their turn are asleep.

Among the Kabaïl of Northern Africa a rather curious version is current: An expert thief dies, leaving two sons, who prove themselves true "chips of the old block." They seek out their father's old comrade in thieving, who had "retired from business," but consents to accompany them in their adventures. They come upon a hawk's nest, and the old man shows his dexterity by taking away the sleeping bird without waking it, and putting it into his sack—an incident which resembles the exploit of one of the Four Clever Brothers in stealing the eggs from beneath a sitting-bird, in the German story: see vol. i. p. 277. The elder brother contrives to steal the still sleeping bird from the old man without his knowledge, and the younger in his turn performs the same exploit with his brother. They resolve to rob the king's house; and scaling the wall, one of the youths breaks through the roof and "conveys" from the house a quantity of valuables. The king misses his property, consults an old man, who advises him—as in the 'Dolopathos' version—to discover the place by which the thieves had gained entrance by burning faggots and observing whence the smoke issued. This being successful, he fixes a trap; one of the youths is caught by it on their next visit (their father's comrade is now dead); his brother cuts off his head and takes it home. The king finds the headless body, and consults his mentor again—

to be brief, he does nothing in the case without his advice. The body, with nails stuck into it, is publicly exposed; and the youth bids his mother take a vessel of oil, on going to view the body, and spill it before beginning to cry, which she does accordingly. When the king observes her crying, he asks the reason; she points to her spilt oil, and the king, pitying her case, gives her gold and tells her to go home. At night the youth disguises himself; mixes among the soldiers guarding the body; they take him for the angel of death, Azrael, and flee in dismay, when he carries the body away. Next day the king scatters gold on the road, expecting the thief would come to pick it up; but the clever youth hires some camels, smears their feet with a sticky substance, and drives them past the place, so the gold pieces stuck to their feet, and once more the craft of the old expert was baffled. Then a gazelle is let loose, and runs into the youth's house unobserved by the watchers. The king offers a large sum for gazelle's flesh, and an old woman goes through the town in search of some, and procures a small quantity from the youth's mother; but just as she is quitting the house in secret triumph, the youth himself comes up, and learning from her that she had just got some gazelle's flesh, "which was good for a fever," he invites her to return and he would give her some more. The busybody re-entered the house, and the youth at once slew her. Next the king gives a general feast, and, as his mentor told him, the man who selected certain dishes would be the thief. The youth goes, selects the dishes, and is immediately pounced upon by a soldier, who cuts off half his moustache; but he contrives to do likewise to the other guests, and once more escapes. After this the king proclaims that if the clever man would declare himself, he should marry his daughter and have the kingdom—the king undertaking to act as his prime minister. The youth now goes boldly before the king, who faithfully implements his promises.[8]

Turning to the Far East, we find an almost unique form of the story current in Mongolia, in which, however, the fundamental outline of the original is still traceable:

A simple-minded khán had among his subjects a man renowned for the acuteness of his intellect. He sent for him one day to try whether his name of "Bright Intellect" (Gegéu Uchátu) became him: "To this end let us see if thou hast the wit to steal the khán's talisman, defying the jealous care of

---

[8]'Recueil de Contes populaires de la Kabylie du Djurdjura,' recueillis et traduits par J. Rivière. Paris, 1882.

the khán with all his guards. If thou succeedest, I will recompense thee with presents, making glad thy heart; but if not, I will pronounce thee unworthily named, and in consequence will lay waste thy dwelling, and put out both thine eyes." Now the khán bound the talisman to the marble pillar of his bed-chamber, against which he lay, leaving the door open, the better to hear the approach of the thief, and the palace was surrounded by a strong guard of soldiers. Bright Intellect takes store of rice and brandy, and after chatting freely with the guards, gives them abundance and goes away. An hour later he returns, and finding the guards before the gate fast asleep on their horses, sets them astride a ruined wall and carries off the horses.[9] He then goes into the kitchen, where the cooks are about to light the fire: he draws over the head of one a cap woven of grass; into the sleeve of another he puts three stones. After this he proceeds to the khán's chamber, and draws over his head and face a dried bladder, hard as a stone; and then, having tied the guards together by their hair, he takes down the talisman from the pillar to which it was bound and makes off with it. The khán calls out, "Hey! a thief has been here!" But the guards can't move, and their exclamations of "Don't pull my hair," one to another, drowned the khán's cry of "Stop the thief!" "Hey!" roars the khán, "bring me a light. Not only is my talisman stolen, but my head is enclosed in a wall of stone!" One of the cooks, in a hurry, begins to blow the fire—his cap blazes up and burns his hair off; the other, trying to put out the fire, the stones fall from his sleeve and hit him on the head— too much engrossed with his own concerns to go after the thief. The khán, out of breath with his shouting, now calls to the outer guards, who should have been on horseback at the gates. Waking up at his voice, they begin spurring at the old wall; and thus Bright Intellect makes good his escape. Next day he presents himself before the khán, who is seated on his throne full of wrath. "Be not angry," says the clever man; "here is your talisman. I only took it according to the word of the khán." Quoth the khán, "I will not take back the talisman. But for drawing the stone-like bladder on my face last night, you shall have your head cut off." Hearing this, Bright Intellect, thinking to himself, "This is not just," dashed the talisman against a stone, and lo! blood poured out of the khán's nose, and he died.[10]

[9]This absurd incident reappears in Berni's 'Orlando Innamorato'; and in 'Don Quixote' by a similar device Sancho's ass Dapple is stolen from him.

[10]The khán proved himself an arrant noodle by refusing to take back his talisman, on the preservation of which his life depended. In another of the Tales of Siddhí Khúr a similar life-charm figures prominently; and these may be added to those I have mentioned in the Note on Life depending on an extraneous object.—See vol. i. pp. 167–171.

ᘒ

The Tibetan story of the Clever Thief (which was derived from India) bears a closer resemblance to the legend of Herodotus: An orphan and his uncle, a weaver, betook themselves to housebreaking. Once, when they had made a hole into a house and the weaver was going to pass his head through the opening, the youth said, "Uncle, although you are a thief, yet you do not understand your business. The legs should be put in first, not the head. For if the head should be cut off, its owner would be recognised, and his whole family plunged into ruin. Therefore put your feet first."[11] When the weaver had done so, attention was called to the fact, and a cry was raised of "Thieves! thieves!" At that cry a great number of people assembled, who seized the weaver by his legs and began to pull him in. The youth all by himself could not succeed in pulling him out, but he cut off the weaver's head, and got away with it. The king hears of this, and orders the trunk to be exposed at the crossing of the main street, and sets a party of soldiers to guard it. The youth assumes the appearance of a madman, goes up to the headless body and embraces it, unmolested by the guards. He then disguises himself as a carter, and drives a cart laden with wood past the body, where he contrives to upset it, and having unyoked the bullock from the cart, he set the wood and the cart on fire and went away; so the body of his uncle was consumed. Next he went disguised as a Bráhman from house to house collecting food; made five oblation cakes and left them at the place where he had burned the body. Then having assumed the appearance of a Kápálika (skull-carrying Siva worshipper), he went back to the place, smeared his body with ashes, filled a skull with the bones and ashes of his uncle and flung it into the Ganges. Now the king had a garden at a spot where the Ganges formed a bay, and he set men in it to watch its shores, and his daughter also, who was to cry out should any one touch her, and the watchmen were to hasten to the spot as

---

[11]It is not only customary at the present day in India and other Asiatic countries for thieves to gain access to a house by digging through the clay walls and beneath the floor, but it was their *modus operandi* in the time of the patriarch Job, who says (chap. xxiv. 16), "In the dark days they dig through houses." As an illustration of this practice, the following amusing Chinese anecdote may be cited: A literary man, while reading during the night, perceived that a thief was digging under the wall of his house. He happened to have before the fire a teapot full of boiling water. He took it, put it beside the wall, and awaited the thief. The opening made, the thief first put in his feet; the literary man caught them and watered them well with the scalding contents of his teapot. The thief uttered a piercing cry, and asked pardon. But he answered him in a grave tone, "Wait till I have emptied the teapot."

soon as they heard her voice calling for help. The thief went thither with an empty pitcher and began to draw water, when the watchmen struck him and broke the pitcher; the like happens to him a second time, and the watchmen conclude he is not a thief but a water-carrier, and take no more notice of him. After this he covered his head with a pot, swam down the river, and came ashore. He went up to the king's daughter and threatened her that if she called out he would instantly kill her. The consequence of this meeting was that the princess had a son. The thief would not but be present at his son's birth-feast, so he goes to the palace as a courtier, and tells the king's servants to plunder the merchant's quarter—by order of the king—which they do accordingly, supposing it to be in honour of the birth of the king's grandson, and there was a great outcry. Then the king orders public proclamation to be made that all men in the kingdom assemble within an enclosure he had caused to be formed, under pain of death. All assemble, and the king gives his grandson a wreath of flowers which he is to present to the man who is his father, and watchmen are instructed to lay hands on him when thus discovered. "As the boy walked with the wreath through the assembled crowds and closely observed them, he caught sight of the thief, and in accordance with the incomprehensible sequence of human affairs, handed him the wreath." The watchmen at once seized the thief, and brought him before the king, who gave his daughter to him as his wife, and half of the kingdom.[12]

Several of the incidents in the Gaelic, Breton, Sicilian, Kabaïl, and Russian versions reappear in the following Bengalí popular tale, which also has a close affinity with the Norse tale of the Master-Thief, and other European stories of the same class:

There was a past master in thievery who had a son that bade fair to rival himself, and in order to test the lad's skill he told him to steal the queen's gold chain and bring it to him. The youth contrives, by a series of clever stratagems, to pass unnoticed through four doors, each of which was guarded by a number of soldiers, and enter the royal bed-chamber, where a maid-servant was drowsily reciting a story, and the king and queen were apparently asleep. He went stealthily behind the girl and seated himself.

[12]'Tibetan Tales, derived from Indian Sources.' Translated from the Tibetan of the 'Kah-Gyur,' by F. Anton von Schiefner. Done into English from the German by W. R. S. Ralston, M.A.

The queen was lying down on a richly furnished bed of gold beside the king. The massive chain of gold round the neck of the queen was gleaming in the candle-light. The thief quietly listened to the story of the drowsy girl, who was becoming more and more sleepy. She stopped for a second, nodded her head, and again resumed her story; it was evident she was under the influence of sleep. In a moment the thief cut off the head of the girl with his sword, and then himself went on reciting for some minutes the story she had been telling. The king and queen were unconscious of any change of the story-teller, for they were both sound asleep. He stripped off the girl's clothes, put them on himself, tied his own clothes in a bundle, and, walking softly, very gently took off the chain from the queen's neck. He then went through the rooms down-stairs, ordered the inner guard to open the door, as 'she' was obliged to go out of the palace on urgent business. The guards, seeing it was the queen's maid-servant, readily allowed her to go out. In the same manner he got through the other doors, and at last out into the street. When he put into his father's hand the gold chain of the queen, the old thief's joy knew no bounds. "Well done, my son," said he; "you are not only as clever as your father, but you have beaten me hollow. The gods give you long life, my son!"

Great was the astonishment of the king and the queen to discover in the morning that the gold chain of the queen had been stolen and the poor maid-servant murdered. The king learned from his guards that a person calling herself the queen's maid-servant had gone out of the palace some hours before daybreak. All sorts of inquiries were made, but in vain. At last the king ordered a camel to be brought to him. On the back of the animal he caused to be placed two large bags filled with gold mohurs. The man taking charge of the bags upon the camel was ordered to go through every part of the city making this challenge: "As the thief was daring enough to steal a gold chain from the neck of the queen, let him further show his daring by stealing the gold mohurs from the back of this camel." Two days and nights the camel paraded through the city, but nothing happened. On the third night, as the camel-driver was going his rounds, he was accosted by a religious mendicant (*sannyasi*), who sat on a tiger's skin before a fire, and near him was a huge pair of tongs. This individual was none other than the thief in disguise. He said to the camel-driver, "Brother, why are you going through the city in this manner? Who is there so daring as to steal from the back of the king's camel? Come down, friend, and smoke with me." The camel-driver alighted, tied the camel to a tree, and began smoking. The thief not only supplied him with tobacco, but also with *ganja* and other narcotics, so that in a short time he became quite intoxicated, and fell asleep. Then the young thief led away the camel with the treasure on its back in the dead of night, through narrow lanes and bypaths, to his own house. That very night the camel was killed, and its carcase buried in deep pits in the earth. And the thing was so managed that no one could discover any trace of it.

Next morning, when the king heard that the camel-driver was lying drunk in the street, and that the camel had been stolen, together with the treasure, he was almost beside himself with rage. Proclamation was made in the city, that whoever caught the thief should get a reward of a lakh of rupees. The son of another thief now came forward and said he would apprehend the thief. In the evening of the following day he disguised himself as a woman, and coming to that part of the town where the young thief lived, began to weep very much, and went from door to door, saying, "Oh sirs, can any of you give me a bit of camel's flesh? For my son is dying, and the doctors say nothing but eating camel's flesh can save his life." At last he came to the house of the young thief, who happened to be out, and begged of his wife to tell him where he could get some camel's flesh in order to save his son's life. The woman, saying, "Wait, and I will try to get you some," went secretly to the spot where the carcase of the camel was buried, cut off a piece, and gave it to the pretended mother. He then went and told the king that he had traced the thief, and would be ready to deliver him up at night if the king would send some constables with him. At night the old thief and his son were captured, the body of the camel was disinterred, and all the treasure in the house seized. Next morning the king sat in judgment. The son of the old thief confessed that he had stolen the queen's gold chain, killed the girl, and taken away the camel; but he added that the person who had detected him and his father were also thieves and murderers, of which he gave proofs. As the king had promised to give a lakh of rupees to the person who discovered the camel-thief, he placed that sum before the youth. But soon after he ordered four pits to be dug in the earth, in which were buried alive, with all sorts of thistles and thorns, the two young thieves and their fathers.[13]

༄

---

[13]Abridged from "Adventures of Two Thieves and their Sons," in Rev. Lal Behari Day's 'Folk-Tales of Bengal,' pp. 174–181.

brother, and they did The first part of the foregoing Bengalí story closely resembles a tale in the 'Bahár-i Dánush,' which may be termed an Indo-Persian version. A king possesses a great golden fish encrusted with the most precious jewels, and this coming to the knowledge of a bold and expert thief, he determines to steal it, and one night he contrives to escape the vigilance of the royal guards who surrounded the palace, and, by means of a rope and a hook, climbs to the parapet. Entering the chamber of the king, he found him asleep. A lamp burned on the floor, and the fish lay under his pillow. A beautiful slave-girl was rubbing the king's feet with her hand.[14] The thief, advancing lightly, concealed himself behind a curtain till sleep overpowered the girl, when he removed the veil from her head, and covering himself with it, began to perform her office on the king's feet (lest he should awake upon the sudden cessation of the rubbing); and when the king happened to turn himself on his side, he drew the fish from under his pillow, and quitting the palace in the same manner as he had entered, escaped unobserved by the drowsy guards. Reflecting that the king would cause a thorough search to be made for the golden fish, and that the city gates would be kept carefully closed, he devised a plan for effectually concealing it till the search was abandoned. Wrapping the fish with the veil which he had taken from the sleeping slave-girl in the form of a shroud over a dead infant, and covering it with wreaths of white flowers to which he had helped himself from a neighbouring garden, the thief proceeded like one afflicted by sore calamity to the city gates. Telling the guards that his infant having died of an infectious disease, he wished to bury it at once, he prevailed upon them to let him go out of the city. Another thief, who had heard his pretended complaints as he went past his house, and readily suspected the true object, resolving to watch his movements, presently went up to the guards and begged them to open the gates for him also, in order that he should accompany his bereaved brother, and they did so.

[14]"The Arabs," says Lane—and, he might have added, Persians and Indians—"are very fond of having their feet, and especially the soles, slowly rubbed with the hand; and this operation, which is one of the services commonly required of a wife or a female slave, is a usual mode of waking a person, as it is also of lulling a person to sleep." Thus in the story of Maaroof (Lane's 'Arabian Nights,' vol. iii. p. 271), "the damsel then proceeded to rub and press gently the soles of his feet till sleep overcame him." Sometimes young boys are employed in this office. Thus in the story of Abú Temám (Persian Romance of Bakhtyár) we read: "When it was night the boys were engaged as usual in their office of rubbing the king's feet; and when they perceived his eyes to be closed," and so on.

The first thief went directly to the place of execution, where he saw three robbers impaled upon stakes, and a fourth stake vacant, close by. From this last, having counted a few paces, he buried the fish in the ground, and taking a stone clotted with blood from beneath one of the pales, placed it as a talisman upon his treasure, that he might readily know the spot. The thief who had followed, while the first was employed in digging the hole and burying the fish, climbed up the vacant stake and seated himself upon it. The first thief, when he had finished his business, by way of making sure, again came to the stakes, where he now saw also a man upon the fourth. Astonished at this, he thought at first that his eyesight must have deceived him, but on reflection becoming alarmed, he "exercised his wits to obtain certainty and cut the knot of such a mystery. First he felt the breast and temples of each criminal, that he might distinguish if they breathed, and find out the living from the dead. But they proved alike to his feeling, without the least difference. Overcome with surprise, he considered a while; then advancing to the suspicious stake, and holding for a full quarter of an hour the thief's nose, tried his breath. But the artful rogue so held his breath that it would have been impossible even for the finger of Afflatún (Plato) to perceive the motion of his veins. The first thief, after he had used all this trial and caution, according to the axiom, that the sword is the last resource, drawing a short sabre, struck it with all his force at the cheek of the second, who shrank not a hair's breadth or moved the least, though he received a severe wound. The first thief, now dismissing suspicion from his mind, became eased of apprehension, and, self-secure from mischief, went his way. Then the second thief descended from the stake, and going to the spot where the golden fish was buried, dug it up, and having deposited it in another place, bound up his wound and returned home." Next day it was proclaimed through the city: "A thief last night stole the king's fish set with jewels. Whosoever will recover it shall be distinguished by the royal favour, and may take the phœnix of riches in the snare of attainment." The first thief, having already discovered the trick that had been played upon him by some equally clever thief, went to the palace, and on condition of pardon, told everything, adding that the wound which he had inflicted on the face of the man on the stake would be the means of his detection. The king commanded the chief of police to afford him every assistance, and he set out to examine all the streets, and whenever he saw a surgeon visiting patients he insisted upon accompanying him in his rounds. At length he followed

the right person into the house of the thief, whose wound was fast healing, and caused him to be brought before the king, who had him
instantly executed.[15]

A different form of the legend is found in the 'Kathá Sarit Ságara': Two
thieves, Ghata and Karpara, one night break into the king's palace to
plunder his treasure-chamber; and while Ghata watches without, the
other enters the inner apartments, where he is seen by the king's daughter, who falls in love with him. She bestows on him much wealth in jewels and gold, which he passes out to his companion, and returns to the
princess, where he is surprised by the guards, and by the king's order led
off to execution. On the way, Ghata, who was alarmed at his friend's
absence, and had returned to look for him, sees him led to the gibbet.
Karpara, by secret signs, commends the princess to his care, and he, in
like manner, answers that he should effect her rescue. Accordingly at
night Ghata enters the palace, and releasing the princess from the fetters
with which she was bound, carries her off. When the king heard of this,
he concluded that it must have been the work of some accomplice of his
daughter's paramour. So he set a party of soldiers to watch the body of
Karpara, with orders to arrest any one that came thither lamenting, in
order to burn the corpse and perform other rites. Ghata, as the king had
anticipated, resolved to obtain the body of his friend, and so, disguising
himself as a drunken villager, with one of his servants dressed as a bride,
and another carrying a pot of sweetmeats, in which the narcotic juice of
the *dhatura* had been infused, he came reeling along past the guards,
entered into familiar conversation with them, and invited them to partake of his sweetmeats, of which they all ate, and were speedily stupefied.
He then took the body of Karpara and burnt it. When the king was
informed of this new exploit, he placed other guards to watch that no one
carried away the ashes; but Ghata by another device contrived this also,
and the king at length caused it to be proclaimed that he would give his
daughter and his kingdom to the man who had performed these clever
deeds. Ghata is persuaded, however, by the princess that no confidence is
to be placed in the king's word, and he departs with her and a religious
mendicant, by both of whom he is afterwards murdered.

ॐ

---

[15]Scott's translation of the 'Bahár-i Dánush,' vol. ii. pp. 225–248.

An interesting variant is current in Ceylon: A father and son are both very expert thieves. The son proposes to his father that they should steal the king's jewel-box, which was always kept, for safety, at the foot of his bed. There was a tunnel leading to the royal palace from a certain part of the town. It was only large enough for a man of ordinary size to creep through: when, by whom, and for what purpose this tunnel had been constructed, were facts quite unknown. At dead of night the father and son got into the tunnel, the former leading the way. Having entered the palace, the father's first care was to eat as much as his stomach could contain, after which he takes the casket, and, handing it to his son, whispers him to recede—the king and queen being still fast asleep. Then he began himself to creep back through the tunnel, but had not gone more than two or three cubits when he stuck fast—his stomach being so distended with food that he could neither get back nor forward; upon which he told his son to cut off his head, for if caught, he and his wife and the youth would be impaled alive. The son accordingly cuts off his father's head, and on his way home ties a heavy stone to it and throws it into the river. He acquaints his mother of the catastrophe, and the treasure is concealed. In the morning the headless body is discovered in the tunnel by the king's servants, and the casket is also missing. An old counsellor advises the king to cause the body to be drawn through the town, and to order every one, on pain of death, to be outside their houses when it passes; and on being seen by the wife, mother, or other relatives of the dead thief, they would give way to grief, and thus betray themselves. This was done accordingly, and the son planned with his mother that he should climb a tree, and just as the body came past, drop down, as if he fell by accident, when she should rush up to him, and her weeping would be mistaken for concern at his supposed injury by falling from the tree. The plan succeeded, and the king did not recover his jewels.[16]

The general likeness which these versions of the Robbery of the King's Treasury bear one to another is very striking, and some resemble others still more remarkably in the incidents. Thus, the king acts by the advice of a wise old man in 'Dolopathos,' the modern Greek, the Gaelic, Dutch, Tyrolese, Kabaïl, and Sinhalese; and the device of burning a straw-fire in the treasury occurs in 'Dolopathos,' Giovanni, the modern Greek, Dutch,

---

[16]'The Orientalist,' vol. i. pp. 56–61 (March, 1884).

and Kabaïl. The self-wounding of the hand occurs in the 'Seven Wise Masters,' the Breton, the Gaelic, and the Dutch. The stolen animal and the quest for some of its flesh is found in the Sicilian, the modern Greek,[17] Breton, Gaelic, Tyrolese, Kabaïl, and Bengalí. For the wine in Herodotus and several versions, we have whisky in the Gaelic, *ganj* in the Bengalí, and *dhatura* in the Sanskrit. There seems a close affinity between the modern Greek and the Kabaïl versions; for example, in one the woman, in viewing her husband's body, spills some glasses of sour milk to account for her lamentation, and in the other she spills oil; while in the Sinhalese version, the lad pretends to fall from a tree with the same purpose, when the body of his father is drawn past. For the child and the wreath in the Tibetan version we have more naturally the child and the apple in the Gaelic.[18] Many other points of resemblance are readily observable on a comparative analysis of the several versions.

The well-known Arabian tale of Ali Baba and the Forty Robbers also presents some analogy to our story: For the loose stone in the latter we have the magical "open sesame" and "shut sesame" in the former, which enable the poor woodcutter to enter the robber's cave and carry off assloads of gold: and the stealing of the avaricious brother's quartered body; the discovery, through the man who sewed the parts together, of Ali Baba's house; the marking of the door,—all bear some analogy to the exploits of the clever young treasury-thief, who foiled every attempt to entrap him.

Sir George Cox, in his 'Mythology of the Aryan Nations,' includes among parallels to, or variants of, the Robbery of the King's Treasury, the Adventure of the Poor Mason in Washington Irving's 'Tales of the Alhambra.' It seems to me the resemblance is very remote; but however this may be, Irving's story has its analogue in a Persian legend related by J. Baillie Fraser in his interesting 'Narrative of a Journey into Khorassam' (pp. 458, 459), regarding the founder of a medressa called Paen Pah.

[17]The fact of the animal being a camel in the modern Greek version indicates its Asiatic origin.

[18]It is a common notion in the East that a child instinctively knows its parents; hence in the Tibetan story the thief is readily recognised by his own offspring! The incident is much better related (according to European ideas) in the Gaelic version, where the child is to give the thief an apple, and the thief having provided himself with two things which amuse children, a carpenter's shaving and a musical instrument, the child naturally came up to him with its apple.

"There is a tradition," he says, "that the founder of this college, having, like other adventurers, gone to India [from Persia] in the hope of bettering his fortune, continued for a long time so unlucky that he was forced to solicit charity in the public streets. One day he was accosted by an old Hindú, who told him that, if he would submit to be blindfolded and led to his house, he would have work and good pay. The poor man, reflecting that his condition could not well be made worse, but might be improved, consented to the terms; and after a very circuitous course, his eyes being uncovered he found himself in a place surrounded by lofty walls, where he was ordered to dig a large hole, in which the Hindú buried a great quantity of gold mohurs and other money. This operation occupied several days, during which time he bethought himself of an expedient by which he might discover whither he had been conveyed. A cat came into the place, which he caught and killed; and stuffing the skin with gold, he took an opportunity, when not observed, to throw it over what he believed to be the boundary wall of the premises. He listened to the sound, and judged that it fell upon clay, or some moist substance. When his work was done, he received a present of a few rupís, was again blindfolded, and led to the place whence he had been brought. He immediately began to search for his cat, which, after some time, he found lying in a dirty pond beside a high wall, which he recognised for the enclosure of the Hindú's dwelling. The gold he thus obtained enabled him at the old man's death, which took place some time after, to purchase the house from his heir, and he thus became possessed of the wealth which the Hindoo had buried. With this he returned to Persia, and with a portion of it he built this college."

Irving's tale is to this effect: There was once in Grenada a mason who, in spite of his piety, grew poorer and poorer, and could hardly earn bread for his family. One night he was roused from sleep by a knocking at the door, and on opening it beheld a lean, cadaverous-looking priest, who asked him if he would undertake a job, for which he would be well paid, but he must submit to be blindfolded. The mason willingly consented to this proposal, and after being hoodwinked, was led through many tortuous passages to the portal of a house, which the priest opened with a key, and when they had entered, again locked and bolted. When the bandage was taken from his eyes, the mason found himself in a spacious hall, in the centre of which was the dry basin of a Moorish fountain, beneath which the priest desired him to form a small vault, bricks and mortar being at hand for the purpose. The mason worked all night, and being again blindfolded was conducted back to his own house, promising to return next night and complete the job, which having done, the priest asked him to help him to bury some dead bodies in the vault. Trembling with terror, the mason followed the priest, but was relieved to find, instead of ghastly corpses, a number of jars in a corner, which, from their weight, were evidently filled with money. The jars were conveyed into the vault, which was then closed, and all traces of the work removed: the priest gave the mason two pieces of gold, and having blindfolded him again, he conducted him out of the house. Years passed on, and still the mason continued poor. One day a man, who was known to be the owner of many houses in Grenada, came to him, saying he wanted to repair an old house that was fallen into decay. On entering the house, the mason recognised the Moorish fountain in the hall, and inquired of the landlord who had formerly lived there. "An old miserly priest," quoth he, "who died suddenly; and when the friars came to take away his wealth, they found only a few ducats in his purse. The people say that his ghost haunts the house, and that they often hear him clinking his gold: whether this be true or false, no tenant will remain here." The mason offered to keep the house in repair, if allowed to live in it rent-free, to which the landlord gladly consented. So the mason removed to it with his family, and soon increased in wealth, of which he gave largely to the church, and on his deathbed revealed the secret of the vault to his son.

The only points of resemblance which I can discover between this tale and that of Rhampsinitus' Treasury, as related by Herodotus, are, the vault in the former, and the loose stone in the latter,—but the Spanish mason had no clue to the vault; and in both, the father's revealing the secret to his son on his deathbed. I am disposed to consider Irving's story as a Spanish survival of some Moorish legend, of which the tradition related by Baillie Fraser seems a variant.

NOTE

MARKING A CULPRIT (p. 341)

This device is often met with in popular stories. In Nov. 2, Day III, of the 'Decameron,' King Agiluf, having ascertained that one of his household had been with the queen, goes into the gallery where they all slept, and discovering the guilty person by the palpitation of his heart, in order to distinguish him in the morning, cuts off a lock of his hair above the ear; but the groom escapes punishment by clipping off a corresponding lock from the heads of all his companions.

Boccaccio probably derived this idea from some Eastern story; at all events, a similar incident is found in a collection of Canarese tales, entitled 'Kathá Manjarí,' which was published, with an English translation, at Bangalore, in 1841: A merchant, who was travelling on business, put up one night at a lodging-house. While he slept, some one stole from him a jewel which he had tied up in his cloth. He awoke in the night, and missing the jewel, thought he might ascertain who had stolen it, by feeling at every one's breast, and seeing whose heart palpitated the hardest. He did so, and finding one man amongst them whose heart beat rapidly, he cut off the knot of his hair, that he might know him next day, and again went to sleep. The fellow whose hair he had cut awoke also, and discovering what had been done to him, cut off the knot of hair from every one in the place, that all should be alike. The merchant was, of course, ignorant of this, and arose early in the morning, and desired the landlord to search for the thief, and apprehend the man whose knot of hair was cut off, as he was the person who had stolen the jewel. Accordingly he roused all who were asleep, and on looking at their heads found that all had been deprived of their knots of hair, consequently the thief was unknown. He then took them before the magistrate, to whom the affair was related. The magistrate suspected that the thief must be a tailor, as the hair had been cut off with much exactness; so he asked each man what his business was, and apprehended and punished the man who said he was a tailor, who gave up the jewel, and the merchant was dismissed.

The marking of the door of Ali Baba's house by the leader of the Forty Thieves, in the well-known Arabian story, and Ali's clever servant Morgiana's marking similarly all the other houses in the street, has been already referred to as a parallel to the incident in versions of the 'Treasury' legend; and the same device is adopted in the Albanian tale of the Wonderful Box, No. 13 of M. Dozon's collection; and in the German story of the Blue Light, an attempt made to discover the house of the hero by scattering peas all the way thither is frustrated by the "slave" of the Blue Light scattering peas in all the other streets of the city.

⟡ LLEWELLYN AND HIS DOG GELLERT, OR KILLHART ⟡

IN his 'Curious Myths of the Middle Ages,' Mr Baring-Gould has conclusively shown that the tradition of Llewellyn and his faithful hound—so glibly related to credulous tourists in North Wales by the officious guides, who show, moreover, the very grave of the dog Gellert, or Killhart—has no more foundation in fact than the story of William Tell's shooting at an apple on his son's head. I purpose, in the present paper, going somewhat more fully into the literary history of this widely-diffused tale, tracing it, if not to its original, at least to an older form than is referred to in Mr Baring-Gould's useful and interesting work.

The Dog Gellert.

"There is a general tradition in North Wales," says Edward Jones, in his 'Musical Relics of the Welsh Bards,' vol. i., "that a wolf had entered the house of Prince Llewellyn. Soon after, the prince returned home, and going into the nursery, he met his dog Killhart all bloody and wagging his tail at him. Prince Llewellyn, on entering the room, found the cradle where his child lay overturned and the floor strewed with blood. Imagining that the greyhound had killed the child, he immediately drew his sword and stabbed it; then turning up the cradle, found under it the child alive, and the wolf dead. This so grieved the prince that he erected a tomb over the faithful dog's grave, where afterwards the parish church was built, and goes by the name Bedd Gelhart (the Grave of Killhart), in Caernarvonshire. From this incident is derived a very common Welsh proverb, 'I repent as much as the man who slew his greyhound.' "Prince Llewellyn ab Jowerth," adds our author, "married Joan, a daughter of King John, by Agatha, daughter of Robert Ferrers, Earl of Derby, and this dog was a present to the prince from his father-in-law, about the year 1205."[1]

---

[1] The legend of Gellert has been finely versified by Mr Spencer: when Llewellyn had slain the faithful dog and immediately after discovered his child unhurt—

Ah, what was then Llewellyn's pain!
　　For now the truth was clear:
The gallant hound the wolf had slain,
　　To save Llewellyn's heir.

Such is the Welsh tradition; but the story was current in Europe, with a snake instead of a wolf, before Prince Llewellyn was presented with his faithful hound. It is the first tale in the oldest Latin prose version of 'The Seven Wise Masters,' entitled 'Dolopathos; sive, de Rege et Septem Sapientibus,' written by Johannes, a monk of the Abbey of Alta Silva (Dan Jehans of Haute Seille), in France, about the year 1184. Nearly a century previous to that date—*circa* 1090—it had existed in 'Syntipas,' a Greek version of the Book of Sindibád, the Eastern prototype of 'The Seven Wise Masters'; and it is probable that it was current orally at a much earlier period. From the Latin 'Dolopathos,' or from oral tradition, the story was taken into subsequent versions of the Wise Masters, and also into the 'Gesta Romanorum.'[2] It reappears in the 'Historia Septem

> Here never could the spearman pass,
>   Or forester, unmoved;
> Here oft the tear-besprinkled grass
>   Llewellyn's sorrow proved.
>
> And here he flung his horn and spear,
>   And oft as evening fell,
> In fancy's piercing sounds would hear
>   Poor Gellert's dying yell.

Vain, vain was all Llewellyn's woe:
    "Best of thy kind, adieu!
The frantic deed which laid thee low
    This heart shall ever rue."

And now a gallant tomb they raise,
    With costly sculpture decked;
And marbles storied with his praise
    Poor Gellert's bones protect.

[2] The story also occurs in the 'Liber de Donis' of Etienne de Bourbon (No. 370). "After giving a version of this story, which has become in several places a local legend, Etienne proceeds to say that the dog was considered as a martyr, and its grave was visited by the sick, just like the shrines of wonder-working saints. Sick children especially were brought to the place, and made to pass nine times through an aperture formed in the trunks of two trees growing over the hound's grave, while various pagan rites were performed, and the child was finally left naked at the foot of the tree until two candles an inch long were consumed. Etienne, by virtue of his office as inquisitor [of heresy in the south of France], had the dog exhumed, its bones burnt, and the grove cut down."—Professor T. F. Crane: 'Mediæval Sermon-Books and Stories.'

'Sapientum Romæ,' from which was derived our English version of the 'History of the Seven Wise Masters of Rome,' first printed by Wynkyn de Worde, about 1505, and reprinted by W. Copland, about 1550. And here I may remark that Sir G. Dasent, following Des Longchamps and others, is in error when he states, in the introduction to his 'Popular Tales from the Norse,' pp. lxi, lxii, that the 'Historia Septem Sapientum Romæ' was derived from the work of Dan Jehans, that is, the Latin 'Dolopathos.' These two works are very different: In 'Dolopathos' there are eight sub-ordinate stories, seven of which are related by the Wise Masters, and the eighth by the prince's tutor; in the 'Historia' there are fifteen stories, seven by the Wise Men, seven by the queen, and one by the prince, and only three of these—the Snake, the King's Treasury, and the Husband Shut Out—are found in 'Dolopathos.' Moreover, the 'Historia' was not composed till after the invention of printing (say, in the latter years of the fifteenth century), while the French 'Roman des Sept Sages,' written about 1284, has all the tales save one which are found in the 'Historia,' and *that* one does not occur in 'Dolopathos.'

The story of the Dog and the Snake is thus related in a black-letter copy of the 'Seven Wise Masters,' preserved in the Glasgow University Library:

The Knight and the Greyhound

There was a certain valiant knight which had only one son, the which he loved so much, that he ordained for his keepers three nourishers (*i.e.*, nurses). The first should give him suck, and feed him; the second should wash him, and keep him clean; and the third should bring him to his sleep and rest. The knight had also a greyhound and a falcon, which he also loved right well. The greyhound was so good that he never run at any game, but he took it and held it till his master came. And if his master disposed him to go into any battel, if he should not speed therein, anone as he should mount upon his horse, the greyhound would take the horse-tail in his mouth, and draw backward, and would also howl and cry marvellouslie loud. By these signs, and the due observation thereof, the knight did always understand that his journey should have very ill success. The falcon was so gentle and hardy, that he was never cast off to his prey but he took it. The same knight had much pleasure in justing and tourney, so that upon a time under his castle he proclaimed a tournament, to the which came many great lords and knights. The knight entered into the tourney, and his ladie went with her maidens to see it: and as they went out, after went the nourishers, and left the child lying alone there in the cradle in the hall, where the greyhound lay near the wall, and the hawk or falcon standing upon a perch. In this hall there was a serpent lurking, or hid in a hole, to all of them in the castle unknown, the which when he perceived that they were all absent, he put his head out of the hole, and when he saw none but the child lying in the cradle, he went out of his hole towards the cradle, for to have slain the child. The noble falcon perceiving that, made such a noise and rustling with her wings presently, that the greyhound awoke and rose up: and when he saw the serpent nigh the child, anone against him he leapt, and they both fought so long together, until that the serpent had grievously hurt and wounded the greyhound, that he bled so sore, that the earth about the cradle was all bloody. The greyhound, when that he felt himself grievously hurt and wounded, starts fiercely upon the serpent, and fought so sore together, and so eagerly, that between them the cradle was overcast with the child, the bottome upward. And because that the cradle had four pomels like feet falling towards the earth, they saved the child's life and his visage from any hurt. What can be more exprest to make good the wonder in the preservation of the child? Incontinently thereafter, with great pain the greyhound overcame and slew the serpent, and laid him down again in his place and licked his wounds. And anon after the justs and turney was done, the nourishers came first into the castle, and as they saw the cradle turned upside down upon the earth, compassed round about with blood, and that the greyhound was also bloody, they thought and said among themselves that the greyhound had slain the child, and were not so wise as to turn up the cradle again with the child, for to have seen what was thereof befallen; but they said, Let us run away, lest that our master should put or lay any blame upon us, and so slay us. As they were thus running away, they met the knight's wife, and she said unto them, Wherefore make ye this sorrow, and whither will ye run? Then said they, O lady, wo and sorrow be to us, and to you. Why, said she, what is there happened? show me. The greyhound, they said, that our lord and master loved so well, hath devoured and slain your son, and lyeth by the wall all full of blood. As the lady heard this she presently fell to the earth, and began to weep and cry piteouslie, and said, Alace, O my dear son, are ye slain and dead? What shall I now do, that I have mine only son thus lost? Wherewithal came in the knight from the tourney, and beholding his lady thus crying and making sorrow, he demanded of her wherefore she made so great sorrow and lamentation. She answered him, O my lord, that greyhound that you have loved so much hath slain your only son, and lyeth by the wall, satiated with the blood of the child. The knight, very exceeding angry, went into the hall, and the greyhound went to meet him, and did fawn upon him, as he was wont to do, and the knight drew out his sword, and with one stroke smote off the greyhound's head, and then went to the cradle where the child lay and found his son all whole, and by the cradle the serpent slain; and then by diverse signs he perceived that the greyhound had killed the serpent for the defence of the child. Then with great sorrow and weeping he tare his hair, and said, Wo be to me, that for the words of my wife I have slain my good and best greyhound, the which hath saved my child's life, and hath slain the serpent, therefore I will put myself to penance. And so he brake his sword in three pieces, and went towards the Holy Land, and abode all the days of his life.

How many generations, "gentle and simple," old and young, have pored over, or listened to, this story of the Knight and his Greyhound! In the pedlar's pack, among his stock of ballads and chap-books, the 'History of the Seven Wise Masters of Rome' was never wanting; and the reading of it aloud by the "farmer's ingle" has cheered many a winter's night. Görres, in his 'Folksbucher,' bestows extraordinary praise on this Book of the Seven Sages. "It sprang originally," says he, "from the Indian mountains, whence from primeval days it took its course as a little rivulet, and flowed in a westerly direction through Asia's wide field, and, while it proceeded for thousands of years through space and time, always spreading more and more in reaching us. Out of it whole generations and many nations have drank; and, having passed to Europe with the great tide of population, is now also in our day and generation supplied to such a considerable portion of the public, that in regard to its celebrity and the magnitude of its sphere of influence, it reaches the Holy Book, and surpasses all classical works." But there is much exaggeration in all these fine phrases. It is utterly absurd to assert that the tales of the Seven Sages are as old as the Aryans in Europe. There are no grounds for supposing the original Indian work to date much farther back than two thousand years.

The story of the Dog and the Snake occurs in all the Western group of the Book of Sindibád, known commonly as the Seven Wise Masters; and of Eastern texts, or versions directly derived from Eastern texts, it is found in the Syriac, Persian, Greek, Hebrew, Latin (the 'Directorium Humanæ Vitæ' of John of Capua), and the Old Spanish, translated from an Arabic version, now lost. It does not occur in the modern Arabic version (the Seven Vazírs) which is incorporated with the 'Book of the Thousand and One Nights.' In the Persian metrical version, 'Sindibád Náma,' written in 1374, but representing probably a much earlier text, of which a unique, but unfortunately imperfect, MS. copy is preserved in the library of the India Office, a cat is substituted for a dog, and the following is an abstract of the story as related in this text:

The Snake and the Cat

In a city of Cathay there dwelt a good and blameless woman and her husband, who was an officer of the king. By-and-by she bore him a son, and thereupon died, and the officer procured a nurse to bring up the child. Now he had a cat, of which he was very fond, and to which his wife had also been very much attached. One day he went out on some business, and the nurse also had left the house, no one remaining but the infant and the cat. Presently a frightful snake came in and made for the cradle to devour the child. The cat sprang upon it, and after a desperate fight succeeded in killing it. When the man returned, he was horrified at seeing a mangled mass lying on the floor. The snake had vomited so much blood and poison that its form was hidden, and the man, thinking that the cat, which came up to him, rubbing against his legs, had killed his son, struck it a blow, and slew it on the spot. But immediately after he discovered the truth of the matter, how the poor cat had killed the snake in defence of the boy, and his grief knew no bounds.

But we have a much older form of the story in the Sanskrit collection of tales and apologues entitled 'Panchatantra' (five sections), which, according to Dr H. H. Wilson, bears internal evidence of having been composed not later than the fifth century, as follows (sect. v. fab. 2):

The Snake and the Ichneumon

There was a Bráhman, named Déva Sarmá, whose wife had one son; she had also a favourite ichneumon that she brought up with the infant, and cherished like another child. At the same time she was afraid that the animal would, some time or other, do the child a mischief, knowing its treacherous nature, as it is said, "A son, though ill-tempered, ugly, stupid, and wicked, is still the source of delight to a father's heart." One day the mother, going forth to fetch water, placed the child in the bed, and desired her husband to guard the infant, especially from the ichneumon. She then departed, and after a while the Bráhman himself was obliged to go forth to collect alms. When the house was thus deserted, a black snake came out of a hole, and crawled towards the bed where the infant lay: the ichneumon, who saw him, impelled by his natural animosity, and by regard for his foster-brother, instantly attacked him, and after a furious encounter, tore him to pieces. Pleased with his prowess and the service he had rendered, he ran to meet his mistress on her return home, his jaws and face besmeared with blood. As soon as the Bráhman's wife beheld him, she was convinced that he had killed her child, and in her rage and agitation she threw the water-jar at the ichneumon with all her force, and killed him on the spot. She then rushed into the house, where she found the child still asleep, and the body of a venomous snake torn in pieces at the foot of the bed. She then perceived the error she had committed, and beat her breast and face with grief for the unmerited fate of her faithful little favourite. In this state her husband found her on his return. When he had told her the cause of his absenting himself, she reproached him bitterly for that greedy desire of profit which had caused all the mischief.[3]

In this Sanskrit version, it will be observed, the mother is represented as avenging the supposed death of her child; [4] and instead of reproaching

[3]Near akin to the story of the Bráhman and the Ichneumon is that of the King and his Falcon, which is found in the 'Anvár-i-Suhaylí;' or Lights of Canopus, a Persian version of the Fables of Bidpaï, composed by Husain Vaïz. In this tale a king, while hawking, chanced to ride ahead of his followers, and feeling thirsty, he sought about for water. Coming to the foot of a mountain, he discovered water slowly trickling from a rock, and taking a little cup from his quiver, he held it to catch the drops as they fell. When the cup was full, and the king was about to drink, his hawk flapped his wings so as to spill the water, and this occurring a second time, the king in a rage dashed the bird to the ground, and it instantly expired. It was afterwards found that a monstrous serpent lay dead at the fountain-head, and his poisonous foam was mingling with the water. The king then reflected on the evils of precipitancy and thoughtlessness, and during the remainder of his life the arrow of regret was continually rankling in his breast.—A variant of this is interwoven in No. 9 of Lal Behari Day's 'Folk-Tales of Bengal,' p. 154, in which a king, hunting in a dense forest and becoming very thirsty, looks about for water, and at last saw something dripping from the top of a tree. Thinking it to be rain-water which had fallen into a cavity of the tree, he stood up on the back of his horse and caught the drops in a small cup. But it was not rain-water. His horse knew better. A huge cobra on the top of the tree was dashing its fangs against it, and its poison was falling in drops. And when the king was about to drink from the cup, the horse, to save his master, so moved about that the cup fell from his hand to the ground. The king with his sword struck the horse on the neck, and killed his faithful steed.

[4]In a Sinhalese variant, it is a widowed mother who leaves her child alone in the house, while she pounds rice for her wealthy neighbours.

her husband for his "greedy desire of gain," she should rather have blamed her own precipitation. In the 'Seven Wise Masters,' the man bitterly blames himself for having listened to the words of his wife. In the 'Hitopadesa' (Friendly Advice), an abridgment of the 'Panchatantra'—though it has a number of tales peculiar to itself—the woman leaves the house to make her ablutions, and during her absence the rájá sends for her husband to perform for him some religious rite. The Persian 'Sindibád' Náma is the only version in which the mother is represented as having died in giving birth to her child. It is a *dog* that kills the snake in the Syriac, Greek, Hebrew, and Old Castilian versions, and also in the 'Seven Wise Masters.' In the 'Panchatantra' it is a *mungoose,* or *ichneumon;* and in the 'Hitopadesa' it is a *weasel,* of which the ichneumon is a species. "The fierce hostility of the mungoose to snakes," says Dr H. H. Wilson, "and its singular power of killing them, are in India so well known as to have become proverbial, and are verifiable by daily observation. It is doubtful," he adds, "if a dog has either any instinctive enmity to snakes, or any characteristic dexterity in destroying them."

A very curious example of the modifications which a written story sometimes undergoes after it has once more passed into oral tradition, is furnished in the following version of the Snake and Mungoose story, current among the natives of the North-West Provinces, from 'Past Days in India':

Current Indian Version

In a certain village there lived a poor family, consisting of the man and his wife and several children. One day, when her husband and elder children had gone out to work and the younger ones to play, the mother put her infant son on the ground, and by his side she placed a *thálee* (a metal plate of different sizes, having a deep rim of half an inch, or an inch) of water to amuse himself with, while she went about some necessary household duties. Before setting about cleaning the rice and so forth in the adjoining room, as they had a tame mungoose about the house, she caught and tied it up not far from the child, thinking that if loose it might hurt the boy. When the mother had left the room, a cobra-snake, hearing the splashing of the water, came out of its hole to have a drink. The little child, not knowing what it was, stopped playing with the water, intently watching the snake as it came up and began to drink. Having satisfied its thirst, the reptile was gliding back to its hole, when the little innocent put out its hands and caught it, thinking to amuse himself with the pretty new toy. The snake made no resistance, and in turn amused itself with twining in and out of the boy's arms and legs, until somehow the child accidentally hurt the snake, when it turned round and bit him in the neck. On feeling the bite, the child let go of the snake, and very soon became motionless, the snake gliding off to its hole. The mungoose, directly the snake (which is its natural enemy) came out of its hole, began making fruitless efforts to break the string with which it was tied, and failing in that, succeeded in biting the string through, just as the snake had slipped into its hole. Having seen what the snake did to the child, the mungoose ran off quickly into the jungle to get some snake-root.

Meanwhile the mother, alarmed at his unusual silence, coming into the room at that moment, and seeing the child motionless, ran and took him up and tried her best to restore animation, crying heartily all the time. Having found the antidote, the mungoose ran back quickly with it in his mouth into the room, and the mother, turning her head in that direction, seeing the mungoose loose, and having remarked a wound on the child's neck, immediately concluded that the mungoose had bitten and killed her little son. Without reflecting a moment, she seized the mungoose, and in a rage dashed it on the ground with all her strength. After one or two convulsive motions the pet mungoose died, and then, too late, the mother discovered something in the animal's mouth, and, examining it closer, recognised the snake-root. Intuitively divining all the circumstances, she instantly reduced the root to powder, and administering it to the child at once, had the happiness of seeing her darling returning to consciousness. The mungoose having been a great pet with all the children, the news of its death caused general grief, to no one more than the mother, who resolved never to let her anger master her again.[5]

Thus far we have traced the Welsh tradition of the Dog Gellert to an ancient Sanskrit source, and we can even go a step farther, and show that

---

[5] "The natives of India," adds the author, "have an idea that when the mungoose, in its encounter with a snake, happens to be bitten by it, it immediately runs off in search of an antidote to counteract the virulent poison of the snake. This supposed antidote, the root of a plant, hence called snake-root, is regarded by all classes of the natives as a certain specific against snake-bite. That it is a foolish belief is proved by continual failure."—This version is also given in Vermieux' collection of Indian Tales appended to his story of 'The Hermit of Motee Jhurna' (second edition, pp. 101, 102).

371

the story is of Buddhist origin, dating from before Christ. But first I shall take leave to correct some errors which Mr Baring-Gould has unaccountably fallen into, in the following passage, referring to this story:

"It occurs in the 'Seven Wise Masters' and in the Calumnia Novercalis' as well, so that it must have been popular throughout medieval Europe. Now the tales of the Seven Wise Masters are translations from a Hebrew work, the 'Kalilah and Dimnah' of Rabbi Joel, composed about 1250, or from Simeon Seth's Greek 'Kylile and Dimne,' written in 1080. These Greek and Hebrew works were derived from kindred sources. That of Rabbi Joel was a translation from an Arabic version made by Nasr-Allah in the twelfth century, whilst Simeon Seth's was a translation of the Persian 'Kalilah and Dimnah.' But the 'Kalilah and Dimnah' was not either an original work; it was in turn a translation from the Sanskrit 'Panchatantra,' made about 540."[6]

These statements are very misleading. The 'Calumnia Novercalis' is a Latin version of the 'Seven Wise Masters.' But to say that the tales of the Seven Wise Masters are translations from a Hebrew work, the 'Kalilah and Dimna' of Rabbi Joel, or from Simeon Seth's Greek 'Kylile and Dimne,' is absolutely incorrect. 'Kalíla and Dimna' is the title of the Arabic version of the Fables of Bidpaï, or Pilpay. The history of this remarkable work is briefly as follows: About the year 531 a Sanskrit collection of tales and fables was translated into Pahlaví, the ancient language of Persia, under the title of 'Kalílag and Damnag,' the names of two jackals that play leading parts in the first section. From Pahlavi, the work was translated into Syriac, about 570, and into Arabic, under the title of 'Kalíla and Dimna,' by Ibn-Almukaffa, about the year 754. From the Arabic a Greek translation, entitled 'Ichnelates and Stephanites,' was made by Simeon the son of Seth, in 1080. Two Hebrew translations were made from the Arabic or Syriac, both in the thirteenth century, one of which is anonymous, the other is by Rabbi Joel. And here we come to another gross inaccuracy: Rabbi Joel's version was *not* "a translation from an Arabic version made by Nasr-Allah in the twelfth century." The work of Nasr-'ulláh was a *Persian* translation from the Arabic, made in 1168. But in the concluding sentence of the above-cited passage Mr Baring-Gould has contrived to reach a climax of confusion: "Simeon Seth's [Greek version] was a translation of the Persian 'Kalilah and Dimnah.' But the 'Kalilah and

[6]'Curious Myths of the Middle Ages,' p. 138.

Dimnah' was not either an original work; it was in turn a translation from the Sanskrit 'Panchatantra,' made about 540." The 'Panchatantra' was *not* the Sanskrit work translated into Pahlaví (called Persian by Mr Baring-Gould), although it is the oldest extant Sanskrit form of the Fables as a separate work; and the Pahlavi text, which was translated into Arabic, is now lost.[7] How Mr Baring-Gould could derive the tales of the 'Seven Wise Masters' from any version of the Fables of Bidpaï is matter for profound wonder: with exception of the story of the Snake and another, the Fables of Bidpaï are quite different from the Tales of the Wise Masters. I have thought it advisable to correct such misleading statements, since the work in which they are found ('Myths of the Middle Ages') is so generally read and esteemed as reliable for the information it affords regarding the popular legends and fictions of which it treats.

The learned Benfey has pointed out the Buddhist origin of the tales and apologues in the 'Panchatantra,' and in the case of the story of the Snake and the Ichneumon, the proof seems conclusive. Dr S. Beal, of the British Museum, published in 'The Academy' for Nov. 4, 1882, the following translation of a version from the 'Vinaya Pitaka' of the Chinese Buddhist collection of books:

The Bráhman and the Nakula.

In years gone by there was a certain Bráhman who, being very poor, had to beg daily for food enough to keep him alive. This Bráhman's wife had borne him no child, but there was a young Na-ku-lo (Nakula, or mungoose) in the house, of which the master had made a pet, as if it was his own son. After this, it came to pass that the wife of the Bráhman bore him a son, on which he thought thus: "Certainly it was lucky for me when I took this mungoose as my child, for, in consequence of this, my wife has borne me a child." Now on one occasion, the Bráhman wishing to leave home to beg some food, enjoined on his wife, if she went out, to be sure to take the child with her, and not to loiter about, but return home quickly. It happened, however, that, having fed the child, she went to grind at the mill,[8] and forgot to take the baby. In her absence a snake,

[7] See Professor Max Müller's 'Chips from a German Workshop,' vol. iv. pp. 145–209; and the introduction to the Hon. Keith Falconer's English translation of the later Syriac text of 'Kalíla and Dimna.'

[8] See p. 369, note 4.

attracted by the smell of the cream which the child had eaten, came towards the spot, and was about to kill it with its fang, when the mungoose, seeing the danger, thought thus with itself: "My father has gone out and my mother, and now this poisonous snake would kill my little brother;" and so it is said:

> The poisonous snake and the nakula,
> The little (flying) bird and the hawk,
> The Shaman and the Bráhman,
> The step-mother and the child of a former wife—
> All these are mutually opposed and at enmity,
> And desire, as with poison, to destroy one another.

At this time the mungoose attacked the poisonous snake and killed it, and tore it into seven pieces. Then the mungoose thus thought: "I have killed the snake, and preserved the child. I ought to acquaint my father and mother of this, and rejoice their hearts." So he went out of the door and stood there, with his mouth covered with blood. At this time the Bráhman, coming home, saw his wife in the outside house [where the mill was] without the child. On this he was angry, and expostulated with her. And now, as he entered the door, he saw the mungoose there with his mouth covered with blood. On this he thought: "Alas, this creature, being hungry, has slain and eaten the child!" Whereupon, taking up a stick, he beat the mungoose to death. On entering his house, he saw the little child sitting upright in his cradle and playing with his fingers, while the dead snake in seven pieces lay by his side. Beholding this, he was filled with sorrow, and said: "Alas, for my folly! This faithful creature has preserved the life of my child, and I have hastily, and without consideration, killed it!"

Dr Beal considers this as probably the oldest form of the 'Panchatantra' story. The Chinese book from which it is rendered dates, he says, from the time of Fa-hien (A.D. 412), who translated it from an Indian original, which he had procured at Patáliputra, where it was supposed to date from the time of Asoka's Council, say, B.C. 230.—And now we may leave the Welsh guides to continue to recite their veritable story of Prince Llewellyn and his Faithful Hound!

❧ THE LOVER'S HEART ❧

THE ninth novel of the fourth Day of Boccaccio's 'Decameron' is a ghastly story of a jealous husband's revenge: Two noble gentlemen, who were intimate friends, lived in neighbouring estates in Provence. The name of one was Gulielmo Rossillione, that of the other Gulielmo Guardastagno. At length the former, suspecting that a criminal intercourse subsisted between his wife and his friend, invited him to his residence, but waylaid and murdered him in a wood, through which the road between the two castles passed. He then opened the breast of his victim, drew out his heart, and carried it home, wrapped in the pennon of his lance. When he alighted from his horse, he gave it to his cook as the heart of a wild boar, commanding him to dress it with his utmost skill, and serve it up for supper. At table the husband pretended want of appetite, and the lady ate the whole of the monstrous repast. When not a fragment was left, he informed her that she had feasted on the heart of Guardastagno. The lady, declaring that no other food should profane the relics of so noble a knight, threw herself from a casement which was behind her, and was dashed to pieces in the fall.

Dunlop, who gives the foregoing outline of the story in his 'History of Fiction,' remarks that some of the commentators on Boccaccio have supposed it to be taken from the well-known story of Raoul de Couci; "but as Boccaccio himself informs us that his tale is given according to the relation of the Provençals ('secondo de che raconti i Provenzals'), it seems probable that it was taken from the story of the Provençal poet Cabestan, which is told by Nostradamus in his 'Lives of the Troubadours.' Besides, the story of Cabestan possesses a much closer resemblance to the novel of Boccaccio than the fiction concerning Raoul de Couci and the lady of Du Fayel. Indeed it precisely corresponds with the 'Decameron,' except in the names, and in the circumstance that the lady starves herself instead of leaping from the window." It will be seen from the following version of the story of De Couci, from Bougier's 'Historical Memoirs of Champagne,' that it varies considerably from Boccaccio's tale:

The Lord de Couci, vassal to the Count de Champagne, was one of the most accomplished youths of his time. He loved with an excess of passion the lady of the Lord du Fayel, who felt a reciprocal affection. With the most poignant grief, his lady heard from her lover that he had resolved to accompany the king and the Count de Champagne to the wars in the Holy Land; but she would not oppose his wishes, because she hoped that his absence might dissipate the jealousy of her husband. The time of departure having come, these two lovers parted with sorrows of the most lively tenderness. The lady, in quitting her lover, presented him with some rings and diamonds, and with a string of her own hair, intermixed with silk and buttons of large pearls, to serve him, according to the fashion of those days, to tie a magnificent hood which covered his helmet. In Palestine, at the siege of Acre, in 1191, De Couci, in gloriously ascending the ramparts, received a wound which was declared mortal. He employed the few moments he had to live in writing to the Lady du Fayel; and he poured forth the fervour of his soul. He ordered his squire to embalm his heart after his death, and to convey it to his beloved mistress, with the presents he had received from her hands on quitting her. The squire, faithful to the dying injunction of his master, returned to France, to present the heart and gifts to the Lady du Fayel. But when he approached the castle of the lady, he concealed himself in the neighbouring wood, watching some favourable moment to complete his promise. He had the misfortune to be seen by the husband of the lady, who recognised him, and immediately suspected he came in search of his wife with some message from his master. He threatened to deprive him of his life if he did not divulge the occasion of his return. The squire assured him that his master was dead; but Du Fayel, not believing it, drew his sword on him. The squire, frightened at the peril in which he found himself, confessed everything, and put into his hands the heart and the letter of his master. Du Fayel was maddened by the fellest passions, and he took a wild and horrid revenge. He ordered his cook to mince the heart, and having mixed it with meat, he caused a ragout, which he knew pleased the taste of his wife, to be made, and had it served to her. The lady ate heartily of the dish. After the repast, Du Fayel inquired if she had found the ragout according to her taste, and she answered that she had found it excellent. "It is for that reason that I caused it to be served to you, for it is a kind of meat which you very much liked. You have, madam," continued the savage Du Fayel, "eaten the heart of the Lord de Couci." But this the lady would not believe till he showed her the letter of her lover, with the string of her hair and the diamonds she had given him. Shuddering in the anguish of her sensations, and urged by the utmost despair, she said to him, "It is true that I loved that heart; for never could it find its superior. And since I have eaten of so noble a meat, and my stomach is the tomb of so precious a heart, I will take care that nothing of inferior worth shall ever be mixed with it." Grief and passion choked her utterance. She retired to her chamber; she closed the door for ever; and refusing to accept of consolation or food, the amiable victim expired on the fourth day.[1]

The story was the subject of an English chap-book in the last century: "The Constant but Unhappy Lovers; being a full and true Relation of one Madam Butler, a young Gentlewoman, and a great Heiress, at Hackney Boarding School, who, being forced by her father to marry Mr Harvey, a Rich Merchant's Son, near Fanchurch Street, against her Will, one Per-point, a young Gentleman of Considerable Estate, who had courted her above two years, grew so Discontented that he went a Volunteer to the Wars in Spain, where being Mortally Wounded, at the Battle of Almanza, he writ a Letter with his own Blood, therein putting a Bracelet of Madam Butler's Hair, and then ordering his Servant to bake his Heart to powder, after his death, he charged him to deliver them in a Box to the above-said Gentle-woman. His man came to England, and went on the 6th June to deliver the Present to Madame Butler, but it was took away by her Husband, who gave her the Powder in a Dish of Tea; which when she knew what she had Drank, and saw the bloody Letter and Bracelet, she said it was the last she would ever Eat and Drink, and accordingly going to Bed, she was found dead in the Morning, with a copy of verses lying by her on a Table, written with her own Blood (London: Printed by E. B., near Ludgate, 1707)."

It is probable the story was brought to Europe by the Crusaders, or by pilgrims returned from the Holy Land, whither it may have migrated from India, through Persia, since it is a very old and favourite legend in the Panjáb, where it is still recited by the Bháts, or minstrels, of Rasálú, son of Rájá Sálbúhan, *circa* A.D. 78. Rájá Rasálú is to the Panjáb what Antar is to Arabia, Rústam to Persia, and Arthur to England. The fol-lowing version is from a little work by General James Abbott, printed, for private circulation, at Calcutta, in 1851:

Rasálú educated the young Rání Kokilán,[2] apart from her father, and at an early age married her. The rájá, however, proposed to himself a life of rigorous self-denial and hardihood, without reflecting upon the claims a young wife possesses on the tenderness and attention of her husband. Left alone in his palace of Múrut (since so-called), whilst he followed

---

[1] Cited in D'Israeli's 'Curiosities of Literature.'

[2] Queen Cooing-Dove. Kokilán (Kokla is her name in some versions) may be interpreted as cuckoo, cooing-dove, or simply darling, according to Captain R. C. Temple, in an inter-esting paper on Legends of Rájá Rasálú in the 'Calcutta Review' for 1884.

the chase at Dumtúr, and little cherished or fondled on his return, a dangerous void was left in her young and inexperienced heart. The Rájá Hodí-who seems to have resided in Sohat, Peshawar, and the Yúsúfzaie, and whose castle is still shown on the hill opposite Attuk, Trans-Indus—whether allured by her reputation for beauty, or accidentally led thither, came to Múrut to hunt or hawk. He saw the Rání Kokilán looking from the window of her palace, and was violently enamoured of her. She saw him, and he took the place which Rasálú had left vacant in her heart. Rasálú was hunting at Dumtúr; but he had left behind him two guardians of his honour, a hill *maina* (or starling) and a parrot, both of which could talk. Hodí approached the window of the palace, looked around, and saw no one in the court. But the beautiful Rání Kokilán sat at the window looking northward, and there was no approach to her chamber excepting through the hall, where were the menials of the palace. So she threw him down a rope, which she tied firmly to the balcony, and Rájá Hodí climbed up by it and entered her chamber. The *maina,* in great indignation, exclaimed, "What wickedness is this?" and Hodí went to the cage and wrung the bird's neck. Then the parrot, taking warning, said: "The steed of Rasálú is swift; what if he should surprise you? Let me out of my cage, and I will fly over the palace, and will inform you the instant he appears in sight." The Rání Kokilán said, "O excellent bird! do even as thou hast said;" and she released the parrot from its cage. And the parrot flew swift as an arrow to Dumtúr, alighted upon Rasálú's shoulder as he hunted the stag, and exclaimed: "O Rájá, may your shadow never be less! A cat is at your cream." So Rasálú wheeled round his wonderful horse and galloped back to Múrut, seventy miles, without drawing rein, and the clang of his horse's hoofs in the court was the first notice of his approach. Rájá Hodí in dismay retreated down the rope into the court, where he met Rasálú, who made him follow into the wilderness, and there slew him after a brief combat, and cut out his heart and liver,[3] and

---

[3]"His heart and liver."—Asiatics, like the old Greeks and Romans, place the seat of love in the liver. Thus the Arabian poet-hero Antar exclaims: "Ask my burning sighs that mount on high; they will tell thee of the flaming passion in my liver." Theocritus says of Hercules (13th Idyll), "In his liver love had fixed a wound." Anacreon tells how the god of Love drew his bow, and "the dart pierced through my liver and my heart." An epigram in the 'Anthologia' is to the same effect:

Cease, love, to wound my liver and my heart;

If I must suffer, choose some other part.

had them fricas seed and set before the Rání that day at dinner.[4] The Rání ate the fricassee with great relish, and when she had finished, Rasálú said, "Do you know whose heart and liver you have eaten?" The Rání replied, "Doubtless they belonged to some dear little pet of a calf." Then said Rasálú, "True, O Kokilán, that heart was beating two hours ago in the breast of that pet-calf Rájá Hodí." This was said as they stood in the balcony; and Rání Kokilán clapped her hands and shrieked, "Then will I die with him;" and leaping from the balcony, she fell into the paved court, and was taken up, apparently lifeless. And Rasálú bound the bodies of Rájá Hodí and Rání Kokilán together by a strap, flung them over Hodí's steed, so that one body hung on one side and one body on the other side; then he cropped the ears, mane, and tail of the horse, and drove him forth into the jungle. It so happened that the horse took the route towards Ghayb, a district on the left bank of the Indus, far below Atuk. The prince of that country was a Chandala, and the horse was brought to him with his strange burthen. He ordered the bodies to be unbound, and perceiving that life was still left in the body of Rání Kokilán, with care she revived. The prince was struck with her beauty and married her; and the Ghayb race are descendants of this pair. But remorse fell upon Rasálú: probably he reflected that he had needlessly exposed his young and inexperienced wife to temptation; and he caused her form to be carved in stone, and set it up over that fountain at which they had so often sat together to enjoy the evening breeze.[5]

General Abbott adds that he saw this statue of the Rání Kokilán in 1848; but it had fallen under the ban of a bigoted Moolah, who had defaced the features. The place is called Múrut (the statue), after the effigy of Kokilán. "The tale is on the lips of every bard of the Panjáb; and the ascent of Rájá Hodí to the balcony is one of the favourite subjects for painters, and may be seen in fresco on the panels of palaces and temples."

And Horace: "Burning love . . . doth in thy liver rage." Our own Shakspeare seems to have had the same notion:

> Alas, then, love may be called appetite,
> No motion of the liver, but the palate.

[4]According to tradition, Rasálú himself never tasted flesh-meat, being a Jallú Rájá.

[5]See also 'Legends of the Panjáb,' by Captain R. C. Temple, published at Bombay, 1884—London: Trübner & Co.—where this story may be found, with other traditions of Rájá Rasálú.

❧ THE MERCHANT, HIS WIFE, AND HIS PARROT ❧

APARALLEL to the device of the Rájá Rasálú, of leaving behind him two talking birds to watch over, and report to him on his return home, the conduct of his young wife during his absence (cited in the last paper), is found in the frame, or leading story, of the Persian 'Túti Náma,' Tales of a Parrot: A merchant, before setting out on a long journey, purchased, for a large sum of money, a wonderful parrot that could discourse eloquently, and a *sharyk*, a species of nightingale, says Gerrans, "which imitates the human voice in so surprising a manner, that if you do not see the bird you cannot help being deceived," and put both in the same cage. In taking leave of his young and beautiful wife, he charged her, whenever she had any affair of importance to transact, to first obtain the advice and consent of the two birds. Some time after his departure, she was one day on the terrace of her house when a handsome young prince with his attendants passed, and having observed her beauty, he sent an old go-between to the lady, soliciting an interview with her at his palace. The *sharyk* forbade her to go, upon which the lady flew into a rage, seized the virtuous bird, and dashed it on the ground, so that it died. She then represented her case to the parrot, who, having witnessed the fate of his companion, prudently resolved to temporise with the amorous dame, "quenched the fire of her indignation with the water of flattery, and began a tale conformable to her temperament, which he took care to protract till the morning." In this way the parrot prevents the lady's intended intrigue by relating, night after night, until her husband returns, one or more fascinating tales, which he does not bring to an end till it is too late for the assignation.[1]

This plan of the 'Túti Náma' is faintly reflected in the Mongolian tales of "Ardshi Bordshi" (the second part of 'Sagas from the Far East'), where

---

[1] The 'Túti Náma,' or Parrot-Book, was written by Nakhshabí about A.D. 1320, according to Pertsch, after an older Persian work, now lost, which was made from a Sanskrit book, also no longer extant, of which the 'Suka Saptati,' Seventy (Tales) of a Parrot, is a representative. A similar Indian work is the 'Hamsa-Vinsati,' written in Telegu: twenty tales related by a hamsa, or goose, to prevent the wife of Vishnudâs from carrying on a criminal intrigue during his absence; by Agala Rájá Narayana, son of Suráppá. Nakhshabí is the pen-name

a merchant buys a parrot for a hundred ounces of silver, and leaves it to watch over his wife during his absence. The wife resolves to go out and visit her acquaintances, and indulge in pleasures from which she had hitherto been debarred. But the parrot detains her all night by telling her the story of the wife of a king who swore falsely, and yet spoke the truth, to which reference has already been made in vol. i. p. 178, note.

The story seems to have found its way to the south of Europe in the fourteenth century, and it may perhaps have been diffused among the people of Italy through some Oriental collection which is now lost, since versions have long been current in Piedmont and Tuscany, and also in Sicily. In a very interesting and valuable paper on Italian Popular Tales, in the 'North American Review' for July 1876, Professor T. F. Crane gives abstracts of three of the versions, as follows:

The most simple version is from Pisa (Professor Comparetti's collection), under the title of "Il Pappagallo," and is to this effect: There was once a merchant who had a beautiful daughter, with whom the king and the viceroy were both in love. The former knew that the merchant would soon have to depart on business, and he would then have a chance to speak with the girl. The viceroy knew it too, and considered how he could prevent the king from succeeding in his design. He was acquainted with a witch, and promised her immunity and a large sum of money if she would teach him how to change himself into a parrot. This she does, and the merchant buys him for his daughter, and then departs. When the parrot thought it was about time for the king to come, he said to the girl, "Now to amuse you, I will tell you a story; but you must attend to me, and not see any one while I am telling it." Then he began his story, and after he had gone a little way in it, a servant entered and told her mistress that there was a letter for her. "Tell her to bring it later," said the parrot; "and now listen to me." The mistress replied, "I do not receive letters while my father is away," and the parrot continued. After a while there was another interruption—a servant announced the visit of an aunt of her mistress: it was not an aunt, however, but an old woman who came from the king. The parrot said, "Do not receive her—we are in the finest

---

(*takhalus*) of Ziyá-ed-Dín, the author of the 'Túti Náma,' from his birthplace, Nakhshab, a city in Turkestan, where they say there is a well named Cháhí Nakhshab, from which an appearance of the moon, called Mahi Nakhshab, was produced by a notorious impostor named Mukanna—the "Veiled Prophet of Khorassan" of Moore's 'Lalla Rookh.'

part of the story;" and the young girl sent word that she did not receive any visits while her father was absent; so the parrot went on. When his story was ended, the girl was so pleased that she would listen to no one else until her father returned. Then the parrot disappeared, and the viceroy visited the merchant, and asked his daughter's hand. He consented, and the marriage took place that very day. The wedding was scarcely over when a gentleman came to ask the girl's hand for the king, but it was too late. And the poor king, who was much in love with her, died of a broken heart, and the girl remained the wife of the viceroy, who had been more cunning than the king.

Another version from Piedmont (De Gubernatis' 'Zoological Mythology,' vol. ii. p. 322—Comparetti's collection, No. 2), differs materially from the one just given: A king is obliged to go to war, and leave behind him his wife, with whom another king is in love. Before departing, he forbids his wife to leave the palace during his absence, and presents her with a parrot. No sooner had the king left than the other king attempted to obtain an interview with the queen, by giving a feast and inviting her to it. The parrot prevents her from going, by relating the same story which is contained in the first version. They are interrupted in the same manner by an old woman, sent by the royal lover, but to no purpose. When the story is finished the husband returns, and the parrot becomes a young man, whom the king had engaged to watch over his wife's fidelity.—The story told by the parrot is of no special interest, except that it is in the main also the one given in the Sicilian version, and has some resemblance to a story in the 'Pentamerone,' vol. ii. p. 22—"Verdo Prato."

The Sicilian version is the most interesting as well as the most complete; the single story in the Italian versions has here been expanded into three, and the frame is more artistic. It is the second in the collection of Pitrè: A merchant is obliged to leave his wife, of whom he is insanely jealous. She advises him to shut her up in the house with plenty to eat. One day, to amuse herself, she looks out of the single window which has been left open. At this moment a gentleman and a notary happen to pass, and see her. They immediately make a bet of a hundred ounces as to which of them will speak to her first. The notary summons an evil spirit, and sells him his soul, on condition that he wins the bet. The devil then changes him into a parrot, who plays the same *rôle* as in the Italian versions, but relates, as we have said, three stories. When the merchant returns, the parrot is placed on the table at dinner, and splashes some of the soup into the husband's eyes, flies at his throat and strangles him, and then escapes through the window. The parrot, of course, resumes his human form, obtains the widow's hand and his hundred ounces from the *cavalari;* and afterwards tells his wife the whole story, her only comment being, "I am astonished!" (*Io restu allucuta*).[2]

The well-known story, in the 'Arabian Nights,' of the Merchant, his Wife, and his Parrot, which properly belongs to the Book of Sindibád, may have been adapted either from the legend of Rájá Rasálú and his fair young wife, or from the frame of the original Indian Parrot-Book. It occurs in the Breslau printed text of the 'Thousand Nights and One Night,' and also in the text of the first Two Hundred Nights, edited by Shaykh Ahmed bin Muhammad Shirwání el-Yemení, printed at Calcutta, 1814–18. But in the text printed at Bulák, and in that edited by Sir W. Macnaughton and printed at Calcutta, 1839–42, in place of it is the story of the King and his Falcon, which will be found in a former paper—see note on page 369. Lane, in his translation of a portion of the Bulák text of the 'Nights,' has substituted the story of the Parrot, although it occurs also in its proper place in his work, namely, the romance of the 'King and his Seven Vazírs.'

With a magpie instead of a parrot, the story forms one of the tales of the 'Seven Wise Masters.' According to the oldest extant English version of that famous work (in the Auchinleck MS., and printed in Weber's 'Metrical Romances'), a merchant had a clever magpie: in his absence his wanton wife had an intrigue with a young man, and the magpie, on seeing him enter the house, cried out that he would tell of this to his master on his return. The wife, with a ladder, removed a tile or two from the roof, placed a basin of water so that it should drop on the bird, and make a clear light dazzle its eyes. The youth goes away in the morning, and when the merchant comes home the magpie tells him of the lover, and how it rained and lightned during the night. His wife bids him not credit the magpie's story, but ask the neighbours what sort of a night it had been. He learns that the night was fair, upon which he wrings the magpie's neck. But soon after he finds the ladder against the wall of his house, and the basin, etc.; and thus discovering how the bird had been tricked, he drove his wife out of doors.

[2]See also Crane's 'Italian Popular Tales' (London: 1885), pp. 167–183, where the stories related by the parrots are given in full.

ᔓ

An analogous legend is told by Ovid in his 'Metamorphoses,' which has been adapted by Chaucer for his Manciple's Tale, and has also been taken by Gower into the third book of his 'Confessio Amantis.' In the latter, after relating, out of Ovid, the story of the dispute between Jupiter and Juno, which began "as it were in borde (jest)," which of the two is the more amorous, man or woman, and they referred the question to Tiresias, who gave his decision in favour of man, at which Juno was so incensed that she deprived him of his eyesight; to compensate him, Jupiter bestowed on him the gift of prophecy: but though he was ever after a soothsayer, he had much rather have had his eyesight;—the Confessor warns his "son" to guard his speech, and to keep to himself whatever he might hear or see against other men, and relates this tale:

> Phebus, which maketh daies light,
> A love he hadde, which tho hight[3]
> Cornide, whom aboven alle
> He pleseth. But what shall befalle
> Of love, there is no man knoweth.
> But as fortune her happes throweth,
> So it befell upon a chaunce
> A yonge knight toke her acqueintaunce
> And had of her all that he wolde.
> But a fals bird, which she hath holde
> And kept in chambre of pure youthe,
> Discovereth all that ever he couthe.[4]
> The briddes name was as tho
> Corvus, the which was than also
> Well more white than any swan,
> And he the shrewe [5] all that he can
> Of his lady to Phebus saide.
> And he for wrath his swerd out-braide,[6]
> With which Cornide anone he slough,[7]
> But after him was wo inough
> And toke a full great repentaunce,

[3]Then called.   [4]Knew.   [5]Calumniated.
[6]Drew out.   [7]Slew.

Wherof in token and remembraunce
Of hem,[8] whiche usen wicke[9] speche,
Upon this bird he toke his wreche,[10]
That there he was snow-white to-fore[11]
Ever afterward cole-black therfore.
He was transformed, as it sheweth.
And many a man yet him beshreweth
And clepen[12] him unto this day
A Raven, by whom yet men may
Take evidence, whan he crieth,
That some mishap it signifieth.
Beware therfore and say the best,
If thou wolt be thy self in rest,
My gode sone, as I the rede.[13]

The story as told in all the versions, Eastern as well as Western, of the 'Seven Wise Masters,' was certainly not derived from any Greek or Roman source, and it is probable that the classical legend is of Indian extraction. This is how it is related in the Persian 'Sindibád Náma':

There once lived in Egypt a confectioner, who had a very beautiful wife, and a parrot that performed, as occasion required, the office of watchman, guard, policeman, bell, or spy, and flapped his wings did he hear a fly buzzing about the sugar. This parrot was a great annoyance to the wife, always telling the suspicious husband what took place in his absence. One evening, before going out to visit a friend, the confectioner gave the parrot strict injunctions to watch all night, and desired his wife to make all fast, as he should not return till morning. No sooner had he left than the woman went for her lover, who returned with her, and they passed the night together in mirth and feasting, while the parrot observed all. In the morning the lover departed, and the husband, returning, was informed by the parrot of what had taken place; upon which he hastened to his wife's apartment and beat her soundly. She thought to herself, who could have informed against her, and asked a woman who was in her confidence whether she had done so. The woman protested, "by what is hidden and what is open," that

---

[8]Them.   [9]Wicked   [10]Revenge..
[11]Before; hitherto.   [12]Called; named   [13]I thee advise.

she had not betrayed her; but informed her that in the morning her husband, on his return, stood some time before the cage, and listened to the talking of the parrot. When the wife heard this, she resolved to plot the destruction of the bird. Some days after, the husband was again invited to the house of a friend, where he was to pass the night. Before departing, he gave the parrot the same injunctions as before. His heart was free from care, for he had his spy at home. She and her confidante then planned how they might destroy the credit of the parrot with its master. For this purpose they resolved to counterfeit a storm, which they effected by means of a hand-mill placed over the parrot's head, which the lover worked—by a rush of water, by blowing a bellows, and by suddenly uncovering a taper hid under a dish. Thus did they raise such a [sham] tempest of rain and lightning that the parrot was drenched and immersed in a deluge. Now rolled the thunder, now flashed the lightning—the one from the noise of the hand-mill, the other from the reflection of the taper. "Surely," thought the parrot to itself, "the deluge has come on, and such a one as perhaps Noah never witnessed." So saying, he buried his head under his wing, a prey to terror. The husband, on his return, hastened to the parrot to inquire what had happened during his absence. The bird replied that he found it impossible to convey an idea of the deluge and tempest of last night; it would take years to describe the uproar of the hurricane and storm. When the shopkeeper heard the bird talk of last night's deluge, he said, "Surely, O bird, you are gone mad. Where was there—even in a dream—rain or lightning last night? You have utterly ruined my house and ancient family. My wife is the most virtuous woman of the age, and all your accusations of her are false." In anger he dashed the cage upon the ground, tore off the parrot's head, and threw it from the window. Presently his friend, coming to call upon him, saw the parrot in this condition, with head torn off, and without wings or plumage. Being informed of the circumstances, he suspected some trick on the part of the wife, so he said to the husband, "When your wife leaves home to go to the bath, compel her confidante to disclose the secret." As soon, therefore, as his wife went out, the husband entered his harem, and insisted on the woman telling him the truth. She detailed the whole story, and the husband now bitterly repented having killed the parrot, of whose innocence he had proof.

In the Hebrew version of the Book of Sindibád ('Mishlé Sandabar') the husband "slew the parrot, and sent to bring his wife, and gave her presents"; in the Arabic, he kills the parrot, and afterwards discovering the bird's innocence and his wife's guilt, according to one text he divorces her, but in the others he kills both the woman and her paramour. In the Syriac ('Sindban') and the old Spanish ('Libro de los Engannos et los Asayamientos de las Mugeres,' Book of the Deceits and Tricks of Women), as in the Hebrew text, he kills the parrot, and is reconciled to his wife. The story also occurs in the Turkish romance of the Forty Vazírs ('Qirq Vezír'), with some variations: A piece of bullock's hide is beat from time to time to imitate thunder; water is sprinkled on the bird through a sieve; and a looking-glass is flashed now and again: in this version the husband does not kill the parrot, which is also the conclusion of the Greek text of the Book of Sindibád ('Syntipas').—The story was very popular in the thirteenth and fourteenth centuries, forming one of the tales and fables in John of Capua's 'Directorum Humanæ Vitæ,' a Latin version of the Fables of Bidpaï; and it is also found in the 'Discorsi degli Animali' and the 'Giorni' of Sansovini.

The story related by the parrot on the first night in some texts of the Persian 'Túti Náma' is a variant of the tale of the Merchant and his Parrot: Once on a time, in days of yore, a merchant having occasion to travel, left his goods and chattels and his wife in charge of a cockatoo. While he is absent, his wife entertains a young man every evening; but when he returns home, the discreet bird, in giving him an account of all other transactions, says not a word about the lady's merry pranks. The merchant, however, soon hears of them from a "good-natured friend," and reproaches and punishes his wife. Suspecting the cockatoo to have blabbed, the lady goes at night to the cage, takes out the bird, plucks off all its feathers, and throws it into the street. In the morning, when her husband misses his favourite bird, she tells him that a cat had carried it off; but he discredits her story, and thrusts her out of doors. Meantime the cockatoo has taken up its abode in the burying-ground, to which the poor woman also retires; and the cockatoo advises her to shave her head and remain there fasting during forty days, after which she should be reconciled to her husband. This she does, and at the end of the prescribed period the cockatoo goes to his old master and upbraids him for his cruel treatment of his innocent wife, who had been fasting forty days in the burying-ground. The husband hastens to seek his wife, asks her forgiveness, and they live together afterwards in perfect harmony. "In like manner," adds the story-telling parrot, "shall I conceal your secret from your husband, or make your peace with him if he should find it out."[14]

Whether the leading story of the Parrot-Book suggested the incident of the two birds left by Rasálú to watch his wife's conduct, is a question which cannot well be decided in the absence of any knowledge of the approximate date of the original Sanskrit work. The resemblance is certainly too close to be merely fortuitous; and the legend of Rájá Rasálú and Rání Kokilán has been current in the Panjáb time out of mind. It is the opinion of some scholars that the 'Sindibád' story of the Merchant and his Parrot was adapted from the frame of the 'Suka Saptatí,' and that the other (*second*) tales of the Vazírs in the several existing representatives of the Book of Sindibáad were also taken from that work. Others, again, contend that these tales were taken into the Parrot-Book from the Book of Sindibád.

In Indian tales and fables the parrot is a favourite character, probably from the remarkable facility with which that bird imitates the human voice, as also from the belief in metempsychosis, or transmigration of human souls after death into other animal forms. Stories of wise parrots frequently occur in the 'Kathá Sarit Ságara'; sometimes they are merely birds, but often they are men or women who have been re-born in that form. The third of the Twenty-five Tales of a Vetála, or vampyre ('Vetála Panchavinsatí'), relates how a king had a parrot that was "possessed of a god-like knowledge, versed in all the 'Sastras,' having been born in that condition owing to a curse"; and his queen had a hen-maina "remarkable for knowledge." They are put into the same cage, and "one day the parrot became enamoured of the maina, and said to her, "Marry me, fair one,

---

[14]The 68th chapter of the Continental 'Gesta Romanorum' seems near akin to the story of the Woman and the Parrot: A certain noble had a fair but vicious wife. It happened that her husband, having occasion to travel, was from home, and the lady sent for her gallant, and rioted in every excess of wickedness. Now one of her handmaids, it seems, was skilful in interpreting the song of birds; and in the court of the castle were three cocks. During the night, while the gallant was with his mistress, the first cock began to crow. The lady heard it, and said to her servant, "Dear friend, what says yonder cock?" She replied, "That you are grossly injuring your husband." Then said, the lady, "Kill that cock without delay." They did so; but soon after the second cock crew, and the lady repeated the question. "Madam," said the handmaid, "he says, 'My companion died for revealing the truth, and for the same cause I am prepared to die.'" "Kill him," said the lady, which they did. After this the third cock crew. "What says he?" cried the lady again. "'Hear, see, and say nothing, if you would live in peace.'" "Oh," said the lady, "*don't* kill him."

as we sleep, perch, and feed in the same cage." But the maina answered him, "I do not desire intimate union with a male, for all males are wicked and ungrateful." The parrot answered, "It is not true that males are wicked, but females are wicked and cruel-hearted." So a dispute arose between them, until at length they agreed each should relate a story, the one to show that men are all wicked and ungrateful, the other that women are wicked and cruel-hearted; and if the maina won, the parrot should be her slave, but if the parrot won, then he should have the maina for his wife. In a Gujeratí metrical version of the 'Sinhásana Dwatriusatí' (Thirty-two Tales of a Throne), by Samala Bhata, this story reappears in an extended form, and with two parrots in place of a parrot and a maina—tale of the Twenty-second Statue. In the Bahár-i Dánush (Spring of Knowledge), composed by 'Inayatu-'lláh of Delhi, a wise parrot inflames the hero with love for a princess whose beauty it describes eloquently, and accompanies him as guide on his travels in quest of the lady. And in the story of 'Nala and Damayanti,' a swan incites love between the hero and heroine by praising to each the personal charms and good qualities of the other. This beautiful tale—which is an episode of the 'Mahábhárata'—was translated from the Tamil by Kindersley in the end of last century; and the Sanskrit original has been rendered into graceful English verse by Dean Milman.

⤳ THE ELOPEMENT ⤳

ALTHOUGH the frame, or leading story, of the romance of the 'Seven Wise Masters,' in its European versions—Latin, French, Spanish, German, Italian, English, etc.—generally corresponds with that of its Indian prototype, the Book of Sindibád, as represented by several Eastern texts, yet the subordinate tales for the most part belong exclusively to this Western group. One of these, the Robbery of the King's Treasury, has been traced in a former paper through a great variety of versions (*ante,* p. 334 ff.), and in the present paper I shall endeavour to throw some new light on the history of another, which is commonly known as "The Two Dreams," or "The Elopement," of which the outline is as follows:[1]

A certain noble knight of Hungary dreamt of seeing a very beautiful lady, but knew her not; and it so happened that the lady whom he saw in his dream that same night dreamt also of him.[2] Next day the knight of Hungary took horse and arms, and proceeded in quest of the lady. Three weeks and more did he ride, sorely sighing for his lady-love, till he came to a town where was a fair castle, strongly fortified. He took up his abode at the inn, and on questioning the landlord regarding the castle and its owner, learned that it belonged to a lord who had a fair jewel of a wife, of whom he was so jealous that two years ago he built a strong tower at one end of the castle, in which he confined her, with one maiden as her companion; and he always carried the key of the tower, which was never opened save when he himself visited her. Now the knight had already seen the lady looking out of the tower window, and recognised her as the object of his dream. The following day he went to the castle and offered his services to the old lord, who heartily bade him welcome; and the knight, being a good and valiant warrior, conquered all his enemies for him, so that the old lord loved him fondly, and made him steward of his lands.

One day, when the knight chanced to be under the tower, the lady perceived and recognised him as the same she had seen in her dream, and contrived to communicate with him by means of a rope of rushes let

---

[1] English metrical MS. text of 'The Seven Sages'—composed probably about the end of the fourteenth century—edited by Wright, and printed in vol. xvi. of the Percy Society's publications.

[2] See note at the end of this paper: "Falling in love through a Dream."

down from the window. The knight now planned a crafty device, by which he should enjoy the society of his lady-love unknown to the old lord. He built a tower at some distance from the castle, and caused an underground passage to be made, leading direct from it to the lady's chamber. When all was completed, he visited the lady, who gave him a ring as a keepsake, telling him, should her husband see it and appear suspicious, to bring it back to her at once. The old lord does one day recognise his wife's ring on the knight's finger, "as he sat at meat," and after examining it, hastens to the tower; but the knight having reached the lady's chamber by the private way, and restored the ring, on the husband demanding to see it she at once produces the ring, to his great satisfaction.[3]

At length the lovers resolve to elope, and the lady counsels the knight to tell the old lord that, having slain a great man in his own country, he had been banished, and that his lady-love was coming to him with tidings of his heritage. The old lord would, of course, ask to see the lady, and she herself would play her part. The knight accordingly tells his lord this story, and invites him to a banquet at his house. Before he arrives, his wife, dressed in the costume of the knight's country, has reached the banqueting-hall by the secret passage, prepared to enact the part of the knight's leman. The old lord, on seeing her, thinks she is remarkably like his own wife; but then he recollects the affair of the ring, and there might also be two women exactly alike. At this juncture the lady pretends to swoon, is taken out, and returns with all speed by the private way to her chamber, where, having changed her dress, she is found by her husband, whom she embraces with every token of affection. He was "blythe as bird on bough," says our author, and remained with her all night.

On the day following the knight sends all his property on board a ship, and goes to take leave of the old lord, as he is to return at once, with his lady-love, to his own country. The knight and the old lord's wife—who had now resumed the character of the supposititious lady of Hungary—are accompanied by the deceived husband "into the sea a mile or two,

---

[3]The husband is a king in the 'Historia Septem Sapientum Romæ' (a later prose version), and he and the knight, while hunting, having dismounted in order to repose during the heat of noontide, the king recognises the ring on the knight's finger while the latter is asleep. On awaking, the knight suspects from the king's countenance that the ring has betrayed him, and, feigning illness, obtains leave to return home. This incident may be compared with the first part of the legend of St Kentigern—see vol. i. p. 400—in which the queen's gift to her paramour is discovered by her jealous husband under similar circumstances.

with minstrelsy and many manner of melody," and then bids them farewell. On his return home, he proceeds, as usual, to the tower, and finds his bird has flown:

> Then sayed he, walaway!
> That ever was he man boren!
> Than was all his myrthè lorne.
> He lepe out of the tour anon,
> And than brake hys neke boon.[4]

Dunlop has pointed out the resemblance which this story bears to the "Miles Gloriosus" of Plautus; he also states that it coincides with "Le Chevalier à la Trappe," one of the 'Fabliaux' (Le Grand, vol. iii. p. 157); with a tale in the fourth part of the 'Novellino' of Massuccio Salernitano; and with the adventures of the Old Calender in Gueulette's 'Contes Tartares.'[5] But he does not notice the version in Berni's 'Orlando Innamorato':

Folderico, who had won the damsel,[6] carried her to a tower which he possessed upon the sea-shore, called Altamura, where he kept her, together with his treasure, under lock and key, and utterly secluded from the sight of man. But what will not love? Ordauro, who was also rich, though not so wealthy as Folderico, purchased a sumptuous palace in the immediate neighbourhood of Altamura, and at an immense cost made a subterraneous passage from his palace to the damsel's prison, by which he visited her and enjoyed her society without danger. At last, however, the lovers, tired of the restraint under which they carried on their intercourse, and emboldened by success, determined to make a desperate effort to escape.

With this view Ordauro communicates to Folderico news of his approaching nuptials with another daughter of Monodontes—for so was called the king of the Distant Isles—and invites him, as his brother-in-law, to the marriage feast. Folderico having carefully secured the gates of

---

[4]From the Appendix to my (privately printed) versions of the 'Book of Sindibád,' from the Persian and Arabic: 1884.—This story is related by the Seventh Wise Master in two old English metrical versions, and in the French metrical text, 'Roman des Sept Sages' (about 1284); but by the queen on the seventh night in our prose English version, derived (through the French probably) from the 'Historia Septem Sapientum.'

[5]Dunlop's 'History of Fiction.'

[6]Namely, the Daughter of the King of the Distant Isles, having distanced her in a foot-race in the same manner as was Atalanta by Hippomenes, the son of Macareus.

his tower, goes thither, and finding his wife installed as bride, becomes ferocious at the sight. Ordauro, however, with great difficulty, succeeds in appeasing him, by the assurance that she was a twin-sister of his own wife, to whom she bore a perfect resemblance; and by bidding him return to his tower and satisfy himself of the fact. The means of proof appeared decisive, and accordingly Folderico accepts them. He finds his locks as they were left, and his wife (who had returned by the subterraneous passage and changed her dress) alone and overcome with melancholy. He again takes the way, which was somewhat circuitous, to the palace of Ordauro, and again finds her there, shining in all the festivity of a bride. He can no longer resist the conviction that the two persons whom he had seen were different women, lays aside his distrust, and even offers to convoy the bridegroom and his bride on a part of their journey towards Ordauro's natural home, to which he was returning.

A certain advantage was thus gained, since Folderico never left his tower, though locked, for above an hour, and consequently would have soon discovered his loss if the lovers had eloped in secret. The party set out together; and at the end of the first day's journey, Folderico turns back and gallops to his tower. He is now first assured of his disgrace. Full of rage, he pursues his rival, but does not dare make any attempt to recover his wife till he has separated Ordauro from his adherents. Having effected this by a stratagem, he attacks his retainers and repossesses himself of the lady. He is destined to a short possession of the prize; for he is, on his return, beset by giants, who seize her and all his treasure, which the lady was carrying off as a dowry to her new lord. He himself escapes.[7]

A version current among the common people of Rome furnishes an interesting example of the curious transformations which stories undergo in being transmitted by oral tradition:

There once lived in a small cottage a poor woman and her daughter, a very pretty girl. At the death of her mother the girl was rendered homeless, and was wandering aimlessly about when an ugly hunchbacked tailor chanced to see her, and being struck with her beauty, he asked her name.

---

[7]'The Orlando Innamorato.' Translated into prose from the Italian of Francesco Berni, and interspersed with extracts in the same stanza as the original. By William Stewart Rose. Edinburgh and London: 1823. Pp. 125–128.—This story, of the Daughter of the King of the Distant Isles and her lover and husband, she herself relates to the brave knights Orlando and Brandimart, who had rescued her from the giants. The princess is afterwards reunited to her lover Ordauro, and they pursue their journey to his home.

"They call me," said she, 'La Buona Grazia' (the Good Grace). "Come," said the hunchbacked tailor, "and be my wife." The girl consents, and so he takes her to his house. Thinking to himself, "She's too young and pretty to care for me," he keeps her carefully locked up in a room up-stairs, and whitened all the windows, so that she should not be seen by any passers-by in the street. But there was a small window in a dirty lumber closet that had not been thus obscured, and she was looking out of it one day when a stranger happened to pass and discovered her. He enters into conversation with the lovely girl, and learning from her that there was a large picture on the wall adjoining his room in the next house, he arranges that he should break through the wall on his side, and she on hers, which being done, they meet. The gentleman asks her if she would like to marry him, and she very readily consents, upon which he tells her that he will have a dress made for her, even by the hunchbacked tailor himself. So he takes her to the tailor, who, on seeing her, thinks she is very like La Buona Grazia. After he had taken her measure, the gentleman gives him some money to get himself breakfast, in order that the girl might get back and replace the picture. Soon after, the tailor comes into the girl's room, and tells her that she has got to work hard to make a travelling dress for the wife of a gentleman staying at the inn, who is exactly like herself. "Going to travel?" asks La Buona Grazia with an air of innocence. "Yes," says the hunchback; "they said they should start as soon as the dress was ready." "Oh, let me see them drive off!" "Nonsense; get on with your work." So she went on, but teased him till he consented for that day to take the whitening off one of the windows. The dress was duly finished, and taken to the inn, and while the tailor was absent on this errand, the girl got out by the hole behind the picture, and joined her lover. She had previously dressed a great doll to look like herself, and placed it at the window. The tailor stood below to see the couple drive off; looked up and saw the doll, which, supposing to be La Buona Grazia, he made signs to her not to stay there too long. Presently the gentleman and his lady came out of the inn. The hunchbacked tailor was standing at the door of the carriage, and near him were two of the inn-stablemen. "You give me your good grace?" said the gentleman to the tailor. "Yes, yes!" "You say it sincerely and with all your heart." "Yes, with all my heart." And the hunchback, more than delighted with the gentleman's condescension, put out his hand, and the two stablemen were looking on all the time. As soon as the carriage had driven off, the tailor looked up at the window to see if the girl had gone in, but the doll was still there. "Go in, go in," cries he, waving his hand.

He then goes into the girl's room, and discovers how he had been tricked. He complains to the judge, and demands that soldiers should be sent after the fugitives. But the stablemen had had their orders, and were there before him, and deponed that they were witnesses to his having given his *Good Grace* up to the gentleman with all his heart, and his hand upon the bargain. So the hunchbacked tailor got no redress.[8]

The story is also found in Pitrè's Sicilian collection, "where it is told of a tailor who lived next to the king's palace (*sic*), with which his house communicated by a secret door, known only to the king and the tailor's wife. The tailor, while at work in the palace, imagines he sees his wife there, and pretending that he has forgotten his shears, etc., rushes home, to find his wife there. She finally elopes with the king, leaving at her window an image that deceives her husband until she is beyond pursuit."[9]

The principal part of the intrigue in the "Miles Gloriosus" of Plautus, which properly commences with the second act, is thus sketched by Dunlop:

While residing at Athens, the captain had purchased from her mother a young girl—whose lover was at that time absent on an embassy—and had brought her with him to his house at Ephesus. The lover's slave entered into the captain's service, and seeing the girl in his possession, wrote to his former master, who, on learning the fate of his mistress, repaired to Ephesus, and there went to reside with Periplectomenes, a merry old bachelor, who had been a friend of his father, and who now agreed to assist him in recovering the object of his affections. The house of Periplectomenes being immediately adjacent to that of the captain, the ingenious slave dug an opening between them, and the keeper, who had been entrusted by the captain with charge of the damsel, was thus easily persuaded, by her rapid, and to him unaccountable, transition from one building to the other, that it was a twin-sister who had arrived at the house of Periplectomenes, and who possessed an extraordinary resemblance to her. Afterwards, by a new contrivance, a courtesan is employed to personate the wife of Periplectomenes, and to persuade the captain that she is in love with him. To facilitate this amour, he allows the girl whom he had purchased at Athens to depart with her "twin-sister"—her lover having assumed the character of

[8]"The Good Grace and the Hunchback:" Miss M. H. Busk's 'Folk-Lore of Rome,' p. 399.
[9]Crane's 'Italian Popular Tales,' p. 167.—This Sicilian variant is ludicrously garbled, judging from the above outline.

the master of the vessel in which she sailed. The captain afterwards goes to the house of Periplectomenes to a supposed assignation, where he is seized and beat, but does not discover how completely he has been duped till the Athenian girl had got clear off with her lover.[10]

While Dunlop did not, apparently, know of the existence of the story in Berni's 'Orlando Innamorato,' Rose, on the other hand, seems to have been ignorant of its forming the main part of the plot of the "Miles Gloriosus"; since, in a note to his outline of Berni's version of the story, he says that, "as the author was indebted to Greek fable for the beginning,[11] so was he indebted to Norman story for the subsequent adventure;" adding, "the story would seem to be of Eastern origin." What reason he had to conjecture that the story is of Asiatic extraction does not appear: it is certain he could not have known of any Eastern form of it; and indeed but one is known even at the present time, namely, an Arabian version, which is found in the Breslau-printed text of the 'Thousand and One Nights,' and of which the following is a translation:

There was once in a certain city a woman fair of favour, who had to lover a trooper. Her husband was a fuller, and when he went out to his business, the trooper used to come to her and abide with her till the time of the fuller's return, when he would go away. On this wise they abode awhile, until one day the trooper said to his mistress, "I mean to take me a house near unto thine, and dig an underground passage from my house to thy house, and do thou say to thy husband, 'My sister hath been absent with her husband, and now they have returned from their travels; and I have made her take up her sojourn in my neighbourhood, so as I may foregather with her at all times. So go thou to her husband the trooper and offer him thy wares [for sale], and thou wilt see my sister with him, and wilt see that she is I and I am she, without doubt. So, Allah! Allah! go to my sister's husband and give ear to that which he shall say to thee.'" Accordingly the trooper bought him a house near at hand, and made therein an underground passage communicating with his mistress' house.

When he had accomplished this affair, the wife bespoke her husband as her lover had lessoned her, and he went out to go to the trooper's

[10] 'History of Roman Literature. From its Earliest Period to the Augustan Age.' In Two Volumes. By John Dunlop, author of 'The History of Fiction.' London: 1823. Vol. i. pp. 212, 213.

[11] That is, the foot-race—à *la* Atalanta—between Folderico and the princess—see *ante*, p. 391, note 6.

house, but turned back by the way, whereupon quoth she to him, "By Allah, go forthright, for that my sister asketh of thee." So the dolt of a fuller went out, and made for the trooper's house, whilst his wife forewent him thither by the secret passage, and going up, sat down by her lover. Presently the fuller entered and saluted the trooper and his [supposed] wife, and was confounded at the coincidence of the case. Then doubt betided him, and he returned in haste to his dwelling; but she forewent him by the underground passage to her chamber, and, donning her wonted clothes, sat [waiting] for him, and said to him, "Did I not bid thee go to my sister and salute her husband, and make friends with them?" Quoth he, "I did this, but I misdoubted the affair, when I saw his wife." And she said, "Did I not tell thee that she resembleth me and I her, and there is nought to distinguish between us but our clothes? Go back to her." So, of the heaviness of his wit, he believed her, and turning back, went in to the trooper; but she had foregone him, and when he saw her beside her lover, he fell to looking on her and pondering. Then he saluted her, and she returned him the salutation; and when she spoke he was bewildered. So the trooper said to him, "What ails thee to be thus?" And he answered, "This woman is my wife, and the voice is her voice." Then he rose in haste, and returning to his own house, saw his wife, who had foregone him by the secret passage. So he went back to the trooper's house and saw her sitting as before; whereupon he was abashed before her, and sitting down in the trooper's sitting-chamber, ate and drank with him, and became drunken, and abode without sense all that day till nightfall, when the trooper arose, and, shaving off some of the fuller's hair [which was long and flowing], after the fashion of the Turks, clipped the rest short, and clapped a tarbosh on his head. Then he thrust his feet into boots, and girt him with a sword and a girdle, and bound about his middle a quiver and a bow and arrows. Moreover, he put money in his pocket, and thrust into his sleeve letters-patent addressed to the governor of Ispahán, bidding him assign to Rustam Khemartekeni a monthly allowance of a hundred dirhams[12] and ten pounds of bread and five pounds of meat, and enrol him among the Turks under his commandment. Then he took him up, and carrying him forth, left him in one of the mosques.

The fuller gave not over sleeping till sunrise, when he awoke, and finding himself in this plight, misdoubted of his affair, and imagined that he

---

[12]About fifty shillings.

was a Turk, and abode putting one foot forward and drawing the other back. Then said he in himself, "I will go to my dwelling, and if my wife know me, then am I Ahmed the Fuller, but if she know me not, I am a Turk."[13] So he betook himself to his house; but when the artful baggage, his wife, saw him, she cried out in his face, saying, "Whither away, O trooper? Wilt thou break into the house of Ahmed the Fuller, and he a man of repute, having a brother-in-law a Turk, a man of high standing with the sultan? An thou depart not, I will acquaint my husband, and he will requite thee thy deed." When he heard her words, the dregs of the drunkenness wrought in him, and he imagined that he was indeed a Turk. So he went out from her, and putting his hand to his sleeve found therein a scroll, and gave it to one who read it to him. When he heard that which was written in the scroll, his mind was confirmed in the false supposition; but he said in himself, "May be my wife seeketh to put a cheat on me; so I will go to my fellows the fullers, and if they know me not, then am I for sure Khemartekeni the Turk." So he betook himself to the fullers, and when they espied him afar off, they thought that he was one of the Turks who used to wash their clothes with them without payment, and gave them nothing. Now they had complained of this aforetime to the sultan, and he said, "If any of the Turks come to you, pelt them with stones." So when they saw the fuller, they fell upon him with sticks and stones, and pelted him; whereupon quoth he [in himself], "Verily, I am a Turk and knew it not!" Then he took of the money in his pocket and bought him victual [for the journey], and hired a stout hack-

---

[13]This recalls the favourite nursery rhyme of the little old woman who "went to market her eggs to sell," and falling asleep on the road, a naughty pedlar cut her petticoats "up to the knees":

> When the little woman first did wake,
> She began to shiver and she began to shake;
> She began to wonder, she began to cry—
> "Lawk-a-mercy on me, this is none of I!"

> "But if this be I, as I do hope it be,
> I've a little dog at home, and he'll know me;
> If it be I, he'll wag his little tail,
> And if it be not I, he'll loudly bark and wail."

[14]'Tales from the Arabic of the Breslau and Calcutta (1814–18) editions of the "Book of the Thousand Nights and One Night," not occurring in the other printed texts of the work. Now first done into English by John Payne.' London (privately printed), 1884. Vol. i. p. 261.—This version of The Elopement forms one of twenty-eight tales related to Shah Bakht by his vazír Er-Rahwan, a romance found only in the Breslau-printed text of "The Nights;"—see an account of this romance, pages 302 and 303 of the present volume.

ney, and set out for Ispahán, leaving his wife to the trooper.[14]

In a prologue to the second act of the "Miles Gloriosus," the plot of the drama is said to have been taken from the Greek play Ἀλαζών, but whether the Greek dramatist was the inventor of the intrigue, or borrowed it from some popular tale of Eastern extraction, is not known. Whatever may have been the source whence the Arabian version was derived—and the circumstance that it is found only in a text of the "Nights" which is said to have been made in Tunis would seem to point to a Turkish one—it is very unlikely that it was adapted from the comedy of Plautus. True, in Berni and the Arabian version, as in Plautus, the damsel is represented to the husband as a twin-sister of his wife; but, on the other hand, the Arabian story corresponds with the version in the 'Seven Wise Masters' in at least one particular, namely, in the lover's house being situated at some distance from the house of his mistress. The Italian and Sicilian versions seem to be distorted reflections of Plautus; at all events, in all three the house of the damsel adjoins that of her lover. It is probable, on the whole, that the original story is best preserved in the 'Seven Wise Masters': the incident of the two dreams with which the version in that work commences is essentially Oriental; and many parallels to it are known to exist in the fictions of India and Persia.

NOTE

FALLING IN LOVE THROUGH A DREAM (p. 389)

In the Hindú romance entitled 'Vásavadattá,' by Subhandhu (7th century), as analysed by Colebrooke in vol. x. of 'Asiatic Researches,' Candaspascétu, a young and valiant prince, saw in a dream a beautiful maiden, of whom he became enamoured. Impressed with the belief that a person such as he had seen in his dream had a real existence, he resolves to travel in search of her, and departs, attended only by his confidant Macaranda. While reposing under a tree in a forest at the foot of the Vindhya mountains, where they halted, Macaranda overhears two birds conversing,[15] and from their discourse learns that the princess Vásavadattá, having rejected all the suitors who had been assembled by the king

---

[15]This may be added to the other examples of secrets learned from birds, adduced in vol. i, p. 104.

her father for her to make choice of a husband, had seen Candaspascétu in a dream, in which she had even learned his name. Her confidante, Samálika, sent by her in search of the prince, has arrived in the same forest, and is discovered there by Macaranda. She delivers the prince a letter from the princess, and conducts him to the king's palace. He obtains from the princess the avowal of her love, and her confidante reveals to him the violence of her passion.

ᔐ LITTLE FAIRLY ᔑ

THIS is the title of an Irish legend, related with much humour by Samuel Lover, which is even as widespread as the story of the Robbery of the King's Treasury, to which indeed it is closely allied:

Once upon a time there was a farmer who had two wives—for in those days a man could have more than one wife at a time—by one of whom he had a son, who was very sharp-witted, and was called, from his diminutive size, Little Fairly; by the other he had a son of huge dimensions, and as stupid as his half-brother was clever. The old man left all his possessions to his big son, with the exception of one poor cow, which he bequeathed to Little Fairly, desiring his favourite son to allow it to graze on his land. The big brother, however, grudging even this small concession, contrives to cause the death of Little Fairly's cow, for he bore him a bitter hatred. Then Little Fairly takes off the skin of the wretched animal, and splitting it in a few places puts into them some shillings, and goes away to market, where he demands a hundred guineas for it, which soon brings a jeering crowd about him. But he tells the people that the skin has the wonderful property of producing any quantity of shillings whenever it is beat with a stick; and in proof of this he thrashes the skin at a place where he had slipped in a coin, when, sure enough, out drops a shilling, to the admiration of the onlookers, and he repeats the process several times, until a greedy old farmer calls out to him to stop, and handing him a hundred guineas, folds up the magical skin and hastens home with his prize. Next day Little Fairly sends to his big brother to borrow his scales, and he is engaged ostensibly in weighing his gold, when the brother pops in, and seeing what he is about, asks him where he got so much money. Little Fairly tells him that he had got a hundred guineas for the old cow's hide at the market, and he at once goes home and slaughters all his kine and calves, and takes their skins to market, where he demands a hundred and *ten* guineas for each. But by this time the folks had heard of Little Fairly's trick, and conceiving this to be another attempt to impose on them, they set upon him with their sticks, and left him with aching bones.

When he got home he went to Little Fairly's but with a big stick, and while attempting to fell him, he accidentally struck his old mother and killed her on the spot. But Little Fairly determines to make profit even out of this misfortune. His old mother had been a nurse in the squire's family, and the children were still fond of her, for she often visited at the mansion, and brought them gingerbread. So he carried the body to the squire's, and having propped it close by the well in the garden, went into the house, and told the squire's children that "old mammy nurse" was in the garden with gingerbread for them. Hearing this, they all scampered out, and in their race to be first they came bump against the body, which tumbled into the well. Little Fairly sets up a great cry at this *fatal* accident, and the squire gives him fifty guineas, and undertakes to bury the old woman "dacently." Returning home, he again borrows his brother's scales, telling him that he had got a "thrifle" of fifty guineas for the corpse of the old woman. So the big brother kills his old mother, and takes her body to the same doctor who had bought the other, as Little Fairly pretended. The doctor, however, was horror-struck at the offer, and bade him be off, or he would give him into custody as a murderer.

Enraged at being again tricked by the little "spalpeen," he vows that he will throw him into the deepest hole in the Bog of Allen; and so he stuffs Little Fairly into a sack, and rides off with him. On the way he alights at a public-house, and sets the sack against the wall outside. While he is drinking his whisky, a farmer comes up with a great drove of cattle, and hearing groans from something in the sack, he asks who is there, when Little Fairly calls out that he is going straight to Paradise in this holy sack. The farmer offers his horse, his drove of cattle, and five hundred guineas, if Little Fairly will allow him to get into the sack in his place, to which he agrees; and after the blockhead has set him at liberty and is himself secured in the sack, Little Fairly mounts his horse and drives the cattle away. At length the big brother comes out of the tavern, and taking up the sack, which he found much heavier than before, but without suspecting its changed contents, he proceeds to the Bog of Allen, into the deepest hole of which he throws the unlucky farmer. On his way home he sees Little Fairly on horseback and driving a fine lot of cattle. Inquiring where he had got the beeves, Little Fairly tells him that he took them from amongst many thousands that grazed in the meadows at the bottom of the big hole into which he had been thrown, adding that there was an easy way from the place to upper-earth. Upon this the big brother gallops off and casts himself into the hole—and he never came back to persecute clever Little Fairly.

There is another Irish version, in which a poor fellow called Darby Daly puts some coins in his grey horse's dung, and pretends that he thus produces money. Mr Purcell buys the horse of him; and when he comes to revenge himself for the cheat, and have the rascal hung, Darby pretends that he has come to contention with his wife, and, having previously fastened a sheep's stomach full of blood round her neck (concealed by her dress), he stabs her, and she falls apparently dead. Then he reanimates her by blowing in her ear with a ram's horn. Purcell is appeased, and buys the horn. He goes home and stabs his wife, and in vain attempts to resuscitate her. Purcell then stuffs Darby in a sack, intending to drown him; but while the persons he has engaged to do this piece of business turn into a tavern, a pedlar passes by, and changes places with Darby, who makes him believe he has to marry Purcell's daughter and doesn't like her. So the pedlar is drowned. Darby goes round with his wares, and after some time he comes to Purcell, who is much frightened at seeing him. Darby pretends that he is a blest spirit, and brings greeting from Purcell's wife in purgatory, and in her name asks for money, which Purcell readily gives him.[1]

The Norse tale of "Big Peter and Little Peter" is own brother to the Irish legend of Little Fairly, but varies somewhat in the earlier details. Little Peter's sole possession is a calf, which his big brother kills, because it grazed in his field. Having taken off the skin and dried it, Little Peter goes away to sell it, but no one would buy such a tattered thing. Coming at night to a farm-house, he asks for lodgings, but the farmer's wife refuses him, saying that she is quite alone, and could not admit any one in the absence of her husband. But Little Peter, peeping in at the window, sees the dame and the parish priest at supper together, regaling themselves on a great bowl of custard, and having plenty of ale and brandy besides. Presently the farmer is heard approaching, upon which the good dame locks the priest in a great chest, and hides the bowl of custard in the oven and the liquors in the cellar. The farmer being admitted, Peter again knocks at the door, and is heartily welcomed by the good

---

[1]This last incident is the subject of a quite different story, which is widely spread. For instance: in the Norse tale (Dasent) entitled "Not a Pin to choose between them," an old fellow sets out in quest of three greater fools than his own wife, and, among other curious adventures, persuades a simple-minded woman that he has come from Paradise, where one of her husbands (for she had been thrice married) is in rather sad case as to clothes and food, and gets from her good store of both to take back to him.—This tale is also current in Brittany, and similar stories are found in Miss Busk's 'Folk-Lore of Rome' and Natésa Sástri's 'Folk-Lore in Southern India.' Moreover, the story is well known in Ceylon—see my 'Book of Noodles.'

man. Sitting down with his calf's skin at his feet, he thus addresses it, "What are you saying now?" The farmer asks him who he is talking with. "It is a spae-maiden I've got in my calf's skin," he replies. "And what does she spae?" "She says there's a bowl of custard in the oven." The farmer, on searching, discovers it, and also, by the directions of the "spae-maiden," the ale and brandy hidden in the cellar.[2] Amazed at this, the farmer offers to buy the calf's skin, and Peter says he will sell it for the great chest [in which the priest is locked], to which the farmer readily agrees. The dame, secretly alarmed, declares she has lost the key, but Peter will take it notwithstanding; and so, shouldering his bargain, he trudges off. When he comes to a bridge he sets down his burden on the parapet, exclaiming, "This is too heavy for me to carry farther; I will throw it into the river." On hearing this the priest implores him not to do so, but to set him free, and he should have for his reward 800 dollars and his gold watch. So Peter takes a stone and breaks the lock, and the priest got out and went home, *minus* his watch and money. When Peter reached home, he said to his big brother, "There was a good sale for calf-skins in the market to-day. I got 800 dollars for my tattered one, but bigger and stouter ones fetch twice as much," and shows his dollars. "'Twas well you told me this," answered Big Peter, who went and slaughtered all his kine and calves, and set off on the road to town with their skins. So when he got to the market, and the tanners asked what he wanted for his hides, Big Peter said he must have 800 dollars for the small ones, and so on, more and more for the big ones. But all the folk laughed and made game of him—he'd better turn into a madhouse for a better bargain; and so he found out how things had gone, and that Little Peter had played him a trick.

After this he determined to make short work of Little Peter; but the latter, suspecting as much, got his mother to exchange places with him in bed, and Big Peter with his axe cut off her head, thinking he had done for

---

[2] Although this incident does not occur in the story of Little Fairly, a variant of it is found in another Irish popular tale, current in the county of Kerry, which the Hon. J. Abercrombie has published in the 'Folk-Lore Journal' for 1885. A poor lad enters the service of a farmer, and he is not at liberty to leave until (among other stipulations) the cat can speak. The farmer's wife is in love with the landlord, and had one day concealed in her bedroom a dish of fowls which she designed for him. In the evening the lad takes up the cat and pretends to converse with her. His master asks what the cat is saying. "She says, there's a dish of fowls in the bedroom," quoth the lad. So the farmer goes thither, and finds "the cat" has told nothing but the truth. In the sequel, both the wicked landlord and the farmer's wife come to well-merited punishment through the poor lad's clever devices.

his brother. But next morning Little Peter shows him what he had done, and gets 800 dollars from him as hush-money. Then he set his mother's head on her body again, put her on a hand-sledge, and so drew her to market. There he set her up with an apple-basket on each arm and an apple in each hand. By-and-by came a skipper, walking along; he thought she was an apple-woman, and asked if she had apples to sell, and how many he might have for a penny. But the old woman made no answer. So the skipper asked again. No! she hadn't a word to say for herself. "How many may I have for a penny?" he bawled the third time, but the old dame sat bolt upright, as though she neither saw him nor heard what he said. Then the skipper flew into such a rage that he gave her one under the ear, and so away rolled her head across the market-place. At that moment up came Little Peter with a bound; he fell a-weeping and bewailing, and threatened to make the skipper smart for it for dealing the old woman her death-blow. "Dear friend, only hold your tongue about what you know," said the skipper, "and you shall have 800 dollars." And so they made it up.

Big Peter, having learned that Little Peter had got 800 dollars for the body of his old mother, went and killed his mother-in-law, then tried to sell the body, and narrowly escaped being handed over to the sheriff. Then he threatens to strike Little Peter dead, but Little Peter suggests that he should rather put him in a sack and throw him in the river. On the way Big Peter found that he had forgotten something, so he set down the sack by the road-side, and went back for it. Just then came by a man driving a flock of fat sheep, and Little Peter roars out lustily—

> "To kingdom-come, to Paradise!
> To kingdom-come, to Paradise!"

The shepherd asks leave to go with him, and Little Peter bids him untie the sack, and he can creep into it in his stead—for his own part, another time will do as well. Big Peter throws the man in the sack into the river, and returning home overtakes Little Peter with the flock of sheep; and being told that he had got them at the bottom of the river, where they were in thousands, Big Peter gets his wife to tie him in a sack and throw him in;—should he not return soon, it would be because the flock was bigger than he could manage, so she must jump after him, which she does. And so Little Peter got rid of them both.[3]

[3]Dasent's 'Popular Tales from the Norse,' second ed., p. 387 ff.

A considerably amplified version of the droll incident of Little Peter and the priest in the chest is found in the once-popular 'History of Friar Rush,' as follows:

"Rush got up earely in the morning and went to the field, and about his worke; so soone as his master was ready, he tooke his man's breakfast and came to the field, thinking to helpe Rush. (But he was no sooner come from his house but the priest came to see his wife, and presently she made ready some good meate for them to be merry withall, and whyle it was a dressing, they sate sporting together—who had beene there should have scene many loving touches.) And when the goodman came to the field, he found that Rush had done all that which he appointed, whereof he had great marvaile; then they sate downe to breakfast, and as they sate together, Rush beheld his master's shoone, and perceived that for fault of greasing they were very hard: then said Rush to his master, Why are not your shooes better greased? I marvaile that you can goe in them, they be so hard. Have you no more at home? Yes, said his master, I have another payre lying under a great chest at home in my chamber. Then said Rush, I will goe home and grease them, that you may put them on to-morrow; and so he walked homeward merrily and sung by the way. And when he approached neare the house he sung out very loude; with that his dame looked out at the window, and perceiving that it was her servant, shee said unto the priest, Alas, what shall we doe? Our servant is come home, and my husband will not be long after; and with that she thrust the meate into the oven, and all that was upon the table. Where shall I hyde me? said the priest. Goe into the chamber, and creepe under the great chest, among the olde shoone, and I shall cover you: and so she did. And when Rush was come into the house, his dame asked him why he came home so soone? Rush answered and said, I have done all my busines, and my master commaunded me to come home and grease his shoone. Then he went into the chamber and looked under the chest, and there he found the priest, and tooke him by the heeles and drew him out, and said, Thou whoreson priest, what doest thou here? With that, the priest held up his hands and cryed him mercy, and desired him to save his honesty, and he would never more come there; and so Rush let him goe for that once."

The priest broke his word, however, returned, and was again surprised by Rush, who found him hidden under some straw in the stable. A second time he was permitted to escape, though not till after he had received "three or four good dry stripes," and had solemnly promised never to return. Yet the priest ventured to break his word again, and in a visit to the farmer's wife their merriment was a third time interrupted by the familiar song of Rush, who was returning from his labours.

"Then wringing her hands she said unto the priest, Goe hyde you, or else you be but dead. Where shall I hyde me? said the priest. Goe up into the chamber and leape into the basket that hangeth out at the window, and I shall call you when he is gone againe. Then anon in came Rush, and she asked him why he came home so soone? Then said Rush, I have done all my busines in the field, and my master hath sent me home to wash your cheese-basket; and so he went into the chamber, and with his knife he cut the rope that the basket hung by, and downe fell the priest and all into a great poole of water that was under the window: then went he into the stable for a horse and rode into the poole, and tooke the rope that hung at the basket, and tying it to the horse's tayle, rode through the poole three or four tymes. Then he rode through the towne to cause the people to wonder at him, and so came home againe. And all this while he made as though he had known nothing, but looking behinde him, espyed the priest. Then he alighted downe, and said unto him: Thou shalt never more escape me; thy life is lost. With that the priest held up his hands and said, Heere is a hundred peeces of gold, take them and let me goe. So Rush tooke the golde and let the priest goe. And when his master came home, he gave him the half of his money, and bad him farewell, for he would goe see the world."[4]

---

[4]'The Historie of Frier Rush: How he came to a House of Religion to seeke service, and being entertained by the Priour, was first made Under-Cooke. Being full of Pleasant Mirthe and Delight for Young People. Imprinted at London, by Edw. All-de, dwelling neere Christchurche, 1620.'—This work seems to have had a common origin with an old Danish poem of 'Brother Rus; how he did service as a cook and monk in the monastery of Esserom.' The tricky friar was known to Reginald Scot before the history of his pranks was published in this country.

"Friar Rush," says the writer of an interesting article on the Popular Mythology of the Middle Ages in the 'Quarterly Review,' No. XLIV., "is Puck under another name. Puck is also found under the character of Robin Goodfellow, or Robin Hood—the outlaw acquired his by-name from his resemblance to the unquiet wandering spirit. The Robin Hood of England is also the Scottish Red Cap and the Saxon spirit Hudken or Hodeken, so called from the hoodiken, or little hood or hat, which he wore, and which also covers his head when he appears in the shape of the Nisse of Sweden. Hoodiken was ever ready to aid his friends and acquaintances, whether clerks or laymen: A native of Hildesheim, who distrusted the fidelity of his wife, said to him, when he was about to depart on a journey, 'I pray thee have an eye upon my wife whilst I am abroad: I commend my honour to thy care.' Hoodiken accepted the trust without anticipating the nature of his labours. Paramour succeeded paramour. Hoodiken

In a Danish variant of our story, entitled "Great Claus and Little Claus," the hero and his enemy are not brothers, merely neighbours. Little Claus has but one horse, and Great Claus has four horses. All the week Little Claus ploughed for Great Claus, and on Sunday he had leave to plough his own land with all the five. But he was wont to call out, "Gee up! *my* five horses!" at which Great Claus was so enraged that he killed his only horse. Instead of a priest it is a sexton who is locked in the chest; Claus gets a bushel of money from the sexton to let him free, and goes home. Then he sent a boy to Great Claus to borrow a bushel measure. "What can *he* want that for?" thought Great Claus; so he smeared the bottom of the measure with tar, that some of whatever was put into it might stick there and remain. And so it happened; for when the measure was returned, three new silver florins were sticking to it.[5] Great Claus, having killed his four horses, offered their skins for sale, asking a bushel of money a-piece, but only got his own skin well marked by the people, so he re solved to kill Little Claus. Now it happened at this time that the old grandmother of Little Claus died, and he laid the body on his bed, and seated himself in a chair for the night. Great Claus comes in, and groping his way to the bed, strikes the corpse with his hatchet, supposing he had done for Little Claus. In the morning Little Claus dresses his dead grandmother in her best clothes, borrows a horse, which he harnesses to a cart, and drives off to town. Stopping at a wayside inn, he tells the landlord to take a glass of mead to his grandmother in the cart. The landlord offers the mead repeatedly, but the old lady makes no sign; at last in a rage he flings the glass at her, and she falls back into the cart. "Oh!" says Little Claus, "you've killed my old grandmother! Look at the big hole in her forehead!" The landlord gives him a bushel of money, and promises to bury her respectably. As in the other versions, Great Claus kills *his* grandmother, and offers, without success, to sell the body to an apothecary. The rest of the story exactly agrees with the conclusion of the

---

broke the shins of the first, led the second into the horse-pond, and thrust the third into the muck-heap; and yet the dame had wellnigh evaded his vigilance. 'Friend,' exclaimed the merry devil to the husband when he returned to Hildesheim, 'take thy wife back: as thou leftest her even so thou findest her; but never set me such a task again: sooner would I tend all the swine in the woods of Westphalia than undertake to keep one woman constant against her will.'"

[5]The reader will here be reminded of the similar device adopted by the sister-in-law of Ali Baba in the Arabian tale. This incident occurs in other variants of our story which follow the present one; also in the Norse tale of the Magic Quern—see vol. i. p. 28.

Norse variant, excepting only that Great Claus on his way to drown Little Claus comes to a church, and thinks he "may as well go in and hear a psalm," and while thus engaged, an old cattle-driver comes up, and so on.

In a second Norwegian version, the king one day asks the hero ("Peik") to show him some of his tricks, but he says he has left his "fooling-rods" at home. The king lends him his horse to go and fetch them, and the trickster rides off to the next town and sells the horse and the saddle. He afterwards persuades the king to buy a boiler that could boil porridge without a fire; and when the king discovers he has been again tricked and goes to punish him, he induces him to buy the chopping-block to set the boiler on in place of a fire. After this the king vows he will have the rogue's life, but he fills a bladder with sheep's blood and hangs it round his sister's neck, and, having instructed her what to do when the king comes, lies down in his bed. On the arrival of the justly incensed king, he asks the girl where her brother is, and she replies that he is ill and confined to his bed, and she dare not disturb him; but the king insisting upon her awaking her brother at once, she does so, upon which he stabs the bladder suspended from her neck and she falls down as if dead. The king is horror-struck at this, but the rogue blows a horn, and immediately the girl rises up as well as ever. For a large sum the king purchases this wonderful horn, and returning to his palace picks a quarrel with the queen and his daughter, and having slain them both, blows his horn in vain to restore them to life—dead they were, and dead they continued to be, in spite of all the horn-blowing. The story concludes like the preceding version, with a cask substituted for the sack.[6]

As might be expected, the story is also current among the people of Iceland, but in a form so different from any of the versions already cited, that a pretty full abstract of it is necessary for comparison with variants that are to follow. The hero of the Icelandic legend is a young smith named Sigurdr, who had in his early youth been a playmate of the king's two sons, but when the princes grew up they treated him harshly, for which he paid them off with clever tricks. They burned down his smithy one night, and next day Sigurdr filled two sacks with the ashes, and hanging one on each side of his horse, went off into the forest. Coming

[6]Dasent's 'Tales from the Fjeld,' pp. 94–104.

to a farm belonging to the king, he asked and obtained leave to stop there for the night, and consigned to the manager's care his two sacks of ashes, saying they contained rare and costly things. Now the housekeeper, over-hearing this conversation, became curious to see the contents of the two sacks; so at night she took one of them and emptied it outside the house, and the wind blew all the ashes away, and she was no wiser than before; then she emptied the other sack, with the like result. Thinking that this might be a hanging matter for her, she secretly filled the two sacks with the king's gold, and put them in their former place. In the morning, Sig-urdr takes his new load home, and pretends to the king's sons that he got all the money by the sale of the ashes of his old smithy. So they burned down the forge of their father's goldsmith, and gathering the ashes, went about offering them for sale, but they only got laughed at for their trou-ble. Then they swore to be revenged on Sigurdr, but he suspected they meant him no good, and going to the stable, he scattered a lot of gold about his mare, and was busy picking it up when the king's sons came. They asked him if it was the mare that had produced all that money, and when he said it was, they bought the mare for a great sum; and Sigurdr told them to put her in a stable by herself, give her no meat for a fort-night, then go to the mare—and they should see what they should see. But at the end of a week they went to the stable, and found the mare stone-dead, with a heap round her of something different from gold coins. Sigurdr next takes a big lump of butter, and spreads it over a hillock with his cudgel, when up came the king's sons and scolded him for the mare-business; but he told them all had happened because they did not wait the fortnight out. When they discover the butter on the hillock, they ask him how that was, and he says that his cudgel has the magic power of turning hillocks that were beaten with it into butter. So they buy his cudgel for an unheard-of price, and on the way home they begin turning the hillocks into butter, but only knocked the clods and stones about their own ears. After this they induce the king to promise he will put Sigurdr to death. But he is not to be taken unawares, so he says to his mother, "The king is coming here. Dress as well as you can, and sit down in the middle of the floor, and I will cover you over with a heap of rags; and when the king comes to the window and looks in, I shall tell you that I am going to make you shed your age-shape.[7] I will

---

[7] In Norse folk-lore, certain men, after living a hundred years, shed their "age-shape," and became young and vigorous again.

take a bag full of wind and thump you with it, and at the blow I will tell you to get up and shake yourself. Then you will stand up at once, and the rags will fall off you, so that you will look younger than before in the king's eyes." So when the king comes to the window, he hears some one inside saying, "Now I will have you shed your age-shape, my mother"; and then walking into the cottage, he says to Sigurdr, "If you show me how it is done, I will spare your life." And Sigurdr did all with his old mother that he had before arranged. So the king tries the plan on his son's foster-mother, but as he put stones in the sack, he broke her skull. "Get up, old woman, and shake yourself," says the king; but she moved neither leg nor limb, and then he saw that he had been duped by Sigurdr. After this the king was having one of his oxen slaughtered, and Sigurdr came to beg some of the entrails, when the king roundly abused him for his trick, but Sigurdr explained, the king should not have put stones in the sack; and then the king asked what he meant to do with the entrails of the ox, so Sigurdr replied he should drink the liquor from them through a reed, and then he should have knowledge of future events. The king gave him a part but kept the remainder for his own use, and the result of the experiment he made was that he died. The king's sons had now his death to avenge, so they went to Sigurdr's cottage, and broke his mother's neck because she would not tell them where Sigurdr was to be found. When Sigurdr comes home and discovered his dead mother, he dressed her up in fine clothes, saddled a horse, and fastening the body to it, led it into the forest, where he met with a man who had charge of the king's oxen; and the oxen surrounded the horse and made it shy, and the body of the old woman fell to the ground. "Oh, oh," cries Sigurdr, "you're the cause of my poor mother's death—you'd better cut and run, if you'd save your own life." So the man ran off, and Sigurdr drove the oxen to his own place. Next day he tells the king's sons that he had exchanged the old woman's body for these oxen, so they drown their old mother in the bath, and go to the king, who, Sigurdr pretended, had bought the other body, and offered him the corpse for sale; but he bade them be off for a brace of villains. Meanwhile Sigurdr had visited their sister, who asked his advice as to how she might get her rights from her two brothers; so he told her to keep an easy mind, for he did not think her brothers would live long. When they come home, they seize Sigurdr, put him in a sack, and hang him over a rock that stretched up from the sea, saying that there he should hang till he died, and went away. It happened that Sigurdr had his harp with him, and he was playing on it for amusement, when up comes a herdsman and asks him that was in the sack what he was doing. "Let me alone," cries Sigurdr; "I'm drawing money out of the rock." Then the herdsman hauled him up, drove him out of the sack, jumped into it himself, and set to work with the harp to draw money from the rock, while Sigurdr took the herdsman's sheep and drove them home. But the king's sons had gone to the rock and tossed the herdsman in the sack into the sea, thinking they had done for Sigurdr, and were returning home when they overtook Sigurdr himself with his flock of sheep. "It was well done, your throwing me over a rock, for I've got all these sheep in a cave under the sea, and there are many more." On hearing this, they went to the rock, cast themselves into the sea expecting to find lots of sheep, and were both drowned. Then Sigurdr wooed and married the king's daughter, and was made king over the whole kingdom—and here ends the story.[8]

A great many versions are known in Germany, some of which are rather important. In Valentin Schumann's 'Nachtbüchlein,' No 6, a peasant, called Einhirn, has made himself detested through his knavery. His neighbours destroy his oven. He pounds the red clay small, puts it into a sack, and goes to Augsburg. The hostess of an inn believes there is gold in the sack, and substitutes a sackfull of pence. Einhirn relates at home that he obtained money for the earth of the oven. His neighbours then smash all their own ovens and try to sell the earth in Augsburg. Finding how they had been tricked, they kill Einhirn's cow. He takes off the hide and sells it in Augsburg. From the tanner's wife, with whose amorous desires he had complied, but whom he threatened to betray to her husband, he extorts 100 florins, and pretends at home that he received them for the cow's hide. Then his neighbours slaughter their cows and carry the hides to Augsburg. Once more deceived, in revenge they kill his mother. He lays the corpse in the highway, where a wagoner drives over it, whom he accuses of the murder, and who in his fear gives up to him his wagon and horses. Finally, the peasants put him in a sack to drown him; but before they do this they hear a mass. Einhirn screams in the sack, "I won't learn it," and palms off upon a passing swineherd that his father wants him to learn the goldsmith's craft. The herd allows himself to be put in the sack, and is drowned. In the evening Einhirn appears in the village with the swine. The peasants now determine to throw one of

---

[8]Powell and Magnusson's 'Legends of Iceland,' second series, p. 581–595.

themselves also into the water, and' if he sees swine at the bottom, he must throw up his hands. The drowning man does this, and they all spring in after him.

In 'Volkssagen, Märchen, and Legenden,' edited by J. G. Büsching, p. 296 ff., the hero is a peasant named Kibitz (Lapwing). As he at his ploughing one day heard a lapwing crying continually "kibitz," he thinks the bird is mocking his own name, and throws a stone at him, but the stone hits one of his yoke of oxen and kills it. Then he strikes the other ox also, for he can't do anything with it alone, kills it, and carries the hides to the town for sale. He has an opportunity to observe how a tanner's wife conceals her lover in an old chest; buys the chest of her husband for the hide, and then extorts from its occupant a large sum of money. To the peasants of his village he says he has got the money for the hides, where-upon they all kill their oxen and drive off to the tanners with the hides, and finding the cheat that had been put upon them, they try to kill Kibitz, but instead of him they kill his wife, with whom he had exchanged clothes. Kibitz now sets the body with a basketful of fruit against a paling in the town, where the servant of a noble house, who wants to buy fruit, and whom she does not answer, pushes her, so that she falls into the water. Kibitz hastens up, crying, and the servant's master gives him a carriage and horses by way of compensation, with which he returns to the village. The envious peasants now put him in a barrel, and so on. He cries in the barrel, "I won't be burgomaster!" and exchanges places with a shepherd, and so on. Afterwards he says to the peasants that only the white bubbles in the water will turn out to be sheep. The bailiff springs in first, and when the peasants begin to be afraid he will take too many, they all jump in and are drowned.

A Westphalian variant more closely resembles the Norse story (Stahl, 'Westphälische Sagen und Geschichten,' s. 34): A poor peasant named Hick through necessity kills his only cow. He carries the hide to Cologne. Caught in a thunderstorm on the way, he wraps himself up in the hide, and by this means catches a raven, which settles upon him. In Cologne he spies a hostess entertain a monk and eat with him. When her husband arrives unexpectedly, she conceals the food and drink and the

---

[9]Here, again, we have Little Peter's adventure at the farmhouse, which indeed occurs in many European versions of this story. It is the subject of the poetical tale entitled "The Friars of Berwick," ascribed to William Dunbar, the eminent Scottish poet, who died about the year 1525, which was imitated by Allan Ramsay, under the title of "The Monk and the Miller's

monk. Hick says to the husband that his raven can divine, and discovers to him the hidden articles and the monk, whereupon the husband purchases the bird of him.[9] At home Hick tells his neighbours that he has got all his money for the cow's hide, and so on. After the disappointment of the peasants with their cow-hides, immediately follows the incident of the tun (or sack), the turning of the peasants into the tavern, the exchange with the passing shepherd, and lastly, the leap of the peasants into the Rhine. Hick sings in the tun, as it were but to ease his misery, the commencement of a popular song, "I must be Bishop of Cologne, and have little joy." The shepherd takes this seriously, and thus Hick succeeds in his device. Subsequently Hick drives his sheep to the Rhine, and their reflections in the water are taken by the peasants for real sheep at the bottom.[10] The first who leaps in has to stretch his arms upward if he sees the sheep.

In a Tyrolese version (Zingerle, vol. ii. p. 414), an old blind butcher has a cow he had bought replaced by other neighbouring butchers by a goat. For this he has his revenge when, in concert with some innkeepers, he makes them believe he has an old hat which always pays the score, and sells it to them for a large sum of money. When he hears the victims of his deception afterwards crowding into his house, he concerts with his wife and pretends to be dead, but the wife revives him by a thrice-repeated touch with a stick. The butchers at sight of this marvel forget their wrath, buy the stick, and endeavour to revive the king's dead daughter with it. Then the story runs as usual: sack, tavern, pig-driver—"I won't have the king's daughter," and so on.[11]

An interesting version, taken, it is said, from a manuscript of the eleventh century, is found in Grimm and Schmeller's collection of mediæval Latin poetry, published, at Göttingen, in 1838, from which the German

---

Wife." Between the time of Dunbar and Ramsay, the story of the concealed lover was produced in the third part of a curious work by Francis Kirkman, a voluminous scribbler, "The English Rogue," published in 1674, pp. 182–188, where a soldier is billeted in the house of an old mercer, lately married to a pretty young woman, who scrupled to admit him in the absence of her husband. The soldier spies, through a crack in the floor of the garret, the virtuous young wife about to sit down to a sumptuous supper with her lover, a young lawyer, when the husband returns unexpectedly, and there is barely time to conceal the lover and the food before he comes into the room. When the soldier introduces himself, he pretends to be a magician, and causes the hidden supper to be produced, as in the case of the little trickster of our tale.

[10]In a Hessian version found in Grimm, No. 61, the reflections of the fleecy clouds in the water are taken for lambs.

[11]These form but a small selection from the German and other variants, cited by Dr Reinhold Köhler, in a valuable review of Campbell's Gaelic tales in 'Orient and Occident,' vol. ii. p. 488 ff.

story of The Little Farmer (Grimm's 'Kinder und Haus Märchen') was perhaps derived: The hero, Unibos, who was so named because he constantly lost all his cattle but one, had enemies in the provost, mayor, and priest of the town. At length his last bullock dying, he took the hide to a neighbouring fair and sold it, and on his way home accidentally discovered a treasure. He thereupon sent to the provost to borrow a pint measure. The provost, curious to know the use to which this is to be applied, watches through the door, sees the gold, and accuses Unibos of robbery. The latter, aware of the provost's malice, determines to play a trick upon him, which leads him into farther scrapes than he expected, though they all turn out in the end to his advantage. He tells the provost that at the fair which he had visited, bullocks' hides were in great request, and that he had sold his own for the gold which he saw there. The provost consults with the mayor and the priest, and they kill all their cattle and carry the hides to the fair, where they ask an enormous price for them. At first they are only laughed at, but in the end they become involved in a quarrel with the shoemakers of the town, are carried before the magistrates, and obliged to abandon their hides to pay the fine for a breach of the peace.

The three enemies of Unibos return in great wrath, to escape the effects of which he is obliged to have recourse to another trick. He smears his wife with bullock's blood, and makes her lie down, to all appearance dead. The provost and his companions arrive, and are horror-struck at the spectacle offered to their eyes; but Unibos takes the matter coolly, and tells them that, if they will forgive him the trick he had played upon them, he will undertake to restore his wife to life, and make her younger and more handsome than she had been before. To this they immediately agree, and Unihos, taking a small trumpet out of a wooden box, blows on it three times over the body of his wife, with strange ceremonies, and when the trumpet sounds the third time, she jumps upon her feet. She then washes and dresses herself, and appears so much more handsome than before, that the three officials, who had each a wife that was getting old and ill-favoured, give a great sum of money to possess the instrument, and each of them goes immediately and kills his wife; but they find that the virtue of the trumpet has departed.

Again they repair to the hut of Unibos, who averts their vengeance by another trick, and extorts a large sum of money as the price of his mare. In this they find themselves equally cheated, and seize upon Unibos, whose tricks appear to be exhausted, and give him only the choice of the manner of his death. He requests to be confined in a barrel and thrown into the sea. On their way to the coast, his three enemies enter a public-house to drink, and leave the barrel at the door. A herdsman passes at this moment with a drove of pigs, and hearing a person in the barrel, asks him how he came there. Unibos answers that he is subjected to this punishment because he refused to be made provost of a large town. The herdsman, ambitious of the honour, agrees to change places with him, and Unibos proceeds home with the pigs. The three officials continue their journey, and in spite of the exclamations of the prisoner in the barrel that he is willing to be provost, they throw him into the sea; but what was their astonishment on their return at meeting their old enemy, whom they supposed drowned, driving before him a fine drove of pigs. He tells them that at the bottom of the sea he had found a pleasant country where were innumerable pigs, of which he had only brought with him a few. The greedy officials are seduced by his tale, and throw themselves from a rock into the sea, and Unibos is thus delivered of his enemies.[12]

In Burgundy (Beauvois' 'Contes populaires de la Norvége, de la Finlande, et de la Bourgogne') the story is told of one called Jean Bête, who, on the way to market with his cow-hide, was overtaken by a thunderstorm, and climbed a tree under which a gang of thieves presently came and seated themselves to divide their booty. Jean Bête lets his hide fall, and the thieves run away in great fright, leaving the money lying there, which Jean appropriates. Returning home, he borrows of his lord a bushel to measure the money with, and leaves some pieces sticking to it, for the lord had put a little pitch inside of it. Being told that the money was obtained by the sale of the skin, the lord kills all his cows and carries the hides to market with the usual result. Then follows the incident of the sack: Jean cries out in the sack that he won't be a bishop, and changes places with a passing cattle-dealer.

In Gascony the story (according to Cenac Moncaut's 'Contes populaires de la Gascogne') is thus told: A youth called Capdarmère is sent by his mother to sell her only pair of oxen, and get as much as possible for them. Two merchants give him a little tobacco and a bean. When he

---

[12]From an article on Mediæval Stories in the 'Foreign Quarterly Review,' No. LXX., July 1845, pp. 434–436.—The hero's trick with his mare, so obscurely referred to by the modest reviewer, was doubtless similar to that employed by Sigurdr the Sack-knocker in the Icelandic version.

comes home with these articles his mother scolds him, and says he will never "catch the wolf by the tail." Capdarmère goes into the forest, catches a sleeping wolf with a noose, and leads him to his mother. Then he puts the fleece of a sheep round the wolf, and sells it to the two merchants who had cheated him out of the oxen, in whose stalls the wolf soon makes great havoc. When the merchants hasten in a rage to Capdarmère, who sees them coming, they find him just as he has apparently stabbed his dog with a knife, and then reanimated him with certain words. He pretends that refractory animals pierced with this knife, and revived with the words, become tame. The merchants buy the knife of him, and when they have found out the trick, they pounce upon him, and stuff him in a sack, and so on. Capdarmère tells a passing pig-dealer that he has to marry a princess. The swine are to rise from the bottom of the lake. For the rest, neither the pig-dealer nor the two merchants are drowned in this Gascon version, but are saved by Capdarmère, which may, perhaps, as Dr Köhler has remarked, be an alteration of the collector. The introduction, which is quite peculiar to the Gascon tale, probably belongs to a different one; while the knife which tames refractory animals is certainly no improvement on the reanimating or rejuvenating horn in other versions.

One of the four Gaelic versions given by Campbell in his 'Popular Tales of the West Highlands' (vol. ii. p. 218) is rather inaptly entitled "The Three Widows," since they are only mentioned in the opening sentence: "There were three widows, and every one of them had a son apiece. Dòmhnull was the name of the son of one of them." He had four stots, and the others had but two each. They kill his animals, and he takes the skin of one of them to sell in "the big town." At night he goes into a wood, and puts the hide about his head; and a flock of birds come and light on the hide, and he put out his hand and caught one of them. At daybreak he resumed his journey, and arrived at the house of a gentleman, "who came to the door himself." Dòmhnull tells him that his bird is a soothsayer, and that it says he has a wish to buy it, and would give two hundred pounds Saxon for it. So the gentleman buys the bird and pays the money, and Dòmhnull went home, "but never a pinch of divination did the bird do after." The two envious neighbours of Dòmhnull believing that he had got his money by the sale of a stot's skin, killed their stots, with the same result as is related in the preceding versions, and returning home, they kill his mother on her way to the well. Dòmhnull adopts a similar device to that of Little Fairly to make profit out of the misfortune, only in place of a squire it is the king's house that he visits. The conclusion corresponds with that of the versions already cited.

In the second Gaelic variant, "Ribin, Robin, and Levi the Dun" (vol. ii. p. 229), we find Little Fairly's trick of slitting the cow's hide and putting pieces of money inside. Levi the Dun takes his cow's hide to market, and meeting with a man who made him an offer, he invited him to go into the inn and "have a dram." When the liquor was brought, Levi the Dun struck the hide with his stick and said, "Pay this, hide," whereupon the required sum fell on the floor. So the gentleman bought the hide. When his mother is killed by the two others, Ribin and Robin, Levi the Dun takes the body to the town and props it against a well; a boy, the son of the provost, topples it into the well, and the father gives him 500 marks by way of compensation, and promises to see her "decently buried." After getting home, his two envious neighbours observe him counting his money, and learning from him that "there is a high price given for dead old women, to make powder of their bones," they will try the same thing. And "he who had no mother had a mother-in-law; so they killed an old woman each," but without producing the expected result. Levi the Dun, suspecting they meant to do him an injury, invited them to a grand feast, and before they came, "he filled a portion of a sheep's gut with blood, and tied it round his wife's neck. 'Now,' said he, 'when they come, I will call you to place more upon the table, and when you don't lay down enough, I will rise and take my knife, and stick it into the piece of gut that is around your neck, and I will let you fall gently to the ground. Afterwards I will sound a horn, and you will then rise and wash yourself, and be as you were—living and well.'" All this took place at the feast, and when Ribin and Robin saw the strange things that Levi the Dun could do, they went away, saying to each other, "Our own wives might very well provide us with such a feast as we had from Levi the Dun; and if they do not, we will treat them just as he did his wife." When they had returned home, "they told their wives that they must prepare them a feast, and a better one than Levi the Dun had given them. 'Oh,' said the women, 'Levi the Dun has sent you home drunk, and you don't know what you are saying.' Both of the men rose and cut the throats of their wives at once. They fell down and were shedding their blood. The men then rose and sounded a horn to raise them again. Though they should sound the horn till this very hour, the wives wouldn't rise. When they saw that their wives would not rise, they resolved to pursue Levi the Dun. When he saw them coming, he took to his heels and ran away. They looked at nothing else; but after him they ran, determined to have his life. He hadn't run far on his way when he met with a man having a flock of sheep. He said to the man, 'Put off your plaid and put on what I am wearing; there are two men coming who are resolved to have your life. Run as fast as you can, or you will be a dead man immediately.' The man ran away as he was bidden, and they ran hard after him. They didn't halt until they had pushed him into the deep pool of Ty-an leòban. The man fell in, and he was never seen afterwards. They returned home. Next day, what did they see on looking out but Levi the Dun herding a fine flock of sheep. They came to the place where he was. 'Levi the Dun,' said they, 'the whole world won't satisfy you; didn't we think that we had pitched you last night into the pool of Ty-an leòban?' 'Don't you see the sheep I found there?' said he. 'Would we find the same if we went in?' said they. 'Yes, if I were to put you in,' said he. Off Ribin and Robin set, and off Levi the Dun set after them. When they were got to the hole they stood still. Levi the Dun came behind them, and pushed them both into the pool. 'Fish for sheep there,' he said, 'if you choose.' Levi the Dun came home, and got everything in the place for himself."

The third of the Gaelic versions is entitled "Brian Briagach," Bragging Brian (vol. ii. p. 233). The hero is visited by a merchant, and pretends to him that he has a mare that coined gold and silver. Brian secretly "gave the mare money among her food, and the merchant found it when he looked for it, and he gave thousands for the mare, and when he got her she was coining money. He took her with him, and he had her for a week, but a penny of money she did not coin. He let her alone till the end of a month, but money she did not make." Then he went to talk to Brian "for the lie," and to send the mare back again. Brian adopts the same device as Levi the Dun in the preceding version, of tying a gut full of blood to his wife's neck, and in presence of the merchant begins to scold her, and ultimately knocks her down for dead, and the blood ran about the floor. Then he takes *two* horns and blew into his wife's throat, and brought her alive again. "The merchant got the horns, and promised to say no more about the mare, and went home and killed his wife, and his sister, and his mother, and he began to blow into their throats with the horns; but though he were blowing for ever, he had not brought them alive. Then he went where Lying Brian was, to kill him. He got him into a sack, and was to beat him to death with flails, but Brian asked a little delay, and got out [it is not said how], and put in two little dogs. The men threw the sack into the sea when they were tired of beating it.—What was more wonderful for the merchant at the end of a fortnight than to see Brian and a lot of cattle with him! 'Oh my reason!' said the merchant, 'halt thou come back, O Brian?' 'I came,' said Brian. 'It was you that did the good to me: when you put me into the sea, I saw thy mother, and thy wife, and thy sister, since I went away, and they asked thee to go out on the sea in the place where thou didst put me out, and said that thou thyself shouldst get a lot of cattle like this.' The merchant went and cut a caper on the spot where he had put out Brian, and he was drowned, and Brian got his house for himself."

Something is evidently omitted in this version, which leaves Brian's escape from the sack and his herd of cattle unexplained. The fourth Gaelic version given by Campbell (vol. ii. p. 235) comprises incidents in the second and third, and may be passed over, as it has nothing peculiar to itself.

In his notes to the Gaelic variants Campbell points out that the story occurs in the 'Pleasant Nights' (Piacevoli Notti) of the Italian novelist Straparola, first published, at Venice, in 1550. In this version three rogues outwit a priest, who is very profitably revenged on them in his turn: First, they persuade him that a mule which he has bought is an ass, and get it (an incident adapted from the story, in the Fables of Bidpai, of the Bráhman and the Goat); then he sells them, as a bargain, a goat which is good for nothing. He next pretends to kill his housekeeper by sticking a knife into a bladder filled with blood, as in the third and fourth Gaelic versions, and brings her alive again by something which he sells to them for two hundred gold florins, and they kill their wives in earnest. They are enraged, catch the priest, and put him into a sack, intending to drown him in the river. They set him down, and a shepherd comes, who hears a lamentable voice in a sack saying, "They wish to give her to me, and I don't want her." The priest explains that the lord of that city wants to marry him to his daughter, and thus entices the shepherd to exchange places with him, and he is drowned. The priest takes the sheep, and the rogues, when they find that he had got them (according to his own account) in the river, beg also to be put into sacks. They get in, and are thrown into the river, after which the priest, rich in money and flocks, returns home and lives very happily.

Mr Campbell remarks that "it seems worthy of inquiry by what process the story got from Italian into Gaelic, or who *first* invented it." But the story did not come to the West Highlands from Italy, but through the Norsemen; moreover, there is reason to believe that it was also carried to the south of Europe by the same hardy and adventurous race, since there is a Sicilian popular version, in Pitrè's collection, which presents some points of resemblance to incidents in the second Norse variant (cited on page 407), not found in any other version, the substance of which is as follows:

There was a crafty old fellow called Uncle Capriano, who had a wife and a daughter, and lived on his own property near a certain town. One day thirteen robbers happened to pass his house; they dismounted, made friends with him, and often afterwards came to see him, and even do work for him. Uncle Capriano at length says to his wife that he has devised a plan for getting money out of the simple-minded robbers, and instructs his daughter how she is to act when they next come to the house. So one day Uncle Capriano brings the thieves home with him, and his daughter, as she had been previously instructed, bathes a rabbit privately, and bringing it into the room wet from its bath, exclaims to her father, "Is this the way you load the poor little thing, that it comes home tired to death, and all covered with sweat?" The robbers, believing that the rabbit had been taught to fetch and carry, buy it of Uncle Capriano for a large sum of money, and take it away. "Let us," said one, "send a bag to each of our houses. First carry a bag to mine;" and giving the rabbit a stroke, it ran off and was seen no more.[13] So they went to Uncle Capriano and complained of the trick he had played them. "Did you beat it?" "Of course we did." "Oh, where?" "On the left side." "That's why it ran away. You should have beat it on the right." And so they became good friends as before. Another day Uncle Capriano said to his wife, "To-morrow you must buy a new pot, and then cook some meat in an old pot somewhere in the house; and at Ave Maria, just before I come home, you must empty the contents of the old pot into the new one, and I will tell them that I have a pot that cooks without fire." When the thieves see this new wonder they buy the pot, to find they have been duped once more; and they broke the pot in their rage. Going to Uncle Capriano with their fresh complaint, "What kind of a hearth did you set it on?" he asks—"high or low?" "It was rather high." "Ah, you should have set it on a low hearth," says Uncle Capriano; and the thieves go off, satisfied that it was all their

[13] In the "Merry Tales of the Mad Men of Gotham," one of the exploits of those wittols is to put their rents into a purse, which they fasten to a hare's neck, and send her off with it to their landlord.

own mistake. Some days after this, Uncle Capriano fastens a bladder of blood under his wife's dress, and when the thieves come to dine with him, he stabs his wife, who falls down, apparently weltering in her life's blood. Uncle Capriano then blows a whistle three times, upon which she starts up, to the astonishment of the simpletons, who, having purchased the whistle, go home and kill their wives, and find the whistle's blasts powerless to restore them to life. They now resolve to put Uncle Capriano to death for his repeated villainies; so they stuff him in a sack, and set off to throw him into the sea. On their way they stop at a country house to eat, leaving him in the sack outside. A herdsman comes past, and Uncle Capriano begins to cry, "They want to marry me to the king's daughter, and I won't, for I'm married already." The herdsman says, "I'll take her myself—I'm single." So he readily exchanges places with Uncle Capriano, who drives off the herdsman's sheep and oxen. The thieves having thrown the sack containing the unlucky herdsman into the sea, they overtake Uncle Capriano driving his flocks and herds, and when they learn that he found them at the bottom of the sea, they all entreated to be thrown in also. They returned to the sea, and Uncle Capriano began to throw them in, and each cried out, "Quick, Uncle Capriano, throw me in before my comrades get them all!"[14]

In M. Legrand's collection of modern Greek popular tales we find a rather unsatisfactory version, which must be taken for what it is worth:

Three brothers, Spazio, Antonuccio, and Trianniscia, inherit from their father, the two first, each a fine ox, and the youngest, who was thought a little silly, a lean cow. Trianniscia, the youngest, kills his cow, flays it, and stretches the skin to dry on a wild pear-tree. When it is very dry he binds it round him with a cord and goes off, beating on it like a drum. He frightens some thieves, while they are dividing their spoil, who, thinking the soldiers are coming, run away, and Trianniscia takes all the money they leave behind them, and returning home, tells his brothers he got it for the dried skin. They kill their oxen, dry the skins, and go to market, crying, "Who wants skins for 100 ducats each?" The police put them in prison, and on their being set at liberty, they determine to kill their brother. Trianniscia next takes a basket and goes away again. Coming to a village, he enters the inn, where he leaves it, saying, "Let no one touch this basket. I'm going to

---

[14]Crane's 'Italian Popular Tales,' pp. 303–308.

hear mass." On his return, the basket could not be found, so he begins to scold the folk of the inn, and the landlord pacifies him with a present of 100 ducats and he goes home. Another time he conceals himself in the confessional of the church: an old lady is being buried there; after the people are all gone, he takes up the body, puts it on his horse, and brings it to Lecce. He enters the inn there, and having laid the body in a bed, goes to mass, leaving orders not to disturb the lady. When he comes back, he makes a great outcry at her death, and the innkeeper offers him one of his three pretty daughters for his wife. He chooses one, and takes her home with him. The brothers are envious of his good fortune, and exclaim, "What trick have you played us? One and one, *two,* and one, *three:* let us take him, bind him in a sack, and throw him into the sea." Accordingly they put him in a sack, carry him to a wall, throw him over, and leave him till their return from mass. Meantime a shepherd playing the flute comes by, and Trianniscia persuades him to open the sack and exchange places with him. When the brothers return they take up the sack and throw it into the sea, saying, "We have got rid of him now!" But they soon see Trianniscia sitting on a wall playing the flute, and say to each other, "What a miserable lot is ours! This Trianniscia is a demon who plays us tricks!"[15]

The story of the Young Calender in Gueulette's so-called 'Contes Tartares' may have been partly adapted from Straparola: The hero, having been cheated by three sharpers in a manner similar to the story of the Sharpers and the Simpleton—see *ante,* p. 281 ff.—is eager to be revenged, and having two white goats resembling each other, he goes with one of them to the market where he had been cheated. The three men, who are there seeking opportunities of depredation, immediately enter into conversation with him, and in their presence he buys various articles of provision, and placing them in a basket on the goat's back, orders the animal to inform his servant that he had invited some friends to dinner, and to give her directions how each of the different articles is to be cooked, and then he turns it loose. The sharpers laugh at him; but in order to con-

[15]Had M. Legrand known the story in a number of forms, it is possible that, by jogging the memory of his story-teller, he might have obtained a much better version. As it is, the brothers say that the hero had played them *three* tricks, yet only one is mentioned—the cows' hides. The youth must have pretended that his basket contained something valuable, to induce the host to give him 100 ducats as compensation. The incident of the sack is also very obscurely told.

vince them he was in earnest, he asks them to accompany him home. There, to their astonishment, they find the dinner prepared exactly according to the Calender's directions; and, in their presence, the mother of the Calender, who was in the secret and acted the servant, tells her son that his friends had sent to excuse themselves, and that the goat had delivered his orders and was now feeding in the garden, where, in fact, the other white goat was browsing on the plants. The Calender invites the sharpers to join in his dinner, and ends by cheating them of a large sum of money in exchange for the supposed miraculous goat.

Finding the animal endowed with none of the properties they expected, they return to take revenge on the Calender. He receives their reproaches with surprise, calls in his pretended servant, and asks why she neglected to give them a particular direction relating to the goat which he had forgotten, and she makes an excuse. In a feigned passion he stabs her, and she falls down covered with blood, and apparently dead. The three men are horrified at this catastrophe; but the Calender tells them not to be alarmed. He takes a horn out of a little casket, blows it over the body, and his mother, who only pretended to be dead, arises and leaves the room unhurt. Seeing this, the three sharpers buy the horn for a great sum of money, and returning home, sup with their wives. After supper, anxious to try the virtue of the horn, they pick a quarrel with the ladies and cut their throats. The horn proves as great a failure as the goat; and the police, who had been attracted by the noise, force their way in and seize two of the sharpers, who are hanged for the murders, while the third escapes.

The surviving sharper, some time afterwards, meets with the Calender, puts him in a sack, and carries him off with the intention of throwing him into a deep river. But on his way he hears the approach of horsemen, and, fearing to be discovered, throws the sack into a hole beside the road, and rides off to a distance. A butcher arrives with a flock of sheep, and discovering the Calender in the sack, proceeds to question him. The Calender says he is confined there because he will not marry the kází's daughter; a beautiful damsel, but who has been guilty of an indiscretion. The butcher, allured by the prospect of advancement, agrees to take his place in the sack, and the Calender marches off with the sheep. The sharper returns, and, in spite of the promises of the butcher to marry the kází's daughter, throws him into the river. But on his way back he is astonished to meet the Calender with the sheep. The latter tells him that when he reached the bottom of the river he found a good genie, who gave him these sheep, and told him that if he had been thrown farther into the river he would have obtained a much larger flock. The sharper, allured by the love of gain, allows himself to be confined in a sack and thrown into the river.[16]

The Kabaïl, or wandering tribes of Algeria, have a very curious version of the story, which they probably obtained from some Muslim (Arabian) source:

An orphan boy tends a calf of his own and two oxen belonging to his uncle. He puts the calf to feed in the meadow, and fastens up the oxen so that they cannot feed. At the end of a month the oxen are lean and the calf is bursting with fatness; and when the uncle asks the reason of this, the boy professes ignorance, but the old man secretly discovers the trick. One day he asks the lad to come out to hunt, and gives him a gun. He contrives to cover the calf with dust, in order to alter its appearance, and drives it towards his nephew, who shoots it by mistake; but he says nothing, and makes a grand feast with the flesh. The skin of the calf he keeps till it is sour, and then sells it at market for one pierced coin. Meeting two men who had sold goods for 100 francs, the youth slyly puts his coin among theirs, and then shouts that they have robbed him, upon which they are apprehended. The youth states to the judge that they took 100 francs and a pierced coin from him. The men are searched, and this sum is found in their possession. In vain they disown the pierced coin; the judge decrees that the money belongs to the youth, so home he goes with the 100 francs, which he gives to his uncle. The nephew then advises him to kill his oxen, keep the skins till they have become sour, and then take them to market, which he does, but finds no purchasers. Seeing how he has been tricked, the old man takes his nephew out one day to cut wood, gets him up an ash-tree, and leaves him hanging there. By-and-by an aged man and his daughter-in-law come riding past on a mule, and the youth, seeing them, exclaims, "Oh, oh, an old man once I was; now I'm a youth again!" So the old man wishes a similar change in his own person, liberates the boy, puts the rope round his own neck, and is speedily strangled. The boy goes home with the young woman and the mule, and replying to his uncle's expressions of astonishment, he says, "Had you hung me on the very top of the tree, I should have been luckier still." So the uncle takes one of his own sons and hangs him to the tree-top; awaits his return in vain; then goes and finds him

---

[16]Gueulette's 'Contes Tartares' are imitations of Eastern fictions, though the incidents are for the most part traceable to Asiatic sources.

dead. More than ever bent on revenge, the uncle next invites the youth to go and fish with him. On the way the youth persuades a shepherd to take his place, pretending that his uncle is going to be married. He takes the shepherd's flock of 100 sheep home to his uncle's house. Now the uncle had in the dusk thrown the shepherd into the sea, supposing him to be his nephew, saying to himself, "This time he is drowned, and won't come back any more." When he reaches home, he is surprised to see his nephew alive and well. "You threw me," says the lad, "into the sea near the shore, and I have got only 100 sheep for you; if you had thrown me farther out I should have been more lucky." The uncle, with this hope, throws his only remaining child into the sea—and he never returned. After this the uncle, his wife, and the nephew set out on a journey, and coming to a precipice, "Let us sleep here," says the uncle. The youth arranges a cord, carefully covered with earth; he is placed nearest the precipice, then the uncle, and his wife farthest from it. At night the uncle says he must have more room; the youth replies there is plenty, and slips aside. The old man feels after him, and the youth pulls the cord and sends his uncle and aunt to the bottom of the precipice. He then returns home and inherits his uncle's property.

The original source of this favourite story of the cunning fellow who always contrived to profit by his misfortunes has not yet been ascertained. It belongs obviously to the same class of tales as those of the Cobbler and the Calf and the Robbery of the King's Treasury, and may, perhaps, like the latter, be of Egyptian extraction. The story is known popularly in India in several forms, each of which presents some points of resemblance to European versions. Under the title of "The Farmer who outwitted the Six Men," Mr C. H. Damant published, in the 'Indian Antiquary,' vol. iii., the following legend of Dinajpur (Bengal):

There was once a farmer's wife who had a tame paddy-bird, and when the farmer went to plough, his wife used to fasten a hookah, cleaning stick, tobacco, chillum, flint and steel to the body of the bird, and it would fly with them to the field where the farmer was working, and he unfastened all the things and smoked his hookah. One day six men, who were passing that way on their road to the cutcherry, saw the bird thus act, and offered the farmer 300 rupees for it, and he agreed to sell it. And the six men took it and tied 300 rupees to its body, and said, "You, paddy-bird, take these 300 rupees to the cutcherry." But the bird, instead of going to the cutcherry, went to the farmer's house, and he took all the money, and made a cow eat 100 rupees of it. In the meantime the men went to the cutcherry, and not finding the paddy-bird, returned to the farmer's house, where they saw the cow relieving herself of the rupees she had eaten, and forgot all about the paddy-bird.[7] Seeing the extraordinary virtue the cow possessed, they offered the farmer 5000 rupees for her; and he agreed, and they took her away. The farmer came a little way after them, and called out, "Feed her well, and she will give you plenty of rupees." So they fed her well, but not a rupee, nor even a pice, did they get from her; so they determined to take her back to the farmer's house and to return her.

When they arrived, they told the farmer about the cow, and he said, "Very well; have something to eat first." So they consented, and all sat down to eat, and the farmer took the stick with which he drove his plough-bullocks in his hand and began to eat, and when his wife went out to bring more food he struck her with the stick and said, "Be changed into a girl, and bring in the curry," and so it came to pass; and this happened several times. When the men saw this wonderful thing, they forgot all about the cow; but the truth of it was that the farmer had a little daughter, and she had been sent in with the food. The men offered 150 rupees for the stick, and he sold it them, and told them that when their wives came to bring their food they must beat them well, and they would recover their former youth and beauty.

When they were near home, they all began to quarrel as to which should first test the stick. At last one of them took it home, and when his wife was bringing his food he struck her so violently with it that she died; but he told no one about it. And this happened to them all, so they all lost their wives. After that they all went in a body and burnt down the farmer's house, and he collected a large quantity of ashes and put them in bags and placed them on a bullock's back and went away. On his road he met a number of men driving bullocks laden with rupees, and asked them where they were going, saying he wished to go with them; they said they were going to the house of a certain banker at Rangpur, and he said he was taking his bullock to the same place. So they went together for some

---

[7]In the 'Kathá Sarit Ságara' an ape is trained to bring up from his stomach as many pieces of money as might be asked for, the ape having been made previously to swallow a quantity. And in the Albanian tale of the Cock and the Hen (No 23 of Dozon's French collection) the cock, being found in the king's garden, is taken and locked up in the royal treasury, where it ate as many gold pieces as it could contain, and afterwards making its escape, deceived the old woman who owned the hen by voiding the money.

distance, and then cooked their food under a tree and went to sleep. But the farmer put two bags of rupees on the back of his bullock, leaving the two bags of ashes in their place, and took to flight.

After that he sent the first of the six men with the bags to take home to his wife, and he put some gum underneath one of the bags, so that some of the rupees stuck to it, and so he found out the contents. The six men then went to the farmer's house, and asked him how he had obtained the money; he said he had got it by selling ashes, and that, if they wished for money, they had better burn down their houses and fill bags with the ashes, and open a shop in the bazaar, and every one would buy them. So they went home and burned down their houses, but the only result was that a great number of people seized them and kicked them and beat them with shoes. They were extremely enraged at this, and went to the farmer's house and tied him hand and foot, and put him into a sack, and threw him into the river Ghoradhuba, and then ran away, thinking he would surely die this time. But he went floating downstream till he struck against a post. Now a man happened to pass by on horseback, and he called out to him, "If you come and open the mouth of this sack, I will cut grass for your horse without pay." So the man came and opened the mouth of the sack, and the farmer, stepping out on the clear, said, "If you will give me your horse, I will take him for an airing." The man gave him the horse, and went home, but when the farmer had gone a little way he mounted the horse and rode past the houses of the six men, so that they could see him. They were exceedingly surprised at the sight, and asked him where he had found the horse. He said he had found it in the river Ghoradhuba, and added, "I was alone, and could only catch this small one, as I could not run very fast; there are a great many fine horses there, and if you were to go you could catch them."

When they heard this they asked what they must take with them, and he said they must each bring a sack and some strong rope; but when they had brought them, he said he was going home. However, they persuaded him to stop, and he told them all to go into the sacks, and he threw them one after the other into the river, but took care to avoid the place where the post was. When the other five heard the bubbling of the water they asked what it was, and he said it was only the other man catching a horse. Directly they heard that they all entreated him, and began to quarrel, saying, "Throw me in first—throw me in first!" So he threw them all in, and in this way they all perished, and the farmer ever after that spent his time in happiness.

Another Indian version, entitled "The Six Brothers," is found in the little collection of tales translated from Urdú, Hindí, and Bengalí by Mr C. Vernieux,[18] of which this is an abstract:

Once upon a time there were six brothers, the youngest of whom had very defective eyesight, in consequence of which the other five cast him off, giving him a half-ruined hut and a wretched bullock as his portion. Near his hut was a large tree, and beneath it a gang of robbers were used to assemble to divide their spoil. The youth overheard them one night saying to each other, "He who does not make a just division, God's thunder will descend on his head." In order to work upon their superstitious minds to his own advantage, he slaughters his poor bullock, dries the skin in the sun, and next night climbs with it into the tree, and awaited their coming. When they were all assembled under the tree, and had repeated their formula about the thunder, he dropped the dried skin, which fell on them with a dreadful noise. Appalled at this, they all leapt up and ran off in different directions, leaving their ill-gotten wealth behind them, which the youth gathered up and took into his hut. In the morning he desired his mother to go to his brothers and borrow their *coonkee* (or measuring basket), that he might ascertain the amount of money he had got by his trick on the robbers; and before returning it he slipped a few rupees between the rattan ties. When his brothers saw the coins they hastened to him, and inquired how he had procured so much money as to require to measure instead of count it. So he told them it was by the sale of the hide of his poor bullock; but had he as many cows as they possessed, he could make ten times as much money. On this the brothers went home, killed all their cows, dressed their skins, and went to market to dispose of them. But they found they could get only four annas for each hide, and seeing they had been fooled by their despised half-blind brother, when they came home they set fire to his house. Next morning he gathered all the ashes into sacks, and, hiring a bullock, went ostensibly to sell them. On his road he fell in with a party of merchants near sunset, who had oxen laden with bags of gold and silver. He obtained permission to remain under their protection all night, and to place his bags of ashes—which he pretended to contain the same precious metals—along with their goods. Early in the morning he crept stealthily from his place, and

---

[18]'The Hermit of Motee Jhurna, or Pearl Spring; also Indian Tales and Anecdotes, Moral and Instructive.' By C. Vernieux. Second Edition. Calcutta: 1872.

putting his bags of ashes among their sacks, he dragged two of them near his bullock, and when all were awake and preparing to resume their journey, he got them to help him to lift the sacks on his animal, saying that he had a long way to go, and must be off at once; so they helped him to load his bullock with their own property, and he went away. When he reaches home he tells his brothers he had got all his new wealth by the sale of the ashes of his house, upon which they burn down their houses, to find themselves once more deceived. They now determine to put him to death; so, tying his hands and feet, they stuff him in a sack and throw him into a tank, and to elude detection decamp in hot haste. Some cowherds, who were watching their cattle close by, having seen this, ran quickly to the tank and drew him out, after which they all went off to get some food. Meanwhile the half-drowned brother, having recovered from his stupor, drove the herds to his own house, on seeing which his brothers were astonished, and inquired where he had got such fine cattle. At the bottom of the tank, he tells them; and, anxious to obtain some for themselves, they allow him to tie their hands and feet, put them in sacks, and throw them all into the tank.

In the second part of the Santálí story of the brothers Kanran and Guja, translated by the Rev. F. T. Cole in the 'Indian Antiquary,' vol. iv. pp. 257–259, of which the first part has been already cited—see vol. i. pp. 148, 149—is found a rather singular version, which, however, in the catastrophe is similar to several European variants:

After the stupid tiger has been killed, Kanran takes for his share the best portions of the flesh, and Guja takes simply the entrails. Then they resumed their journey, and as it drew near nightfall, they found a suitable tree on which to rest. It so chanced that a king's son was just passing on the way to his father-in-law's house, in order to fetch home his wife, and he lay down to repose under the same tree. All this time Guja had been holding the entrails of the tiger in his hands. At last he said to his brother, "I can't keep this any longer." Kanran replied, "What shall we do, then? If you let it fall we shall be discovered, and shall certainly be killed." But Guja, unable to hold it any longer, let it fall on the king's son, who was lying fast asleep at the foot of the tree. Awakened by the blow, he arose, greatly dismayed at seeing blood, etc., upon his body, and imagined that some accident must have happened to himself; he therefore hastened from the spot. His servants, seeing him run at a mad pace, immediately followed. The two brothers quickly came down from the tree and began to plunder the baggage which had been left behind in the fright. Kanran seized upon the finest garments, while Guja selected a large drum. Being upbraided by his brother for thus losing such a splendid opportunity of enriching himself, he replied, "Brother, this will suit my purpose." They now proceeded on their journey. Guja was so much pleased with his drum that he kept on beating it all day long, till the drum-head split, and it was rendered useless. But Guja, instead of throwing it away, carried it about with him. They found a bee's nest, and Guja refreshed himself with the honey, and filled his drum with bees. Continuing their journey, they arrived at a river ghát. When the villagers came out at eventide to draw water, Guja let fly some of the bees amongst them. The people, being much stung, ran home and told how two strangers had arrived, and had greatly annoyed them by allowing bees to sting them. The villagers, headed by their chief and armed with bows, advanced to the attack, determined to be avenged upon the strangers. They commenced shooting, but the brothers, hidden behind their drum, remained unharmed. After all the arrows had been shot, Guja opened the hole of his drum, and the bees streamed out like a cart-rope. The villagers now prayed to be released from this plague of bees, and their chief promised to give one of them his daughter in marriage, also a yoke of oxen and a piece of land. Guja then calling his bees forced them into the drum. The chief performed his promise. Kanran was married to his daughter, and he cultivated the land which his father-in-law gave him.

One day, for some reason, Kanran was obliged to leave home for a short time, and upon his departure gave Guja this injunction: "If," said he, "the plough becomes at any time entangled in the ground, and the ox be unable to get along, strike it with your axe." Guja imagined that his brother was speaking of the ox; so when the plough became entangled he struck the ox with his hatchet and killed him, instead of cutting away the obstacle as his brother had intended. Kanran, returning home about this time, was informed by his wife of what had happened. Upon hearing it he became greatly enraged, and ran to the spot intending to kill his brother. Guja, however, becoming aware of his brother's intentions, immediately snatched up the entrails of the ox and fled. Seeing a tree having a large hole in the trunk, he got inside, having first covered himself with the entrails. Kanran, arriving at the spot, thrust his spear into the hole repeatedly, and when he drew it out, perceived that it was smeared with blood. He exclaimed, "I have speared him to death, and now he won't kill any more of my oxen," and returned home. Guja, however, was not at all hurt, the spear not having touched him—the blood was not his, but that of the ox. Having satisfied himself that no one was near, he came out of the hole, crept secretly into his brother's house, and climbing to the top, he sat there perched upon one of the beams. A little while after Kanran entered, bringing with him portions of the slain ox, and also some rice. After closing the door, he commenced to offer a sacrifice to his brother Guja's memory. The usual ceremony being performed, he addressed the soul of his departed brother in the following manner: "O Guja, receive these offerings. I killed you indeed, but don't be angry with me for doing so. Condescend to accept this meat and rice." Guja, from his hiding-place, replied, "Very well; lay them down." Kanran, hearing the voice, was greatly astonished, but was afraid to look in the direction from which the sound proceeded. Going out, he inquired of the villagers whether it was possible for a dead man to speak. They told him that such was sometimes the case. While Kanran was talking to the neighbours, Guja escaped secretly by a back door, taking with him the meat and rice. He had not gone far before he encountered some men who, he afterwards learned, were professional thieves. He divided his meat and rice with them, and they were at once great friends. Guja became their companion in their plundering expeditions. However, afterwards coming to words, they beat him severely, tied his hands and feet, and were carrying him off to the river with the intention of drowning him, when they were compelled by hunger to go in search of food, and not wishing to be burdened with him, they set him down bound under a tree. A cowherd passing that way was attracted by his crying, and asked who he was, and why he was lamenting. Guja answered, "I am a king's son, and am being taken against my will to be married to a king's daughter, for whom I have not the slightest affection." The cowherd said, "I am indeed sorry for you; but let me go instead of you. I will gladly marry her." So the cowherd quickly released Guja, and allowed himself to be bound in his place. The thieves returning soon afterwards, took up the supposed Guja, and, in spite of the cowherd's protestations that he was not Guja, threw him into the river. In the meanwhile Guja drove away the cowherd's cattle. The thieves afterwards meeting him again, and seeing the cows, inquired of him whence he had procured them. Guja answered, "Don't you remember you threw me into the river? There it was I got all these. Let me throw you in too, and you will get as many cows as you wish." This proposition meeting with general approbation, they suffered themselves to be bound and thrown into the river, where, as a natural consequence, all were drowned.

From a comparative analysis of the foregoing versions, I am disposed to consider them as representing, more or less closely, two distinct variants of a common original—that the story was brought to Europe in two different forms. In the Indian tale of the Farmer who outwitted the Six Simpletons the first incident is that of the carrying paddy-bird, for which we have the hare in the Sicilian popular version (Uncle Capriano), and the goat in Straparola and Gueulette. (2) For the cow that was supposed to produce rupí there is the horse in the second Irish, the Icelandic, the Latin, and the third Gaelic variants; while the cow's skin plays a similar part in all the others. (3) The incident of the farmer's wife being (apparently) changed into a young girl has its equivalents in the Icelandic story, where the hero pretends to make his old mother throw off her "age-shape," in the second Irish, the second and third Gaelic, in Straparola, the Sicilian, and in Gueulette, where the hero makes believe that he restores the woman to life by blowing a horn or a whistle; in the Kabaïl, the lad suspended from a tree persuades an aged passer-by that he has been changed from an old man to a young lad. The trick with the ashes of the burned house occurs in the Icelandic as well as in two of the Indian stories; but the Icelandic has, exclusively, the incidents of the hillock of butter and the cow's entrails. The stove (or boiler) that required no fire to cook meat is found in the second Norse and the Sicilian variants. Only in European versions does the adventure with the dead body occur—first Irish, first Norse, Danish, Icelandic, first and second German, and the first and second Gaelic. The device of the hero in the second Indian tale, of letting his cow's hide fall upon a party of thieves dividing their booty under a tree, has its parallel in the Burgundian version, and others which are not cited in this paper.[19] The borrowing of the *coonkee* and the sacks of ashes changed for sacks of money reappear in European variants. Not less interesting is the Indian story of the brothers Kanran and Guja, since in it we find the incident of killing the plough-ox, which also occurs in a modified form in the second German version (p. 250), and the trick of the hero in order to get out of the sack, his saying that they want to marry him to a great lady whom he doesn't like, which occurs in many of the Western versions.

[19]In the third Indian tale, Guja drops the tiger's entrails on a sleeping prince.

The different tricks with the skin may perhaps be considered as characteristic of the localities where the story is domiciled; that of the Kabaï hero seems to be so especially, for the wandering tribes of Algeria do not regard theft as dishonourable, and are noted for being expert thieves; while the device of Little Fairly, of putting coins between the cow's skin, reappears in the second of the Gaelic variants. Finally, in the Irish, first Norse, Danish, old Latin, three Gaelic, the Kabaïl and second Indian stories the hero contrives that his enemies should slaughter their cattle, in the vain expectation of obtaining a great price for their hides, a device which seems adapted in the following story from the Talmud:

An Athenian while on a visit to Jerusalem openly ridiculed the citizens, some of whom devised a plan for punishing his impertinence. They despatched one of their number to Athens in order to induce him to revisit Jerusalem. Arriving there, he soon found out the man's house and bought of him a new shoe-string (for the man was a shoemaker), and paid for it a greater sum than the value of a pair of shoes. Next day he went to him again, and bought a second shoe-string, paying for it a similar sum. "Why," cried the Athenian, in amazement, "shoes must be very dear in Jerusalem, when you give so much for a mere shoe-string!" "You are right," quoth the Hebrew, "they are rather dear: they generally cost ten ducats a pair, and the cheapest sort cost seven or eight ducats." "In that case," said the Athenian, "it would be more profitable for me to sell my stock of shoes in your city." The stranger replied that he would doubtless make a much greater profit, and find a ready market for his goods; after which he took his leave, returned to Jerusalem, and acquainted his complotters of the probable success of his mission. Soon after this the Athenian, with a large stock of shoes, entered the Holy City, and was accosted by a number of respectable citizens, who desired to know his business. Suspecting nothing sinister on the part of a people whom he so much depised, he informed them that, understanding that shoes were very dear in Jerusalem, he had brought with him a considerable quantity, in hopes of profitably disposing of them. The citizens pretended to warmly approve of his object, assuring him that he would readily find purchasers for his whole stock; but being a foreigner, it was absolutely necessary, in order to qualify himself to offer his goods for sale in the Holy City, that he should shave his head and blacken his face, after which he would be entitled to take his stand among the merchants in the great square. The greedy Athenian ("covetousness sews up the eyes of cunning!") willingly consented to this initiatory ceremony, which being completed to the satisfaction of the plotters, he then, with blackened face and shaven head, took up his stock-in-trade, and proceeded to "the place where merchants most do congregate." The loungers soon observed the strange-looking merchant, and flocking round him, inquired the price of his shoes. "They are ten ducats a pair," said he, "and certainly not less than seven or eight ducats." On hearing this preposterous demand, the people laughed at him; and at length discovering that he had been cleverly hoaxed, he was glad to make his way out of the city with all speed; but he was accompanied to the gate by a great crowd, jeering and hooting him, until he escaped through the gateway, and set off for Athens, "a sadder and a wiser man."

↜ THE LADY AND HER SUITORS ↜

THERE is a widespread class of tales, in which a virtuous wife is beset by importunate suitors, and cleverly entraps and exposes them to ridicule, or gets rid of them by imposing unpleasant or dangerous tasks as the condition of her love. The *fabliau* of 'Constant du Hamel' is probably the earliest European version: A lady is violently solicited by a priest, a provost, and a forester, who, on her refusal, persecute her husband. To stop their attacks, she gives them a meeting at her house immediately after one another, so that when one is there and stripped for the bath, another comes, and, pretending it is her husband, she conceals them successively in a large tub full of feathers. Finally, they are turned out into the street, well feathered, with all the curs of the town barking and snapping at their heels.

In the 69th tale of the Continental 'Gesta Romanorum' a carpenter receives from his mother-in-law a shirt, having the wonderful quality of remaining unsoiled so long as he and his wife were faithful to each other. The emperor, who had employed him in the erection of a palace, is astonished to observe his shirt always spotless, and asks him the cause of it; to which he replies, that it is a proof of his wife's unsullied virtue. A soldier, having overheard this, sets off to attempt the wife's chastity, but she contrives to lock him in a room, where she keeps him on bread and water. Two other soldiers successively visit her on the same errand, and share their comrade's fate. When the carpenter has finished his job, he returns home and shows the unsullied shirt to his wife, who in her turn exhibits to him the three soldiers, whom he sets free on their promising to reform their ways.

We have a much better version than that of the 'Gesta,' in which there is also a test of chastity, but of a more dignified nature than a shirt, in the old English metrical tale of 'The Wright's Chaste Wife,' written about the year 1462, by Adam of Cobsam, which was published for the Early English Text Society in 1865, under the editorship of Dr F. J. Furnivall. The story runs thus:

A wright marries the daughter of a poor widow, whose sole dower is a rose-garland that will remain fresh and blooming as long as she continues chaste, but will wither the moment she becomes unfaithful. He is delighted with his garland and his wife, and takes her home. After a time, thinking that men would likely come to tempt his wife when he was absent, he constructs in his house a lower room, the walls of which he makes as smooth as a mirror, and in the floor above a trap-door, which would give way when a man put his foot upon it, and precipitate him into the room below, out of which it was impossible to escape. Just at that time, the lord of the town sent for him to build him a hall—a two or three months' job. The lord observes the wight's garland, and learning that it is a token of his wife's chastity, he determines to visit her. So off he goes, and offers her forty marks. She asks him to lay the money down, and then conducts him to the place with the cunningly contrived trap-door, on which having stepped, down he tumbles into the lower room. The lord begs and prays the dame to have pity on him, but she says, "Nay, you must wait till my husband comes home." Next day he asks for food, but she says he must first earn it. "Spin me some flax," she says. The lord consents; so she throws him the tools and the flax, and he works away for his meat. The steward next sees the wright's garland, and he too must visit the goodwife, whom he offers twenty marks, which she pockets, and then leads him into the same trap, where, after suffering hunger for several days, he also spins flax for his food. Then the proctor, seeing the garland, asks the wright all about it, and, in his turn, having given the dame other twenty marks, he joins the lord, and the steward in the trap which the wright had so craftily constructed for men of their sort. There the three spin and spin away, as if for their very lives, until at length the wright has finished his three months' job and comes home. His wife tells him of her prisoners, and then sends for their wives, each of whom takes away her shamefaced husband.[1]

It is possible that 'The Wright's Chaste Wife' suggested to Massinger the idea of the plot of his comedy of 'The Picture' (printed in 1630), which is as follows: Mathias, a Bohemian knight, about to go to the wars, expresses to his confidant Baptista, a great scholar, his fears lest his wife Sophia, on whom he doted fondly, should prove unfaithful during his absence. Baptista gives him a picture of his wife, saying,

[1] With 'The Wright's Chaste Wife' may be compared the old ballad of "The Fryer well-fitted; or,

A pretty jest that once befel,
How a maid put a Fryer to cool in the well,"

which is found in 'Wit and Mirth, an Antidote to Melancholy,' 1682, and has been reprinted in the Bagford and other collections of ballads.

"Carry it still about you, and as oft
As you desire to know how she's affected,
With curious eyes peruse it. While it keeps
The figure it has now entire and perfect,
She is not only innocent in fact
But unattempted; but if once it vary
From the true form, and what's now white and red
Incline to yellow, rest most confident
She's with all violence courted, but unconquered;
But if it turn all black, 'tis an assurance
The fort by composition or surprise
Is forced, or with her free consent surrendered."

On the return of Mathias from the wars, he is loaded with rich gifts by Honoria, the wife of his master Ferdinand, king of Hungary; and when he expresses his desire to return to his fair and virtuous wife, Honoria asks him if his wife is as fair as she, upon which he shows her the picture. The queen resolves to win his love—merely to gratify her own vanity—and persuades him to remain a month at court. She then despatches two libertine courtiers to attempt the virtue of Mathias' wife. They tell her Mathias is given to the society of courtesans—moreover, not young, but old and ugly ones; so poor Sophia begins to waver. Meanwhile the queen makes advances to Mathias, which at first he repels; but afterwards, seeing a change in his wife's picture, he consents, when the queen says she will think over it and let him know her decision. Sophia, at first disposed to entertain her suitors' proposals, on reflection determines to punish their wickedness; and pretending to listen favourably to one of them, she causes him to be stripped to his shirt and locked in a room, where he is compelled to spin flax (like the suitors in 'The Wright's Chaste Wife'), or go without food. The other fares no better, and the play concludes with the exposure of the libertines to the king and queen, their attendants, and the lady's husband.

The identity of the 'Gesta' story with that of 'The Wright's Chaste Wife' is very evident, and they have a close parallel in the fourth story of Nakhshabí's 'Túti Náma.' The following is a translation of the tale, according to Káderí's abridgment of that entertaining work:[2]

[2]Although an abstract of this tale has been given in the first vol., in connection with Tests of Chastity, it is necessary to present it here more fully, for the purpose of comparison.

In a certain city dwelt a military man who had a very beautiful wife, on whose account he was always under apprehension. The man being indigent, his wife asked him why he had quitted his profession and occupation. He answered, "I have not confidence in you, and therefore do not go anywhere in quest of employment." The wife said, "This is a perverse conceit, for no one can seduce a virtuous woman; and if a woman is vicious, no husband can guard her. It is most eligible for you to travel, and to get into some service. I will give you a fresh nosegay, and as long as it shall continue in this state, be assured that I have not committed any evil action; but if it should wither, you will then know that I have done something wrong." The soldier listened to these words, and resolved on making a journey. On his departure his wife presented him with a nosegay. When he arrived in a certain city he engaged in the service of a nobleman of the place. The soldier always took the nosegay along with him. When the winter season arrived the nobleman said to his attendants, "At this time of the year a fresh flower is not to be seen in any garden, neither is such a thing procurable by persons of rank. It is wonderful from whence this stranger, the soldier, brings a fresh nosegay every day." They said that they also were astonished at this circumstance. Then the nobleman asked the soldier, "What kind of nosegay is this?" He answered, "My wife gave me this nosegay as a token of her chastity, saying, "As long as it continues fresh and blooming, know you of a truth that my virtue is unsullied."" The nobleman laughingly remarked that his wife must be a conjuror or a sorcerer.

Now the nobleman had two cooks, remarkable for their cunning and adroitness. To one of these he said, "Repair to the soldier's country, where, through artifice and deceit, contrive to form an intimacy with his wife, and return quickly with a particular account of her; when it will be seen whether his nosegay will continue fresh or not." The cook, having accordingly gone to the soldier's city, sent a procurers to the wife, who, through treachery and deceit, waited on her, and delivered the message. The wife did not give any direct assent to the procurers, but said, "Send the man to me, in order that I may see whether he will be agreeable to me or not." The procurers introduced the cook to the soldier's wife, who said in his ear, "Go away for the present, and tell the procurers that you will have nothing to say to such a woman as I am; then come along to my house without apprising the procurers, for persons of her sort cannot keep a secret." The cook approved of her plan and acted accordingly. The soldier's wife had in her house a dry well, over which she placed a bedstead, very slightly laced, and covered it with a sheet. When the cook returned, she desired him to sit down on that bed; and he, having placed himself thereon, fell through, and began to bawl out. The woman then said, "Tell me truly who you are, and from whence you came." Thereupon the forlorn cook related all the circumstances about her husband and the nobleman; but she kept him confined in the dry well. And when some time had passed and the cook did not return, the nobleman gave the other cook a large sum of money, with abundance of goods, and sent him to the soldier's wife in the character of a merchant. He pursued the like course with the other, and was caught in the same whirlpool. The nobleman, astonished that neither of the two cooks came back, began to suspect that some evil had befallen them, so he at length resolved to go himself.

One day, under pretence of hunting, he set out, attended by the soldier. When they arrived at the soldier's city, he went to his own house, and presented his wife with the nosegay, still fresh and blooming, and she informed him of all that had occurred. Next day the soldier conducted the nobleman to his dwelling, and prepared for him a hospitable entertainment. He took the two cooks out of the well and said to them, "Guests are come to my house; do you both put on women's clothes, place the victuals before them, and wait upon them; after which I will set you at liberty." The cooks accordingly put on women's apparel, and served up the victuals to the nobleman. From their sufferings in the well and their poor food, the hair had fallen from off their heads, and their complexion was very much changed. Quoth the nobleman to the soldier, "What crimes have these girls been guilty of, that their heads have been shaved?" The soldier answered, "They have committed a great fault—ask themselves." And having examined them more attentively, the nobleman recognised them as his own cooks, while they, having, in their turn, recognised their master, began to weep grievously, fell at his feet, and testified to the woman's virtue. The wife then called out from behind a curtain, "I am she whom you, my lord, suspected to be a sorceress, and sent these men to put me to the proof, and laughed at my husband. Now you have learned my character." Hearing this, the nobleman was abashed, and asked forgiveness for his offences.

Such is the Persian form of the story; and although the 'Túti Náma' of Nakhshabí is probably not of earlier date than the 'Gesta Romanorum,' yet it represents a very much older work, now lost. Moreover, in the 'Kathá Sarit Ságara' we have a version of the story which dates as far back as the 6th century of our era:

A merchant named Guhasena is compelled to leave his wife, Devasmitá, for a season, on important business matters. The separation is very painful to both, and the pain is aggravated by fears on the wife's part of her husband's inconstancy. To make assurance doubly sure, Siva was pleased to appear to them in a dream, and giving them two red lotuses, the god said to them, "Take each of you one of these lotuses in your hand; and if either of you shall be unfaithful during your separation, the lotus in the hand of the other shall fade, but not otherwise." The husband set out on his journey, and, arriving in the country of Katáha, he began to buy and sell jewels there. Four young merchants, learning the purport of his lotus and the virtue of his wife, set off to put it to the proof. On reaching the city where the chaste Devasmitá resided, they bribe a female ascetic to corrupt the lady; so she goes to her house, and adopting the device of the little she-dog—see chap. xxviii. of Swan's 'Gesta Romanorum'[3]—which she pretends is her own co-wife in a former birth, re-born in that degraded form, because she had been over-chaste, and warns Devasmitá that such should also be her fate if she did not take her pleasure in her husband's absence. The wise Devasmitá said to herself, "This is a novel conception of duty; no doubt this woman has laid a treacherous snare for me," and so she said to the ascetic, "Reverend lady, for this long time I have been ignorant of this duty, so procure me an interview with some agreeable man." Then the ascetic said, "There are residing here some young merchants who have come from a distant country, so I will bring them to you." The crafty old hag returns home delighted with the success of her stratagem.

In the meantime Devasmitá resolves to punish the four young merchants. So calling her maids, she instructs them to prepare some wine mixed with *datura* (a stupefying drug), and to have a dog's foot of iron made as soon as possible. Then she causes one of her maids to dress so as to resemble herself. The ascetic introduces one of the young libertines into the lady's house in the evening, and then returns home. The maid, disguised as her mistress, receives the young merchant with great courtesy, and, having persuaded him to drink freely of the drugged wine till he becomes senseless, the other women strip off his clothes, and, after branding him on the forehead with the dog's foot, during the night push him into a filthy ditch. On recovering consciousness he returns to his

[3]Taken into the 'Gesta,' probably, from the 'Disciplina Clericalis' of P. Alfonsus. The incident is also the subject of a *fabliau,* and occurs in all the Eastern versions of the Book of Sindibád.

companions, and tells them, in order that they should share his fate, that he had been robbed on his way home. The three other merchants in turn visit the house of Devasmitá, and receive the same treatment. Soon afterwards the pretended devotee, ignorant of the result of her device, visits the lady, is drugged, her ears and nose are cut off, and she is flung into a foul pond. In the sequel, Devasmitá, disguised in man's apparel, proceeds to the country of the young libertines, where her husband had been residing for some time, and going before the king, petitions him to assemble all his subjects, alleging that there are among the citizens four of her slaves who had run away. Then she seizes upon the four young merchants, and claims them as her slaves. The other merchants indignantly cried out that these were reputable men, and she answered that if their foreheads were examined they would be found marked with a dog's foot. On seeing the four young men thus branded the king was astonished, and Devasmitá thereupon related the whole story, and all the people burst out laughing, and the king said to the lady, "They are your slaves by the best of titles." The other merchants paid a large sum of money to the chaste wife to redeem them from slavery, and a fine to the king's treasury. And Devasmitá received the money, and recovered her husband; was honoured by all men, returned to her own city, and was never afterwards separated from her beloved.

We now come to versions in which, as in the *fabliau,* there is no magical test. In the Arabian text of the Book of Sindibád, commonly known as the 'Seven Vazírs,' the story is to this effect:

A lady, whose lover has been arrested and carried to prison, earnestly solicits his release, first, of the chief of police; next, of the kází, or magistrate; then, of the chief vazír; and, lastly, of the governor of the city; each of whom promises to grant her request on condition that she permit him to visit her at her own house. She professes willingness, and appoints a different hour for each to wait upon her the same evening. As they arrive in turn, she shuts them up unknown to each other in a large cabinet, with separate compartments, on the pretence that her husband is at the door. By-and-by her lover, having been released from prison, comes to the house, and she decamps with him, leaving the amorous officials locked up, safe enough. In the morning the owner of the house, finding the gate open, enters, and hearing the voices of the imprisoned dignitaries clamouring to be released, causes the cabinet to be carried to the sultan's palace, where it is opened in his presence; and the shamefaced officials come forth amidst the derision of the whole court.

The story is told very differently in Jonathan Scott's edition of the 'Arabian Nights,' vol. vi., where the lady is represented as virtuous. Her suitors are the judge, the collector-general of port-duties, the chief of the butchers, and a wealthy merchant. She informs her husband of her plan to punish them, and at the same time reap some profit. The judge comes first, and presents her with a rosary of pearls. She makes him undress and put on a robe of yellow muslin, and a parti-coloured cap—her husband all the while looking at them through an opening in the door of a closet. Presently there is heard a loud knock at the street-door, upon which she affects to think it is her husband, and the judge is pushed into an adjoining room. The three other suitors, as they successively arrive, bring each also a valuable present, and are treated in like manner. The husband now enters, and his wife tells him—to the consternation of the suitors—that in returning from the bazaar that day she had met four antic fellows, whom she had a great mind to bring home with her for his amusement. He pretends to be vexed that she had not done so, since he must go from home on the morrow. The lady then says that they are, after all, in the next room, upon which her husband insists on their being brought before him, one after another. So the judge is dragged forth in his ludicrous attire and compelled to dance and caper like a buffoon, after which he is made to tell a story, and is then dismissed. The three other suitors go through the same performance in succession, each making himself ridiculous to please the lady's husband, and prevent scandal.

In the Persian tales of the 'Thousand and One Days,' by the Dervish Mukhlis of Ispahán, Arúya, the virtuous wife of a merchant, in like manner entraps, also with her husband's consent, a kází, a doctor, and the city governor; but they do not relate stories. And in the 'Bahár-i Dánush,' or Spring of Knowledge, by 'Ináyatu-'lláh of Delhi, a lady named Gohera, whose husband is in the hands of the police, makes assignations with the kutwal (police magistrate) and the kází, one of whom is entrapped in a large jar, the other in a chest, which next morning she causes porters to carry into the presence of the sultan, who punishes the suitors and sets her husband at liberty.

In Miss Stokes' charming little work, 'Indian Fairy Tales,' the wife of a merchant, during his absence on a journey, having spun a quantity of beautiful thread, takes four hanks to market. There she is accosted successively by the kutwal, the vazír, the kází, and, lastly, by the king himself, to each of whom she grants an interview at her own house at different hours, and, as they arrive, shuts them in separate chests. In the morning she hires four stout coolies, who take the chests on their shoulders. She first goes to the kutwal's son, and asks him to give her 1000 rupís for one of the chests, which, she says, contains something he would value far beyond that sum; he gives the required sum, opens the chest when it has been taken into the house, and finds his father crouching in it, full of shame; in like manner from the vazír's son she receives 2000 rupís, from the kází's son 3000, and from the king's son 5000. With the money thus cleverly acquired she builds a fine well, to the admiration of her husband on his return home.

In a legend of Dinajpúr, by G. A. Damant ("Folk-Lore of Bengal"—'Indian Antiquary,' 1873), a woman plays somewhat similar tricks upon four admirers: A king having promised that he would give every one whatever he wished during the space of two hours, when the family priest had distributed all the king's possessions, he asked a present for himself, and said he should like to have a touchstone. The king was grieved at being quite unable to comply with this request; but his son undertook to bring him a touchstone, in order that he might keep his word. After a long and toilsome journey, the prince receives a touchstone from a pair of birds, who inform him that they had brought it from over the sea, because the shells of their eggs would not burst until they were rubbed with a touchstone. On his way homeward he falls in with a party of robbers, whose practice it was to decoy their victims into an inner room by means of the blandishments of the chief's daughter. But the girl falls in love with the prince, and they both escape from the robbers' den. When the prince arrived at his father's capital he first placed his bride in the care of a garland-maker, and then went to his father's palace, where he gave his wife the touchstone to keep in the meantime. She, however, was in love with the kutwal of the city, and gave him the touchstone. The prince became distracted on learning that it had been "stolen"; but the robber-chief's daughter found by magical arts that it had fallen into the hands of the kutwal, and formed a plan to recover it. She went on the roof of the house, where the kutwal passing by saw her, and spoke to the garland-maker about her beauty, saying that he would visit her that night. The man (having been prompted by the damsel) said that his "sister" had made a vow to receive no one unless he presented her with a touchstone. To this the kutwal consented, and an hour was appointed for his visit. Shortly after this the king's counsellor in passing saw the girl on the house-top, and the garland-maker arranged that he should come to converse with her at the second watch of the night. Next comes the king's prime minister, and the garland-maker appoints the third watch of the night for his visit. Lastly, the king himself, happening to observe the damsel, is to come at the last watch. At the due time the kutwal comes, delivers up the touchstone, and sups with the damsel. When the king's counsellor comes, the kutwal, on being informed of it, urgently requests to be concealed somewhere. She smears him over with molasses, pours water on him, covers his whole body with cotton-wool, and fastens him in a window. On the minister's knocking at the door, the counsellor is concealed beneath a seat. The minister, when the king comes, is placed near the kutwal, behind a bamboo screen. The king, having observed the frightful figure of the kutwal, inquires what was fastened in the window. She answers that it is a rákshasa (a species of demon), whereupon the king, counsellor, and prime minister flee from the house in mortal fear of the monster, after which the kutwal is allowed to make the best of his way home, in his strange garb of molasses and cotton-wool. Next morning the damsel gives the touchstone to the prince, who recovers his wits, presents the treasure to his father, puts to death his wife and the wicked kutwal, and takes the clever damsel for his wife. The king abdicates in favour of his son, and retires to the forest as a hermit.

One of the exploits of the Indian jester, Temal Ramakistnan (the Tyl Eulenspiegel, or the Scogin, of Madras), is akin to the various stories already cited; Temal Ramakistnan, fearing that the rájá and his priest, who were angry with him on account of his frequently ridiculing them, would one day deprive him of his head, thought his only safety lay in obtaining an oath of protection from them. For this purpose he went first to the rájá's priest, and, after speaking a while, informed him that a certain man was come from a distant country to his house, accompanied by his wife, who was as bright as the moon, but he was unable to tell him her quality, adding that he did not think such another beautiful woman could be found throughout the whole fifty-six kingdoms of India. The priest desired him to make him acquainted with this beautiful lady; but Ramakistnan said that her husband was so jealous that he seldom allowed her out of his sight, and advised the priest to disguise himself in woman's garb, and come to his house at ten o'clock that night, when he would comply with his request. Having made this arrangement with the priest, the jester then went to the rájá, gave him a similar account of the lady's charms, and agreed to introduce him to her at one o'clock that night, disguised as a woman. Ramakistnan then returned home and prepared a room for their reception. The priest and the rájá arrived each at the hour appointed, and were conducted one after the other into the room, and the door was locked on them. They soon discovered each other, and being heartily ashamed, softly requested to be let out; on which Ramakistnan demanded, as a condition, that they should first swear to him by a solemn oath that they would pardon him one hundred offences every day. The rájá and his priest, fearing that if they refused he would publish their disgrace to the world, had no alternative but to comply, and Ramakistnan then sent them home with all possible marks of respect.

The original of all the foregoing versions in which there is no magical test is probably found in the story of the virtuous and wise Upakosa in the 'Kathá Sarit Ságara,' which has been thus translated by Dr H. H. Wilson:

Whilst I [Vararuchi] was absent, my wife, who performed with pious exactitude her ablutions in the Ganges, attracted the notice and desires of several suitors, especially of the king's domestic priest, the commander of the guard, and the young prince's preceptor, who annoyed her by their importunites, till at last she determined to expose and punish their depravity. Having fixed upon the plan, she made an appointment for the same evening with her three lovers, each being to come to her house an hour later than the other. Being desirous of propitiating the gods, she sent for our banker to obtain money to distribute in alms; and when he arrived he expressed the same passion as the rest, on her compliance with which he promised to make over to her the money that I had placed in his hands, or on her refusal he would retain it to his own use. Apprehending the loss of our property, therefore, she made a similar assignation with him, and desired him to come to her house that evening, at an hour when she calculated on having disposed of the first comers, for whose reception, as well as his, she arranged with her attendants the necessary preparations.

At the expiration of the first watch of the night the preceptor of the prince arrived. Upakosa affected to receive him with great delight, and after some conversation desired him to take a bath, which her attendants had prepared for him.[4] The preceptor made not the slightest objection, on which he was conducted into a retired and dark chamber, where his bath was ready. On undressing, his own clothes and ornaments were removed, and in their place a small wrapper given to him, which was a piece of cloth smeared with a mixture of oil, lamp-black, and perfumes. Similar cloths were employed to rub him after bathing, so that he was of a perfect ebon colour from top to toe. The rubbing occupied the time till the second lover (the priest) arrived, on which the women exclaimed, "Here is our master's most particular friend—in, in here, or all will be discovered"; and hurrying their victim away, they thrust him into a long and stout wicker basket,[5] fastened well by a bolt outside, in which they left him to meditate upon his mistress.

The priest and the commander of the guard were secured, as they arrived, in a similar manner, and it only remained to dispose of the banker. When he made his appearance, Upakosa, leading him near the baskets, said aloud, "You promise to deliver me my husband's property?" And he replied, "The wealth your husband entrusted to me shall be yours." On which she turned towards the baskets and said, "Let the gods hear the promise of Hiranygupta!" The bath was then proposed to the banker. Before the ceremony was completed the day began to dawn, on which the servants desired him to make the best of his way home, lest the neighbours should notice his departure; and with this recommendation they forced him, naked as he was, into the street. Having no alternative, the banker hastened to conceal himself in his own house, being chased all the way by the dogs of the town.[6]

So soon as it was day, Upakosa repaired to the palace of Nanda, and presented a petition to the king against the banker, for seeking to appropriate the property entrusted to him by her husband. The banker was summoned. He denied ever having received any money from me.

---

[4] It is curious that the *fabliau* alone agrees with this Hindú story in disrobing the suitors by the plea of the bath.

[5] This will probably remind the reader of the buck-basket in which Sir John Falstaff was thrust by Mrs Ford and her gossip Mrs Page.

[6] The *fabliau* has also this incident, the only difference being that *all* the lady's suitors are turned naked, or rather, well-feathered, into the street, are hunted by the townsfolk and the dogs, and reach their homes "well beaten and bitten."—So, too, in the Dinajpurí story (p. 442), the kutwal is sent away, covered from head to feet with molasses and cotton-wool, and such a figure must have maddened all the dogs of the quarter, though nothing is said about them.

Upakosa then said, "When my husband went away he placed our household gods in three baskets; they have heard this man acknowledge his holding a deposit of my husband's, and let them bear witness for me." The king, with some feeling of surprise and incredulity, ordered the baskets to be sent for, and they were accordingly produced in the open court. Upakosa then addressed them, "Speak, gods, and declare what you overheard this banker say in our dwelling. If you are silent I will unhouse you in this presence." Afraid of this menaced exposure, the tenants of the baskets immediately exclaimed, "Verily in our presence the banker acknowledged possession of your wealth." On hearing these words the whole court was filled with surprise, and the banker, terrified out of his senses, acknowledged the debt and promised restitution.

This business being adjusted, the king expressed his curiosity to see the household divinities of Upakosa, and she very readily complied with his wish. The baskets being opened, the culprits were dragged forth by the attendants, like so many lumps of darkness. Being presently recognised, they were overwhelmed with the laughter and derision of all the assembly. As soon as the merriment had subsided, Nanda begged Upakosa to explain what it all meant, and she acquainted him with what had occurred. Nanda was highly incensed, and, as the punishment of their offence, banished the criminals from the kingdom. He was equally pleased with the virtue and ingenuity of my wife, and loaded her with wealth and honour. Her family were likewise highly gratified by her conduct, and she obtained the admiration and esteem of the whole city.

Part of the Norse story of the "Mastermaid" (Dasent) presents some analogy to the several tales of the Lady and her Suitors:

The heroine takes shelter in the but of an old cross-grained hag, who presently meets with her death by an accident. Next morning a constable, passing the hut and seeing a beautiful maiden there, instantly falls over head in love with her, and asks her to become his wife. She requires him to state how much money he possesses, and he at once goes away and returns with a half-bushel sack full of gold and silver. So she consents to marry him; but they have scarcely retired to their nuptial couch when she says that she must get up again, as she has forgotten to make up the fire. The loving constable, however, would not hear of her getting out of bed, so he jumped up and stood on the hearth. Says the lady, "When you have got hold of the shovel, let me know." "Well," says he, "I'm holding it now." Then the damsel said, "God grant that you may hold the shovel, and the shovel hold you; and may you heap hot burning coals over yourself till morning breaks." So there stood the constable all that night, heaping hot coals upon himself till dawn, when he was released from the spell and sped home, dancing with pain, to the amusement of all who saw him on the way. Next day the attorney passed by the hut, and fell in love with the damsel. In answer to the question, had he much money, he went off and brought a whole bushel-sack full of gold and silver. Just as they had got into bed, she said she must rise and fasten the door of the porch. The attorney would not allow her, but gets up himself; and when she learns from him that he has grasped the handle of the porch-door, she expresses the wish that the handle might hold him, and he the handle, till morning. Such a dance the attorney had in struggling to free himself from the door-handle till dawn, when he, too, runs home, leaving his money behind him. On the third day the sheriff passes, and falls in love with the damsel; he goes and brings a bushel and a half of money. When they have got into bed, she says that she has forgot to bring home the calf from the meadow; so the sheriff gets up, and she utters a spell, by which he holds the calf's tail, and the calf's tail holds him, until daybreak, when the breathless sheriff is released, and returns home in a sorry plight.[7]

Closely allied to the tales in which a lady entraps objectionable suitors are those which represent the lady as appointing them disagreeable tasks in order to be rid of them:

The first novel of the Ninth Day in Boccaccio's 'Decameron' tells of a widow lady who had two lovers, one called Rinuccio, the other Alexander, neither of whom was acceptable to her. It happened that while she was pestered by their solicitations, a man named Scannadio, of reprobate life and hideous aspect, died and was buried. His death suggested to the lady a mode of getting rid of her lovers, by asking them to perform a service which she felt sure they would not undertake. She informed Alexander that the body of Scannadio was to be brought to her dwelling by one of her kinsmen, for a purpose which she would afterwards explain, and feeling a horror at such an inmate, she would grant him her love if, attired in the dead garments of Scannadio, he would occupy his place in the coffin, and allow himself to be conveyed to her house instead of the corpse.

[7]In an Icelandic variant, entitled "Story of Geirlaug and Groedari," two pages and a prince, who come as suitors to two daughters of a farmer and the heroine, are tricked by means of the calf's tail only.—Powell & Magnusson (Second Series).

She then sent a request to Rinuccio that he would bring the body of Scannadio at midnight to her house. Contrary to her expectations, both lovers agree to comply with her desires. During the night she watches the event, and soon perceives Rinuccio coming along bearing Alexander, who was equipped in the shroud of Scannadio. On the approach of some watchmen with a light, Rinuccio throws down his burden and runs off, while Alexander returns home in the dead man's shroud. Next day he demands the love of his mistress, which she refuses, pretending to believe that no attempt had been made to execute her commands.—*Dunlop*.

The old English metrical tale of 'The Lady Prioress and her Three Wooers,' ascribed to John Lydgate, a monk of Bury (*circa* 1430),[8] bears a strong resemblance to the great Florentine's novel:

The suitors are a knight, a parish priest, and a merchant. As the condition of her love, the lady prioress imposes on the young cavalier the task of lying all night in a chapel as a dead body, wrapped in a sheet. She next sends for the churchman, and, telling him a feigned story, induces him to go to the chapel and secretly bury the body. Then beguiling the merchant with another fictitious tale about the body, she persuades him to array himself as the devil and prevent the burial. The priest on seeing, as he imagines, the arch-fiend, throws down his book and leaps through the chapel window; the knight rises and takes to his heels; the merchant, equally affrighted, seeing the dead come back to life, flies from the chapel in a different direction from the others; and the fugitives spend a terrible night in hiding from each other. Next day the priest comes to tell the lady prioress how, just as he was about to bury the body, the devil appeared, and the dead man came to life again. "I never," quoth the lady, "had a lover that died a good death." "Then," says Mass John, "that will serve for ale and meat; thou wilt never be wooed by me." The cavalier is dismissed because he did not remain all night in the chapel, according to the condition she had imposed. When the merchant comes to tell her of his misadventures, she threatens to disclose his wicked designs to his wife and to all the country; and he purchases her silence by giving twenty marks a year to the convent. Thus the good lady prioress punished her three profligate suitors, and freed herself from their importunities.[9]

[8]Ritson, in his 'Biographia Literaria,' unjustly calls honest Lydgate "a voluminous, prosaic, drivelling monk."

[9]If this most diverting tale was imitated from Boccaccio's novel (which I doubt), the author deserves credit for his invention, since it is a great improvement on his model.

ᘒ

Lastly, under the title of "The Wicked Lady of Antwerp," in Thorpe's 'Northern Mythology,' we find a very singular variant of the two preceding stories, in which the catastrophe is tragical:

A rich lady in Antwerp led a very licentious life, and had four lovers, all of whom visited her in the evenings, but at different hours, so that no one knew anything of the others. The Long Wapper[10] one night assumed the form of the lady. At ten o'clock came the first lover, and the Wapper said to him, "What dost thou desire?" "I desire you for a wife," said the gallant. "Thou shalt have me," replied the Wapper, "if thou wilt go at once to the Churchyard of Our Lady, and there sit for two hours on the transverse of the great cross." "Good," said he, "that shall be done"; and he went and did accordingly. At half-past ten came the second lover. "What dost thou want?" asked the Wapper. "I wish to marry you," answered the suitor. "Thou shalt have me," replied the Wapper, "if thou wilt go previously to the Churchyard of Our Lady, there take a coffin, drag it to the foot of the great cross, and lay thyself in it till midnight." "Good," said the lover, "that shall be done at once"; and he went and did so. About eleven o'clock came the third. Him the Long Wapper commissioned to go to the coffin at the foot of the cross in Our Lady's Churchyard, knock thrice on the lid, and wait there till midnight. At half-past eleven came the fourth gallant, and Wapper asked him to take an iron chain from the kitchen and drag it after him, while he ran three times round the cross in the Churchyard of Our Lady. The first had set himself on the cross, but had fallen dead with fright on seeing the second place the coffin at his feet. The second died with fright when the third struck thrice on the coffin. The third fell down dead when the fourth came along rattling his chain. The fourth knew not what to think, when he found the three others lying stiff and cold around the cross. With all speed he ran from the churchyard to the lady, to tell her what had happened, and to hold her to her word. But she, of course, knew nothing of the matter. When, however, on the following day she was informed of the miserable death of her three lovers, she put an end to her own life.

[10]A Flemish sprite, whose knavish exploits resemble those of our Robin Goodfellow, or of Friar Rush.

HOW A KING'S LIFE WAS SAVED BY A MAXIM

IN the 'Gesta Romanorum' we read of a king who bought of a merchant three maxims, the first of which was, "Whatever you do, do wisely, and think of the consequences"; and it saved his life on one occasion, when his barber had been hired by the prime minister to cut the king's throat while engaged in shaving him, but observing these words engraved on the bottom of the basin he was about to use, the razor dropped from his hand, and he fell on his knees and confessed his guilty design.—This story was probably taken into the 'Gesta' from No. 81 of the 'Liber de Donis' of Etienne de Bourbon, where a prince buys for a large sum of money the advice, "In omnibus factis tuis considera antequam facial, ad quem finem inde venire valeas," which he causes to be written on all the royal linen, etc.; and it was the means of saving his life, as above related.

An Arabian version is given in Beloe's 'Oriental Apologues': A king obtains from a dervish, seated by the wayside, the maxim, "Let him who begins a thing consider its end." This he had engraved on all the dishes of the royal household, and painted on the walls of the palace. One day he sends for his surgeon to bleed him. The prime vazír gives the surgeon a handsome lancet to use in place of his own, but on reading the maxim engraved on the basin, he substitutes his old lancet. After the operation the king inquires why he had changed lancets, to which the surgeon replies so as to awaken the king's suspicions, and he commands the grand vazír to approach and submit to be bled with the lancet he had given the surgeon, which being poisoned, the vazír dies on the first puncture.

In the Turkish romance of the 'Forty Vazírs,' where the same story also occurs, instead of the chief vazír plotting against the king's life, it is another king, his mortal enemy, who disguises himself, goes to the king's barber, presents him with much gold, and gives him a poisoned lancet to be used when he is next called to bleed the king. The conclusion is the same as that of the version in the 'Gesta Romanorum.'—The story is also found in several collections of Italian tales, and in the 'Sicilianische Märchen' of Laura Gonzenbach.

In a Kashmírí variant, a holy man sells to a king, for a hundred rupís, certain words, which he is to repeat three times every night. One of the ministers resolved to bring about the king's death, and to this end had caused an underground passage to be made between his house and the king's palace. It happened one night that the minister had gone into the passage to remove the foot of earth that yet remained, when he heard the king mutter the holy man's charm, and saying to himself, "I am discovered," he hastened back.[1]

It has not hitherto been pointed out—to English readers, at least—that this story is of Buddhist extraction. The incident of the king and his barber occurs in 'Buddhaghosha's Parables,' under the title of the "Story of Kulla Panthaka":

This youth, on quitting his teacher to return home, received from him a charm, consisting of these words: *Ghatesi ghatesi kim kárana? tava karman aham gánámi,* "Why are you busy? why are you busy? I know what you are about!" His teacher advised him to repeat these words frequently, so that he should not forget them. "It will," he added, "always provide you with a living, wherever you may be—you have only to mutter the charm." The young man duly arrived at the house of his parents in Benáres. It happened that the king went out one night in disguise,[2] "to discover whether the actions of his subjects were good or evil." As he was passing the house where the youth resided, he overheard him repeat the words of the charm; and it so chanced that a party of thieves, who had burrowed under the walls of a neighbouring house,[3] and were about to enter it, also heard the words, and saying one to another, "We are discovered," they made off in all haste. The king saw them as they fled away, and knowing that it was in consequence of the charm, noted the place very carefully and returned to his palace. Next morning he despatched a messenger to bring the youth into his presence; and when he stood before him, the king desired him to impart to him the charm he had repeated on the previous evening. The youth willingly did so, and the king rewarded him with a thousand pieces of gold.

"At this time," the narrative proceeds, "the prime minister, having formed the design of taking the king's life, went to the king's barber and

---

[1] Knowles' 'Dictionary of Kashmírí Proverbs and Sayings.'

[2] Like the renowned Khalíf Harún-er-Rashíd and King James the Fifth of Scotland, both of whom, according to tradition, were wont to go about disguised among their subjects.

[3] See *ante,* p. 351, note 11.

said to him, 'When you shave the king's beard, take a very sharp razor and cut his throat. When I am king I will give you the post of prime minister.' He made the barber a present worth a thousand [pieces of gold], and the man agreed to do it. Accordingly, after he had soaked the king's beard with perfumed water, and was just going to cut his throat; at that moment the king, thinking of the charm, began to recite it. The barber no sooner heard this than he said, 'The king has discovered my intention!' Then he dropped the razor and fell trembling at the king's feet. The king exclaimed, 'O you, barber! do you not know that I am the king?' 'Your majesty,' said the barber, 'it was no plot of mine: the prime minister gave me a present worth a thousand [pieces of gold] to cut your majesty's throat while I was shaving you. It was he indeed who induced me to attempt it.' The king said to himself, 'It is owing to this young man who taught me the charm that my life has been saved.' Then he sent for the prime minister, and banished him from the country, saying, 'Since you have plotted against my life, you can no longer live within my territory.' After this, he called the young man who had given him the charm, and making him a very handsome present as an acknowledgment for his services, conferred on him the post of prime minister."

Here we have another example of the influence of Buddhism on the literature of Europe during the Middle Ages. The story had evidently assumed the form in which it is found in the Arabic long before it was brought to Europe, with many others that occur in the monkish collections of *exempla*.

✑ IRRATIONAL EXCESS OF SORROW ✑

THE celebrated Dr Isaac Barrow, in a sermon on Contentment, has the following anecdote: "When once a king did excessively and obstinately grieve for the death of his wife, whom he tenderly loved, a philosopher, observing it, told him that he was ready to comfort him by restoring her to life, supposing only that he would supply what was needful towards the performing it. The king said he was ready to furnish him with anything. The philosopher answered that he was provided with all things necessary except one thing. What that was, the king demanded. He replied that if he would, on his wife's tomb, inscribe the names of three persons who never mourned, she presently would revive. The king, after inquiry, told the philosopher that he could not find one such man. 'Why then,' said the philosopher, smiling, 'O absurdest of all men, art thou not ashamed to moan as if thou hadst alone fallen into so grievous a case, whereas thou canst not find one person that ever was free from such domestic affliction?'"

The editor of Barrow's Sermons conjectures that this was derived from the Epitome of Julianus. However this may be, it occurs in Lucian's 'Demonax': Herod was grieving for the death of his son Pollux, and the philosopher Demonax offered to raise up his shade, provided Herod produced three men who had never grieved for anything.

To the same purpose is the tale related in the collection of Ser Giovanni: A son, on his deathbed, writes to his mother to send him a shirt made by the most happy woman in the city where she resided. The mother finds that the person whom she selects is utterly wretched, and is thus consoled for her own loss, as her son intended. Dunlop remarks that Giovanni's tale has given rise to 'The Fruitless Enquiry, or Search after Happiness,' by Mrs Heywood, one of the earli est of our English novelists. And an analogous story is related of Iskandar, or Alexander the Great, by the Arabian historian Abu-'l-Faráj: Alexander's last words to his mother had been to request that a banquet should be set out on the occasion of his death, and that proclamation should be made, at the beginning of the feast, that none should partake of it but those whose lives had been uniformly prosperous. When this was announced, every hand was drawn back, all sat silent, and the unhappy mother saw, in this tacit and affecting confession of the troubled lot of humanity, a melancholy consolation for her own individual loss.

A much more beautiful version—if it be not indeed the original form—occurs in 'Buddhaghosha's Parables' (Mr Edwin Arnold has reproduced it in his grand poem, 'The Light of Asia,' being an account of the life and teachings of Gautama. the illustrious founder of Buddhism):

A wealthy man of the Savatthi country married a young girl, whose name was Kiságotamí. In course of time she gave birth to a son. When the boy was able to walk by himself he died. The young girl, in her love for it, carried the dead child clasped to her bosom, and went about from house to house asking if any one would give her some medicine for it. When the neighbours saw this, they said, "Is the girl mad, that she carries about on her breast the dead body of her son?" But a wise man, thinking to himself, "Alas, this Kiságotamí does not understand the law of death; I must comfort her," said to her, "My good girl, I cannot myself give medicine for it, but I know of a doctor who can attend to it." "If so, tell me where he is." The wise man continued, "Pará Taken[1] can give medicine; you must go to him." Kiságotamí went to Pará Taken, and doing homage to him, said, "Lord and Master, do you know any medicine that will be good for my boy?" Pará Taken replied, "I know of some." She asked, "What medicine do you require?" He said, "I want a handful of mustard-seed." The girl promised to procure it for him, but Pará Taken continued, "I require some mustard-seed taken from a house where no son, husband, parent, or slave has died." The girl said, "Very good," and went to ask for some at the different houses, carrying the dead body of her child upon her hip.[2] The people said, "Here is some mustard-seed, take it." Then she asked, "In my friend's house has there died a son, a husband, a parent, or a slave? " They replied, "Lady, what is this you say? The living are few, but the dead are many." Then she went to other houses; but one said, "I have lost a son;" another, "I have lost my parents;" another, "I have lost my slave." At last, not being able to find a single house where no one had died, from which to procure the mustard-seed, she began to think, "This is a heavy task that I am engaged in. I am not the only one whose son is dead. In the whole of the Savatthi country everywhere children are dying, parents are dying." Thinking thus, she

[1] Pará Taken: Lord, or Master, *i.e.*, Gautama (Buddha) himself.
[2] Still a common mode of carrying young children in India.

acquired the law of fear, and putting away her affection for her child, she summoned up resolution and left the dead body in the forest. Then she went to Pará Taken and paid homage to him. He said to her, "Have you procured the handful of mustard-seed?" "I have not," she replied. "The people of the village told me, 'The living are few, but the dead are many.'" Pará Taken said to her, "You thought that you alone had lost a son;—the law of death is, that among all living creatures there is no permanence."

Buddhist teaching had begun to spread westward before the time of Lucian. It is possible that the story of his friend Demonax and the sorrowing Herod had foundation in fact; on the other hand, Lucian was not the man to be scrupulous about appropriating to his own purposes any tales or legends he chanced to hear, and he may have heard some modified form of the Buddhist story of Kiságotamí.

ᔕ THE INTENDED DIVORCE ᔕ*

IN one of Mr Ralston's 'Russian Folk Tales,' Semiletka is chosen for his wife by a civil governor (Voyvode), with the stipulation that if she ever meddled with the affairs of the law-court, she should be sent back to her father, but allowed to take with her whatever thing belonging to her which she most prized. One day she tells him that he had decided a certain case unfairly. The governor, enraged at her interference, demands a divorce. "After dinner, Semiletka was obliged to go back to her father's house. But during dinner she made the Voyvode drink till he was intoxicated. He drank his fill, and went to sleep. While he was sleeping, she had him placed in a carriage, and then she drove away with him to her father's. When they arrived there, the Voyvode awoke, and said, 'Who brought me here?' 'I brought you,' said Semiletka. 'There was an agreement between us that I might take away whatever I prized most, and so I have taken you.' The Voyvode marvelled at her wisdom, and made peace with her. He and she returned home, and went on living prosperously."

This beautiful little story has perhaps been derived (indirectly, of course) from a similar one in the Talmud, which is somewhat as follows:

A certain man brought his wife before Rabbi Simon the son of Jochoe, stating his desire to be divorced from her, since he had been married over ten years without being blessed with children.[1] The rabbi at first endeavoured to dissuade the man from his purpose, but finding him resolute, he gravely addressed the pair thus: "My children, when you were married, did ye not make a feast and entertain your friends? Well, since you are determined to be divorced, do likewise; go home, make a feast, entertain your friends, and on the following day come to me and I will comply with your wishes." They returned home, and, in accordance with the reverend father's advice, the husband caused a splendid feast to be prepared, to which were invited their friends and relations. In the course of the entertainment, the

---

[1] According to Jewish law, the want of children is sufficient to justify the dissolution of the marriage tie, though the Rabbins, it is said, are not generally in favour of divorces, unless on very grave grounds. Throughout the East the want of offspring is considered as a great disgrace. Readers of the 'Arabian Nights' must be familiar with the numerous instances which occur in that most fascinating work of khalífs, sultans, vazírs, etc. being childless, and of the pious and often magical means they adopted to obtain the blessing of a son and heir. An Asiatic considers his sons as the light of his house.

husband, being gladdened with wine, said to his wife, "My beloved, we have lived many happy years together, it is only the want of children that makes me wish for a separation. To convince thee, however, that I still love thee, I give thee leave to take with thee out of my house whatever thou likest best." "Be it so," said his wife. The wine-cup was freely plied among the guests, and all became merry, until at length many had fallen asleep, and amongst these was the master of the feast, which his wife perceiving, she caused him to be carried to her father's house and put to bed. Having slept off the effects of his carouse, he awoke, and, finding himself in a strange house, he exclaimed, "Where am I? How came I here?" His wife, who had placed herself behind a curtain to await the issue of her little stratagem, came up to him, and told him that he had no cause for alarm, since he was in her father's house. "In thy father's house!" echoed the astonished husband. "How should I come hither?" "I will soon explain, my dear husband," said she. "Didst thou not tell me last night that I might take out of thy house whatever I most valued? Now, my beloved, believe me, amongst all thy treasures there is none I value so much as I do thyself." The sequel may be easily imagined: overcome by such devotion, the man affectionately embraced his wife, was reconciled to her, and they lived happily together ever afterwards.[2]

It is curious to find a historical anecdote which presents a close resemblance to these stories of devoted wives: In the year 1141, during the civil war in Germany between the Ghibellines and the Guelphs, it happened.that the Emperor Conrad besieged the Guelph count of Bavaria in the castle of Weinsberg. After a long and obstinate defence, the garrison was obliged at length to surrender, when the emperor, annoyed that they had held out so long and defied him, vowed that he would destroy the place with fire, and put all to the sword except the women, whom he gallantly promised to let go free, and pass out unmolested. The Guelph countess, when she heard of this, begged as a farther favour that the

---

[2] A variant of this is found in Crane's 'Italian Popular Tales:' "The Clever Girl," p. 311. In the same story is another incident which also occurs in the Talmud: A youth, who is the guest of a householder, is given at supper a capon to carve; to the master he gave the head, because (as he afterwards explained) he was head of the house; to the mistress, the inward part, as typical of her fruitfulness; to the two daughters, who were marriageable, each a wing, to indicate that they should soon fly abroad; to the two sons, who were the pillars of the house, the legs, which are the supporters of the animal; and to himself, he took that part of the capon which most resembles a boat, in which he had come thither, and in which he intended to return. This is also the subject of a story in Boccaccio's 'Decameron.'

women might be allowed to bear forth as much of their valuables as they could severally manage to carry. The emperor having pledged his word and honour that he would grant this request, on the morrow at daybreak, as the castle gates were opened, he saw, to his amazement, the women file out one by one, every married woman carrying her husband with their young ones upon her back, and the others each the friend or relation nearest and dearest to her.[3] At sight of this the emperor was tenderly moved, and could not help according to the action the homage of his admiration. The result was, that not only were life and liberty extended to the Guelphs, but the place itself was spared and restored in perpetuity to its heroic defenders. The count and his countess were henceforth treated by the emperor with honour and affection, and the town itself was long after popularly known by the name of "Weibertreue," *i.e.*, the Abode of Womanly Fidelity.—Heywood, in the Third Book of his 'History of Women,' reproduces this anecdote; he says that the emperor "not only suffered them [*i.e.*, the women] to depart with their first burdens, but granted every one a second, to make choice of what best pleased them amongst all the treasure and wealth of the city," but he does not state that the place was spared.

[3] The women of Weinsberg must have been stronger than London draymen, when each could carry "her husband with their young ones upon her back"!

᧰ THE THREE KNIGHTS AND THE LADY: THE THREE HUNCHBACKS, ETC. ᧰

IN the old English prose version of the 'Seven Wise Masters' we have a kind of tragi-comical story—related by the sixth sage—such as our mediæval ancestors seem to have keenly relished:

An old knight had a young and beautiful wife, who sang so melodiously that many persons were attracted to her house, several of whom came as lovers. Among the latter were three young and gallant knights, great favourites of the emperor. She promised each of them an interview, unknown to one another, for which she was to receive twenty florins. Having received the money, she causes her husband to murder them, one by one, as they come into the house; and then sends for her brother, who was a city sentinel, and, telling him that her husband had killed a man in a quarrel, prevails upon him to take the body of one of the murdered knights and throw it into the sea. When the brother returns, she proceeds to the cellar (where the bodies had been temporarily concealed), on the pretence of drawing some wine, and suddenly cries out for help. The sentinel hastens to the cellar, when she tells him that the body has come back again, at which he is naturally much astonished; but stuffing the second body into his sack, and tying a stone round the neck, he plunges it into the sea. The same trick is played upon him with the third body, which he takes away, believing it to be the one that he had first thrown into the sea, and burns it in a great fire which he had kindled in the middle of a wood, to make sure that it should not again return. Presently a knight on horseback, who was going to a tournament, approached the fire to warm himself, and the sentinel, supposing him to be the dead man, throws him and his horse into the midst of the fire, and remains until they are reduced to ashes. He then goes back to his sister and obtains the promised reward. Some time after this the woman, in a fit of rage, accuses her husband of the triple murder, and both are put to death.[1]

Precisely the same story is found in the 'Gesta Romanorum,' into which it was taken immediately from the 'Seven Wise Masters,' according to

[1] See Note at the end of this paper; "Women betraying their Husbands."

461

Douce, the eminent literary antiquary; but in this conjecture he was mistaken, as also in believing the 'Gesta' to have been first composed in Germany, and another version made from it in England some time afterwards. Oesterley has shown, on the contrary, that the 'Gesta' was originally written in England, towards the end of the thirteenth century, and that what is now distinguished as the Continental 'Gesta' was composed after it. As the 'Historia Septem Sapientum Romæ,' from which was derived our prose version of the 'Seven Wise Masters,' was not written till near the end of the fifteenth century, it follows that the story in question was taken from that work into the 'Gesta.' It does not occur in any earlier version of the Wise Masters, such as the French 'Roman des Sept Sages,' thirteenth century; the 'Liber de Septem Sapientibus' (in the 'Scala Cœli' of Johannes Junior, a Dominican monk who lived in the middle of the fourteenth century), and our Early English metrical texts of the 'Seven Sages.' In the 'Historia' two stories which are separate in these earlier texts are fused together in order to make room for this tale of the Three Knights and the Lady.

The *fabliau* of 'Estourmi,' by Hugues Piaucelle, of which Le Grand gives only an *extrait*, is probably the source of the 'Gesta' story. The outline of it is as follows:

Three canons enamoured of Yfame, wife of Jean, offer her each a considerable sum of money for her love-favours. She feigns to consent, and assigns to each of them a different hour. As they successively arrive, Jean, her husband, whom she has forewarned, kills them, and takes the money they had brought, but he is presently much perplexed about the disposal of the bodies. He goes to his brother-in-law, Estourmi, a sort of bandit and frequenter of low taverns, confesses to him that he has killed a priest, and asks him if he has enough courage to take away the body and bury it somewhere. Estourmi, with many horrid oaths, answers that he wishes he was the last of the priests, in order to have the pleasure of freeing the world from them; and he goes to inter this one in a field. But when he returns, and Jean shows him the second body, he appears to be astonished at seeing the dead man come back, and swears dreadfully; nevertheless he carries it away and buries it in another place. The same thing happens in the case of the third. As Estourmi is returning, he meets a good priest on the way to church, to sing matins, and, with the idea that it is always the same man, kills him on the spot.[2]

[2]Le Grand's 'Fabliaux,' ed. 1781, tome iv. pp. 250, 251; Barbasan (Méon's eel. 1808), t. iii. p. 245 ff.

There are no fewer than five of the *fabliaux* in Le Grand and Barbasan that recount droll adventures with dead bodies, of which the most amusing is that of the Three Hunchbacks ('Les Trois Bossus'), by Durant, which Dunlop has thus rendered:

Gentlemen (says the author), if you choose to listen, I will recount to you an adventure which once happened in a castle that stood on the bank of a river, near a bridge, and at a short distance from a town, of which I forget the name, but which we may suppose to be Douai. The master of this castle was humpbacked. Nature had exhausted her ingenuity in the formation of his whimsical figure. In place of understanding, she had given him an immense head, which, nevertheless, was lost between his two shoulders; he had thick hair, a short neck, and a horrible visage. Spite of his deformity, this bugbear bethought himself of falling in love with a beautiful young woman, the daughter of a poor but respectable burgess of Douai. He sought her in marriage, and, as he was the richest person in the district, the poor girl was delivered up to him. After the nuptials, he was as much to pity as she, for, being devoured by jealousy, he had no tranquillity night or day, but went prying and rambling everywhere, and suffered no stranger to enter his castle.

One day during the Christmas festival, while standing sentinel at his gate, he was accosted by three hump-backed minstrels. They saluted him as a brother, as such asked him for refreshments, and at the same time to establish the fraternity, they ostentatiously displayed their humps. Contrary to expectation, he conducted them to his kitchen, gave them a capon with some peas, and to each a piece of money over and above. Before their departure, however, he warned them never to return, on pain of being thrown into the river. At this threat of the chatelain the minstrels laughed heartily, and took the road to the town, singing in full chorus, and dancing in a grotesque manner in derision. He, on his part, without paying any farther attention to them, went to walk in the fields.

The lady, who saw her husband cross the bridge, and had heard the minstrels, called them back to amuse her. They had not been long returned to the castle when her husband knocked at the gate, by which she and the minstrels were equally alarmed. Fortunately the lady perceived, on a bedstead in a neighbouring room, three empty coffers. Into each of these she stuffed a minstrel, shut the covers and then opened the gate to her husband. He had only come back to spy the conduct of his wife, as usual, and after a short stay went out anew, at which you may believe his wife was not dissatisfied. She instantly ran to the coffers to release the minstrels, for night was approaching, and her husband would not probably be long absent. But what was her dismay when she found them all three suffocated! Lamentation, however, was useless. The main object now was to get rid of the dead bodies, and she had not a moment to lose. She ran then to the gate, and seeing a peasant go by, offered him a reward of 30 livres, and leading him into the castle, she took him to one of the coffers, and showing him its contents, told him he must throw the dead body into the river. He asked for a sack, put the carcase into it, pitched it over the bridge into the stream, and then returned quite out of breath to claim the promised reward. "I certainly intended to satisfy you," said the lady, "but you ought first to fulfil the conditions of your bargain; you have agreed to rid me of the dead body, have you not? There, however, it is still"; saying this, she showed him the other coffer, in which the second hunchback had expired. At this sight the clown was perfectly confounded, saying, "How the devil! come back! a sorcerer!" He then stuffed the body into the sack, and threw it, like the other, over the bridge, taking care to put the head down, and to observe that it sank.

Meanwhile the lady had again changed the position of the coffers, so that the third was now in the place which had been successively occupied by the two others. When the peasant returned she showed him the remaining body. "You are right, friend," said she, "he must be a magician, for there he is again." The rustic gnashed his teeth with rage: "What the devil! am I to do nothing but carry about this accursed hunchback?" He then lifted him up, with dreadful imprecations, and having tied a stone round the neck, threw him into the middle of the current, threatening, if he came out a third time, to despatch him with a cudgel. The first object that presented itself to the clown on his way back for the reward was the hunchbacked master of the castle returning from his evening walk, and making towards the gate. At this sight the peasant could no longer restrain his fury: "Dog of a hunchback, are you there again?" So saying, he sprang on the chatelain, stuffed him into a sack, and threw him head-long into the river after the minstrels. "I'll venture a wager you have not seen him this last time," said the peasant, entering the room where the lady was seated. She answered that she had not. "Yet you were not far from it," replied he. "The sorcerer was already at the gate, but I have taken care of him—be at your ease, he will not come back now." The lady instantly comprehended what had occurred, and recompensed the peasant with much satisfaction.[3]

The second tale of the seventh sage in the 'Mishlé Sandabar'—the Hebrew version of the Book of Sindibád—written about the middle of the thirteenth century, seems to have been derived from the same source as Durant's *fabliau:*

There was a young and beautiful woman married to an old man, who [was so jealous of her that he] would not allow her to walk in the street, and she submitted to this only with impatience. One day she said to her maid, "Go outside; perhaps thou wilt meet some one who will be able to amuse us." The maid went out and met a hunchback, who had a tambourine and a flute in his hand, and was dancing and beating the tambourine, so that the people might give him some reward. The maid brought this man to her mistress, who gave him to eat and to drink, which caused him great pleasure. He then rose and danced and leaped about, at which the young woman was much pleased, and having dressed him in fine clothes, and given him a present, she sent him away. The friends and comrades of the hunchback saw him, and asked him where he had met with such good luck, and he told them of the beautiful wife of the old man. They then said to him, "If thou dost not take us with thee, we will make the whole affair public." Now the young woman sent [her maid] again to the hunchback, that he might come to her. He said to her, "My companions also wish to come and amuse thee;" and she replied, "Let them come." The lady offered them all sorts of things; so they set to eating and drinking, and got drunk, and fell from their seats. Presently the master of the house came back, and the lady immediately rose with her maid and carried the men into another part of the house. There they quarrelled and fought, and strangled each other, and died. Meantime the husband, having taken some food, went out again, and then the lady ordered her maid to bring the hunchbacks out, but they were all dead. Then said she, "Go out quickly, and find some simpleminded porter," and she put the dead bodies into sacks. The maidservant chanced to meet a black man, and brought him to her mistress, who said to him: "Take this first sack and throw it into the river; then come back to me and I will take care to give thee all thou mayest require."

[3] Le Grand's 'Fabliaux' (ed. 1781), tome iv. p. 241; Barbasan (Méon's ed. 1808): "Du Trois Boçus," tome iii. p. 245.

The black did so, then he returned and took the second sack; and in that way he took them all, one after the other, and threw them into the river.

Wright, in his introduction to an early English metrical version of the 'Seven Sages,' printed for the Percy Society, gives a somewhat confused abstract of the Hebrew story: he says that the lady, hearing her husband at the door, "hurriedly concealed the hunchbacks in a place full of holes and traps, into which they fell and were strangled," as if it had been her purpose thus to get rid of them; yet no sooner is her husband gone than "she opens the door to release them, and is horrified to find them all dead." It does not appear from the Hebrew text that the number of the minstrels was only three, or indeed that all were hunchbacks; but it is very probable that the version as we now possess it is imperfect, and that it originally concluded in the same manner as the *fabliau* of 'Estourmi.' It is not to be imagined, surely, that the lady could have the hardihood to exhibit, even to a black, all the bodies at once and ask him to dispose of them.

The 'Mishlé Sandabar' is the only Eastern text of the Book of Sindibád that has the story of the Hunchbacks, a circumstance which may have led Wright to make the very erroneous statement that from it was derived the 'Historia Septem Sapientum Romæ,' which "served as the groundwork of all other mediæval versions." This is not the case: with the exception of the story of the Three Knights and the Lady, which was almost certainly derived from the 'Gesta,' the 'Historia' possesses no more in common with the Hebrew than with any other Eastern version.

That Durant's *fabliau* of 'Les Trois Bossus' and its Hebrew analogue are both of Indian extraction seems probable from a circumstance which has, I believe, hitherto escaped notice. In the appendix to Scott's translation of the 'Bahár-i-Dánush,' vol. iii. p. 293, there is the following outline of one of the tales which he omitted from the text for reasons of his own: A princess, having fallen in love with a young man, had him brought into her palace disguised as a female. While she was enjoying his society the king came to pay her a visit, and she had barely time to put her gallant into a narrow dark closet to prevent his discovery. The king stayed long, and on his departure the princess found her lover dead from suffocation. In order to have the body conveyed away, she applies to an ugly negro, her domestic, who refuses, and threatens to disclose her abandoned conduct unless she will receive his addresses, and she is forced to submit. Wearied with his brutality, she, with the assistance of her nurse, one night hurls him headlong from the battlements, and he is dashed to pieces by the fall.—As the rest of the story belongs to another cycle, we may suppose the incidents of the disguised youth, the unexpected visit of the lady's father, the hurried concealment of the lover, and his suffocation, together with the negro's stipulation before removing the body (which occurs in the Hebrew tale), to have been adapted from an Indian story from which the *fabliau* of 'Les Trois Bossus' was indirectly derived. Through Persia the story would reach Syria, where doubtless the author of the 'Mishlé Sandabar' heard it, and whence some *trouvère* or pilgrim brought it to Europe.

Douce thought that the original of the Three Knights and the Lady, and the different *fabliaux* which resemble it, is the story of the Little Hunchback in the 'Arabian Nights.'[4] I consider this as very far from being probable—indeed as almost impossible. In the tale of the Three Knights and the Lady, and in the *fabliau* which is most likely its model, the bodies are represented to the watchman as being one and the same body, having returned to the place whence it had been taken; while in the Arabian tale, the body of the hunchbacked buffoon is moved about from one place to another—first, by the Tailor to the house of the Jewish Physician, who, having stumbled against it in the dark and believing he had accidentally killed his patient, to save himself, carries it to the store-room of the Sultan's Purveyor, who, mistaking it for a thief, beats it till he thought he had slain him, takes it to a shop and props it against the front wall, after which the Sultan's Broker, returning home from an orgie, staggers against it, and is accused of having murdered the hunchback.

Lane was of opinion that, while very many of the tales in the 'Arabian Nights' are of Indian origin, those of a humorous character are distinctly of Arab invention, and perhaps such is the case. But that celebrated collection, according to Baron de Sacy and other competent judges, was not composed before the middle of the 15th century, and consequently could not have furnished the *trouvères* with materials for those *fabliaux* which are similar to Arabian tales—both must have been derived independently, and, in the case of the *fabliaux*, probably from oral sources. The story of the Little Hunchback finds a parallel in a *fabliau* by Jean le Chapelain, entitled 'Le Sacristan de Cluni,' the substance of which is as follows:

---

[4] 'Illustrations of Shakespeare,' vol. ii. pp, 378, 379.—"Little Hunchbacked *Tailor*" Douce calls him; but he was the Sultan's buffoon, and it was while supping with the Tailor and his pretty wife that he was choked with a fish-bone.

Hugues, a citizen of Cluni, was a money-changer and merchant. One day as he was returning from a fair with different kinds of goods, and amongst other things, with cloth from Amiens, he was attacked in a forest by robbers, who took from him his wagons. Obliged, in order to satisfy his creditors, to sell the little property which he possessed, he found himself thus entirely ruined. Then his wife Idoine proposed that they should withdraw into France,[5] where they had some friends, and they fixed their departure on the third day. But the sacristan of the monastery, who loved Idoine, wished to profit by the circumstance in order to obtain one of those nice little agreeable favours which he had hitherto solicited in vain. He offered Idoine 100 livres, a sum which he could very readily give, since he was treasurer of the abbey. The wife, tempted by so considerable a sum, which in a moment would have repaired the embarrassments of the family, feigned to yield, and, by concert with her husband, made an assignation with the monk for the evening. The monk secretly escaped by the door of the church, of which he had the keys. He hands over to the lady the stipulated money, and claims her fulfilment of the other half of the bargain, when suddenly the husband appears armed with a stick. Hugues, intending to strike the monk in order to frighten him and cause him to fly away, unfortunately dealt him a blow on the head that killed him on the spot. Upon this Hugues and his wife were in despair. "What shall we do," say they, "when day appears, and this is discovered?" They were so much alarmed, that if the gate of the town had been open they would have saved themselves by flight at once. Presently, necessity reanimating their courage, Idoine proposes to carry back the body into the abbey, which they could enter by means of the sacristan's keys. Hugues accordingly takes the body upon his shoulders and sets off, followed by his wife to open the door of the church, and deposits it in an appendage to the monastery. During the night the prior visited this place, and pushing the door open hastily, overturned the dead sacristan, who fell to the ground with a heavy thud. The prior believed he had killed the sacristan, and this misfortune was augmented by the fact that he had quarrelled the evening before with him, and so it would be universally concluded that he had murdered him out of revenge. What he

---

[5]It is to be observed that this manner of speaking distinguishes France from Burgundy. The author understands by the first country the provinces which were domains of the king, as distinct from those which were only suzerain, and which, like Burgundy, had their particular sovereign. The people say even to-day, "St Denis en France."—*Note by Le Grand.*

conceived the best he could do in the circumstances was to carry the body outside of the abbey and place it at the door of some beautiful lady, in order to cause suspicion to be thrown upon her husband. The house of Idoine being nearest, he went thither, placed the body near the door, and then retired. The prior's purpose would undoubtedly have been accomplished had Hugues and his wife been asleep, but anxiety kept them both awake, and Idoine having heard a noise at the door, caused her husband to rise. When the body is discovered they believe themselves lost, and that the devil had carried it to their house to bring about their death. In order to foil this purpose of the evil spirit, the lady gave her husband a billet in which was written the name of God. Armed with the sacred talisman, Hugues recovered his courage, and lifted the body of the sacristan a second time, with the design of depositing it elsewhere. In passing before the house of Thebaut, the farmer of the convent, he perceived a heap of dung, and the idea occurred to him that here he might conceal the monk, since the sacristan was in the habit of frequently visiting Thebaut, and so they would suspect him of the murder. He was preparing a place among the straw, when he felt a sack which seemed to contain a body. "Oh, oh," he exclaimed, "is it possible that this fellow has also killed a monk? Ah, well, they will keep one another company, and he will have the honour of both." Then Hugues untied the sack, and was very much astonished to find therein a pig. Thebaut, in fact, as Christmas was approaching, had killed one of his pigs, but two thieves had come in the evening to carry it off, and while waiting till night should enable them to take it away without risk, they had concealed it in the fireplace, and gone to drink at the tavern. Hugues, without troubling himself as to whom the pig belonged, drew it out of the sack, and having substituted the monk, went off with his booty. The two thieves had found at the tavern other men of their own kidney, with whom they drank. One of the company, in order to improve the flavour of the wine, said he wished to have a rasher or two of fresh pork, upon which one of the thieves offered to treat them all to rashers, and immediately went to fetch the pig. At the appearance of the sack they all expressed their pleasure—it was evidently a large pig; and while one thief goes for firewood the other goes for a gridiron. Meantime the servant-girl unties the sack, and raises up the other end in order to drop the pig on the floor. Suddenly the monk appears, and the girl utters a fearful scream. All present are stupefied. The host enters, and asks where is the murderer. "I have killed no one," said one of the thieves. "I had only stolen a pig, and the devil, to play me a trick, has made a monk of it. For the rest, it belongs to Thebaut. I wish the villain had it again." The thief then returns with the body to Thebaut's house, and hangs it from the same cord that had been used to suspend the pig before it was stolen. All this could not be done without some noise. Thebaut awoke and rose up in order to go and feel if his pig was still in its place. But the cord, too weak for its new weight, suddenly breaks, and the monk's body falls on the farmer, whom it overturns. The farmer cries for help; his wife and servants come with a light, and find him caught under the robe of the sacristan. Thebaut was not long before recognising the dead body, and fearing that if they found it at his house they would accuse him of the murder, he sought means for getting rid of it, for it was already day. In his stable there was a young colt which had not yet been broken in, and was therefore very wild. He causes it to be led out, places on its back the sacristan's body, which he ties to the saddle to prevent it from falling off, and after having put in the right hand an old lance, and suspended a shield from his neck, as if it was a knight, he struck the horse with his whip, when it at once rushed madly through the town, followed by Thebaut and his men, calling out, "Stop the monk! "Their cries, joined to those of the townsfolk, frightened the horse still more. It ran till out of breath, and rushed into the garden of the convent, the gate of which was open. The prior, who happened to be there, and had not time to get out of the way, was struck with the lance and thrown down. The monks save themselves and shout, "Take care! take care! the sacristan has become mad!" Twenty times the frightened horse runs through the garden and cloister. He even penetrates into the kitchen, where he breaks everything, striking lance and shield against the walls. At last he comes to a large hole which they had dug for a well and falls headlong into it, with the cavalier-monk. As no one knew his adventure, the sacristan's death was ascribed to the fall. As to Hugues, he gained by it a fine pig and 100 livres. Thebaut alone was a loser, but he caused the monks to compensate him for the loss of his colt, and it was they who paid everything.[6]

Under the title of "The Fair Lady of Norwich," Heywood, in his 'History of Women,' gives a variant of the *fabliau* of the Sacristan of Cluni:

[6] Le Grand (ed. 1781), t. iv. pp. 252–260; Barbasan (Méon's ed. 1808): "Du Segretaine Moine," t. i. p. 242 ff.—The poet Longfellow, in his 'Outre Mer; or, a Pilgrimage Beyond Sea,' has turned this *fabliau* into an excellent prose tale, entitled "Martin Franc; or, the Monk of St Anthony."

In the time of Henry the Fifth there resided at Norwich a worthy knight and his lady, whose beauty was such that "she attracted the eyes of all beholders with no common admiration." This brave knight, "for the good of his soul," erected near his own house a church, and between them a religious house capable of accommodating twelve friars and an abbot. Two of the friars, John and Richard, were at continual enmity, and nothing could reconcile them. It was the custom of the knight and his lady to attend matins in the church, and Friar John, becoming enamoured of the lady, had the audacity to write her a letter, in which he declared his passion. The lady showed her husband this letter, at which he was naturally enraged, and caused her to write a reply to the monk, stating that, her husband being about to ride to London, she would receive and entertain him. Friar John is punctual to the appointment; the lady conducts him into a private chamber, where the knight and his man strangle him. After this the man takes up the body, and by means of a ladder scales the convent wall and deposits the body in an outhouse. Friar Richard gets up during the night and perceiving his enemy in that place, addresses him, and receiving no answer, in a rage picks up a brick-bat and throws it at him, whereupon Friar John falls to the ground. Believing that he had slain him, and aware that their enmity was well known, Friar Richard takes the body, climbs over the wall and leaves it at the door of the knight, of whose lady he had heard it whispered Friar John was enamoured. The knight's conscience so pricked him that he could not sleep, and he sent his man out to listen about the convent walls and ascertain whether there was any uproar about the murder. When the man opens the door, he is terror-struck to discover Friar John sitting in the porch, and returns to inform his master, who, when he has recovered from his astonishment, quickly devises another plan to get rid of the body. He causes his man to bring out an old stallion he had used in the French wars; to put an old suit of armour on the monk and a rusty lance in his hand; then to bind him on the horse, seated like a cavalier; which being done, the horse is turned out into the highway. Meantime Friar Richard is ill at ease, and at length resolves to escape from the monastery. With this object he wakes up the man who had charge of the mare that was employed to carry corn to the mill, bids him saddle her, and he would himself go and bring back their meal. The man, glad to be saved the trouble, brings out the mare, which Friar Richard mounts and rides out of the convent gate, just at the time when the knight and his man had turned out Friar John upon the horse. To be brief, the horse scents the mare and rushes after her. Friar Richard looking back, and perceiving the horse and its armed rider, is in mortal terror. The citizens awake at the noise and come out of their houses. Friar Richard, finding himself still pursued, cries out that he is guilty of murder, and is arrested and thrown into prison. The runaway horse is caught; Friar John is dismounted and buried. Friar Richard is tried for the murder, and condemned on his own confession. But the knight, knowing him to be innocent, posts to the king, confesses his guilt, and, on account of his former services, is pardoned, and Friar Richard is released.[7]

In this version, it will be observed, a knight is substituted for the broken merchant of the *fabliau*, and the incident of the carcass of the pig is omitted. Kirkman, however, who lived about the same time as Heywood, has introduced the story with all the details of the *fabliau* and some additional incidents, and with a "little lawyer" in place of a monk in his translation of the French rendering of 'Erasto,' an Italian version of the 'Seven Wise Masters.' It is fused with the story of the Three Knights and the Lady, which does not occur either in the original Italian text or the French translation, but which Kirkman gives, as being "to the same purpose" as the story, told by the sage Agathus, of the lady who killed her husband out of love for a young man. In this curious variant, the lady having got rid of the bodies of her three murdered lovers, as related in the 'Seven Wise Masters' (*ante*, p. 458), the tale goes on to say that "after this manner she served several wooers, and among the rest came a little lawyer." He is knocked on the head by the husband, who carries the body and deposits it in an outhouse, where it is discovered by the little lawyer's bedfellow, who, thinking him asleep, pulls him by the sleeve, when down drops the lawyer on the floor. The lawyer's friend, suspecting who was his murderer (he does not believe himself to have killed him), takes the body and leaves it at the knight's house. It is discovered by the knight, who carries it off, intending to throw it into the river, but on his way, he sees some thieves hide a sack full of stolen goods under a stall, and then retire to a tavern to drink, so he opens the sack and finding it contains two flitches of bacon, he takes them out and puts the body in their stead. The thieves offer to sell the host of the

---

[7]This story has somehow got into Blomfield's 'History of Norfolk,' with the addition of the name of the murderer, which is strangely said to be Sir Thomas Erpingham. From Blomfield's version it is probable George Coleman the Younger derived the materials of the metrical tale of "The Knight and the Friar," which is found in his 'Broad Grins.'

tavern some bacon, to which he consents, and one of them fetches the sack. When its contents are discovered, they resolve to carry it to the chandler's back-shed, whence they had stolen the bacon, and they do so. The chandler sends his man to drop the body in the mill-dam, and on coming to the mill he sees a cart loaded with sacks of meal ready for the market, and, it being dark, he lays the sack with the lawyer on the cart, and, taking one of the sacks of meal on his horse, returns home. At daybreak the miller's cart is driven to market, whither come the knight and his lady to buy meal. The lady desires a sack to be opened in order to judge of the quality of the meal. It chanced that the one containing the body was opened, and the lawyer's head appearing, the lady cried out, "O Lord, husband, the lawyer you killed is come again!" They were taken before a magistrate, and, confessing the murders, were duly executed.[8]

Both Heywood and Kirkman may have derived their stories from an old English metrical version, a unique copy of which is preserved in the Bodleian Library, at Oxford, entitled 'Here beginneth a mery Jest of Dane Hew,[9] Munk of Leicestre, and how he was foure times slain and once hanged': printed at London by John Allde; no date. Dibdin, who has reprinted it in vol. ii. of the 'British Bibliographer,' edited by Sir Egerton Brydges, says the first notice of Allde as a printer is in 1554, but from the rudeness of the language it is probably a century earlier. In this version we are told that Dan Hew, a young and lusty monk of the abbey of Leicester, was deeply in love with the fair wife of a tailor. At length, by concert with her husband, she feigns to consent. The tailor is locked in a chest, and when the monk arrives and presents her with 20 nobles, she opens the chest to put them in it: out leaps the tailor, and

He hit Dane Hew upon the head.
Thus was he first slain indeed.

When it is dark, the tailor takes the monk's body and places it near the abbey-wall. The abbot sends his man to look for Dan Hew; he discovers

---

[8] From Kirkman's 'Erastus' was evidently taken the version of the Three Knights and the Lady which is found in an edition of the 'Seven Wise Masters' printed at Glasgow in 1772, since it has this addition of the Little Lawyer in almost the identical words.

[9] Dan (Master) Hugh. Dominus: monkish Latin, Domnus; abbreviated in Fr., Dom; Sp., Don; English, Dan.

and addresses him; then goes back and tells his master that Dan Hew will not answer him. So the abbot goes himself, and finding he will not speak, gives him a rap on the sconce, when down he tumbles. Thus was Dan Hew a second time slain. The abbot gives his man forty shillings to get rid of the body. He takes it to the tailor's house. The tailor tells his wife that he dreamt Dan Hew had come back again. She laughs at him, saying dead men don't. He gets up, and, armed with a pole-axe, goes and opens the door, where he sees Dan Hew, sure enough. He cleaves the monk through the head; and thus was Dan Hew a third time slain. The wife advises him to put the monk in a sack and throw it in the mill-dam. Near the mill he perceives two thieves with a sack; they take him for the miller, and throwing down the sack, run away. The tailor opens the sack, and substitutes Dan Hew for the bacon he found it contained. After a time the thieves return to seek their bacon, and finding a dead man instead of it, they hang the body in the place from which they had taken the bacon.

> The Miller's wife rose on the morning erly,
> And lightly made herself redy,
> To fetch some Bacon at the last,
> But when she looked vp she was agast,
> That she saw the Munk hang there;
> She cryed out, and put them all in fere;
> And said, Heer is a chaunce for the nones,
> For heer hangeth the false Munk, by cocks bones.

"It must have been the devil," she thinks, "that has thus requited him. But our bacon is stolen; this is a scurvy trick;—I wonder what we shall eat this winter?" Quoth the miller, "Don't fret yourself about that, but advise me as to how we shall get quit of the monk." She details a plan.

> When the Miller this vnderstood,
> He thought his wiues counsail was good,
> And held him wel therwith content,
> And ran for the horse verament.
> And when he the horse had fet at the last,
> Dane Hew vpon his back he cast;
> And bound him to the horse ful sure,
> That he might the better indure,
> To ride as fast as they might ren;

Now shall ye knowe how the Miller did then.
He tooke the horse by the brydle anon,
And Dane Hew sitting theron;
And brought him that of the mare he had a sight,
Then the horse ran ful right.
The Abbot looked a little him beside,
And saw that Dane Hew towarde him gan ride;
And was almoste out of his mind for feare,
When he saw Dane Hew come so neere,
He cryed, Help, for the looue of the trinitie,
For I see wel that Dane Hew auenged wil be.
Alas I am but a dead man!
And with that from his mare he ran;
The Abbots men run on Dane Hew quickly,
And gave him many strokes lightly,
With clubs and staues many one,
They cast him to the earth anone;
So they killed him once again.
Thus was he once hanged and foure times slaine;
And buried at the last as it was best,
I pray God send vs al good rest.
                              Amen.

Such is the "merry jest of Dan Hew," which must, I think, have been directly derived from Jean le Chapelain's *fabliau* of 'Le Sacristan de Cluni,' which is also the original of the first novel of Massuccio de Salerno (*circa* 1470), as Dunlop has pointed out. The early Italian novelists, it is well known, drew largely on the compositions of the trouvères for their materials; but how came this *fabliau* to Norway? For in that country it is popularly known; the story of "Our Parish Clerk" in Sir G. Dasent's 'Tales from the Fjeld' having been evidently adapted from the Sacristan of Cluni.

NOTE

WOMEN BETRAYING THEIR HUSBANDS (p. 458)

Churchmen of mediæval times had seldom a good word to say about women. In their writings, at least, they appear to have been arrant misogynists; albeit, if we may credit contemporary lay authors, they were the very reverse, constantly intriguing with honest men's wives under cover of their religious profession. No follower of Muhammed could speak with more contempt of women than the monks in their sermons; and they commonly illustrated their unjust remarks with some story representing women as naturally vindictive and cruel. The lady denouncing her husband at the end of the tale of the Three Knights (by which, however, she was herself also a sufferer) has many parallels in mediæval tales. Thus in one text of the 'Gesta Romanorum' it is related that a noble having offended his king, he is to be pardoned on condition that he bring to court his best friend, his best comfort, and his worst enemy. At this time a pilgrim comes to his castle to claim his hospitality, and after he has retired to his chamber the noble says to his wife that pilgrims often carry much gold, and proposes to rob and murder their guest, of which she approves. But the knight, rising early in the morning, dismisses the pilgrim, then kills a calf, and cutting it into pieces, he puts them in a sack, which he gives his wife, telling her that it contains only the head, legs, and arms of the pilgrim—the rest he had buried in the stable. On the appointed day he appears before the king, accompanied by his dog, his little son, and his wife. The dog, he tells the king, is his most faithful friend; his little son is his greatest solace, for he amuses him with his mimicry; and his wife is his worst enemy. Hearing this, the lady exclaims, "Dost thou forget that thou didst slay a pilgrim in thy house, and that I know where I placed the sack containing parts of the murdered man, and that the rest lies in the stable?" But when messengers are despatched to search the places she indicated, and return with the bones and flesh of the calf, the king bestows rich gifts on the knight, and ever afterwards held him in great esteem.[10]

An earlier version of this story is found in 'Dolopathos,' from which it was taken into the 'Cento Novelle Antiche': A king, during a protracted siege, orders all the old men and women to be killed, as they consumed food, and were useless for the defence of the city. One wise old man was concealed in a cave by his son, whose wife was aware of the fact, but swore to keep it secret. The enemies of the young man suspected that his father was still alive, but dared not openly to say so. Thinking to entrap him, they induced the king to appoint a time for feasts and games, and to require every one to bring forward (1) his best friend; (2) his most faithful servant; (3) his best mimic; (4) his worst enemy. The youth presents his dog, his ass, his little son, and his wife. The woman, in a rage, cried

[10]Hans Sachs has made this story into a *Spiel;* the woman says:
"Thou murderer and villain,
Broken on the wheel thou'rt bound to be:
Art thou going to murder me too,
As thou murderedst the man yesterday?"

out, "Oh, most ungrateful of men, have I not shown kindness to your father, whom you saved, and have for years kept concealed in a cave?" The youth then asked the king whether he was not right in calling his wife his worst enemy, since for a single word she had both betrayed his concealed father, and brought himself under sentence of death? The king, admiring his wisdom and filial piety, told him that the lives of himself and his father were safe.

Akin to these stories is an anecdote of Hajáj, a great captain, and harsh Arabian governor, in the 7th century, which is told in a Persian work entitled 'Akhlák-i Jelalí' (15th century), in illustration of the truly Muslim maxim that "a man should not consult his wife on matters of paramount importance: let him not make her acquainted with his secrets, or their weakness of judgment will infallibly set them wrong":

We are told in history that Hajáj had a chamberlain with whom, having been long acquainted, he was on very familiar terms. In the course of conversation, he happened one day to remark that no secrets should be communicated and no confidence given to a woman. The chamberlain observed that he had a very prudent and affectionate wife, in whom he placed the utmost confidence, because, by repeated experiment, he had assured himself of her conduct, and now considered her the treasurer of all his fortunes. "The thing is repugnant to reason," said Hajáj, "and I will show you that it is." On this he bade them bring him a thousand dinars in a bag, which he sealed up with his own signet, and delivered to the chamberlain, telling him the money was his, but he was to keep it under seal, take it home, and tell his wife he had stolen it for her from the royal treasury. Soon afterwards Hajáj made him a farther present of a handsome maiden, whom he likewise brought home with him. "Pray oblige me," said his wife, "by selling this handsome maiden." The chamberlain asked how it was possible for him to sell what the king had given. At this the wife grew angry, and coming in the middle of the night to the door of the palace where Hajáj resided, desired it might be told him that the wife of the chamberlain such-a-one requested an audience. On obtaining access to Hajáj, and after going through the preliminary compliments and protestations, she represented that, long as her husband had been attached to the royal household, he had yet been perfidious enough to peculate upon the privy purse, an offence which her own sense of gratitude would not allow her to conceal. With this she produced the bag of money, saying it was the same her husband had stolen, and there was the prince's seal to prove it. The chamberlain was summoned, and soon made his appearance. "This prudent, affectionate wife of yours," said Hajáj, "has brought me your hidden deposit; and were I not privy to the fact, your head would fly from your shoulders, for the boys to play with and the horses to trample under foot."

⤳ THE ADVANTAGES OF
SPEAKING TO A KING ⤳

IDARESAY our worthy ancestors had many a laugh over this oft-told tale in the 'Jests of Scogin,' and greatly admired the cleverness of the imaginary jester:

"On a certain time Scogin went to the King's Grace, and did desire that he might come to him divers times and sound [query—'round,' that is, 'whisper,'] in his ears *Ave Maria gratia plena Dominus tecum.* The king was content he should do so, except he were in great business. Nay, said Scogin, I will mark my time. I pray your Grace that I may do thus this twelvemonth. I am pleased, said the king. Many men were suitors to Scogin to be good to them, and did give him many gifts and rewards of gold and silver, and other gifts, so that within the year Scogin was a great, rich man. So when the year was out, Scogin desired the king to break his fast with him. The king said, I will come. Scogin had prepared a table for the king to break his fast, and made a goodly cupboard of plate of gold and silver, and he cast over all his beds and tables and corners of his chamber full of gold and silver. When the king did come thither and saw so much plate and gold and silver, he asked of Scogin where he had it, and how he did get all his treasure. Scogin said, By saying *Ave Maria* in your ear; and seeing I have got so much by it, what do they get that be about your Grace daily, and be of your counsel, when that I with six words have gotten so much? He must needs swim that is held up by the chin."

A similar story occurs in the Italian novels of Morlini (the 4th), in which a merchant, who is deeply in debt, gives a considerable sum of money to the king for the privilege of riding by his side through the city; and his creditors, believing him to be on the high road to fortune, henceforth cease from importuning him.—It is not unlikely, however, that the tale was taken into Scogin from one of the mediæval Latin collections.

The following variant is from an old French collection of anecdotes: A gentleman who had been long attached to Cardinal Mazarin, reminded him of his many promises and his dilatory performance.

Mazarin, who had a great regard for him, and was unwilling to lose his friendship, took his hand, and explained the many demands made upon a person in his situation as minister, which it would be politic to satisfy previous to other requests, as they were founded on services done to the state. The cardinal's adherent, not very confident in his veracity, replied, "My lord, all the favour I now ask of you is, that whenever we meet in public, you shall do me the honour to tap me on the shoulder in a familiar manner." The cardinal smiled, and in the course of two or three years his friend became a wealthy man on the credit of these attentions to him.

The story is of Eastern extraction. In a Kashmírí version, a poor wood-cutter is observed by the king from a window of his palace, half-clad and shivering from cold, for it was winter-time, and pointing him out to his queen, he remarks that it was a pity to see such a wretched creature. The queen replies that the poor man had not got a wise minister; and her royal consort, supposing that this remark was a reflection upon himself and his prime minister, in a rage orders her to quit the palace and become a ser-vant to the woodcutter. She at once obeys his command, and, in the hum-blest of humble capacities of servant to the woodcutter, manages his household affairs admirably, is friendly with his wife, and induces him to practise economy even with his scanty income. When the woodcutter had saved some money, and was able to wear respectable clothes, the queen advised him one day to go with bread and water into the jungle when the king was likely to be done with the chase; offer them to him, and he would be so grateful for the timely and unexpected refreshment that he would ask what the woodcutter wished in requital. He should answer that he simply wished the king to grant him a few private interviews at the palace. The man follows this advice, and the king grants his request. "Frequently did this man visit the king privately, and the king appeared to welcome his visits. When the nobles and courtiers saw this they were very jealous, and afraid that this man would impeach them. So they began to give him handsome presents by way of bribes to check his tongue concerning them-selves. The woodcutter had now become the king's intimate companion, and having amassed much wealth, the queen thought it would not be amiss if he made a great feast and invited the king and many of the nobles to grace it by their presence. The king readily accepted the invitation. The dinner was served on a most magnificent scale, and everybody seemed pleased. Before the company retired, the queen went up, unperceived, to the king, and told him that his host was the poor woodcutter of former years, and that she was his 'wise minister.' Admiring her astuteness, the king was there and then reconciled to his queen."[1]

The original form of the story is perhaps found in the 'Kathá Sarit Ságara,' Book x. chapter 66, where it is thus related, according to Professor C. H. Tawney's translation (vol. ii. pp. 121, 122):

There was a certain king in a city in the Dekkan. In that city there was a rogue who lived by imposing upon others. And one day he said to himself, being too ambitious to be satisfied with small gains, "Of what use to me is this petty rascality, which only provides me with subsistence? Why should I not do a stroke of business which would bring me great prosperity?" Having thus reflected, he dressed himself splendidly as a merchant, and went to the palace-gate and accosted the warder. And he introduced him into the king's presence, and he offered a complimentary gift, and said to the king, "I wish to speak with your majesty in private." The king was imposed upon by his dress, and much influenced in his favour by the present, so he granted him a private interview, and then the rogue said to him, "Will your majesty have the goodness every day, in the hall of assembly, to take me aside for a moment in the sight of all, and speak to me in private? And as an acknowledgment of that favour I will give your majesty every day five hundred dínars, and I do not ask for any gift in return." When the king heard that, he thought to himself, "What harm can it do? What does he take away from me? On the contrary, he is to give me dínars every day. What disgrace is there in carrying on a conversation with a great merchant?" So the king consented, and did as he requested, and the rogue gave the king the dínars as he had promised, and the people thought he had obtained the position of a cabinet minister. Now one day the rogue, while he was talking with the king, kept looking again and again at the face of one official with a significant expression. And after he came out, that official asked him why he had looked in his face so, and the rogue was ready with this fiction: "The king is angry, because he supposes that you have been plundering his realm. This is why I looked at your face, but I will appease his anger." When the sham minister said this, the official went home in a state of anxiety, and sent him a thousand gold pieces. And the next day the rogue talked in

[1] Knowles' 'Dictionary of Kashmírí Proverbs and Sayings,' pp. 210–212.

the same way with the king, and then came out and said to the official, who came towards him, "I appeased the king's anger against you with judicious words. Cheer up; I will now stand by you in all emergencies." Thus he artfully made him his friend, and then dismissed him; and then the official waited upon him with all kinds of presents. Thus gradually this dexterous rogue, by means of continual conversation with the king, and by many artifices, extracted from the officials, the subordinate monarchs, rajputs, and the servants so much wealth, that he amassed together fifty millions of gold pieces. Then the scoundrelly-sham minister said in secret to the king, "Though I have given you every day five hundred *dinars,* nevertheless, by the favour of your highness, I have amassed fifty millions of gold pieces. So have the goodness to accept of this gold— what have I to do with it?" Then he told the king his whole stratagem. But it was with difficulty that the king could be induced to take half the money. Then he gave him the post of a cabinet minister, and the rogue, having obtained riches and position, kept complimenting the people with entertainments.

"Thus," adds the story-teller, "a wise man obtains great wealth without committing a very great crime, and when he has gained the advantage, he atones for his fault in the same way as a man who digs a well."

If we may judge from popular tales, Oriental potentates frequently select sharpers, thieves, and highway robbers for their vazírs and treasurers; in the present case, however, since the king's ministers were all corrupt, perhaps he acted wisely in thus "setting a thief to catch thieves." Yet this clever man's conduct, after all, was not quite such as to justify his being called a scoundrel by the story-teller. When he had amassed an immense sum, by practising on the fears of the ministers, he certainly showed himself an honest fellow by explaining all to the king, and offering to restore the whole of the money to him. Few Eastern monarchs would refuse such an offer; the general practice of an Asiatic potentate being to allow his ministers and provincial governors to amass wealth for a few years, and then, on some frivolous pretext—or without any at all— cut off their heads and transfer their riches into his own treasury. As it was, this king received from the rogue 500 dínars every day, and in the end, one half of his gains!

﹌ THE LOST PURSE ﹌

A VERY common story in our old English jest-books is that of a merchant who, having lost his purse, caused it to be proclaimed, stating the sum it contained, and offering a reward, which he afterwards refused when the purse was found, alleging that it contained more money than was advertised, in consequence of which he loses it all. The following version (spelling modernised) is from 'Tales and Quick Answers': A certain merchant, between Ware and London, lost his budget and £100 therein, wherefore he caused to proclaim, in divers market towns, that whosoever found the said budget, and would bring it again, should have £20 for his labour. An honest husbandman that chanced to find the said budget, brought it to the bailie of Ware, according to the cry, and required his £20 for his labour, as it was proclaimed. The covetous merchant, when he understood this, and that he must needs pay £20 for the finding, he said that there was £120 in his budget, and so would have had his own money and £20 over. So long they strove, that the matter was brought before Master Vavasour, the good judge. When he understood by the bailie that the cry was made for a budget with £100 therein, he demanded where it was. "Here," quoth the bailie, and took it unto him. "Is it just £100?" said the judge. "Yea, truly," quoth the bailie. "Hold," said the judge, to him that found the budget; "take thou this money into thine own use, and if thou hap to find a budget with £120 therein, bring it to this honest merchantman." "It is mine; I lost no more but £100," quoth the merchant. "Ye speak now too late," quoth the judge. By this ye may understand that they that go about to deceive others be oftentimes deceived themselves; and some time one falleth in the ditch that he himself made.[1]

There are innumerable variants of the story in French and Italian collections of tales and facetiæ. Cinthio, one of the Italian imitators of Boccaccio, who flourished in the sixteenth century, relates it in his 'Hecatommithi' (ninth of the First Decade): A merchant loses a bag containing 400 crowns. He advertises it, with a reward to any one who finds it; but when brought to him by a poor woman, he attempts to defraud her

---

[1] In 'Pasquil's Jests and Mother Bunch's Merriments,' 1604, the tale is reproduced, with the variation that the greedy merchant lost his purse between Waltham and London.

482

of the promised recompense, by alleging that besides the 400 crowns it contained some ducats, which he had neglected to specify in the advertisement, and which she must have purloined. The Marquis of Mantua, to whom the matter is referred, decides that, as it wanted the ducats, it could not be the merchant's, advises him again to proclaim his loss, and bestows on the poor woman the whole of the contents of the purse.

The tale is also domiciled in Turkey. Prince Cantemir, in his 'History of the Othman Empire,' gravely relates it as a case that was decided by the celebrated Chorluli Ali Pasha.[2] A merchant of Constantinople went to a bath before morning prayers, and on his way to the mosque lost in the street his purse out of his bosom. On coming out of the mosque he for the first time became aware of his loss, and at once got the crier to proclaim a reward of one half its contents, or one hundred pieces of gold, as a reward to the finder on his restoring the purse with the two hundred gold pieces intact. It happened that a marine found the purse, and took it to the crier, who sent for the merchant, who, finding the money complete, tried to back out of his bargain, and pretending there were also in the purse emerald ear-rings, demanded these of the marine. The man stoutly denied this; but the merchant brought him before the kází, and accused him of theft. The magistrate, probably having been bribed, acquitted the man of the charge of theft, but dismissed him without a reward, because of his carelessness in losing such valuable articles. The poor marine presented his case in a petition to Chorluli Ali Pasha, who summoned the merchant, with the money in dispute and the crier, to appear before him. After hearing the case, the pasha first asked the crier what it was the merchant had requested him to make inquiry after; and he replied that it was for two hundred pieces of gold. The merchant thereupon said that he had caused no mention to be made of the emerald ear-rings, fearing that if the purse had fallen into the hands of some person who knew not the value of the gems, when he should discover what a great treasure he had found, it might be a temptation to him to keep it all. The marine, on the other hand, making oath that he had found nothing in the purse but the money, Ali Pasha passed the following judgment: "Since the merchant, besides two hundred pieces of gold, has lost also emerald ear-rings in the same purse, and since the marine

---

[2]Chorluli Ali Pasha, *temp.* Ahmed III., the 24th Sultan, early in the last century.

has deposed upon oath that he found nothing but the money, it is plain that the purse and money which the marine found were not lost by the merchant, but by some one else. Let the merchant, therefore, have his things cried till some God-fearing person, having found them, restore them to him; and let the marine keep the money he found for the space of forty days, and if no one comes and claims it within that period, then let it be his own."

When the reader learns that the story is found in the 'Disciplina Clericalis' of Peter Alfonsus, he will readily perceive that neither "Mayster Vavasour, the good judge," nor the Marquis of Mantua, nor the Chorluli Ali Pasha ever had the "case" to decide, any more than Attorney-General Noy defended the Alewife in the case of the Three Graziers. It is the sixteenth tale of Alfonsus: A man loses a purse of gold, and a golden serpent with eyes of hyacinth, and endeavours to defraud a poor man who had found it of the promised reward, by asserting that the purse contained *two* serpents. The dispute being referred to a philosopher, the purse is adjudged to the finder. As the tales of Peter Alfonsus were avowedly derived from the Arabian fabulists, the Turkish version was doubtless adapted from the same source.

↝ THE UNGRATEFUL SON ↝

THE story of a man who neglected and even ill-used his old father, and was brought to a sense of his iniquity by his own little child, has long been "familiar in our mouths as household words." It was from Bernier's *fabliau* of 'La Housse Partie,' according to Dunlop, that the Italian novelist Ortensis Lando, who flourished in the sixteenth century, derived his 13th tale:

A Florentine merchant, who had been extremely rich, becoming sickly and feeble, and being no longer of service to his family, in spite of his intercessions, was sent by his son to the hospital. The cruelty of this conduct made a great noise in the city, and the son, more from shame than affection, despatched one of his children, who was about six years of age, with a couple of shirts to his grandfather. On his return he was asked by his parent if he had executed the commission. "I have taken only one shirt," replied he. "Why so?" asked the father. "I have kept the other," said the child, "for the time when I shall send you to the hospital." This answer had the effect of despatching the unnatural son to beg his father's pardon, and to conduct him home from his wretched habitation.

Etienne de Bourbon, in No. 161 of his 'Liber de Donis,' cites a version of the story from a sermon by Nicolas de Flavini, Archbishop of Byzantium (who occupied the See of Besançon from 1227 till 1235):

A certain man, who had married his son well and made over to him all his great wealth, when he became old and decrepit, at the instigation of his wife, was put into a wretched place, and with difficulty obtained from his son two ells of borel[1] in order that he might cover himself in the winter. The son's child, a little boy, observing this, wept bitterly, and said he would not cease unless his father would give him also two ells of borel as he had given his grandfather. After it had been given to him, the boy carefully folded it together and laid it aside, saying that he himself would do the same to his father when he became old as he had done to his grandfather, giving him two ells of borel to cover him.

[1] In the original, "de burello": *borel* (Fr. *bureau*), coarse cloth of a brown colour—see Du Cange, *s.v.* Burellus. Chaucer employs the word *borell,* or *burel,* to denote an ignorant, rude, clownish person.

The following is quoted in Cobbett's 'Advice to Young Men': "In Heron's collection of 'God's Judgments on Wicked Acts,' it is related of an unnatural son, who fed his father upon oats and offal, lodged him in a filthy and crazy garret, and clothed him in sackcloth, while he and his wife and children lived in luxury, that sackcloth enough for two dresses for his father having been bought, his children took away the part not made up and hid it, and on being asked what they could do this for, they told him they meant to keep it for him when he should become old and walk with a stick."

With slight modifications, this touching little tale is popular throughout Europe. In the following Albanian version, from M. Dozon's French collection, it is considerably amplified, and, as I think, improved:

There was in a certain town a very honourable merchant, who had commercial relations with many friends in the same city. Being afraid that his partners would waste the capital which he had acquired, he withdrew from them, and took the wise step of leaving that town and setting up his business in another. He took his wife and son with him. After having chosen a suitable position, he commenced a small business, which prospered by degrees and gave him the means of living comfortably. When he had been twenty years in the new establishment, and was intending to retire from business, his wife died suddenly. They had lived together for thirty years, and neither of them had ever given the other the least cause of reproach. It is easy to conceive how sad a loss was her death to the merchant. However, seeing that his son was also afflicted, he tried to overcome his own grief in order to console him. "Thy mother is no more," he said; "the loss is irreparable. All we can do is to pray to God for her soul, for our tears will not restore her to life. Here I have no one but thee to love me, for my friends remain in the city where we formerly dwelt. If thou dost wish to be wise and to conduct thyself well, labour, and I will try to marry thee to some girl of our rank." And indeed the old man set about seeking a wife for his son.

In their neighbourhood lived three brothers, the eldest of whom had a daughter. Formerly rich, they were at that time living in a condition bordering on poverty; and the old man had often thought of their daughter. One day he made up his mind, put on his new clothes, and went to ask her in marriage for his son. He thought that, being poor, she must be honest. The first question of the three brothers was this: "What does your son possess?" He replied, "All my wealth, goods and money may amount to a thousand pounds; I give now the half of it to the young couple, and the rest will be theirs after my death." They came to an agreement, and the marriage took place. After some time a child was born to the couple, who showed himself intelligent, and endowed with many good qualities.

But, unhappily for the old man, his daughter-in-law did not love him. At first she had still some regard for him, but soon she lost all respect: she spared no outrage, and even went so far as to refuse him bread.[2] The unfortunate one concealed his grief, and dared not speak of it to any one. At last he once heard his daughter-in-law say to her husband, "I can no longer endure to live under the same roof with that man"; and one day his own son desired him to look out for another abode, saying that he should support himself at his own charge. At these words the poor man changed colour, and his whole body trembled. "What, my son," said he, "is it you who speak thus to me? From whom have you received all that you possess? Nevertheless, do not drive me away—no, no, leave me a shelter till I die; reflect, my dear son, on what I have suffered in order to bring you up!" This address of the old man deeply moved his son, but his daughter-in-law would no longer bear the sight of him. Then he said to the former: "Where do you wish me to go? How can I approach strangers when my son drives me away?" And as he spoke the tears ran down his face. He ended, however, by taking his staff, and rising, prayed to God to pardon the ungrateful son; and then he said: "Winter approaches, if God does not pity me, but leaves me in life till that time, I shall have nothing to cover me. I conjure you, give me some old garments—something you no longer wear." The daughter-in-law, who heard him make this request, replied that she had no clothes to spare. Then he prayed that they would give him one of the horse-rugs, and the son made a sign to his little boy to bring one of them. The child, who had lost none of the conversation, went to the stable, and having taken the best of the rugs, he cut it in two, and brought one half to his grandfather. "Everybody, it seems, desires my

[2]Something seems omitted just before this—probably that the old man had been induced to surrender to his son the remainder of his property, else how should he be without bread?

death," he cried, "since even this young child wishes it!" The son growled at the boy for not executing the order as he had given it. "I was wrong, father," said the child; " but I had something in my mind: I wish to keep the other half for you, when you will become old in your turn." This reproach made him see himself; he understood all the extent of his crime, sent away his wife, and falling at the old man's feet, he begged him still to stay with him.

The story would appear to be of Indian extraction; at all events, it is found in a form closely resembling the version sometimes given in English schoolbooks, in the Canarese collection of tales entitled 'Kathá Manjarí,' as follows:

A rich man used to feed his father with *congí* from an old broken dish. His son saw this, and hid the dish. Afterwards the rich man, having asked his father where it was, beat him [because he could not tell]. The boy exclaimed, "Don't beat grandfather! I hid the dish, because when I become a man I may be unable to buy another one for you." When the rich man heard this he was ashamed, and afterwards treated his father kindly.

Quite a different story is No. 145 of the Brothers Grimm's collection, "Der Undankbare Sohn:"

Once upon a time a man and his wife were sitting before their house-door, with a roast fowl on a table between them, which they were going to eat together. Presently the man saw his old father coming, and he quickly snatched up the fowl and concealed it, because he grudged sharing it, even with his own parent. The old man came, had a draught of water, and then went away again. As soon as he was gone, his son went to fetch the roast fowl again; but when he touched it he saw that it was changed into a toad, which sprang upon his face and squatted there, and would not go away. When any one tried to take it off, it spat out poison and seemed about to spring in his face, so that at length nobody dared to meddle with it. Now this toad the ungrateful son was compelled to feed, lest it should feed on his flesh; and with this companion he moved wearily about from place to place, and had no rest anywhere in this world.

Professor T. F. Crane, in his paper on 'Mediæval Sermons and Story-Books,' states that this story is found in Etienne de Bourbon, No. 163; Bromyard's 'Summa Prædicantium,' F 22; Pelbartus, 'Serm. de Temp.

Hiem.,' B 22; and in other works of the same class referred to by Oesterley in his notes to Pauli, 'Schimpf und Ernst,' and by Doúhet, 'Dictionnaire des Légendes,' col. 305, n. 158. He adds that there are probably other versions which have not yet been collected.

↝ CHAUCER'S "PARDONER'S TALE" ↝

READERS of the "well of English undefiled," as Spenser styles the writings of Chaucer, must be familiar with the striking story which he represents the Pardoner as relating to his fellow-pilgrims on the way to the shrine of Thomas à Becket:

A pestilence was raging in a certain city, and people were dying in great numbers every day. Three youths, drinking and dicing in a tavern, inquired of the host the reason why the church bell was tolling so constantly, to which he replied that a "privie thefe" had come amongst them, and was busy taking away the folk's lives. Hearing this, they resolved to seek out this "false traitour," and slay him without fail. They meet an "old chorle," and after mocking his grey beard and bent form,[1] demand to know of him where they should find Death. The old man replies:

> "Now sirs, if that it be to you so lefe
> To findin Deth, tourne up this crokid waie,
> For in that grove I left him, by my faie,
> Undir a tre, and there he woll abide,
> Ne for your boste he n'ill him nothing hide:
> Se ye that oke, right there ye shal him finde;

---

[1] The "old chorle" says:

> "Thus walke I like a restlesse caitiffe,
> And on the ground, which is my mother's gate,
> I knocke with my staffe both erliche and late,
> And sayin thus, Leve mother, let me in!"

In the Bedouin romance of Antar, the hero and his half-brother Shibúb, traversing the wilds and deserts by secret paths, one day came upon a single tent pitched beside a spring, and near it was an aged shaykh, bent with years:

> An old man was walking along the ground,
> And his beard almost swept his knees.
> So I said to him, "Why art thou thus stooping?"
> He said, as he waved his hands towards me,
> "My youth is lost somewhere in the dust,
> And I am stooping in search of it."

In a Talmudic variant of the Seven Stages of Man's Life, the final stage is thus described: "He now begins to hang down his head towards the ground, as if surveying the place where all his schemes must terminate, and where ambition and vanity are finally humbled to the dust."

And God you save that bought ayen mankinde,
And you amende," thus sayid this olde man.

The three "riottours" set off as directed, and find a great treasure at the
foot of a tree, and, resolving to wait on the spot till darkness should
enable them to carry it off unseen by any, they draw lots, and the
youngest, on whom the lot falls, is sent to the town for some wine. During his absence the two others plot his death when he returns, in order
that they should have his share of the treasure. The youth, on his way to
the town, determines to poison his companions, and so have all the treasure for himself. He goes first to an apothecary and buys strong poison,
then to a wine-shop where he purchases three bottles of wine, and having put the poison into two of them, returns to his comrades:

> What needith it thereof to sermon more?
> For right as thei had cast his deth before,
> Right so thei han him slain, and that anone.
> And whan that this was doen, than spake that one,
> Now let us sit and drinke and make us mery,
> And aftirward thei wolne his body bury.
> And aftir that it happid one, per caus,
> To take the bottle there the poison was,
> And dronke, and yave his fellowe drinke also,
> Through whiche anon thei stervin[2] bothè two.

This fine story was very popular in Europe during mediæval times, and
while it has not been ascertained whence Chaucer derived it, I think we
can now guess pretty approximately. In the oldest Italian collection of
short stories, 'Cento Novelle Antiche,' which is generally believed to have
been made in the 13th century, and was first printed, according to Panizzi,
at Bologna in 1525, the 73rd tale is as follows:

Christ was one day walking with his disciples through a desert place,
when they who were following him, saw shining there on the wayside a
quantity of gold piastres; whereupon they, calling to Christ and wondering why he did not stop, said to him, "Lord, let us take this gold, for it
will make amends to us for many labours." And Christ turned and

---

[2] *Stervin,* died; were killed; perished.

rebuked them, and said, "Ye desire such things as rob our kingdom of the greater part of souls. And that is true; on our return, ye shall perceive an example thereof," and passed on. A little after, two intimate companions found it, whereat they were joyous, and agreed [one should go] to the nearest village to get a mule, and the other remain on guard. But hearken how evil deeds followed on evil thoughts, for the enemy gave them. The one returned with the mule, and said to his companion, "I have eaten at the village, and thou must also be hungry; eat these two fair loaves, and then we will load [our mule]." Replied the other, "I have no great mind to eat now, so we will do our loading first." Then they set to loading. And when they had nearly done, he who had gone for the mule bent down to make the burden fast, and the other fell upon him treacherously from behind with a sharp knife and killed him. Then he took one of the loaves and gave it to the mule. The other he ate himself. The bread was poisoned; he fell down dead, and the mule also, before they could move from the spot; and the gold remained free as at first. Later in the same day our Lord passed with his disciples, and pointed out to them the example of which he had spoken.

Here we have but two men, and the other details vary considerably; but in a later edition of the 'Novelle Antiche,' printed at Florence in 1572, a different version is substituted—it is No. LXII. of this edition, which is entitled 'Libro di Novelle, et di bel Parlar Gentile,' Book of Stories, and of fine Courtly Speaking—and one which much more closely resembles the Pardoner's Tale:

A hermit, walking one day in a desert place, found a very large cave, which was much hidden from view, and retiring thither for sleep (for he was very weary), saw, as soon as he entered the cave, something shining in a certain place very brightly; for much gold was there. And no sooner had he perceived it than he incontinently departed and began to run through the desert as fast as he could go. Thus running, the hermit met with three great ruffians, who haunted that wild place (*foresta*), to rob whoever passed thereby. Nor were they ever aware this gold was there. Now seeing, as they lay hid, this man flee without a soul behind to chase him, they were somewhat afraid, but yet stopped him, to know what he was fleeing for, because at this they marvelled much. And he replied and said, "My brothers, I am fleeing from Death, who comes after me in chase." They, seeing neither man nor beast that chased him, said, "Show us what is chasing thee, and lead us unto where it is." Then said the hermit to them, "Come with me and I will show it to you"; beseeching them all the time not to go to it, for he himself was fleeing for that reason. And they, desiring to find it, to see what manner of thing it was, demanded of him nothing else. The hermit seeing that he could do no more, and fearing them, led them to the cave, whence he had departed, and said to them, "Here is Death, which was chasing me"; and showed them the gold that was there; and they began to mightily congratulate themselves, and to have great fun together. Then they dismissed that good man, and he went away about his own affairs; and they began to say one to the other, how simple a person that was.

These three ruffians remained all three together, to guard this wealth, and began to consider what they must do. Replied one and said, "Meseems that God has given us this so high fortune, that we should not depart from here until we carry away all this property." And another said, "Let us not do so. Let one of us take somewhat thereof and go to the city and sell it, and buy bread and wine, and whatsoever we need; and in that let him do his best, so that we be furnished." To this they all agree. The Devil, who is crafty and bad enough to contrive to do whatever evil he can, put in this one's heart to go to the city for supplies. "When I am in the city," said he to himself, "I will eat and drink what I want, and then provide me with certain things whereof I have need at the present time; and then I will poison what I bring to my comrades, so that when the pair of them are dead I shall then be lord of all this property; and, as it seems to me, it is so much that I shall be the richest man of all this country for possessions." And as it came into his thought, so he did. He took for himself as much victual as he needed, and then poisoned the rest, and so he brought it to those his companions. But while he went to the city, as we have said, if he thought and contrived ill, to slay his companions, that every thing should remain for him, they, on their part, thought no better of him than he of them, and said one to the other, "As soon as this our comrade shall return with the bread and the wine and the other things we need, we will kill him, and then eat as much as we desire, and then all this great wealth shall be between us two. And the less in number we are the more shall each of us have." Now came he who had gone to the city to buy the things they needed. The moment his companions saw he had returned, they were upon him with lances and knives and killed him. When they had made a dead man of him, they ate of what he had brought; and so soon as they were satisfied both fell dead. And so died all three; for the one slew the other, as ye have heard, and had not the wealth. And thus may the Lord God requite traitors; for they went seeking death, and in this manner they found it, and in a way which they deserved. And the sage wisely fled it, and the gold abode free as at first.[3]

Tyrwhitt was the first to point out the likeness between this version and that of Chaucer; and Wright, in his edition of the 'Canterbury Tales,' says that the Pardoner's Tale appears to have been taken from a *fabliau*, now lost, but of which the outline is preserved in No. 72 of the 'Novelle Antiche.' That the story was the subject of a *fabliau* is likely enough, and certainly a number of the tales in the 'Novelle Antiche' are also among the *fabliaux* of the trouvères. From the 'Novelle Antiche' perhaps the tale of the Hermit who found a Treasure was taken into one of the old Italian miracle-plays, that of St Antonio,[4] published in D'Ancona's 'Rappresentazione Sacre,' vol. ii. p. 33, of which the following is the outline of the part referring to our story:

The Spirit of Avarice places a silver dish in the way of St Antonio, to corrupt his virtue, "for such a springe will snare the wisest bird." Antonio walks in the desert and finds the basin. He at once perceives the trick and its origin. Avarice, finding his device unavailing, then sets forth a great pile of gold (*monte d'oro*), resolved, should this attempt fail, to give up the game. Antonio finds the gold, and roundly rails at the enemy, whose cunning has in this instance again been foiled.

Two robbers, Tagliagambe and Scaramuccia,[5] meet; the latter asks the news. Trade is so bad that Tagliagambe has not a groat in his purse. Scaramuccia has been robbed of a thousand ducats at Reggio fair. He proposes that they join hands and take to the road. At this juncture Carapello, an old acquaintance, comes on the scene; they welcome him, and it is agreed that the three shall share equally all that they "convey."

---

[3]Hans Sachs made this story the subject of a 'Meisterlied' and also of a 'Spiel,' the first of which was written in 1547, the second in 1555; the only variations being that the hermit discovers the treasure in the hollow trunk of a tree, and that the robbers, when he tells them he has seen Death in the trunk of a tree, thinking he is mocking them, slay him on the spot.— In another German version, three robbers murder a merchant for his money; and in yet another, three men of Balkh find a treasure, and so on. And Professor Adalbert Kuhn, in his 'Westfälische Sagen, Gebräuche, und Märchen,' cites the same story, of three Jews who commit a robbery.

[4]"Antonio (San), of Padua, a relative of Godfrey of Bouillon, was born in Lisbon in 1195; preached with such fervour that even the fishes rose to the surface of the sea to listen to him; and died in Padua, 1231. The splendid basilica in which his ashes rest was not completed until two centuries later. His chapel, with its *alti relievi* by Lombardi, Sansovino, and others, still attracts the student of art."—From Bayard Taylor's Notes to his 'Faust,' ed. 1871, vol. i. p. 319.

[5]Legslasher and Skirmisher.

The Devil (Satanasso) is introduced, ordering his fiends to soundly cudgel Antonio, whom pain, if not pleasure, may move. They do his bidding. Antonio is comforted by the appearance of Jesus, who promises him world-wide fame and an eternal reward. Healed of his wounds, Antonio walks into the desert, and meets with the robbers, whom he counsels to turn back from the death in their way. They take him for a madman, and go on. Finding the pile of gold, they laugh at the hermit's simplicity, who had called it Death.

The three robbers agree to draw lots for one of them to go to Damascus for food and flasks of wine, and a pair of balances to weigh the gold. The lot falls on Scaramuccia, who sets off, but on the way reflects on his folly in leaving the others in possession of the gold, and resolves to have it all for himself. He changes his lump for two and twenty ducats, purchases ratsbane of an apothecary, and plenty of victuals and wine; and having poisoned the viands, he returns. Meanwhile the two others have concerted his death, and as soon as he appears they pick a quarrel with him and despatch him. They then sit down to their meal and dine heartily, particularly commending their late comrade's taste in wine; and while they are considering how they shall extract the most enjoyment from their treasure, the poison begins to work, and speedily makes an end of them.

Avarice, delighted at his success, returns to Satan, full of confidence, and makes his report. He is promised a crown as his reward for having brought three souls below instead of one. An angel closes the show, and dismisses the spectators with a solemn injunction to take warning by the catastrophe, and to direct their eyes upward, seeking God, who is the true riches.

An ancient Portuguese version is given by Theophilus Braga ('Contos tradicionæs do povo portuguez,' No. 143) from the 'Orto do Sposo' of Frei Hermenegildo de Tancos, 14th century: Four robbers open a grave in Rome, and find in it gold and silver, precious stones, and vessels and cups of gold. One of them goes to the town to procure food, for which he gives the largest and finest gold cup, and so on, as in Chaucer.

Four is also the number of the rascals in a version cited by M. Paulin Paris, in his 'Les Manuscrits français,' vol. iv. p. 83, from a treatise on the Holy Scripture, "blaming the vices and praising the virtues" therein, of the 15th century: They find a golden stone, and agree that when they have breakfasted they will share it. Two keep watch over the treasure while the other two go to buy bread, and so on. "Thus may we understand how things of earth are death to those who know not how to use them well: for a hundred men may damn themselves for an inheritance, and the inheritance remain in its place to this day. It is the golden stone which does not die."

In the novels of Morlini a singular version occurs—Nov. XLII. "De illis qui in Tiberi reperto thesauro, ad invicem conspirantes, venemo et ferro periere": A magician learns from the spirits that a great treasure lies hid in the Tiber. On its being found, some of his companions go to a neighbouring town to fetch food and liquor, and they resolve to buy poison to kill the others. Those who remain meanwhile conspire to kill them, which they do on their return, and then eating of the poisoned food themselves perish. "This story teaches that evil should not be thought of; for he who sows, reaps."

We now proceed towards the very ancient original of this oft-told tale. In a form which is already familiar to us, it is found in the Breslau-printed Arabic text of the 'Thousand and One Nights,' where it forms one of the twenty-eight tales related to King Shah Bakht by his Vazír Er-Rahwan.[6]

Three men once went out in quest of riches, and came upon a block of gold weighing a hundred pounds. When they saw it, they took it up on their shoulders and fared on with it till they drew near a certain city, when one of them said, "Let us sit in the mosque whilst one of us goes and buys us what we may eat." So they sat down in the mosque, and one of them arose and entered the city. When he came therein, his soul prompted him to play his fellows false, and get the gold for himself alone. So he bought food and poisoned it; but when he returned to his comrades they fell upon him and slew him, so they might enjoy the gold without him. Then they ate of the [poisoned] food and died, and the gold abode cast down over against them.

Presently Jesus, son of Mary (on whom be peace!), passed by, and seeing this, besought God the Most High for tidings of the case. So He told him what had betided them, whereat great was his wonderment, and he related to his disciples what he had seen.[7]

ﺵ

---

[6] See *ante*, p. 302.

[7] 'Tales from the Arabic,' &c. Now first done into English by John Payne. London (Privately Printed), 1884. Vol. i. p. 282.—Muslims, while denying the divinity of Christ, being essentially Unitarians, yet regard Him with great reverence, as the "Spirit" or "Breath" of God, as they are taught by the Kurán and by their traditions.

Very different from all the preceding versions, and possibly composed from memory, is the story as found in the Calcutta and Búlák printed texts of the 'Arabian Nights,' which Sir R. F. Burton has thus rendered (in vol. ii. p. 158, of his complete translation):

In a city called Sindah there was once a very wealthy merchant, who made ready his camel-loads and equipped himself with goods, and set out with his outfit for such a city. Now he was followed by two sharpers, who had made up into bales what merchandise they could get; and, giving out to the merchant that they also were merchants, wended with him by the way. So, halting at the first halting-place, they agreed to play him false and take all he had; but at the same time each inwardly plotted foul play to the other, saying in his mind, "If I can cheat my comrade, times will go well with me, and I shall have all these goods to myself." So after planning this perfidy, one of them took food, and putting therein poison, brought it to his fellow; the other did the same: and they both ate of the poisoned mess, and they both died. Now they had been sitting with the merchant; so when they left him, and were long absent from him, he sought for tidings of them, and found the twain lying dead, whereby he knew that they were sharpers who had plotted to play him foul, but their foul play had recoiled upon themselves. So the merchant was preserved, and took what they had.

Peculiarly interesting and suggestive is a version given by Muhammad Casim Siddi Lebbe, in his "Account of the Virgin Mary and Jesus, according to Arabian Writers," published in the first volume of 'The Orientalist':

Jesus was once journeying in company with a Jew, and the Lord proposed that they should put their stock of food together and make common property of it. Jesus had but one loaf and the Jew had two loaves. In the absence of Jesus (to perform his devotions), the Jew ate one of the loaves, and afterwards persistently denied that he had done so. After Jesus had performed several miracles, each time conjuring the Jew to declare who had ate the loaf, and the Jew persisting there were originally but two loaves, the narrative thus proceeds: They came to a lonely place, where Jesus made three heaps of earth, and by his word turned them into three massive blocks of gold. Then addressing the Jew, he said, "Of these three blocks, one is for me, one for you, and the other for the man who ate the loaf." The Jew immediately exclaimed, "It was I that ate the loaf, and therefore I claim the two blocks." Jesus gently rebuked him for obstinately adhering to a falsehood, and making over to him all three blocks, left him and went away. The Jew then endeavoured to take away the blocks of gold, but found them too heavy to be moved. While he was thus wasting his strength in trying to move the blocks, Jesus returned to the spot and said to the Jew, "Have nothing to do with these heaps of gold. They will cause the death of three men; leave them and follow me." The man obeyed, and leaving the gold where it lay, went away with Jesus.

Three travellers happened soon afterward to pass that way, and were delighted to find the gold. They agreed that each should take one. Finding it, however, a matter of impossibility to carry them, they resolved that one of them should go to the city for carts and food for them to eat, whilst the other two should watch the treasure. So one of the travellers set out for the city, leaving the other two to guard the gold. During his absence the thoughts of his companions were engrossed in devising some means whereby they should become the sole sharers of the treasure, to the exclusion of the one who had gone to the city. They finally came to the diabolical resolution of killing him on his return. The same murderous design had entered into the mind of him who had gone to the city in reference to his companions. He bought food and mixed poison with it, and then returned to the spot to offer it to them. No sooner had he arrived than, without a word of warning, his companions fell upon him and belaboured him to death. They then began to eat the food which was in its turn to destroy them; and so, as they were partaking of the poisoned repast, they fell down and expired. A little after, Jesus and the Jew were returning from their journey along that road, and seeing the three men lying dead amidst the gold, Jesus exclaimed, "This will be the end of the covetous who love gold!" He then raised the three men to life, upon which they confessed their guilt, repented themselves, and thenceforward became disciples of Jesus. Nothing, however, could make the Jew overcome his avarice. He persisted in his desire to become the possessor of the gold; but whilst he was struggling to carry away the blocks, the earth opened and swallowed him up, and the gold with him.

It is much to be regretted that Mr Siddi Lebbe did not give the names of the Arabian writers from whom he compiled his narrative, or afford some other clue to its date. But, thanks to the learned Dr F. Rückert, a similar Persian version, though differing in some important details, is known to European scholars, regarding the authorship and date of which there need be no doubt. From a Persian manuscript in the Library at Gotha, entitled 'Kitáb-i Masíbatnáma,' or Book of Misfortunes, by the

celebrated Súfí poet Shaykh Farídu-'d-Dín Attár, who died in 1229 (a
century old, it is said, on good authority), Dr Rückert published the text
of a version of our tale, together with a translation in German verse, in
the 'Zeitschrift der Deutschen Morgenländischen Gesellschaft' (Journal
of the German Oriental Society) for 1860, Bd. xiv. s. 280–7. My esteemed
friend Mr Chas. J. Pickering has favoured me with the following translation of the same Persian poem, in which he has preserved the original
form of verse, called *masnaví*, or rhymed couplets:

Upon a road fared 'Ísá, bathed in light;
The fellow of his far way a caitiff wight.
Three wheaten loaves alone were 'Ísá's cheer;
One loaf he ate, another gave his fere;
So one of those three loaves whereof they ate
Remained between the two uneaten yet.
For water 'Ísá walked a space before;
His fellow ate the loaf in that same hour.
When to him ' Ísá, Marím's child, returned,
No wheaten loaf beside him he discerned.
Said he, "Where is that wheaten loaf, my son?"
Replied he, "Never have I heard of one."
Thence fared the two still onward, side by side,
Till on their path appeared a river-tide:
Straightway his hand caught ' Ísá, as he stood,
And walked with him across the running flood.
When o'er that stream at last he'd passage given,
"Ah, fere," said he, "by the just Judge in heaven,
That Sovereign Lord who has this wonder shown,
Such wonder as man had never wrought alone—
This moment tell me true, O traveller,
Who yonder ate the wheaten loaf to spare?"
"Thereof I've not an inkling," answered he.
"When I know not, why dost thou question me?"

So onward, inly loathing, 'Ísá fared,
Till from afar a little fawn appeared.
To him did 'Ísá call that nimble roe,
Then with its life-blood made earth rosy grow.
The flesh he broiled, thereof a little ate;

Full to the throat that sinner feasted yet.
Then 'Ísá, Marím's child, the several bones
Gathered, and breathed into their midst but once.;
New life the fawn snatched from that breath's impress,
Worshipped, and sprang into the wilderness.[8]
That hour Messiah, guide in ways untrod,
Spake, "O companion, by the truth of God,
Who of His power hath shown thee such a proof,
Let me but know of that one wheaten loaf."
"I never set my eyes on it," said he.
"How long wilt thou object this thing to me?"

Yet all the same that man with him he bore,
Until three mounds of earth appeared before;
When a pure prayer by 'Ísá's lips was told,
And the three heaps of earth were yellow gold.
"Man of good faith," said he, "one heap is thine;
This other heap thou seest here is mine;
And that third heap is at this moment his
Who ate in secret that one loaf we miss."
The man, soon as he heard the name of gold
(Strange, that mutation should so swiftly hold),
Cried, "That one loaf of bread I've eaten—I,
A-hungered, I devoured it secretly."
When 'Ísá heard him so confess the sin,
He said, "I care not; all the three are thine.
My fellow-traveller thou'rt not fit to be;
I'll none of thee, although thou wished for me."
So spake he, and, in sorrow for his sake,
Forsook him, far away his path to take.

A brief time fled, and two men passed thereby;
Both see the gold, and burn with enmity.

---

[8]Muslims believe that the breath of the Messiah had the virtue of restoring the dead to life. In the Persian romance of the 'Four Darweshes' a very skilful physician is called 'Ísá in allusion to this notion. And in the Persian 'Sindibád Náma' we read: "Sweet is the air of Ja'farabád [a suburb of Shiráz], whose breezes perform the work of the Messiah"—that is, are health-giving, like his breath. For parallels to the above incident of the resuscitation of the roe from its bones, see Note at the end of this paper: "On Resuscitation in Folk-Lore."

The one said, "Mark you, all this gold's mine own."
"Not so," the two replied; "'tis ours alone."
Much babble and contention thence arose,
Till tongue and hand were tired of words and blows.
The quarrelling trio came to terms at last,
That all the gold should in three lots be cast.
By this time all the three were hungering sore;
They were so beaten they could breathe no more.
The one said, "Life is more to me than gold:
I'll go to the city and buy where bread is sold."
Quoth the other two, "If thou but bring us bread,
To failing bodies bring'st thou life indeed.
Go thou for bread: when thou return'st in glee,
We will that moment share that gold in three."

Now to his friends the man his gold resigned,
Set out, and to his business gave his mind.
To the city he came, bought bread, and ate awhile;
Then mid the rest put poison in his guile,
So the other two might eat and die, and he
Survive, and all the gold be his in fee.
But those two made a compact in their stay
That they would put that one out of the way,
Then into two divide those portions three;
As this was settled came the man in glee.
Incontinent the couple struck him dead,
And erelong perished as they ate his bread.

When 'Ísá, Marím's child, came there again,
He saw the dead men there, he saw the slain.
Said he, "If here unmoved this treasure stay,
Uncounted throngs of creatures will it slay."
A prayer that pure soul offered up once more;
The gold became the earth it was before.
Though gold be better than the earth we tread,
Gold is the best when earth lies overhead.[9]

[9]Dr Reinhold Köhler has informed me that Fabricius, in his 'Codex Apocryphus Novi Testamenti,' ed. 1739, iii. 395, cites a brief prose version from 'Proverbiorum et Sententiorum

From the "Happy Valley" of Kashmir we have yet another version, which differs materially from those already cited: Four men left their country together to seek their fortune. As they journeyed on, it came to pass that Allah, according to His power and wisdom, caused a large golden tree to spring up suddenly, which was loaded with rich clusters of golden fruit.[10] Seeing this miracle, the travellers were astonished, and at once resolved to proceed no farther, but to take the tree home with them, and be glad for ever. In order to fell the tree, and cut it up into pieces of convenient size, it was arranged that two of the party should go to the nearest village and procure saws and axes, while the two others should remain to guard the precious treasure; and they went accordingly. The two who were left to watch the tree began to consult together how they might kill their partners, and they resolved to mix poison with their bread, so that, when they ate thereof, they should die, and they themselves should have a double share of the treasure. But the other two, who were going for the tools, had also plotted that they might get rid of their partners left behind by the tree, and they resolved to slay them with one stroke of the axe, and thus have a double share of the treasure. And when they returned from the village they immediately slew them with one stroke of the axe. Then they began to hew down the tree, and soon cut up the branches and made them into bundles convenient for carrying away; after which they sat down to eat and sleep. They ate of the poisoned bread, and slept the fatal sleep of death. Some time afterward, a party of travellers chanced to pass that way, and found the four bodies lying cold and stiff beneath the golden tree, with the bundles of golden branches ready for carrying away.[11]

In Mr Ralston's 'Tibetan Tales from Indian Sources,' pp. 286, 287, we find our story assume a form which is unique, while curiously reflecting the source whence it was derived:

Persicarum Centuria, collecta, et versione notisque adornata, à L. Warner,' Leyden, 1644, p. 31. (It is not in the first edition of Fabricius.) Warner, he says, gives also the Persian original, but without stating the source: Three travellers find a treasure. One goes to procure food, and so on. Jesus comes by with his disciples, and seeing the three dead bodies, he says, "Hæc est conditio mundi! Videte quomodo ternos hosce tractaverit, et ipse tamen post eos in statu suo perseveret. Vae illi qui petit mandum ex mundo!"—This is evidently a different version from the above.

[10]In the 'Kathá Sarit Ságara' we read of trees with golden trunks, branches of jewels, the clear white flowers of which were clusters of pearls—a very old and very wide-spread myth.

[11]'Dictionary of Kashmírí Proverbs and Sayings. Explained, and illustrated from the rich and interesting folk-lore of the Valley.' By J. Hinton Knowles. Bombay, 1885. Pp. 45, 46.

In long past times a hunter wounded an elephant with a poisoned arrow. Perceiving that he had hit it, he followed after the arrow and killed the elephant. Five hundred robbers, who had plundered a hill-town, were led by an evil star to that spot, where they perceived the elephant. As it was just then a time of hunger with them, they said, "Now that we have found this meat, let 250 of us cut the flesh off the elephant and roast it, while 250 go to fetch water." Then those among them who had cut the flesh off the elephant and cooked it said among themselves, "Honoured sirs, now that we have accomplished such a task and collected so much stolen property, wherefore should we give away part of it to others? Let us eat as much of the meat as we please, and then poison the rest. The others will eat the poisoned meat and die, and then the stolen goods will be ours." So after they had eaten their fill of the meat, they poisoned what remained over. Those who had gone to fetch water, likewise, when they had drunk as much as they wanted, poisoned what they were to take with them. So when they came back, and those who had eaten the flesh drank the water, and those who drank the water ate the flesh, they all of them died.

And now we have reached the original source of all the foregoing stories. It is the 'Vedabbha Játaka'—the 48th of Fausböll's edition of the Páli text of the Játakas,' or (Buddhist) Birth-Stories.[12] The first to point out—in this country, at all events—the identity of Chaucer's Pardoner's Tale with one of the Buddhist Birth-Stories was the Rev. Dr Richard Morris, in a paper in the 'Contemporary Review' for April 1881. Mr Francis, of Cambridge University Library, published an abstract of the story in 'The Academy' for 1882. A year later Professor C. H. Tawney contributed a full translation to the 'Journal of Philology,' 1883, vol. xii. pp. 202–208. In 1884 the Bishop of Colombo published, in the 'Journal of the Ceylon Branch of the Royal Asiatic Society,' a translation of the first fifty 'Játakas,' one

---

[12]"According to the Buddhist belief, every man living has entered on his present life in succession to a vast number of previous lives, in any one of which he may have been a man—king, monk, or goatherd—an animal, goblin, or deity, as the case might be. For the mass of men, these previous lives have left no trace on memory, but a Buddha remembers them all, and not his own only, but the previous births also of other men. And Gotama, so the tradition runs, was in the habit of explaining the facts of the present in the lives of those about him, by what they had been or done in other births, and of illustrating his own teaching by what he had done himself in earlier births. Of the stories which he has thus told of his own previous existences, 550 are supposed to have been collected immediately after his decease." —The Bishop of Colombo, in the 'Journal of the Ceylon Branch of the Royal Asiatic Society,' 1884, vol. viii. part 2, p. 100.

of which is our original. Another rendering—slightly abridged—appeared in 'The Orientalist,' published at Kandy, Ceylon, 1884, which is as follows:

In times gone by, when King Bráhmadatta reigned in the city of Benáres, there lived a Bráhman who was skilled in alchemy and knew a certain charm (*mantra*) called "Vedabbha." When this charm was repeated at a lucky hour, with the eyes of the reciter turned up to the sky, it had the effect of bringing down showers of treasure from the heavens. This Bráhman set out once for the Cetiyan country with the Bódhisat,[13] his pupil, and on their way they fell into the hands of a band of robbers, called "sending thieves," from a practice they had of sending one of their captives for a ransom, while they detained the rest as hostages till its arrival. Of father and son, they were wont to detain the son; of mother and daughter, the daughter; of two brothers, the younger; of teacher and pupil, the teacher. In conformity with this practice they detained the Bráhman, and sent the Bódhisat to fetch the ransom. On taking leave of his teacher, the Bódhisat entreated him not to avail himself of the charm, although there was to be a lucky hour that very day, at which the *mantra* might be repeated with effect, warning him at the same time that a disregard of this advice would result in the death both of himself and of the five hundred robbers. So saying, he went away, promising to return in a day or two with the ransom. The Bráhman, however, unable on the one hand to bear his confinement, and on the other to resist the temptation which the approach of the lucky hour presented, gave way to his weakness, and informed the robbers of his resolution. Thereupon he performed the ablutions enjoined preparatory to the recital of the *mantra*, bedecked himself with flowers, and at the advent of the lucky hour muttered the *mantra*, when, to the amazement and gratification of the robbers, a shower of gems fell from the heavens. The robbers helped themselves to as much of the treasure as they could carry, and, releasing the Bráhman, set out thence. Whilst they were on their march another band of robbers more powerful than they met them and made them captives. The captives informed their captors how they got the wealth, whereupon they were released, and the Bráhman was seized. On being told by the Bráhman that they must wait for a lucky hour, the robbers were so much incensed that they cut the Bráhman into two, and throw-

[13]A potential Buddha; in the present case, Gautama himself before attaining Buddhahood (see last note).

ing the two pieces on the way, pursued the five hundred robbers whom they had just released, killed them all, and took possession of the treasure. After this they divided themselves into two factions, not being able to agree in the division of the spoil. Each faction attacked the other, and all were killed except two.[14]

Now these two surviving robbers carried the treasure and buried it in a woody place near a village, and one sat with a sword guarding it while the other went into the village to get rice and other food cooked. Covetousness is indeed the root of destruction! The man who was sitting by the treasure thought, "When he comes, the treasure will be divided into two parts. Suppose I strike him a blow with the sword just as he comes, and kill him." And he drew the sword and sat watching for his arrival. And the other thought, "That treasure will have to be divided into two parts. Suppose I put poison into the food, and give it to that man to eat, and so kill him, and take all the treasure for myself." And so, as soon as the food was prepared, he ate of it, and then put poison in the rest and took it to the place. He had hardly set down the food and stood still, when the other cleft him in two with the sword, and threw him in a covered place. Then he ate the food, and himself died on the spot.

In the meantime the Bódhisat collected some money for ransoming his tutor the Bráhman, and entering the forest to offer it to the robbers, found the corpse of his teacher cut into two pieces. He at once knew that his teacher must have disregarded his advice, and caused a shower of treasure to descend. Advancing farther, he saw the mangled corpses of the thousand but two robbers lying scattered on the ground, and he finally discovered the corpses of the two who were the last possessors of the ill-fated treasure. The Bódhisat then, reflecting upon the consequences of covetousness, removed the treasure and spent it in charitable purposes.[15]

"Thus far, and no farther," in the case of Chaucer's well-told tale of the

---

[14]In the Tibetan version we have a curious reflection of this absurdity, in the five hundred robbers, one half of whom went to fetch water and poisoned it, while the other half remained to cook the elephant's flesh, and poisoned what they did not eat themselves.

[15]The story assumes a very different form in the 'Avadánas,' Indian tales and apologues, translated from the Chinese into French by M. Stanislas Julien (3 vols., Paris, 1859), in which it occurs twice, No. xi. tome i. p. 60, and No. ci. tome ii. p. 89. In this Chinese-Buddhist form we have no longer three travellers or robbers slaying each other; but still the leading idea, that "covetousness is the root of destruction." The two 'Avadánas' are so nearly alike that it will suffice to cite No. ci. as follows:

The ambition of riches exposes us to a danger as formidable as a venomous serpent. We should neither look at them nor attach ourselves to them. One day Buddha, journeying in the three "riottours" and their treasure-trove? Perhaps not. Then in what quarter should we expect to find an earlier form of this world-wide story? In the Egyptian papyri? Possibly. Or, failing these, in the 'Mahábhárata'? The great Hindú epic has not, I think, been thoroughly examined by special students of the genealogy of fiction. It is as yet only known to such from episodes of it which have been translated into English and other European languages—Nala and Damayanti, Dushwanta and Sakúntala, the Bráhman's Lament, etc. There is, however, a complete English translation of the 'Mahábhárata' now in course of publication at Calcutta,[16] a considerable portion of which has already appeared—would that the paper and typography were more worthy of the noble work!—and it should be searched for this and other ancient stories. We ought to be cautious in giving Buddhism all credit for the invention of tales which are traceable to Páli writings. There can be no doubt that the early Buddhists adopted for their purposes many fictions of Hindú origin, as well as tales and apologues which, even in their time, were the common property of the world.

The version which most closely resembles Chaucer's tale is the second of those cited from the 'Novelle Antiche.' True, there is nothing in the Italian story about a pestilence—which renders the old English poet's narrative the more impressive—but the "olde chorle" who tells the "riot-tours" where they may find Death is the counterpart of the Hermit, and of Saint Anthony in the Italian miracle-play. If Chaucer, like Shakspeare after him, used materials which he found ready to his hand, it must be allowed that he has in every instance used them as the statuary does a

---

province of Prasirajit, saw a place where a treasure had been deposited by some one, which was composed of a quantity of precious things. Buddha said to Ananda, "Do you not see that venomous serpent?" "I see it," replied Ananda. At this moment there was a man walking behind Buddha. On hearing these words, he resolved to go and see the serpent. Having observed precious and beautiful objects, he bitterly blamed the words of Buddha, and considered them vain and foolish. "These are very precious things," said he, "and yet he said that it was a venomous serpent!" Straightway he brought all the people of his house to the spot, and by their assistance conveyed away that treasure, so that his wealth became immense. But there was a man who presented himself before the king, and told him that that person had lately found a great treasure, and had not brought it to the judge. So the king immediately caused him to be cast into prison, and demanded from him the treasure which he had found. He declared that he had spent it all. But the king would not believe him; he caused him to be stunned with blows, and put him to the most cruel tortures. This man recognised too late the truth of the words of Buddha.

[16]'The Mahábhárata of Krishna Dwaipayana Vyasa. Translated into English Prose by Protap Chundra Roy.'

block of marble; and of all the variants of the Robbers and their Treasure-trove there is none, I think, to compare with the Pardoner's Tale.

Regarding the other versions, it is observable that three is the usual number of the robbers or travellers who perish through their own cupidity and treachery; although in the original it is but two, which, curiously enough, is also the number in our second Arabic version. With a few insignificant exceptions, the several versions all run in the same groove: a treasure is found, or stolen, by three men, one of whom goes away to fetch food; the other two plan to murder him on his return; and he puts poison in the food he is bringing to them. The Persian poem points to an Indian source. There must, it seems to me, have been a Hindú version in which the number of the men was three. From India the story would get to Persia, thence to the Arabs, from some of whose possessions on the Mediterranean it would get to Italy, and from Italy spread throughout Europe; or, "another way," to employ the formula of the immortal Mrs Glasse, let us say that it was brought by some minstrel or palmer from Syria, and through a *fabliau* became current from England to Italy.

NOTE

ON RESUSCITATION IN FOLK-LORE (p. 496)

Legends similar to the incident, in the Persian tale, of the resuscitation of an animal from its bones have been popular time out of mind in Europe as well as in Asia. A very curious analogue of it is found in the Older Edda (the compilation of which is ascribed to Sæmund Sigfusson, a learned Icelander, who was born A.D. 1056), in the narrative of Thor's journey to Utgard:

Thor and Loki once set out, in chariots drawn by buck-goats, for Yötenheim, or giant-land. Towards evening they arrived at the house of a farmer, where they took up their quarters for the night. Thor took and killed his goats, broiled their flesh, and invited his host and his children to partake of the feast. When it was ended Thor spread the goat-skins on the ground, and desired the children to throw the bones into them. The farmer's son Thialfi had broken one of the bones to get out the marrow. In the morning Thor got up and dressed himself, and then laying hold of Miölner (his wonder-working hammer) swung it over the skins. Immediately the goats stood up, but one of them limped on the hind leg. The god exclaimed that the farmer and his family had not dealt fairly with the bones, for the goat's leg was broken. The farmer was terrified to death when he saw Thor draw down his eyebrows and grasp the handle of Miölner till his knuckles grew white. He and his children sued for grace, offering any terms, and Thor, laying aside his anger, accepted Thialfi and his sister Rosko for his servants, and left his goats there behind him.

I shall not, I trust, be charged with irreverence by any reader, in referring to mediæval Christian and Muhammedan legends of miracles ascribed to Christ: it is necessary that I should do so, in order to illustrate an interesting and curious feature of folk-lore. Legends of the miracles of 'Ísá, son of Maryam,[17] found in the works of Muslim writers seem to have been derived from the Kurán and also from early Christian, or rather quasi-Christian traditions, such as those in the apocryphal gospels, which are now for the most part traceable to Buddhist sources. Thus the Muslim legend which relates that when 'Ísá was seven years old, he and his companions made images in clay of birds and beasts, and 'Ísá, to show his superiority, caused his images to fly and walk at his command—this is also found in the gospel of Pseudo-Matthew and in that of the Infancy.

Another Muslim legend of 'Ísá, son of Maryam, is of his healing the sick by laying his staff on them. A man, thinking the virtue lay in the staff, begged and obtained it of him, and hearing of a king who was sick unto death, he undertook to heal him. Being admitted to the king, he laid such a stroke upon him that he immediately expired. In his distress he applied to 'Ísá, who came and restored the king to life.[18]

---

[17]Maryam (Mary) is regarded with much reverence by Muslims. Muhammed himself has said, that although many men had attained moral excellence, yet among *women* only four had arrived at that dignity, namely, 'Áshiyáh, wife [query-daughter?] of Pharaoh; Maryam (Mary), the daughter of Imrán [mother of Jesus]; Khadíja, the first wife of Muhammed; and Fátima, Muhammed's daughter—*M. Cassim Siddi Lebbe,* in 'The Orientalist,' 1884.

El-Mas'údí, the Arabian traveller and historian, in his 'Meadows of Gold and Mines of Gems' has the following: "When Maryam was seventeen years of age, God sent the angel Gabriel to her, and he breathed the Spirit into her. She was pregnant with the Masíh [Messiah], Jesus the son of Maryam, and she gave him birth in a country town called Beit Lehm [Bethlehem: the House of God], which is some miles from Jeru.salem. His history is related in the Kurán [3d sura and *passim*], and the Christians believe that Jesus observed the old religion of his nation. He lectured on the Pentateuch and other ancient books twenty-nine or thirty years in the province of the Jordan, in a synagogue called el-Madras [the college]. A certain day he was reading the Book of the prophet Esaias, and he saw in it the passage, "Thou art my prophet and my elect; I have chosen thee for me." He closed the book, gave it to the minister of the synagogue, and went out, saying, 'The word of God is now fulfilled in the Son of Man.' Some say Christ lived in a town called Názarah [Nazareth], in the district of el-Lajjún, in the province of the Jordan; hence the Christians have [in Arabic] the name of Nazáraníya."

[18]This seems reflected in those versions of 'Little Fairly' (*ante,* p. 399 ff.) in which the hero pretends to make his wife young by striking her with a cudgel, or to reanimate her by sounding a horn over her.

A parallel to this is found in the tale of the Master-smith, which is equally current in Sicily and Italy, and in Germany, Norway, and Russia: There was a blacksmith who boasted that he was without an equal in his craft. One day Christ appeared in his smithy and transformed the smith's aged and bedridden mother into a young woman, by burning her in the furnace. The smith attempted to do likewise with an old beggar-woman, and burned her to a cinder. But the Lord, coming back, restores her to life—thus rebuking the pride of the boastful smith.

This legend appears to have been formerly popular in England, since it is the subject of an old black-letter tract (in verse), entitled, 'Of the Smyth that burnt his Wyfe, and after forged her againe by the helpe of our blessed Lord,' printed by William Copland, probably about 1550, and privately reprinted in 1849, by Mr Halliwell-Phillipps, in his 'Contributions to Early English Literature.'

The indecent Jewish author of the 'Toldoth Jeśu,'[19] while admitting that Christ performed many wonders, ascribes them to his having abstracted from the Temple the Ineffable Name[20] and concealed it in his thigh—an idea which is evidently of Indian origin, and which had doubtless found its way, with other magical nonsense, into Syria long before the time of this most scurrilous writer. In the first story of the Tamil romance 'Madana Kámáraja Kadai,' the son of Lókádhipa, king of Udayagiri, longs to obtain the daughter of Indra for his wife. In the course of his wanderings he comes to a cottage, where he takes up his abode with an old woman, and herds her cattle. One day he observes the beautiful daughter of Indra bathing in a tank, and having stolen her garment takes it home. The old woman cuts open his thigh, puts the celestial garment in the opening, and then sews it together. The daughter of Indra—like others of the Bird-Maiden class—had no alternative but to follow him and become his wife. In the 'Toldoth Jeśu,' we have an incident similar to that related in the Persian tale, of the resuscitation of the roe: When Jesus was challenged to give public proof of his divinity (according to the recension in Wagenseil), he said, "Bring hither to me a dead man, and I will restore him to life." The people hasten to a certain sepulchre, and finding there nothing but bones, they return and report this, whereupon Jesus said, "Bring them hither in our midst." And when the bones were brought, he put them together, and lo! there rose up a living man.

---

[19] Not the recension published, with a Latin translation and *castigation*, by Ulrico, 1705—see *ante*, p. 318—but the version, also with a Latin translation, at the end of the second volume of Wagenseil's 'Tela Ignea Satanæ,' 1681.

[20] In the Arabian tale of Hasan of Basra, it is said of a shaykh of the seed of 'Azáf bin Barkhiyá (vazír of Solomon), "he knoweth the most Great Name of Allah."

This legend was probably current in Syria during the time of Muhammed, since he apparently alludes to it in the Kurán, "See how I restored the carcase after it was separated;" and he may have obtained it from the Christian who is said to have had a hand in the composition of the Kurán, for many tales of the same kind were known among the different so-called Christian sects in Egypt and Syria, in the earlier centuries of our era.

Stories of the resuscitation of animals from their bones are common in Indian fiction, one of which occurs in the 'Vetála Panchavinsatí' (Twenty-five Tales of a Demon): Four brothers, after agreeing to go into the world in order to acquire magic knowledge, and fixing upon a trysting-place at which to meet, separate, each going in a different direction. In course of time they met again at the appointed spot, and asked one another what each had learned. Then one of them said, "I have learned this magic secret: if I find a bit of a bone of any animal, I can instantly produce on it the flesh of that animal." The second said, "When the flesh of any animal has been superinduced upon a piece of bone, I know how to produce the skin upon it." Then the third said, "And I am able to create the limbs of the animal." And the fourth said, "When the animal has its limbs properly developed, I know how to endow it with life." Then the four brothers went into the forest to find a piece of bone on which to display their skill. There it happened that they found a piece of a lion's bone, and they took it up, without knowing to what animal it belonged. And when the four brothers had successfully exercised their magical arts on the piece of bone, it rose up a very terrible lion, and rushing upon them, it slew them on the spot.—The story is somewhat differently told in the 'Panchatantra' (Book v. fab. 14): Of the four brothers, three possess knowledge, and one possesses only common sense. The first joins the bones of the lion; the second covers them with flesh and skin; and the third is about to give the animal life, when the man of common sense says, "If you raise it to life it will kill us all." Seeing the third brother will not desist from his purpose, he climbs up a tree, and thus saves his life, while the others are torn to pieces.—In the 'Túti Náma,' four friends, journeying through a desert, discover the bones of a monstrous serpent. One of them, being a magician, takes out a book from which he reads certain words, when the bones are joined and covered with skin. He then proposes to his friends that he should endow the carcase with life, but they advise him not to do so, and when they see he is obstinate, they run away. The magician then takes out another book, and on reading therefrom the serpent becomes alive, and instantly devours him.—In No. 20 of Lal Behari Day's 'Folk-Tales of Bengal' four friends learn their several arts by overhearing a hermit recite the magical formulæ, but all escape up a tree, and the tiger, having devoured their horses, rushes into the jungle.—In a

Burmese version (No. 10 of 'Decisions of the Princess Thoo-dhamma Tsari') the friends are three, and having resuscitated a tiger from its bones, which they find in a forest, the tiger follows them, ostensibly to furnish them with food, but in three nights he eats up the three learned but foolish friends. This last version would seem to indicate that the story is of Buddhist extraction.—In the 'Bahár-i Dánush' (vol. ii. p. 290 of Scott's translation) a hermit put together the bones of a cow, then sprinkled water on the skeleton, and at once it was covered with flesh and skin, stood up, and began to low.

All these stories cannot fail to remind the reader of the sublime parable in the Book of Ezekiel, chap. xxxvii. 1–10:

"The hand of the Lord was upon me, and carried me out in the Spirit of the Lord, and set me down in the midst of the valley which was full of bones, and caused me to pass by them round about: and, behold, there were very many in the open valley; and, lo, they were very dry. And He said unto me, Son of man, can these bones live? And I answered, O Lord God, thou knowest. Again He said unto me, prophesy upon these bones, and say unto them, O ye dry bones, hear the word of the Lord. Thus saith the Lord God unto these bones: Behold, I will cause breath to enter into you, and ye shall live; and I will lay sinews upon you, and will bring up flesh upon you, and cover you with skin, and put breath in you, and ye shall live; and ye shall know that I am the Lord. So I prophesied as I was commanded: and as I prophesied, there was a noise, and behold a shaking, and the bones came together, bone to his bone. And when I beheld, lo, the sinews and the flesh came up upon them, and the skin covered them above: but there was no breath in them. Then said He unto me, Prophesy unto the wind, prophesy, son of man, and say to the wind, Thus saith the Lord God, Come from the four winds, O breath, and breathe upon these slain, that they may live. So I prophesied, as He commanded me, and the breath came into them, and they lived, and stood up upon their feet, an exceeding great army."

✌ THE LUCKY IMPOSTER ✌

THE story of the Charcoal-Burner is certainly not one of the least entertaining of Dr Dasent's 'Tales from the Fjeld': A bibulous charcoal-burner, on returning from the market-town where he had been to sell a few loads of his charcoal, is asked by his friends what he had seen there, and replies that all he had observed was, that the people paid great deference to the priests, but took no notice whatever of him. They advise him to go to the sale of their dead priest's effects, buy his gown and cape, and set up for a priest himself. He does so, and is upbraided by his wife for his folly. Next day he sees a party of priests go past his house, so, putting on his gown and cape, he joins them, and they all proceed to the palace, where the king informs them that his ring having been stolen lately, he had sent for them to see whether they could find out the thief, and whoever did so should be suitably rewarded: if a rector, he should be made a dean; if a dean, he should be made a bishop; if a bishop, he should be made the first man in the kingdom. He went round them all, without success, till he came to the charcoal-burner, of whom he demanded, "Who are you?" Our impostor boldly answered, "I am the wise priest, and the true prophet." "Then," said the king, "can you tell me who has stolen my ring?" He replied that he must have time and some paper, for it required a good deal of calculation in order to track the thief through many lands. With paper, pen, and ink he was accordingly locked up in a room of the palace, and having spent many days in merely making pot-hooks on the paper (for he could not write), at length the king told him that if he did not discover the thief within three days he should be put to death. This was certainly a sore dilemma, but his good luck saved him. For it happened that his meals were served to him successively by three of the king's servants, who had jointly stolen the ring; and in the evening, when the man who waited on him took away his supper dishes, the poor charcoal-burner, thinking only of the lapse of one of his three days of life, sighed and exclaimed, "This is the *first* of them!" and the fellow believing himself detected, reported this to his comrades. Next day, when another of the trio performed the same service, the sham priest said, "This is the *second* of them!" When the other rogue, on the following day, heard him say, "This is the *third* of them!" he hastened to the others, and consulted with them what they had best do to save themselves. In short, they offered him each a hundred dollars if he would not denounce them to the king. Surprised but glad at this, the charcoal-burner consented, provided they brought him the ring and a great bowl of brose, which they did very willingly, at the same time giving him three hundred dollars. He stuffed the ring in the brose, and bade them give it to the biggest of the king's pigs: and when the king came to see whether he had discovered the thief, or the whereabouts of his ring, the charcoal-burner told him that the thief was not a man, but one of his own pigs—the biggest and fattest of them. The king, albeit thinking this a mere subterfuge, caused the pig to be killed and cut open, and, behold, the ring was found in its inside, upon which the sham priest was presented with a living. In his capacity of rector he performed some queer antics, which, however, were explained by his superiors to have a mysterious spiritual meaning, and he was extolled as a wise priest. But farther trials awaited him. The king's consort having been pronounced to be in "an interesting condition," he sent for his priests to ascertain from them whether she should present him with an heir to the crown; but they all confessed their ignorance, and suggested the wise priest as the most likely person to afford him the desired information. The king, by way of preliminary test of the wise priest's gift of prophecy, takes a big silver tankard, and goes to the sea-shore, where he picks a crab, which he puts in it, closing down the lid. Then he calls for the wise priest, and asks him to declare what is in the tankard. Believing his last hour was come, the poor man, addressing himself aloud, said, "Oh you most wretched crab and cripple on earth! this is all your backslidings and side-long tracks have brought on you!" Admiring his sagacity, the king lifted the lid of the tankard and showed that it contained a crab. Then he commanded him to go into the queen's presence, and declare whether she was to present him with a son or a daughter. In a state of mortal agitation, the wise priest paced the chamber to and fro, exclaiming, "Whenever I come near the queen I think it will be a girl, and whenever I go at some distance from her I am sure it will be a boy." As the queen was shortly after this safely delivered of *twins*, a boy and a girl, the sagacity of the whilom charcoal-burner was placed beyond farther question.

There is a well-known German version of this story in Grimm's collection: A poor peasant, named Krebs, sets up as a doctor who knows everything (*Allwissend*), and a great robbery having taken place in the house of a nobleman, Dr Know-all is requested to assist in the recovery of the stolen property. He consents to visit the nobleman, on condition that his wife be allowed to accompany him. When they are seated at the nobleman's table, the first servant brings a dish, upon which the Doctor says to his wife, "Grethel, that is the *first*," meaning the first dish; and he makes similar remarks when the second and third servants come in; but when the fourth enters, the nobleman, to test the Doctor's skill, desires him to say what is under the cover. Now it happened to be a crab, which the Doctor, of course, did not know; so he looked at the covered dish, and felt that he was in a great dilemma, from which he could not escape; and so he said in a low tone to himself, "O Krebs, Krebs, what will you do?" The nobleman said, "Yes, it is a *crab;* I see you know everything, and will be able to tell me where my money is, and who has stolen it." The servants, alarmed, winked at the Doctor to come out to their offices. They there confessed that they had stolen the money, and offered him wealth to any amount if he would not betray them. He promised, on condition that they would show him where they had hidden the money; so they took him to the spot at once. On returning to the table, he said he would consult his book, and ultimately conducted the nobleman to the place where the money was concealed.

In a popular version current in Mantua, after the pretended astrologer—whose name, as in the German story, is Crab—has been shut up in a room for a month, his wife comes to visit him, and he makes her hide under the bed and cry out when a servant enters, "That is one," and so on. The servants confess they stole the king's ring, and Crab says to them, "Take the ring and make the turkey-cock swallow it; leave the rest to me." At the impostor's suggestion, the king has the turkey killed and the ring, of course, is found in its inside, and the "astrologer" is richly rewarded. Then follows the test of the crabs in a covered dish.[1]—It is evident that this version was not derived from the German story of Dr Know-all, in which the servants reveal to the impostor the spot where they had concealed the stolen money; while in the Italian story, as in the Norse tale of the Charcoal-Burner, an animal is made to swallow the lost article, which is not merely fortuitous, but rather an instance of the influence of the Norsemen in the south of Europe.

The story is current in Persia, and was related to Sir John Malcolm by the Shah's own story-teller. In this version a poor but contented cobbler

[1] Crane's 'Italian Popular Tales,' p. 314.—Mr W. J. Thomas, in the notes to his 'Lays and Legends of Tartary,' refers to an English story of "The Conjuror and the Turkey-Cock" which is probably similar to this Italian version.

named Ahmed is induced by his vain and ambitious wife to set up as an astrologer, who knew the past, the present, and the future. By chance he discovers a fine ruby that had been stolen from the king's jeweller, and a valuable necklace, which a lady had lost in the public baths. After this it happened that the royal treasury was robbed of forty chests of gold and jewels, and the king's astrologer having failed to discover either the robbers or the treasure, his majesty threatened him with death if he did not find out the thieves within the next day. Ahmed is sent for by the king's astrologer, who conducts him before the king. On being desired to discover the robbers of the treasury, Ahmed declares there were forty robbers concerned in the affair, and that he should require forty days to discover them all; intending to escape to another country before the expiry of that period. When he returns home and acquaints his wife of his having but forty days more to live, unless he made good his escape out of the land, she threatens to inform the king at once of his meditated flight if he does not set to work to find out the robbers. "Well," says the unhappy cobbler, "so be it. All I desire is to pass the few remaining days of my life as comfortably as I can. You know that I am no scholar; so there are forty dates, give me one of these every night after I have said my prayers, in order that I may put them in a jar, and by counting them, may always see how many of the days I have to live are gone." The wife, pleased at carrying her point, took the dates and promised to be punctual in doing what he desired. Meanwhile the thieves who had stolen the king's treasure, having been kept from leaving the city by fear of detection and pursuit, had received information of every measure taken to discover them. One of their number was among the crowd before the palace on the day the king sent for Ahmed, and hearing the cobbler had immediately declared there were forty robbers concerned in the affair, he ran in a fright to his comrades and exclaimed, "We are all found out! Ahmed, the new astrologer, has told the king there are forty of us." The captain of the band replied, "It needed no astrologer to tell that: this Ahmed, with all his simple good-nature, is a shrewd fellow;—forty chests having been stolen, he naturally guessed that there must have been forty thieves, and he has made a good hit, that is all. Still, it is prudent to watch him, for he certainly has made some strange discoveries. One of us must go tonight and listen to his conversation with his handsome wife, for he is said to be very fond of her, and will, no doubt, tell her what success he has had in his endeavours to detect us." Every one approved of this proposal; and soon after nightfall one of the thieves repaired to the terrace of Ahmed's house. He arrived there just as the cobbler had finished his evening prayers, and his wife was giving him the first date. "Ah," said Ahmed, as he took it, "there, my dear, is one of the forty." The thief, supposing Ahmed was aware of his presence, hastened back to his comrades, and told them what he had heard. Next night two men went to Ahmed's house, and heard him say to his wife, as he received the second date, "Now there are two of them, my dear." Three men went the next night, and so on, till the fortieth night, when the whole gang went, and heard Ahmed exclaim, "The number is complete, my dear; to-night the whole forty are here," upon which the robbers knocked at the door, and when Ahmed opened it, expecting to see the king's guards come to lead him off to execution, to his surprise and relief, the robbers confessed their guilt, and conducted him to the place where they had concealed the king's treasure, he having promised not to betray them to the king. In the morning he appeared before the king, who asked him if he had succeeded in discovering the robbers, and also the whereabouts of the treasure they had stolen. Ahmed replied that he could either direct him to the robbers or the treasure, but not to both. The king thought hanging the thieves would do no good to himself if he lost his treasure, so he chose to have the chests recovered, even though the rogues should get off scot-free. Then Ahmed made his calculations, and finally led the way to the place where the treasure was hidden, after which the king gave him his own daughter in marriage; and his vain and foolish wife was no gainer, but a loser, by her having urged the honest cobbler to set up as an astrologer.[2]

A Mongolian variant occurs in the 'Relations of Siddhí Kúr,' under the title of the Magician with the Sow's Head, in which, in place of stolen treasure, the pretended soothsayer recovers a lost talisman on which the welfare of the country depended, and cures a khán who was bewitched by evil spirits. His folly is shown by the paltry reward he asks for his services; but his wife afterwards goes to the khán, and obtains costly gifts.[3]

The oldest and best form of the story is found in the 'Kathá Sarit Ságara,' Book vi. chapter 30, and it is here given in full, from Professor C. H. Tawney's translation of that work:

There was a certain Bráhman in a certain village, named Harisarman [*i.e.*, says Benfey, "Blockhead"]. He was poor and foolish, and in evil case

[2] Sir John Malcolm's 'Sketches of Persia,' chap. xx.
[3] 'Sagas from the Far East': Tale iv. of Siddhí Kúr.

for want of employment, and he had very many children, that he might reap the fruits of his misdeeds in a former life. He wandered about begging with his family, and at last he reached a certain city, and entered the service of a rich householder called Sthúladatta. He made his sons keepers of this householder's cows and other possessions, and his wife a servant to him, and he himself lived near his house, performing the duty of an attendant. One day there was a great feast on account of the marriage of the daughter of Sthúladatta, largely attended by many friends of the bridegroom and merry-makers. And then Harisarman entertained a hope that he would be able to fill himself up to the throat with *ghí* and flesh and other dainties, together with his family, in the house of his patron. While he was anxiously expecting that occasion, no one thought of him. Then he was distressed at getting nothing to eat, and he said to his wife at night, "It is owing to my poverty and stupidity that I am treated with such disrespect here; so I will display, by means of an artifice, an assumed knowledge, in order that I may become an object of respect to this Sthúladatta, and when you get an opportunity, tell him that I possess supernatural knowledge." He said this to her, and after turning the matter over in his mind, while people were asleep he took away from the house of Sthúladatta a horse on which his son-in-law rode, and placed it in concealment. And in the morning the friends of the bridegroom could not find the horse, though they searched for it in every direction. Then, while Sthúladatta was distressed at the evil omen, and searching for the thieves who had carried off the horse, the wife of Harisarman came and said to him, "My husband is a wise man, skilled in astrology and sciences of that kind, and he will procure for you the horse; why do you not ask him?" When Sthúladatta heard that, he called Harisarman, who said, "Yesterday I was forgotten; now the horse is stolen I am called to mind." And Sthúladatta then propitiated the Brahman with these words, "I forgot you; forgive me," and asked him to tell him who had taken away the horse. Then Harisarman drew all kinds of pretended diagrams, and said, "The horse has been placed by thieves on the boundary-line south from this place. It is concealed there; and before it is carried off to a distance, as it will be at close of day, quickly go and bring it." When they heard that, many men ran and brought the horse quickly, praising the discernment of Harisarman, who was honoured by all men as a sage, and dwelt there in happiness, honoured by Sthúladatta.

Then, as days went on, much wealth, consisting of gold and jewels, was carried off by a thief from the palace of the king. As the thief was not known, the king quickly summoned Harisarman on account of his reputation for supernatural knowledge. And he, when summoned, tried to gain time, and said, "I will tell you to-morrow"; and then he was placed in a chamber by the king, and carefully guarded. And he was despondent about his pretended knowledge. Now in that palace there was a maid named Jihvá,[4] who, with the assistance of her brother, had carried off that wealth from the interior of the palace. She, being alarmed at Harisarman's knowledge, went at night and applied her ear to the door of his chamber, in order to find out what he was about. And Harisarman, who was alone inside, was at that very moment blaming his own tongue, that had made a vain assumption of knowledge. He said, "O Tongue, what is this you have done through desire of enjoyment? Ill-conducted one, endure now punishment in this place." When Jihvá heard this, she thought in her terror that she had been discovered by this wise man, and by an artifice she managed to get in to where he was, and falling at his feet, she said to that supposed sage, "Brahman, here I am, that Jihvá [*i.e.,* Tongue] whom you have discovered to be the thief of the wealth; and after I took it I buried it in the earth in a garden behind the palace, under a pomegranate tree. So spare me, and receive the small quantity of gold that is in my possession." When Harisarman heard that, he said to her proudly, "Depart! I know the past, the present, and the future. But I will not denounce you, being a miserable creature that has implored my protection; but whatever gold is in your possession you must give up to me." When he said this to the maid she consented, and departed quickly. But Harisarman reflected, in his astonishment, "Fate, if propitious, brings about, as if in sport, a thing that cannot be accomplished; for in this matter, when calamity was near, success has been unexpectedly attained by me. While I was blaming my tongue [*jihvá*] the thief Jihvá suddenly flung herself at my feet. Secret crimes, I see, manifest themselves by means of fear." In these reflections he passed the night happily in his chamber, and in the morning he brought the king, by some skilful parade of pretended knowledge, into the garden, and led him up to the treasure which was buried there; and he said that the thief had escaped with a. part of it. Then the king was pleased, and proceeded to give him villages.

But the minister, Devájnánin, whispered in the king's ear, "How can a man possess such knowledge unattainable by man, without having studied treatises? So you may be certain that this is a specimen of the way he makes a dishonest livelihood, by having a secret intelligence with thieves;

---

[4]The name, or word, means "tongue."

therefore it will be better to test him by some new artifice." Then the king, of his own accord, brought a new covered pitcher, into which he had thrown a frog, and said to Harisarman, "Bráhman, if you can guess what is in this pitcher, I will do you great honour to-day." When the Bráhman heard that, he thought his last hour had come, and he called to mind the pet name of Frog which his father had given him in sport; and, impelled by the deity, he apostrophised himself by it, lamenting his hard fate, and exclaimed, "This is a fine pitcher for you, Frog, since suddenly it has become the swift destroyer of your helpless self in this place." The people there, when they heard that, made a tumult of applause, because his speech chimed in so well with the object presented to him, and murmured, "Ah, a great sage! He knows even about the frog!" Then the king, thinking that this was all due to knowledge of divination, was highly delighted, and gave Harisarman villages, with gold, umbrella, and vehicles of all kinds. And immediately Harisarman became like a feudal chief.

This Sanskrit version is for us the oldest form of the story, and, as Tawney has pointed out, the German version of Grimm is nearest to it, in the exclamation of Doctor Know-all—whose name is Krebs—when the covered dish with a crab inside is set before him, "O crab, crab! what will you do?" The name of the sham-priest in the Norse version was evidently also Krebs, else there would be no appositeness in his exclamation, "O you most wretched crab!" And this version corresponds with the Sanskrit in the locking-up of the pretended priest. The story is also found, says Tawney, in the 'Facetiæ' of Henricus Bebelius, 1506. Here a poor charcoal-burner, as in the Norse version, represents the Bráhman. He asks three days to consider. The king gives him a good dinner, and while the first thief is standing at the window, he exclaims, "*Jam unus accessit,*" meaning, "one day is at an end." The next day the second thief comes to listen. The charcoal-burner exclaims, "*Secundus accessit,*" and so with the third; whereupon all confess. This seems to have been derived from the same source as the Norse story. Benfey conceives the incident of the horse to be found in the 'Facetiæ' of Poggius, where a doctor boasts a wonder-working pill. A man who has lost his ass takes one of these pills, and it conducts him to a bed of reeds, where he finds his ass! The version of the story in 'Siddhí Kúr' differs greatly from all the others. Benfey considers that collection as a comparatively late work, and thinks that the Mongols brought the Indian story to Europe in a form more nearly resembling that in the 'Kathá Sarit Ságara' than does the tale in the 'Siddhí Kúr.'[5]

Incidents similar to that of the chance-discovery of the thieves in the several versions of the story above cited are found in other tales. In the 'Pleasant Nights' of Straparola, xiii. 6, a mother sends her booby-son to find "good day." The lad lies down by the roadside near the city gate, where he could see all that went in or out of the city. It so happened that three men had gone into the fields to take away a treasure they had found, and on their return, when one of them greeted the booby with "good day," he exclaimed, "I have one of them," meaning that he had met one of the good days; and so on with the second and third. Believing they were discovered, the men shared the treasure with the booby in order to secure his silence.

In Pitrè's Sicilian collection, among the stories of Giufà, the typical noodle of Sicily, it is related that he went out one day to gather herbs, and it was night before he returned. On his way home the moon rose through the clouds, and Giufà sat down on a stone and watched the moon appear and disappear behind the clouds, and he exclaimed alternately, "It appears! it appears!" "It sets! it sets!" Now there were near by some thieves, who were skinning a calf which they had stolen, and when they heard, "It appears! it sets!" they feared that the officers of justice were coming, so they ran away and left the meat. When Giufà saw the thieves running away, he went to see what it was they had left behind, and found the calf skinned; so he took his knife and cut off flesh enough to fill his sack, and went home.[6]

An elaborate variant of the incident is known among the Sinhalese, of which a translation is given by Mr W. Goonetilleke in 'The Orientalist' for February 1884, to this effect: A blockhead said to his wife that he wished to receive *sil*[7] so she bade him go to the priest and repeat after him the words he should pronounce. Before break of day next morning he set out for the priest's house, and arriving there, knocked at the door. The priest called out, "Kavuda?" (Who's there?) The noodle, following literally the instruc-

---

[5]The Mongolian form of the story is so different from the European versions and their Indian original that I have thought it needless to give an abstract of it. The hero does not, as in all other versions, at first pretend that he is a soothsayer or astrologer; it is only after he has by chance seen where the talisman is deposited that he undertakes to recover it; and in the case of the sick khán, he overhears two demons—one, in the shape of a buffalo, the other in that of a woman who had become the khán's wife, and had caused his sickness—conversing together about the means by which they might be destroyed, and next day, acting upon the information thus obtained, the khán is cured, honours and wealth are bestowed upon himself and his relations, and he is ever after regarded as a most skilful magician.

[6]Crane's 'Italian Popular Tales,' p. 293.

[7]*Sil* is a religious observance: vowing to follow the Five Precepts of Buddha—see *ante*, p. 320, note 4.

tions of his wife as to repetition, replied, "Kavuda?" The priest could not understand how any one should be in the mood for jesting at such a time and place, and drawing near the door, said, "Mokada?" (What's the matter?) "Mokada?" repeated the blockhead. The priest was bewildered: he could not for the life of him understand the meaning of so strange a proceeding, so he called out, "Allapiya!" (Lay hold!) And "Allapiya!" was quickly echoed. Upon this the priest went into one of the rooms to wake up his servant, and in the meantime the simpleton, hearing nothing more, concluded that the ceremony was over, and returning home, told his wife that the words he must repeat were, "Kavuda? Mokada? Allapiya!" His wife replied that if he had not already lost his small wits he was pretty near it. The man, however, paid no attention to her remarks, believing her to be in jest, but kept repeating the words all night long at frequent intervals, to the serious disturbance of his wife's rest. This went on for several nights, and nothing that the wife could think of had the effect of convincing the man of his mistake. About this time three thieves broke into the king's treasury at night, and stole from it much wealth, consisting of gold, silver, and jewels of price. Carrying off their booty, they came to the back part of the simpleton's house and began to divide it, when they were startled by the words, "Who's there? What's the matter? Lay hold!" uttered in a loud tone from within the house. "We are undone!" said one of the thieves. "Discovered most certainly we are," said another. "Hush, hush!" said the third; "the words may have been addressed to somebody else." So they made up their minds to go on with the division, but had scarcely recommenced before the same words fell on their ears, "Who's there? What's the matter? Lay hold!" Then they took to their heels, leaving the treasure behind. The man, hearing the clatter outside, went to the back part of the house with a light, and saw, to his amazement, three heaps of treasure. He immediately awoke his wife and took her to the spot. Her eyes beamed as she beheld the unexpected wealth: husband and wife together conveyed the heaps into the house, and all was secure before day dawned. "Now," said the wittol to his wife triumphantly, "was it not my observance of *sil* that brought us this luck?" "Yes," said she; "I am glad you have been so earnest in its practice."

These three stories are not only closely allied to the chief incident of the story of the Lucky Impostor, but may be farther considered as having near affinity with the cycle of tales (see *ante,* p. 449 ff.) in which a certain maxim saves a king's life. "Thus conscience does make cowards of us all!"

ꙮ "DON'T COUNT YOUR CHICKENS UNTIL THEY ARE HATCHED!"ꙮ

THIS proverb, or maxim, had its origin in the favourite tale of the Milkmaid and her Pail of Milk, which, in her day-dream, was to form the basis of her fortune: With the profit obtained from her milk she would purchase a hundred eggs, the eggs would produce chickens, which, when grown up, she would sell, and then buy a pig, and finally a cow and a calf; then she would have many suitors for her hand in marriage, but she would scorn them every one; hereupon she tossed her head, and her pail fell, and all the milk was spilled on the ground.—In this form it was adapted from La Fontaine's fable of "La Latière et le Pot au Lait," but it was well known throughout Europe long before the great French fabulist's collection of apologues and tales was published—in 1678. In the 'Contes et Nouvelles' of Bonaventure des Periers (sixteenth century) it is thus related:

A good woman carried a pot of milk to market, making her reckoning thus: she would sell it for two liards; with these two liards she would buy a dozen of eggs; she would hatch them, and obtain a dozen chickens; these chickens would grow up and become fat fowls, selling at five sols apiece, which would make a crown or more; with which she would buy two little pigs, male and female; which would grow up, and produce a dozen others; which she would sell for twenty sols apiece, which would be twelve francs; with which she would buy a mare, which would bring a beautiful colt, which would grow up and become quite gentle: it would leap and cry *hin!* And in saying *hin!* the good woman, with the joy she had attained from her reckoning, made a kick as the colt would do, and so doing the pot of milk was kicked over, and the milk flowed away. And there were her eggs, her chickens, her fat fowls, her pigs, her mare, and her colt—all on the ground!

The story seems to have been familiar in France in the 15th century, with a shoemaker, however, in place of the milkmaid, since it is thus referred to by Rabelais, in his 'Gargantua,' "I have great fear (said Echephron) that all this enterprise will be like the farce of the *pot of milk*, with which the shoemaker made himself rich in his day-dream, and then broke the pot, and had not wherewithal to dine"—a version which does not seem to have survived.

ॐ

The Infante Don Manuel, who died in 1347, gives it as follows, in cap. 29 of 'El Conde Lucanor':

There was a woman called Dona Truhana [*i.e.,* Gertrude], rather poor than rich. One day she went to the market, carrying a pot of *honey* on her head. On her way she began to think that she would sell the pot of honey and buy a quantity of eggs; that from those eggs she would have chickens; that she would sell them and buy sheep; that the sheep would give her lambs; and thus calculating all her gains, she began to think herself much richer than her neighbours. With the riches which she imagined she possessed, she thought how she would marry her sons and daughters, and how she would walk in the street surrounded by her sons and daughters-in-law, and how people would consider her very happy from having amassed so large a fortune, though she had been so poor. While she was thinking over all this, she began to laugh for joy, and struck her head and brow with her hand. The pot of honey fell down, and was broken, and she shed hot tears because she had lost all that she would have possessed if the pot of honey had not been broken.

In the 14th century it was also related in 'Dialogus Creaturarum optime Moralizatus,' by Nicolaus Pergamenus, which was rendered into English under the title of 'Dialogues of Creatures Moralised,' where it thus appears:

"For as it is but madnesse to trust to moche in svrete, so it is but foly to hope to moche of vanyteys, for vayne be all erthly thinges longynge to men, as sayth Davyd, Psal. xciiii: Wher of it is tolde in fablys that a lady uppon a tyme delyvered to her mayden a galon of mylke to sell at a cite, and by the way, as she sate and restid her by a dyche syde, she began to thinke that with the money of the mylke she wold bye an henne, the which shulde bring forth checkyns, and when they were growyn to hennys she woude sell them and by piggis, and exchaunge them in to shepe, and the shepe in to oxen, and so whan she was come to richesse she sholde be maried right worshipfully unto some worthy man, and thus she rejoycid. And whan she was thus mervelously comfortid and ravisshed inwardly in her secrete solace, thinkynge with howe greate ioye she shuld be ledde towarde the chirche with her husbond on horsebacke, she sayde to her selfe, 'Goo we, goo we.' Sodaynlye she smote the ground with her fote, myndynge to spurre the horse, but her fote slyppid, and she fell into

the dyche, and there lay all her mylke, and so she was farre from her purpose, and never had that she hopid to have."

But the same form of the story is found in the 'Liber de Donis' of Etienne de Bourbon, which was written a century before the 'Dialogus
Creaturarum,' and, still earlier, in the 'Sermones' of Jacques de Vitry, who
seems to have been its originator, or rather, he was the first thus to adapt
the ancient Eastern original,[1] which is one of the celebrated Fables of
Bidpaï, the Arabian version of which, entitled 'Kalíla wa Dimna' (8th
century), derived from the Pahlaví, is probably the closest representative
of the Sanskrit original. This is how the story is told in the Arabic version, according to Knatchbull's translation:

A religious man was in the habit of receiving every day from the house
of a merchant a certain quantity of butter and honey, of which having
eaten as much as he wanted, he put the rest into a jar, which he hung on
a nail in a corner of the room, hoping that the jar would in time be filled.
Now as he was leaning back one day on his couch, with a stick in his
hand, and the jar suspended over his head, he thought of the high price
of butter and honey, and said to himself, "I will sell what is in the jar, and
buy with the money which I obtain for it ten goats, which, producing
each of them a young one every five months in addition to the produce
of the kids, as soon as they begin to bear, it will not be long before there
is a large flock." He continued to make his calculations, and found that
he should, at this rate, in the course of two years have more than 400
goats. "At the expiration of this term, I will buy," said he, "a hundred black
cattle, in the proportion of a bull or a cow to every four goats. I will then
purchase land, and hire workmen to plough it with the beasts, and put it
into tillage, so that before five years are over I shall no doubt have realised
a great fortune by the sale of the milk which the cows will give, and of
the produce of my land. My next business will be to build a magnificent
house, and engage a number of servants, both male and female, and when
my establishment is completed, I will marry the handsomest woman I
can find, who, in due time becoming a mother, will present me with an
heir to my possessions, who, as he advances in age, shall have the best

---

[1] In Jacques de Vitry's version it is "a certain little old fellow" who is carrying milk to the
market in an earthen pitcher; but in Etienne de Bourbon it is a maid-servant who has
received as a gift a quantity of milk which she carries on her head to sell in the city. The story
of the shoemaker referred to by Rabelais was doubtless taken from Jacques de Vitry.

masters that can be procured, and if the progress which he makes in learning is equal to my reasonable expectations, I shall be amply repaid for the pains and expense which I have bestowed upon him; but if, on the other hand, he disappoints my hopes, the rod which I have here shall be the instrument with which I will make him feel the displeasure of a justly-offended parent." At these words, he suddenly raised the hand which held the stick towards the jar, and broke it, and the contents ran down upon his head and face.[2]

Here we see, in what is perhaps the oldest form of the tale, instead of a maiden and her pail of milk, it is a religious man and a pot of oil and honey, and thus it is also in the Greek version, made from the Arabic, in 1080, by a Jew named Symeon, the son of Seth.[3] In the oldest extant Sanskrit form of the Fables of Bidpaï, the 'Panchatantra,'[4] the story is told somewhat differently, and has been translated as follows, by Dr H. H. Wilson (Book v. fab. 9):

There was an avaricious Bráhman, named Soma Sarmá, who had collected during the day as much meal in alms as filled an earthen jar. This jar he suspended to a peg immediately at the foot of his bed, that he might not lose sight of it. During the night he lay awake some time, and reflected thus: "That jar is full of meal. If a scarcity should take place I shall sell it for a hundred pieces at least. With that sum I will buy a pair of goats. They will bear young, and I shall get enough for their sale to

---

[2] This tale is somewhat altered in the conclusion of the following version, which occurs in a manuscript text of the Turkish romance of the 'Forty Vazírs,' preserved in the India Office Library: They relate that there was a devotee in the province of Fars, and that this devotee had a friend who loved him exceedingly. And that man was by trade a grocer, and sold oil and honey; and every day he gave the devotee a sufficient quantity of oil and honey. The devotee ate a little of it, and put the rest into a jar, and kept that jar in a corner of his house. One day the jar became full, and the devotee said in himself, "Now shall I take this oil and honey and sell it; and I shall buy five head of sheep with the money; and these sheep with their lambs will in time become a flock; and I shall grow very rich, and wear new clothes, and marry a virgin; and I shall have a son and heir by her, and I shall teach him all things polite." Then he took the staff in his hand, and put the jar on his head, and went to the bazaar; but as he was leaning his staff against the wall, he forgot the jar, and it struck against the wall, so that it was broken, and all that oil and honey ran down his beard.—From Mr Gibb's translation of the 'Forty Vazírs,' recently published (London: Redway). Appendix, p. 393.

[3] It is also a pot of honey in 'El Conde Lucanor,' from which we might suppose that this version was adapted from the Arabic or the Greek, did we not find a woman in place of the religious man, which, as we shall presently see, occurs in no Eastern version of the tale.

[4] The oldest extant *Sanskrit* form; but it was not from the 'Panchatantra' that the Pahlaví translation was made, from which was derived the Arabic 'Kalíla wa Dimna' (see *ante*, pp. 372,).

purchase a pair of cows. I shall sell their calves, and will purchase buf-
faloes; and with the produce of my herd I shall be able to buy horses and
mares. By the sale of their colts I shall realise an immense sum; and with
my money I will build a stately mansion. As I shall then be a man of consequence, some wealthy person will solicit my acceptance of his daughter, with a suitable dower. I shall have a son by her, whom I will call by
my own name Soma Sarmá. When he is able to crawl, I shall take him
with me on my horse, seating him before me. Accordingly, when Soma
Sarmá sees me he will leave his mother's lap, and come creeping along,
and some day or other he will approach the horses too near, when I shall
be very angry, and shall desire his mother to take him away. She will be
busy with her household duties, and will not hear my orders, on which I
shall give her a kick with my foot." Thus saying, he put forth one of his
feet with such violence as to break the jar. The meal accordingly fell to
the ground, where, mingling with the dust and dirt, it was completely
spoiled; and so ended Soma Sarmá's hopes.

In the 'Hitopadesa,' which is commonly considered as an abridgment
of the 'Panchatantra,' although it has some tales not found in the latter, we find other variations (Professor Johnson's translation; Book iv.
fab. 8):

In the city of Devakotta lived a Bráhman, whose name was Deva Sar-
man. At the entrance of the sun into the equinoctial line, he obtained a
dish of flour, which when he had taken, he laid himself down overpowered with heat in a potter's shed filled with pots. And as he held a staff
in his hand to protect the flour, he thus thought within himself: "If by
selling this pot of flour I gain ten cowries, then with those cowries having presently purchased a stock of pots, pans, etc., I will dispose of them
at a profit. With the money thus greatly increased, having repeatedly purchased betel-nuts, cloth, and the like, and having sold them again, and in
this manner carried on traffic, until I have realised a fortune amounting
to a lack of rupís, I will contract four marriages. Among those wives there
will be one young and beautiful, and on her I shall bestow my affection.
Afterwards, when those rival wives, grown jealous, shall be bickering
among themselves, then, being inflamed with anger, I will thrash them
all with a stick"—saying which, he flung his stick, whereby the dish of
flour was dashed in pieces, and many pots were broken. He was consequently seized by the throat and turned out of the shed by the potter, who
came out on hearing the pots broken.

The tale of Alnaschar (properly, En-Nashshár) must be familiar to all readers from our common version of the 'Arabian Nights,' which was derived from Galland's French translation, 'Les Mille et une Nuits':

With a hundred pieces of silver, it will be remembered, he purchased all kinds of articles of glass, and having put his stock in a large tray, he sat upon an elevated place to sell it, leaning his back against a wall. "And as he sat he meditated, and said within himself, 'Verily, my whole stock consisteth of glass. I will sell it for two hundred pieces of silver; and with the two hundred I will buy other glass, which I will sell for four hundred; and thus I will continue buying and selling until I have acquired great wealth. Then with this I will purchase all kinds of merchandise and essences and jewels, and so obtain vast gain. After that I will buy a handsome house, and mamlúks, and horses, and gilded saddles; and I will eat and drink; and I will not leave in the city a single female singer, but I will have her brought to my house that I may hear her songs.' All this he calculated with the tray of glass lying before him." He then proposes to demand as his wife the daughter of the chief vazír, and the marriage is to be a very grand affair. But he will treat his wife with disdain: refuse to take the proffered cup of wine from her hand, albeit she humbly kneels before him in presenting it. Her mother will order her to put the cup to his mouth, but he will shake his hand in her face and spurn her with his foot, and do thus—so saying, he kicked the tray of glass, which fell to the ground, and all that was in it broke—there escaped nothing.[5]

Yet another variant is found in Miss Stokes' 'Indian Fairy Tales'—a charming collection. The Foolish Sachalí is promised four pice to carry a jar of *ghí* for a sepoy. As he goes along he says to himself, "With these four pice I will buy a hen; and I will sell the hen and her eggs, and with the money I get for them I will buy a goat; and then I will sell the goat and her milk and her hide, and buy a cow, and then I will sell her milk. And then I will marry a wife; and then I shall have some children, and they will say to me, 'Father, will you have some rice,' and I will say, "No,

---

[5]Sir Richard F. Burton, in a note to this story (The Barber's Fifth Brother), in his excellent unabridged translation of the 'Book of the Thousand Nights and a Night,' would "distinctly derive it from Æsop's market-woman who kicked over her eggs, whence the Latin proverb, *Ante victoriam canere triumphum:* to sell the skin before you have caught the bear." But it is probable this proverb had a very different origin, like our "don't halloo till you are out of the wood." Moreover, what proof is there that Æsop composed that fable—or any others that are ascribed to him?—Tyrwhitt compares Malvolio, in Shakspeare's 'Twelfth Night,' act ii. scene 5, to Alnaschar.

I won't have any rice.'" At this he shook his head, when down came the jar and was smashed, and the *ghí* was all spilled.

On comparing these different Eastern versions, it is curious to find that the day-dreamer purposes punishing his potential son in the Arabian 'Kalíla wa Dimna,' and his wife in the 'Panchatantra,' 'Hitopadesa,' and the tale of Alnaschar. "It seems a startling case of longevity," remarks Professor Max Müller, "that while languages have changed, while works of art have perished, while empires have risen and vanished again, this simple children's tale should have lived on and maintained its place of honour and its undisputed sway in every schoolroom of the East and every nursery of the West."

Some passages in Lucian's tract of 'The Wishes' present a resemblance to these versions of a day-dream of opulence. For example: Adimittus tells his friends that, having learned that the annual profit earned by a large vessel, then lying in the harbour of Athens, could not be less than twelve Attic talents (over £2000), he thought to himself, "If some god now should put me in possession of this ship, what a happy life I should lead, and how well could I serve my friends; sometimes going to sea myself, and sometimes sending my servants.' I then, with my twelve talents, began at once to build a house in a good situation, bought slaves, fine clothes, horses, and chariots. I then set sail, and was considered the happiest of men by the passengers, dreaded by the sailors, and respected like a little king by every one of them—when, behold! just as I was settling my naval affairs, and looking out at a distance for the haven, whilst my ship moved on with a propitious gale, you came in, and sank all my treasures to the bottom!" This may very possibly be a mere coincidence; but the Indian fictions had already begun their westward travels in the time of Lucian, who was a diligent collector as well as a skilful adapter of current tales, regardless of their origin.

THE FAVOURITE
WHO WAS ENVIED

SCARCELY any story of Eastern origin has attracted more admiration, if we may judge from the number of versions which exist, than that of the favourite of a king whose death was plotted by an envious courtier who fell into his own snare. This is the well-known tale of Fulgentius, in the 98th chapter of the Anglican 'Gesta Romanorum.' Its first appearance in Europe, according to Dunlop, was in the 'Contes Dévots,' under the title of "D'un Roi qui voulut faire brûler le fils de son Seneschal," from which it was adapted in the earliest Italian collection of tales, 'Cento Novelle Antiche,' No. 68, where an envious knight is jealous of the favour a young man enjoys with the king. As a friend, he bids the youth hold back his head while serving this prince, who, he says, was disgusted with his foul breath, and then acquaints his master that the page did so from being offended with his Majesty's breath. The irascible monarch forthwith orders his kilnman to throw the first messenger he sends to him into the furnace, and the young man is accordingly despatched on some pretended errand, but, happily passing near a monastery on his way, tarries for some time to hear mass. Meanwhile the contriver of the fraud, impatient to learn the success of his stratagem, sets out for the house of the kilnman, and arrives before his intended victim. On inquiring if the commands of his master have been fulfilled, he is answered that they will be immediately executed, and, as the first messenger on the part of the king, is forthwith thrown into the furnace.[1]

The story reappears in the 'Liber de Donis' of Etienne de Bourbon,

---

[1] Walter Mapes, one of the most remarkable of the literary men at the court of Henry II. (latter part of the 12th century—he is lost sight of after 1196), has this story in his 'Nugæ Curialium,' which exists in only one manuscript, preserved in the Bodleian Library, and that a very incorrect one. The 'Nugæ Curialium' was printed for the Camden Society, in 1850, edited, with an introduction and notes, by Mr Thomas Wright, the well-known literary antiquary, and the story will be found on pages 124–131 of the work. The 'Contes Dévots' were first composed in Latin, in the 12th century, by Hugues Farsi, a monk of St Jean des Vignes, from which selections were rendered into French verse, by Coinsi, or Comsi, a monk (afterwards prior) of St Médard de Soissons, who died in 1236, including some tales of his own invention or adaptation. It is impossible to say whether Walter de Mapes derived his story from the 'Contes Dévots'; most probably it was orally current in his time—or he may have heard it related by some monkish preacher in the course of a sermon.

13th century; John of Bromyard's 'Summa Prædicantium,' 14th century; and the 'Dialogus Creaturarum' of Nicolaus Pergamenus; and, under the title of "Les deux Pages," it is also found in 'Anecdotes Chrétiennes de l'Abbé Reyre.' Schiller has made it the subject of a fine ballad, 'Der gang nach dem Eisenhammer," which must be generally known to English readers from Mr Bowring's translation, entitled "Fridolin; or the Walk to the Iron Foundry." Schiller's ballad differs in some of its details from other versions: Robert the huntsman, having long cherished in vain a guilty passion for the wife of his master the Count Savern, in revenge falsely accuses the page Fridolin of the very crime which he had himself designed:

> Then two workmen beckons he,
>   And speaks thus in his ire:
> "The first who's hither sent by me,
>   Thus of ye to inquire—
> 'Have ye obeyed my lord's will well?'
> Him cast ye into yonder hell,
>   That into ashes he may fly,
>   And ne'er again torment mine eye."

The catastrophe is identical with that of the Italian version.—Mr J. Payne Collier states, on the authority of M. Boettiger, that Schiller founded his ballad upon an Alsatian tradition which he had heard at Mannheim.

In the Turkish romance of the 'Forty Vazirs' (the Lady's 22d tale), the favourite companion of a king is envied by the other courtiers, one of whom tells the monarch that his favourite said he had leprosy. The envious courtier cooks a Tartar pie strongly seasoned with garlic, and invites the favourite to his house. They eat together, and afterwards go to the king. On their way the favourite is warned by his "friend" not to go near the king, because of his garlic-tainted breath; so he holds his sleeve to his mouth, and stands a little way off. The king, believing this conduct confirmed the report, gives him a letter to take to the chief magistrate, telling him to keep whatever he is offered. The envious man persuades the favourite to give him the letter, for the sake of the present, since he would always be in the king's favour. So he gave him the letter, which ordered the magistrate to seize the bearer, "flay him alive, stuff his skin with grass, and set it upon the road that I may see it there when I pass." When the king recognises the stuffed skin of the envious courtier, he sends for his favourite, who explains why he had held his sleeve to his mouth in his presence.

Through the Ottoman Turks this incident may have reached Northern Africa; at all events, it occurs in the Kabaïl story of the Good Man and the Bad Man (Rivière's French collection), the first part of which is a variant of the German tale of the Three Crows—see vol. i. p. 50. The good man, who had married the king's daughter, feeling unwell one day, his false friend advises him to eat an onion as medicine, but he must take care that the king does not smell his tainted breath. Then the wicked man tells the king that his son-in-law despises him; and when he comes into his presence the king observes that he keeps his face turned away from him. So he gives him a letter to the sultan, and on the way the good man meets his false friend, who offers to do his errand, which he does, and is burnt to death in place of the king's son-in-law.

The story is also found, but in a different form, in the Arabian romance of the 'Seven Vazírs,' but in no other version of the Book of Sindibád:[2]

A sultan adopts a male infant whom he saw exposed on the highway, and when he is grown up appoints him keeper of the royal treasury. It happened one day that Ahmed (such was the foundling's name), having occasion to pass through the chamber of the king's favourite concubine, he discovered her with a male slave, but did not tell of this misconduct to his master. The woman, convinced that she had been seen by Ahmed with her paramour, and that he would not long keep the matter a secret, resolved to anticipate him by complaining to the king that his base-born treasurer had made improper proposals to her. The king told her to conceal the affair, and in an hour he should bring her Ahmed's head. Then sending for one of his slaves, he privately instructed him to go to a certain house and remain there: "When any one shall say to thee, 'Thus saith the sultan, Do that which thou wast commanded to execute,' strike off his head, place it in this basket, and fasten over it the cover. When I shall send to thee a messenger, who will say, 'Hast thou performed the business?' commit to

---

[2]And, so far as I am aware, only in two Arabic texts of the 'Seven Vazírs,' viz., that translated by Dr Jonathan Scott (see vol. i. p. 188, note 16), and that in the imperfect manuscript of the 'Thousand and One Nights' preserved in the British Museum: Rich. MSS. Nos. 7404, 7405, and 7406—the story of the 'Seven Vazírs' is in the third volume.

him the basket." When the slave had retired, the king called to Ahmed, and said, "Hasten to such a house, and say unto such a slave, 'Execute the commands of the sultan.'" On the way Ahmed saw the woman's paramour sitting with some of his fellow-slaves feasting and drinking. The guilty slave, thinking that by detaining Ahmed from the king's business he might procure his death, invited him to join them. Ahmed replied that he had been sent by the king with a message to a certain house, and the slave offered to carry the message in his stead, if he would remain with his companions till he returned. Then Ahmed said, "Be it so, and say to the slave whom thou wilt find there that he must execute the orders of the sultan." When the wicked slave arrived at the house, he said to the person there, "Thus saith the sultan, 'Complete thy orders.'" "Most willingly," he replied, and drawing his sword, struck off his head, and then placing it in the basket, he tied the cover on it, and sat down. Ahmed, having waited some time for the messenger's return, proceeded to the house, and inquired of the man, "Hast thou performed thy orders?" He answered that he had, and committed the basket to him. Ahmed, ignorant of the ghastly contents, took the basket to the sultan, who was greatly astonished to see him, and lifting the lid, discovered the head of the slave. The sultan then inquired into the whole affair, and being convinced of the guilt of his concubine, caused her to be put to death.

Several versions of this widespread story are current in different Indian countries. Mr Vernieux gives two in his collection of Indian tales and anecdotes (Calcutta, 1873). In one of these, a prince who had spent all his wealth resolves to leave his country, with his wife, and before departing he receives from a fakír four maxims: (1) Act according to circumstances; (2) Never forsake ready food; (3) Clothe the naked; (4) Never proceed without premeditation. Coming to a foreign country, he acts upon the first maxim, and takes service as a field-labourer, continuing in that capacity for some months. One day he saw the body of a devotee floating on the river, and drew it to land in order to bury it, as was the custom of the place, when he found a ball of gold entwined in the long knotted hair of the corpse. With part of this wealth he procured better clothes, and then applied to the rájá for employment, who, seeing him to be a person of refinement, kept him about his own person for a time, and finally appointed him prime minister. Now it was the rájá's custom to go out very early in the morning to the river for ablution, and the new prime minister observed that no sooner had he quitted the palace than the queen also went out, but whither he did not know. One morning he saw, by chance, the queen in the apartment of the gate-keeper and entirely nude; and recalling to mind the second maxim of the fakír, he threw his upper garment over her with averted face, and then went away. The faithless queen, dreading the disclosure of her crime, accused the prime minister to the rájá of having attempted her dishonour, showing his garment as evidence. The rájá, full of rage, despatched the minister with a letter to his brother, in which he was desired to put the bearer to death.

As he was about to depart on his fatal errand, his wife suggested that he should take the food prepared for him; and so, acting on the third maxim of the fakír, he postponed his journey till he had breakfasted. Meanwhile the profligate paramour of the queen came in about some business, when the minister informed him of the letter he had to deliver to the king's brother, which the gate-keeper undertook to do, as he was going in that direction. When the brother of the king had read the letter, the bearer was immediately beheaded. The minister arriving soon after this, and learning the fate of the gate-keeper, he thought of the fourth maxim, and related the whole affair to the prince, who, being convinced that it was a clear case of retributive justice, gave him a letter to the king, disclosing the queen's guilt. The king, on reading the letter, banished his wicked queen, and, having resigned the throne in favour of his faithful minister, spent the remainder of his days in pious meditation.

The second version translated by Vernieux relates how a fakír obtained from a pious rájá an allowance of two rupís daily, but, living at a distance, he came only every third or fourth day to receive his money. He had thus enjoyed the rájá's bounty for some time when the rájá's gúrú, or chaplain, becoming envious of the fakír's good fortune, resolved to bring about his destruction. With this object, he said to the fakír one day, after he had received his allowance, "Why do you bring your face so near the king? It is very disrespectful. Next time you come, take care to turn away your face from the king." The gúrú then went to the king and said to him privately, "O Mahárája, you are too easily imposed upon by any rascal who tells you a plausible story of his distress. That fakír who was here to-day is a great drunkard. I saw him go into one of the drinking-houses after leaving here, and spend all the money you gave him. Observe whether he turns his face from you when next he comes to receive your bounty." On hearing this the king felt much grieved to think that he should have bestowed money on such an unworthy person.

When the fakír came again, he spoke to the rájá with his face averted from him, which convinced the rájá that the gúrú's account of his drunken habits was true; and to punish him for his roguery, he gave the fakír a letter to his (the rájá's) brother, ordering the bearer to be soundly scourged. The gúrú, learning that the fakír had received a letter from the king for his brother, and supposing his stratagem to have failed, and that the king designed him still farther favours, said to him, "The rájá has written to his brother to pay you the sum due to you for the last three days; here are the six rupis, give me the letter and I will deliver it myself." The gdru, on taking the letter to the rájá's brother, was treated kindly, received water to wash his hands and feet, got a bath, and then some refreshments. But when he had opened and read the letter, he had no alternative but to execute the rájá's order. So he caused one of the gúrú's cheeks to be marked with *chunan,* and the other with lamp-black, and, with a string of old shoes suspended from his neck, he was paraded through the streets of the city and the market-place, with beat of drum. It happened that while he was thus being made the object of public ridicule the queen saw him and informed the rájá of the treatment to which his gúrú was subjected. The gúrú and the fakír were both brought to the palace, and the facts of the case being ascertained, the rájá dismissed the gúrú from his service, and appointed the fakír a residence in the royal garden.

In a Bengalí folk-tale, entitled "The Minister and the Fool," translated by Damant in vol. iii. of the 'Indian Antiquary,' the rájá, having heard three birds conversing, desired his prime minister to interpret to him what they had said to each other. A young man in the minister's service, who was thought to be little better than crazy, knowing the language of birds, gave his master the required information, which he at once communicated to the rájá. Afraid lest it should transpire that the fool had solved the question for him, the minister determined to have him put to death, and accordingly gave him a letter to the executioner. In passing through the garden, on the way to deliver his own death-warrant, he encountered the minister's son, who desired him to pick a nosegay of flowers for him, which he promised to do after he had delivered his letter; but the minister's son would brook no such delay, and told the fool to remain and pick the flowers, while he himself delivered the missive. The fool, therefore, remained in safety, while the minister's son was put to death in his stead.

⤫

To the same effect is the story of Phalabhúti in the 'Kathá Sarit Ságara' (Tawney's translation, vol. i. pp. 162, 163). A king is persuaded by his wife, in order that he should acquire magic power, to consent to practise the horrid rite of eating human flesh, and the story goes on thus: Having made him enter the circle, previously consecrated, she said to the king, after he had taken an oath, "I attempted to draw hither, as a victim, that Bráhman named Phalabhúti, who is so intimate with you; but the drawing him hither is a difficult task; so it is the best way to initiate some cook in our rites, that he may himself slay and cook him. And you must not feel any compunction about it, because by eating a sacrificial offering of his flesh, after the ceremonies are complete, the enchantment will be perfect, for he is a Bráhman of the highest caste." When his beloved said this to him, the king, though afraid of the sin, consented—alas! terrible is compliance with women! Then that royal couple had the cook summoned, and after encouraging him and initiating him, they both said to him, "Whoever comes to you to-morrow morning and says, 'The king and queen will eat together to-day, so get some flesh ready quickly,' him you must slay, and make for us secretly a savoury dish of his flesh." The cook consented, and went to his own house.

Next morning, when Phalabhúti arrived, the king said to him, "Go and tell the cook in the kitchen, 'The king, together with the queen, will eat to-day a savoury mess, therefore prepare as soon as possible a splendid dish.'" Phalabhúti said, "I will do so," and went out. When he was outside, the king's son, whose name was Chandraprabhá, came to him and said, "Have made for me this very day, with this gold, a pair of earrings like those you had made before for my noble father." Phalabhúti, in order to please the prince, immediately proceeded, as he was ordered, to get the earrings made, and the prince went readily with the king's message, which Phalabhúti told him, alone to the kitchen; and when he delivered the king's message, the cook, true to his agreement, at once put him to death with a knife, and made a dish of his flesh, which the king and queen ate, after performing the ceremonies, not knowing the truth. After spending the night in remorse, the king saw Phalabhúti arrive with the ear rings in his hand. So, being bewildered, he questioned him about the earrings immediately; and when Phalabhúti had told him his story, the king fell on the earth and cried out, "Alas, my son!" blaming the queen and himself; and when the ministers questioned him, he told them the whole story, and repeated what Phalabhúti had said every day, "The doer of good will obtain good, and the doer of evil, evil."

Though the details are more or less varied in each of these versions, yet the catastrophe is identical in them all, except the two last: he who plotted the death of an innocent man falls into his own snare; or the innocent is saved from death by the cupidity of the guilty, who justly suffers in his stead. The story, we have seen, was known in Europe in the 12th century, or three hundred years before the Turkish romance of the 'Forty Vazírs' was composed; yet it is curious to find that in the Ottoman version, as in the 'Contes Dévots,' the 'Gesta,' and the 'Novelle Antiche,' the envious man pretends to the king that his favourite says he has a foul breath: in the second Indian version from Vernieux the envious gúrú tells the king that the fakír turns his face away in order that his majesty should not discover from his breath that he is a drunkard. On the other hand, Schiller's "Fridolin," in which the huntsman falsely accuses the page of criminal intimacy with the countess, seems a reflection of the Arabian story, where the king's favourite damsel accuses Ahmed of having attempted her chastity—an incident which finds a parallel in the first of the Indian versions from Vernieux' collection. The Turkish and second Indian versions agree in the incident of the envious man falling a victim to his own cupidity by undertaking to deliver the letter, in hopes of obtaining a present; and doubtless the lady's paramour in the first Indian version was actuated by a similar motive. The catastrophe of the Bengalí version resembles that of the story of Phalabhúti, which is probably of Buddhist extraction.

❧ THE MILLER'S SON; OR, DESTINY ❧

IT would be a hard task to find among the folk-tales of any country one more pleasing than that of "Rich Peter the Pedlar," in Dasent's 'Popular Tales from the Norse,' a story which, besides being admirably suited to the minds of the young, illustrates a peculiar article of ancient popular belief—that it is vain to attempt to oppose the decrees of destiny, as they are foretold by the aspect of the heavenly bodies:

Rich Peter the Pedlar hears from the "star-gazers" that the miller's son is to marry his daughter. In order to prevent such a disgrace, he buys the lad from his parents, puts him in a box, and throws it into the river. But the boy is found and adopted by a miller who lives lower down the river. Peter discovers this by the skill of the "star-gazers," and procures the youth as his apprentice by giving the second miller 600 dollars. "Then the two travelled about far and wide with their packs and wares till they came to an inn, which lay by the edge of a great wood. From this the pedlar sent the lad home with a letter to his wife, for the way was not so long if you take the short cut across the wood, and told him to tell her she was to be sure to do what was written in the letter as quickly as she could. But it was written in the letter that she was to have a great pile made then and there, fire it, and cast the miller's son into it. If she didn't do that, he'd burn her alive when he came back. So the lad set off with the letter across the wood, and when evening came on, he reached a house far, far away in the wood, into which he went; but inside he found no one. In one of the rooms was a bed ready made, so he flung himself across it, and fell asleep. The letter he had stuck into his hat-band, and the hat he pulled over his face. So when the robbers came back—for in that house twelve robbers had their abode—and saw the lad lying on the bed, they began to wonder who he could be, and one of them took the letter and broke it open and read it. 'Ho! ho!' said he, 'this comes from Peter the Pedlar, does it? Now will we play him a trick. It would be a pity if the old niggard made an end of such a pretty lad.' So the robbers wrote another letter to Peter the Pedlar's wife, and fastened it under his hat-band while he slept; and in that they wrote that as soon as ever she got it she was to make a wedding for her daughter and the miller's son, and give them horses and cattle and household stuff, and set them up for themselves in the farm which he had under the hill, and if he didn't find all this done when he came back she should smart for it. Next day the robbers let the lad go; and when he came home and delivered the letter, he said he was to greet her kindly from Peter the Pedlar, and to say that she was to carry out what was written in the letter as soon as ever she could." This was accordingly done, to the great chagrin of Peter the Pedlar.[1]

The 20th chapter of Swan's 'Gesta Romanorum' presents a striking analogy to the Norse tale: A king, belated while hunting, takes shelter for the night in the hut of a disgraced courtier, whom he does not recognise. During the night the courtier's wife gives birth to a fine boy, upon which the king hears a voice telling him that the child just born should be his son-in-law. In the morning the king orders his squires to take the infant from his mother and destroy it; but, moved to compassion, they place it upon the branches of a tree, to secure it from wild beasts, and then kill a hare, and convey its heart, as that of the infant, to the king. A duke, passing through the forest, hears the cries of the child, and discovering it, wraps it in the folds of his cloak, and takes it to his wife to bring up. In course of time, when the child is grown a handsome youth, the king suspects him to be the same who was predicted to be his son-in-law, and despatches him with a letter to the queen, commanding her to put the bearer to death. On his way he goes into a chapel, and there having fallen asleep, a priest, seeing the letter suspended from his girdle, has the curiosity to open it; and after learning the intended wickedness, he alters its purport thus: "Give the youth our daughter in marriage"; which the queen does accordingly.

But the thirteenth of M. Dozon's Albanian Tales comprises the principal incidents which occur in our series of stories of 'The Favourite who was Envied' and in the foregoing: A couple who had long been childless had at length a son born to them; and on the third night after, three women came to declare his destiny. It so happened that a pasha had that night taken refuge in the cottage from a fearful storm, and lay in a corner, but awake, for he had thousands in money with him; and he overheard the first woman declare, "The child will be short-lived, and die soon"; the second woman said, "The child will live for years, and then perish by the hand of his father"; and the third woman predicted, "This child will live

[1] See also Thorpe's 'Yule-Tide Stories,' p. 315 of Bohn's edition.

to kill this pasha, deprive him of his authority, and marry his daughter."
Next day the terrified pasha persuaded the parents to give him the child
for 9000 piastres. In journeying he threw the child and cradle into a river,
and they were stranded lower down. Hearing the child's cries, one of a
flock of goats, which were brought down to drink, went and suckled the
child, and the same occurring next day while the goatherd was watching,
he took the infant home. He soon found out to whom it belonged, and
gave it to the old man, to be returned to him when it grew up. The boy
showed great intelligence, and was sent to the man who had rescued him.
The pasha came to the village, and, lodging in the goatherd's house, took
a fancy to the boy, but was terrified on learning his history. He sends the
boy to his wife with a letter, ordering his death, which was to be
announced to him by a volley of cannon. On the way the youth becoming
tired, goes to a spring, drinks, and falls asleep. A negro comes, takes the
letter and reads it, then writes another, requiring the pasha's wife to receive
the youth with all honour, provide a feast, and marry him to their daughter, announcing the completion by a volley of cannon; and substitutes this
for the pasha's letter. The youth delivers the forged letter, and all comes off
as it directed. When the pasha returns and finds how matters stand, he
once more determines to have the youth put to death. He sends for a
blacksmith, and tells him that a youth whom he will send to him next day
he is to kill with his big hammer, and to send him his head in a handkerchief. On the following day the youth, having been requested by the pasha
to go to the smith's shop, was about to rise at an early hour, but his wife
persuaded him to rest a little longer. By-and-by the pasha sent his own son
to see whether his son-in-law had started on his fatal errand, who, finding him still at home, went himself, and was killed by the smith, his head
being sent to the pasha by his son-in-law when he arrived and learned the
fate that he had so narrowly escaped. Next day the pasha orders his groom
to take a spiked-club, allow the horses to fight in the stable, and when his
son-in-law comes out to separate them, to kill him on the spot. When
night comes the pasha calls to his son-in-law to go and quell the disturbance in the stable, but his wife detains him, and soon the horses become
quiet. Thinking his son-in-law now dead, the pasha goes out to see, and
is killed by the groom with his club. The son-in-law becomes pasha, and
thus is the prophecy of the third woman fulfilled.

M. Dozon, in his "rapprochements," gives the opening of a similar tale
in Hahn's modern Greek stories: A rich man had no children. It was

foretold that the youngest son of a poor man would spend his fortune. He finds the man, and offers to buy his son, is refused, but allowed to adopt him. He throws the child from a bridge into the river; a shepherd finds him on the sands, and so on. The negro is replaced by a priest. The boy grows up, and encounters only one danger, when the merchant is killed instead of himself, by a shot from a vineyard guard, who had been ordered to shoot one who should come to eat raisins.[2]

A very close Indian parallel to the Norse tale of Peter the Pedlar is found in the 'Kathá Kosa,' a Jaina collection, the conclusion of which, like that of the Albanian variant, is similar to the catastrophe of the "Favourite who was envied":

There was formerly, in the town of Rájagriha, a merchant named Ságarapota, who was told by an astrologer that a young beggar named Damannaka—he was, however, the son of a merchant who had died of the plague—would inherit all his property. He made over the youth to a Chandála (outcast) to be killed. But the Chandála, instead of killing him, cut off his little finger; and Damannaka, having thus escaped death, was adopted by the merchant's cowherd. In course of time the merchant recognised the youth, and, to ensure his being put out of the way, he sent him with a letter to his son Samudradatta. But when he reached the outskirts of the town of Rájagriha he felt fatigued, and fell asleep in the temple. Meanwhile the daughter of the merchant came to that temple to worship the divinity. "She beheld Damannaka with the large eyes and the broad chest." Her father's handwriting then caught her eye, and she proceeded to read the letter, in which was the following distich:

> "Before this man has washed his feet, do thou with speed
> Give him poison [*visham*], and free my heart from anxiety."

The damsel concluded that she herself (Visha) was to be given to the handsome youth, and that her father in his hurry had made a slight mistake in orthography. She therefore made the necessary correction and

[2]Hahn cites another parallel from Grimm, in which the prophecy threatens a king.—This inevitable destiny recalls the story of the Second Calender, in the 'Arabian Nights'; the story of the Second Dervish, in the Persian romance of the Four Dervishes ('Kissá-i Chehar Darwesh'); the "Fulfilled Prophecy," in Ralston's translation of 'Tibetan Tales from Indian Sources'; the Netherlandish legend of Julian the Ferryman, in Thorpe's 'Northern Mythology'; and the story of the King and his Son, in the Persian romance, 'Bakhtyár Náma.'

replaced the letter. The merchant's son carries out his father's order—"as amended"—and Ságarapota returns home to find Damannaka married to his daughter Visha. The implacable merchant once more attempts the life of the young man. Knowing that the bride and bridegroom must perform the customary worship at the temple, he despatched a man to lie in wait for him there. But his own son met them and insisted upon performing the worship in their stead. "Having taken the articles for offering, he went off, and as he was entering the temple of the goddess he was slain by Khadjala, who had gone there before." Thus was the proud merchant justly punished for his impious efforts to thwart the decrees of Heaven.

Sending a person with a letter containing his own death-warrant is a very common incident in popular tales. The letter which David king of Israel gave to Uriah to deliver to Joab is the prototype of that carried by Bellerophon in the classical legend. An instance in ancient Arabian tradition is found in the story of the letters which Tarafa and Mutalammis, two celebrated pre-Islamite poets, received from the king of Híra, whom they had offended by their lampoons, addressed to the governor of Bahrayn, commanding him to put the bearers to death. It seems neither of the poets could read, since we are told that Mutalammis, suspecting the design of the king, broke open his letter and showed it to a friend, who read it to him, and on learning the fatal contents, Mutalammis destroyed it and advised his companion to turn back with him. But Tarafa, perhaps thinking that his friend had been deceived by the reader of the letter, declined his advice and continued his journey. On delivering his letter, the governor of Bahrayn, carrying out the order of the king, cut off Tarafa's hands and feet, and then caused him to be buried alive.

ॐ "LUCKILY, THEY ARE NOT PEACHES" ॐ

MANY proverbs and sayings, it is well known, are derived from popular tales and apologues, although the latter may not be themselves "original." Thus we have seen that the saying "Don't count your chickens until they are hatched" originated in the tale of the Maid and the Pot of Milk, which is of Indian extraction. The Arabian saying, "The Boots of Hunayn," when a person has lost more than he has gained by a transaction, had its origin in a tale (see *ante*, p. 294) which has its parallels in Europe and in India.

Isaac D'Israeli, in a paper on the Philosophy of Proverbs, gives the following story as being the origin of the Italian popular saying, "Luckily, they are not peaches," employed in reference to any person who has received a beating quietly:

The community of Castle Poggibonsi, probably from some jocular tenure observed on St Bernard's Day, pay a tribute of peaches to the court of Tuscany, which are usually shared among the ladies-in-waiting and the pages of the court. It happened one season, in a great scarcity of peaches, that the good people of Poggibonsi, finding them rather dear, sent, instead of the customary tribute, a quantity of fine juicy figs, which were so much disapproved of by the pages that as soon as they got hold of them they began in a rage to empty the baskets on the heads of the ambassadors of the Poggibonsi, who, attempting to fly as well as they could from the pulpy shower, half-blinded, and recollecting that peaches would have had stones in them, cried out, "Luckily, they are not peaches!"[1]

Whether there ever was such a "tribute" paid to the court of Tuscany (and it is, to say the least, very doubtful), the story is evidently, like that of the Pot of Milk, a mere localised variant of an Asiatic tale. As an example of the folly of following a woman's advice—a favourite subject of Oriental jests—it is related in the Turkish collection of blunders and jokes ascribed to the Khoja Nasr-ed-Dín Efendi, that the citizens of Yenisheher (where the Khoja lived) prepared to defend their city when

---

[1] 'Curiosities of Literature,' second series, ed. 1823, vol. i. pp. 461, 462.

they heard that Tímúr (Tamerlane) was coming against it. The Khoja earnestly dissuaded them, and offered to go himself as ambassador to the emperor. As he was about to leave his house, he had some doubts regarding the kind of present best calculated to appease Tímúr and render him benevolent towards both himself and his fellow-citizens.[2] At last he resolved on fruit; but reflecting that advice is good in times of difficulty, he went to his wife and asked her, "What should be more grateful to Tímúr—figs or quinces?" She replied, "Oh, quinces, of course; being more beautiful as well as larger, they are, in my opinion, more likely to prove acceptable." But the Khoja thought within himself, "However good advice may be in general, a woman's advice is never good,[3] and therefore I will present figs, not quinces." So, having gathered a quantity of figs in a basket, he hastened to Tímúr. When the emperor was apprised of the Khoja's arrival at his camp, he ordered him to be brought before him bareheaded, and his figs to be thrown at his bald pate. The servants obeyed the order with great alacrity, and the Khoja, at every blow he received, exclaimed very composedly, "Praised be Allah!" On the emperor demanding to know the reason of this exclamation, the Khoja replied, "I thank Allah that I followed not my wife's advice; for had I, as she counselled me, brought quinces instead of figs, my head must have been broken."

The same incident forms the second part of the rabbinical tale of the Emperor and the Old Man, as related in the Talmud:

The emperor Hadrian, passing through the streets of Tiberias one day, observed a very aged man planting a fig-tree, and thus addressed him, "Why are you thus engaged? If you had laboured in your youth, you should now have had ample store for your old age; and surely you cannot hope to eat of the fruit of that tree?" "In my youth I laboured," replied the old man, "and I still labour. With God's pleasure, I may even partake of the fruit of this tree which I plant: I am in His hands." "What is thine age?" asked the emperor. "I have lived a hundred years." "A hundred years old, and yet expect to eat of the fruit of this tree!" exclaimed Hadrian. "If

---

[2] All great men in the East expect a present from a visitor, and look upon themselves as affronted, and even defrauded, when the compliment is omitted. See 1 Samuel ix. 7 and Isaiah lvii. 9.

[3] "Bear in mind," says Thorkel to Bork, in the Icelandic saga of Gisli the Outlaw—"bear in mind that a woman's counsel is always unlucky."—And see vol. i. pp. 65–66 for the Muslim estimate of women's advice.

such be God's good pleasure," answered the old man; "if not, I will leave it for my son, as my father left the fruit of his labour for me." "Well," said the emperor, "if thou dost live until the figs of this tree are ripe, I pray thee let me know of it." The aged man actually lived to partake of the fruit, and, remembering the emperor's words, he resolved to visit him. So, taking a small basket, he filled it with the choicest figs from the tree, and proceeded on his errand. Telling the palace-guard his purpose, he was admitted into the presence of the emperor. "Well," said Hadrian, "what is thy wish?" "I am the old man to whom thou didst say on the day thou sawest him planting a fig-tree, 'If thou live to eat of the fruit, let me know;' and behold, I have brought thee of the fruit, that thou mayest also partake of it." The emperor was greatly pleased, and, emptying the basket of the figs, he ordered it to be filled with gold coins. When the old man had departed with his treasure, the courtiers asked Hadrian why he had thus signally honoured the old Hebrew. "The Lord has honoured him," answered he; "and why should not I?" Now, next door to this old man there lived an envious and foolish woman, who, when she heard of her neighbour's good fortune, desired her husband to try his luck in the same quarter. She filled for him an immense basket with figs, and, bidding him put it on his shoulder, said, "Carry this to the emperor; he loves figs, and will fill thy basket with gold coins." When her husband reached the gates of the palace, he told his errand to the guard, saying, "I have brought these figs for the emperor; empty my basket, I pray, and fill it up again with gold." On this being told to the emperor, he ordered the man to be placed in the balcony of the palace, and all who passed pelted him with figs. Returning home crestfallen, his wife eagerly asked him what good luck he had. "Have patience, wretched woman," he replied, "have patience, and I will tell thee. I have had both *great* and *good* luck: my great luck was that I took the emperor figs instead of peaches, else I should have been stoned to death; and my good luck was that the figs were ripe, for had they been unripe, I must have left my brains behind me."[4]

It is not at all likely, I think, that the Ottomans derived the story ascribed to their typical noodle, Nasr-ed-Dín, from a Jewish source. But the Italian version may have come through the Ottomans. The incident of the old man and the emperor is of common occurrence in Asiatic

---

[4] 'Hebrew Tales,' etc. By Hyman Hurwitz, London: 1826. Pp. 5–100.

story-books, and the sequel is also a separate popular jest in the East: the two seem to have been fused into one story by the talmudist.

Here, for the present, end my examples of the migrations and transformations of popular tales and fictions—not that materials have "run short," for they are practically inexhaustible. Many other interesting features of folk-lore—many other popular stories—have I carefully traced through different countries, and the results may assume form at no very distant date, though probably not *book*-form in the first instance. Meanwhile perhaps my good friend—the friend of all authors—the "intelligent reader" will condescend to "ponder and inwardly digest" what is set down in these two volumes. For my own part, I can truly say, modifying the words of Spenser—

> The ways through which my wearie steps I guyde,
>   In this researche of olde antiquitie,
> Are so exceeding spacious and wyde,
>   And sprinckled with such sweet variety
>   Of all which pleasant is to eare or eye,
> That I, nigh ravisht with rare thoughts delight,
>   My tedious travail doe forget thereby.

⁓ APPENDIX ⁓

I.

"ASS OR PIG?"—*p. 286*

THIS Roman popular story, together with the Norse variant, "This is the Lad who sold the Pig" (p. 286, note 8), finds a modern Egyptian analogue in J. A. St John's 'Tales of the Ramad'han,' vol. iii. pp. 33–47:—

A youth in the city of Cairo, named Mansúr, having captured two nightingales and placed them in a wicker cage, which he suspended outside of the window, their sweet warbling one day attracted the attention of an officer of the khalíf's guard, who offered two or three dirhams for them, and on being told that the birds were not for sale, rose gradually in his offer to two gold dínars, for which the lad consented to part with them. "Take the cage," said the officer, "and follow me; I am now going home, and will be your guide." On arriving at his house the officer knocked at the door, and, taking the cage from Mansúr, stepped in, bidding him tarry a moment for the money. He waited a long time, and at last knocked, upon which a soldier came out and demanded his business. The youth told him that he had sold the officer two nightingales and waited for payment. "You had better be contented with your loss," said the soldier, "and make the best of your way home, for you may otherwise deliver up the camel to him who has stolen the saddle."—"What is your master's name?" asked Mansúr. "Abú Sefí," replied the soldier; "but he is more commonly known by the appellation of Ibn Shaytan" [the Son of the Devil]. "Well," said Mansúr, "were he the Devil's father, he should pay me for my birds. Tell him this from me; but add, at the same time, that I am willing to take them back if he does not consider them worth what he offered me."—"Be advised, friend," answered the soldier, "and push this business no farther. It is better to lose ten ardebs of dhourra than set fire to the granary. You know not Ibn Shaytan: he is dreaded throughout Cairo as a blood-drinker, whom no man can offend with impunity. There is, in fact, not a merchant in the bazár who would not prefer taking a lion by the mane to beholding the moustachios of Ibn Shaytan stiffening, like a cat's tail, with indignation against him."—"Yet," said Mansúr, "I am determined to have my birds, or the price agreed upon between us. Tell him this, and I will remain here in the meantime." Surprised at the lad's resolute air, the soldier proceeded towards the apartment of his master, followed by Mansúr, who had slipped into the house unperceived.

On hearing the importunate demands of the youth, Ibn Shaytan grew angry, or pretended to be so, and in a harsh, intimidating manner exclaimed, "Where is the impertinent fellow? Bring him hither that I may chastise him."—"Here I am, bimbashi," said Mansúr, springing out from behind the soldier, who started at the sharp sound of his voice—"here I am, to receive two gold dínars for the nightingales you purchased of me about an hour ago." For a moment Ibn Shaytan himself was disconcerted by the youth's intrepidity, but recovering his self-possession, told him that he chose to owe him nothing, and if he did not be off, the soles of his feet should be quickly made acquainted with the bastinado. The youth, seeing there was no remedy, left the house, resolved to revenge the injury he had suffered.

Near the residence of the officer there was a deep well, to which the young women of the neighbourhood daily resorted to draw water. Disguising himself as a girl, Mansúr proceeded one day with a neat wooden vessel in his hand towards this well, and waiting patiently until Ibn Shaytan appeared, purposely dropped his vessel into the water, and then wringing his hands, and affecting extreme grief, as if he had suffered a great loss, attracted the notice of his enemy, who, being an unprincipled man, came up and offered his services, in the hope of deriving some advantage from the gratitude of the supposed young woman. "Ah," exclaimed Mansúr, in a soft feminine voice, "I am undone! Having lost an antique carved vessel in the well, I shall be scourged to death." The officer pretended to compassionate the young slave, and then leaned over the parapet, bent down his head, and hung so nicely balanced that the slightest touch would have sufficed to precipitate him into the well. Drawing near on tiptoe, Mansúr caught him by the feet, and bidding him remember the widow's son whom he bad so cruelly wronged, hurled him down headlong, and immediately making his escape, removed with his mother to another quarter of the city. Contrary to all probability, Ibn Shaytan, though much bruised and lacerated, was not killed by the fall; and, the water being shallow, likewise escaped drowning. After long shouting in vain, he at length heard the voices of women above, and his heart began to entertain hopes of effecting his escape; so mustering all his strength, he vociferated as loud as he could, and entreated them to draw him up. Hearing an indistinct and broken murmur arising out of the bowels of the earth, the women started back with terror, imagining they had arrived by mistake at the mouth of Jehennam, and that the father of devils, with a legion at his back, would presently be amongst them. Observing, however, that the voice, to whatever it might belong, still continued at a respectful depth, one of the women, more adventurous than the rest, plucking up her courage and approaching the well, inquired, in the name of Allah, whether it was Shaytan or the son of Shaytan who made so fearful a clamour below. Abú Sefí, supposing she alluded to the *sobriquet* he had acquired, and not caring by what name they called him, provided he could effect his escape, replied that he was Ibn Shaytan [the Devil's son], begging, at the same time, that they would lower the bucket and draw him up. "God forbid!" exclaimed the woman; "we have devils enough on earth already. If the Prophet, therefore, hath condemned thee to cool thyself in this situation, remain where thou art until the day of judgment. The water, however, can be none of the most savoury where so foul an imp is confined; and for this reason we must warn our neighbours no more to draw from this well—curses light on thee!" It was in vain that the officer, perceiving the blunder he had committed, sought to convince her that he had not the honour of belonging to the family of Iblís, and was a simple officer of the khalíf's guards. The only answer he obtained was a large stone, which, being thrown at random, fortunately missed him; after which all the women took to their heels, looking back apprehensively over their shoulders to see whether the fiend was following them. The news of Ibn Shaytan's being in the well quickly spread; and at length some Arabs, more acute than the rest, proceeded to investigate the mystery, on the clearing up of which Abú Sefí was released from his uncomfortable situation, and carried home more dead than alive.

Mansúr, who thought he had killed him outright, was greatly vexed on learning of his escape, and at once began to cast about him for some means of completing the work he had commenced; being convinced that should Ibn Shaytan recover, he would leave no stone unturned to avenge himself on his youthful enemy. For the present, however, there was little danger. The officer, though attended by many doctors, lay groaning on his couch, suffering the most excruciating pains, and unable to enjoy a moment's sleep night or day. Nevertheless, instead of regarding the present affliction as the just chastisement of Heaven and learning mercy from the lessons of calamity, he only grew more implacable; his sole consolation being derived from the projects of revenge which his imagination was employed in devising. One morning, as he lay awake on his couch anticipating the satisfaction he should derive from hanging Mansúr upon his mother's door-post, a soldier entered the apartment to inform him that a remarkable little hunchbacked physician, with a long white beard, was at that moment passing by, inviting all persons who were suffering from any disorder to have recourse to his art, and he would heal them. Persons in Ibn Shaytan's situation are always open to delusion. Conceiving a sudden confidence in the unknown doctor, chiefly on account of the deformity of his person—as if Heaven must necessarily disguise wisdom and genius in an uncouth exterior— he ordered him to be called in, and, even before he appeared, began to amuse himself with hopes of the most flattering kind. Presently the physician, preceded by the soldier, entered, and, drawing near the patient's bed, inquired in a cheerful voice the nature of his case. Ibn Shaytan related what had befallen him, dwelling particularly on the frightful dreams which disturbed the short imperfect slumbers procured by *datura;* at which the doctor smiled, and when he had made an end replied, that if he would place himself entirely under his care, and take without reluctance whatever medicines he should prescribe, he might reasonably expect a speedy recovery. Greatly rejoiced at these consolatory expressions, Ibn Shaytan promised to do whatever was enjoined him; and so complete was the confidence inspired by the hunchbacked doctor, that even before any medicines had been administered, much of the cure appeared to be already effected.

Having thus enlisted the imagination of the patient on his side, the doctor despatched his attendants in different directions for various medicines; and when they were all out of doors, approaching the bed with flashing eyes, he said, "Ibn Shaytan, I have with me two potions, both very bitter, but productive of very different effects. Thou sayest that Mansúr, the son of Esmé, is thine enemy, and even now, while on the brink of the grave, the rancour of revenge curdles round thy heart. Know, however, that the unforgiving are abandoned by Allah, and that, while their souls are thus diseased, no mortal mixture can heal their bodies. Forgive, therefore, and it shall be well with thee. Say thou wilt not prosecute thy feud with the young man, and I will answer for thy recovery. The first potion I offer thee is Repentance. Wilt thou drink it?"—"Nay, hakim," replied the patient, alarmed at the manner of the old man, but resolved not to listen to his advice—"nay, presume not beyond thy art. I will never forgive him, by Allah! or cease to pursue my just revenge until both he and the beldam who bore him shall be trampled beneath my feet. Indeed, it is chiefly this consideration that renders me desirous of life."—"Slave! dog! infidel!" exclaimed Mansúr, tearing off his disguise, and seizing him by the throat—"hadst thou been capable of mercy, I would have spared thee; but since thy savage revenge meditates not only my destruction, but also that of my parent, who never injured thee or thine, take the second potion I have provided for thee!" So saying, he smote him with a dagger in the breast, and, having slain him, made his escape from the house.

II.

THE TALE OF BERYN (*p. 325*)

Mr Thomas Wright, in a note to this poem, which he reprints from Urry's Chaucer in his edition of the Canterbury Tales published for the Percy Society,

says: "From the manner in which the Seven Sages are introduced at the beginning of the Tale of Beryn, it is evident there must have been some version of that
romance [the 'Seven Sages'] in Europe differing from the usual one, which does
not contain this story." (Vol. xxvi. p. 243, of the Society's publications, vol. iii. of
the Canterbury Tales.) I do not think such a conjecture—Wright even considers
it an "evident" fact—has much foundation. The Tale begins by stating that once
upon a time the city of Rome was the most honoured in the world; but, like all
other cities, it has gone down, for all things get worse, and man's life grows
short. So Rome has lost its honour. After Romulus, Julius Caesar ruled Rome [a
long time after!], and subdued all lands. After him the Douzepairs held sway.
Then came Constantine; then his son Philippus Augustinus:

> In whose tyme sikerlich[1] the vii. sagis were
> In Rome dwelling dassently; and if ye lust to lere.[2]
> How they were y-clepid,[3] or I ferther goon,
> I woll tell you the names of hem every choon.[4]

After the names and qualities of the Seven Sages of Rome (the two last, Scipio
and Cicero, being skilful astrologers) follow these lines:

> But now to othir purpose: for here I woll departe
> As lightly as I can, and draw to my matere;

and then the author proceeds to relate that during the time of those seven sages
there dwelt in the suburbs of Rome a rich senator, "Faunus was his name," and
so on.

Now the Seven Sages figure but once in the subsequent narrative, namely,
after Faunus has lost his wife and is plunged in grief, the emperor consults with
them and the senators how he might console Faunus. Wright seems to have
overlooked (for he could hardly be ignorant of) the fact that this Tale of Beryn
is taken from the first part of the old French romance 'L'Histoire du Chevalier
Berinus;' the second part of which, as I have before mentioned—p. 340, note 3,
of the present volume—recounts the adventures of his son Aigres; and the third
part the robbery, by Berinus, of Philip's treasury; and in this last part the Seven
Sages appear but once again—see p. 341—when they are consulted about the

[1]Surely, certainly.
[2]If you please to learn.
[3]Named, called.
[4]Every one of them.

barons being all similarly marked. There is not the faintest indication either in the old English Tale of Beryn or in the French romance from which it was taken that the Seven Sages related stories to the emperor, which they do, and nothing else, in the romance of the Seven Sages, or Wise Masters. The fact is, in medieval romances kings and emperors are often represented as having seven counsellors—a notion borrowed, doubtless, from the story-book which was then so popular throughout Europe. Moreover, the 'Historia Septem Sapientum Romæ' itself has two stories, in each of which seven sages figure prominently: in one they are evil-minded men, who by their magical arts render the king blind whenever he goes out of the palace, in order that they might increase their own wealth by defrauding him and the people; in the other, Rome being besieged by three Saracen knights, its defence is undertaken by seven wise men, one of whom, by a device with a mirror, causes the Saracens to decamp in mortal terror. The circumstance that a story like that of Beryn's adventures in Falsetown is found in the Greek, Hebrew, and other Eastern versions of the Book of Sindibád, and that the Robbery of the Treasury occurs in all the versions of the 'Seven Wise Masters,' goes for nothing: both are not found in either of the two groups.

III.

ROBBERY OF THE KING'S TREASURY (p. 335)

A very curious modern Egyptian adaptation of this world-wide story is found in J. A. St John's 'Tales of the Ramad'han,' vol. iii. p. 67 ff., in which, "amidst all the multiplications of masquerade," we can still discern the fundamental outline of the original:

Mansúr having slain the vindictive and unprincipled officer of the khalíf's guards, rather for the preservation of his own life than in revenge, as related *ante*, p. 546, and foreseeing the danger he stood in, placed his mother in an obscure but safe retreat, and leaving in her hands nearly all the money he possessed, took refuge among the *harami*, or robbers, a formidable body of men who inhabited a particular quarter of Cairo, and under command of a shaykh elected by themselves, maintained a species of independence, often setting the government at defiance, and spreading terror through the whole community. He was heartily received by the chief of the robbers, and next day commissioned to set out with a band of fifty picked men to waylay the guards escorting the camels coming to the city laden with revenue from the provinces. A dozen of the more youthful of the band, whose beards were not yet grown, disguised their persons as almé; two, putting on a ragged brown blanket, provided themselves with a pipe and drum, like the Dancing Dervishes; while the remainder, armed at all points, took their station in the hollows of the rocks commanding the entrance to the ravine through which the camel-train must pass. About two hours after sunset Mansúr was informed by his scouts that their expected booty was approaching. Upon this a large fire was kindled near the tents, and the piper and drummer, blowing and thumping with all their might, set the twelve almé in motion. Still more surely to reach the ears of the Bedouins, they all began to sing; and so agreeably did they acquit themselves in their new calling and so musical were their voices, that even their own companions, forgetting the purpose of their merriment, listened with pleasure to the songs. The snare was not set in vain, for as soon as the Arabs arrived opposite the mouth of the ravine, and saw the red reflection of the fire gleaming upon the rocks, they gave orders to halt, resolving to enjoy themselves at the expense of the strangers. Fatigued with their long marches across the desert, they, moreover, heard with delight the sound of the pipe and drum, and the intermingling voices of the singers; little suspecting that those notes might be the prelude to their own death-shriek, and scatter mourning over the land of their forefathers.

Immediately the camels, kneeling under their light burdens, which are never taken off on such occasions, were ranged in a circle, and the horses, in their saddles and bridles, picketed round them on the sand; and while a part of the escort performed these duties, the others, impatient for pleasure, hastened up the valley, directed by the fire and merriment of the robbers. They were received with extraordinary glee by the almé, who laughed, clapped their hands, sang, and danced for their amusement; but, to avoid exciting suspicion, they pretended to be too poor to entertain so great a number of people. It was therefore agreed that the Bedouins should provide the entertainment; and being so near Cairo, in their own deserts, where they considered all danger at an end, they brought two or three of their sumpter camels up the valley with their utensils and provisions, in order to enjoy the performances of the dancers, at the same time they superintended their cooking. As a show of precaution, eight or ten men were left with the revenue camels and horses; but, influenced by the same motives as their comrades, and considering their situation perfectly safe, they soon deserted their post and joined the revellers in the glen.

This was more fortunate than could possibly have been anticipated. Mansúr, therefore, without a moment's delay, descended from the rocks, roused the camels, and delivering them to a part of his followers, directed them to push forward with all speed, while he remained to secure the horses and extricate their companions in arms. To prevent pursuit, the beasts of the enemy were tied together in long strings, and despatched after the sumpter animals; which being done, they led forth their own horses out of the valley, and stationing them at a convenient spot, crept up the rocks overlooking the fire, to observe what was going forward, that they might regulate their own movements accordingly. Part of the Bedouins, having collected a quantity of camel's dung and kindled several large fires, were engaged in preparing their evening meal; others amused themselves with the performances of the dancers, whose effrontery somewhat surprised them; but, in the entire absence of suspicion, all appeared intent on the enjoyment of the present hour. They were crouching on their heels in a large circle, and the glare of the flames falling on their swarthy visages, exhibited many a double row of white teeth grinning with delight. Having advanced to within a short distance of them without being discovered, Mansúr and his party suddenly raised a loud shout, and discharged several arrows, but without hitting any one. The pretended almé, affecting extreme terror, ran off with loud shrieks, and disappeared among the small glens and fissures of the cliffs; the musicians followed, and the Bedouins, rushing down the valley towards their encampment, allowed them ample time to join their comrades and effect their escape. No words can express the amazement and fury of the outwitted escort on discovering the trick that had been put upon them. They stamped on the ground, tore their beards, and cast dust upon their heads; but at length, perceiving that these manifestations of rage brought back neither horse nor camel, they exclaimed, as all wise people do on such occasions, "Allah kerím!" (God is merciful) and proceeded on foot towards Cairo, inventing by the way a fearful account of their combat with fifteen hundred robbers, who ultimately overpowered them.

Mansúr effected his return with the same spirit and success, and was congratulated on his boldness and ingenuity by the chief of the robbers; who, however, observed that his exploit could not fail to arouse the anger of the khalíf, and great pains would be taken to trace it home to them. He therefore advised Mansúr to take up his abode in an uninhabited house close to a certain mosque, where he should easily discover the steps taken by government to detect the authors of the achievement in the desert. Mansúr accordingly proceeded to the residence indicated to him, and, taking his mother to manage his household affairs, began to live in the style of a private gentleman. Meanwhile the authorities were indefatigably employed in pursuing every trace, real or imaginary, of the robbery committed on the royal treasury, but without success. At length the khalíf, Biamrillah, who has been celebrated by historians for the extravagance of his fancies and the recklessness with which he set aside the established usages of the people, conceived a means of fathoming the mystery, that never could have presented itself to any other mind than his own. Learning that among the camels captured by the robbers there was one beautiful animal, marked in an extraordinary manner with black and white stripes, he informed the kázís and learned men that he would give the aga of police a lesson in his business, and make the very triumph of the robbers the means of betraying them into the hands of justice.

In order to carry this sagacious plan into execution, he commanded thirty of his courtiers to send him each one of the ladies of his family; and when they had arrived at the palace, they were seated on so many handsome mules, and directed to traverse the various streets of the city, with a crier going before them, proclaiming their intention of becoming the harem guests of the person who would entertain them with the flesh of a striped camel. It was in vain that they expressed their reluctance to execute the disgraceful commission; the khalíf was inexorable—indeed, considering the idea wholly new, as it really was, the scruples they exhibited surprised and provoked him, not being able to comprehend how any person should value the preservation of honour above the satisfaction of fulfilling his commands. The cavalcade set out, therefore, each lady attended by two slaves; but the crier, amused at his whimsical employment, could scarcely perform his duty for laughter. Though, on regarding the ladies, who were all unveiled, there was many an honest man that, not knowing what he prayed for, besought the Prophet to bestow on him a striped camel, it seemed probable that the wisdom of the prince would no more prove efficacious than the vigilance of the chief of the police; for the fair ensnarers had already paraded in vain the greater part of the city, and no person invited them to alight. At length, having passed the mosque of Shaykh Hussayn, they saw Mansúr seated before his house. The crier, wishing to divert the young man, immediately repeated the khalíf's proclamation, dwelling with malicious emphasis on the happiness proffered to the possessor of a striped camel. He even caused the mules to stand still, to allow the beauty of his charges to be seen; but, having been hitherto unsuccessful, was not a little surprised to perceive the young man advance towards the ladies with a profound obeisance, and express the joy he felt at being able to entertain them as they desired.

It should have been before observed that Mansúr was extremely handsome, and possessed of manners in the highest degree engaging. "Ladies," said he, "I am your slave. You may enter my house with safety; for while you honour it with the light of your presence, I swear by the Prophet that your will shall be the will of the khalíf. Pray suffer your slave to aid you in alighting." Somewhat reassured by the suavity of his demeanour, the ladies descended from their mules, and were conducted with becoming ceremony into a saloon of spacious dimensions, spread with Persian carpets, and furnished with divans of crimson cloth, fringed with gold. The mild, rich light of sunset, streaming through the numerous windows of painted gypsum, cast a flood of purple and deep orange colour over the fretted roof, luxuriant arabesques, and pillared recesses; and its effect, blending with that of the most costly perfumes, cast a soft spell over the imagination, which Mansúr was careful to maintain by a language and behaviour in keeping with the place, now bestowing his attention on one, and now on another, with as scrupulous a politeness as if each had been a princess, and he the meanest of her slaves. A number of the thieves, disguised as merchants, performed all the household offices—killed the camel, and bringing in its striped skin, according to their desire, spread it before them on the carpet, and waited on Mansúr's mother, who undertook to superintend the preparations for the banquet.

When the ladies had alighted from their beasts, and were about to enter the house, part of the attendants, under pretence of not incommoding the host by their numbers, endeavoured to make their escape, for the purpose of informing the khalíf of the success of his stratagem, and to guide thither the troops for the apprehension of Mansúr. But, perceiving the drift of the whole scheme, he affected to take offence at the supposition which the movement implied, that he was too poor to entertain the whole company, and took particular care that not a single individual, not even the crier, should absent himself from the feast he had provided for all. The slaves, therefore, being secured in the apartments appropriated to persons of their class, and their beasts provendered in the stables, nothing remained but to enjoy the passing hour. Several of the superior robbers, happening to be that evening on business with Mansúr, were invited to be of the party; and being men of prudent and discreet manners, their company greatly contributed to the amusement of the guests. Finding themselves treated with extraordinary respect, the ladies began gradually to dismiss their fears, and to say within themselves that, after all, it might not be absolutely necessary to their happiness to live secluded in the recesses of the harem. The supper, which, in addition to the camel's flesh, consisted of every delicacy that could be procured, tended to strengthen this persuasion. And presently when, under the name of sherbet, the most exquisite wines were brought in, every vestige of reserve disappeared; and forgetting their strange position, they talked and laughed with their host and his friends as familiarly as if they had been among their brothers and cousins. But, being wholly unaccustomed to wine, it was not long before they imagined themselves in Paradise. Everything floated around them in pleasing disorder. Now they were the húrís of the Prophet's heaven; and the thieves seemed, by the ministry of fancy, to be converted into beautiful youths, with whom they could be content to pass an eternity. To give fresh force to this delusion, a company of almé, with several musicians, were introduced into the apartment; and their performances, with the music, the songs, and the rapturous applause of the spectators, and their own bewildered imaginations, completing what the wine had begun, at length plunged them into absolute intoxication, which ended in a profound sleep. When Mansúr perceived they were no longer conscious of what was going on around them, he ordered his companions to take each a lady in his arms and follow him into the street, where, selecting a large recess in front of the house of a pious man, sufficiently out of the track of passengers to secure them from being trodden on by mules or asses, he laid the whole sleeping bevy side by side, and then returned to dispose of their attendants, who had likewise been reduced to the same condition.

Next morning, at peep of day, as Mustapha the cake-seller was going his usual rounds, bawling, as he trudged along, "Mashallah! cakes! nicely-buttered, fresh, hot cakes!—who will buy my cakes?" he discovered a number of white bundles packed close against the wall. "Aha!" thought he to himself, "here hath fortune been at work for thee, Mustapha, before thy own mustachios were awake! Wallah! a whole caravan of muslin! Let me see: I hope none of my neighbours are stirring. No, not a soul. Well, I will take the first bale that comes to hand and run home with it. Who knows? perhaps no one may pass before I can return; and then, if I secure a second, my fortune is made." So saying, he threw down the baking apparatus, spilling in his hurry a quantity of the liquid paste that constituted the whole of his property, and springing forward in the imperfect light, caught hold of something extremely heavy, which moved as he endeavoured to lift it. Horror-stricken and trembling in every limb, he started back, exclaiming, "May the devil singe my beard, but I have stumbled on the warehouse of some magician! Allah kerím! See, the bales begin to move! Imps of Jehennam, as I am a cake-seller!" The lady, who had been roused by his seizing her rudely round the waist, now raised her head, still confused with the fumes of wine, and perceiving, instead of her curtained chamber and female slaves, the dark outline of a suite of ruinous houses, and the ragged cake-seller snatching up his baking apparatus and preparing to run away, she rubbed her eyes, supposing she was still in a dream. But, on making a second trial with the same result, a sudden fear and faint recollection of what had taken place came over her, and she started on her feet with an exclamation of distress. Upon this, her morning visitor, apprehending it was all over with him, took to his heels and plunged headlong down the street, shrieking like an ogre, his pan of liquid paste splashing over his back and descending in streams to his travel-stained babúshes, so that he appeared an overgrown baboon which some mischievous barber had covered with soap ready to be shaved. It was in vain that the lady, who really stood in need of some assistance, conjured him to come back. The louder she called the more he ran; and it was not until he had proceeded the length of five streets that he considered it safe to pause a moment for breath. An aged fakír, supporting his tottering steps with a staff, now approached, and made as if he would pass on; but the lady, emboldened by his age and the sacredness of his character, besought him to have pity on her and her companions, and guide them to the palace. "Daughter," said the holy man, "what dost thou here?"—"Be my guide to the palace," replied the lady, "and I will satisfy thy curiosity." She then awakened her companions, while the fakír, who seemed to have compassion on them without knowing who they were, called a number of ass-drivers, and assisting them into the saddles, led the way in the direction she desired. After traversing a large portion of the city, just as the gates of the royal residence appeared in sight, the fakír, who had attentively listened to her relation, stopped at the entrance into a dark alley, and stepping up close to her beast, whispered softly in her ear, "Speak favourably of me to the khalíf, and, above all, commend the flavour of my striped camel and my wine"; and gliding down the obscure winding alley, vanished in a moment.

The khalíf, enraged at being thus foiled, vows vengeance on the young robber, but is prevented from executing any other scheme for entrapping Mansúr by his negro guards breaking into insurrection, and clamouring for the khalíf's head. By the advice of an Arab shaykh, who chanced to be the guest of the khalíf, the aid of Mansúr and his followers (for he had now become chief of the robbers) is requested to chastise the rebels, who are effectually subdued; after which Mansúr obtains the khalíf's daughter in marriage, and is declared heir-apparent to the khalífate.

In this sprightly story (much of which I have had to omit for want of space) we find two incidents reappear which occur in most versions of the Robbery of the Treasury, though in very different forms: the quest of camel's flesh; making the ladies and their attendants all intoxicated; and placing the former in a ridiculous situation, which in Herodotus and other versions is done to the soldiers who guarded the headless body; while we may consider the khalíf's offering the ladies as harem guests to the person who should give them flesh of a striped camel, as derived from Rhampsinitus' device of sending his daughter abroad in the capacity of a kuttiní.

IV.

FALLING IN LOVE THROUGH A DREAM (p. 398)

In the 'Túti Náma' the Emperor of China becomes violently enamoured of a beautiful damsel whom he saw in a dream, and his prime minister undertakes to go in quest of the creature of his dreaming fancy. After much toilsome journeying he at length discovers her in the person of the Princess of Rúm (the Western Empire), and ascertains that she is averse from marriage in consequence of having seen in her garden a peacock basely desert his mate and their young when the tree on which their nest was built had been struck with lightning, which incident she considered as typical of the inherent selfishness of all men. The vazír provides himself with a number of paintings of animals, and among these was a picture of a male deer sacrificing his life to save his mate and their fawn, which on being shown to the princess fills her with astonishment. Then the vazír shows the portrait of his master, the emperor, who, he tells her, has an aversion from women on account of having witnessed the incident depicted in the painting. This conquers the dislike of the princess, and the emperor is made happy. The frame of the Persian story-book, 'Hazár ú Yek Rúz' (the Thousand and One Days—see p. 56), seems to have been adapted from this tale; and Mr J. A. St John gives a story which has also some resemblance to it, in his 'Tales of the Ramad'han,' vol. ii. p. 164 ff., under the title of "The Princess who was changed into a Gazelle." The tales comprised in Mr St John's entertaining volumes he professes to have heard related in Egypt by a ghawazi (singing and dancing girl) and by minstrels and story-tellers in the evenings of the great Muhammedan Fast.

V.

LITTLE FAIRLY (p. 399)

In a paper on Aberdeenshire Folk-Lore, contributed to the 'Folk-Lore Journal,' vol. ii. (1884), pp. 70, 71, by the Rev. Walter Gregor, there is a story, entitled "Mally Whuppie," communicated to him by Mr James Moir, rector of the Grammar School, Aberdeen, who heard it told by his mother, which presents points of resemblance to versions of the Robbery of the King's Treasury, and in the conclusion bears some analogy to the incident of the sack in the variants of Little Fairly:

The heroine, Mally Whuppie, first steals a giant's sword from the back of his bed, next, his purse from below his pillow, and each time escapes; but in stealing the ring from off his finger the giant awakes and grasps her by the hand. "Now," says the giant, "I hae catcht you, Mally Whuppie; and if I had deen as muckle ill to you as ye hae deen to me, what wad ye dae to me?" Mally considered what plan she would fall upon to escape, and she said, "I wad pit you into a pyock (poke),[1] and I wad pit the cat inside wi' you, and the dog aside you, and

---

[1] The *y* in this word is pronounced as in "yoke," "yard," etc.

a needle and thread and a sheers, and I wad hang you upon the wa', and I wad gang to the wood and wile (choose) the thickest stick I could get, and I wad come hame and tak you down and lay upon you till ye were dead." "Well, Mally," says the giant, "I'll just do that to you." So he gets a pyock and puts Mally into it, and the cat and the dog beside her, and a needle and thread, and shears, and hings her up upon the wa', and goes to the wood to choose a stick. Mally sings, "O gin ye saw faht (what) I see!" "O faht div ye see, Mally?" says the giant's wife. But Mally never said a word but "O gin ye saw faht I see!" The giant's wife pleaded that Mally would take her up into the pyock till she would see what Mally saw. So Mally took the shears and cut a hole in the pyock and took out the needle and thread with her, and jumpt down, and helpit the giant's wife up into the pyock, and sewed up the hole. The giant's wife saw nothing, and began to ask to get down again, but Mally never minded, but hid herself at the back of the door. Home came the giant, and a great big tree in his hand, and he took down the pyock and began to lay upon it. His wife cried, "It's me, man"; but the dog barkit, and the cat mewt, and he did not know his wife's voice. But Mally did not want her to be killed, so she came out from the back of the door, and the giant saw her and he after her; and he ran and she ran, till she came to the "Brig o' the ae hair," and she wan (got) ower, but he coudna (couldn't), and he said, "Wae worth you, Mally Whuppie! let you never come again!" "Never mair, carle," quo' she, "will I come again to Spain." So Mally took the ring to the king, and she was married to his youngest son, and never saw the giant again.

Another analogue of the sack-trick of Little Fairly is found in the Norwegian tale of the Master-Smith (Thorpe's 'Yule-Tide Stories,' p. 272), in which the hero, personating an angel, persuades the priest that be will take him to heaven in a holy sack: "On Monday the Master-Smith appeared again as an angel, and the priest fell on his knees and returned thanks previous to being put in the sack; and when he was well in, the Master-Smith pulled and hauled him over stock and stone. 'Oh, oh,' cried the priest in the sack, 'where are you taking me to?' 'This is the narrow way that leads to the kingdom of heaven,' said the Master-Smith, dragging him on till he had almost killed him. At length he threw him into the Amtman's goose-house, and the geese began to hiss and peck at him so that he was more dead than alive. 'Oh, oh, where am I now?' said the priest. 'Now you are in purgatory for the purpose of being purged and purified for ever-lasting life,' said the Master-Smitb, and went his way, taking all the gold, silver, and valuables which the priest had collected together in his large parlour. Next morning, when the maid came into the goose-house to let out the geese, she heard the priest in the sack wailing and lamenting bitterly. 'In the name of Jesus, who are you and what do you want?' said she. 'Oh,' cried the priest, 'if thou art an angel from heaven, let me out and allow me to go back to earth again, for here it is worse than hell itself; little devils are pinching me with their tongs.' 'God mend us,' said the girl, helping the priest out of the sack, 'I am no angel; I tend the Amtman's geese, and they are the little devils that have been pecking at you, father.' 'Oh,' cried the priest, 'this is the work of the Master-Smith! Oh my gold and silver and all my fine clothes!' and he ran home lamenting so woefully that the girl thought he had lost his senses."

VI.

THE MAXIM THAT SAVED A KING'S LIFE (p. 449)

From the story of Kulla Panthaka in 'Buddhaghosha's Parables,' the version orally current among the Sinhalese was probably derived: The favourite minister of a king was foolish, timid, and illiterate, and the other ministers, out of envy of the favour he enjoyed, devised a plan for exposing his ignorance. They proposed to the king that each of them should compose a stanza in his honour and present it to his majesty on a certain day. The stupid minister went home, and taking a style and a palm leaf, sat down on the floor to the task of verse-making. His children, wondering at their fathers novel occupation, crowded round him and began shouting out their childish rhymes. The poor man fearing the anger of the king, and finding himself unable to write anything in the presence of his noisy children, left the house, perched on a rock in a neighbouring field, and began to meditate very deeply. At last, when he despaired of writing anything fit to offer to the king, a buffalo came up and began rubbing his neck against the rock, a circumstance which inspired the minister with a brilliant idea. Starting up and seizing his style he wrote the following line: "Do I not know the reason why you are coming rubbing your neck against the rock?"[1] Now this line in the original means also, "Do I not know the reason why you are whetting your razor?" After writing this down the minister spent the whole of the night in attempting to get up three more lines to complete the stanza. He tried very hard, but in vain; and when the time came for him to present himself before the king, he at length wrote down the same line four times over in imitation of a stanza, and with this he went to the palace. After all the other ministers had presented each his stanza to the king, it came to the turn of the stupid man, who tremblingly handed it to his majesty. The stanza was expressed in

[1] Karagalagagá enavá, mama nodanindá.

such simple language, one line four times repeated, that the king at once committed it to memory, in spite of its forming the subject of general laughter among the jealous courtiers. The simplicity of the piece made the king keep repeating it when at leisure, so much was he taken up with it. This stirred the jealousy of the ministers afresh, and the king also incurred their displeasure to such an extent that they entered into a conspiracy and planned to take away his life. To this end, they bribed the king's barber, who promised to cut his majesty's throat when he went to shave him. Early in the morning of the day fixed for this wicked act, the barber went up with his razors and other things to the king. It so happened that the king was as usual repeating the foolish minister's line, on hearing which the barber at once thought his design on the king was alluded to in the stanza, and that the plot had been discovered; so prostrating himself on the ground before the king, he made a full confession of the conspiracy. The king was shocked, and on inquiry ascertained the fact. Then he caused the conspirators to be executed; and the stupid minister, whose simple line had saved his life, he raised to the position of his chief adviser.[2]

VII.

THE CAPON-CARVER (p. 456, note 2)

In M. Legrand's 'Contes Albanais,' No. 4, as in the Italian version, a prince is the guest of a poor man. A cock, having been killed and dressed, is placed on the table, and the host's clever daughter carved it, giving the head to her father, the body to her mother, the wings to the prince, and the flesh to herself and the young children. The old man seeing his daughter share the food in this manner, turned and looked at his wife, for he was ashamed to speak of it before the stranger. But when they were going to bed, he said to his daughter, "My child, why did you cut up the fowl so badly? Our guest has gone supperless to bed." She replied, "Ah, my father, let me explain it. The head I gave to you, because you are the head of this house; to my mother I gave the body, because, like the body of a ship, she has borne us in her sides; the wings I gave to the stranger, because to-morrow he will take flight and leave us; and lastly, the flesh to us the children, because we are the true flesh of the house." The prince having overheard this explanation greatly admired the girl's cleverness, and ultimately married her.

[2] J. P. Panabokke in 'The Orientalist,' 1885, pp. 174, 175.

VIII.

NORSE VERSION OF
'THE SACRISTAN OF CLUNI' (p. 465)

An abstract of "Our Parish-Clerk," as given in Dasent's 'Tales from the Fjeld,' referred to in p. 472 as a variant of the *fabliau* 'Le Sacristan de Cluni,' may find a place here, although I did not consider the analogy between them sufficiently close to require its insertion among the other versions:

There was once a parish-clerk of whom all the folks said that his brains were in his belly; for while he was fond of pretty girls and buxom wives, he liked good meat and drink still better. It so happened that his next-door neighbour married a rich young lass, and the parish-clerk made friends with him, and something more than friends with his wife. Whenever the husband was from home on business—at the mill, in the wood, or floating timber—she would send for the clerk, and they spent the day in mirth and jollity. By-and-by the ploughboy discovers their on-goings, and one day he tells his master how his wife and the parish-clerk, in his absence, lived as if there was a bridal in the house every day, while his master and himself scarce got the leavings of their good cheer. The master wouldn't credit this story, and the boy offered to wager ten dollars that he would soon prove it to him. "Done!" said the master. So when they got home he told his wife that he must be off to the river and land timber—and off he and his boy went; but when they had gone about half a mile they returned to the house, and found the door locked. By means of a trapdoor they got from the cellar into the kitchen, and striking a light, there they saw the clerk and the goodwife both sound asleep, and the clerk lay snoring with his mouth wide open. The boy got some lead bullets from his master and melted them in a saucepan. Then they poured the molten lead down the clerk's throat, after which they went out by the way they got in, and began to thunder at the front door. The wife, waking up, and perceiving that her paramour was as dead as a doornail, dragged him by the legs and hid him among the heap of wood behind the stove, and then opened the door to her husband. While he and his boy were at supper, he got up and went to the wood-pile for a few faggots, and there he saw the clerk lying stark and stiff. "Who's this?" asks the man. "Only a beggar-man who came here and asked for a night's lodging." "A fine beggar," said the husband, "with his silver buckles in his shoes, and silver buttons at his knees! I see what you've been about; and by rights I should hand you over to the sheriff. As it is, get rid of the body the best way you can." So the goodwife promised to reward the boy handsomely if he would but get the clerk buried; and the boy, taking the body on his back, went away. Seeing some horses in a meadow, he caught one of them and bound the clerk fast to his back, and off he trotted, till he came near a barn where two men were watching for thieves who came to steal the hay. One of them called out, "Who's there?" but there came no reply, of course, and after calling again, he fired his gun, at which the horse gave a sudden jump, and off tumbled the clerk to the ground. When the two men found the supposed thief was killed outright, they were in a great fright, but at length resolved to bury him in the meantime among the hay, which they did accordingly. Presently up came a man bearing a heavy load on his back, all out of breath, and he sat down to rest on the door-step. He had been killing pigs at a farm a few days before, and thinking he was but poorly paid for his work, had stolen the biggest and fattest of them, which he had then with him in a sack. Suddenly recollecting that he had forgotten his gloves, and knowing that if they were found at the farm he would be at once detected, he rose up hastily to get them. The two men in the barn thought this a capital opportunity of getting rid of the dead man, so they drew out the porker and put the clerk in the sack. The man came back with his gloves, and taking up the sack, carried it home. What was the surprise of his wife on opening the sack to find, instead of the fat porker her man had bragged so much about, the body of the parish priest! However, they must get rid of the body, and that without a moment's delay. So Mary, their daughter, a stout, strapping wench, undertakes to carry it off and bury it in some out-of-the-way place, where nobody would ever find it. As she was tramping along she came near a house where

> The sound of flute and fiddle
> Gave signal sweet in that old hall
> Of hands across and down the middle;

for there was a dance going on; and so she quietly set the clerk down on the back-stairs of the house, with his hat in his hand, as if he was asking charity, and then hid herself. Not long after this a girl comes out, and seeing what she supposed to be a beggar-man, she dropped twopence in his hat, but never a "Thank you" said he in return. So she went into the house and told this to the guests, and the young sheriff's officer goes out and bawls in the dead man's ear, "Why are you sitting here, sir?" But not a word did he get in reply; so at last, in a rage, he fetched the parish-clerk one under the ear, when down he fell across the staircase. Out jumps Mary from her hiding-place, and makes a great outcry over the murder of her poor father. So the sheriff's officer gave her ten dollars to say no more about the accident, and Mary once more shoulders the parish-clerk and jogs off, till she came to another farm, and there she placed him on the brink of the well, as if he was looking down into the water. At daybreak the ploughboy comes to the well, and calls to the dead man, "Get out of this; I want to draw some water. What are you looking at?" Receiving no reply, the lad gave him a stroke that sent him plump into the well. When the body was drawn out and recognised, the farmer sent for the sheriff, and when he came and inquired into the affair it was found that the parish-clerk had been killed three times before: first with boiling lead, then with a bullet through his forehead, and lastly his neck was broken.

The affinity of this story with the *fabliau* and its English derivatives is very evident, notwithstanding the variations in the earlier incidents: that of the horse comes first, yet it is curious to find the tumbling of the body into the well the final incident, as in the case of the dead sacristan; while in both the dead man is substituted for the porker in the sack.

IX.

WOMEN BETRAYING THEIR HUSBANDS (p. 472)

As another example of the stories related by the mediæval ecclesiastics at the expense of women, the following tale of the "Physician in spite of himself" may be cited from Jacques de Vitry's 'Sermones':

I have heard (says he) of a certain woman who always contradicted her husband. When she and her husband were coming from the market, a hare crossed the road before them and escaped. Then the husband said, "How sleek and fat it is! If we had caught it, we should have eaten it roasted with onions and stuffing." But the wife said, "I would relish it more heartily with pepper." "Nay," said the husband, "it is better when prepared with onions and stuffing." "It is not," said the wife, wishing in no way to humour her husband. The latter, very angry, beat her severely. And she began to reflect and consider in what manner she could avenge herself on her husband. Having heard that the king was in very delicate health, she went to the servants of the king and said, "I have a husband who is an excellent physician, but conceals his skill, and will not assist any one unless moved by terror and blows." And when her husband was brought before the king, he was commanded to diligently apply his skill on the king and cure him of his infirmity. But he refused, saying, "I am not a doctor." The servants of the king told him the words of his wife, and the king ordered him to be smartly whipped; and when he could not be persuaded he was beaten again and again, and cast out from the presence of the king. And so the wicked wife caused her husband to be beaten.

RESUSCITATION IN FOLK-LORE (p. 503)

According to the ancient and wide-spread myth, the Water of Life had not only the virtue of endowing whosoever drank of it with immortality, but also of reviving the dead. In No. 18 of Prym and Socin's 'Syrische Märchen,' the bones of a man who had been killed ten years ago are collected and the water of life poured over them, upon which the man rose up alive as he was before. In the second of the Twenty-five Tales of a Demon, an ascetic entered as a guest the house of a Bráhman, who received him courteously, and he sat down to rest. Meanwhile a child there began to cry. When, in spite of all efforts, it would not stop, the mistress of the house fell into a passion, and taking it up in her arms, threw it into the blazing fire. The moment the child was thrown in, as its body was soft, it was reduced to ashes. When the ascetic saw this his hair stood on end, and he exclaimed, "Alas, alas! I have entered the house of a Bráhman-demon. So I will not eat food here now, for such food would be sin in a visible and material shape." But the Bráhman said to him, "See the power of raising the dead to life inherent in a charm of mine, which is effectual as soon as it is recited." Then he took a book containing the charm and read it, and threw on to the ashes some dust, over which the charm had been recited, whereupon the child rose up alive and well. When the Bráhman was asleep the ascetic got up quietly, took the book, and quitted the house. By means of the charm, he raised to life from her ashes his beloved Mandáravatí.

In the 47th tale of the 'Pentamerone' of Basile, one of the five sons raises the princess to life and then demands her in marriage. Satú, in the ancient Egyptian romance—see vol. i. p. 170—is revived by means of a certain liquid. And in the 'Rámáyana, Hanuman, the monkey-deity, procures four different kinds of herbs in order to resuscitate his dead subjects: the first kind restores the dead to life; the second drives away all pain; the third joins broken parts; the fourth cures all wounds. Mr Ralston, in a note to his 'Russian Folk-Tales,' p. 232, says that in a Kirghis (Siberian) story a golden-haired hero finds, after long search, the maiden to whom he had in very early life been betrothed. Her father has him murdered. She persuades the murderer to show her the body of her dead lover, and weeps over it bitterly. A spirit appears, and tells her to sprinkle it with water from a neighbouring well. It is very deep, but she induces the murderer to allow her to lower him into it by means of her remarkably long hair. He descends and hands up to her a cup of the water. Having received it, she severs her hair, and the murderer drops and is drowned. Then she sprinkles her lover's corpse with the water, and he revives, but lives only three days. She resolves not to survive him, and is buried by his side. From the graves of the lovers spring two willows, which intertwine their boughs as if in an embrace.[1]

In the 'Kathá Sarit Ságara,' ch. 59, a husband and wife, who are re-born as swans, and reunited, after the rainy season take up their abode on the top of a mountain. There the female is shot by a fowler, on which her mate flies away, distracted with grief. The fowler takes up the dead female swan and goes off. On the way seeing many armed men at a distance coming towards him, and thinking they might take the bird from him, he cuts some grass with his knife, and covering up the bird with it, leaves her on the ground. After the men had gone, the fowler returns for the bird. But it happened that among the grass he had cut was an herb which possessed the power of raising the dead to life, and by means of its juice the female swan was resuscitated, and before his eyes she flung off the grass, flew up into the sky, and disappeared.—Readers who desire farther instances will find many in Grimm's 'Teutonic Mythology,' p. 185, note, where, among other parallels, he refers to the myth of Zeus and Tantalus.

XI.

WOMEN WHOSE LOVE IS SLIGHTED

Analogues of the Incident of Joseph and Potiphar's Wife. (Vol. i. pp. lii, lxxxvi; ii. 527, 529.)

Near akin to stories of women betraying their husbands are those in which an amorous dame, having found her advances repulsed by the object of her passion, avenges herself by accusing him of having attempted to violate her chastity. The oldest recorded instance is found in the Egyptian romance of the brothers Anapú and Satú, to which reference is made in vol. i., p. lxxxvi, and again in p. 170. On a similar incident is based the frame, or leading story, of the 'Seven Wise Masters,' and of the several versions of the 'Book of Sindibdád'—see vol. i. p. lii, note; and it is not only found in the tales and legends of many lands, but doubt-less has often occurred in real life. Among classical tales it forms the old story of Hyppolyte, the wife of Acastus, and Peleus; that of Antea and Bellerophon; and that of Phædra and Hyppolytus; while in European traditions it reappears in the story of Fausta and Crispus. There is scarcely a single Asiatic story-book of any note which does not contain an analogous tale: it occurs in the 'Túti

---

[1] Readers familiar with our old ballad poetry will remember more than one love-ditty which concludes in this manner.

Náma,' in the 'Forty Vazírs,' and in the Persian romance which purports to recount the adventures of Hatim Tai.

In the 'Kathá Sarit Ságara' it is found again in the story of King Mahásena and his virtuous minister Gunasarman, as related to King Súryaprabha, one night when he was sleepless,[1] by his minister Vítabhíti. Queen Asokavatí is desperately enamoured of Gunasarman, the faithful minister of Mahásena, king of Ujjayiní, who had saved his royal master's life on five occasions, one of which was when the cook had put poison in the king's food. The king desired Gunasarman to teach his queen to play on the lute; and while he was instructing her, the queen indulged in perpetual coquetry, laughter, and mirth. One day, wounded with the arrow of love, she said to the chaste Gunasarman, "It was yourself that I asked for, handsome man, under the pretext of learning to play the lute, for I am deeply in love with you, so consent to my wishes." Gunasarman replied, "Do not talk so, for you are my master's wife, and such a one as I am should not commit such treason; desist, therefore, from this reckless conduct."[2] The queen continued, "Why do you possess in vain this beauty and skill in accomplishments? How can you look with a passionless eye on me who love you so much?" Gunasarman answered sarcastically, "You are right. What is the use of that beauty and skill which is not tarnished with infamy by seducing the wife of another, and which does not in this world and the next cause one to fall into the ocean of hell?" Then the queen, pretending to be angry, said, "I am determined to die, if you do not do what I say; so, being despised by you, I will slay you before I die." Gunasarman replied, "By all means do so. For it is better to live for one moment bound by the bonds of righteousness than to live unrighteously for hundreds of crores of *kalpas*.[3] And it is far preferable to die without reproach,

---

[1] It is still a common practice of Asiatic monarchs, when they cannot sleep o' nights, to cause a story-teller to recite some entertaining narratives. In the case of Ahasuerus, as related in the Book of Esther, that potentate preferred more solid stuff, and well was it for the captive Israelites that he did so: "On that night could not the king sleep; and he commanded to bring the book of records of the Chronicles; and they were read before the king,"—ch. vi. 1.

[2] The young Hebrew slave gave a more pious reason to the wife of Potiphar: "How can I do this great wickedness, and sin against God?—"Gen. xxxix. 9.

[3] So, too, in the 'Dhammapada,' or (Buddha's) Path of Virtue: "He who lives a hundred years vicious and unreflecting, a life of one day is better if a man is virtuous and reflecting." And in Addison's 'Cato' we read—

A day, an hour, of virtuous liberty
Is worth a whole eternity of bondage.

And Bishop Heber—

Swell, swell the bugle, sound the fife;
To all the sensual world proclaim—
One crowded hour of glorious strife
Is worth an age without a name.

having done no wrong, than for me to have done wrong and to be put to death by the king, with reproach attaching to my name." In short, Queen Asokavatí did not cease from importunately soliciting Gunasarman day and night; but he would never consent to that crime: good men prefer death to immodest conduct. Then Asokavatí, finding that he was resolved, one day, out of enmity to him, affected to be unhappy, and remained with tearful countenance. And Mahásena, coming in and seeing her in that condition, said, "What is this, my beloved? Who has offended you? Tell me the name of the man whose life and property I am to take by way of punishment." Then the revengeful queen said, with affected reluctance, "You have not the power to punish the man who has injured me; so what is the good of revealing the injury?" But when the king pressed her, she said, deceitfully, "My husband, if you are very anxious to know, listen, and I will tell you. Gunasarman came into my presence to-day, and said, 'Queen, I am consumed with passion for you, so consent to my wishes, otherwise I cannot live; bestow on me life as a Bráhman's fee.' When he had said this, as the room was empty, he fell at my feet. Then I drew away my foot and rose up in bewilderment, and he, rising up, embraced me, a weak woman, by force. And my maid Pallaviká, came in at that very moment. The instant he saw her he fled out alarmed. If Pallaviká had not come in, the villain would certainly have outraged me. This is the injury he has done me to-day." When the queen had told this false tale, she stopped and wept. For in the beginning wicked women sprang from Lying Speech. And the moment the king heard it he was all on fire with anger, for reliance upon the words of women destroys the discrimination even of the great. And he said to his dear wife, "Be comforted, fair one; I will certainly punish that traitor with death."—In the sequel, the king and his other ministers attempt to kill Gunasarman, but he wards off their sword-cuts by his cunning of fence, makes his way out of the palace by force, and putting on his eyes an ointment which rendered him invisible, leaves the country and proceeds towards the Dekkan, reflecting on the way, "Surely that foolish king was set on by Asokavatí. Alas! women whose love is slighted are worse than poison!"

"Our happiness," said Speroni to Francis Maria II., Duke of Rovere, "is to be measured by its quality, not by its duration; and I prefer to live for one day like a man, than for a hundred years like a brute, a stock, or a stone."

INDEX

About the Editor

Christine Goldberg has adapted the comparative (or historic-geographic) method to investigate various folktales. She is the author of *Turandot's Sisters* (1993) and *The Tale of the Three Oranges* (1997), and is a regular contributor to the *Enzyklopädie des Märchens*.